THE FEDERAL JUDICIARY

THE FEDERAL JUDICIARY

Strengths and Weaknesses

RICHARD A. POSNER

HARVARD UNIVERSITY PRESS

CAMBRIDGE, MASSACHUSETTS

LONDON, ENGLAND

2017

First printing

LIBRARY OF CONGRESS CATALOGING-IN-PUBLICATION DATA
Names: Posner, Richard A., author.
Title: The federal judiciary : strengths and weaknesses / Richard A. Posner.
Description: Cambridge, Massachusetts : Harvard University Press, 2017. |
Includes bibliographical references and index.
Identifiers: LCCN 2017010498 | ISBN 9780674975774 (hardcover : alk. paper)
Subjects: LCSH: Courts—United States. | Judicial process—United States. |
Judges—United States.
Classification: LCC KF8700 .P674 2017| DDC 347.73/1—dc23
LC record available at https://lccn.loc.gov/2017010498

For Charlene

Contents

Preface

Let [not] the dead bury the living.

NIETZSCHE, 1874[1]

Not fare well, / But fare forward, voyagers!

T. S. ELIOT, 1941[2]

Remember less and forget more.

HEW STRACHAN, 2016

I HAVE BEEN A FEDERAL JUDGE for thirty-five years and before that I had been a law professor for twelve years and before that had worked in government in Washington for six years following my graduation from law school. But it is only relatively recently that I have become fully aware that the federal judiciary is laboring under a number of handicaps, many though not all self-inflicted because arising from a traditional legal culture that has to a significant degree outlived its usefulness. Full realization of this was slow in coming to me; but in a series of books, all published by the Harvard University Press since I became a federal appellate judge in 1981 (not to mention countless articles), I have addressed deficiencies in our judicial culture and performance. The books are *The Problems of Jurisprudence* (1995); *Overcoming Law* (1995); *Frontiers of Legal Theory* (2001); *Law, Pragmatism, and Democracy* (2003); *How*

---

1. The original quotation is "Let the dead bury the living"—Nietzsche's sarcastic characterization of historians. He of course thought the dead should *not* bury the living.

2. From "The Dry Salvages," Quartet 3 of Eliot's *Four Quartets*. There is much else in this vein in *Four Quartets*. In Quartet 2, "East Coker," for example, we read that "there is, . . . at best, only a limited value in the knowledge derived from experience; the knowledge imposes a pattern, and falsifies, for the pattern is new in every moment."

Judges Think (2008); *The Behavior of Federal Judges: A Theoretical and Empirical Study of Rational Choice* (coauthored with Lee Epstein and William M. Landes) (2013); *Reflections on Judging* (2013); and, most recently (and cited several times in this book), *Divergent Paths: The Academy and the Judiciary* (2016). The present book continues, and perhaps completes, my critical reflections on the judiciary that I've served and written about for so many years. It emphasizes, as did *Divergent Paths,* that our judicial system is excessively backward-looking. The emphasis I've placed for many years on pragmatism as a guide to judicial decision making implies a forward as opposed to a rearward focus, since pragmatism focuses on consequences, and the consequences of a judicial decision lie in the decision's future. So neither *Divergent Paths* nor this book should surprise readers familiar with my earlier work.

I cover a lot of ground in this book, but the book is more a *macédoine* than a treatise (see next paragraph). I acknowledge the strengths of our judicial system, but only briefly, emphasizing instead the weaknesses because it's they that require critical attention, improvement, and reform. Moreover, they are far more numerous than the strengths.

The book is somewhat unconventional in format. It contains a good deal of quoted material—some of it from my articulate critics, such as Michael Dorf and Akhil Amar, some from allies (principally my good friend and frequent collaborator Professor Eric Segall of the Georgia State University College of Law), some from judicial opinions—my own and others', and other official legal documents—but all intended to give the reader a better feel for today's federal judiciary. The book is blunt, though also in places light. It spares none of the law's sacred cows (including Justices of the Supreme Court) and indeed is relentlessly critical and overflowing with suggestions for reform. It is not the kind of book one expects from a judge. But I am a judge who besides acknowledging an affinity with the legal realists of the 1920s and 1930s (such as Benjamin Cardozo, Roscoe Pound, Felix Cohen, Karl Llewellyn, Jerome Frank, and Leon Green), aligns himself with the nineteenth-century painters of whom Edmund Wilson wrote, "They swore, if they had any spirit, that they were going to work at their craft even though nobody wanted their wares."[3]

For readers interested in learning more about me ("where I'm coming from," as the cliché has it), I can recommend William Domnarski, *Richard Posner*

---

3. "Notes on Babbitt and More" (1930), reprinted in *Edmund Wilson: Literary Essays and Review of the 1920s & 30s* 367, 374 (2007).

(2016); Lincoln Caplan, "Rhetoric & Law: The Double Life of Richard Posner, America's most Contentious Legal Reformer," *Harvard Magazine,* February 2016, p. 49; Joel Cohen, "An Interview with Judge Richard A. Posner," *ABA Journal,* July 1, 2014, www.abajournal.com/magazine/article/an_interview_with _judge_richard_a._posner; Larissa MacFarquhar, "The Bench Burner," *New Yorker,* December 10, 2001, p. 78; and Jeffrey Rosen, "Overqualified," *Washington Diarist,* April 3, 1994. I have a flippant side, most recently exhibited in @Posner_Thoughts, https://twitter.com/Posner_Thoughts?ref_src=twsrc%5E google%7Ctwcamp%5Eserp%7Ctwgr%5Eauthor. (My critics, who are numerous, can be found by Googling me.)

Admirers and critics agree on one thing: I'm not a typical federal judge. In Jeffrey Rosen's words,[4]

> [Posner's] cheerful contempt for dimmer judges, including several of the worthies on the Supreme Court, seems less a mark of arrogance than of candor. "I say outright what other judges prefer to keep under their hat," he told the Chicago Council of Lawyers. "That is why my opinions strike some lawyers as being outside the professional groove." . . . [T]he Lawyer's Council tabulated the number of times other circuits have cited Posner's opinions. By this standard, Posner is easily the most influential judge in the nation, averaging 273 citations each year, or more than four times the national average of 66 citations. In a perfectly meritocratic world, a delegation of Senators from both parties would fly to Chicago with a signed Supreme Court commission and lay it respectfully at Posner's feet.

Rosen continues:

> But in the middle of a star-struck swoon, I remembered a reservation. It's hard to avoid the suspicion, after reading and talking to Posner, that he does not believe very wholeheartedly in law. He prefers the "cynical acid" of empirical analysis to abstractions about legal rules and legal rights. (Posner notes that Holmes, too, believed in policy analysis, but lacked the patience to do it.) The Chicago Council of Lawyers puts it mildly

4. Jeffrey Rosen, "Overqualified," *Washington Diarist,* April 3, 1994.

when it calls Posner a "legal realist who gives little weight to history and is famously derisive of original intent." (See Posner's "What Am I, A Potted Plant?," *New Republic,* Sept. 28, 1987, p. 23.) In *The Problems of Jurisprudence* (1990) Posner confesses that "political factors, and sometimes social visions, are decisive in the most difficult cases"; and he endorses Holmes's dark aphorism: "The prophecies of what the courts will do in fact, and nothing more pretentious, are what I mean by the law."

Critics and admirers have noted the affinities between Posner's no-nonsense pragmatism and the radical skepticism of the critical legal studies movement, although Posner disavows the "left-of-center politics" characteristic of the crits. But there's something exhilarating and unsettling about the image of Posner, presiding by day over the Seventh Circuit and squirreling away hours at night to pound out his subversive books on the indeterminacy of law. When I asked Posner about the irony, he chuckled and then demurred, with surprising tentativeness. Judges are restrained by law in two senses, he said. They have to be impartial, in that they can't decide even close cases on the basis of personal sympathy for the parties; and unlike moral philosophers, they have to try, for reasons of efficiency if nothing else, to maintain a legal fabric that includes considerations of precedent, legislative authority, and the facts of each case. (Posner stressed, however, that the gray area where precedents give no clear answers is wider for him than for other judges.) On this score, Posner's next book may not be entirely reassuring. The working title is *Overcoming Law.* [The book was published under that title in 1995.]

A note on timing. A few words about dates of composition and publication. I began work on the book in late May 2016, and by early June had a draft of about two hundred pages. By early November it exceeded four hundred pages. I thought I had finished, but the dramatic and largely unexpected outcome of the Presidential election on November 8, which gave rise to frenzied speculation concerning the implications for the Supreme Court (handicapped by the vacancy in its ranks caused by the death of Justice Scalia in February 2016), led me to make additions to Chapter 2, the chapter that deals with the Supreme Court. The election, as distinguished from its possible consequences for the federal judiciary, is not my subject, but I take this opportunity to note my agreement with Yale political science professor Eitan Hersh that Donald Trump's election was largely due to the ineptitude of the Democrats, beginning with the choice of Hillary Clinton to be the Democratic standard-bearer. Hersh explains, "I wonder[,] if there [had been] a smoke-filled room of Democratic Party elites, whether they would have chosen Hillary Clinton. I think they would have chosen Vice President Biden. Clinton had too many obvious vulnerabilities going into this."[5] Democratic leaders, thinking back to Barry Goldwater's unsuccessful Presidential campaign in 1964, doubtless thought Trump too much the demagogue to win. But Trump, unlike Goldwater, was not running against a President.

Hersh's final sentence is worth pondering: "I think [Trump's] voters will turn against him because I don't think this was a thoughtful move [voting for him]. It was an emotional move and one in which the voters misperceived the stakes."[6] Yet what Hersh leaves out is the imperative need of the Democratic Party to reorganize, to jettison its current incompetent leadership that played a critical role in Clinton's defeat, to marginalize the shrillest voices in the party—such as those of Senator Schumer and Senator Warren—and to campaign vigorously among the kind of voters who were drawn to Trump: the "deplorables," as Clinton called them in the dumbest sally of the 2016 campaign.

My book was largely complete, and submitted to the publisher, Harvard University Press, on December 10, 2016, a month and two days after the election. A shorter version of Chapter 1 had been published even earlier, as an article entitled "Response to Michael C. Dorf's Book Review of *Divergent Paths: The Academy and the Judiciary,*"[7] though it appears in this book in expanded form with a number of changes, some motivated by Dorf's alliterative reply—"Parsing Posner's Peevishness"[8]—to my article. Yet even after December 10, a growing preoccupation with the consequences for the federal judiciary, especially the Supreme Court, of the Trump Presidency, a preoccupation reflected in countless academic and journalistic articles and Internet postings, along

5. Mike Cummings, "Understanding Trump's Triumph: Q&A with Eitan Hersh," *Yale News,* November 10, 2016, http://news.yale.edu/2016/11/10/understanding-trump-s-triumph-qa-eitan-hersh?utm_source=YNemail&utm_medium=email&utm_.campaign=ynalumni-11-10-16.

6. Id.

7. 66 *Journal of Legal Education* 203 (2016), © 2016 Association of American Law Schools; Dorf's review is in the same issue.

8. In *Dorf on Law,* September 30, 2016, www.dorfonlaw.org/2016/09/parsing-posners-peevishness.html.

with judicial opinions, and culminating in the nomination of Judge Neil M. Gorsuch to succeed Scalia, required continued revision and amplification of the book well into February and early March; the text of the book has now been updated through March 6.

The year 2016 marked not only Scalia's death and the outsized attention that it received but also the nomination of Merrick Garland to fill the Scalia vacancy—a nomination left twisting in the wind because of the Republican-controlled Senate's refusal to hold a confirmation hearing for him, and finally killed by Trump's election to the Presidency—and the impact on the Court of its being evenly divided between Republicans and Democrats because of Scalia's death and the Senate's refusal to consider his nominated successor Garland. It was also of course the year of a Presidential election bound to be critical for the Court and indeed for the Constitution because of the Scalia vacancy and candidate Donald Trump's public vow to fill the vacancy with a Scalia clone, and finally it was the year of continued decline in public support for and approval of the Court, owing in part at least to the disarray brought about by Scalia's death and the unfilled vacancy that it created. The Epilogue brings the book up to February 2017, although there are also numerous February additions in the earlier chapters.

I need to acknowledge the many debts that I have incurred in writing this book. I thank my wife, Charlene, for insightful comments on and careful proofreading of my error-laden first draft, and Erwin Chemerinsky, Steven Eisman, Christopher Hampson, Dennis Hutchinson, John L. Kane, Jr., Gary Peeples, Eric Segall, Mary Schnoor, and Julia Schwartz for helpful suggestions regarding my project. I thank Lee Epstein for sources I have used in my analysis of the length and readability of Supreme Court opinions, Tom Ginsburg for his penetrating insights into foreign constitutions that I discuss in Chapter 2, Peter Heidenberger for helpful comparison of the German and American judicial systems, Thomas LeBien of Harvard University Press for his critical comments on the structure and substance of earlier drafts of the book, Cheryl Lincoln for her careful editing of my final draft, Jennifer Nou for insights into administrative regulation, which I discuss in Chapter 3, and my chief research assistant at the University of Chicago Law School, Theresa Yuan, and her team of law-student research assistants—Makar Gevorkian, Jacob Grossman, Jacob Mazzarella, John McAdams, Benjamin Meyer, Emma Thurber Stone, Noah Weeks-Brittan, and Robert Zhou—for their careful citechecking of the entire manuscript and their stylistic suggestions, and Meyer in addition for his helpful formatting suggestions. And finally Paul Rogerson deserves special thanks for reformatting the entire draft after the numerous changes I had made that had disfigured the previous formatting, and for repaginating the book after I had managed to scramble the page numbers.

This is a big book, though not huge—not in a class with *Moby-Dick*, for example. It's been said that "a big book is forbidding, but at the same time it carries a challenge in its very pretension. It seems to say, 'This is a serious project and demands serious attention from serious minds.'"[9] I can hope.

---

9. "A Note on the Hamlet of Thomas Wolfe," in Robert Penn Warren, *Selected Essays* 170 (1958).

THE FEDERAL JUDICIARY

Introduction

Noting Weaknesses and Strengths, and
Proposing A New Research Agenda

I HAVE A MOTTO, borrowed from Tennyson's poem "Ulysses":

> Match'd with an aged wife, I mete and dole
> Unequal laws unto a savage race,
> That hoard, and sleep, and feed, and know not me.

The aged wife, in my appropriation of Tennyson, is not Charlene Posner, my wife and the mother of my children, but the federal judiciary, much in need of improvement—the principal subject of this book is what can be done to improve it. It needs *many* improvements, from top (the Supreme Court) to bottom (the immigration court and the social security disability office—in my experience the two weakest federal administrative agencies that by engaging in adjudication of matters of federal concern are realistically though not officially parts of the federal judiciary).

By way of introduction, interdisciplinary legal fields such as law and psychology and law and economics, and statistical studies of the legal system, have a major role to play—have already played a major role—in the design and evaluation of potential improvements in the system. Much of my full-time academic career (which began in the summer of 1968 and ended on December 4, 1981, when I was appointed to the court of appeals for the Seventh Circuit) was devoted to such studies, and as recently as 2013 I coauthored a book (*The Behavior of Federal Judges: A Theoretical and Empirical Study of Rational Choice*, with Lee Epstein and William M. Landes) that relied heavily on statistical and economic analysis. But I'm troubled by the fact that the faculties of the leading law schools are increasingly populated by refugees from the humanities and social sciences who have little or no legal experience. Beginning in the 1960s, economic analysis of law, and Critical Legal Studies, along with other "law and" fields, attracted people into law teaching who differed from the traditional or aspiring lawyer in being interested in theory rather than in legal practice. Critical Legal Studies faded, but economic analysis of law thrived, as did the application to law of other social sciences as well, including sociology and political science, history and philosophy, race and gender studies, statistics and finance.

These interdisciplinary invaders have come to dominate the faculties of the elite law schools and to influence a great many of the other law schools. The interdisciplinarians are valuable additions to law faculties, but they should not be allowed to displace faculty who bring to the teaching of and research into law a rich background of legal practice in lieu of expertise in a scholarly field or fields outside of law. And the interdisciplinarians would be well advised to obtain some practical legal experience. Although my primary interest when I was a law professor was in economic analysis of law, both before and after becoming a professor I had extensive practical legal experience as a Supreme Court law clerk, a Federal Trade Commission lawyer, an assistant to the Solicitor General, the general counsel of a Presidential task force on telecommunications policy, and (after I became a law professor) a legal consultant and advocate. That experience has served me in good stead as a judge. Those who teach lawyers law should as a rule have been lawyers themselves.

An additional feature of the recent evolution of academic legal research worth noting has been the increased emphasis placed on constitutional law—a distinctly marginal field when I was a law student (1959–1962). The increase was a result initially of the Supreme Court's move to the Left in the late 1950s and especially in the 1960s, the heyday of the "Warren Court." In the late 1970s, with most members of the Warren Court gone, a political surge from the Right, stimulated by the formation of the Federalist Society but also by a wide-ranging national conservative impulse that would propel Ronald Reagan into the White House at the beginning of the next decade, kept the judicial-political pot boiling—and it hasn't cooled yet. But as we'll see, particularly in the next chapter, the academic study of constitutional law seems not to have progressed very far; no consensus seems to have emerged from it, and its influence on the Supreme Court and the other federal courts is slight. Indeed at this writing the Court is weak and constitutional law in disarray—a major theme of Chapter 2.

The contrast between constitutional law, but also criminal law and civil and criminal procedure (all troubled fields of law), and the areas of law strongly influenced by economic analysis and business and financial expertise generally (such as bankruptcy law, securities law, patent and other intellectual-property law and banking law, contract law, and commercial / financial law generally) explains the imbalance that the reader will soon begin to notice between the discussion in the book of the "strengths" of the judiciary and of its "weaknesses." The former will receive far less attention than the latter simply because commercial / financial law is on a more even keel than constitutional law and civil and criminal procedure. It is those other fields that urgently need to be revitalized and so receive the bulk of my attention in this book and that as we'll see can't be revitalized by academic interdisciplinarians alone. Lawyerly experience remains vital to both understanding and reforming the weak areas of the law.

So, to repeat, the elite law schools, which incubate a disproportionate number of judges, law clerks (especially Supreme Court law clerks), and other legal practitioners, should be hiring not only and indeed not mainly "law and" professors (such as professors of law and economics, legal history, law and medicine, law and sociology, law and philosophy, law and psychology, law and literature, and foreign law) but also—and many more than at present—law professors who intend to base their research and teaching primarily on their practical experience rather than on the social or natural sciences, or on history or other humanities. A great deal of worthwhile legal research is grounded in practical experience rather than in the natural or social sciences; the biographies of judicial luminaries such as Holmes, Brandeis, Hand, and Friendly reveal the rich fruits of practical study that owes nothing to extralegal training or experience.

At the same time, and in undoubted tension with what I just said, too much law is taught in law school. A modern lawyer has to be familiar with first-rate literature in order to be able to write briefs or opinion drafts, or even just memos to superiors, that will be literate, eloquent, fully intelligible, and persuasive—for most good writers begin as good readers. The modern lawyer has also to be familiar with technology and with economics, because these subjects loom large in many cases, particularly big, important cases. Some law students will have mastered these subjects in college or in graduate programs preceding law school; most will not have and so will require remedial training in law school.

This is not to say that all law school faculty, let alone all law school graduates, must be learned in literature, technology, and economics, as well as in law. And there are other promising methods of legal research, besides the authorship of judicial biographies, that do not require mastery of fields outside law. One such method consists of interviews of federal judges, for which the interviewer needn't have any extralegal training; and let me describe two such studies in which I've participated, both of which identified weaknesses in the federal judiciary. And it is with weaknesses that I begin my analysis of the strengths and weaknesses of the federal judiciary because it is the weaknesses that predominate.

WEAKNESSES OF THE FEDERAL JUDICIARY

The first of the interview studies mentioned in the preceding paragraph was conducted by Professor Mitu Gulati and me and concerned the management by federal court of appeals judges of their tiny staffs.[1] The study was based on phone interviews of seventy-five such judges, selected more or less at random, and we discovered to our surprise that only three and a half judges (4.7 percent of our sample), of whom I am one, tell their law clerks to call them (the judges, that is) by their first name. The half is a judge who tells her clerks to call her by her first name—but only outside the courthouse, as she believes that her colleagues would be furious with her if they discovered she was allowing such liberties of address.[2]

What is odd about such judicial formality (and illustrative of the general problem of inefficient judicial management of staff that I'll be exploring in this Introduction) is that modern businesses tend to require *all* their professional employees to be on a first-name basis with each other, even to the point where a company's CEO is addressed by his or her underlings by first name.[3] This is done not out of warmth or affection or kindness but rather in order to create an egalitarian atmosphere believed to elicit greater loyalty, commitment, and effort from junior professional employees, who will feel that their views are val-

---

1. Mitu Gulati and Richard A. Posner, "The Management of Staff by Federal Court of Appeals Judges," 69 *Vanderbilt Law Review* 479 (2016).

2. Although my information about law clerks' being or not being on a first-name basis with their judges derives from my study with Gulati, it is not discussed in the article but rather in my book *Divergent Paths: The Academy and the Judiciary* 372–373 (2016).

3. See id. at 373; also Jodi Glickman, "What's in a (First) Name" (*Harvard Business Review,* Career Planning, November 1, 2011), https://hbr.org/2011/11/the-power-of-a-first-name.html.

ued by their bosses. Fifty years ago, probably twenty years ago, such informality would have been unthinkable by businesspeople as well as by judges.[4] The former have changed; why not the latter? The only reasons I can think of are that the judiciary is habituated to formality, resistant to change, backward-looking, even stodgy, as I'll be arguing throughout this book, though with a qualification in Chapter 3.

The insistence of virtually all federal judges that their law clerks call them "Judge" rather than addressing them by name is only one example of the poor management practices common in the federal judiciary.[5] Another example, almost equally widespread, is requiring law clerks to write bench memos. A bench memo is a written analysis of a case composed before the case is argued (or submitted without argument) to the appellate panel, or, if it's a district court case, composed before the case is tried. It is useful to judges to have their law clerks do research on a case before trial or oral argument and then brief them on the fruits of the research. But there is no reason for the briefing to be written up. That takes up a lot of a law clerk's time, as most law clerks try to impress their judge with their diligence and energy. Worse, should a clerk's bench memo become, as is common, the basis or even the first draft of a judicial opinion (because the case was assigned to the clerk's judge by the judge presiding at the argument of the appeal), the authenticity of the opinion will be diminished. For the author of the first draft of any document is likely to remain the strongest voice in it even if it's edited carefully; moreover, while some judges do edit carefully, others do not.

An important reform, though hopeless, would be to require the judges to write their own opinions. As it is, almost all federal judicial opinions are drafted by law clerks (or staff attorneys, who are law clerks hired by court staff rather than by individual judges and pooled rather than assigned to particular judges) in the first instance, and edited more or less heavily by the judge. When you read an opinion drafted by a judge rather than by a law clerk you connect with the judge's mind rather than with the mind of an inexperienced assistant, a novice. But nowadays there are few such opinions. This is partly attributable to the decline in the prestige of writing, as typified by the fact that nowadays U.S. Presidents and other prominent people usually delegate the writing of their speeches to anonymous staff—and generally are frank to admit it.

4. Not all; my law clerks, at my insistence, have at my invitation been calling me "Dick" since my first day on the job, thirty-five years ago.

5. Others are discussed in the *Vanderbilt* article cited in note 1 above, at 488–490.

My contention that judges should write their own opinions is challenged by David Lat in his article "How Should a Judge Be: In Defense of the Judge as CEO."[6] He quotes a statement by a federal court of appeals judge that "even the justices [of the Supreme Court] don't write their own opinions! Judges today aren't writers, but managers. I am the CEO of this chambers: I use my expert judgment and accumulated wisdom to make the big, important decisions. As the president who appointed me famously said, 'I am the decider.' The president, as commander in chief of the armed forces, decides whom we fight and when, but we don't expect him to drive a tank. Similarly, I decide how a case should come out . . . and my team executes." This is not reassuring. "I'm the decider" was the slogan of the second President Bush, who made a number of bad decisions. Nor does one get the impression that the "I am the decider" judge had ever been a CEO or studied how to be an effective one.

That judge's bluster implies that novels, short stories, plays, law review articles, treatises—all—should be written by novices; the writing is nothing. A big shot just makes "the big, important decisions." One imagines Dante saying to some fourteenth-century scrivener, "I've got this idea about a guy with my name who gets scared by a lion, goes down into Hell, then climbs up into Purgatory and finally enters Paradise where he's reunited with his old girlfriend, Beatrice. Go execute." I prefer what Judge Friendly said when asked why he wrote his own opinions: "They pay me to do that."[7] I write my own opinions too. Not many federal judges do.

The principal benefit of requiring that judges write their own opinions, which has been completely overlooked, is that it would winnow out the weakest judges. Imposing a requirement to do one's own writing would induce many of the weakest judges to resign or (if eligible) retire. Even more important, it would eliminate from the pool of prospective judges the ones who can't write or would find writing a painful challenge and probably an embarrassment; they would not seek a judicial appointment, and if offered one would decline it. The result both of the resignations and of the declinations would be to increase the average quality of the judiciary—markedly, I should think.

Another questionable judicial practice that is common is the judge's dis-

6. See 69 *Vanderbilt Law Review en Banc* 151 (April 6, 2016). In 2013, 95 percent of federal judges surveyed said their law clerks wrote at least the first drafts of their opinions. Todd C. Peppers, Micheal W. Giles, and Bridget Tainer-Parkins, "Surgeons or Scribes? The Role of United States Court of Appeals Clerks in 'Appellate Triage,'" 98 *Marquette Law Review* 313, 326 (2014) (tab. 2).

7. William Domnarski, "Judges Should Write Their Own Opinions," *New York Times*, May 31, 2012. www .nytimes.com/2012/06/01/opinion/judges-should-write-their-own-opinions.html [https://perma.cc/GL8L-RR29].

cussing a case, both before and after argument, with only one of his or her law clerks (invariably the one who wrote the bench memo for that case). As a result the judge gets less help from his clerks than he would if he discussed each case with all of them—and the clerks learn less about the cases heard by the court during their clerkship.

There is also a well-nigh universal insistence by federal judges on largely pointless, and potentially improper, secretiveness by law clerks: "what goes on in chambers stays in chambers" is the standard mantra. It is largely pointless because law clerks would rarely want to defame or embarrass their judge or fellow clerks by nasty gossip, and it is potentially improper because the clerks are government employees rather than the judges' personal servants and so have a duty to disclose any improprieties that they observe or hear in their job. Judges should remind their law clerks of that duty, rather than inducing them to violate it. I make clear to my law clerks that there is no code of *omertà* in my office (which I don't call my "chambers"—a pompous and antiquated term for a judge's office suite, derived from the Latin word for a room, *camera,* via the Old French variant, *chambre*). Oddly, despite being plural, the word "chambers" is used to denote a judge's or a lawyer's own office, as well as his or her suite of offices. Why does such antiquarian silliness persist? What does it tell us about our judges, and the legal profession more broadly?

Moving on, I don't understand why most of the federal courts of appeals, including mine, take a three-month summer recess from hearing cases, like the Supreme Court (except that in my court, at least, a few cases are heard during the summer—but very few). One reason given for the long break is that the judges have to devote time to the cases that were heard but not decided when the summer recess began. But that's a bad reason, because all throughout the nine-month period that follows one summer recess and precedes the next the judges are simultaneously hearing and issuing opinions or orders resolving appeals heard during the period. Why can't they do this in the summer, minus one month for a vacation? Except for judges in very busy district courts or in courts with many unfilled vacancies, a federal judgeship isn't so demanding a job that a judge, unless old and infirm, needs to take the entire summer off from work. And if he is old and infirm he should retire.

Still another problematic practice of many federal judges is requiring all their law clerks to start their clerkship on the same day, which means they don't overlap with the last term's clerks (who must leave when all their replacements are on board)—from whom they could learn a lot about the job were the start dates staggered. The only reason I've heard given for the practice is one judge's fear that the new clerks will be "poisoned" by contact with the old ones. That seems an absurd fear.

Compounding the folly of the same-day rule is the requirement imposed by many judges that the changeover day shall be the day after Labor Day—the day in which, in my court at any rate, hearings resume after the summer break. The consequences of this timing are that staff preparation for the early hearings in the fall term is done by inexperienced clerks and that there is a surge of opinion issuance at the very end of the summer by the judges whose law clerks rushed to complete their work before Labor Day lest they not be allowed to quit when their term ends do. That surge (I call it "Labor Day Bunching") places a lot of pressure on the other judges on a panel, faced as they are with a sudden rush of last-minute opinions that they need to decide whether to join or dissent from or suggest changes in.

I am also troubled by the practice of some federal judges of employing "career clerks" as well as the one-year clerks that continue to be the norm. Usually only one career clerk is employed (though sometimes two), often being made responsible for supervising the judge's one-year clerks. I don't think career clerks are a good idea, at least for appellate judges.[8] Though there are exceptions, lawyers who have decided to make a career of being a law clerk are generally less motivated and more bureaucratic in outlook than one-year clerks hired straight out of law school—and being more experienced are more likely to be deferred to by their judge, to the point sometimes of becoming the de facto judge. As for the career clerk who supervises the judge's two (more commonly three) one-year clerks, this distances the short-term clerks from the judge and may dampen their enthusiasm for the job. Hiring career clerks also diminishes the clerkship opportunities of law school graduates, depriving them of valuable experience should they become litigating lawyers. Suppose a judge has two career law clerks, both of whom remain employed by the judge for twenty years (this is not unheard of). The consequence is to reduce the number of one-year clerkships by forty and the number of one-year clerks of this judge by thirty-eight.

The way in which most federal appellate judges use their law clerks increases the average interval between when a case is argued (or submitted on the briefs,

---

8. District judges with heavy caseloads often find they need experienced clerks to deal with the procedural and managerial complexities of trial-level case processing, and so sensibly will hire one or more career clerks.

without oral argument) and when it is decided. Remember that the first draft of the opinion is almost certain to be done by a law clerk, who being inexperienced and wanting to make a good impression on his judge is likely to take his or her time in completing the draft. The judge will read it and may spend additional time editing it, which may result in more work for the law clerk (if the judge asks the law clerk to check up on the judge's revisions, which is common) and thus more delay.

Also worth noting is the widespread practice of judges of making "exploding offers" to prospective law clerks, forcing the interviewee to accept or reject the offer of a clerkship on the spot, thereby curtailing the applicant's employment opportunities. I consider that an evil practice, and likewise the practice of some law schools of instructing their students that they *must* accept the first offer of a clerkship they receive even if it isn't an exploding offer, lest turning down the offer offend the judge and turn him against the school. This practice also leads to gamesmanship by prospective law clerks—trying to arrange their interviews with the best judges first.

There are some interesting variants of the standard methods of judicial staff management. I'll mention one: requiring one's law clerks to write *very* elaborate bench memos, any of which can be rapidly converted to an opinion if the case is assigned to the law clerk's judge. I have to admit (despite my dislike of bench memos) that this variant has the advantage of minimizing the time between oral argument and decision. It is a corrective to the remarkable lags one sometimes observes between the argument of an appeal and the issuance of the opinion—in my court a year is not uncommon and we once had a case that took four years to be decided and was not decided until our circuit justice (Justice Stevens at the time) issued a mandamus to our court. Procrastination (about which more shortly) is a serious problem in many federal courts, both trial and appellate. Sometimes it is unavoidable, but sometimes it reflects a weak work ethic or a psychological compulsion to procrastinate.

I am surprised not that some judges are poor managers of their tiny staffs but that so many are.[9]

I want now to consider the tier of federal judicial management above the judge's management of his staff. Every federal court has a chief judge, who pre-

9. See further, on judicial use of law clerks, Todd C. Peppers, Michael W. Giles, and Bridget Tainer-Parkins, "Inside Judicial Chambers: How Federal District Court Judges Select and Use Their Law Clerks," 71 *Albany Law Review* 623 (2008), and Stephen L. Wasby, "Clerking for an Appellate Judge: A Close Look," 5 *Seton Hall Circuit Review* 19 (2008).

sides at meetings of the court's judges, presides at any trial or appeal in which he or she participates (that is, the chief judge is *ex officio* the court's senior active judge), and supervises the court's nonjudicial staff (in principle—usually most of the supervision is delegated to professional staff: in the case of a court of appeals the relevant staff consists primarily of the Circuit Executive, the Court Clerk, and the Senior Staff Attorney). The chief judge also represents the court at the semiannual meetings of the Judicial Conference of the United States, which is composed of the chief judges of each of the thirteen federal circuits plus one district judge from each circuit (so a total of twenty-six judges).

The chief judge of a court of appeals is simultaneously chief judge of the entire circuit, which includes district courts, bankruptcy courts, and other judicial elements of the circuit, though his or her supervision of courts other than the court of appeals usually is largely nominal. Each district court in the circuit also has a chief judge and, unsurprisingly, chief district judges do not take kindly to efforts by circuit chief judges to impose their views on the district court; consequently such efforts are rare. This hands-off policy may be a mistake. The chief circuit judge decides whether a senior judge, district or circuit, may continue to hear cases. These are important decisions, because senior judges,[10] whether district or appellate, not infrequently want to continue hearing cases even if (as they may not be aware) they are too old or infirm. In addition, some district judges impose idiosyncratic rules of their own invention on the lawyers and litigants before them, and unless the circuit chief judge is firm the court of appeals may be reluctant to invalidate the rules even when they violate federal procedural rules.

I was chief judge of the Seventh Circuit from 1993 to 2000, so participated in the semiannual meetings at the Supreme Court that I mentioned earlier. I didn't think they had much value; nor have I been impressed by the Judicial Conference's ambitious-seeming projects, such as its September 2015 Strategic Plan for the Federal Judiciary. They are basically just talk.

My most vivid recollection of the semiannual meetings is of Chief Justice Rehnquist's insistence on conformity to Robert's Rules of Order, which, I learned, require that any question intended for a speaker (for example, the chairman of a Judicial Conference committee giving a report to the judges attending the meeting) be directed not to the speaker but to the chairman of the session, namely Rehnquist—though, after rebuking the questioner for having violated Robert's Rules, he would refer the question to the speaker.

---

10. Senior judges are judges who though eligible to retire instead take "senior status," which allows them to continue judging but with a reduced caseload.

What nonsense.

My second most-vivid recollection of the semiannual meetings is of the breakfasts that Rehnquist had before the day's meeting with the circuit chief judges attending the conference. The breakfasts were catered by the Supreme Court cafeteria, whose food, I noted, was just as bad as it had been when I had eaten there, as infrequently as possible, many years previously, first as a Supreme Court law clerk and later as an assistant to the Solicitor General (*plus ça change, plus c'est la même chose*). Rehnquist's principal contribution to the breakfasts was to chain-smoke. Apparently none of the chief judges was a smoker; for Rehnquist's chain-smoking provoked a good deal of coughing, to which he, a genuine sourpuss, remained utterly indifferent.

Altogether a strange bird was Rehnquist; for remember that in the Senate trial of President Clinton following his impeachment by the House of Representatives, Rehnquist presided in the traditional judicial robe—but with four bright yellow braids on each sleeve, a fashion idea he'd picked up from Gilbert and Sullivan's comic opera *Iolanthe*.

Now why do I recite such trivia? Because I want readers to have some sense of what the federal judiciary looks like from within. I shall be presenting an unvarnished inside look throughout this book. I have started with management because the often lax management by the federal district and appellate judges of their tiny staffs is a danger sign mirrored by the frequently lackluster management at the circuit or court level. The principal duties of a chief judge— and there aren't many—would include, one would think, efforts to maintain collegiality among the judges of his or her court and to help slowpoke judges speed up their issuance of opinions. Without such prodding, some appellate judges will take a year or more from the oral argument, or submission, of the appeal to issue an opinion and some trial judges will let their cases drag on for years. Nevertheless many chief judges are ineffectual even at these modest management tasks, one reason being that the selection of a chief judge is based on seniority rather than aptitude. When the chief judgeship of a federal district or circuit court becomes vacant, normally because of the expiration of his or her seven-year term (or because he or she has reached the age of seventy— whichever comes first), the most senior judge who is not yet sixty-five years old becomes the chief judge unless refusing the appointment, and such refusals are infrequent even by judges who should know they're not able managers. The result is that some chief judges, though bound to be experienced judges, are not fit for a leadership position—a problem compounded by the long, though fortunately nonrenewable, term of a chief judge.

I mentioned slowpoke appellate judges—the judges who take an inordinate amount of time to issue an opinion assigned to them at the panel conference that follows oral argument. There appear to be only two feasible ways in which a chief judge can deal with such judges. One is to have two or three court meetings a year at which a list of each judge's backlog is passed around and the judge asked to explain it. (Other issues of common concern may also be discussed at such meetings.) I know that one chief judge asks that only backlogs of more than three months be disclosed at the conference, the thinking behind this rule being that three months is not an inordinate amount of time to issue an opinion. True, but not all judges take as long as three months, and it is good for the conference to be able to identify the speedy judges as well as the slow ones, and for that one needs the dates of all the oral arguments and submissions that have occurred but have not yet resulted in a published opinion.

The second method of dealing with slow-moving judges is for the chief judge to speak individually to each of them, seeking to understand why they are slow and to explore possibilities of getting them to speed up without undue sacrifice of quality. I don't think this method is commonly employed, or would be likely to be effective. To the extent that delay in the issuance of opinions by a court of appeals is considered a significant problem, the solutions, according to the leading analysis of the issue, would include such measures as increasing the number of circuits and thus reducing the average size of each (thus reducing travel time for the judges), increasing the total number of judges in order to reduce the average caseload per judge, reducing delay in filling vacancies, and depoliticizing judicial appointments by basing the appointments on the quality of prospective appointees.[11] But none of these measures is likely to be adopted in the foreseeable future.

A curious feature of the allocation of duties between a chief judge and the other judges of the court is that while normally the senior judge on an appellate panel who is in active service presides over the panel and allocates among its members the assignment of the opinions in the cases heard by the panel, the court's chief judge is, by statute (28 U.S.C. § 45 (b)), *ex officio* the presiding and therefore assigning judge on any panel on which he or she sits (ordinarily participation in panels is randomly assigned). Because chief judges are selected on

11. Robert K. Christensen and John Szmer, "Examining the Efficiency of the U.S. Court of Appeals: Pathologies and Prescriptions," 32 *International Review of Law and Economics* 30 (2012). However, a study I conducted some years ago found that increasing the number of judges of an appellate court *reduces* judicial quality. See Richard A. Posner, "Is the Ninth Circuit Too Large? A Statistical Study of Judicial Quality," 29 *Journal of Legal Studies* 711 (2000).

the basis not of capability but of the accident of being the senior judge in active service who has not already served as chief judge when the chief judgeship becomes vacant, there is little reason to suppose them abler than the judges whom they sit with on the appellate panels and therefore more fit to preside and make opinion assignments than whoever is the senior (hence most experienced) active judge on the panel. In one court at present five of the judges in active service have served longer on the court than the current chief judge and three of them are former chief judges of the court. But a note in favor of giving the presiding role at oral argument to the current chief judge when he or she is a member of the panel is that the judges with greater seniority may be rather long in the tooth and less fit to preside than the chief judge.

Because of how chief judges are selected (by seniority), and because they are merely *primus inter pares,* lacking well-defined authority (as far as I know, the statutory provision that I cited in the preceding paragraph is the only binding specification of their powers), they don't often assume a strong leadership role. A recent example is the response of a chief judge to a request by C-SPAN to be allowed to televise a pair of back-to-back en banc oral arguments. Rather than saying "yes" or "no" (presumably after consultation with the head of the court's technical staff and relevant personnel at C-SPAN), the chief judge asked the other active judges of the court for their views, and the predominant response was that they needed more than the two weeks between the request and the date scheduled for the en banc arguments to decide the issue. The chief judge yielded to that request, which had the effect of rejecting C-SPAN's request. The chief judge did this without consulting the court's senior-status judges who continue to hear cases, even though those judges would be affected by whatever policy the court adopted regarding the televising of oral argument. But that's a detail. The proper approach would in my view have been for the chief judge to rule that the issue was within a chief judge's administrative authority.

I recall that the issue had arisen in my court many years ago, and that there had been concern that if judges were seen on television they might be recognized and harassed (or worse) on the street by hostile viewers. In 1996, however, the Judicial Conference of the United States had authorized the televising of appellate proceedings,[12] and the Ninth Circuit, later followed by the Second Circuit, and, very recently, the Third Circuit, had accepted the offer. As far as I can determine, there has never been an adverse incident resulting from such

12. See U.S. Courts, *About Federal Courts,* "History of Cameras in Courts," www.uscourts.gov/about-fed eral-courts/cameras-courts/history-cameras-courts.

televising. Judge Alex Kozinski of the Ninth Circuit has assured me that in the twenty years that his court has been televising appellate proceedings there has never been an incident and in fact, he tells me, the public has grown closer to the court as a result of the opportunity to see the judges in action. I return to the issue of televising judicial proceedings later in this book.

But as I said, chief judges tend not (though there are exceptions) to lead their courts with a strong hand. For example, it never occurred to me when I was chief judge, and I am pretty sure it never occurred to my predecessors or successors either, to advise the members of my court on the management of their staffs, or to discuss delay in issuing opinions with the slowpokes. (I recall backing away from my proposal that out-of-town members of the court be allowed to participate in oral argument by video, when a couple of the judges objected.) I imagine that such discussion would have been resented and in any event ignored.

I did make efforts, with modest success, to improve collegiality among the judges of my court. And I tried, though without much success (and in truth without much effort), to persuade judges of my court who had not been trial judges to volunteer to conduct occasional trials in the district courts of the circuit. When I was appointed to the Seventh Circuit in 1981 not only had I not been a trial judge, I had not been a trial lawyer, although I had some experience with trials as a consultant and occasional expert witness. A senior Seventh Circuit judge told me shortly after I was appointed that in view of my inexperience I should volunteer to conduct trials in the district courts of the circuit. I took his advice and have been conducting trials, many of them jury trials, ever since, plus pretrial proceedings and settlement negotiations. Most of the trials have been civil trials but lately I've been conducting criminal trials. I think it tells us something about the current Supreme Court that only one of the Justices, Justice Sotomayor, is a former trial judge; and as far as I know none of the other Justices has ever volunteered to conduct a trial.

I don't think it's possible for an appellate judge to have a full understanding of the job without some experience as a trial judge, because the transcript of a trial, and other written records, simply do not convey the emotions, the challenges, of a trial, the role of witnesses and of pretrial discovery, the strengths and weaknesses of the jury system; it should therefore be *mandatory* for appellate judges to obtain trial experience if they had none before their appointment to the appeals court. Some federal appellate judges who had never been trial judges—I for example—have done this, but not many. Five of the judges of my court were not trial judges before becoming appellate judges, and of those I am the only one to have conducted both bench and jury, civil and criminal trials. One of the others conducted a few civil bench trials some years ago, but not recently. Of the ten judges of my court at this writing, four have never conducted jury trials and three of the four have conducted no bench trials either.

Enough about judicial staff management. Obviously it needs to be improved. Maybe someday the Federal Judicial Center will examine the subject, but I am not holding my breath. It is very difficult to change any established practice of our legal system. That is because our judges and lawyers tend to look backward rather than forward. Their motto might be "We've always done it this way."

Moving on: fruitful interviews of federal judges need not be limited to management issues. At this writing Professor Abbe Gluck of the Yale Law School, a formidable expert on statutory interpretation, and I have interviewed a number of federal court of appeals judges with respect to their beliefs and practices concerning statutory interpretation. The thirty-five judges whom we've interviewed can be divided into three groups. One consists of what I'll call curmudgeons—judges who are merciless regarding imperfections in the legislative process. Suppose for example that an ordinance states "no vehicles in the park." A visitor to the park falls into a pond, an onlooker calls 911, an ambulance roars into the park to rescue the flailing visitor—and a police officer gives the ambulance driver a ticket for violating the ordinance. Most judges would consider the officer to have erred, because surely the authors and enactors of the ordinance didn't intend "no vehicles" to mean "no vehicles, even emergency vehicles." (Likewise a sign in the park that says "keep off the grass" should not be interpreted to forbid park employees to cut the grass.) But the curmudgeons would say an ambulance *is,* as a matter of "plain meaning" (a favorite judicial phrase—one of many common judicial phrases that I avoid), a vehicle, and therefore the ordinance applies to ambulances, and though the result is silly it was the writers and issuers of the ordinance who screwed up and it is for them to clean up the mess they made.

What the example actually shows is the importance of context in interpreting statutes (or ordinances, regulations, or other documents). Obviously text is an important clue to the meaning of a written communication. But the full meaning is to be inferred from text *and* context. The context of the "no vehicles in the park" ordinance is an intention to exclude ordinary traffic from the park because of crowding, noise, or other disamenities. Ambulances, which rarely enter parks, are not part of *that* context; the context applicable to them is the need to provide for the rescue of people in danger. The problem with plain meaning is that it excludes context, leading in the ambulance case to the absurd interpretation by the curmudgeons. "Plain meaning" is the first of numerous legal clichés that I'll be whacking in this book.

Context is not a novel recourse for judges asked to interpret a statute or a regulation. We mustn't forget the medieval law regarding "bloodletting" in the streets of the Italian city of Bologna—the law famously "deconstructed" in William Blackstone's *Commentaries on the Laws of England*, which stated that "whoever drew blood in the streets should be punished with the utmost severity." Blackstone asked whether the law should have been interpreted to make punishable a surgeon "who opened the vein of a person that fell down in the street with a fit." He thought not, saying that "the fairest and most rational method to interpret the will of the legislator, is by exploring his intentions at the time when the law was made, by signs the most natural and probable. And these signs are either the words, the context, the subject matter, the effects and consequence, or *the spirit and reason of the law*. . . . As to the effects and consequence, the rule is, where words bear either none, or a very absurd signification, if literally understood, *we must a little deviate from the received sense of them*."[13] The law didn't mention surgeons, but Blackstone thought it obvious that the legislators, who must have known something about surgeons, had not intended the law to apply to them. And so it is with ambulances in parks that prohibit vehicles.

Judges whom Professor Gluck and I interviewed who had had firsthand experience with the enactment of legislation, whether as legislators themselves, members of legislative staffs, or members of agencies, such as the Office of Legal Counsel in the Department of Justice, that work with legislatures, were confident of their ability to interpret statutes. For example, they felt they knew which kinds of legislative history provide reliable clues to the legislators' intentions and which not. These judges tend to be eclectic in their use of the various aids (many however spurious and thus to be avoided) to statutory interpretation. There is an argument for requiring federal judges to spend some time learning their way around Congress and speaking to the members and to the legislative staff; but there is no such requirement and probably never will be.

The remaining judges whom we interviewed—neither literalists nor legislative experts—also tend to be eclectic, because they lack any firm ground to stand on. They rely on such dubious interpretive aids as dictionaries, all types of legislative history, the "canons of construction" (a pompous term for interpretive principles both linguistic and policy, the latter illustrated by the ever-

13. William Blackstone, *Commentaries on the Laws of England*, vol. 2, p. 60 (1765) (emphases added).

popular—though actually rarely invoked—"rule of lenity" in criminal cases), precedents, literal meanings of statutory terms ("plain meaning" again), implicit statutory purpose, and the meaning of related statutes. But within this group of eclectic judges there are discernible differences along a spectrum that runs from highly deferential judges who believe their duty is to discern concrete legislative intent with reference to the particular issue of interpretation that the court is confronted with and who therefore can be described as "textualist" or "originalist" judges, to "pragmatists," "purposivists," and "contextualists" at the other extreme, who (especially the pragmatists) try to give the statute they're interpreting a meaning that will have socially beneficial effects (pragmatic judging is simply judging based on the likely consequences of alternative outcomes). Another way to understand the eclectic spectrum, therefore, is as stretching from passive to active, or from rule-bound to creative (that is, to lawmaking).

Some eclectic judges rely heavily on common sense (I am one of them), and a few (again including me) are skeptical about statutory "interpretation" altogether, noting that issues that arise in litigation relating to the meaning or application of statutes often had not been foreseen by the enacting legislature. In such cases there is no intended legislative meaning to be recovered, thus compelling the judges to play a lawmaking role—to become in effect ad hoc interstitial legislators. As Holmes famously remarked, "I recognize without hesitation that judges do and must legislate, but they can do so only interstitially; they are confined from molar to molecular motions."[14] Few judges would have the courage to say that today. Holmes's *aperçu* would have been more accurate, however, had he said, ". . . judges do and must make law. . . , but . . . only interstitially. . . ." For to say that judges "legislate," while correct in a sense, obscures the very considerable differences between legislatures and courts.

A problem that needs to be considered in evaluating the results of interviewing judges about their methods of statutory interpretation is the difference between what one does and what one says. I have no doubt that what the judges told us in the interview study of judicial staff management that I did with Professor Gulati was candid; I know enough judges, and former law clerks of judges (some of whom clerked for me after their clerkships for other judges), to be confident that the judges were leveling with us. But regarding my study with Professor Gluck of judges' approaches to statutory interpretation, while I'm confident that they were frank with us I can't be confident that what they said

---

14. *Southern Pacific Co. v. Jensen*, 244 U.S. 205, 221 (1917). See Thomas C. Grey, "Molecular Motions: The Holmesian Judge in Theory and Practice," 37 *William & Mary Law Review* 19, 33 (1995).

coincided with what they do. I am not accusing them of duplicity. It is a matter of the influence of priors. Maybe when a judge scanning the briefs in a case or discussing the case with a law clerk first encounters the issue of statutory interpretation that the case presents, he or she has an unconscious reaction to how the issue should be resolved—a *Gestalt* reaction, which means a reaction to a whole rather than to its components (which the judge has not studied). But it is then the law clerk who supplies the formal apparatus of text and canons and so forth for demonstrating in a judicial opinion the compliance of the judge's instinctual reaction with the "law" of statutory interpretation—a "law" that may however just be window dressing.

A closely related concern in considering the judicial as distinct from the staff role in statutory cases is the tendency of some judges to equate staff with self. A judge who says that he consults legislative history, or a treatise on canons of statutory construction, as an aid to deciding a statutory case may actually mean that he expects his law clerks to do the research and analysis and incorporate the results in a bench memo or opinion draft. The result is likely to be to merge the law clerk's research with the judge's *Gestalt* reaction.

Enough for the time being about statutory interpretation, which I discuss elsewhere in this book as well, with constitutional as distinct from statutory interpretation a major topic in Chapter 2.

A final point to be noted about judicial-interview research is the utility of having a judge on the interview team. There is a certain clubbiness among federal judges, which tends to make them more comfortable if an interviewer is also a federal judge.

As should be obvious by now, I am critical of many features of the American legal system, with emphasis on characteristic practices and attitudes of the judiciary, particularly (in this book exclusively) the federal judiciary. I am a federal judge who was never a state judge or practiced law in a state court, and I have limited familiarity with the state courts of today as distinct from those of yore in their glory days, such as the Supreme Judicial Court of Massachusetts (the court of Lemuel Shaw, Horace Gray, Oliver Wendell Holmes, Jr., and Benjamin Kaplan), the New York Court of Appeals (Benjamin Cardozo), and the supreme courts of California (Roger Traynor), New Jersey (Arthur T. Vanderbilt), and Oregon (Hans Linde).[15] I confine my discussion in this book to to-

---

15. So little regarded are most state supreme courts today that there is no Google entry for "great state supreme court justices" or similar phrases. If one Googles "great state supreme court justices" all one gets are lists of U.S. Supreme Court Justices, many of whom do not measure up to the greatest state supreme court justices. If I were better versed in the state judiciaries, my list of great state court judges would be much longer.

day's federal courts and to the persons and institutions on which those courts depend, which include the lawyers who practice in them, the law schools, the federal administrative agencies, and the President and Senate.

Unfortunately many of the weaknesses of the federal judiciary that I've mentioned and will be elaborating in this book have no chance of being remedied in the near or for that matter the distant future. Consider the appointment of federal judges by politicians—the President who nominates and the Senators who confirm—for whom, we now know, quality is almost always secondary to political advantage. One can't rightly criticize politicians for being politically motivated in regard to the appointment of officials, but such motivations make it inevitable that most Justices will lean either liberal or conservative in their judging, depending on whether the President who appointed them was liberal or conservative. True, if the Senate is in the hands of a different political party from the President's party this may force compromise that creates room for a politically neutral appointment, but examples of this are rare. *All* the current Justices and many lower-court federal judges display in many of their judicial opinions a distinct political cast—which makes the federal judiciary and especially the Supreme Court not so different from what many judges refer to as the "political branches" of the federal government, namely the President (indeed the entire executive branch) and the Congress. So one hears Justices described as "politicians in robes," and while this is an exaggeration it has a kernel of truth. Realistically the federal judiciary is a political branch of government along with the President and Congress, albeit one that employs dramatically different procedures. The legal profession should either stop using the term "political branches" or acknowledge that there are not two but three federal political branches, one of which is the federal judiciary.

Judges including Supreme Court Justices don't *have* to be appointed by politicians. For consider England, from which our legal system descended. The judges, including the Justices of the recently created Supreme Court of the United Kingdom, are appointed not by the Prime Minister or the Chancellor of the Exchequer or the Parliament but instead by a commission composed of judges and senior government legal officials. Our system of appointing federal judges and Justices is not going to give way to the British system, or to appointment by popular election, which is common in state judicial systems and is of course the method used for choosing Presidents and the members of Congress. Another alternative to our current system of judicial appointments would be, as in the German judiciary, to base all federal judicial appointments on law school performance, qualifying exams, and other objective criteria of merit.

But there are serious problems with that approach too: namely that being a good student or a successful practitioner is often not predictive of judicial ability or at least of outstanding judicial ability and that performance-based promotions often are based not on superior competence but on successful maneuvering within a bureaucratic promotion system.

Another deeply rooted weakness of the federal judiciary, this one readily curable though unlikely ever to be cured, is the lack of salary uniformity among Article III judges—there's no reason that all such judges aren't paid the same base salary, though judges who live in parts of the country in which the cost of living is abnormally high, such as New York and San Francisco, should receive a cost of living supplement. They don't and doubtless won't.

Still another weakness is the dearth of *relevant* diversity in the backgrounds of federal judges, by which I mean diversity consisting of a variety of career experiences, such as having been a trial lawyer or even a state trial judge, working in a law office whether as an advisor, litigator, or negotiator, obtaining and utilizing technical and other background knowledge, and having a rich educational background. I say "relevant" diversity because I don't think that racial or sexual diversity has much significance for federal judges. I've known many federal judges and haven't noticed systematic differences between black and white, or male and female, or native and immigrant. It might be different if the appointing authorities gave positive weight to a candidate's having overcome an impoverished childhood or serious physical or mental illness or "gone straight" after an early career in crime, but I believe that such factors rarely are given positive weight.

Here's an esoteric but important source of weakness of the federal judiciary. A federal statute—28 U.S.C. § 44(c)—states that "in each circuit (other than the Federal judicial circuit) there shall be at least one circuit judge in regular active service appointed from the residents of each state in that circuit."[16] The Seventh Circuit—my court—complies: there is one circuit judge in regular active service from Wisconsin, two from Indiana (plus two Indiana judges who are senior but still hear cases), and the rest from Illinois (six—making a total of eleven judges on the court of appeals), those being the states that comprise the circuit. Though not required by the statute, it is customary for the President to appoint as successor to a circuit judge who has quit, retired, or died, a resident of the same state as the judge whom he or she is replacing. Neither the statute

16. See www.law.cornell.edu/uscode/text/28/44.

nor the custom makes good sense. With random assignment to appellate panels, which is the custom, and with most appeals in my circuit coming from the
federal district courts in Illinois, our one Wisconsin judge and our four Indiana judges hear mainly cases from Illinois, cases to which familiarity with Wisconsin or Indiana law rarely has any relevance.

The Wisconsin and Indiana judges in question happen to be excellent judges,
but not because they are residents of the least populated states in the circuit.
The population of Illinois—about 13 million—slightly exceeds the population
of Indiana (6.5 million) and Wisconsin (5.7 million) combined. Illinois has the
major universities in the three-state area and the principal law firms. There are
forty-five federal district judges in Illinois, compared to nineteen in Indiana
and only eight in Wisconsin. These differences reflect the much greater federal
load in Illinois.

Should the non-Illinois judges resign or retire they would *have* to be replaced by Hoosiers (that is, Indianans) and a Wisconsinite; the statute I cited
requires that. A current vacancy in my court is the result of a Hoosier member
of the court having resigned last year. Only custom, not law, requires the President to nominate another Hoosier to replace him, since there is already a Hoosier on our court (in fact four Hoosiers). The custom makes no sense, and so I
hope the President will ignore it.

Other weaknesses of the federal judiciary worth noting here (many others
will be noted later in the book) are judges' lack of candor; their heavy reliance
on open-ended multifactor tests to decide complex cases; the canons of statutory construction; the verbosity of so many judicial opinions; the overuse of
jargon; the pretense of apolitical judicial objectivity; the Supreme Court's deciding to maintain a very light caseload yet at the same time failing inexplica-
bly to allow sufficient oral-argument time in every case that the Court agrees to
hear; and the fact that the Court's term is too short because of the long summer
recess, which results in an awkward bunching of opinions in late June. There is
also the judicial staff mismanagement that I discussed earlier in this chapter,
the weak overall management of the federal judiciary (not just by the Judicial
Conference of the United States but also by the Chief Justice), and the obsessive use by judges and their law clerks of citation manuals, notably the grossly
overblown *Bluebook*.

But I need to qualify my criticism of judges' lack of candor. The great philosopher Immanuel Kant thought lying never excusable, but did not think
there was a moral duty always to speak one's mind. He was right; there are oc-

casions on which the benefits of candor are outweighed by its costs. One of those occasions was *Brown v. Board of Education*, the Supreme Court decision that held racial segregation in public schools to be a denial of the equal protection of the laws and therefore unconstitutional. The cause of racial segregation was racism, and the reason the Court voted unanimously to invalidate it was the Justices' hostility to racism. But the Court's opinion does not say that, as to do so would have inflamed the South even more than the opinion did; instead the opinion makes it seem as if by accident the South simply had failed to realize the adverse psychological effects of public school segregation on black children. Readers weren't fooled; but the Court was prudent, in the fevered sociopolitical climate of the 1950s, to avoid denouncing racism.

So far as legal jargon and judicial verbosity are concerned, the immediate villains are for the most part the law clerks, as most judges (and Justices) require their law clerks to write the initial opinion draft, which the judge then edits (sometimes perfunctorily). The judges are ultimately responsible for what their law clerks do or don't do, but the writing role of the clerks is and will continue to be large. Too large, in my opinion. I write and edit my own opinions, though I rely on my law clerks to correct errors and make suggestions for improvements both substantive and rhetorical. But I'm not typical; I've been writing steadily since my parents bought me my first typewriter, when I was thirteen years old—sixty-five years ago!

Recognizing rather than applauding the dominant writing role played by most law clerks today, Judge John Kane, a very able, independent-minded, and experienced district judge in Denver, requires his clerks upon arrival to read George Orwell's famous 1946 essay "Politics and the English Language" (available online as well as in countless books). That strikes me as an excellent suggestion—as I greatly admire Orwell's writing style—and a suggestion I intend to emulate. Let me in imitation of Judge Kane try to convey the flavor of Orwell's prose, so superior to that of our legal profession, with quotations from "Politics and the English Language" and a minimum of comment from me.

> Modern English, especially written English, is full of bad habits which spread by imitation and which can be avoided if one is willing to take the necessary trouble. If one gets rid of these habits one can think more clearly, and to think clearly is a necessary first step toward political [and here I—Posner—would add legal] regeneration: so that the fight against bad English is not frivolous and is not the exclusive concern of professional writers.

Orwell then quotes five very badly written passages appearing in books, essays, or in one instance a letter to a newspaper; a quotation from that letter will give the flavor of the quotations:

> The British lion's roar at present is like that of Bottom in Shakespeare's *A Midsummer Night's Dream*—as gentle as any sucking dove. A virile new Britain cannot continue indefinitely to be traduced in the eyes or rather ears, of the world by the effete languors of Langham Place, brazenly masquerading as "standard English." When the Voice of Britain is heard at nine o'clock, better far and infinitely less ludicrous to hear aitches honestly dropped than the present priggish, inflated, inhibited, schoolma'amish arch braying of blameless bashful mewing maidens!

Orwell remarks that "two qualities are common to all" five passages that he quotes and criticizes:

> The first is staleness of imagery; the other is lack of precision. The writer either has a meaning and cannot express it, or he inadvertently says something else, or he is almost indifferent as to whether his words mean anything or not. This mixture of vagueness and sheer incompetence is the most marked characteristic of modern English prose. . . . As soon as certain topics are raised, the concrete melts into the abstract and no one seems able to think of turns of speech that are not hackneyed: prose consists less and less of *words* chosen for the sake of their meaning, and more and more of *phrases* tacked together like the sections of a prefabricated hen-house.

Among the different verbal vices that Orwell names and denounces one stands out as particularly relevant to legal, including judicial, writing: "Pretentious Diction," "used," he explains, "to dress up a simple statement."

To illustrate how badly English has deteriorated, Orwell translates "a passage of good English into modern English of the worst sort." A famous verse from Ecclesiastes in the King James Version of the Bible is "I returned and saw under the sun, that the race is not to the swift, nor the battle to the strong, neither yet bread to the wise, nor yet riches to men of understanding, nor yet favour to men of skill; but time and chance happeneth to them all." Orwell's translation into modern English reads: "Objective considerations of contemporary phenomena compel the conclusion that success or failure in competitive activities exhibits no tendency to be commensurate with innate capacity, but that a considerable element of the unpredictable must invariably be taken into account." Orwell points out that

> the whole tendency of modern prose is away from concreteness. Now analyze these two sentences a little more closely. The first contains forty-nine words but only sixty syllables, and all its words are those of everyday life. The second contains thirty-eight words of ninety syllables: eighteen of those words are from Latin roots, and one from Greek. The first sentence contains six vivid images, and only one phrase ("time and chance") that could be called vague [I don't agree that it's vague]. The second contains not a single fresh, arresting phrase, and in spite of its ninety syllables it gives only a shortened version of the meaning contained in the first. Yet without a doubt it is the second kind of sentence that is gaining ground in modern English.

Orwell distills his advice for good writing into six rules:

1. Never use a metaphor, simile, or other figure of speech which you are used to seeing in print.
2. Never use a long word where a short one will do.
3. If it is possible to cut a word out, always cut it out.
4. Never use the passive where you can use the active.
5. Never use a foreign phrase, a scientific word, or a jargon word if you can think of an everyday English equivalent.
6. Break any of these rules sooner than say anything outright barbarous.

All good advice! But what of Orwell's own writing? In my opinion he wrote better than any later writer (he died in 1950) of English that I can think of except Saul Bellow at his best (not that he wrote better than Orwell—merely that at his best he wrote as well).

Here is the concluding paragraph of "Politics and the English Language": a model of good writing for judges and lawyers and law clerks to imitate:

> I have not here been considering the literary use of language, but merely language as an instrument for expressing and not for concealing or preventing thought. Stuart Chase and others have come near to claiming

that all abstract words are meaningless, and have used this as a pretext for advocating a kind of political quietism. Since you don't know what Fascism is, how can you struggle against Fascism? One need not swallow such absurdities as this, but one ought to recognise that the present political chaos is connected with the decay of language, and that one can probably bring about some improvement by starting at the verbal end. If you simplify your English, you are freed from the worst follies of orthodoxy. You cannot speak any of the necessary dialects, and when you make a stupid remark its stupidity will be obvious, even to yourself. Political language—and with variations this is true of all political parties, from Conservatives to Anarchists—is designed to make lies sound truthful and murder respectable, and to give an appearance of solidity to pure wind. One cannot change this all in a moment, but one can at least change one's own habits, and from time to time one can even, if one jeers loudly enough, send some worn-out and useless phrase—some *jackboot, Achilles' heel, hotbed, melting pot, acid test, veritable inferno,* or other lump of verbal refuse—into the dustbin where it belongs.

I have given the reader only a taste of Orwell's writing; my excerpts amount to only one-fifth of his essay. You must read the rest, and you must read a fair sample of the hundreds of his writings reprinted in the *Collected Essays, Journalism and Letters of George Orwell,*[17] if you seek a marked improvement in your own writing.

Among other weaknesses of the federal judiciary I would include the judicial administration of federal criminal law, noting among many other deficiencies (some discussed in the Epilogue to this book) the substitution of supervised release for parole, the conditions of supervised release (postrelease conditions imposed at the time not of release but of sentencing, often many years earlier),[18] the inadequacy of medical care in many state prisons, the brutality with which prison inmates are frequently treated by guards,[19] the excessive length of many prison sentences, and the insufficient use of alternative forms of punishment to imprisonment, such as fines and probation.

The conduct of both civil and criminal trials also leaves much to be desired,

17. Sonia Orwell and Ian Angus eds. (1968).

18. I discussed supervised release and its conditions at some length in *Divergent Paths,* note 2 above, at 197–221.

19. For a horrendous recent example, see Eli Hager and Alyxia Santo, "On Private Prisoner Vans, Long Road of Neglect: Dangers in a Business Largely Overlooked by Regulators," *New York Times,* July 7, 2016, p. A1.

as also discussed in later chapters. There are unresolved issues regarding demeanor cues (such as body language, volume and rapidity of speaking, relaxed or nervous affect) as a way of determining the truthfulness or falsity of a witness's testimony. There is uncertainty regarding the propriety of Internet research, and whether to allow jurors to ask questions. There is lawyer imbalance, especially in criminal cases, where the prosecution usually outguns and often even outnumbers the defense (there is usually just one defense lawyer but often there are two prosecutors and sometimes there is *no* defense lawyer—the defendant is pro se).

These problems illustrate the federal judiciary's overinvestment in the traditional Anglo-American adversary system versus the Continental European inquisitorial system, which we should consider borrowing from though not adopting. Our vaunted adversary system has a variety of problems—problems with jury instructions, with the utilization or more commonly the failure to utilize Federal Rule of Evidence 706 (authorizing the appointment of neutral expert witnesses by the judge, but little used because it doesn't comport with our adversarial system, in which all witnesses are selected by the parties to the litigation or the parties' lawyers), with the mishandling of class actions and exaggerated concern with the hearsay rule—all issues that I take up later in this book along with the controversy over independent judicial research, such as Internet searches for evidence to be used in a trial or an appeal—searches criticized as inconsistent with the traditional Anglo-American adversary system, in which the submission of evidence is the prerogative of the lawyers.

In an inquisitorial judicial system, such as that of Germany, the judge is all-powerful. He or she chooses the witnesses and questions them; the lawyers' role in litigation is peripheral. German judges are appointed at younger ages than our judges, on the basis of more elaborate screening than our new judges receive, with emphasis on academic performance and apprenticeship, and they rise from tier to tier of the judiciary as they become more deft and experienced. My friend Peter Heidenberger, who was a lawyer in Germany before immigrating to the United States, reports that it took him one year of law school to be able to take the District of Columbia bar exam, compared to six years in Germany including two day-long oral exams; unsurprisingly he found American judges to be much more down-to-earth than the abstract-thinking German judges.

It is impossible to envisage our adopting the German system, which largely though not entirely banishes politics from the appointment and promotion process and by appointing most judges at a young age diminishes the role and stature of trial lawyers—who constitute a large and influential slice of our professional class and therefore wield significant political power.[20] A narrower alternative to our present system would be to base appointment and promotion of judges on objective criteria of professional success as lawyers or law professors, but such a system would doubtless be rejected as insufficiently democratic, or rather (but this would not be admitted) insufficiently political.

Amplifying my earlier reference to jargon, I note that the federal judiciary is heavily overinvested in a specialized but mostly confusing and useless legal vocabulary, some of it still in Latin, which in America as in most of the world is an almost totally dead language. Appellate briefs and judicial opinions alike fairly bristle with terms that, even when they are in English rather than Latin, have no clear meaning, such as "actual innocence," "arbitrary and capricious," "abuse of discretion" [insulting to district judges and confuses error correction with mere disagreement], "rational basis" [can't be taken seriously, given that the antithesis is irrational—an inappropriate synonym for a mistake or disagreement], "deliberate indifference," "clear and convincing" [evidence], "suspect class," "narrow tailoring," "extraordinary circumstances." (I discuss these and other monstrosities in Chapter 3; each of them is what Polonius in *Hamlet* would have called "an ill phrase, a vile phrase.") Holmes's aphorism "To rest upon a formula is a slumber that, prolonged, means death"[21] has been forgotten. There is even *comical* linguistic insensitivity, illustrated by "*Roe* and its progeny." (What *are* the progeny of abortions?)

And there is the war, a century or more old, between formalism and realism, that continues to divide the judiciary. The distinction is between real or pretended interpretation and common sense, and also between looking backward (what Nietzsche sarcastically called "let the dead bury the living") and looking forward. I go so far as to suggest that there is room for executive defiance of judicial decisions. Though it is small, there are notable examples—such as Lincoln's defiance of Chief Justice Taney's grant of habeas corpus to a southern sympathizer at the outset of the Civil War—that I applaud.

I shall have much to say throughout this book, especially in the early chap-

20. For a comprehensive comparison of German and American judicial appointment processes, see Fiona O'Connell and Ray McCaffrey, "Judicial Appointments in Germany and the United States," Northern Ireland Assembly Research and Information and Service Research Paper, March 2012, www.niassembly.gov .uk/globalassets/Documents/raISe/Publications/2012/justice/6012.pdf.

21. See http://quotes.yourdictionary.com/author/quotes/138102. Oliver Wendell Holmes, Jr., "Ideals and Doubts," 10 *Illinois Law Review* 3 (1915).

ters, about the legal profession's current fawning regard for formalism parading under such names as "textualism" and "originalism." The meanings of these two words are similar but not identical. As most commonly used, textualism means deciding constitutional cases in strict conformity to the text of the applicable constitutional provision, while originalism allows consideration of contextual factors that might have influenced the understanding of the constitutional provision at the time of its enactment or ratification. "Textualism" is thus a synonym for the term more commonly used in legal interpretation to denote strict adherence to the literal meaning of a text—"plain meaning."

Whether ideological, heartfelt, or feigned, formalism is a compounding sin because it not only slights the real-life concerns of litigants by burying its head in ancient doctrine and conceals the actual motives and thinking of judges, but also understands law to be about words rather than about action or conduct and to be a gift from the past rather than a challenge in the present and preparation for the future. It refuses to engage realistically with twenty-first century challenges. It *might* acknowledge that a judge or a Justice whose gaze was fixed over his hip rather than over his backside would be en route to improving the legal system, but unfortunately examples of successful advances sideways into the future are rare. If we get wrong how twenty-first century judges and Justices *should* think, the current celebration of formalism in the wake of Justice Scalia's demise (see Chapter 2) will leave a bitter taste.

Formalist judges tend to be politically conservative, realist judges politically liberal, but there are exceptions. One that I'll discuss in Chapter 5 is my colleague David Hamilton, a liberal democrat yet committed to a formalist conception of the adversary system that excludes independent judicial research—a position that led Judge Hamilton to urge (fortunately in dissent) denial of a very ill inmate's right to necessary medical treatment arbitrarily withheld by prison medical staff. The formalist often is a curmudgeon (though Judge Hamilton is not), opposed to any change in legal practices brought about by judges and largely indifferent to the social and human consequences of adherence to outmoded doctrines and practices.

What drives judges into these different camps? Politics, sometimes flavored with religious belief or disbelief; sensitivity or insensitivity to human suffering; leisure preference (refusal to innovate is a time-saver); shyness, timidity, deference, insecurity, ambition, temperament, intellect, culture, patience or impatience, energy, self-importance; and other "priors" (such as attitudes, inclinations, and the like that a person brings to an issue or problem before seeking evidence bearing on it and that may guide the person's actions without regard to evidence). Deference deserves particular emphasis. Judges respectful of authority, especially the authority of their judicial colleagues, legislative bodies, and higher courts, may suppress many of their personal reactions to the cases they're asked to rule on.

In general one expects judges, like most people, to be "utility maximizers," that is, to take positions that increase their overall welfare, and because the utility function differs across persons even in the same line of work one can't assume uniformity among judges even of the same court.[22]

Another problem of the federal judiciary, this one examined at length in my recent book *Divergent Paths: The Academy and the Judiciary* but deserving some consideration in this book as well, is that legal education is lagging behind the needs of a modern judiciary. I don't mean because it's failing to iron out the differences in judges' priors that I noted in the preceding paragraph. Legal education couldn't do that. What it can and should do is provide more clinical, as distinct from casebook or treatise, teaching of procedure and evidence; have faculty take over management of law reviews and moot courts; abandon the *Bluebook;* and recognize the costly superfluity of casebooks in this era of online research, where in lieu of a more than $200 casebook a teacher could simply give the students a list of the opinions the teacher wanted them to read which they could then read online (they also could read online the briefs in the cases, which Westlaw cites at the end of each opinion), plus a list of comments or questions to help them get the most out of reading the opinions. This is an obvious, cheap, simple reform that is *long* overdue, but of course will be resisted by the authors of the expensive casebooks (and treatises), and by the force of inertia, which is a powerful force in the legal system, and by lawyers' love of the printed word; for there was no Internet when the Code of Justinian, or even the U.S. Constitution, was compiled.

Bad writing is a related bane of the judiciary, the literary culture in America being either dead already, or rapidly dying from the rapid rise in texting and other forms of electronic transmission that paralyze the brains of the young. Good writing seems rarely to be taught in schools or colleges any longer, or if it is, to make an impression on the youthful brain. Most Americans write badly

---

22. See, for example, my article "What Do Judges and Justices Maximize? (The Same Thing Everybody Else Does)," 3 *Supreme Court Economic Review* 1 (1994); my book *Economic Analysis of Law* § 20.6 (What Do Judges Maximize?) (9th ed. 2014); and an excellent recent article (as yet unpublished) by Alain Marciano, Alessandro Melcarne, and Giovanni B. Ramello, "Justice without Romance: The History of the Economic Analyses of Judges' Behavior."

and many judges don't like to write, let alone try to improve their writing—they have law clerks to do their writing. The President uses ghostwriters—why not the judges? Forget eloquence in high places; that ended with Lincoln and Churchill, though in fairness I must acknowledge that even today there are some good academic writers, good brief writers, and even some good judicial writers (names of federal court of appeals judges, not in my court, who come immediately to mind are Ambro, Katzmann, Kozinski, O'Scannlain, Sutton, and Wilkinson—and that is a very partial list). There are even some quite accomplished ghostwriters (law clerks). Not many though. Many law clerks learned bad writing in law school, where they imbibed the law's repulsive jargon, and they cling to it as to flotsam and jetsam in a rough sea, whence it seeps into judicial opinions.

Above all—my most fundamental criticism, the main theme of this book—is that our legal culture is backward-looking, constitutional originalism being a prime example. How can eighteenth-century thinkers be thought to have foreseen twenty-first century conditions? Of course they did not. Chapter 2 addresses this important issue at length.

I have no respect for a number of entrenched legal doctrines (not limited to textualism and originalism). I consider *Chevron*[23] (the Supreme Court's decision commanding appellate courts to bestow deference on interpretations by federal administrative agencies of the statutes they administer) profoundly misconceived, and likewise standards of appellate review in general (thus not limited to the *Chevron* doctrine), methods of constitutional and statutory interpretation, and much else besides. For the most part what a judge does or should do is to try to decide a case in a way that will comport with common sense and the fundamental ethical norms of society and have overall good consequences consistent with governing legislative (including constitutional) rules and with recognition of the reliance often placed by the legal community and its clientele on settled (even if imperfect) judicial decisions or other judge-made rules and results. The implication, which I do not shrink from despite its unconventionality, is that the judicial role is to a considerable extent legislative even outside the domain of the common law, an area of explicit and accepted judicial creation of legal rules, principles, and standards.

Some readers will recognize that I am invoking the creed of legal realism (equivalently of legal pragmatism), the creed embraced and refined by Holmes,

---

23. *Chevron U.S.A. Inc. v. Natural Resources Defense Council, Inc.*, 467 U.S. 837 (1984), discussed at some length in Chapter 3 of this book.

Brandeis, Cardozo, Jackson, Hand, Friendly, Traynor, and other great judges, and by great academics such as Karl Llewellyn, Edwin Patterson, Felix Cohen, Grant Gilmore, and Edward Levi, as well as great philosophers who dabbled in law such as John Dewey and Richard Rorty.[24] It is a considerable but at least slightly reassuring paradox that despite the rise of originalism and its cognate doctrines, the most admired American judges are still the realists, the pragmatists, of yore—those who heeded, or heed, the following dictate of Holmes: "We must think things not words, or at least we must constantly translate our words into the facts for which they stand, if we are to keep to the real and the true."[25]

Indeed, as explained in an excellent recent book by Allen Mendenhall,[26] we owe legal pragmatism mainly to Holmes, though his debts—to the great philosophers of his era: Ralph Waldo Emerson, Charles Sanders Peirce, William James, and John Dewey—were also considerable. Pragmatic adjudication emphasizes the consequences of judicial decisions, not only or even mainly the consequences for the litigants and their lawyers and judicial reputations but the consequences for society of decisions that establish or confirm or modify rules of conduct by persons, firms and other private agencies or associations, and government. Thus, as Mendenhall explains,

> it was not relativism that Holmes welcomed. It was a method of debate and exchange; the coordination of human action toward dispute resolution; the distillation and dispersal of power; and the benefit of society writ large. . . . Courts were not designed to referee or legislate moral tendencies but to ensure that the consequences of human action are reasonable and practicable in the workaday social sphere. . . . The classical pragmatists [the reference is to Emerson, Peirce, James, and Dewey] sought to strip philosophy—in Holmes's case, the philosophy of law—of its extraneous modes of reasoning and its abstract or dogmatic moralizing and to avoid attenuated lines of thinking that did not comport with commonsense empiricism. . . . They examined ideas in light of human expectations concerning causes and effects, actions and consequences. They expressed these expectations in terms of probability. And whatever meaning they took from these expectations depended upon what practical dif-

24. See my book *Law, Pragmatism, and Democracy* (2003).
25. Oliver Wendell Holmes, "Law in Science and Science in Law," 12 *Harvard Law Review* 443, 460 (1899).
26. Allen Mendenhall, Oliver Wendell Holmes Jr., *Pragmatism and the Jurisprudence of Agon: Aesthetic Dissent and the Common Law* (2017).

ference it made to interpret the expectations in one manner as opposed to another.[27]

Unfortunately, few modern judges think about judicial lawmaking in these classical terms.

True, it was also Holmes who liked to say that he deemed a statute unconstitutional only if it made him want to throw up—a proposition often and understandably criticized as lawless. But it should be understood rather as a striking affirmation of one brand of realism or pragmatism—that which acknowledges and accepts the role of emotion in judicial decision making. Because much of the Constitution is vague or obsolete or simply incomplete, judges are often left at large in interpreting it; and if one is democratically inclined, as Holmes was, one may seek guidance in emotion, and intervene only if one's emotional reaction to a statute challenged as unconstitutional is strongly negative.

There is a prime example of constitutional incompleteness in the First Amendment, where we read that "Congress shall make no law . . . abridging the freedom of speech." Taken literally this would preclude laws punishing defamation, copyright infringement (if the copyright was of written matter rather than of a painting or sculpture, unless "speech" is understood to encompass visual as well as verbal expression, which would bring all pornography within the scope of the First Amendment), child pornography (with the same proviso regarding visual as distinct from verbal matter), death threats, shouting "fire" in a crowded theater, lies on employment forms, and so forth. Instead these things are forbidden but burning the American flag as a protest is deemed constitutionally protected "speech." You may like or dislike this panoply of dos and don'ts, but it can't be referred to the First Amendment. Constitutional law is to a great extent the scratches made by judges on the defenseless text of the Constitution.

The most criticized scratch made by the great Holmes was his Supreme Court opinion in *Buck v. Bell*,[28] upholding (with no dissenting opinion and only one dissenting vote, that of Justice Peirce Butler, the only Catholic on the Court), against a challenge based on the Fourteenth Amendment, a Virginia law that authorized the sterilization of "mental defectives" who were confined to institutions for epileptics and feebleminded persons. The opinion has a passage, much criticized, in which Holmes combined enthusiasm for the Virginia law with a note of levity, saying:

27. Id. at 127.
28. 274 U.S. 200 (1927).

We have seen more than once that the public welfare may call upon the best citizens for their lives. It would be strange if it could not call upon those who already sap the strength of the State for these lesser sacrifices, often not felt to be such by those concerned, in order to prevent our being swamped with incompetence. It is better for all the world if, instead of waiting to execute degenerate offspring for crime or to let them starve for their imbecility, society can prevent those who are manifestly unfit from continuing their kind. The principle that sustains compulsory vaccination is broad enough to cover cutting the Fallopian tubes. *Jacobson v. Massachusetts*, 197 U.S. 11. Three generations of imbeciles are enough.[29]

The first sentence in the quoted passage echoes Holmes's military experience; he served for three years in the Union army as an infantry officer during the Civil War and was wounded three times, all three wounds being serious yet seemingly without any durable effects on him. The sentence beginning "It is better for all the world . . ." reflects Holmes's enthusiasm for the eugenics movement, which flourished in the United States as in many other countries in the 1920s, but was later discredited.[30] The opinion is a striking illustration of a persistent judicial tendency to base decisions on personal experiences and values, as well as—or in place of—conventional legal reasoning.

Moving on: Judge John Shepard Wiley, Jr., of the Superior Court of California in Los Angeles, published a short review[31] of my last book before this one, *Divergent Paths,* that describes accurately and succinctly what I am trying to do in this book as well, and with his permission I reprint the review here:

Every judge seeking to improve should read "Divergent Paths: The Academy and the Judiciary" (Harvard University Press, 2016), a new book by Judge Richard A. Posner of the 7th U.S. Circuit Court of Appeals. Posner critiques the American judicial profession, broadly and deeply, and offers constructive suggestions. Nominally Posner writes about federal appellate courts, but this book is hardly so narrow. It offers something worthwhile for every bench officer. Posner has standing to appraise the whole

29. Id. at 207. The three generations were Carrie Buck, the plaintiff, her mother, and Carrie Buck's daughter; apparently none were mental defectives, though this could not have been known by Holmes or the other Justices.

30. See, e.g., "Eugenics in the United States," Wikipedia, https://en.wikipedia.org/wiki/Eugenics_in_the _United_States. (On the two key passages in Holmes's opinion, see also Mendenhall, note 26 above, at 131–132.)

31. "Read Before That Novel Case Arises," *Los Angeles Daily Journal,* February 19, 2016.

profession. He is our nation's most influential living judge. In 1973, he wrote his pathbreaking book "Economic Analysis of Law" (now in its ninth edition) and he has written dozens of other books. He has published more than 3,100 judicial opinions and has scrutinized our judicial pantheon, which here he ticks off by name and virtue. Worthies hail Posner as a "wonder" and "the most cited legal scholar of all time."

Posner's number one criticism of the judiciary is "legal formalism." What is that? It is the notion "that cases can be decided only by a two-step process. The first step is interpretation—guided by dictionaries and by interpretive principles special to law (such as 'canons of construction')—of authoritative legal materials. The second step is the application to the facts of the case of a legal rule or standard derived by interpretation."

What is wrong with formalism? "I'm denying [Posner says] merely the formalist premise that there is no such thing as a novel case—that every case can be decided by reference to some earlier decision or some otherwise authoritative document. I'm denying that all that there is or should be or can be to legal analysis is interpretation." Posner writes that formalists ask how the authors of the past authority (be it a statute, a constitution, or a legal opinion) would have applied it to the facts at hand. "But since the authors can't be asked what they meant, what is called interpretation is actually creation." Posner pointedly examines the judicial act of creation. Posner acknowledges that "certainly formalism in the sense of respecting statutory text, well-settled legal doctrines, and binding precedents is a vital element of the judicial process, and indeed suffices to decide most cases correctly—just not the important ones, the ones that change or advance the law."

Devotion to legal authority is vital to the rule of law. It creates predictability. People plan with the law in view. When human conflicts arise, our predictable law allows parties to resolve most conflicts well short of court. Posner appreciates predictability better than most. After all, in the *Khan v. State Oil* episode, Circuit Judge Posner encountered a 1968 Supreme Court antitrust opinion he criticized as resting on "increasingly wobbly, moth-eaten foundations." Yet Posner applied the governing rule he ridiculed. The Supreme Court granted cert, praised Posner for following Supreme Court precedent in a predictable way—and then overruled its moth-eaten rule. See *Khan v. State Oil*, 522 U.S. 3, 20–22 (1997).

Novel cases do arise, however, and each one tests the judge. Appellate judges encounter more novel cases than do trial judges, yet every experienced trial judge knows the sensation of longing for, but not finding, a clearly decisive legal authority. For me and the many trial judges with whom I discuss work, this sensation is unwelcome. Trial judges apply rules for a living. The job is easier when the rules are clear. Los Angeles generates a never-ending stream of disputes. The longer a case takes to figure out, the more our groaning dockets will lag. Even Hamlet bemoaned "the law's delay."

When a judge has plumbed all relevant authorities and still none resolves the case, what is the alternative to formalism? Posner calls it "everyday pragmatism" or, alternatively, "legal realism." Posner's realist judge "asks what is a sensible result in a case—in light of common sense but also of likely consequences and the general legal culture—and is it blocked by an authoritative piece of constitutional or statutory text, or by a precedential decision that even if questionable as an original matter has been relied on so extensively that overruling it would cause more harm than good." Posner writes that "if the sensible result, all things considered (including reliance on previous decisions), is not blocked by an authoritative enactment or binding precedent, the realist judge says: go with it!" Posner describes his realist approach as "arch heresy" and "radical." Yet he also labels himself as a "conservative" appointed by President Reagan, "although today I am a moderate rather than a conservative."

Judges face no obligation to adopt or reject Posner's "pragmatism" in one fell swoop. As we tackle one case after another, we ordinary judges have whole careers to assess Posner's invitation. But Posner has primed the pump in a way we should consider. It might be helpful to read this book *before* that novel case arrives.

Legal interpretation is central to Posner's analysis. He writes that interpretation "is a natural human act, but it is intuitive, and trying to bound it by rules, though a natural ambition of lawyers and judges, has always failed." Posner argues the "interpretive canons are worthless" and defends his argument in depth. Posner proves legal interpretation can be fun to read. One much-mooted case is *United States v. Gayle*, 342 F.3d 89 (2d Cir. 2003) (not a case Posner was involved in) which interpreted a statute forbidding gun possession by one convicted of a felony "in any court." Defendant Gayle was convicted of a felony by a Canadian court.

Does "any court" include a foreign court? This interpretative poser split appellate courts and then the Supreme Court, but Posner makes short work of the supposed puzzle. "It is *ridiculous* to think that a conviction in one of the world's 194 countries—a club with so many dubious members (such as North Korea)—of a crime punishable by imprisonment for more than a year would make it a crime to possess a gun in the United States without regard to which country had convicted the person of what crime. Depending on the country, the crime might be insulting a dictator, might be sorcery, might be apostasy, might be advocating vaccination, might be adultery, might be blasphemy, might be refusing to commit a crime against humanity. . . . [T]herefore would Solzhenitsyn, who spent eight years in the gulag . . . for writing a postcard that made fun of Stalin . . . have been a felon had he bought a gun to kill moles during his sojourn in Vermont?"

This book catalogs a list of other problems plaguing the judiciary, and issues a call for the legal academy to address them. Posner is skeptical that law professors will listen.

Charmingly, Posner identifies his own past errors. At 77, Posner proves he is still considering the big issues, still intrigued by new ideas, still evolving. He is the revered elder who remains young at heart. This book challenges judges to strive after his inspiring example.

I am grateful to Judge Wiley for his generous assessment of my work. But I need to acknowledge that, long as this book is, it does not cover all the weaknesses of the federal judiciary—as I am reminded by an article by Jed Rakoff, a very distinguished federal district judge in New York,[32] entitled "Why You Won't Get Your Day in Court."[33] The principal weaknesses that Rakoff discusses and that I do not (not because I disagree with him, but because I either have nothing to add or do not want to lengthen the book further, or because they are weaknesses of the state judiciaries rather than of the federal judiciary—he discusses both), or that I touch on only glancingly, are a steep increase in the cost of hiring a lawyer (which has compelled a growing number of litigants to represent themselves in litigation—which they are almost certain to lose, and which therefore often induces them to agree to paltry pretrial settlements of their claims) because average billing rates have soared since the 1980s, and in litigation costs generally; the decline of unions and other organizations

---

32. See note 6 in Chapter 1.
33. *New York Review of Books,* November 24, 2016, p. 4.

that provide their members with free legal representation; the Supreme Court's *Chevron* doctrine, which as we'll see in Chapter 3 limits judicial protection of parties to litigation before administrative agencies; the severity of criminal sentences for many crimes, which induces many defendants to plead guilty in exchange for a lighter sentence, rather than go to trial and risk conviction (often a near certainty) and a heavier sentence; and judicial tolerance of mandatory arbitration clauses and prohibitions of class actions, in contracts that employers and sellers frequently impose on employees and customers with the intention and effect of denying judicial relief to those individuals.

The greatest weakness of the federal judiciary is one that receives no attention at all: the judges and Justices are nominated and confirmed by politicians—the President and the Senators. The politicians are unlikely to try to pick the very best candidate for a judgeship or Justiceship. Rather they want a candidate that is likely to support the policies of the appointing authorities or attract political support (factors in the appointment for example of the Italian-American Scalia, and the Hispanic-American Sotomayor, to the Supreme Court); a rare exception being President Hoover's appointment of Benjamin Cardozo to succeed Holmes. Cardozo's being Jewish was not a plus for Hoover, since there was already a Jew on the Court—Brandeis—and since Cardozo was a Democrat and liberal, and Hoover of course a Republican and conservative.

The situation is different in other countries, notably the United Kingdom, where appointments to its recently created Supreme Court (as well as to lower courts) are made not by politicians but instead by Justices and other judges and other legal officials. The Justices as well as the other U.K. judges are subject to compulsory retirement at age seventy if first appointed to a judicial office after March 31, 1995, or at seventy-five otherwise. Sounds like a big improvement over our system.

STRENGTHS OF THE FEDERAL JUDICIARY

Because so much of my recent writing about the federal legal system has been critical—and this book is no exception—I need to make clear my belief that the system has definite strengths. One is that it provides important though as I'll argue in Chapter 4 incomplete protections for persons accused of crime. These protections include the requirement of proof beyond a reasonable doubt for conviction, the right to a jury trial, the right to counsel, the right to invoke habeas corpus as a remedy against unjust convictions, the constitutional protections found in the Fourth and Fifth Amendments (the Fourth limits searches and arrests and the Fifth guarantees due process of law and forbids compelled self-incrimination and double jeopardy), and the *enormous* number of American lawyers (some 1.3 million, though most are not criminal lawyers), of whom an unknown though undoubtedly small percentage are well trained, experienced, very smart, and employed by first-class law firms, or by government agencies, or by business or other private organizations, or by law school clinics often dedicated to the defense of persons accused of crime, or who teach part time in law schools.

The federal judiciary is large, though dwarfed by the number of state court judges. There are almost nine hundred Article III federal judgeships (comprising district judges, circuit judges, Supreme Court Justices—and vacancies), and Article III judges are well though not lavishly compensated, with salaries above $200,000 a year and generous benefits (including retirement at full pay). They have life tenure (more precisely, they are assumed to have and accepted as having) and thus are independent of the other branches of the federal government, though they (or should I say we) have to worry about Congress's willingness to give us occasional raises. A number of federal adjudicators, however, are not Article III judges. They include administrative law judges, who are employed by federal agencies, and bankruptcy and magistrate judges, who are district court adjuncts.

Elite law schools provide the Article III judges with first-rate staffs of law clerks, and the independence of the judges is guaranteed by the life tenure believed (though perhaps erroneously) to be conferred on them by Article III.[34] There are enough federal judges to handle the caseload with minimal delay (though there are a number of procrastinating federal judges), in part because of respect for the importance of principles of finality in litigation—cases must not be allowed to linger indefinitely, as in such countries as India and Brazil, where lack of a culture of finality in litigation has resulted in staggering caseloads that include cases hundreds of years old. But important as finality is to a well-run judicial system, I am sympathetic to Judge Jack Weinstein's belief in playing "fast and loose with a lot of procedure."[35] Procedure, worshipped to excess by American judges, mustn't be allowed to strangle justice. Such aposta-

---

34. Actually it's unclear whether Article III, or any other provision in the Constitution, confers life tenure on federal judges. All that Article III says that bears on the issue is that the judges "shall hold their Office during good Behaviour," and good behavior is not a synonym for life. Judges like other federal officials can be impeached by the House of Representatives and tried by the Senate and if convicted they are removed from office, but it is unclear whether that is the only procedure whereby a judge can be removed for bad behavior.

35. Quoted in Jeffrey P. Morris, *Leadership on the Federal Bench: The Craft and Activism of Jack Weinstein* 113 (2011).

sies, disdainful of conventional legal doctrines, will crop up from time to time throughout this book. Toward the end of the Epilogue I discuss briefly another important federal judicial concept—that of "standing to sue"—that like finality provides a sensible limit on federal litigation.

The federal judiciary has benefited from (though it's also, as we'll see, been hurt by) a legal tradition commonly traced back to the ratification of the U.S. Constitution in 1788,[36] more than two and a quarter centuries ago, but in fact rooted in English law derived originally from Roman and particularly Anglo-Saxon (Germanic) law but evolving continuously after the Norman conquest of England in 1066. There is a fairly high level of public respect for our judiciary, though it has been declining, at least with regard to the Supreme Court, as we'll see in Chapter 2, in tandem with increased public disillusionment with the federal government in the current era of political turmoil (I write this on the eve of the 2016 Presidential election), unprecedented since, and probably worse than, the 1960s.

Special recognition must be accorded to a roster of outstanding judges (though they are a small minority of all judges), not all federal by any means, who brighten the history and reputation of the American judiciary with their contributions to legal justice. These bright stars—John Marshall, Joseph Story, Lemuel Shaw, Oliver Wendell Holmes, Louis Brandeis, Benjamin Cardozo, Charles Evans Hughes, Charles E. Clark, Jerome Frank, Charles Wyzanski, Earl Warren, William Brennan, Hugo Black, the two Harlans, Learned Hand, Robert Jackson, Roger Traynor, Henry Friendly, and others (I omit living judges)— have shaped much of American law and raised law's prestige to a level probably attained in no other country and dramatically reflected in the remarkable number of lawyers who have become U.S. Presidents—twenty-five of the forty-five Presidents (56 percent), including Thomas Jefferson, James Madison, Abraham Lincoln, William Howard Taft, Woodrow Wilson, Franklin Roosevelt, Richard Nixon, and most recently Bill Clinton and Barack Obama. Law professors and law deans, and latterly economists and other social scientists, and also legal journalists such as Emily Bazelon, Linda Greenhouse, Adam Liptak, and Dahlia Lithwick, have contributed to the improvement of federal law and its administration, although I am troubled by the self-satisfaction expressed by many law school deans and law professors.[37]

36. Actually it was ratified in 1788, but there was agreement that government in accordance with the rules laid down in the Constitution would not begin until the following year.

37. See, for example, David F. Levi, "From Judge to Dean: Reflections on the Bench and the Academy," 70 *Louisiana Law Review* 913, 922 (2010); Cass R. Sunstein, "In Praise of Law Books and Law Reviews (and Jargon-Filled Academic Writings)," 114 *Michigan Law Review* 833 (2016).

Any discussion of the strengths of our federal legal system would be incomplete without further reference to economic analysis of law, mentioned in passing earlier in this Introduction, and to the social sciences in general. The application of economic analysis to law goes back to Aristotle, received an enormous boost from Jeremy Bentham in the eighteenth and early nineteenth centuries, languished for quite a while, began a comeback in the 1920s and 1930s, surged in the 1950s through 1970s, and remains strong. The economic analysis of law, the joint creation of economists such as Ronald Coase, George Stigler, Gary Becker, Harold Demsetz, William Landes, and Steven Shavell, and of law professors such as Guido Calabresi, Henry Manne, Louis Kaplow, and yours truly (these are very partial lists), has transformed such statutory fields of law as antitrust, administrative regulation, commercial law, bankruptcy law, and patent law (and the other fields of intellectual property law, notably copyright law), as well as common law fields such as torts, contracts, and property. Economic analysis has infiltrated other fields of law as well, ranging from constitutional law to civil procedure and evidence, criminal law, domestic-relations law, labor law, discrimination law, damages law (and remedies more broadly), and comparative and international law. Its scope is indicated by the three-volume *New Palgrave Dictionary of Economics and the Law* (1998), my thousand-page treatise *Economic Analysis of Law*, the *Journal of Law & Economics,* now in its fifty-ninth year of publication, and the *Journal of Legal Studies,* which I founded in 1972 and edited until my appointment to the court of appeals, and which now, in its forty-fifth year, is still going strong.

Much of this research is conducted in law schools by law professors with strong backgrounds in the social sciences, sometimes in collaboration with social scientists, an example being *The Behavior of Federal Judges,* which I coauthored with Lee Epstein (political scientist) and William Landes (economist). But important as interdisciplinary legal research is, it receives little attention in this book. My focus is on the basic structure of the federal judiciary, a structure that has remained largely impervious to the rise of interdisciplinary research and for this and other reasons is rife with weaknesses. Areas of strength in the judiciary, such as interdisciplinary research, can take care of themselves; and so despite my book's title the focus is the judiciary's weaknesses.

But because I'm so closely identified with economic analysis of law—it was the focus of my entire career as a law professor (summer 1968 to December 4, 1981, when I was appointed to the court of appeals for the Seventh Circuit) and is still the primary field of interdisciplinary legal research, I feel a need to say something about my gradual estrangement from it. One factor was the death, retirement, or resignation of the great economists (such as Aaron Director, George Stigler, Milton Friedman, Ronald Coase, and Gary Becker), and of economically sophisticated law professors (such as Donald Turner, William Baxter, and Guido Calabresi)—the two groups of academics from whom I learned economics and its application to law. (The lists of names I've given is only partial, however.) Another factor was that my judicial duties have concerned cases most of which have not presented significant economic issues.

But I want to stress a third factor in my estrangement from economic analysis of law—a growing sense that I might have exaggerated the pertinence of economics to law. I was reminded of this possibility by a recent piece in the *New York Times Book Review* by Professor John Fabian Witt of the Yale Law School.[38] What struck me was the remark in the review that "Notoriously, Posner entertained the idea (though he thought it implausible) that it might be best not to punish the crime of rape if the rapist enjoys the act of rape enough to outweigh the harm to the victim." My reaction was: had I really said that? It turns out, as I discovered searching through my books for anything I'd ever written about the economics of rape, that I hadn't said that. What I had said, in my book *Sex and Reason,* published in 1992, was that

> the rational model has been said to imply . . . contrary to our unshakable moral intuitions, that a man who derives a special pleasure, sexual or otherwise, from the coerciveness of rape ought to be permitted to rape, provided only that he derives more pleasure from the act, over and above all substitutes (such as sex with a prostitute who will, for a price, consent to the man's abusing her physically), than the pain suffered by his victim. [There is a footnote at the end of the preceding sentence that cites three articles, one by me, plus a book I coauthored with William Landes. Both the book and my article criticize the "ought to be permitted to rape" argument.] This example points to a familiar problem of utilitarianism— the problem of the "utility monster," who by virtue of having a capacity for enjoyment vastly greater than that of the average person in the society appears to stake a utilitarian moral claim to engross a disproportionate share of the society's goods. Only here the utility monster really is a monster, who by virtue of having a capacity for sadistic pleasure greater

38. John Fabian Witt, "Court Provocateur: A Biography of the Unconventionally Opinionated Judge Richard Posner," October 9, 2016. The biography, entitled *Richard Posner,* was written by William Domnarski.

than his victim's capacity for pain stakes a moral claim to be allowed to torture, rape, and kill.

The rational model of human behavior is indeed related to utilitarianism, for both approaches are based on the assumption that people act in accordance with the balance of pleasures and pains. But to suppose that the rational model stands or falls with utilitarianism is to confuse positive with normative analysis. In any event it should be plain that licensing utility monsters such as Bluebeard or de Sade to rape would not really be utility-maximizing, if only because of the fear that it would engender in the community as a whole and the expense of the self-protective measures that this fear would incite.

Notice my statement in the first two lines of the quotation that to give a pass to the rapist who is a "utility monster" insofar as he derives more pleasure from his act than his victim suffers from it would be "contrary to our unshakable moral intuitions," and that I didn't criticize those intuitions or claim not to share them. And I said that the utility monster in the rape setting "really *is* a monster." The reasons I gave for not "licensing utility monsters such as Bluebeard or de Sade to rape [because the rapes] would not really be utility-maximizing" were that it would engender fear and create costs in the form of additional self-protective measures. The second of these reasons ("the costs of additional self-protective measures") states the issue in explicitly economic terms: given those additional costs, rape may be (in fact clearly is) "inefficient" from an overall social standpoint even if the rapist's pleasure often exceeds his victim's pain.[39]

I need particularly to emphasize, with regard to the strengths of the federal judiciary, the substantial independence that federal judges have from the other branches of the federal government, namely the President (and the executive branch of the government, which he presides over) and Congress. The President nominates federal judges, but cannot appoint them, for his nominees cannot take office until they are confirmed in their judicial positions by the Senate; the Congress's power to appoint federal judges is limited to Senate confirma-

---

39. In an earlier book, *Sex and Reason* 384–395 (1992), I had discussed rape and rape law at length without invoking the model of rational choice. But in a still earlier book, *Economic Analysis of Law* 202 (3d ed. 1986), I had invoked the model, saying, "Suppose a rapist derives extra pleasure from the coercive character of his act. Then there would be no market substitute for rape and it could be argued therefore that rape is not a pure coercive transfer and should not be punished criminally," but I had added that "the argument would be weak" and had explained why.

tion of the President's nominees; and Congress can remove a federal judge only if the House of Representatives impeaches the judge and the Senate convicts him (the impeachment is thus the counterpart of an indictment in a conventional criminal prosecution). See Article I, sections 2 and 3, of the Constitution. Impeachment and conviction have been very rare; and so for most federal judges, although Congress determines their salaries, once determined the salaries can't be reduced. In addition the judges "shall hold their offices during good Behaviour," which has been assumed to equate to life tenure, though perhaps mistakenly.

So the judges have been granted considerable independence from the other branches of the federal government and they do not hesitate to exercise it, sometimes to the dismay of those branches. A current example, which I discuss in Chapter 2, is the refusal (at this writing, February 10, 2017) of the federal courts to buckle under to President Trump's executive order barring entry of persons from seven predominantly Muslim nations.

Reader, read on; and as you near the end of the Conclusion notice something unusual: my attempt to give a grade to the federal judiciary, as if it were a collection of students.

ONE

Some Weaknesses of Our Legal System
Mistakenly Denied by a Critic

THE CRITICISMS I'LL BE MAKING of the federal judiciary and the institutions that buttress it, such as the law schools, the President and Congress, and the bar, amplify and extend criticisms that I've made in previous books, such as *Divergent Paths*. A number of those criticisms have been criticized in turn both in a review of that book by law professor Michael Dorf and in a later piece by him responding to my criticisms of his review and intensifying his earlier criticisms.[1] Dorf's criticisms of *Divergent Paths* contrast strikingly with Judge Wiley's praise of the book[2] and provide a springboard for a discussion of views that I advance in the present book.

A reader for the Harvard University Press criticized my discussing "small matters," specifically Dorf's criticism of my criticism of misspelling by lawyers and judges of the Latin phrase *de minimis non curat lex* (the law doesn't concern itself with trifles) as *de minimus non curat lex*. If *minimis* were the only word, or one of a handful, that lawyers and judges frequently misspell, my drawing attention to the misspelling would indeed be petty. But actually it's one of a number of words and phrases widely used by the legal profession (including its judicial branch) that I criticize on page 250 of *Reflections on Judging* and in this book as well,[3] all being words and phrases that appear frequently in briefs, judicial opinions, and law review articles.

My criticisms of bad legal writing are not "cranky," as Dorf contends; for no

---

1. Michael C. Dorf's Book Review of "Divergent Paths: The Academy and the Judiciary" by Richard A. Posner, 66 *Journal of Legal Education* 186–202 (2016), and "Parsing Posner's Peevishness," in *Dorf on Law*, September 30, 2016, www.dorfonlaw.org/2016/09/parsing-posners-peevishness.html.

2. John Wiley, "Read Before That Novel Case Arrives," *Los Angeles Daily Journal*, February 19, 2016.

3. See note 16 in Chapter 3.

profession gives more weight to writing than the law does. Nor my criticisms of the *Bluebook*. I would like to see him try to defend that monstrosity—its length (560 pages in the current [20th] edition), its cost ($36), its unintelligible abbreviations (guess what words "Auth.," "Auto.," "Broad.," "Bhd.," "Ent.," "Prot.," "Res.," and "Unif." are *Bluebook* abbreviations of), its opacity, its clotted history of wasted effort by very intelligent professors and students,[4] its superfluity, and its ambiguity, which led the *Harvard Law Review* staff to create the *Blackbook* to provide answers to citation questions ignored or left opaque in the *Bluebook*. The handbook that I give my law clerks contains five pages on citation format; that's plenty. I reproduce those pages as an addendum to this chapter.

Recently the *Berkeley Journal of Gender, Law & Justice* decided to abandon the *Bluebook*. What makes that a notable event is the journal's comprehensive and convincing statement of its reasons for the abandonment:

> First, the Bluebook presents an enormous and unnecessary barrier to publication in law journals for scholars from other disciplines, young scholars, legal practitioners, and others without access to students and clerks to Bluebook their work. The 20th Edition of the Bluebook is 560 pages long, a Russian doll of rules within rules. It strictly regulates when to use small-caps, when to italicize commas, and how to abbreviate the proper names of over 1000 law journals. Conforming citations to the Bluebook is an immense undertaking, even for attorneys who have presumably been trained to use it. For the non-attorney, reading the hundreds of pages of legal rules and then applying them is daunting. To the extent that the Bluebook citation style privileges the publication of work created by authors of a particular, narrow background or those with access to more resources, adherence to that style is inconsistent with the mandate of the Journal.
>
> Second, conforming to Bluebook citation style requires an investment

---

4. See Fred R. Shapiro and Julie Graves Krishnaswami, "The Secret History of the *Bluebook*," 100 *Minnesota Law Review* 1563, 1566–1568 (2016). For other criticisms see my article "*Goodbye to the* Bluebook," 53 *University of Chicago Law Review* 1343 (1986). Recently I came across this priceless interchange between two law review editors concerning internal quotation marks in a judicial opinion quoted in a law review article: "{XE: I was uncertain about whether to put the internal quotation marks omitted parenthetical here because the internal quotation marks are only omitted in the first quotation where they were co-extensive with the quoted material.} {XE2: I know we've been all over this one but see the SB 5.2(c) as requiring them to stay in there; am I right about that?} {XE1: I see BB/SB as requiring them to stay in the second quotation, but not the first, which I think was DE's question.}{DE: See XE2's response}." How ridiculous can one get?

of editorial time and effort which is wildly disproportionate to the utility of the style. Rules regarding the use of small-caps versus italics, or whether commas are italicized, underlined, or neither, give no substantive guidance to the reader regarding how to locate the particular source or how the source is being used. These stylistic fixes, however, are immensely time-consuming for the editor. Highlighting each comma in an eighty-page article to determine its formatting can easily consume an hour or more. An editor working on an interdisciplinary or cutting-edge piece citing non-traditional sources, such as tweets, podcasts, internet videos, may spend hours of their time looking up the particular obscure formats required. This time could be spent checking for accuracy or, even better, testing the argument and improving its structure. It is the substance of a piece—rather than its use of punctuation—which can introduce innovative ideas and further productive discussion. It is, therefore, our conclusion that the primary responsibility of editors should be working with authors to build the strongest possible version of that substance. It is our opinion that following the Bluebook is an obstacle to fulfilling that responsibility.

Thirdly, the Bluebook citation system is inaccessible to the unfamiliar reader. Any reader not trained in Bluebook citation—which is to say, any reader who has not attended law school—is unlikely to understand a citation to J. Mar. L. & Com (with our apologies to the convenient example of the Journal of Maritime Law and Commerce). Is it a publication? Which one? Instead of immediately understanding the source of the author's claim, the reader must run a search on the unfamiliar abbreviation before returning to the text. Citation form should help readers trace the author's intellectual process, not place unnecessary roadblocks in their way. Focusing on this purpose is particularly important for the Journal because it is central to our mission to promote voices, perspectives, and research subjects which have historically been excluded from legal and academic discourse. We have an obligation to produce a publication which is as accessible as possible to a wide range of readers, including non-lawyers.

In Judge Posner's memorable words, the Bluebook has become "a monstrous growth, remote from the functional need for legal citation forms, which serves obscure needs of the legal culture and its student subculture." The Bluebook is difficult to master—1L courses spend a significant amount of time teaching new law students its minutia and many professors employ students specifically to Bluebook their pieces for publication. Moreover, practicing attorneys almost never use the Bluebook, using simplified, court or office-specific citation forms instead. Perhaps the last bastion of the Bluebook, outside of the academic publications that created it, is in federal judicial chambers, but a critique of the Bluebook is emerging from this corner as well as exemplified by Posner's article "The Bluebook Blues."

Uniformity of style is an admirable goal and one for which the Journal will continue to strive. However, we believe that uniformity is not the only goal of citation, and is in fact only a minor one. The most important goal for a system of legal citation is to allow a reader to trace an author's intellectual process. Clear, accessible, simple, and consistent citations serve this goal. The Journal will be using a seven-page citation guide, borrowing heavily from the system Judge Posner describes in his article and retaining useful elements of the Bluebook. The citation guide will be available on our website. We will revise the articles we publish with this guide, but will continue to accept articles in any (consistent) citation style.[5]

Right on!

While not defending the *Bluebook,* Dorf describes my criticizing it at length in *Divergent Paths* as "out of proportion" because the *Bluebook* is not a "serious issue[s]." I beg to differ. Among other reasons to think it serious that are discussed by the *Berkeley Journal,* the *Bluebook* not only is expensive but its mastery is time consuming if only because of its length. Even at the University of Chicago Law School, whose law review uses a different and much simpler citation manual (the *Maroonbook*), first-year law students are required to master the *Bluebook.* That is a complete waste of time and money. There is no need for 560 pages of confusion where 5 lucid pages will do. But alas, the legal profession has never considered brevity a virtue. The original explanation was that

5. "BGLJ Says Goodbye to the Bluebook," October 7, 2016, https://genderlawjustice.berkeley.edu /bglj-says-goodbye-to-the-blue-book/.

lawyers charged their clients by the page for the documents they drafted for them, so the more words and therefore the more pages, the higher the pay. The current explanation is that lawyers now charge by the hour, so the more hours, the more words, and the more words, the more money.

Dorf says that reputable legal writing instructors advise students in first-year writing courses to avoid "jargon." I wonder what he means by the word. A typical dictionary definition of jargon is "special words or expressions used by a particular profession or group that are difficult for others to understand." That is an exact description of many of the words and expressions that are drilled into law students and show up later in their briefs and oral arguments when they embark on the practice of law. Now it's true that the word "jargon" is sometimes used as a synonym for words having specialized, technical meanings; so one might speak for example of sociological jargon or philosophical jargon. But law could get by very nicely with little in the nature of a specialized vocabulary. Not nothing: there are terms like "diversity" (jurisdiction), "consideration" (in contract law), "reverse and remand," "res judicata," and "supplemental jurisdiction" that mean nothing to laypersons but that lawyers have to learn. But there are also lots of terms thrown around in law that are either superfluous or confusing, as I will be pointing out from time to time—beginning in just a couple of pages.

Dorf says that on page 325 of *Divergent Paths* I had argued that clinical teaching should be done by tenured faculty. No, what I had said was that "I would like to see the clinical professors do more teaching because, as I've suggested, fields like civil and criminal procedure, evidence, and trial advocacy are practical," making "doctrine in such fields . . . for the most part simple, secondary, and often ignored by both the lawyers and the judge." Rightly ignored, I should add.

Oddly Dorf implies that I tried but failed through "pointed criticisms" of Justice Scalia "during the last years of Scalia's life" (does Dorf think I was trying to hasten his death?) "to turn Scalia into a Posner-style legal realist." That's absurd. I could no more have done that, and so would have been wasting my time trying, than I could turn my cat into a dog. I would like my books to have *some* impact on the profession, but I know it will be modest, in part because of the complacency of many judges and professors, in part because professors are reluctant to criticize judges, in part because of immovable barriers to reform such as that most state judges are elected rather than appointed and that federal judges are appointed by politicians (the President and Senators), in part because I am reputed in some quarters to be a maverick,[6] and above all because of the stodginess of the legal profession—a major theme of this book. The profession marches forward with its head screwed on backward—transfixed by an eighteenth-century Constitution of limited relevance to the twenty-first century (I will be giving many examples of that limited relevance in this book), and by an antiquated professional vocabulary still sprinkled with Latin words and opaque verbal formulas (such as "clear and convincing," "actual innocence," "rational basis," "strict scrutiny," "intermediate scrutiny," "substantial evidence," "arbitrary and capricious," and "abuse of discretion"—terms that I discuss disapprovingly in Chapter 3), transfixed too by countless obsolete precedents, by the pretense of "interpreting" statutes and constitutional provisions that have to be loosely construed in order to read on current issues, and by much else besides as I'll show throughout the book.

Documents, the older the better, not current understandings, are the gold coin of conventional and still dominant legal research and analysis outside of financial and other commercial areas of law. One is put in mind of the background to "the rise of science and secular philosophy [in the seventeenth century, which] required a new conception of knowledge in which observation, not authority, was the source of knowledge. The learned man . . . had hitherto been conceived [of] as someone steeped in sacred texts, whether biblical or

6. I wish there were more judicial mavericks than there are. I'm just a semi-maverick. One of the few federal appellate judges who I know qualifies as a total maverick is Judge Alex Kozinski of the Ninth Circuit. I can think of three federal district judges who fit the bill as well—Judges Weinstein and Rakoff in New York and Judge Kane in Denver—the last particularly colorful and outspoken critic of our legal system. All four are *excellent* judges who write and speak clearly and boldly. Kane is the least well known of the four, but by no means the least forthright and colorful. He says such things as "any judge who says he is unbiased is delusional"—which is true. Kirk Mitchell, "Feisty Federal Judge in Denver Knows All About Challenging Authority," *Denver Post*, August 12, 2014, www.denverpost.com/2014/08/12/feisty-federal-judge-in-den ver-knows-all-about-challenging-authority/. About the sentencing guidelines Judge Kane has said, "I couldn't see how you could look at a chart and sentence somebody without regard to their individual circumstances" —though in fact federal judges are not allowed to impose a guidelines sentence without first satisfying themselves that such a sentence will comport with the sentencing factors in 18 U.S.C. § 3553(a). He calls the "war on drugs" "crap." And when "Colorado legislators complained about the millions of dollars his court orders would cost the state he told them to melt the gold in the Capitol's dome to fund statewide prison improvements." In high school, when he corrected his history teacher who had said that our war with Mexico followed our Civil War, the teacher said to him: "If you know so much why don't you teach?" To which Kane replied, "OK." And finally, in the interview from which I've been quoting he spoke "while petting a purring, black cat in his lap." I know of no other judge who has ever been interviewed with an animal in his lap, although very occasionally the official portrait of a judge will include an animal. I happen to be a cat nut myself, so hats off to Judge Kane. And to Oliver Wendell Holmes, who said in a letter to Alice Stopford Greene, "Nature is an aristocrat or at least makes aristocrats, e.g. the cat." Quoted in *The Essential Holmes: Selections from the Letters, Speeches, Judicial Opinions, and Other Writings of Oliver Wendell Holmes, Jr.* 22 (Richard A. Posner ed. 1992).

Hellenic; his knowledge was essentially derivative and second hand. He knew what he knew because he'd learned from someone in authority, generally from books. But the new mode of knowledge was not textual: it was sensory. To find out about the world you had to observe it with your senses and then make inferences using your faculty of reason, not study ancient texts."[7] A similar adjustment is necessary for today's legal culture, which remains preoccupied if not with ancient, then with very old, texts.

I connect the backward-looking character of legal analysis to an influential current in legal thinking that claims the same metaphysical standing for law as scientific realists claim for science or moral realists for morality. Good legal reasoning, according to these thinkers, tells us what the law really is, just as science tells us what nature really is and religion or moral theory tells us what the correct answer to any moral question really is. A critical difference, however, is that scientists do not believe that old scientific documents can be relied on as sources of scientific knowledge.

And there is an inconsistency in the veneration of the old texts, especially the old opinions. There is a willingness, even eagerness, to deem decisions that offend current values to have been decided incorrectly, yet that is an approach that ignores historical context. So take *Plessy v. Ferguson*,[8] which held that a state could, without thereby violating the federal Constitution, forbid whites and blacks to be allowed to occupy the same railway cars, provided the cars assigned to each race were of equal quality. The Supreme Court upheld the state law by a vote of 7 to 1 (the ninth Justice did not participate; the lone dissenter was John Marshall Harlan), even though of the seven Justices in the majority six were Northerners. Although most modern Americans, including the Supreme Court Justices, consider such racial segregation abhorrent, it is difficult to imagine the Court having ruled differently back in 1896. It is unlikely that the Southern states would have obeyed such a ruling, and beyond unlikely that the federal government would have attempted to use force to enforce the ruling, in what the South would have regarded as a reopening of the Civil War. The ruling was "right" for its time.

And likewise *Korematsu v. United States*,[9] the decision that upheld (over three dissents—Roberts, Murphy, and Jackson) the constitutionality of a federal order that forced Japanese Americans living on the West Coast into intern-

7. Colin McGinn, "Groping Toward the Mind," *New York Review of Books,* June 23, 2016, pp. 67, 68.
8. 163 U.S. 537 (1896).
9. 323 U.S. 214 (1944).

ment camps inland during World War II even if they were U.S. citizens. The order (which Korematsu had been arrested and prosecuted for violating) was issued and executed just a few months after the Pearl Harbor attack, which had given rise to fears that the Japanese might invade the West Coast and be aided by Japanese Americans living there. There was of course, as things turned out, no Japanese invasion and no Japanese American fifth column; in fact a number of Japanese Americans fought in the American army, though they were assigned to the European rather than the Asian theater of operations. And by 1944, when *Korematsu* was decided, it was obvious that Japan was going to lose the war, and soon. Nevertheless the Court held that the executive order had been valid, and so Korematsu lost.

Not only did the executive order prove to have been mistaken, but the order seems never to have had a convincing basis in what was known about the loyalty of Japanese Americans and about Japanese military capacity and intentions to invade the United States, an operation that was in fact clearly beyond Japanese power even at its height after Pearl Harbor. But I imagine that the motive behind the order was not fear of a Japanese invasion but a desire to demonstrate to the American people that the government would stop at nothing to defeat the enemy. The Pearl Harbor attack—a complete and shocking surprise—did severe damage to the U.S. battle fleet at a time when the nation was not fully mobilized for war, and Hitler declared war on the United States just four days after the attack. We were on the defensive, and the government (led of course by President Roosevelt) was (I am guessing) demonstrating by its unprecedented action in interning a significant number of American citizens an absolute commitment to war and victory. Churchill had made, and Stalin was to make in a few months when attacked by Hitler, similar demonstrations of an absolute commitment to total victory.

And so *Korematsu*, though like *Plessy* a much-criticized decision,[10] is saved from obloquy when understood in its historical context.

We see in these examples, moreover, further evidence of the unsoundness of the backward focus that is so conspicuous a feature of our legal culture. We read the eighteenth-century Constitution and Bill of Rights for guides to the present, though today's world was invisible to the eighteenth century, and likewise we read *Plessy* and *Korematsu* as if their authors should have known how

---

10. See, e.g., Jacobus tenBroek, Edward N. Barnhart, and Floyd W. Matson, *Prejudice, War and the Constitution* (1968), and Jamal Greene, "The Anticanon," 125 *Harvard Law Review* 379 (2011), criticizing both decisions.

we moderns would think about racial segregation and the internment of U.S. citizens, rather than how their contemporaries thought about those practices. In the next chapter, however, we'll see the courts resisting President Trump's executive order—a descendant of the order to intern Japanese Americans in World War II—forbidding entry to the United States of persons from seven predominantly Muslim countries.

The problems created by the rearward focus of so much legal reasoning are compounded by the profession's delight in complexity. I do not mean the complexity of the subject matter of legal cases. Litigation over medical, financial, scientific, psychological, religious, and criminal issues often requires the lawyers, the judges, witnesses, and staff to deal with complexity. But the complexity of "the law" is an invention. Law is basically dispute resolution. Dispute resolution requires mastery of the facts in dispute and common sense. It does not require analytic complexity, as distinct from comprehension of factual complexity if the dispute to be resolved involves complex facts.

Lawyers want law to be complex in order to impress their clients and sway judges and jurors. Judges want their decisions to be complex in order to impress the litigants, the lawyers, and executive and legislative officials, although most of that decorative complexity comes from the lawyers and the judges' law clerks rather than from the judges themselves. Law professors like complexity because they want to impress their students, the lawyers, judges, and themselves, with their brilliance; law professors consider themselves the intellectual kings and queens of the legal profession. We'll see an example of this in Chapter 3, in Professor Adrian Vermeule's self-regarding sophomoric disparagement of Judge Henry Friendly.

Legal complexity like rearward focus is an impediment to sensible adjudication. This proposition is illustrated by a recent book by Professor William N. Eskridge, Jr., of Yale Law School.[11] Eskridge, along with Abbe Gluck and Victoria Nourse, is at the top of the academic ladder so far as statutory and constitutional interpretation is concerned. He is very intelligent, very experienced, and even very nice. He is the coauthor of a masterful casebook on legislation.[12] But the 470 pages of his new book leave me dizzy, in part, though only in part, because they cover *everything*. The Introduction is entitled "Canons and Norms in Statutory Interpretation." Six chapters follow, entitled respectively "Ordinary

11. *Interpreting Law: A Primer on How to Read Statutes and the Constitution* (2016).

12. William N. Eskridge, Jr., and Philip P. Frickey, *Cases and Materials on Legislation: Statutes and the Creation of Public Policy* (1988), reviewed by me in 78 *Virginia Law Review* 1567 (1988).

Meaning," "Whole Act, Statutory Purpose, and Whole Code," "Statutory Precedents," "Legislative History," "Agency Interpretation and Regulatory History,"
"Constitutional Principles and Background Norms," and then comes the Conclusion—"Canons and Norms in Constitutional Interpretation"—followed by
an Appendix called "The Supreme Court's Canons of Statutory Interpretation
(1986–2016)."

Opening the book literally at random, I found myself on page 235 being introduced to a federal statute I'd never heard of (and can't find any reference to
in Google—and upon inquiry Professor Eskridge told me that it's merely a "hypothetical" statute, not an actual one) called the "Park Safety Act," which the
reader is told "means 'any mechanism' for conveying people from one place
to another" and thus "helps open up the Act to regulating horses as vehicles."
But later the reader learns that Congress (in an amendment to a hypothetical
statute??) changed "any mechanism" to "any thing," which raises the question
"ought this [change] to be treated as a significant change? The answer to that
question, 'by the Rules,' is not at all." Also how can a statute mean a mechanism? And on and on. I can't understand the utility of complexifying legal interpretation in this way.

The still-popular idea, though false, that legal reasoning, even if it is as
opaque as is (to me at any rate) a good deal of Professor Eskridge's latest book,
gives the intelligent lawyer, judge, or professor access to *the* right answer to every legal question is called legal formalism—the umbrella term, mentioned in
the Introduction to this book, under which originalism and textualism huddle
along with other metaphysical legalisms. In the simplest version of formalism
the premises for legal reasoning are given and the correct outcome of particular disputes derived deductively; this was nineteenth-century legal formalism.
In another version, reasoning by analogy is given parity with the syllogism as a
method of apodictic reasoning. But more commonly nowadays interpretation
is substituted for analogy, as by constitutional originalists.

Yet in still another version of formalism, positive law is held to be derivative
by logical methods from natural law, which might be founded on religious belief or, as in the late Ronald Dworkin's influential conception of law, on political
theory.

What ties all these approaches together is that the proponents of each believe that it enables the attainment of certainty. The problem with this belief
system is not only that the proponents of the different approaches do not agree
with one another, but also that there is no analytical method of determining

who is right—no means of forcing agreement or concession. Even worse, the focus of each proponent is on the past—on old decisions, other old documents (such as constitutional provisions), venerable philosophies, religion, logic, political theory. The result is tunnel vision, which is avoided when the focus of legal thinking is on the present and the future.

On another front I am surprised by Dorf's saying that my describing "judges not as interpreters of legislation but as partners of the legislators" is "old hat." The quoted passage has a context that he ignores. I said that "judges have been given the thankless task of 'interpreting' statutes that can't be interpreted in many of the cases to which the statutes apply. Often there is no discernible legislative intent regarding potential cases within the statute's semantic reach. . . . If the legislators did not foresee an issue arising under their statute that has become a subject of litigation, there isn't anything to interpret. . . . Interpretation is recovery of meaning, and there is no meaning to recover in such cases."[13] The result is to make judges legislators. Old hat? Dorf's known it forever? Or is it (*pace* Holmes) heresy? What would Justice Scalia have said?

When Dorf discusses my criticisms of academic legal scholarship he turns defensive—he is after all a legal scholar. Yet I am surprised to find him defending two questionable books on constitutional law, by Professor Laurence Tribe (*The Invisible Constitution*) and Professor Akhil Amar (*America's Unwritten Constitution*), respectively—both of which I've criticized sharply in a book that Dorf does not mention.[14] Although he suggests implausibly that the Tribe and Amar books are read by judges, he doesn't name any, and I'd be surprised if there were any except me—the unfriendly reader.

Dorf waxes particularly wroth at criticisms I leveled in *Divergent Paths* at two articles by Harvard Law Professor Richard H. Fallon, Jr. I quoted passages that I claimed would be unintelligible to judges—and I now add, to lawyers and law students and many law professors as well. I refer the readers of this chapter to my quotations for confirmation of my criticisms.[15] I imagine Dorf would respond that a select circle of law professors could understand Fallon's articles, which undoubtedly is true. But I don't see how the articles (which I don't mean

---

13. *Divergent Paths: The Academy and the Judiciary* 112 (2016). I offer a somewhat broader definition of interpretation in the Conclusion of this book.

14. Richard A. Posner, *Reflections on Judging* 219–233 (2013).

15. *Divergent Paths*, note 13 above, at 42–43, 319–320. To give the flavor, I shall quote here just the first sentence of the first article: "The experience of partly value-based interpretative issues often supplies the trigger for appeals to theories of statutory interpretation including both textualist and purposivist theories." No one should write like that.

to suggest are characteristic of the entire corpus of Fallon's scholarly writing[16]) could be useful to the judiciary, or for that matter to legal education.

Professor Fallon, annoyed by my criticism (who can blame him?—it's not unusual for successful people to be insecure; though later in this book I'll praise some of his work), recently sent me, triumphantly, an article in the *Wall Street Journal* that reports that according to a recent study he is the law professor most cited (actually he's tied with another professor for the title) in Supreme Court opinions in recent years.[17] I don't question the accuracy of the study but I note with interest the reporter's remark that "Chief Justice John Roberts may not think much of legal scholarship coming out of the academy these days, but judges *(or at least their clerks)* do read law reviews" (emphasis added). Since each of the Justices has four law clerks, who draft bench memos and usually the Justices' opinions and work hard and as recent law school graduates tend to be *au courant* with academic commentary on the Court, I suspect that the vast majority of Supreme Court citations to Fallon and other professors are supplied by law clerks rather than by Justices.

I never say, as Dorf suggests I do, that legal scholarship has no value for the judiciary (or for legal education or for the practice of law). I do argue that its value for these enterprises is diminishing as such scholarship, especially at the elite law schools, becomes ever more esoteric because the faculties of those schools are becoming ever more crowded with scholars whose first love and continued loyalty are to other scholarly fields. I know that the librarians in my court are receiving fewer and fewer requests by judges for law review articles, and they tell me also that law review circulation has declined over the past decade. Both data are consistent with my evaluation of current judicial use or rather non-use or diminishing use of legal scholarship, though the decline in law reviews' circulation also reflects the greater availability of research materials online.

Often those other scholarly fields are ones in which some law professors,

16. As Dorf points out, I have cited several of Fallon's articles—intelligible articles—in my opinions, and in Chapter 2 of the present book I cite approvingly his surprising but welcome endorsement of the Supreme Court's controversial decision in *Bolling v. Sharpe* and (with some reservations) his book *The Dynamic Constitution*.

17. Jacob Gershman, Law Blog: "Ranking Law Professors by Judicial Impact," *Wall Street Journal*, August 2, 2016, blogs.wsj.com. Actually Fallon was tied for first with Cass Sunstein, another Harvard Law School professor. Both had fifty-six Supreme Court citations over a nine-year period (2005 to 2014), an average of 6.22 a year. For a study similar to Gershman's but including faculty citations by other courts besides the Supreme Court, see Nick Farris et al., "Judicial Impact of Law School Faculties," http://papers.ssrn.com/sol3/papers.cfm?abstract_id=2826048.

before they had entered law school as students, had obtained advanced degrees, only to realize that the chances of landing secure, well-paying academic
jobs in their fields (especially the humanities, such as classics, English, comparative literature, linguistics, history, philosophy, art, music, and archaeol-
ogy) were slight—a development to which Dorf, in defending legal scholarship,
does not allude.

I don't mean to suggest that legal education should be all law. Indeed Dorf
says that I "persuasively argue[] that a good lawyer should be literate in both
the humanities and the sciences," and thus "that law students who arrive[d in
law school] with a humanities background [should be required to] take undergraduate courses in technical subjects, while those who arrive with a technical
background [should] be required to take humanities courses." But then he
pours cold water on my suggestion, saying that "law schools are already under pressure to add more skills courses, leaving little room to require (admittedly vital) courses outside the law entirely." He doesn't explain, however, why
it's better to have more skills courses than the "admittedly vital" courses that I
suggest.

He claims that I "want[] academics to show that legal realism is correct," a
desire he deems "naïve." No, I want academics to be realistic about judicial behavior—to grasp for example the degree to which it deviates from the formalism that continues to be the official ideology of the judiciary, encapsulated in
John Roberts's eyebrow-raising claim in his Senate confirmation hearing that a
Supreme Court Justice is the equivalent of an umpire or referee, who does not
make rules but merely enforces the rules given to him. The fallacy in the remark is that an umpire or referee can *influence* but does not *decide* the outcome
of the game—for the side with more fouls, or (in baseball) more "outs," called
by the umpire or referee, may nevertheless win—whereas judges, especially appellate judges, as there are no appellate jury proceedings, do decide the outcome of cases. Roberts's larger mistake was to fail to distinguish between, on
the one hand, umpires and referees, who are genuine neutrals—they don't allow themselves to care who wins—and judges, who can and often do disguise
(not necessarily consciously, however) their real reasons for ruling as they do
—reasons that may be political, ideological, religious, or strategic, rather than
legal-doctrinal, and thus are not neutral as between the litigants before them.
The fact that no member of the Judiciary Committee challenged Roberts's inaccurate and irrelevant reference to umpires and referees tells one something
about senatorial competence to evaluate Supreme Court nominees.

It is the rare judge (and Roberts is not that rare judge, nor is any other current member of the Supreme Court) who is a pure *tabula rasa,* bringing nothing to the table when there is a case he has to vote on. Often a judge will not have a political or a religious stake in a case, yet he is bound to have a moral code that may predispose him to one outcome or the other—to make him more receptive to one of the antagonists than to the other, or to the lawyer for one of the parties more than to the lawyer for the other. Even a realist who strains against legal doctrine, who thinks more like an arbitrator than a conventional judge, and who is resolutely apolitical and indifferent to religion, will have priors that predispose him, on grounds perhaps only loosely legal, to side with one party to the case rather than with the other. But he will be less rigid, less predictable, than the ideological judge. Indeed he is likely to be a legal realist.

Dorf discusses legal realism at length, describing me as a legal realist—a label I'm happy to wear—and, less accurately, as someone who wishes to enlist academics in the service of spreading the realist gospel and "banish[ing] all vestiges of formalism"—a crusade I have never thought to embark on, but maybe I should. His thoughts on legal realism lack coherence. On the one hand he quotes approvingly an article in which Brian Leiter, a prominent professor at the University of Chicago Law School, declares that "we are all realists now,"[18] and on the other hand he regards as quixotic what he imagines to be my crusade against formalists, which if they don't exist would be an unlikely target of a crusade. And a tendency to self-contradiction is illustrated by Dorf's unintentionally amusing statement that "Posner does have some good ideas about legal education, but even these seem half-baked." Half-baked ideas are not good ideas. In his second piece contra-Posner he explains that by "half-baked" he just means not adequately developed. Were he to query Google for synonyms for "half-baked," he would discover that they are "foolish, stupid, silly, idiotic, simpleminded, feebleminded, empty-headed, featherbrained, featherheaded, brainless, witless, unintelligent, ignorant." I thank him for not affixing any of those adjectives to me.

One of my suggestions in *Divergent Paths* for reforming law school teaching was that civil procedure and evidence be treated as clinical courses—that instead of being taught as bodies of rules they be playacted. The students, rather than immersing themselves in the rules of civil procedure or of evidence, would draft complaints and conduct depositions in their civil procedure

18. Brian Leiter, "Rethinking Legal Realism: Toward a Naturalized Jurisprudence," 76 *Texas Law Review* 267 (1997).

course and conduct mock trials in their evidence course. I taught evidence at the University of Chicago Law School in mock-trial format for several years in the early 1990s, I thought successfully, using the superbly realistic case files of the Institute of Trial Advocacy.[19]

Dorf objects that such curricular innovations "raise cost questions" because "clinical and simulation courses are more labor-intensive than Socratic or lecture courses" and therefore require larger law school faculties and so greater expense, which many law schools can't afford. But he is wrong about the expense of such a reform. Clinical-style teaching can often be done better by adjuncts—practicing lawyers or judges (me for example)—who receive slight and maybe no compensation for their teaching, than by law professors who have little or no practical experience but command very high salaries. A novice law professor at a leading law school can expect a starting salary of about $200,000, rising gradually to $300,000 or more; and depending on his field of law he may have abundant opportunities to supplement his academic income by consulting, writing books, or engaging in other authorized extracurricular activities. By the last year (1981) of my (officially) full-time academic career, my total income—academic salary, book royalties, lecture fees, modest investment income, and consulting income—exceeded $300,000, which is the equivalent in purchasing power to $868,000 today, a number that, needless to say, greatly exceeds my current income. (I'm not complaining, however; I can still afford my cat's nightly meal of Fancy Feast. And I just learned that my annual judicial salary had been increased from $215,400 in 2016 to $217,600 in 2017. I had thought my current salary was only $213,000—but that's what it was in 2015.)

As for Dorf's suggestion that my criticisms of current legal-writing courses are "misinformed" because such courses enable students to "take poetic license, and their writing begins to flow," I haven't seen any poetry in student writing lately, or for that matter in judicial opinions—most of which are drafted by law clerks recently graduated from law school. Law schools, especially the elite ones, place little emphasis on writing skills; often a first-year course in legal writing is the only such course given and the emphasis is less on writing well than on conforming to the debased standards of legal writing found in today's briefs and judicial opinions and professors' books and articles. The principal vice of professorial writing is excessive length—for which the law reviews are at least partially responsible because the law review editors find it easier to select and edit a handful of very long articles than a larger number of short ones.

19. See Richard A. Posner, "Clinical and Theoretical Approaches to the Teaching of Evidence and Trial Advocacy," 21 QLR 731 (2003).

Although Dorf claims that legal-writing instructors discourage their students from resorting to legal jargon, it would be more accurate to say that a few of the instructors *try* to discourage the use of jargon but that, if one may judge from the number of jargon-ridden student law-review comments and judicial opinions, the instructors who try rarely succeed. I am appalled by Dorf's endorsement of the writing "systems," taught in some law schools often in a first-year writing course, which go by such repulsive acronyms as IRAC (Issue, Rule, Application, Conclusion) and CRAC (Conclusion, Rule, Application, Conclusion). Such courses are straitjackets, putting me in mind of the immortal Holmes's crack that "to rest upon a formula is a slumber that, prolonged, means death."[20] Legal writing is overwhelmingly formulaic.

My court, like the others federal courts of appeals, hires what are called "staff attorneys." These usually are recent law school graduates with good law school records, and although not hired by or assigned to specific judges they provide important assistance to the judges with respect to motions by litigants (which my court receives in great number), many of whom are pro se (that is, have no lawyer). They also advise the judges about a number of the appeals to my court, some orally argued. They do a good job on the whole—but they tend not to write well, and I attribute that deficiency to the failure of the law schools to teach students how to write well, as opposed to how to brandish jargon.

The crowning peculiarity of Professor Dorf's review of *Divergent Paths* is that it has so little to say about the judiciary. Apart from Judge Harry Edwards of the D.C. Circuit (an excellent judge, by the way), I am the only living judge mentioned in the review and even Dorf's references to deceased judges (mainly Holmes, Hand, and Friendly) are few. I infer that his priority is to defend the academy from barbs such as mine because he's an academic and I'm not. He seems little interested in the quality of judicial appointments and judicial opinions, in the failures of judicial management that I discussed in the Introduction to this book, in the lack of relevant diversity on the Supreme Court (a theme of the next chapter), and in my other criticisms. His seeming lack of interest in the judiciary confirms my concern, stressed in *Divergent Paths,* about the growing gap between the academy and the judiciary.

I hope I've persuaded the reader that the sum of the "small matters" discussed in this chapter is not itself a small matter.

20. http://quotes.yourdictionary.com/author/quotes/138102. Oliver Wendell Holmes, Jr., "Ideals and Doubts," 10 *Illinois Law Review* 3 (1915).

ADDENDUM: A MINIATURIZED
SUBSTITUTE FOR THE *BLUEBOOK*

The following is the section on citation formatting from the handbook that I give my law clerks upon their arrival.

Dick doesn't follow the *Bluebook,* the *Maroon Book,* the *Chicago Manual of Style,* or any other style book, and doesn't want you to get hung up worrying about citation form. (He *hates* the *Bluebook* with a passion.) A few simple rules, however, should be kept in mind:

No parallel citations in cases; statutory provisions do not need years, unless the point is to identify an old law.

Case names
- Avoid abbreviations, with a few exceptions such as Ry., RR., Comm'n, Co., Corp., Inc., &, Ass'n, Ins.; sometimes Dist., Mfg., Int'l. Only *obvious* abbreviations should be used.
- Omit *Inc.* or *Co.* when it immediately follows *Co., Ry.,* or *RR.*
- In re Casename, not In the Matter of Casename

The important thing is not to use any nonobvious abbreviation, as otherwise the reader may not know the actual name or other word that is being abbreviated.

State courts
- Highest court: abbreviation for the state (Ill., Cal., N.Y.)
- Intermediate appellate court is Ill. App., Cal. App., etc. New York is an exception: "N.Y. App. Div."
- Regional reporter is preferred, but if the citation is to the official state reporter, do not repeat the state name within parentheses.

Supra cites of cases repeat the full title; *supra* cites of authored materials repeat the author. Use an N-dash (–) for page and date ranges.

Don't just copy blindly a citation from a reporter; reformat it (e.g., by putting a space between court and year, as West does not do: "7th Cir. 2000" not "7th Cir.2000", and by putting in non-breaking spaces where appropriate.).

The usual citation order is reverse chronological order, and, for federal cases, Supreme Court, Seventh Circuit, other circuits, districts; for state cases, governing-law state, then federal cases. Sometimes it makes sense to put a seminal case first. Dick is not a stickler about order. Remember, you are not working on a law review. Substance rather than form is paramount in Dick's chambers (though make sure not to be sloppy!).

The following page contains a sheet of examples. You may note occasional inconsistencies—why name the authors in Nimmer but not McCarthy?—but don't let that bother you. Do not treat these as gospel. When in doubt, check old opinions or ask Dick.

Green v. Bock Laundry Machine Co., 490 U.S. 504, 527 (1989) (Scalia, J., concurring, or just concurring opinion without a judge's name)

Green v. Bock Laundry Machine Co, supra, 490 U.S. at 527 [short citation format for cases]

Outlet Embroidery Co. v. Derwent Mills, 172 N.E. 462, 463 (N.Y. 1930) (Cardozo, C. J.)

Fisher v. Professional Compounding Centers of America, Inc., 311 F. Supp. 2d 1008, 1015 (D. Nev. 2004)

Meyerson v. Harrah's East Chicago Casino, No. 01-1993, 2002 WL 1483222, at *1 (7th Cir. July 11, 2002)

Relational Design & Technology, Inc. v. Brock, No. 91-2452-EEO, 1993 WL 191323, at *6–7 (D. Kan. May 25, 1993) [district court case not published in a reporter]

J&T Hydro Co., 66 F.E.R.C. ¶ 62,138 (1994)

42 U.S.C. §§ 1396a(a)(1), (8), (10)(B)(i), (19), (23)

720 ILCS 5/12-15

Ind. Code § 35-48-4-1(a)

Fed. R. Evid. 408

Fed. R. Civ. P. 10(c)

Fed. R. App. P. 28(a)(9)(B)

24 C.F.R. § 3500.14(c)

57 Fed. Reg. 49600, 49605 (Nov. 2, 1992)

U.S.S.G. § 2G1.1(b)(1) Application Note 2

Restatement (Second) of Torts § 772(a) (1977) [previous opinions reveal uncertainty about the proper date]

2 Fowler V. Harper, Fleming James, Jr. & Oscar S. Gray, *The Law of Torts,* § 7.8, pp. 423–24 (2d ed. 1986)

W. Page Keeton et al., *Prosser & Keeton on the Law of Torts* § 56, p. 376 (5th ed. 1984)

5 Charles A. Wright & Arthur R. Miller, *Federal Practice and Procedure* § 1327, pp. 762–63 (2d ed. 1990) [there are sometimes additional authors—which may make the author "Charles A. Wright et al." (use et al. when there are more than three authors)—it varies by volume]

Richard J. Pierce Jr., *Administrative Law Treatise* § 3.5, pp. 6–7 (4th ed. Supp. 2003)

7 *Collier on Bankruptcy* ¶ 1109.01[1], p. 1109-4 (15th ed. 2002)

2 *McCarthy on Trademarks* § 17:22, p. 17-44 (2002)

4 Melville B. Nimmer & David Nimmer, *Nimmer on Copyright* § 13.03[C], pp. 13-75 to 13-77 (2002)

Matthew C. Stephenson, "Information Acquisition and Institutional Design," 124 *Harv. L. Rev.* 1422, 1434–35 (2011)

Stephenson, *supra,* at 1435–36 [short citation format for periodicals]

David Strauss, *The Living Constitution* 99 (2010) [long citation format for books]

"Making Cocaine Freebase With Ammonia Methods," www.drugs -forum.com/forum/showthread.php?t=30174&page=2 (visited May 21, 2010)

Douglas Hold, "State to Investigate Safety at Zion Park; Asbestos Fears Fuel Madigan Action" *Chicago Tribune,* July 3, 2003, p. 1

Other pointers:
- Abbreviations such as EEOC, FCC, and UCC have no periods.
- Always spell out United States.
- Do not note cert. denied.
- Do not use brackets to indicate when a capital letter has been lower-cased within a quotation.
- Do not use pincites in short opinions or opinions that stand for a single point.
- Insert a space between the "n." and the note number, and if you need to cite both the note and the text on the page, use an "and" instead of an ampersand.

- You can use *Id.* to refer to the last source in a prior stringcite.
- Dick uses two section symbols when he's citing at least two subsections, even if both subsections are within the same section.
- Dick uses et seq.
- Dick places state court cases in reverse chronological order and not alphabetically by state. Within a state, state supreme court citations are placed before intermediate appellate court citations.
- Dick does not insert "the" in the interior of a case name citation, even if the West reporter has it.
- Dick does not include "of [geographical name]" in a case name citation, even if the West reporter has it.
- Dick uses the word "section" in lieu of the section symbol whenever referring to a section in-the text of his opinion (even if it is not the beginning of a sentence), unless he is full-citing the code in-text. For example, "Section 1124 is . . ." and "The language in section 1124 is . . . ," but "The relevant language is in 11 U.S.C. § 1124 . . ."
- In online citations, delete http when it appears right before www.

TWO

Tier One of the Federal Judiciary:

The Supreme Court

The past is a foreign country.
They do things differently there.
L. P. HARTLEY, 1953

That which is not just is not Law.
JOHN FORBES, 1735[1]

Readers of the Constitution need to remember that
writing thrives on a wealth of circumstances and social
assumptions beyond claims about authorial purpose.
ROBERT A. FERGUSON, 2016

SOME PREFATORY REMARKS

I BEGIN AN EXTENDED DISCUSSION of the Supreme Court by sharing with
the reader a fulsome, effusive, hard-to-believe statement by Supreme Court
Justice Elena Kagan that illustrates the absence of realism, or perhaps it's just
the absence of a culture of frank discourse, that characterizes public discussion of the American legal system, especially by judges. After expressing her
"boundless admiration and affection for [the recently deceased—February 13,
2016] Justice Scalia—'I just loved Justice Scalia, and I miss him every day'"
(could that be tongue in cheek?)—Kagan remarks that "I would put this court

1. How then to characterize the jurisprudence of the current Supreme Court, given that "the [Supreme]
Court is awash in an ocean of discretion." Richard A. Posner, *How Judges Think* 272 (2008). See also "The
Court's Constitutional Decisions Pay Lip Service to Legal Doctrine, While the Court's Results Appear to Be
Based on Political Value Judgments." Eric J. Segall, "The Black Holes of Constitutional Law," 17 *Constitutional
Commentary* 425, 445 (2000) (review of Laurence H. Tribe, *American Constitutional Law* [3d ed. 1999], vol. 1).

[the U.S. Supreme Court] as a whole up there with any court that the country has ever had in terms of the kind of legal skills, proficiency and lawyerly aptitude that this court has. . . . Our court is in general a very, very, very lawyerly place. . . . It's natural to have people who have spent lots of years of their lives thinking about legal analysis."[2]

Months later, Justice Kagan was one of a group of Supreme Court Justices and academics who lionized the late Justice Scalia in an article (really a potpourri of comments) entitled "In Memoriam: Justice Antonin Scalia."[3] As in Kagan's earlier statement, her comment includes mawkish invocation of "love," and there is also the dubious claim that "he will go down in history as one of the most significant of Justices—and also one of the greatest," having "transformed our legal culture." There is also a reference to his "splendid prose." All this is over the top, though in fairness he did write well. And what is the reader supposed to understand is the difference between "most significant" and "greatest"? Kagan sounds more like a breathless undergraduate than a Supreme Court Justice.

A former law clerk of Scalia's, writing in the same memorial collection, reports that Scalia "had a contagious laugh that spread pure joy to those who heard it." I knew Scalia off and on for almost forty years, heard him laugh on occasion and did not find his laughter contagious or react with pure joy.

I was stunned to read Professor Cass Sunstein's saying in his contribution to the memorial that "Justice Antonin Scalia was . . . one of the greatest justices in the Court's history, and among its three best writers (alongside Justices Oliver Wendell Holmes, Jr., and Robert Jackson)." Sunstein is a liberal who headed the federal Office of Information and Regulatory Affairs (OIRA) in the Obama Administration. I find it difficult to believe he thought Scalia one of the greatest Justices. Scalia's effort to sell the Court and the profession on "originalism" was a flop as I'll be showing, and as a writer of judicial opinions he was outclassed not only by Holmes (who incidentally—Professor Sunstein, please note—had dropped the "Jr." before his appointment to the Supreme Court) and Jackson, but also by John Marshall, Brandeis, Hughes, Cardozo, Black, Rehnquist, Roberts, and many others. Sunstein adds, "To know him was to love him." I knew him too, I liked him well enough, but *love* him? Ridiculous!

2. Quoted in Adam Liptak, "Supreme Court Is Working Hard to Avoid Deadlocks, Kagan Says," *New York Times,* April 4, 2016, www.nytimes.com/2016/04/05/us/politics/supreme-court-is-working-hard-to-avoid-deadlocks-elena-kagan-says.html?_r=2. I can't make sense of the last sentence of her statement.

3. 130 *Harvard Law Review* 1 (2016).

The best piece in the *Harvard Law Review* issue from which I've been quoting does not appear in the memorial section. The article,[4] entitled "The Age of Scalia," by Jamal Greene, a Columbia Law School professor, is the best as well as the longest article about Scalia that I've ever read. Unfailingly polite, devoid of anger or sarcasm, it makes a convincing case for the failure of Scalia's ambitions to transform constitutional law.

I want to return for a moment to Kagan's remarks, both what she said right after Scalia's death and what she wrote in the *Harvard Law Review*. The views that she expressed about Scalia and the current Supreme Court bespeak both an impoverished conception of the qualifications to be a Supreme Court Justice and an inflated evaluation of the current Court. What needs rather to be acknowledged is that the current Court is a very political place, also not well managed, and that the current set of Justices is deficient in educational and career and even geographical diversity, deficient in understanding science and technology, virtually bereft of trial experience, not good team players, underworked, and in some respects (as I'll argue later in this chapter) ethically challenged.[5] Some of them are downright disagreeable. The current Court is not "up there with any court that the country has ever had."

Whether or not Kagan's remark was (as I doubt) sincere, it was false. Oliver Wendell Holmes was appointed to the Supreme Court in 1902. Robert Jackson, the last of the great Justices, died in office in 1954. The other notable Justices who served during that period were Charles Evans Hughes, Louis Brandeis, William Howard Taft, Harlan Fiske Stone, and Benjamin Cardozo. None of the current Justices measures up to any of them, or—with the possible exception of Justices Ginsburg and Breyer (more likely the latter, in light of Ginsburg's inappropriate remarks, discussed later in this chapter, about Donald Trump and about the black National Football League players who kneeled instead of standing during the playing of the Star-Spangled Banner)—to such lesser though still distinguished Supreme Court Justices of that era as Felix Frankfurter, Hugo Black, Earl Warren, William Brennan, John Marshall Harlan II, Byron White, and even, at his intermittent best, William O. Douglas.

Kagan's encomia that I've been quoting were not her first public paeans to Scalia; three months *before* his death she had said that he would "go down as

---

4. "The Age of Scalia," 130 *Harvard Law Review* 144 (2016).

5. On the lack of relevant diversity, both currently and recently, in the Supreme Court, see, e.g., Adam Liptak, "Obama Has a Chance to Select Justice with Varied Résumé," *New York Times,* May 1, 2009; Emily Bazelon, "How to Bring the Supreme Court Back Down to Earth," *New York Times,* February 15, 2016.

one of the most important, most historic figures on the Court."[6] Colorful, outspoken, disruptive, yes; but likely to be recognized some day as one of the most important Justices in history?—unlikely, and surely it's too soon to tell. He does however deserve credit for his efforts to discredit the overemphasis that the Supreme Court had come to place on legislative history as a guide to statutory interpretation.[7] By the late 1970s the Court was citing legislative history three hundred or four hundred times per term—indeed was citing it in *every* case involving statutory interpretation, and using it as a basis for arguing that statutory language needn't be thought to mean what it says,[8] which is often true but not always. Scalia was not however alone in criticizing the Court for overemphasizing legislative history. Moreover, he was pushing against an open door. He had joined the Court on September 26, 1986, the same day that Rehnquist became Chief Justice, and from then till Scalia's death the Court had a conservative majority, literalist in outlook and receptive therefore to criticisms of legislative history.

Eight months, minus six days, after Scalia's death, Justice Kagan delivered still another public encomium of him, this one on the occasion of the dedication of the Antonin Scalia Law School (formerly called the George Mason University School of Law).[9] She was preceded in the ceremony by the Chief Justice of Virginia (Donald Lemons), who said that Scalia "would fill a room with the enormity of his personality." This was a slip of the tongue, since "enormity" does not mean large; its synonyms are such words as depravity, abomination, monstrosity, turpitude, vice, and villainy. Chief Justice Lemons went on to say that Scalia "was a man on a mission, and his mission involved principled

6. Jonathan G. Adler, "Kagan Discusses Statutory Interpretation at Law School," *Harvard Crimson*, November 18, 2015, www.thecrimson.com/article/2015/11/18/kagan-talk-law-school/. Adler in this piece expresses awe at Kagan's candor; that's pathetic; I very much doubt that she was being candid. Indeed I'm skeptical that she believed what she said. The remark "go down" has an odd ring given how soon after it was uttered he died.

7. See, e.g., *Graham County Soil & Water Conservation District v. United States ex rel. Wilson*, 569 U.S. 280, 302 (2010) (Scalia, J., concurring); *Hirschey v. Federal Energy Regulatory Commission*, 777 F.2d 1, 7–8 (D.C. Cir. 985) (Scalia, J., concurring); Elizabeth A. Liess, "Censoring Legislative History: Justice Scalia on the Use of Legislative History in Statutory Interpretation," 72 *Nebraska Law Review* 569 (1993).

8. See, e.g., *Citizens to Preserve Overton Park, Inc. v. Volpe*, 401 U.S. 402, 412 n. 29 (1971); Patricia M. Wald, "Some Observations on the Use of Legislative History in the 1981 Supreme Court Term," 68 *Iowa Law Review* 195 (1983). See also my book *The Federal Courts: Crisis and Reform* 286 (1985).

9. See Richard Wolf, "Six Justices Turn Out for Dedication of Antonin Scalia Law School," *USA Today*, October 6, 2016, www.usatoday.com/story/news/politics/2016/10/06/supreme-court-antonin-scalia-law-school-dedication/91673686/?utm_source=feedblitz&utm_medium=FeedBlitzRss&utm_campaign=usatoday-news topstories. Actually there was an intermediate renaming—the Antonin Scalia School of Law—but it had an unfortunate acronym (ASSOL), so "School of Law" was replaced by "Law School."

decision-making," and that Scalia cared more about the reasoning behind a ruling than the decision itself. That is very doubtful.

Kagan began her talk at the dedication by saying, "He [Scalia] will go down in history as one of the most important Supreme Court justices ever, and also one of the greatest." [I'm not sure how "most important," like "most significant," differs from "greatest."] She noted that Scalia's "firm belief in originalism and textualism . . . has transformed legal culture." She said his written opinions, full of "wit, dash and verve [sometimes, not always[10]] . . . mesmerized law students" and his visits to campuses had the effect of "exciting students, challenging students, provoking students, charming students, and making them think harder than they had ever thought before. . . . No one was more enthusiastic, more passionate about connecting with law students than Justice Scalia." I can attest that this was not true when he taught at the University of Chicago Law School in the late 1970s and early 1980s, a period in which we were colleagues, and there are doubts that it was true later. It may be significant that he never allowed his talks to students to be videotaped, which may be related to the fact that, I am told, some (maybe many) students found his talks to them off-putting; for he had an aggressive personality and mercurial temperament that he could not or would not control.

But I am reasonably confident that Kagan would at least not take literally the *Economist's* (I assume tongue in cheek) obituary of Scalia, entitled "Always Right" (note pun in "Right") and ending with, "He knew for certain, though, that the Framers were on his side; the Devil was on the other; and that heaven was his portion, for he was always right."[11]

Now here is a genuine curiosity: Professor Dorf, in the second of his two pieces that I discussed in the preceding chapter, accuses me of "a gratuitous insult of Justice Elena Kagan"[12]—namely, questioning the sincerity of her personal affection for Justice Scalia. I doubt that Dorf has the faintest inkling of whether Kagan had any personal affection for Scalia or wanted merely to get on his good side or provide reassurance to the public that disagreements between Justices are impersonal—that Holmes was wrong in calling the Justices

10. Ross Guberman, in his book *Point Taken: How to Write Like the World's Best Judges* (2015), quotes a number of passages from Scalia opinions, and almost all the quotations are pedestrian.

11. "Obituary: Antonin Scalia, 'Always Right,'" *The Economist,* February 20, 2016, www.economist.com /news/obituary/21693161-originalist-chief-devout-and-colourful-end-was-79-obituary-antonin-scalia. And we'll see that Scalia really did believe in the Devil.

12. Michael Dorf, "Parsing Posner's Peevishness," *Dorf on Law,* September 30, 2016, www.dorfonlaw .org/2016/09/parsing-posners-peevishness.html.

"nine scorpions in a bottle." (He was more right than wrong.) But I imagine she did like him, just as Justice Ginsburg did—as I did—because he could turn on the charm when he wanted to, which was often. He didn't in the case of Justice O'Connor, however, and instead made an enemy of her, impairing his ability to command a majority of the Justices. He had a temper that he wasn't able to control.

But what I *know* is that judges on an appellate court, including Justices of the Supreme Court, almost always make *some* effort to get along with each other, since they're engaged in a collective activity. It's difficult for an outsider to determine whether the effort is based on or generates affection. Kagan is a charming person and probably did try to charm Scalia and may have succeeded, though if so it seems not to have affected how he voted in cases. Scalia loved to hunt, and Kagan asked him to teach her to hunt and take her with him on a hunting expedition, and he agreed, enabling her to kill an innocent animal—thereby perhaps ingratiating herself with him. (They went on more than one hunt together; I believe that in toto she bagged one deer and some birds. I do not believe in hunting for sport, which amounts to trying, often with success, to kill innocent animals.)

To help prepare the reader for what is to come in this very long chapter, I need to quote remarks I made at a conference at Loyola Law School in Chicago in 2015 and that Professor Eric Segall of Georgia State University College of Law made on a separate occasion and that are republished here with his permission:[13]

From My Remarks (Edited and Somewhat Amplified)

On the value of text and history. At the risk of being thought a philistine, I confess to not being greatly interested in the eighteenth century, nor in the text of the Constitution (including the Bill of Rights), a product of that century. No document drafted back then can guide our behavior today, because eighteenth-century people couldn't foresee the problems, the culture, the social and economic conditions, the resources and opportunities and problems and dangers, of the twenty-first century. Justice Scalia was the most prominent advocate of the antithetical view—which goes by the name "originalism"—though his ac-

13. My remarks were recorded in "Judge Posner on Judging, Birthright Citizenship, and Precedent," *Josh Blackman's Blog,* November 6, 2015, http://joshblackman.com/blog/2015/11/06/judge-posner-on-judging-birthright-citizenship-and-precedent/. Professor Segall's remarks are from his article "The Constitution Means What the Supreme Court Says It Means," 129 *Harvard Law Review Forum* 176 (2016).

tual adherence to it is a matter of debate. With him gone, the mantle of originalism now covers the shoulders of one of his prominent admirers, my brilliant colleague Frank Easterbrook, who in an aptly named "Scalia Lecture" offered this succinct summary of the version of originalism that he shared with Scalia:

> The evolution of [many constitutional rules declared by the Supreme Court] is problematic . . . because they are largely judge-made in accordance with judicial review, which is meant to be historical, not progressive. Judicial review . . . depends on the belief that rules laid down long ago could remain authoritative in the modern era. Where the decisions of long ago can no longer speak to the problems of today, democracy must fill the gaps. I don't lose sleep over the argument that this leaves us with a wooden Constitution or rule by a dead hand. When there is no definitive decision in the document, we don't have anything dead. We have decision by living majorities, [that is, by legislatures and perhaps by the President].[14]

Judge Easterbrook had said much the same thing in a laudatory foreword to Scalia's book (coauthored with Bryan Garner) on statutory interpretation.[15] His approach implies that constitutional law must shrink over time because it can never be permitted to be "progressive" rather than purely "historical." Eventually, in the radical view that Scalia and Easterbrook shared, the Constitution would have become obsolete and there would then be no judicially enforceable constitutional law until and unless the Constitution was replaced or amended. I do not share that view. I stand with Justice Holmes, who explained in *Missouri v. Holland*,[16] that

> when we are dealing with words that also are a constituent act, like the Constitution of the United States, we must realize that they have called into life a being the development of which could not have been foreseen completely by the most gifted of its begetters. It was enough for them to

14. "Inaugural Scalia Lecture," *Harvard Law Today,* November 17, 2014, http://today.law.harvard.edu/judge-easterbrook-delivers-inaugural-scalia-lecture-interpreting-unwritten-constitution-video/. Judge Easterbrook's originalist views are thus antithetical to Professor David Strauss's "living Constitution" conception of constitutional law, discussed below.

15. Foreword, in Antonin Scalia and Bryan A. Garner, *Reading Law: The Interpretation of Legal Texts* (2012), at p. xxvi.

16. 252 U.S. 416, 433–434 (1920).

realize or to hope that they had created an organism; it has taken a century and has cost their successors much sweat and blood to prove that they created a nation. The case before us must be considered in the light of our whole experience and not merely in that of what was said a hundred years ago. The treaty in question does not contravene any prohibitory words to be found in the Constitution. The only question is whether it is forbidden by some invisible radiation from the general terms of the Tenth Amendment. We must consider what this country has become in deciding what that amendment has reserved.

I go so far as to question Judge Easterbrook's contention quoted above that *democracy* can, let alone is all that should, be called on to fill gaps created by the obsolescence of old rules, such as those found in the text of the original Constitution. For the United States is not correctly described as a democracy, not today and not when the Constitution was adopted, either. Democracy is what Athens had—a direct democracy, in which the people, not politicians, voted for or against proposed legislation, though it was a limited democracy because the franchise was limited to adult male citizens who owned land and were not slaves, and there were many women, many slaves, and many metics (free resident aliens, such as Aristotle), none of whom could vote, who also lived in Athens. In today's United States, politicians such as the Senators and Representatives in the Congress (and indirectly the President, for example in wielding the veto power) make the legislative decisions, as do their counterparts in the state legislatures, and do so largely on the basis of their ambitions, their personal and political beliefs, and the desires of the plutocrats who finance them. The voters do not understand most of the issues in a national election and for that and other reasons many eligible voters don't bother to vote (42 percent in the 2016 Presidential election).

The judges and Justices make obeisance to the "democratic" decisions of Congress, but those decisions are very often not democratic at all—which shows how wrong the NYU political scientist Jeremy Waldron is in his article "The Core of the Case Against Judicial Review"[17] to propose that judicial review of legislation be forbidden altogether, as undemocratic. And crowning all is the extreme poverty, very poor health, frequent early death, and low school enrollment in states of the deep South, notably Mississippi and Louisiana,[18] as a result

17. 115 *Yale Law Journal* 1346 (2006).
18. See, e.g., Arlie Russell Hochschield, *Strangers in Their Own Land* 8–9 (2016).

of which relatively few citizens of those states are competent to participate meaningfully in national elections.

And was Scalia really an originalist? I don't think so. I agree with Professor Segall that "if constitutional law professors are going to write about Scalia's originalism and / or textualism, they should also mention that when it comes to his votes, he was neither. . . . [N]o reasonable person can look at Scalia's votes in affirmative action, takings, 11th Amendment, standing, first amendment, criminal procedure, and commandeering cases, among others, and argue that he voted as an originalist or textualist. He voted his values writ large, like every other Justice."[19]

On the Seventh Amendment. Unsurprisingly given its age, the eighteenth-century constitutional text is rife with anachronisms. The Seventh Amendment states for example that if the matter in controversy in a common-law federal case is at least $20, the parties have a right to insist on a jury trial. (The reference to "common law" was apparently intended to exclude admiralty and patent cases and cases in which the federal government was a party.) But $20 meant something very different in the eighteenth century from what it means today. Twenty dollars back then had a purchasing power equal to $513 today— and even $513 is trivial relative to the present-day costs of litigating a federal case. What the Supreme Court should say about cases in which the matter in dispute is trivial though greater than $20 is that the $20 provision in the Seventh Amendment is hopelessly archaic and simply will not be enforced. The Court could point out that a federal statute (28 U.S.C. § 1332(a)) requires that in a case filed in federal court in which the basis of federal jurisdiction is the diversity of citizenship of the parties the amount in controversy must exceed $75,000 for the case to be litigable. This is squarely contrary to the Seventh Amendment, yet is unchallenged and thus is compelling evidence that some provisions of the Constitution can simply be ignored by the courts—with impunity. And should be and are.

On Article VII of the Constitution. Anyone who doubts what I just said should consult Articles VI and XIII of the Articles of Confederation (1778), which preceded the ratification of the Constitution of the United States by a decade. The

19. Eric Segall, "Justice Scalia 1 and Justice Scalia 2: A Modest Proposal," *Dorf on Law,* September 14, 2016, www.dorfonlaw.org/2016/09/justice-scalia-1-and-justice-scalia-2.html.

Articles were the first American constitution. Article VI stated that "the Articles of this Confederation shall be inviolably observed by every State, and the Union shall be perpetual; nor shall any alteration at any time hereafter be made in any of them; unless such alteration be agreed to in a Congress of the United States, and be afterwards confirmed by the legislatures of every State." Article XIII began with a "pledge of perpetual union" and went on to say that "no alterations can be made to the Articles without the agreement of Congress and the confirmation by each of the state legislatures." Yet Article VII of the Constitution of the United States—the Constitution written in 1787 and ratified by nine states the following year—stated that ratification by nine states would be "sufficient for the Establishment of this Constitution"—thus violating the Articles of Confederation, though the Articles had not been abrogated and by their terms could be abrogated only by unanimous action of the thirteen states.

The ninth state ratified the Constitution in June 1788, thereby activating it under the terms of Article VII, but the thirteenth state (Rhode Island) did not ratify it until 1790. So arguably the Constitution established in 1788 in violation of the Articles of Confederation was illegal. But, very sensibly, no one cares—a lesson in the malleability of American law, including the Constitution: a lesson that recurs again and again in this book.

On birthright citizenship. A constitutional anachronism analogous to the Seventh Amendment is the provision in section 1 of the Fourteenth Amendment that recognizes "birthright citizenship"—meaning that anyone born in the United States is automatically an American citizen. If the provision is read literally, then even a child of foreigners who visit the United States only to have the child born here, so that he or she will have a refuge should things go badly in the family's home country, is an American citizen from birth. (Such children are often referred to as "anchor babies," because birthright citizenship gives them the option of "anchoring" themselves, if they want, in the United States when they grow up, since they are U.S. citizens.) That isn't a necessary construal of the provision, since it seems that what its authors and ratifiers intended was merely that the children of the former slaves, freed in 1866, just two years before the ratification of the Fourteenth Amendment, were entitled to the status of citizens. Otherwise a Southern state would be free to enact and enforce a law that while providing that "there are no more slaves" also provided that "the children of slaves, while lawful residents and free persons, can't become citizens." No one who drafted or voted to ratify section 1 had in mind tourist pregnancies.

On a twenty-one-year-old President. Among other provisions of the Constitution that should not be regarded as justiciable is the requirement in Article II, section 1, that the President be at least thirty-five years old upon assuming the office. The youngest person to become President was Theodore Roosevelt, who was forty-two when President McKinley was assassinated (Roosevelt was his Vice President). The youngest elected President was John F. Kennedy, who was forty-three when he assumed the office. It's not obvious that there's often a great deal of maturing between thirty-five and forty-two—let alone between thirty-four and thirty-five; and it's unlikely that an immature person of any age would be elected President. One of the reasons for the age-thirty-five provision, moreover, having nothing to do with maturity or immaturity, was that the younger the President is when elected, the longer he would be likely to remain in office (there was no Presidential term limit in the original Constitution)—too long, it was feared.

Against this background, imagine that a candidate for President happened to be only twenty years old when elected—the age of Alexander the Great when he succeeded his father as king of Macedonia, or thirty, Napoleon's age when he became the ruler of France—and a suit was filed challenging the election as unconstitutional. The sensible thing for the Supreme Court to do in such a situation would be not to invalidate the election but to declare the age-thirty-five requirement nonjusticiable. That would leave it up to Congress to decide what should be done with an "underage" Presidential candidate. For if the Court invalidated the election, then what? Install the Vice President as President? Continue the incumbent President in office? In either case, order a new election? To be held when? And if a do-over election were held and again resulted in the election of a candidate who was not yet thirty-five (maybe the same candidate whose election the Court had voided), what would the Court do then? Best I think would be for it to ignore the age-thirty-five provision in all circumstances.

It's true that section 3 of the Twentieth Amendment, ratified in 1933, provides that "if the President elect shall have failed to qualify, then the Vice President elect shall act as President until a President shall have qualified." But even if "failed to qualify" includes being under thirty-five, the President-elect could foil the provision by having selected as his running mate a thirty-year-old. The amendment also says that "Congress may by law provide for the case wherein neither a President elect nor a Vice President elect shall have qualified, declaring who shall then act as President." But "qualified" is not defined. I grant that the Court would have to do *something* if the successful candidate were a ten-year-old, or a cat;[20] in such a case "qualified" would come into its own. But only in such extreme cases.

On a President born abroad. The same paragraph in Article II, section 1, that requires that the President be at least thirty-five also requires that he or she be a "natural born Citizen," meaning either born in the United States or born abroad to U.S. citizens. My father as it happens immigrated at the age of three months to the United States with his parents in 1901 from Jassy, Romania, his place of birth. He grew up as a normal American, spoke flawless English, went to college and law school, practiced law, became a successful businessman. My mother immigrated with her parents to the United States from Vienna at the age of five, a few years after my father had immigrated (she was a year older than he), soon spoke flawless English, graduated from Hunter College in New York and then taught high-school English for many years in the New York City public schools. Having been born abroad to foreigners rather than to U.S. citizens, my parents were naturalized U.S. citizens rather than "natural born Citizens" of the United States. Neither of them became politicians, but if they had it would be difficult to understand why their foreign birth, which because of the age at which they'd immigrated to the United States had left no trace on their character, beliefs, speech, or behavior should have barred their eligibility for the Presidency. For just think of the roster of highly distinguished American politicians and statesmen, naturalized citizens all, born abroad to parents who were not U.S. citizens and thus, if Article II section 1 is taken literally, ineligible to be President. The list is long;[21] it includes Madeleine Albright, Michael Blumenthal, Zbigniew Brzezinski, Ted Cruz, John Deutch, Felix Frankfurter, Albert Gallatin, Henry Kissinger, William O'Dwyer, Samantha Power, George Romney, Arnold Schwarzenegger, John Sununu, and Robert

20. Remember Morris, who in 1988 became the first cat to run for President? He was introduced to the electorate by Eleanor Mondale, daughter of Walter Mondale, in a brief though moving talk, which I quote in full: "May I introduce a candidate with the quiet demeanor of a Coolidge, the animal magnetism of a Kennedy, and with the honesty of a Lincoln, a candidate who may shed but never shred, a candidate who stands four square behind the values of life, liberty and the pursuit of din-din." Amy, "Morris the Cat First Feline Presidential Candidate," *LoveMeow,* March 12, 2004, www.lovemeow.com/morris-the-cat-first-feline-presidential-candidate-1608003702.html. I confessed in an earlier note to being a cat nut, and in confirmation of that confession I refer the reader to LawProfBlog and Eric Segall, "Pixie for President: Why Judge Posner's Cat Deserves Your Vote," *Above the Law,* October 11, 2016, http://abovethelaw.com/2016/10/pixie-for-president-why-judge-posners-cat-deserves-your-vote/. As a federal judge, I was not allowed to participate in Pixie's campaign; federal judges are permitted to vote, but not to participate in political campaigns.

21. See "List of foreign-born United States politicians," *Wikipedia,* Wikipedia, https://en.wikipedia.org/wiki/List_of_foreign-born_United_States_politicians.

Wagner. But Ted Cruz's mother was a U.S. citizen (his father was not), which is generally assumed to be enough to have made her child a natural-born citizen of the United States. (Certainly if both parents of a child born abroad are U.S. citizens, the child should be considered a "birthright citizen" rather than an undocumented immigrant.) Perhaps, then, Article II section 1 is undergoing erosion.

On Justice Scalia to the rescue. My suggestion that the judiciary simply ignore patently obsolete provisions of the Constitution derives support from a surprising source: Justice Scalia, who liked to utter such judicial blasphemies as this, from his dissent in *Obergefell*, the same-sex marriage case decided by the Supreme Court in 2015: "A system of government that makes the People subordinate to a committee of nine unelected lawyers [the Supreme Court] does not deserve to be called a democracy." This is a counsel of judicial restraint that could encompass challenges to foreign-born Presidential contenders.

On law versus necessity. A question I've been addressing in this chapter—when should law be overridden by necessity—arose in dramatic form at the time of the 2008 financial crisis, and engaged my attention in a book I wrote entitled *The Crisis of Capitalist Democracy* (2010). I explained that the Federal Reserve, claiming that it lacked the legal authority to save Lehman Brothers from collapsing by lending it the money it would have needed to stave off bankruptcy, had allowed the firm to collapse, precipitating a worldwide financial crisis. The legal claim was unpersuasive. Section 13(3) of the Federal Reserve Act[22] authorizes the Fed to lend money to a nonbank in "unusual and exigent circumstances," provided the loan is "secured to the satisfaction of the Federal reserve bank." Lehman did not have good security for the loan it needed, but in the emergency circumstances created by a collapsing global financial system the Fed could have declared itself "satisfied" with whatever security Lehman could offer. The statutory term "secured to the satisfaction" is defined neither in the statute itself nor in regulations issued by the Fed, and although there is disagreement over its meaning, it is arguable that "the Fed was effectively granted [by section 13(3) of the Federal Reserve Act] complete discretion to accept any types of collateral for a [loan] made in 'unusual and exigent' circumstances."[23]

In national emergencies, moreover—and this is the point I particularly want

22. 12 U.S.C. § 343.
23. See Richard A. Posner, *The Crisis of Capitalist Democracy* 65 (2010), and references cited in id. note 13.

to emphasize—law bends to necessity. Bear Stearns had had lousy collateral, yet had been saved anyway, months earlier, and this created suspicion that the Fed's refusal to save Lehman Brothers must have had some other, hidden motive. Wild rumors, emphasizing Secretary of the Treasury Henry Paulson's past links to Goldman Sachs (he had been its CEO before becoming Secretary of the Treasury), which was a competitor of Lehman Brothers, circulated.

Another example of mistakenly refusing to allow law to be bent by necessity is the refusal of the Illinois Supreme Court, in a case called *Jones v. Municipal Employees' Annuity & Benefit Fund,* decided on March 24, 2016, to interpret a provision of the state's constitution loosely. The case involved two City of Chicago benefits plans for municipal employees. Because the plans were at risk of insolvency, the unions representing the employees agreed with the City to increase gradually the amount of money that participants in the plans were required to contribute and at the same time to reduce, for current participants but also active retirees, the amount and frequency of certain postretirement benefit increases. The state legislature approved the reform package, but the state supreme court invalidated it as inconsistent with a provision of the Illinois constitution of 1970 that states that "membership in any pension or retirement system of the State, any unit of local government or school district, or any agency or instrumentality thereof, shall be an enforceable contractual relationship, *the benefits of which shall not be diminished or impaired*" (emphasis added).

Read literally, the constitutional provision forbade what the legislature did forty-six years (2016 minus 1970) after the provision had been enacted. But in those forty-six years Chicago, and indeed Illinois as a whole, had come close to insolvency, and without the deal with the unions the municipal employees and former employees who were participants in the benefit plans were likely to receive fewer benefits than if the 2016 statute had been upheld, as the unions representing the members of the plans must have believed in supporting the legislative provision. The state supreme court could have ruled that the legislation would not on balance curtail the benefits received by the plan participants, or that there was sufficient doubt about the overall impact of the legislation on them to warrant invoking the constitutional provision—in other words the court could have regarded the issue as nonjusticiable in view of uncertainty concerning the likely impact of the legislation on the plan participants. Instead it relied unimaginatively on a literal reading of "benefits . . . shall not be diminished or impaired" in a constitutional provision almost a half-century old.

On David Strauss's view of the Constitution. If one studies the entire body of constitutional law one will discover that it bears little resemblance to the text of the original Constitution (written in 1787), that text plus the Bill of Rights (1791), or the constitutional text as radically amplified by the ratification of the Fourteenth Amendment in 1868. Professor David Strauss of the University of Chicago Law School has argued convincingly that the Constitution implicitly (or perhaps as a matter of necessity) authorizes the judiciary to create a body of common (that is, judge-made) constitutional law to limit the power of other government officials.[24] He calls this the "living Constitution." But inconsistently he insists that "it is never acceptable [for a judge or a Justice] to announce that you are ignoring the text." He tries to explain away the inconsistency by saying that some structural issues of government need to be settled regardless of whether the settlement is optimal; these include the minimum age of the President, the date of Presidential succession, and the rule that there must be two Senators from every state (to which he could have added other precise provisions in the Constitution, such as the ban on religious tests for public office).[25] But the logic of his position is simply that when the constitutional text is precise, as it sometimes is, it should be followed, and when it's not precise it should be ignored and the common-law aspect of the Constitution allowed to take over. Why doesn't he say that? Because it's heresy to acknowledge that parts of the Constitution are obsolete?

Invented constitutions. Professor Strauss is more interested in the fact that the Supreme Court makes up constitutional law as it goes along than in the variety of constitutions that emerge from the pen of imaginative law professors, who treat the text of the U.S. Constitution as an invitation to press a constitutional theory on the Justices of the Supreme Court. I mentioned Professors Amar and Tribe in earlier chapters and I would add at the very least the late John Hart Ely and the late Ronald Dworkin and the very much still living Richard Epstein. For them as for Strauss the constitutional text is an invitation to judicial creativity, but they take the invitation for granted (as Strauss does not) and create

24. David A. Strauss, "Foreword: Does the Constitution Mean What It Says?" 129 *Harvard Law Review* 1 (2015). My quotation in the next sentence is from page 4 of his Foreword. My criticism of Strauss's contention that the constitutional text must never be ignored echoes pages 40 to 42 of the article by Professor Segall cited in note 13 above.

25. I questioned this proposition above, with reference to the minimum age of the President; I could also question a rigid requirement governing the date of Presidential succession and the requirement of two Senators from every state, regardless of the enormous variance in population among the states.

an imaginary constitution (such as Dworkin's moral constitution and Epstein's libertarian constitution) that bears little relation either to the text of the real Constitution or to constitutional law as it has evolved in the Supreme Court's decisions. Being professors rather than judges, they are free to let their imaginations roam.

On my "aim" as a judge. I'm a pragmatist. I see judges as trying to improve things within certain bounds. The bounds are important; there are practical restrictions on a judge's deciding cases on the basis of his or her political or moral or expedient views, although those views will often have an influence. There are specific laws that bind judges and (as I elaborate in the second part of this chapter) constitutional provisions that bind them too tightly (I just gave some examples). But when judges are free of such restraints their aim should be to try to improve the American society. My approach in judging a case is therefore not to worry initially about doctrine, precedent, and the other conventional materials of legal analysis, but instead to try to figure out the sensible solution to the problem or problems presented by the case. Once having found what I think is the sensible solution I ask whether it's blocked by an authoritative precedent of the Supreme Court or by some other ukase that judges must obey. If it's not blocked (usually it's not—usually it can be got around by hook or by crook), I say fine—let's go with the commonsense solution. I would like to see judicial opinions written by judges rather than law clerks and characterized by brevity and candor and a quest for the sensible result.

One of my mottoes is "Law is made by simple people for simple people." Or as one of the nation's big businessmen said some years ago, "Why make it more complicated? I've always felt that the world is filled with smart people who love complicating stuff."[26] Certainly the legal world is full of such people, and this has led me to suggest that judges should be allowed

> to stretch clauses—even such venerable clauses as the Due Process Clauses of the Fifth and Fourteen Amendments—when there is a compelling practical case for [judicial] intervention. This was Holmes's approach and later that of Cardozo, Frankfurter, and the second Harlan. Holmes said (privately, to be sure) that a law was constitutional unless it made him want to "puke." Of course he was not speaking literally; nor

26. Daniel S. Glaser, "The Challenge of Keeping It Simple," *New York Times,* Sunday Business section, July 17, 2016, p. 2. Mr. Glaser is the CEO of Marsh & McLennon Companies.

am I. The point is only that our deepest values (Holmes's "can't helps") live below thought and provide warrants for action even when we cannot give those values a compelling or perhaps any rational justification. The point holds even for judicial action. The judge knows that he won't have to vote to ratify a law or other official act or practice that he deeply feels to be terribly unjust, even if the conventional legal materials seem not quite up to the job of constitutional condemnation. *He preserves a role for conscience.*[27]

But all four judges I've mentioned were secular. Many federal judges, including Supreme Court Justices, have been religious; at least four of the current Justices (Roberts, Thomas, Kennedy, and Alito) are observant Catholics; when Justice Scalia was alive, there were five. There is a natural suspicion that their opposition (not shared however by Kennedy) to abortion (about which however Kennedy has reservations) and same-sex marriage is (was, in the case of Scalia) motivated by their religious beliefs. The First Amendment states that "Congress shall make no law respecting the establishment of religion," and the Supreme Court has held that the Fourteenth Amendment extends this prohibition to the states. If Congress and the states can't create a church, or require membership in either a specified church or any church, it would be bizarre to think that the Supreme Court could do such things. Yet the four Justices who dissented in the same-sex marriage case *(Obergefell)* were in effect trying to enforce Catholic marriage law. Whether their *motivation* was religious, however, is not known. What is known is that the Catholic Justices on the Court (even setting to one side Kennedy and Sotomayor as the obvious mavericks) do not vote consistently in line with Catholic doctrine.[28]

On consulting precedent only after deciding what is the "best decision." Why would one want to begin a legal-analytical exercise by looking backward—looking at what courts said and did in a different era, dealing with different issues, even if they said things that as a matter of linguistics can be applied to events today, though the judges couldn't have been thinking about such events?

27. Richard A. Posner, "Legal Reasoning from the Top Down and from the Bottom Up: The Question of Unenumerated Constitutional Rights," 59 *University of Chicago Law Review* 443, 446–447 (1992) (emphasis added).

28. See Kevin C. Walsh, "Addressing Three Problems in Commentary on Catholics at the Supreme Court by Reference to Three Decades of Catholic Bishops' Amicus Briefs," 26 *Stanford Law & Policy Review* 411 (2015).

The time to look up precedents, statutory text, legislative history, and the other conventional materials of judicial decision making is *after* one has a sense of what the best decision would be for today's society.

On "interpreting the Constitution." What does it *mean* to interpret the Constitution when trying to resolve an issue that the document does not mention and its framers and ratifiers did not foresee? If the issue was addressed, then there's something to guide, even to govern, decision. But often the judges in the guise of interpretation make up a rule that has some, but maybe accidental and substantively irrelevant, conformity to an old principle, provoking such meaningless speculations as what the framers of the Fourteenth Amendment would have thought of governmental electronic surveillance of people's emails. Or take the free-speech clause of the First Amendment. All it says is that Congress shall not abridge freedom of speech. But defamation is speech, yet is deemed actionable. Likewise child pornography, threats, copyright infringement, lawyers' disclosing confidential conversations that they've had with their clients —all these forms of speech, and more, are actionable. And so an enormous amount of speech is not free, while at the same time some speech that is not speech is classified as free speech and so is protected—burning the American flag as a political protest, for example. Lines have to be drawn, but the lines that separate protected from unprotected speech owe little if anything to the thinking of the framers or ratifiers of the First Amendment. That is a common problem for judges dealing with the Constitution, statutes, or precedents. The resolution by judges of unforeseen issues is not interpretation, at least in a conventional sense of the word; it is an effort to solve a problem left unresolved in statutory or constitutional provisions. It is creation.

As a detail I note that the political-flag-burning cases—*Texas v. Johnson* and *United States v. Eichman*[29]—don't make a great deal of sense. For while it's true that violent acts can be communicative—think of the assassination of Archduke Franz Ferdinand, which triggered World War I—they are a good deal less articulate even than communication in the form of music and art is, which also is often nonverbal (though a great deal of music has a verbal dimension or accompaniment). Music and art are close enough to speech in communicative intelligibility to be assimilated to the first clause of the First Amendment, but it's quite a stretch to interpret freedom of speech to embrace book burning (the book burning the Nazis did, for example) or even flag burning.

---

29. 491 U.S. 397 (1989), and 496 U.S. 310 (1990), respectively.

What is particularly odd about the Supreme Court's two flag-burning cases is their tension with *Turner v. Safley*,[30] decided just two years before *Johnson* and three before *Eichman*. The issue in that case was the free-speech rights of prison inmates, and while holding that there are such rights the Court construed them narrowly by ruling that restrictions placed by prison officials on the free-speech rights of inmates are entitled to deference because the officials have the relevant expertise and prison administration is a legislative and executive rather than a judicial function.[31] Yet Professor David M. Shapiro has shown that the result of this "deference" has been to stifle harmless efforts by prisoners to read, which is a good deal more innocuous than efforts of political agitators to burn. Shapiro lists seventeen senseless, even nutty, prohibitions of prisoners' access to written or pictorial material. Among them: censorship of passages from the Bible on the ground that it was religious literature from home (the prison ultimately backed down under pressure from religious groups); medical books prohibited on the ground that if the prisoner "became more knowledgeable about his medical conditions, he might request more health care"; lunar maps prohibited on the ground that they create an escape risk (!); books authored by President Obama prohibited; also a picture of a cat (!); magazines and newspapers banned in toto; works of Maimonides prohibited (Congress ultimately forbade that prohibition); John Updike novels banned; Joyce's *Ulysses* banned; mail to prisoners prohibited that contained "photo 2 big," "photo 2 small," and "photo of a dog."[32]

Crazy! How can courts permit such nonsense? Some don't, but the Supreme Court seems not to be among them. I don't want to leave the impression that prison censorship is never justified, however. It happens that several years ago I had a case involving such censorship—*Toston v. Thurmer*.[33] The plaintiff, a prison inmate, had with the prison's permission bought three books about the Black Panthers, one being *To Die for the People—The Writings of Huey P. Newton*. Newton was the founder of the Black Panthers, and all three books contained the Panthers' "Ten-Point Program," point eight of which calls for "freedom for all Black men held in federal, state, county and city prisons and jails." I pointed out in my opinion that "the plaintiff is a black man in a state prison, and the Black Panthers were implicated in many acts of violence, including murder. Huey Newton himself may have killed a police officer. . . . The Black

30. 482 U.S. 78 (1987).

31. Id. at 84–85; see also the thorough analysis in David M. Shapiro, "Lenient in Theory, Dumb in Fact: Prison, Speech and Scrutiny," 84 *George Washington Law Review* 972 (2016).

32. See id. at 972–973, 995–1005.

33. 689 F.3d 828 (7th Cir. 2012).

Panther Party is history. But the Ten-Point Program could be thought by prison officials an incitement to violence by black prisoners—especially since there is a 'New Black Panther Party,' active today, which claims descent from the original Black Panthers and like its predecessor both advocates and practices violence."[34]

But I drew a distinction between point eight and the book as a whole. I noted that in the book

> point 8 is much less inflammatory than when read in isolation in the sheet in the plaintiff's cell; for in the book each point is followed by an explanatory passage, and the passage that explains point 8 states rather innocuously: "We believe that all Black people should be released from the many jails and prisons because they have not received a fair and impartial trial." Although Newton's book advocates revolution, it could no more be regarded as a criminal incitement than the Communist Manifesto could be. But this underscores the difference between a book as a whole and an arguably inflammatory nugget plucked from it.

The plaintiff had copied point eight minus the innocuous explanatory passage, and we judges thought the prison authorities were justified in thinking "that the likeliest reason the plaintiff copied the Ten-Point Program was to show it to inmates whom he hoped to enlist in a prison gang, a local cell as it were of the Black Panthers; the Ten-Point Program would be the gang's charter."[35] And so we upheld the prison's confiscation of the copy that the plaintiff had made of point eight. Importantly the prison did not confiscate the books themselves; to do so would probably have been unconstitutional.[36]

From Professor Segall's Remarks

As a descriptive matter, the Justices care less about construing rules of constitutional law to conform to the written Constitution and its history than about balancing contemporary costs and benefits and examining prior cases. But do we want judges to be constructing rules on the basis mainly of their interpretative judgments about what the constitutional text and its history "really mean,"

34. Id. at 830.

35. Id. at 830–831.

36. A brilliant recent article reports the redemptive effect on seemingly hardened criminals of supplying them in prison with classic works of literature, such as works by Shakespeare, Milton, and Voltaire. Larissa MacFarquhar, "Out and Up: Leaving Prison and Going to College," *New Yorker*, December 12, 2016, p. 54.

or primarily on the basis of a careful and prudential analysis of modern-day costs, benefits, and likely consequences (as well as of how prior judges conducted that balancing)? This writer prefers Judge Posner's methods for several reasons. There is no indication in either the text of the Constitution or its history that judges are supposed to interpret the document using backward-looking principles of textual construction. By using so many vague and open-ended words and phrases and not providing any rules of interpretation in the document itself, it is likely that the Framers knew and wanted judges to look forward not backward. This absence of guidance may also partially explain why in virtually every litigated area of constitutional law the Court has reversed itself and altered prior doctrine.

Judge Posner has argued persuasively that there is little sense in asking what eighteenth- or nineteenth-century people believed about modern problems. Whether judges have to decide on the constitutionality of lethal injections, NSA spying on emails, bans on same-sex marriage, or laws requiring government workers to contribute to public-sector unions, constitutional text and the history of that text simply run out before any useful result can be reached. The Second Amendment provides a useful and powerful example of why current conditions should be deemed by judges to be much more important to constitutional law than text and history. Obviously the Framers were not aware of either small, powerful guns that could do great damage or assault-type weapons that could spray hundreds of bullets without reloading. Therefore, even if one believes that the core meaning of the Second Amendment protects the individual right to own guns apart from militia service, many kinds of gun regulations other than total prohibition still require constitutional analysis.

Professor Randy Barnett argues that the resolution of these kinds of Second Amendment issues should be guided by a strong presumption in favor of individual liberty and freedom. But even a "Justice" Barnett would not protect under the Second Amendment the private possession of nuclear weapons, nor would he invalidate all measures designed to make sure guns don't fall into the hands of dangerous criminals. For most gun regulations that are actually likely to be passed by legislatures and then litigated, however, the devil will be in the details, and a background presumption of liberty won't do the real work. Judge Posner would not indulge theoretical posturing and generalizing about the role of guns in the eighteenth century. He would look to see what purposes the law is trying to serve; whether those purposes are likely to be achieved; what consequences result from either upholding or invalidating a particular gun measure; and whether prior cases block the preferred result. Judge Posner adopted exactly that analysis in a decision striking down an Illinois ban on carrying guns outside the home: *Moore v. Madigan*, 702 F.3d 933 (7th Cir. 2012).

Judge Posner's transparent efforts to reach the best results by looking at facts on the ground and anticipated consequences (and prior cases), without regard to the rules and values of yesteryear describe current practice accurately and will lead to better decisions than original-meaning analysis, which runs out in most litigated cases and simply hides the true reasons for judges' decisions.

PART ONE

A politicized court, an antique charter, the mystery of "interpretation." Presidents and members of Congress and the counterpart elected officials in the states (other than judges, who in most states are elected whereas all federal judges are appointed) do not waste time denying they're politicians, as everyone knows they are. But judges, especially federal judges, including the Justices of the Supreme Court, refer to the executive and legislative branches of the federal government as "the political branches," implying that the judicial branch is not political. In actuality political inclinations figure at all levels of the judiciary, including the U.S. Supreme Court. The more it's in play, the more vigorous the denial, which reaches a crescendo among the Supreme Court Justices, their supporters in the "political branches," and, surprisingly, law school faculties. Indeed the entire legal profession, with trivial exceptions, seems committed to trying to conceal from the public the true character of the Court, and indeed of the federal judiciary in general.

It should be obvious that the Supreme Court was predestined to be political to a significant degree. There are two reasons. The first is that the Justices are nominated by a politician (the President) and confirmed by politicians (the Senators). What these politicians want from the Supreme Court is the support and furtherance of the policies that the politicians favor. Quality is relevant, but secondary. A Justice must be competent, but given competence the important thing to the appointing authorities is his or her political inclinations. *Average* competence is enough, moreover, because the Justice will have brilliant law clerks to draft opinions, speeches, and even the questions the Justice asks the lawyers at oral argument. The Justices will vote politically (not always, but often) because their having known and firm political inclinations will have been the *sine qua non* of their appointment. Sometimes the President and the Senate will stumble—will misread the man or the woman they are appointing. More often, a Justice's political inclinations will change unpredictably over time, as illustrated in the careers of Justices Frankfurter, Black, Blackmun, Souter, Stevens, O'Connor, and Kennedy. The first two were liberals when appointed but later became conservative. The other five were conservative (or believed to be conservative) when appointed but grew less conservative during their time on the Supreme Court, with Blackmun, Souter, and Stevens actually becoming liberals.

The second reason the Supreme Court is political—not in every case but in the most important ones—is that it deals primarily with political issues, notably limits on federal, state, and local executive, legislative, and judicial rules, policies, and actions. And the body of "law" that it draws on to resolve these issues has been for the most part created by the Court itself, out of whole cloth. That *has* to be. The Court claims to interpret the Constitution, statutes, and its previous decisions ("precedents"), and sometimes the claim is valid, but very often it is not. For interpretation in its usual (though not invariable) sense means the elucidation of an original meaning, written or spoken, express or implicit, of someone or some group, and rarely is there an original meaning for the Court to draw on to enable it to resolve a constitutional case, given the antiquity of the Constitution and the enormous changes in the nation since its enactment. Hartley's quotation which supplies an epigraph for this chapter is right on target: as a result of the "pastness" of the constitutional text (excluding the most recent amendments), constitutional law is and has to be largely a creation of Supreme Court Justices—virtually a body of common law.

This is not my discovery; but neither is it a fresh insight for me. More than twenty years ago I wrote that "the Constitution is an old document that was drafted by men who despite much civic piety to the contrary were not clairvoyant. Two centuries of amendments have further muddied the waters. A document that as a result is inscrutable with respect to most modern problems has been overlaid by hundreds of thousands of pages of judicial interpretation, much of it internally inconsistent. The sum of all this verbiage is not a directive but a resource,"[37] or as I would now say, "at best a resource."

There is applying law, and there is creating law. Anglo-American judges have done both since time out of mind. The common law, entirely judge-created,

---

37. Richard A. Posner, *Overcoming Law* 207 (1995).

filled an enormous legal vacuum. The Constitution, because of its age and frequent vagueness and the strong disagreements among its framers, filled the political vacuum that the Articles of Confederation had failed to do, but also created something of a vacuum as well, which the Justices of the Supreme Court have tried to fill, with some but only partial success. When judges create law, they are engaged in a political process akin to that of legislators, though procedurally different.

"Statutory interpretation" is a misnomer closely related to "constitutional interpretation." Typically a question of statutory meaning is a question the legislature did not foresee, and so the answer cannot be found in the statute itself but is necessarily a fabrication of the judges and Justices called upon to answer it.[38] And precedents go stale just as constitutional and statutory language does, because issues that arise that are within the semantic scope of a precedent were often not within the understanding of the judges or Justices who decided the case now sought to be applied. The only good reason to "follow precedent" is either agreement with the precedent or reliance interests created by it that outweigh the benefits that would accrue from overruling it.

Everyone knows or should know that there are liberal and conservative Justices, that they frequently disagree, that a majority of liberal Justices will make for a liberal Supreme Court (the Warren Court of the 1950s and 1960s is the best example) and a majority of conservative Justices for a conservative one, well illustrated by the Roberts Court until the death of Justice Scalia. Everyone knows that religious belief or lack thereof plays a role in such hot-ticket judicial items as same-sex marriage and the right of a woman to have an abortion and to government insurance for female contraceptives, while the politics of the Justices play a big—often a dominant—role in the resolution of such issues as gun rights, capital punishment, health care, wealth redistribution, and the regulation of banking and other finance, labor, discrimination, transportation, public investment and regulation, and the environment. If politics, religion, and attitudes pro or con business were taken away from Supreme Court Justices, what tools would they be left with for deciding cases? One can stare at the Constitution till one is blind without finding an answer to most of the questions of constitutional law that the Supreme Court is called upon to decide.

Richard Fallon, the constitutional law professor at Harvard Law School whom I mentioned briefly in the preceding chapter, makes a point similar to

---

38. My use of "fabrication" in this context is a little harsh; I modify it in Chapter 3. Read on!

the one I'm trying to make, in a discussion[39] of the Supreme Court's decision in *Bolling v. Sharpe*,[40] which invalidated racial discrimination in the District of Columbia. No constitutional provision warranted such a result, because the equal protection clause of the Fourteenth Amendment does not apply to the federal government, of which the District of Columbia government is a part. But Fallon writes:

> I would say that the Supreme Court acted morally legitimately in decid-
> ing *Bolling v. Sharpe* as it did, even if the Court's constitutional holding
> was erroneous or possibly even illegitimate as a strictly legal matter, as
> some have argued. Among the relevant considerations, the lack of a con-
> stitutional norm forbidding the federal government from discriminat-
> ing against racial minorities was a serious moral deficiency in the pre-
> existing constitutional regime. In my view, the moral importance of the
> situation would have justified the Court in appealing less to the letter of

39. Richard H. Fallon, Jr., "Legitimacy and the Constitution," 118 *Harvard Law Review* 1787, 1835 (2005) (footnotes omitted). This of course is legal realism, the jurisprudence of noted judges of yore, such as Oliver Wendell Holmes, Karl Llewellyn, Learned Hand, Benjamin Cardozo, Jerome Frank, William O. Douglas, Roger Traynor, and Henry Friendly. I don't think Friendly is commonly described as a legal realist, but that he was is strongly argued in Edmund Ursin, "How Great Judges Think: Judges Richard Posner, Henry Friendly, and Roger Traynor on Judicial Lawmaking," 57 *Buffalo Law Review* 1267, 1338–1349 (2009). (I add that the title of the article is misleading; I am at least one notch below Friendly and Traynor in contributions made to the improvement of American law.) Professor Ursin is the leading academic student of legal realism. See, for example, besides the article just cited, his articles "Judicial Creativity and Tort Law," 49 *George Washington Law Review* 229 (1982); "Holmes, Cardozo and the Legal Realists: Early Incarnations of Legal Pragmatism and Enterprise Liability," 50 *San Diego Law Review* 537 (2013); and most recently, his as yet unpublished article "Chief Justice Traynor's Legal Pragmatism, the Legal Process School, and Enterprise Liability" (University of San Diego School of Law, March 15, 2016).

Further on Judge Friendly: David M. Dorsen, in his excellent biography—*Henry Friendly: Greatest Judge of His Era* (2012)—recounts, see id. at 174–176, an incident in which Friendly, after persuading his colleagues to remand a case to the Social Security Administration, which without adequate evidence had denied disability benefits to an applicant named Philip Kerner, who had a serious heart condition, "did something extraordinary" (Dorsen's characterization)—"talked to a cardiac rehabilitation center with which [Friendly] had [had] some contact when at the bar; they [the center] agreed that they would take Kerner on." Friendly then "communicated with [Kerner's] lawyer suggesting that this [treatment by the rehabilitation center] would be perhaps a more advantageous solution than pursuing the further hearing which we [the appellate panel that Friendly had presided over] had ordered." The lawyer responded that Kerner was "rather a litigious sort"— who indeed refused the suggestion and continued litigating—and lost. Dorsen believes that by trying to help Kerner without notifying the other lawyers in the case of what he was doing, Friendly "might be thought to create an appearance of bias" and therefore may have committed "an ethical violation." It was irregular, what he did, but even apart from the fact that it had no effect on the case, I can't see the harm in it that would justify deeming it an ethical violation. What Friendly had done was the equivalent of independent judicial research, which I for one do not consider forbidden to appellate judges. I discuss this issue at some length in Chapter 5 of this book, in connection with a case in my court named *Rowe v. Gibson*.

40. 347 U.S. 497 (1954).

positive law than to principles of moral right and what Lincoln termed "the better angels of our nature" in calling upon the parties and the nation to accept its decision as deserving of lawful status. This is a controversial and even dangerous form of argument, though I think at once inevitable and justifiable. It might be objected that by forging a new constitutional norm, the Court offended principles governing the fair allocation of political power: the Court should leave the implementation of constitutional change to political majorities acting through the Article V amendment process, not arrogate a power of innovation to itself. It bears emphasis, however, that the status quo ante had been established by political processes from which racial minorities were almost wholly excluded. Under those circumstances, the argument that the Court should have stayed its hand based on concerns about the fair allocation of political power rings slightly hollow.

I agree; it is another example of the principle that law must yield to necessity. But it's interesting to note that after certiorari had been granted in the *Bolling* case but before the case was argued, Chief Justice Warren had sent a memo to the other Justices suggesting that the case could be resolved in favor of forbidding racial discrimination in the District of Columbia public schools by reference to the due process clause of the Fifth Amendment. The key passage in the memo is that "segregation in public education is not reasonably related to any proper governmental objective, and it imposes on these children a burden which constitutes an arbitrary deprivation of liberty in violation of the Due Process Clause."[41] One might call this an acknowledgment of constitutional plasticity. When there are good practical or ethical reasons (as there were in *Bolling*) for deeming a particular law unconstitutional, the Constitution is sufficiently malleable, or at least is treated by the Supreme Court as being so, to yield the desired result. It is curious therefore that notwithstanding Warren's memo, the Court in *Bolling* should have eschewed the constitutional text altogether.

Professor Fallon's willingness, evident in his discussion of the *Bolling* case, to bend the constitutional text where necessary to obtain the result that is "right" in a political or a moral sense, is everywhere evident in his book *The Dynamic*

---

41. Quoted in Dennis J. Hutchinson, "Unanimity and Desegregation: Decisionmaking in the Supreme Court, 1948–1958," 68 *Georgetown Law Journal* 1, 94 (1980).

Constitution: An Introduction to American Constitutional Law and Practice,[42] a work as lucid as some of his articles are opaque. But I think the book mistitled. There is nothing "dynamic" about the Constitution. It's a set of mostly very old documents, some unclear and a great many quite outdated, which the Supreme Court has unhesitatingly revised in application (falsely describing what it does as "interpretation," a word conventionally understood to mean recovering the original meaning of the speaker or writer of a statement, though we'll see that it can take on other meanings as well). And so Fallon remarks that the Supreme Court "typically decides cases in light of what the Justices take to be the Constitution's largest purposes and the values that it presupposes as well as those that it more expressly embodies."[43] Yet elsewhere in his book he remarks inconsistently that "the voting patterns of Supreme Court Justices tend to be relatively (though not perfectly) predictable on the basis of their political ideology. In view of the judgmental character of constitutional adjudication, *it would be astonishing if the results were otherwise.*"[44] This is absolutely correct but doesn't square with his suggestion that Supreme Court decisions are typically based on the Justices' perceptions of the purposes and values of the Constitution.

Even if we pretend that political ideology is not the big factor in constitutional adjudication that Fallon rightly acknowledges it to be, "the Constitution's largest purposes" and "the values that it presupposes" are very vague formulas, and as a practical matter amount to—

42. 2d ed. 2013.

43. Id. at 20. A serious question though is how to identify values that the Constitution presupposes rather than embodying (i.e., enunciating). For example, the text of the Constitution does not authorize the Supreme Court to hold statutes unconstitutional. See Philip Hamburger, *Law and Judicial Duty* (2008). The Court conferred that power on itself in *Marbury v. Madison,* 5 U.S. 137 (1803). This at least is the standard view. Professor Hamburger offers a more complex one in his book, especially in the introduction.

44. Fallon, note 39 above, at 281 (emphasis added). That a good deal of judicial voting at the Supreme Court level is ideological is supported by a compelling study of ideological voting by federal court of appeals judges. See Corey Rayburn Yung, "Judged by the Company You Keep: An Empirical Study of the Ideologies of Judges on the United States Courts of Appeals," 51 *Boston College Law Review* 1133 (2010). Given the differences in cases decided by the courts of appeals and by the Supreme Court, it is a certainty that judicial voting at the Supreme Court level is more ideological than at the court of appeals level, though it is considerable (according to Professor Yung's study) at that level as well. Ideological voting by Supreme Court Justices has been confirmed in numerous studies. See, e.g., Lee Epstein, William M. Landes, and Richard A. Posner, *The Behavior of Federal Judges: A Theoretical and Empirical Study of Rational Choice,* chap. 3 (2013); Robert E. Riggs, "When Every Vote Counts: 5–4 Decisions in the United States Supreme Court, 1900—90," 21 *Hofstra Law Review* 667 (1993). With the realism displayed by Professors Fallon and Yung as well as by the two studies just cited, compare the seventy-six-page article "The Duty of Clarity" by John O. McGinnis, 84 *George Washington Law Review* 843 (2015), arguing for a narrow scope of judicial enforcement of the Constitution without once considering whether such shrinkage of judicial authority would confer net benefits on the American people.

The Court's amending the Constitution.   Professor David Strauss, as I explained earlier, has been emphatic that what we call constitutional law is for the most part not found in the Constitution but rather is a body of common law created by the Supreme Court in an effort to lend precision to constitutional provisions (so often vague) and make the Constitution "speak" (as Edgar Bergen made Charlie McCarthy speak) to issues not envisaged by the drafters and ratifiers of the original Constitution or its numerous amendments. In effect the Court has amended the Constitution—repeatedly, and often clumsily. Fallon appears to agree, and I am surprised therefore not to find Strauss in Fallon's index. But between them Strauss and Fallon have put the kibosh on originalism.

I'll give an example of clumsy judicial amending: the Court's "forums" doctrine, a riff on the First Amendment's freedom of speech and freedom of the press clauses. I gave a critical account of that doctrine in an opinion I wrote for my court years ago[45] and I'll quote from that account here (slightly edited); the reader may notice my reluctance to rely on conventional constitutional doctrine:

> Illinois Beach State Park is a large state park abutting Lake Michigan in northeastern Illinois; it attracts upward of two million visitors in some years. The plaintiff, a nonprofit corporation that helped to create and continues to support the park, filed this suit under 42 U.S.C. § 1983 against state officials involved in its management and the state agency that operates the park, charging infringement of free speech. The agency's officials are . . . sued in their personal capacity . . . and in that capacity are "persons" within the meaning of section 1983 [the agency is not]. The district judge granted summary judgment in their favor; and so the entire suit was dismissed.
>
> The defendants refused to display, in the display racks in various buildings in the park, a scary two-page pamphlet that the plaintiff had prepared entitled "Tips for Avoiding Asbestos Contamination at Illinois Beach State Park." The pamphlet recommends "commonsense approaches . . . for minimizing exposure to you and your family from asbestos contamination while at the beaches of Illinois Beach State Park." It warns that "many pieces of asbestos have been tumbling along the shoreline for years," that "microscopic asbestos can be released from the sand

45. *Illinois Dunesland Preservation Society v. Illinois Dept. of Natural Resources,* 594 F.3d 719 (7th Cir. 2009). I have deleted the citations in the opinion to other, mainly Supreme Court, opinions.

when agitated," and that "disturbing the sand can cause asbestos to become airborne."

The plaintiffs' lawyers have treated us to a barrage of unhelpful First Amendment jargon. A "forum" in that jargon is a piece of public property usable for expressive activity by members of the public ("private speech," in forum jargon). The Supreme Court distinguishes a "traditional public forum" from a "designated public forum" and both from a "nonpublic forum." A traditional public forum is a street or park, or some other type of public property that like a street or park has long ("time out of mind," as some cases put it; "from time immemorial," as others say) been used for expressive activity, such as marches and leafletting. A designated public forum, illustrated by a public theater, is a facility that the government has created to be, or has subsequently opened for use as, a site for expressive activity by private persons. Usually, as in the case of a public theater, it is available only for specified forms of private expressive activity: plays, in the case of a theater, rather than political speeches. Thus the government owner of a theater need not throw it open for political rallies even though it is physically capable of being so used. But the owner is not allowed to discriminate among the plays performed in the theater on the basis of the ideas or opinions that the plays express.

The third category—the "nonpublic forum"—consists of government-owned facilities like the Justice Department's auditorium that could be and sometimes are used for private expressive activities but are not primarily intended for such use. The government can limit private expression in such a facility to expression that furthers the purpose for which the facility was created.

Some decisions recognize a fourth category, a variant of the second, variously called a "limited designated public forum" (what Shakespeare's Polonius would have called "a vile phrase"), a "limited public forum," or a "limited forum." The terms denote a public facility limited to the discussion of certain subjects or reserved for some types or classes of speaker. In *Gilles v. Blanchard* [477 F.3d 466 (7th Cir. 2007)] it was an open space in a state university in which members of the university community and their guests—but not uninvited outsiders—were allowed to give talks.

It is difficult to see what difference there is between such restrictions and the selection that the director of a state theater has to make among theater groups clamoring for access to the stage. Indeed it is rather difficult to see what work "forum analysis" in general does. It is obvious both that every public site of private expression has to be regulated to some extent and that the character of permitted regulation will vary with the differences among the different types of site. Street demonstrations have to be regulated to prevent blocking traffic and the use of a state theater has to be regulated to ration the use of a limited facility and maintain quality, and obviously the regulations will be very different.

The district judge thought the display racks in the Illinois Beach State Park not a public forum but instead "a mini-library of resources for the public, and [the park's management] necessarily made 'editorial' judgments about which materials to include." Indeed there are cases that say that "forum analysis" does not apply to public libraries. But what is the relevant difference between a state theater (a "designated public forum") and a public library or [a] public-college art gallery? In all cases the management of a government facility has to decide which playwright's or author's or artist's work will be allowed to be exhibited, in view of the site's limited capacity.

The defendants argue that "forum analysis" is inapplicable because the materials in the display racks are "government speech." This term would be readily intelligible if it referred just to situations in which a government official made a statement; he would not be required to contradict himself by including a counterstatement urged by a private person. That would have been the situation here had the park display racks still contained the old fact sheet when the plaintiff sought access to the racks for its frightening pamphlet. Most people who read and believed the plaintiff's pamphlet would flee the park forthwith. We don't know what the current fact sheet says, though it must be less alarmist than the plaintiff's, or the park officials wouldn't have excluded the plaintiff's.

But it wouldn't matter if there were no government fact sheet, hence no "government speech" in the literal sense. For there was none in *Pleasant Grove City v. Summum* [555 U.S. 460 (2009)] either, and it is the leading case on "government speech." A city had accepted a Ten Commandments monument donated to it for display in the city's park and had turned down a monument offered to the city by a Gnostic sect. The Court held that the monument selected by the city was the vehicle of the city's expression, just as playing the national anthem at an official function is government expression even though the anthem was composed by a private person.

The materials chosen for the display racks in the Illinois Beach State Park are designed to attract people to the park, and more broadly to Illinois tourist facilities and services. The . . . message is: come to the park and have a great time on the sandy beach. The message of the plaintiff's pamphlet is: you think you're in a nice park but really you're in Chernobyl, so if you're dumb enough to come here be sure not to step on the sand because that would disturb or agitate it, and to scrub under your fingernails as soon as you get home.

The defendants could avoid giving the appearance of endorsing an opinion that they do not believe by resurrecting their old fact sheet and placing it next to the plaintiff's pamphlet in the display racks. But the mere display of that pamphlet would give it a legitimacy, a weight, that the defendants are not obliged to acknowledge.

And so the state prevailed, but there never was a need to invoke "forum analysis."

The dramatic exit of Justice Scalia. The Supreme Court's occasional de facto amending of the Constitution is inevitable, but I see no excuse for the hypocrisy about the Court that reached a crescendo in the encomia for Justice Scalia, who was in very poor health and died suddenly on February 13, 2016, a month short of his eightieth birthday. The encomiasts included, among others (besides Justice Kagan, whose earliest encomia for Justice Scalia I discussed at the beginning of this chapter), the dean of the Harvard Law School and seven other Harvard law professors in a joint celebration of Scalia's career on the Supreme Court. Half the group, including the dean, are liberals, and let me start with them. They fairly tripped over themselves in lauding a deceased ultraconservative Justice of whom they had doubtless strongly disapproved. One of them, who had clerked for Justice Scalia, said that his most meaningful experience as a clerk was to "watch him struggle with what he knew his principles said he should do, and what he wanted as a conservative to do. . . . In every single case where he saw that conflict, Scalia did what his principles said he should do."[46] But the former law clerk gave no examples. And Scalia's principles were notably elastic, which minimized tension between them and his political / religious aims.

Scalia's doctrine of "originalism" (not his invention, by the way, and though

46. "Harvard Law School Reflects on the Legacy of Justice Scalia," *Harvard Law Today,* March 1, 2016, http://today.law.harvard.edu/harvard-law-school-reflects-on-the-legacy-of-justice-scalia/.

he was its most prominent and fervent advocate he was by no means a consistent originalist in his judicial opinions) led him in strange directions. For example it convinced him that flogging is not cruel and unusual punishment because it was a commonplace punishment when the Eighth Amendment was added to the Constitution—yet he joined the two decisions (*Texas v. Johnson,* 1989, and *United States v. Eichman,* 1990) holding that burning the American flag as a political protest is a form of free speech, a decision that could not be referred to any eighteenth-century understanding of freedom of expression. And what civilized principle could lie behind his *rejection* of a constitutional right—easily derived one might think from the cruel and unusual punishments clause of the Eighth Amendment—to judicial consideration of proof of innocence discovered after a defendant had been convicted of murder and sentenced to death but before he'd been executed? Scalia's view was that as long as the trial and the sentencing hearing had been procedurally regular, an innocent defendant could lawfully be executed, and would be unless the state's governor granted clemency.[47] I'd like to see his encomiasts, liberal or conservative, defend that position and the moral outlook that lay behind it. In fairness to Scalia, however, devout Catholic that he was he may have believed that a person executed for a crime he hadn't committed would receive divine clemency.

Another of the liberal Harvard encomiasts said that Scalia had "changed the way lawyers argue cases. He changed our framework."[48] I don't understand the reference to framework, but it's true though trivial that a lawyer arguing a case has to try to address what he knows to be a judge's concerns. A third professor

---

47. The concurring opinion of Justice Scalia, joined by Justice Thomas, states

we granted certiorari on the question whether it violates due process or constitutes cruel and unusual punishment for a State to execute a person who, having been convicted of murder after a full and fair trial, later alleges that newly discovered evidence shows him to be "actually innocent." I would have preferred to decide that question, particularly since, as the Court's discussion shows, it is perfectly clear what the answer is: There is no basis in text, tradition, or even in contemporary practice (if that were enough) for finding in the Constitution a right to demand judicial consideration of newly discovered evidence of innocence brought forward after conviction. In saying that such a right exists, the dissenters apply nothing but their personal opinions to invalidate the rules of more than two-thirds of the States, and a Federal Rule of Criminal Procedure for which this Court itself is responsible. If the system that has been in place for 200 years (and remains widely approved) "shock[s]" the dissenters' consciences. . . , perhaps they should doubt the calibration of their consciences, or, better still, the usefulness of "conscience shocking" as a legal test. *Herrera v. Collins,* 506 U.S. 390, 427–428 (1993).

See also Scalia's dissent in *In re Troy Anthony Davis,* No. 08-1443 (2009), where he said that "this Court has never held that the Constitution forbids the execution of a convicted defendant who has had a full and fair trial but is later able to convince a habeas court that he is 'actually' innocent." Davis was executed in 2011, amidst doubts about his guilt. See "Troy Davis," *Wikipedia,* https://en.wikipedia.org/wiki/Troy_Davis#Trial_and_conviction. Terrible!

48. "Havard Law School," note 46 above.

offered mild criticisms but concluded without elaboration or substantiation that "Justice Scalia was not just a very significant Justice; he was also a superb one. You're blessed to be working in law in the time when Justice Scalia was on the scene."[49] I am dubious. There have indeed been superb Justices: John Marshall, Oliver Wendell Holmes, Louis Brandeis, Charles Evans Hughes, Robert Jackson, maybe others. Scalia was not of their caliber.[50] He had his strengths, but his petulance, his aggressive religiosity that led him to deny evolution and declare his belief in the Devil (see the further discussion of these issues in the Epilogue to this book), his intolerance of disagreement, his pretense of originalism, and his unreflective conservatism placed him well below the most illustrious of his predecessors.

Another professor referred to his "friend Nino" as "an exceptionally gifted man in many ways, of which I stand sometimes almost in awe. . . . I admire his sticking his neck out, putting out on the table a method for judging constitutional cases, a judicial philosophy. . . ."[51] Sticking his neck out? What does it mean for a Supreme Court Justice to stick his neck out? Especially Justice Scalia, a conservative Justice on a conservative Supreme Court. (The Chief Justices in Scalia's time on the Court were first Rehnquist and then Roberts.) The "judicial philosophy" that this professor purports to admire is originalism, which doesn't work. The professor himself goes on to criticize it, thereby undermining the encomium. I knew Scalia for almost forty years. It never occurred to me to "stand sometimes almost in awe" of him.

And finally, ultraliberal Martha Minow, the dean (now the outgoing dean) of the Harvard Law School, *raved* about Scalia, gushing that "his warmth and his willingness to just be genuine were what overwhelmed me."[52] What is true, and I suppose could be thought to have made him "genuine," is that he lacked self-control. He was mercurial. His rages were legendary, but tended to blow over. He and I became friends when we taught at the University of Chicago Law School before either of us became a judge, but latterly, because of a critical review I had written of a book on statutory interpretation that he'd coauthored, whether nominally or not I don't know, with Bryan Garner, he had publicly

49. Id.

50. See my book *Reflections on Judging* 179–219 (2013) for a takedown of Justice Scalia; also my article "The Incoherence of Antonin Scalia," *New Republic,* August 23, 2012, https://newrepublic.com/article/106441/scalia-garner-reading-the-law-textual-originalism.

51. "Havard Law School," note 46 above.

52. Id. She had raved, shortly before Scalia's death, about Chief Justice Roberts, calling him among other thing a "masterful manager." Martha Minow, "Versatile and Nimble," *Harvard Law Bulletin,* fall 2015. Nonsense. What has gotten into these people?

called me a liar and even pretended not to know who I was. Yet later he phoned to tell me that he'd just hired one of my former law clerks to clerk for him in the following year (which happened to be Scalia's last); and we had a perfectly pleasant chat.

The four conservatives in Scalia's Harvard *in memoriam* were somewhat more fulsome than the liberals, though none quite matched Minow. One said Scalia's "ruling virtue" was "courage," and that even his "good humor" (I would say intermittent good humor) was a product of his "courage." I would call him outspoken rather than courageous. To repeat, when did he ever stick his neck out? How *does* a Supreme Court Justice stick his neck out? Who chops it off if he does? Who were or are the "cowardly" Justices?

I am guessing that a principal motive for "HLS Reflects on the Legacy of Justice Scalia" was to associate a Supreme Court Justice closely with the Harvard Law School (of which Scalia was an alumnus), and a conservative Justice with a liberal law school that wants to supply as many law clerks to the Supreme Court as possible irrespective of the political outlook of particular Justices. Almost all Supreme Court clerks are graduates of a tiny handful of premier law schools, such as Harvard.

A more dignified reaction of the Harvard Law School faculty—certainly of the dean and the other liberal members of the faculty—to Justice Scalia's death, a reaction that would have navigated gracefully between candor and falsity, would have been to say nothing, consistently with the Latin maxim *de mortuis nihil nisi bonum* ("of the dead [say] nothing unless good"). The encomia for Scalia were over the top; silence would have been preferable, or a simple *requiescat in pace*. But candor and truthfulness are not common attributes of members of the legal profession. Consider the Court's disposition to engage in occasional plagiarism. Between 1946 and 2013, 9.55 percent of Supreme Court opinions plagiarized briefs filed in cases in the Court,[53] that is, lifted sentences from the briefs without attribution. We expect that sort of thing from students rather than from Supreme Court Justices or their law clerks.

Some realism about the Supreme Court; herein of constitutional "interpretation." What needs especially to be emphasized is the true character of constitutional decision making by the Supreme Court, vividly described in—of all improbable places—a brilliant novel by a law professor at Boston University. In it

---

53. Adam Feldman, "All Copying Is Not Created Equal: Examining Supreme Court Opinions' Borrowed Language," January 1, 2016, p. 3, forthcoming in *Journal of Appellate Practice and Process*. "Borrowed" is not a synonym for "plagiarized," which is what he's describing.

we hear an imaginary Supreme Court Justice say that if "you're a buffoon . . . and you think that every dispute should be decided according to the principle of what a bunch of dead guys would have thought about it in the eighteenth century, then yes, we [the Justices of the Supreme Court] decide cases according to principle. But, you know, judging really involves making the best and most pragmatic decision you can, given all the circumstances. Is that a principle? Maybe. But that's not what I mean when I say that this . . . jerk [another Justice] insists on his principles regardless whether they might ruin some eighteen-year-old girl's life."[54] And later he says: "I never liked constitutional law. It's barely law at all, in my view. It's just politics, filtered through a few vague phrases in an old document written by people who couldn't possibly fathom what the world looks like today."[55] Quite so. Professor Wexler has unwittingly expounded my philosophy of judging.

"Interpretation" of ancient texts and decisions is not the answer to the doubts expressed by imaginary Justice Tuttle concerning the possibility of rigorous, objective judicial decision making at the appellate level. For as I keep emphasizing, in a vast number of the cases in which the lawyers or the judges appeal to interpretation in an effort to shift responsibility for a decision to legislators, regulators, or constitution makers, interpretation in the conventional sense of the word is impossible because the "interpretive" issue had not been foreseen by the authors of the document to be interpreted. Impossible, that is, unless you think that James Madison, the principal drafter of the Constitution, was the reincarnation of the Oracle at Delphi or the Sibyl of Cumae and knew therefore what America would be like in the twenty-first century and drafted the Constitution accordingly.

It thus is silly to ask whether the Fourth Amendment forbids electronic surveillance of suspected terrorists, ordinary crooks, or spies. The amendment's authors and ratifiers had no opinion on wiretapping or other forms of electronic surveillance, because these techniques neither existed nor were foreseen. So the Supreme Court has decided to treat the Fourth Amendment as an open sesame to judges to create rules regulating anything that can be described as a search (or a seizure—which usually means an arrest—but I'll limit my remarks to search warrants). The Fourth Amendment neither says nor suggests that search warrants are *ever* required—all it says about warrants is that *general*

---

54. Jay Wexler, *Tuttle in the Balance* 66 (2015).

55. Id. at 183. "Justice Tuttle" is of course not alone in this view; nor am I his only companion in heresy. There is for example the notable article by Professor Brian Leiter, "Constitutional Law, Moral Judgment, and the Supreme Court as Super-Legislature," 66 *Hastings Law Journal* 1601 (2015).

warrants (warrants that don't specify the place to be searched or the things to be seized), and warrants that are not based *both* on an oath or affirmation by the law enforcement agent applying for the warrant *and* on probable cause to believe that the warrant if executed will yield evidence, or leads to evidence, of illegal behavior, are forbidden. Yet that hasn't stopped the Supreme Court from ruling that a warrant is required—*by the Fourth Amendment*—to search a person's home or to arrest a person in his home: "the Fourth Amendment demonstrates a 'strong preference for searches conducted pursuant to a warrant.'"[56]

Not so; it demonstrates no preference at all for warrants. Search warrants were anathema to the colonists because of their heavy use by British customs officials to enter warehouses owned by colonists and seize tea and other imported goods on which the British tariffs had not been paid, and that anathema is reflected in the restrictions that the Fourth Amendment places on warrants. For the Supreme Court to say the Fourth Amendment shows a preference for warrants over warrantless searches just illustrates the assumption—the inevitable assumption—by courts of a lawmaking role that includes what amounts to judicially amending the Constitution. A perverse consequence, as I pointed out in my dissent in a case called *United States v. Dessart*—a dissent I'll be quoting from at some length in Chapter 4—of the warrant requirement that the Supreme Court has grafted onto the Fourth Amendment in the name of citizen rights has been to reduce those rights. The reason is that the Court insists on judicial deference to magistrates' findings of probable cause to search or arrest. And so the more warrants that are issued, the more searches and arrests that are conducted and upheld, because a search or arrest pursuant to a warrant, having been approved by a magistrate, is less likely to be challenged successfully than a search or arrest without a warrant.

---

56. *Ornelas v. United States*, 517 U.S. 690, 698–699 (1996), quoting *Illinois v. Gates*, 462 U.S. 213, 236 (1983). A recent 146-page article, Laura K. Donohue, "The Original Fourth Amendment," 83 *University of Chicago Law Review* 1181 (2016), argues that the Fourth Amendment forbids not only general warrants and warrants not supported by oath or affirmation and by probable cause, but any searches and seizures that are not emergencies; in other words, if it is feasible to obtain a warrant, a warrant must be obtained for a search or a seizure to be constitutional. The author insists that the text of the Fourth Amendment so requires, see, e.g., id. at 1321; but of course it does not. The amendment does forbid unreasonable searches and seizures, and there are warrantless searches and seizures that are unreasonable. But nothing in the text of the amendment states or implies that all warrantless searches and seizures that are not justified by the existence of an emergency are unreasonable and therefore unconstitutional. Among those that are not are seizures of contraband in plain view, searches consented to by the owner of premises or objects that police want to search, many vehicle searches, stop and frisk (the frisk is a search, the stop a quasi-arrest), and searches incident to a full-fledged arrest. I note in the next paragraph of the text that a warrant requirement can actually reduce the protection of Fourth Amendment rights.

This is not an isolated example of a judicial amendment of the Constitution masquerading as interpretation. As Professor Segall points out,[57] the Supreme Court has interpreted the word "Congress" in the First Amendment to include "the President" (thus forbidding the executive branch to violate the freedoms, notably of speech and of the press, declared in the amendment) and the word "another" in the Eleventh Amendment to mean "the same," and has created out of whole cloth constitutional tests with no basis in text or history. Examples are the "endorsement" test for "Establishment Clause" cases (a government action that amounts to an endorsement of religion is deemed to violate the Establishment Clause of the First Amendment), and the "undue burden" test for cases in which the provision in the Fifth and Fourteenth Amendments that no state shall deny to any person "life, liberty, or property without due process of law" is invoked on the ground that the challenged state law or practice imposes an undue burden on the protected right. And of course there is the Court-created constitutional "right to privacy."

If I'm right, the Constitution is putty in the hands of the judiciary; the judges, especially the Supreme Court Justices, have to a considerable extent re-written it. If that's heresy, at least it is not recent heresy. Twenty-nine years ago, only six years after being appointed to the court of appeals, I published an article proclaiming, though not naming, the heresy;[58] I quote the nub of the article, which I think was correct then and is correct now:

> The framers of a constitution who want to make it a charter of liberties and not just a set of constitutive rules face a difficult choice. They can write specific provisions, and thereby doom their work to rapid obsolescence or irrelevance; or they can write general provisions, thereby delegating substantial discretion to the authoritative interpreters, who in our system are the judges. The U.S. Constitution is a mixture of specific and general provisions. Many of the specific provisions have stood the test of time amazingly well or have been amended without any great fuss. This is especially true of the rules establishing the structure and procedures of Congress. Most of the specific provisions creating rights, however, have fared poorly. Some have proved irksomely anachronistic—for example, the right to a jury trial in federal court in all cases at law if the stakes ex-

57. See note 13 above.
58. "What Am I? A Potted Plant? The Case Against Strict Constructionism," *The New Republic,* September 28, 1987, p. 23.

ceed $20. Others have become dangerously anachronistic, such as the right to bear arms. Some have even turned topsy-turvy, such as the provision for indictment by grand jury. The grand jury has become an instrument of prosecutorial investigation rather than a protection for the criminal suspect. If the Bill of Rights had consisted entirely of specific provisions, it would have aged very rapidly and would no longer be a significant constraint on the behavior of government officials.

Many provisions of the Constitution, however, are drafted in general terms. This creates flexibility in the face of unforeseen changes, but it also creates the possibility of multiple interpretations, and this possibility is an embarrassment for a theory of judicial legitimacy that denies that judges have any right to exercise discretion. A choice among semantically plausible interpretations of a text, in circumstances remote from those contemplated by its drafters, requires the exercise of discretion and the weighing of consequences. Reading is not a form of deduction; understanding requires a consideration of consequences. If I say, "I'll eat my hat," one reason that my listeners will "decode" this in non-literal fashion is that I couldn't eat a hat if I tried. The broader principle, which applies to the Constitution as much as to a spoken utterance, is that if one possible interpretation of an ambiguous statement would entail absurd or terrible results, that is a good reason to adopt an alternative interpretation.

Even the decision to read the Constitution narrowly, and thereby "restrain" judicial interpretation, is not a decision that can be read directly from the text. The Constitution does not say, "Read me broadly," or "Read me narrowly." That decision must be made as a matter of political theory, and will depend on such things as one's view of the springs of judicial legitimacy and of the relative competence of courts and legislatures in dealing with particular types of issue.

Consider the provision in the Sixth Amendment that "in all criminal prosecutions, the accused shall enjoy the right . . . to have the Assistance of Counsel for his defense." Read narrowly, this just means that the defendant can't be forbidden to retain counsel; if he can't afford counsel, or competent counsel, he is out of luck. Read broadly, it guarantees even the indigent the effective assistance of counsel; it becomes not just a negative right to be allowed to hire a lawyer but a positive right to demand the help of the government in financing one's defense. Either reading is compatible with the semantics of the provision, but the first better captures the specific intent of the Framers. At the time the Sixth Amendment was written, English law forbade a criminal defendant to have the assistance of counsel unless abstruse questions of law arose in his case. The Framers wanted to do away with this prohibition. But, more broadly, they wanted to give criminal defendants protection against being railroaded. When they wrote, government could not afford, or at least did not think it could afford, to hire lawyers for indigent criminal defendants. Moreover, criminal trials were short and simple, so it was not ridiculous to expect a person to defend himself without a lawyer if he couldn't afford to hire one. Today the situation is different. Not only can the society easily afford to supply lawyers to poor people charged with crimes, but modern criminal law and procedure are so complicated that an unrepresented defendant will usually be at a great disadvantage.

Is there such a thing as inclusive originalism? A famous phrase in Keats's great poem "Ode to a Nightingale"—a phrase F. Scott Fitzgerald appropriated for the title of his best-known novel—is "tender is the night." I don't think anyone can know what Keats meant in calling night "tender," or can much care. What a poem means to a reader two hundred years after it was published depends on the reader and his surrounding culture more than on the poet. And so it is with the Constitution, and this makes "originalism" nonsense, as the evidence shows[59] and as some originalists are coming close to conceding—notably William Baude, who has taken to advocating what he calls "inclusive originalism."[60] By this he means that any judicial decision that does not flout the original meaning of the Constitution or a constitutional amendment is originalist and therefore lawful. He is thereby enabled to describe the decision that affirmed a constitutional right to same-sex marriage[61] as originalist[62] even though it had no constitutional pedigree and if proposed in the eighteenth century would have led to the proponent's being confined to a loony bin, or worse, and even though the four most conservative Supreme Court Justices (Roberts, Scalia, Thomas, and Alito) dissented—and Baude himself is conservative.

In a subsequent paper, coauthored with Professor Stephen E. Sachs,[63] Baude responds to criticisms that Professor Eric Segall had made of Baude's article "Is

---

59. See, e.g., Eric J. Segall, "The Constitution According to Justices Scalia and Thomas: Alive and Kickin'," 91 *Washington University Law Review* 1663 (2014); Segall, "Originalism on the Ground," in *Dorf on Law*, November 2, 2015, www.dorfonlaw.org/2015/11/originalism-on-ground.html.

60. Baude, "Is Originalism Our Law?" 115 *Columbia Law Review* 2349 (2015).

61. *Obergefell v. Hodges*, 135 S. Ct. 2584 (2015).

62. Baude, note 60 above, at 2382–2383.

63. William Baude and Stephen E. Sachs, "Originalism's Bite," *Green Bag* 2d.

Originalism Our Law?"[64] Here is Segall's and my response to their response (a similar though not identical response by us appears in the same issue of *Green Bag* 2d as the Baude-Sachs paper), and more generally to the unique concept of originalism that Professor Baude is promoting.[65]

He had criticized Segall and me for saying that theories of originalism of the kind promoted by Baude and now by Baude and Sachs "don't matter," are "no different in substance from those of 'living constitutionalists,'" "are "trivial," and don't "tell[] us something important about what the Constitution is [or] how to interpret it." Baude and Sachs riposte that an originalist judge can faithfully interpret the Constitution generally, and the Fourteenth Amendment specifically, in an evolving manner to reach results that the drafters and ratifiers of those provisions hadn't anticipated. But if that's true there is no difference between originalism and Professor David Strauss's "living constitutionalism," generally regarded as the antithesis of originalism.

Baude and Sachs argue that "*Obergefell* [the Supreme Court decision that recognized a constitutional right to same-sex marriage, though of course same-sex marriage, and indeed homosexuality, are nowhere mentioned in the Constitution] made originalist arguments; *Brown* [*v. Board of Education*] made originalist arguments; [and] *Home Building & Loan Association v. Blaisdell*, 290

64. See note 60 above.

65. It's beginning to look as if the back and forth with Professor Baude will never end. For in response to our response to Baude's criticism of us, a law professor named Christopher R. Green has posted on *The Originalism Blog*, "Posner and Segall's Evasion of the Sense-Reference Distinction," December 9, 2016, http://origi nalismblog.typepad.com/the-originalism-blog/2016/12/posner-segall-sense-and-reference.html. I have read Green's response to Professor Segall's and my criticism of Professor Baude's "inclusive originalism," but unfortunately I appear to lack the intellectual sophistication requisite to understanding Green. He renames Baude's "inclusive originalism" "meta-originalism"—and, alas, I don't know what that means. (Hey I'm just a judge, not a professor.) He whacks Professor Segall and me for ignoring the "sense-reference distinction." Unfortunately, I have never heard of the "sense-reference distinction." Green explains it as follows:

> The basic idea is that building cars does not, in itself, change the meaning of the word "car," the "sense" of the word. But building cars *does* change something about the word "car": its "reference," or collection of things picked out by the term. So, if someone asks me how many cars there are, I need to know (a) what he means by "car" and (b) the automotive facts. Both linguistic and automotive facts change all the time, of course, but they do so in different ways and for different reasons. If we want to find out how many cars there are in America, we have to do so (paraphrasing *Brown*) "in the light of [cars'] full development and [their] present place in American life." Current automotive facts are essential, even if we are merely applying a word that someone spoke long ago (e.g., in verifying or falsifying a prediction long ago that someday there will be a certain number of cars in America). . . . My view is that original sense, but not original reference, is interpretively binding. This is how the meaning of words can be both fixed but abstract. The original sense determines a function from possible worlds to outcomes; current facts tell us what possible world we are in, which we then plug into the sense-determined function, producing an outcome.

Sorry, Prof., I still don't get it.

U.S. 398 (1934), a decision, anathema to conservatives, upholding the constitutionality of Minnesota's suspending creditors' remedies during the Great Depression, made originalist arguments." No; all three decisions allowed modern conditions, understandings, values, and needs to trump the firmly held, judicially upheld, beliefs of earlier times. The Court in *Brown* rejected the idea that history mattered when it said that "we cannot turn the clock back to 1868 . . . or even to 1896, when *Plessy v. Ferguson* was written. We must consider public education in the light of its *full development* and *present place* in American life throughout the Nation. Only in this way can it be determined if segregation in public schools deprives these plaintiffs of the equal protection of the laws."[66] If this is originalism, what isn't originalism?

Imagine the Court in *Brown* having taken the opposite position to what it did take by saying, "We know public schools are different today from what they were in 1868 and we know that people's values about race and equality have changed, but the original meaning of the Fourteenth Amendment allows segregated schools and we are bound by that meaning despite fundamental changes in society." That would be originalism, but Baude and Sachs do not accept that understanding of *Brown;* they accept the current, postoriginalist understanding—and merely *call* it originalist.

They argue that Justice Kennedy's majority opinion in *Obergefell* exemplifies originalism because he said that the "generations that wrote and ratified the Bill of Rights and the Fourteenth Amendment did not presume to know the extent of freedom in all of its dimensions, *and so they entrusted to future generations* a charter protecting the right of all persons to enjoy liberty as we learn its meaning."[67] In fact those older generations had said nothing about entrusting the definition or redefinition of constitutionally protected liberties to future generations who might learn the real meaning of liberty; they hadn't said "we don't know what liberty means but what the heck, our descendants may." Baude and Sachs think the passage they quote from the *Obergefell* opinion makes a claim about the law in 1868, yet no one then was thinking that someday homosexuals would and should or might be allowed to marry. Justice Kennedy couldn't have meant that the Fourteenth Amendment *authorized* future generations to decide the constitutional contours of liberty under the standards and conditions prevailing in those generations—in other words that the Fourteenth Amendment had decreed a nonoriginalist method of deciding the

---

66. *Brown v. Board of Education*, 347 U.S. 483, 492–493 (1954) (emphases added).
67. *Obergefell v. Hodges*, note 61 above, at 2598 (emphasis added).

scope, the application—the very meaning—of the amendment. All he could have meant was that the framers and ratifiers of the Fourteenth Amendment had not tried to freeze their understanding of the amendment for eternity, or if they had tried should not be deemed to have succeeded.

Justice Scalia, along with the three other ultraconservative Justices—Roberts, Alito, and Thomas—dissented in *Obergefell*. The implication, if Baude's understanding of originalism is correct, is that none of those four Justices was (and none of the surviving three is) an originalist. Can Baude really have thought that? Can he name a living originalist? Is not he himself an "anything goes" originalist?

Baude and Sachs criticize, among other decisions by the Supreme Court, *Dames & Moore v. Ragan,*[68] which held that executive orders dissolving judgments and suspending pending civil claims against the Iranian government were constitutional; *Wickard v. Filburn,*[69] which held that the federal government could regulate local commerce if it had a potential effect on interstate commerce; and *Lujan v. Defenders of Wildlife,*[70] which held that a court could not order the government to comply with required procedures at the behest of a plaintiff who had suffered no tangible injury as a result of noncompliance with them. (I come back to *Lujan* at the end of the Epilogue.) Baude and Sachs argue that those (and doubtless many other) Supreme Court decisions are inconsistent with the original meaning of the Constitution and that "the fact that originalism brings these cases into doubt, or even disrepute, shows that the theory has real bite." No, for *they* understand the Constitution to authorize the courts to interpret the document in conformity with current needs, and thus to render decisions that the framers of the Constitution would have abhorred, such as *Obergefell*.

They say that "originalism supplies many resources for deciding cases and resolving ambiguities, like precedent and liquidation and common-law backdrops." That can't be right. A precedent is a decision; all decisions interpreting the Constitution postdated it, obviously. They continue: "It's not enough for a judicial opinion to simply avoid [please professors, don't split infinitives!] disparaging originalism while deciding a case some other way; it has to use a methodology that's itself pedigreed to and permitted by the founders' law." I don't know what "pedigreed to" means, but at least "permitted by the founders'

68. 453 U.S. 654 (1981).
69. 317 U.S. 111 (1942).
70. 504 U.S. 555 (1992).

law" is intelligible and Baude and Sachs concede that "the founders' law" permits constitutional decisions that the founders would have considered unconstitutional. None of the decisions cited by Baude and Sachs, from *Blaisdell* to *Brown* to *Lujan* to *Obergefell* and beyond, used the "resources" of originalism to decide cases; nor did they deem themselves bound by "consequences of theory and history." The judges either ignored history (e.g., *Lujan*) or rejected it (e.g., *Brown*). The history of constitutional adjudication by the Supreme Court demonstrates that originalism does *not* supply "resources for deciding cases and resolving ambiguities," because decisions must respond to contemporary —modern—concerns.[71]

The most prominent advocate of originalism was Justice Scalia. But the literal originalism that he displayed, for example in rejecting the suggestion that flogging, a common form of punishment when the Constitution was ratified, could be viewed today as a cruel or unusual punishment, cannot be squared with Baude's "inclusive originalism," which allows the courts considerable latitude to depart from the understanding of the original framers. The original originalists, such as Scalia, were firm in arguing (though not always in ruling) that constitutional decisions were legitimate only if they interpreted constitutional provisions as the people who drafted them, or the population as a whole when they were drafted, understood them. The new originalists (not to be confused with the inclusive originalists such as Baude), some of them liberals, like Yale Professor Jack Balkin, though often disagreeing with other new originalists seem to be at one in thinking that true originalism includes constitutional decisions that are based, as in *Obergefell,* on current understandings of practices, such as same-sex marriage, that the framers of the Constitution and its amendments would have considered far outside the scope of those documents[72] but that legal realists and living constitutionalists would consider within the scope of constitutional understanding and interpretation. What then does the modern, capacious, open-ended originalism add to constitutional decision making? Nothing that I can see.

A disagreement among the few genuine originalists needs to be remarked, however: disagreement over whether the "original" in originalism should be deemed to refer to what the drafters of the original Constitution and the early

71. For further criticism of Professor Baude's version of originalism, see Eric Segall, "Legal Realist Originalism?" in *Dorf on Law,* December 5, 2016, www.dorfonlaw.org/2016/12/legal-realist-originalism.html.

72. On this curious consensus, see Eric Segall, "Originalist Defenses of Overturning Same-Sex Marriage Bans: Really?," *Dorf on Law,* February 9, 2015, www.dorfonlaw.org/2015/02/originalist-defenses-of-overturning.html.

amendments thought the documents meant, or instead to the "public meaning" of the words and sentences constituting the documents—in other words, to how at the time the American people at large would have understood them.[73] It is also worth noting that other forms of nonoriginalist originalism, such as "framework originalism" and "new originalism," the latter proposed by liberals hoping to wrest the originalist mandate from ultraconservatives such as Scalia, are also swamping the academic literature.[74] Originalism is in a state of confusion that may prove permanent.

And let's not forget that such staunch conservatives as Justice Alito and the late Judge Bork embraced a version of originalism very close to the "living Constitution" approach taken by liberals such as Professors Balkin and Strauss.[75] Bork's approach is particularly interesting. Often regarded as the inventor of originalism, he also advocated judicial deference to the democratic process—and the two positions are inconsistent. Originalism, taken seriously, would require the Supreme Court to base interpretation of the Constitution on the understanding of the Constitution by its framers and their contemporaries, while deference to the democratic preference would require the Court to defer to legislation inconsistent with the founders' beliefs. Judge Easterbrook, a protégé of Bork's (Easterbrook was an assistant to the Solicitor General when Bork was Solicitor General [1973 / 1977]), embraced Bork's second position, in his Scalia Lecture discussed earlier in this chapter.

And to cap it all, it's not even clear that the Constitution's framers and supporters were originalists. Certainly Jefferson wasn't. He had written that "some men look at constitutions with sanctimonious reverence, and deem them like the ark of the covenant, too sacred to be touched. They ascribe to the men of the preceding age a wisdom more than human, and suppose what they did to be beyond amendment. . . . But I know also, that laws and institutions must go hand in hand with the progress of the human mind. As that becomes more developed, more enlightened, as new discoveries are made, new truths disclosed,

73. Daniel Farber, "Historical Versus Iconic Meaning: The Declaration, the Constitution, and the Interpreter's Dilemma," 89 *Southern California Law Review* 459, 470–471 (2016).

74. See, for example, Heidi Kitrosser, "Interpretive Modesty," 104 *Georgetown Law Journal* 459 (2016). With Scalia dead, what remains of genuine originalism, rather than its pseudosuccessor? Mainly I think Richard Epstein's scholarly effort to justify genuine originalism on textual and historical grounds. See his book, *The Classical Liberal Constitution* (2014), and his article, "An Unapologetic Defense of the Classical Liberal Constitution: A Reply to Professor Sherry," 128 *Harvard Law Forum* 145 (2015), http://harvardlawreview.org /2015/03/an-unapologetic-defense-of-the-classical-liberal-constitution/.

75. See Farber, note 73 above, at 474–479, discussing *Pleasant Grove City v. Summum*, 555 U.S. 460 (2009), and Robert H. Bork, *The Tempting of America: The Political Seduction of the Law* 168–169 (1990) (judges must "refine and evolve doctrine" provided they are "faithful to the basic meaning" of the constitutional text).

and manners and opinions change with the change of circumstances, institutions must advance also, and keep pace with the times."[76] And in a recent book
a leading legal historian says of the framers "that one of the few original intentions they all shared was opposition to any judicial doctrine of 'original intent.'
To be sure, they all wished to be remembered, but they did not want to be em-
balmed."[77]

Eric Segall has brought to my attention a fascinating article by a long-for-
gotten law professor at the University of Chicago Law School named Arthur W.
Machen[78] that distinguishes between the text of the Constitution, which Machen believed should be construed literally, and the facts to which the text applied, which had changed over time (the article was published 112 years after
the ratification of the original Constitution and 32 years after the ratification of
the Fourteenth Amendment) and would doubtless continue changing. Machen
argued that changes in the facts to which a constitutional provision was applicable were inevitable and would inevitably alter the meaning of the provision.
The Fourth Amendment, for example, might yield (in fact has yielded, though
long after Machen's article) a different rule for the search of a cell phone than
for the search of an office. Such constitutional terms as cruel and unusual punishments and freedom of speech might take on—have in fact taken on—unforeseen meanings as punishments and modes of expression have changed,
which are factual changes. The practical result is judicial revisions of the Constitution—revisions approved by many of today's originalists.

A second transformation of originalism is found, surprisingly, in *The Heritage Guide to the Constitution*.[79] This massive book of more than six hundred
pages—big pages, 9 inches by 5.5 inches—consists of more than two hundred
very well-written short articles by more than one hundred legal scholars, covering every clause in the Constitution and its amendments. The book is the
product of the ultraconservative Heritage Foundation; all the article authors
whose names I recognize are conservative and the book acknowledges having

---

76. *The Jefferson Cyclopedia: A Comprehensive Collection of the Views of Thomas Jefferson* 199 (1900),
quoting a letter that Jefferson wrote in 1733.

77. Joseph J. Ellis, *The Quartet: Orchestrating the Second American Revolution, 1783–1789* 229 (2016). The
massive recent study of the creation of the Constitution—*The Framers' Coup: The Making of the United States
Constitution* (2016), by Professor Michael J. Klarman, amplifies the doubts noted in my text that the framers
labored under the delusion that the Constitution could provide an adequate blueprint for the nation's future.
See, e.g., id. at 628–631.

78. "The Elasticity of the Constitution" (parts 1 and 2), 14 *Harvard Law Review* 200, 273 (1900). See Eric J.
Segall, "A Century Lost: The End of the Originalism Debate," 15 *Constitutional Commentary* 411 (1998), https://
conservancy.umn.edu/bitstream/handle/11299/167780/15_03_Segall.pdf?sequence=1&isAllowed=y.

79. 2d ed. 2014, David F. Forte and Matthew Spalding eds.

an "originalist perspective." Yet the articles are impartial. Each one describes how the clause that is its subject was understood originally, that is, at the time of its enactment or ratification, and how it is understood by courts (mainly of course the U.S. Supreme Court) today. The current understanding (or construal, or application) will often differ radically from the original understanding, and one might expect the articles' authors, as originalists, to criticize the current understanding. But they don't; they describe, they don't make value judgments. The result is a reference work of great value, yet this reader is left to wonder what exactly "originalism" means today.

But the biggest puzzle about originalism is *motivation*. Why would anyone *want* to embrace a theory of judicial decision making that would tether a modern judge to what a subset of the American people (those who were eligible and bothered to vote to ratify the Constitution) thought 228 years ago? Why wouldn't every thinking person want the constitutional text to be the starting point of analysis, as setting forth (as most of the provisions of the original Constitution do) what amount to generalities of good government to be particularized by an evolving political culture? One understands the satisfactions of religion, which are related to a combination of the antiquity and continuity of the major religions and the belief in an unchanging God; but why should conformity to centuries-old political understandings be a source of satisfaction to us moderns? I suspect that the answer is that originalists are conservatives who, unable to prove that the embrace of their values would benefit the American people as a whole, treat the constitutional text as a secular Bible.[80]

And—my parting shot—passages such as the following from a defender of originalism persuade me that among its other vices originalism is confused: "An adjudicator who decides that the meaning of a constitutional provision is supplied by the original meaning of the words is not thereby committed to the view that she should decide cases solely on the basis of that meaning . . . and, less recognized, someone who believes that the subjective intentions of the eighteenth-century Framers should be authoritative in modern interpretation need not adopt any particular theory (nor even believe) that those intentions supply either the linguistic or the legal 'meaning' of constitutional provisions."[81]

Professor Segall, however, deserves the last word on originalism, writing:

80. An equation that is particularly well illustrated by the latest *Cato Supreme Court Review* (15th ed. 2015–2016).

81. Jamal Greene, "The Case for Original Intent," 80 *George Washington Law Review* 1683, 1685 (2012). I cited Greene earlier in this chapter as an articulate critic of Justice Scalia; here I cite him as a defender of originalism, though more of a Baudian than a Scalian originalist.

When Judge Bork and a number of legal academics like Raul Berger and Lino Graglia started advocating for originalism in the 1970's and 1980's, they were reacting to what they perceived to be the excessive judicial activism of the Warren Court in cases like *Roe, Miranda,* and *Baker v. Carr.* Their originalism came with a heavy presumption in favor of legislation whereby in virtually all constitutional cases the plaintiff has the burden of demonstrating that the law violates either clear constitutional text or uncontested history behind the text. This theory is coherent, even if not necessarily persuasive, and if adopted in good faith by judges could dictate results in most constitutional litigation. . . . We will never know if Judge Bork would have actually implemented this type of deference as a Supreme Court Justice. What we do know is no modern Justice has embraced this philosophy. Although Scalia talked the talk before he became a Justice, and continued the rhetoric off the Court when he became a Justice, his votes in constitutional litigation did not come with deference to originalist sources. . . . Justice Scalia (and Justice Thomas) frequently voted to strike down laws where a deferential originalist would have had to uphold them. These were in areas of constitutional law that included litigation over takings, affirmative action, commandeering, sovereign immunity, standing, speech as conduct, and commercial speech, among many other subjects. . . .

Imagine any number of difficult modern cases, such as whether the President may without any judicial process assassinate American citizens who are clearly terrorists, or whether women should have a constitutional right to terminate their pregnancies, or whether gays and lesbians have a legal right to marry. A coherent posture of a judge would be to say to the plaintiffs in all three cases that you have the burden of demonstrating that clear text or history supports your positions and since you can't show that, you lose. Judge Bork's originalism provided a rule for judges in such cases: the government wins in the absence of clear evidence of unconstitutionality, as shown by text or history. But few modern originalists, including Justices Scalia and Thomas as well as Professors Randy Barnett, Jack Balkin, and Will Baude (all self-styled originalists), take that position. Professor Larry Solum's work does not offer this kind of deference either. Solum and Barnett might respond that I am confusing the semantic meaning of the text with the legal meaning. They have argued that what the words meant to the people at the time is a very different question than how judges should apply those words to current modern problems, which requires what they call constitutional construction. The problem is that this dichotomy between semantic and legal meaning renders originalism indistinguishable from living constitutionalism.

Moreover, if, as Randy [Barnett] argues, originalism often "runs out" in hard cases, then the question again becomes who is originalism for? The sad answer, I think, is that originalism is a marketing device for judges and politicians to use to mask personal judgments about what is best for society today.[82]

A note on statutory originalism. Originalist thinking is not limited to constitutional interpretation. There are plenty of old statutes still in force, such as the Sherman Antitrust Act, at this writing in its 126th year and still going strong. The Act prohibits contracts, combinations, and conspiracies in restraint of trade, and also monopolization and conspiracies and attempts to monopolize. The Congress that passed the Act, its supporters, and the judges and Justices who decided the early cases interpreting the Act, did not understand economics and tended to interpret the Act in incoherent populist terms, as protecting consumers from high prices and small competitors of big business from low prices.[83] The current understanding of the Act is that it forbids collusive practices (including mergers to monopoly), in the interest of fostering economic efficiency.[84] That is an understanding forged initially by academics, but by the 1970s embraced by virtually all judges and academics who deal with antitrust issues. It exemplifies the rejection of originalism in the statutory sphere, and can be matched by similar rejections across a wide swathe of federal statutes, one of which (the Civil Rights Act of 1964) I discuss in the Conclusion of this book.

Kagan and Kavanaugh on Scalia, interpretation, and originalism. Given the varied menu of originalisms to choose from, I was not surprised to learn of a talk at the Harvard Law School roughly three months before Justice Scalia's death by the liberal Justice Kagan extolling Scalia's "interpretive" methodology. Here is an account of her talk that appeared in the *Harvard Crimson,* which quoted her at length:

82. Eric Segall, "Who Is Originalism For?," *Dorf on Law,* November 16, 2016, www.dorfonlaw.org/2016/11/who-is-originalism-for.html. I have edited Professor Segall's piece slightly, for reasons of space.

83. See, e.g., my book *Antitrust Law* 34–43 (2d ed. 2001).

84. See id., chap. 2.

"I'm not sure if somebody said to me 'statutory interpretation' I would even quite have known what that meant," Kagan said, referring to her years as a student at the Law School. [That's not to be believed.] "It was not really taught as a discipline." Much has changed since that time, [Professor John] Manning noted, and now courts pay far more attention to the text and wording of statutory law than they ever did before. Kagan ascribed much of this change to her judicial colleague Scalia, who Kagan said had "more to do with this than anybody. . . . Justice Scalia has taught everybody how to do statutory interpretation differently." Following Scalia's example, she went on to say, more legal thinkers consider the meaning, wording, and understanding of statutory texts, in a school of thought known as textualism. She said she believes that Scalia's part in this change in the role of the judiciary will earn her colleague, with whom she has been known to have ideological disputes [for she's a liberal], a place in history. "The fact of the matter is, you wake up in 100 years and most people are not going to know most of our names," Kagan said, referring to herself and her colleagues on the Court. "I think that is really not the case with Justice Scalia, whom I think is [should of course be 'who . . . is'] going to go down as one of the most important, most historic figures on the Court." Audience members who packed into the auditorium . . . where the talk took place said they were struck by Kagan's candor. "It was amazing that she described herself as a textualist," said visiting legal researcher Takahiko Iwasaki. "That was an amazing and candid thing to say."[85]

Candid? Spare me such nonsense, please! Did Iwasaki think Justice Kagan has been *hiding* the fact that she's a textualist, and only now has revealed the awful truth—that she is in thrall to Justice Scalia's textualism? Shouldn't she have been asked to explain how literal interpretation of a text can reveal its meaning with reference to unforeseen events? How for example an ordinance specifying a maximum speed limit of fifty miles an hour for "vehicles" can be "interpreted" (as it invariably is) to create an exception for emergency vehicles, even though the ordinance doesn't mention such vehicles? That is a triumph of common sense over text. Does Kagan allow for such a triumph? Did Scalia? And how can section 1 of the Fourteenth Amendment, which provides that no *state* shall deny to any person within its jurisdiction the equal protection of the

---

85. Adler, note 6 above.

laws, be "interpreted" (as it was in *Bolling v. Sharpe*) to forbid racial discrimination in public education by the District of Columbia, which is not a state or part of a state, but a federal enclave? Realistically, isn't that "interpretation" an invention by the Supreme Court? That doesn't make it bad but does make it nontextualist.

Justice Kagan's late-life conversion to textualism inspired Judge Kavanaugh of the District of Columbia Circuit to pledge his own allegiance to that doctrine[86]—not that anyone would doubt that a conservative D.C. Circuit judge widely thought (whether rightly or wrongly) to have his eyes set on a Supreme Court appointment would pledge such allegiance. In his words, "The text of the law is the law. As Justice Kagan recently stated, 'we're all textualists now.'" (Not all of us, actually; not me, for example.) By emphasizing the "centrality of the words of the statute," Judge Kavanaugh continues,

> Justice Scalia brought about a massive and enduring change in American law. [Only time will tell how enduring it is.] . . . Some may conceive of judging more as a partisan or policymaking exercise in which judges should or necessarily must bring their policy and philosophical predilections to bear on the text at hand. I disagree with that vision of the federal judge in our constitutional system. [You're wrong, Judge.] The American rule of law, as I see it, depends on neutral, impartial judges who say what the law is, not what the law should be. Judges are umpires, or at least should always strive to be umpires. In a perfect world, at least as I envision it, the outcomes of legal disputes would not often vary based solely on the backgrounds, political affiliations, or policy views of judges.[87]

We're not likely to get a perfect world, as Judge Kavanaugh doubtless knows; and if he's right that the American rule of law *depends* on neutral judges— judges as neutral as baseball umpires—then America has never had the rule of law and probably never will. The quoted passage is the standard false rhetoric of judges' asserting their purity, as well as echoing John Roberts's false statement at his confirmation hearing that Supreme Court Justices are just like sports umpires and referees.

But let me pause for a moment to take issue with Judge Kavanaugh's statement that the American rule of law depends on "judges who say what the law is, not what the law should be." Most law, notably most constitutional law, is

---

86. See Brett M. Kavanaugh, "Fixing Statutory Interpretation," 129 *Harvard Law Review* 2118 (2016).

87. Id. at 2118, 2120. Notice his failure to mention judges' religious views.

made by judges, which casts them in a legislative role. Think back to the Fourth Amendment. It neither says nor hints that warrants are required to search a person's home, but the Supreme Court has held that they are required for that purpose because, the Justices must have thought, they *should* be required. That doesn't sound as if they were being neutral.

A car is motionless when in neutral. What is a judge in neutral?

The claim by Justice Kagan and Judge Kavanaugh that Scalia brought about a fundamental change in American law has not been substantiated. He was, after Thomas, the most conservative member of a Supreme Court dominated by conservatives until his death deprived the conservative Justices of their majority. Although the most colorful and outspoken member of the Court, Scalia didn't dominate it, and given the conservatism of a majority of its Justices its decisions would not have been significantly different had he been a clone of Roberts, Thomas, or Alito rather than his own man. And Judge Kavanaugh is mistaken not only to entertain the possibility that judges *are* merely umpires (certainly Scalia wasn't) but also to think it possible that with a little prodding from him and others they will become so.

I don't mean to criticize Kagan and Kavanaugh for their exaggerated conception of Scalia's significance; maybe history will vindicate their assessments of him. And if not, still, no one has ever said that candor is part of the judicial job description. Judges and lawyers are past masters of exaggerated praise of their profession and by implication themselves. But I would have expected Justice Kagan, at least, to be more cautious about uttering extravagant pronunciamentos, in view of questions that have been raised concerning the propriety of her refusing to recuse herself in the Affordable Care Act case.[88] I would also have expected both she and Dean Minow to temper their extravagant praise of Scalia, given that they are liberals. Do they *want* a Scalia clone on the Supreme Court? Of course they were writing before the 2016 Presidential election, and doubtless thought Hillary Clinton a shoo-in and a liberal Supreme Court therefore in the offing.

On the subject of judicial candor I think it worth noting that we can expect it to be inverse to the judge's judicial politicizing. The judge (and *a fortiori* the Supreme Court Justice) whose judicial votes are strongly influenced by his or

88. See Sherrilyn A. Ifill, "Justice and Appearance of Justice," 160 *University of Pennsylvania Law Review PENNumbra* 332, 335 (2012); Eric J. Segall, "Supreme Court Recusal, the Affordable Care Act, and the Rule of Law," id. at 337–339. But I must note in fairness to Judge Kavanaugh his dissenting opinion in *Seven-Sky v. Holder,* 661 F.3d 1, 21–54 (2011), defending the constitutionality of the Affordable Care Act prior to the Supreme Court's upholding it in *King v. Burwell,* 576 U.S. ___ (2015). (The absence of a page number is the result of the Supreme Court's unintelligible delay in publishing its opinions in the *United States Reports.*)

her political leanings is likely to pose as a neutral "umpire" à la John Roberts. The more neutral the judge—the more he sets his political and religious views to one side when judging—the less likely he is to preen himself on being um-pireal—in other words, the less likely he is to feel defensive and therefore in need of shouting "Judges are umpires." (Judge Kavanaugh, beware!) The neu-tral judge has less to hide; and the less one has to hide, the more candid one can be without inviting warranted criticism.

Priors play a big role in influencing—mainly by limiting—judicial candor. A judge who has strong political or religious priors will be at pains to deny that politics or religion (or for that matter personal moral code, emotions, and so forth) plays *any* role in his or her judicial votes, because they're not supposed to though very often they do play a role, and often a decisive one. The truly neutral judges will not have to make such denials—their neutrality will be evi-denced in their opinions—yet they too will not "let it all hang out." They will try to avoid insulting the lawyers and litigants who appear before them, to be polite and considerate rather than brusque and rude, and in other respects as well to maintain the decorum proper to persons publicly engaged in the exer-cise of governmental power. "Let it all hang out" is not a proper slogan for the judiciary; "candor within limits" might be.

And finally though some judges are genuinely neutral all *courts* are political, because they have to make moral or pragmatic judgments all the time owing to the uncertain meaning and frequent obsolescence of statutes, not to mention of precedents and constitutional provisions. You don't hear a judge say to a law-yer, "Sorry, no law to apply to your case, come back tomorrow and maybe we'll have thought of something, or, if not, steeled ourselves to create new law for your case."

And what kind of judge was Scalia, anyway, that he should earn such plau-dits from liberal Justice Kagan? Neither titan nor sweetie, according to Jeffrey Toobin, but instead

> belligerent with his colleagues, dismissive of his critics, nostalgic for a world where outsiders knew their place and stayed there. . . . His revul-sion toward homosexuality, a touchstone of his world view, appeared straight out of his sheltered, nineteen-forties [Roman Catholic] boy-hood. When in 2003 the Court ruled that gay people could no longer be thrown in prison for having consensual sex, Scalia dissented, writing: "Today's opinion is the product of a Court, which is the product of a law-

profession culture, that has largely signed on to the so-called homosexual agenda, by which I mean the agenda promoted by some homosexual activists directed at eliminating the moral opprobrium that has traditionally attached to homosexual conduct." He continued: "Many Americans do not want persons who openly engage in homosexual conduct as partners in their business, as scoutmasters for their children, as teachers in their children's schools, or as boarders in their home. They view this as protecting themselves and their families from a life style that they believe to be immoral and destructive."[89]

But of course there are many things that many Americans do not want; that is not in itself a ground for denial of a constitutional entitlement to those things by the Americans who want them. It is certain that most Americans disapprove of burning the American flag, but Scalia voted to recognize a constitutional right to burn it.

Toobin continues:

It was in his jurisprudence that Scalia most self-consciously looked to the past. He pioneered "originalism," a theory holding that the Constitution should be interpreted in line with the beliefs of the white men, many of them slave owners, who ratified it in the late eighteenth century. [Almost half the signers of the Constitution owned slaves.] During Scalia's first two decades as a Justice, Chief Justice William H. Rehnquist rarely gave him important constitutional cases to write for the Court; the Chief feared that Scalia's extreme views would repel Sandra Day O'Connor, the Court's swing vote, who had a toxic relationship with Scalia during their early days as colleagues. His clashes with her thus were consequential, unlike his much-chronicled friendship with Ruth Bader Ginsburg, which had no effect on either his or her judicial votes.

Not until 2008, after Roberts had succeeded Rehnquist, did Scalia finally get a blockbuster of a case to write: *District of Columbia v. Heller,* the case about Second Amendment gun rights. Scalia spent thousands of words plumbing the psyches of the Framers, to conclude (wrongly, as John Paul Stevens pointed out in a long dissenting opinion[90]) that they

89. Jeffrey Toobin, "Looking Back," *New Yorker,* February 29, 2016, www.newyorker.com/magazine /2016/02/29/antonin-scalia-looking-backward.

90. The dissent, however, was maladroit, because Stevens was playing on Scalia's turf—arguing with him at great length about the historical record in England and America. See *District of Columbia v. Heller,* 554 U.S. 570, 639–670 (2008). Readers would be apt to think that there is no obvious choice between Scalia's reading of

had meant that individuals, not just members of "well-regulated" state militias, had the right to own handguns. Even Scalia's ideological allies recognized the folly of trying to divine the "intent" of the authors of the Constitution concerning questions that those bewigged worthies could never have anticipated. During the oral argument of a case challenging a California law that required, among other things, warning labels on violent video games, Justice Samuel Alito interrupted Scalia's harangue of a lawyer by quipping, "I think what Justice Scalia wants to know is what James Madison thought about video games. Did he enjoy them?"

Scalia described himself as an advocate of judicial restraint, who believed that the courts should defer to the democratically elected branches of government. In reality, he lunged at opportunities to overrule the work of Presidents and of legislators, especially Democrats. Scalia helped gut the Voting Rights Act, overturn McCain-Feingold and other campaign-finance rules, and, in his last official act, block President Obama's climate-change regulations. Scalia's reputation, like the Supreme Court's, is also stained by his role in the majority in *Bush v. Gore.* His crude, oft-repeated advice to critics of that decision was: "Get over it."

Not long ago, Scalia had told an interviewer that he'd cancelled his subscription to the *Washington Post* and received his news from the *Wall Street Journal,* the *Washington Times* (owned by the Reverend Sun Myung Moon's Unification Church), and conservative talk radio. In this, as in his jurisprudence, he showed that he lived within the sealed bubble of contemporary conservative thought.[91]

I'd like to hear a response to Toobin from Kagan and/or Minow. I'm not holding my breath, however. But I'd also like to hear Toobin comment on a curious passage that he quotes from Scalia: "Many Americans do not want persons who openly engage in homosexual conduct as partners in their business." Read literally, Scalia seems to have been saying that as long as homosexuals concealed their homosexual conduct, the straights would be happy to have them as partners in their businesses, etc. I should think the straights' reaction in such a scenario would be the opposite: that if your partner or employee is openly homosexual, at least you know what you're dealing with; if he's a closeted homosexual, watch out!

---

history and Stevens', so the decision (affirming a constitutional right to own a gun for self-defense) must be right, or at least as likely right as wrong.

91. Toobin, note 89 above.

Incidentally, anent *Heller,* Scalia's "blockbuster" opinion, there is more that is wrong with it than Toobin says. For one thing Scalia ignores (contrary to this originalist faith) the language of the Second Amendment: "A well regulated Militia, being necessary to the security of a free State, the right of the people to keep and bear Arms, shall not be infringed." In other words the right is derivative from the need for a well-regulated militia—"keep" as well as "bear" because members of the militia (which is to say, at the time the amendment was ratified, all able-bodied adult males) were expected to have and keep a musket and ammunition at home rather than in arms depots, of which there were few (if any) in the period in which the Second Amendment was adopted. And finally it's been shown that in saying that the amendment created a right of Englishmen (and therefore of Americans, most of whom of course when the Bill of Rights was enacted were of English descent) that had been "secured to them as individuals, according to 'libertarian political principles,' not as members of a fighting force" and thus "was clearly an individual right, having nothing whatever to do with service in a militia,"[92] Scalia was misstating English law and indeed, as Toobin says, "committing a breathtaking inaccuracy."[93]

Why don't our judges and Justices wear a bit of ermine? English judges used to wear a bit of ermine fur on their robes, inspired by the legend that ermines are so proud of their white fur (white only in winter however, and even then there is a black spot on their tail) that if they get a spot of dirt on it they forthwith die of shame. Pondering the likely motives of Kagan and Kavanaugh and Minow and others in praising Scalia, I incline to the view that they may have been wanting to contribute to the endless campaign of the judiciary, symptomatic of defensiveness and abetted by lawyers and law professors and law school deans and the grandees of the American Law Institute, to deny, albeit by methods other than wearing a bit of ermine fur, that personal or political factors play

92. *District of Columbia v. Heller,* note 90 above, at 579.

93. Richard G. Menaker, "How a Historian Changed Gun Law—In 2008, the Supreme Court Radically Expanded Gun Rights—Thanks in Part to a Misreading of Ancient English Laws," *The American Oxonian,* no. 1, p. 3 (winter 2016). A more sophisticated effort to derive a right to individual gun ownership from the Second Amendment can be found in an article years earlier by Don B. Kates, Jr., entitled "Handgun Prohibition and the Original Meaning of the Second Amendment," 82 *Michigan Law Review* 204 (1983), in which, cognizant of the "militia" reference in the first clause of the amendment, the author wrote that "the Founders stated what they meant by 'militia' on various occasions. Invariably they defined it in some phrase like 'the whole body of the people.'" They can't have meant that. The whole body of the people would include women and children, who would not have been considered entitled to own guns. Only able-bodied men were allowed to own guns; all able-bodied men were deemed members of the militia; and there is no indication that the Second Amendment was intended to entitle them to own or use guns for purposes unrelated to their militia duties.

any role in judicial decision making. By claiming (as I noted above) to have "boundless admiration" for Scalia and indeed to "love" him, as well as to have embraced his jurisprudence of textualism, Kagan implicitly denies either personal or political tensions with the most conservative of modern Supreme Court Justices (except for Thomas), though Kagan is a liberal. By expressing "love" for Scalia she dramatizes the false view that politics do not divide judges—do not make enemies—that Justice Holmes's description of the Supreme Court Justices as "nine scorpions in a bottle" was profoundly mistaken; they are a litter of cuddly newborn kittens.

No liberal was he. I find Kagan's effusive "love" and "boundless admiration" for Scalia unfathomable given his many hyperconservative judicial opinions and extrajudicial assertions, such as that there's no principled difference between child molesters and homosexuals—opinions and assertions one would have thought shocking to so liberal a Justice as Kagan. Professor Eric Segall and I discussed some of those assertions in an op-ed[94] prior to Justice Scalia's death, which I take the liberty of quoting from, and editing, with my coauthor's permission:

> The Supreme Court has decided four major cases furthering gay rights. Justice Antonin Scalia wrote a bitter dissent from each. In *Lawrence v. Texas,* for example, where the court invalidated Texas's ban on homosexual relations between consenting adults, Justice Scalia complained that "today's opinion is the product of a Court, which is the product of a law-profession culture, that has largely signed on to the so-called homosexual agenda. . . ." [And] he predicted in his dissent that the court would eventually rule that the Constitution protects the right to same-sex marriage. In June 2015, the Supreme Court's 5–4 decision in *Obergefell v. Hodges* made his prediction came true. His dissenting opinion in that case vented even more than his usual anger, his colleagues' gay rights decisions having it seems driven him to an extreme position concerning the role of the Supreme Court. Thus in the speech to law students at Georgetown in which he denied that there is any principled basis for dis-

---

94. "Justice Scalia's Majoritarian Theocracy," *New York Times,* "The Opinion Pages," December 2, 2015, www.nytimes.com/2015/12/03/opinion/justice-scalias-majoritarian-theocracy.html?_r=0. I have deleted the first three paragraphs of Professor Segall's statement, which discusses the June 2016 end-of-term decisions, from which Scalia of course was absent.

tinguishing child molesters from homosexuals, since both are minorities and, further, suggested that the protection of minorities should be the responsibility of legislatures, not courts, he remarked sarcastically child abusers are also a "deserving minority," as "nobody loves them." That was a statement in poor taste for a Supreme Court Justice to make. I would be interested in Justice Kagan's reaction to it. I would think it difficult for a liberal to "love" a person who had made such a statement. I have to confess that I don't begin to understand Justice Kagan. If she is a liberal, it may be time to retire the word.

Not content with throwing minorities under the bus, Scalia declared that *Obergefell* marked the end of democracy in the United States [wow!] —that "a system of government that makes the People subordinate to a committee of nine unelected lawyers does not deserve to be called a democracy." The implication is that the Supreme Court should get out of the business of enforcing the Constitution altogether, for enforcing it frequently involves overriding legislation, which is the product of elected officials, and hence flouting democracy. He said in his dissent that "to allow the policy question of same-sex marriage to be considered and resolved by a select, patrician, highly unrepresentative panel of nine is to violate a principle even more fundamental than no taxation without representation: no social transformation without representation." [But who, pray tell, are the "patricians" on the Supreme Court? They're all middle class.] The model of government that he was embracing . . . was that of the traditional British Constitution. Until recently Parliament was Britain's "supreme court." It could overrule judicial decisions legislatively, but courts could not invalidate parliamentary legislation. In the words of Lord Tom Bingham, a highly regarded English judge recently deceased, "the British people have not repelled the extraneous power of the papacy in spiritual matters, and the pretension to royal power in temporal, in order to subject themselves to the unchallengeable rulings of unelected judges."[95]

Obergefell obsessed [Scalia]. . . . He said that the decision represents the "furthest imaginable extension of the Supreme Court doing whatever it wants," and that "saying that the Constitution requires that practice"— same-sex marriage—"which is contrary to the religious beliefs of many

95. Bingham, *The Rule of Law* 168 (2010).

of our citizens, I don't know how you can get more extreme than that." The decision, he said, "had nothing to do with the law." Yet his suggestion that the Constitution cannot override the religious beliefs of American citizens is radical. It would imply, contrary to the provision of the Constitution that forbids religious tests for public office, that religious majorities are special wards of the Constitution. Justice Scalia wanted to turn the Constitution upside down when it came to government and religion; his political ideal verged on majoritarian theocracy.

In a talk at the Union League in Philadelphia he criticized the Supreme Court's interpretations of the establishment clause of the First Amendment, which prohibits the government from establishing a religion. He did so, according to the moderator, Robert P. George, an ultraconservative Catholic professor of jurisprudence at Princeton, on the ground that "there is no textual or historical basis for the Court's claim that laws and policies must be neutral not only between different religions, but also between religion and irreligion." The implication is that if a majority of Americans reject same-sex marriage on religious grounds or want Catholicism to be the official U.S. religion, the Supreme Court must bow.

It comes as no surprise that Justice Scalia also said that state and local officials who are not actual parties to Supreme Court cases have no obligation to obey judicial rulings that those officials think lack a warrant in the text or original understanding of the Constitution. He cited Abraham Lincoln's remark concerning the *Dred Scott* ruling that decisions by the Supreme Court are formally binding only on the parties to the case. That's true, but few Americans will agree with Justice Scalia that *Obergefell*, which conferred rights on millions of Americans, is comparable to *Dred Scott*, which denied rights to millions by ruling that slaves were not citizens and could not sue in federal courts.

And can Scalia have wanted his own decisions to have diminished and perhaps negligible force until separate lawsuits were brought in each state to enforce them? That implies that state and local officials should feel free to ignore his gun-friendly decision in *District of Columbia v. Heller*.

Several months after Scalia's death, Professor Segall offered a caustic assessment of Scalia's career as a Supreme Court Justice, from which I quote:

I hope it is appropriate to try and be as honest as possible about the most "ludicrously overrated" Supreme Court Justice of his generation who, in the words of Eric Posner "tragically thought he could take politics out of judging but only made things much worse." Meanwhile, *Judge* Posner has been unsparing in his criticism of Scalia. . . . Justice Scalia was of course best known for his frequent rants about how important text and history (read original meaning) are to judges who have to decide constitutional law cases. But the truth is that he did not come close to voting in an originalist fashion during his long career. . . . In the areas of affirmative action, freedom of speech generally and campaign finance reform specifically, federalism, gun rights, takings, standing, and voting rights, among many others, Justice Scalia voted to strike down laws where neither the text nor the original meaning behind the text supported his votes. Scalia once said he was a "faint-hearted" originalist but later walked that back and then said he was an "honest" originalist. The truth is that he was a snake-oil originalist who sold a product he did not use himself.

One scholarly response to the argument that Scalia voted in a non-textualist, non-originalist way in huge swathes of constitutional law is that in many of the areas of [that] law there are plausible, even if not persuasive, originalist arguments in support of Scalia's votes (arguments excavated by extremely motivated law professors, not Scalia himself). Even if there are such arguments, . . . [they] were not available to Scalia, who never argued for that position. Instead, in most . . . areas of law . . . he simply either ignored or mischaracterized historical evidence while often stridently accusing other Justices of playing fast and loose with the rules of the constitutional game.

. . . In his thirty years on the [Supreme Court], he voted to strike down every affirmative action plan he saw. . . . He always argued that the Constitution is color-blind, and thus the government's using racial criteria to foster diversity and equality was constitutionally indistinguishable from the government's using racial criteria to completely exclude an entire race of people from a government benefit. But at no time in his career did Scalia try to justify this strong policy preference with reference to the original meaning of the text of the Fourteenth Amendment. Given that ambiguous text (which does not mention race) and the fact that from 1868 to 1954 the amendment was not understood to require "color blindness," and given Scalia's dislike of the "living Constitution," when exactly did the meaning of the 14th Amendment change? Scalia never provided an answer, which would be fine for "living constitutionalists" but not for someone who thinks the Constitution frozen in time.

One former Scalia clerk claims he presented originalist evidence to Scalia that the ratifiers would have thought affirmative action to be constitutional (or at least would not have deemed it unconstitutional) only to have that data completely ignored. This tactic of overlooking unhelpful historical evidence was the hallmark of the man who yelled that the Constitution is "dead, dead, dead" while consistently voting to strike down laws based on the Justice's current perspective on what the Constitution should mean today.

Justice Thomas, who seemed very lonely this past term, often dissenting all by himself, ended his dissent in the abortion case [*Whole Woman's Health v. Hellerstedt*] with a quotation from the man whose shadow hung over the term so darkly: "The majority's embrace of a jurisprudence of rights-specific exceptions and balancing tests is a regrettable concession of defeat—an acknowledgement that we have passed the point where 'law,' properly speaking, has any further application." The constant finger-pointing and chest-thumping insistence by Scalia and Thomas over the years that *they* apply "law" and the other Justices are doing something else marginalized both of them. Constitutional law is now and has always been about the clash of values. Maybe Thomas wouldn't have been so lonely this term, and maybe Scalia would have authored a few more majority opinions, if they had been more transparent about their own values.[96]

The Court loses public support. Justice Scalia was atypical in the ferocity of his denunciation of decisions with which he disagreed. More typical is a Justice's defense (e.g., Kagan's defense) of the Supreme Court's objectivity, its apolitical purity, its chumminess—a defense likely to become more intense in reaction to the striking decline in public approval of the Court in the last fifteen years. According to the Gallup Poll, the percentage of Americans who approve of how the Supreme Court is doing its job fell from 62 percent in 2001 to 42 percent in

96. "Supreme Ghosts, Snake Oil Originalism, and the 2015–2016 Term," *Dorf on Law*, June 27, 2016, www .dorfonlaw.org/2016/06/supreme-ghosts-snake-oil-originalism.html. I have edited Professor Segall's statement slightly, with his authorization.

2016, while the percentage disapproving rose from 29 to 52 percent, thus substantially exceeding the percentage approving.[97]

Complementing the growing public disapproval of the Court, a recent article by Brian Christopher Jones discusses a range of challenges to the very legitimacy of the Supreme Court[98]—surprisingly from both Left and Right.[99] He places considerable blame on Scalia's harsh public criticisms of his colleagues' judicial decisions—criticisms formed of such extreme and even rude terms as "absurd," "indefensible," "jiggery-pockery," "argle-bargle," and "pure applesauce" that accused his colleagues of such offenses as being "prepared to do whatever it takes to uphold and assist its favorites" (i.e., its favorite laws) and even to stake a "naked judicial claim to legislative—indeed, *super*-legislative—power."[100] Scalia's "flamboyant attacks . . . often made the Court's work look insignificant or trivial."[101]

Jones goes on to criticize the Court for its failure to accompany each opinion it issues "with a brief and accurate press summary that is easily discernible for the press but also for laypeople."[102] He further remarks that "how some of the Justices behave at both hearings and decisions (being overly and unapologetically sarcastic or going years without ever questioning counsel [the reference of course is to Justice Thomas]) does not exactly align with the behavior of judges from other constitutional courts."[103] He points out that judges of at least one of those courts, the Supreme Court of the United Kingdom, "have abandoned gowns and wigs in favor of formal attire [business clothes]," while our Justices, in the words of Justice O'Connor, believe that wearing a black robe "shows that all of us judges are engaged in upholding the Constitution and the rule of law. We have a common responsibility."[104] It shows nothing; it's just another antiquarian habit. A strip of ermine fur would be an improvement.

97. Gallup, *Supreme Court*, www.gallup.com/poll/4732/supreme-court.aspx. Five percent of the polled took no position regarding approval or disapproval of the Court.

98. Brian Christopher Jones, "Disparaging the Supreme Court, Part II: Questioning Institutional Legitimacy," 2016 *Wisconsin Law Review* 239 (2016).

99. Id. at 249.

100. Id. at 250–251. Justice Scalia "often seems to regard his colleagues with the disdain that one would reserve for people considered unquestionably inferior in intellectual or reasoning abilities." David A. Schulta and Christopher E. Smith, *The Jurisprudential Vision of Justice Antonin Scalia* 208 (1996); see also Daniel A. Farber, "Playing Favorites? Justice Scalia, Abortion Protests, and Judicial Impartiality," 101 *Minnesota Law Review Headnotes* 23, 24 n. 9 (2016). Yet in no period of Scalia's long career as a Supreme Court Justice was he the most intelligent member of the Court.

101. Jones, note 98 above, at 252.

102. Id. at 257.

103. Id. at 258.

104. Id. at 257–259.

The big question, Jones states in conclusion, "is whether the Court will maintain its institutional legitimacy in an era of increased and unrelenting disparagement. . . . [B]y intervening into the political process in such a distinct and resolute manner during recent years, the Court has unquestionably brought this increased disparagement upon itself. After all, the amplified vilification and questioning of the institution's reasoning and proper democratic role comes not only from the media . . . but through the Court's own decisions."[105]

Judge Gorsuch to the rescue? Judge Neil M. Gorsuch, nominated by Trump on the last day of January to fill the vacancy created by Scalia's death, is (at this writing—February 9, 2017) being compared to Scalia. But he is far more sophisticated, better educated, more reasonable, notably more civilized, almost certainly more moderate, and though unquestionably legally and morally conservative he conceivably might drift left as a Supreme Court Justice, as several conservative Justices have done. He lacks Scalia's parade of religiosity, though he is an Episcopalian sympathetic to the legal claims of religious organizations; yet for sure he believes in evolution. At this writing he has not yet had his Senate confirmation hearing—which Democratic Senators have promised to filibuster—but I will be surprised if he is not confirmed. (As a detail, I note with pleasure that he will be breaking the Catholic-Jewish monopoly on the Court. In a predominantly Protestant nation, a Supreme Court devoid of Protestants is anomalous.)

Gorsuch calls himself an originalist and this is taken to indicate a close affinity with Scalia; but as I've pointed out numerous times in this chapter, Scalia was no originalist. Gorsuch may be, if he meant it (I hope he didn't) when he said, "Ours [he means federal judges, including Supreme Court Justices] is the job of interpreting the Constitution. And that document isn't some inkblot on which litigants may project their hopes and dreams for a new and perfected tort law, but a carefully drafted text judges are charged with applying according to its original public meaning. If a party wishes to claim a constitutional right, it is incumbent on him to tell us where it lies, not to assume or stipulate with the other side that it lies, not to assume or stipulate with the other side that it must be in there *somewhere*."[106]

---

105. Id. at 260–261.

106. *Cordova v. City of Albuquerque*, 816 F.3d 645, 661 (10th Cir. 2016) (concurring opinion) (emphasis in original).

That's wrong, as I explain and illustrate numerous times in this book. The Constitution and many of its amendments are obsolete, and while the courts like to say they're basing decision in a constitutional case on this or that constitutional provision, often they are basing the decision on modern beliefs and needs rather than on a true understanding of the provision. And that, for better or worse, is inkblot constitutionalism—and is inevitable given the Constitution's age. (And when will we stop fussing so over an eighteenth-century document!)

Also wrong is the statement in Gorsuch's book *The Future of Assisted Suicide and Euthanasia* (2006) that "All human beings are intrinsically valuable and the intentional taking of human life by private persons is always wrong." Was Hitler "intrinsically valuable"? And is killing in self-defense "always wrong"? The obvious answer to both questions is no.[107]

I wonder whether Gorsuch's strategy in the two examples I just gave is the sensible one. (Of course he can't retract what he said in his book, but he could avoid mention of it or even say he was open to reexamining the issue.) Surely the Republican Senators will vote to confirm him come what may. What he may need (if the filibuster isn't eliminated) are some Democratic votes. So I would think he'd want to throw the Democratic Senators a few bones, perhaps pointing to some liberal decisions that he's written or saying something nice about a Democratic Justice, like Ginsburg or Breyer or his fellow-Coloradan Byron White. He could even say he agreed with (or, more moderately, that he would not vote to overrule) *Obergefell*, which has very strong support, not limited to liberals, throughout the country.

A recent article states that Gorsuch "confessed to having cried on the ski slopes when the news reached him that Scalia had died."[108] I find that hard to believe, even if one ignores the implausibility of someone's accosting Gorsuch on the ski slopes to report Scalia's death. Scalia was a month short of his eightieth birthday when he died, and though the details of his very poor health had not been published he was known to be obese and (despite his age) a heavy smoker, facts that coupled with his age augured a short remaining lifespan. I am likewise skeptical of Peggy Noonan's claim that Gorsuch "loved Antonin Scalia."[109]

107. See, e.g., "Physician-Assisted Suicide—Posner," *Becker-Posner Blog*, February 5, 2012, www.becker-posner-blog.com/2012/02/physician-assisted-suicideposner.html.

108. Leonard Leo, "Trump's Supreme Court Whisperer," *Wall Street Journal*, February 4, 2017, p. A11.

109. Noonan, "In Trump's Washington, Nothing Feels Stable," *Wall Street Journal*, February 4, 2017, p. A13.

I speculated that at Gorsuch's Senate confirmation hearing a Democratic Senator would ask him what he thought about President Trump's calling federal district judge James L. Robart a "so-called judge" on February 4 for his having enjoined part of the President's controversial "keep out the Muslims" order. Gorsuch I imagined would say nothing—not even remind the Senators that there was no basis for the President's calling Judge Robart a "so-called judge," as he was nominated for his judgeship by President George W. Bush in 2003 and confirmed by the Senate by a vote of 99 to 0 six months later—and is a highly regarded judge.[110] Trump added to his abuse of Robart by calling Robart's injunction "ridiculous," but that was a lesser breach of interbranch comity, as it did not question Robart's judicial standing, as "so-called judge" did.

I was wrong about Gorsuch. Just a day or two after I wrote the above paragraph, he did just what he should have done. As reported in the *Washington Post,* "President Trump's escalating attacks on the federal judiciary drew denunciation Wednesday [February 8] from his Supreme Court nominee, Neil Gorsuch, who told a Democratic senator that the criticism was 'disheartening' and 'demoralizing' to independent federal courts."[111] Trump responded by criticizing the Senator, but not Gorsuch, and I assume his confirmation is secure; but it was a courageous statement. Properly Gorsuch has not taken a public position on whether the President's immigration order is unlawful, or made political arguments of any kind. What he was right to do and did do was stand up for the judiciary by declaring that the President of the United States should not attack the integrity of a sitting judge. That was not a political statement but a statement about the Constitution that Judge Gorsuch had already expressed in a judicial opinion in which he pointed out that "the framers lived in an age when judges had to curry favor with the crown in order to secure their tenure and salary and their decisions not infrequently followed their interests. Indeed, the framers cited this problem as among the leading reasons for their declaration of independence. . . . To this day, one of the surest proofs any nation enjoys an independent judiciary must be that the government can and does lose in litigation before its 'own' courts like anyone else."[112]

That President Trump has an imperfect understanding of the role of the federal judiciary is suggested by the results of a recent interview first of two judges

110. See Thomas Fuller, "Judge Denounced by Trump Known for His Independence," *New York Times,* February 5, 2017, p. A13.

111. Abby Phillip et al., *Washington Post,* February 8, 2017.

112. *In re Renewable Energy Corp.,* 792 F.3d 1274, 1278 (10th Cir. 2015).

and then of a third. The two agreed with the unidentified interviewer that the Separation of Powers doctrine is there for a definite reason and purpose and therefore that it's not unusual for members of one branch of government to be frustrated by the disagreement of members of another. The two judges agreed that judges are used to disagreement, frustration, and criticism, having all taken oaths in no way affected or altered by the responses of others to their decisions. The interviewer reports having received a similar "sticks and stones" answer from the third judge.

The day before Gorsuch's courageous statement, the *New York Times* published a rather remarkable editorial about Trump's attack on Judge Robart, which I quote with minor omissions:

> When President Trump doesn't get what he wants, he tends to look for someone to blame—crooked pollsters, fraudulent voters, lying journalists. Anyone who questions him or his actions becomes his foe. Over the past few days, he's added an entire branch of the federal government to his enemies list.
>
> [The day after Judge Robart] blocked Mr. Trump's executive order barring entry to refugees and immigrants from seven predominantly Muslim nations . . . the president mocked . . . Robart, a George W. Bush appointee, . . . as a "so-called judge" who had made a "ridiculous ruling." Later Trump added: "Just cannot believe a judge would put our country in such peril. If something happens blame him and court system. People pouring in. Bad!" . . .
>
> There was, in fact, a terrorist attack shortly after Mr. Trump issued his immigration order: a white supremacist, officials say, armed himself with an assault rifle and stormed a mosque in Quebec City, slaughtering six Muslims during their prayers. Mr. Trump has not said a word about that massacre—although he was quick to tell America on Twitter to "get smart" when, a few days later, an Egyptian man wielding a knife attacked a military patrol in Paris, injuring one soldier.
>
> In the dark world that Mr. Trump and his top adviser, Stephen Bannon, inhabit, getting "smart" means shutting down immigration from countries that have not been responsible for a single fatal attack in the United States in more than two decades. As multiple national security experts have said, the order would, if anything, increase the terrorism threat to Americans. And contrary to Mr. Trump's claim, no one is "pour-

ing in" to America. Refugees and other immigrants already undergo a thorough, multilayered vetting process that can take up to two years. . . .

Judge Robart is not the first judge Mr. Trump has smeared. During the presidential campaign last year, he pursued bigoted attacks on a federal judge presiding over a class-action fraud lawsuit against his so-called Trump University. The judge, Gonzalo Curiel, could not be impartial, Mr. Trump claimed, because he "happens to be, we believe, Mexican," and Mr. Trump had promised to build a border wall and deport millions of undocumented Mexican immigrants. Judge Curiel was born in Indiana, and Mr. Trump settled the lawsuit in November for $25 million. . . .[113]

An article by Michael M. Greenbaum[114] quotes Stephen K. Bannon, President Trump's chief strategist, as saying, "The media should be embarrassed and humiliated and keep its mouth shut and just listen for a while. . . . I want you to quote this," Bannon added: "The media here is the opposition party. They don't understand this country." Is he asking the newspapers to stop publishing and the radio and television news channels to stop broadcasting? Sounds like that. And is there an "or else" implied by his angry words? It's beginning (I am writing this on February 8) to look as if the Trump Administration, though at this writing in office only nineteen days, is already fighting on four fronts: against Muslims, against federal judges, against the press, against some conservatives—such as Sai Prakash and John Yoo, authors of "Trump's 'So-Called' Judgment: It's Legitimate to Criticize the Judiciary, but Unwise to Do It So Injudiciously"[115]—and even, as I'll note in the Epilogue, against police chiefs.

On February 9, the three-judge panel of the Ninth Circuit to which the government's appeal from Judge Robart's order had been taken unanimously affirmed the order in an impressive twenty-nine-page per curiam opinion.[116] President Trump did not immediately comment on the panel's decision, but did denounce Nordstrom for deciding (on grounds of declining sales) to stop carrying the clothing line sold by the President's daughter Ivanka. He was echoed by his sidekick Kellyanne Conway, who said on television "Go buy Ivanka's stuff," in apparent violation of federal law, which forbids federal employees (she is a federal employee, serving in the White House as an adviser to

---

113. "President Trump's Real Fear: The Courts," *New York Times* editorial, February 7, 2017, p. A20.
114. "Media Bashed Again, as Chief Strategist Piles On," *New York Times*, January 27, 2017, p. A1.
115. *Wall Street Journal*, February 13, 2017, p. A15.
116. *Washington & Minnesota v. Trump, et al.*, No. 17, 3105.

President Trump) to promote sales of products of friends. Trump also declared falsely that Senator Blumenthal had misrepresented what Judge Gorsuch had told him (that the President's attacks on Judge Robart were "demoralizing" and "disheartening"), and continued denouncing Senator McCain—while looming over Trump is the threat of a suit against him under the emoluments clause of Article I, section 9, clause 8 of the Constitution, which provides that no federal official shall, "without the Consent of the Congress, accept of any present, Emolument, Office, or Title, of any kind whatever, from any King, Prince, or foreign State." An emolument is a gift, including a gift of money. Trump has business ventures throughout the world, some or many of which are with foreign governmental entities and almost certainly generate profit for the Trump Organization, though how much profit is unknown to the government because he refuses to release his tax returns.[117] Unless he obtains congressional permission to accept emoluments from foreign governments, he will face litigation over his accepting them.

On February 10, the day after the Ninth Circuit's decision upholding Judge Robart's order, an article by David Cole[118] made a number of important points about the President's executive order regarding immigration, which I quote:

> The deficiencies of Trump's executive order are many. It categorically bars entry to all immigrants from seven Muslim-majority countries, even those with lawful permanent residence status in the United States, and even those who have been fully "vetted" and cleared of any concerns relating to national security. It halts *all* refugee entries, again including those who have been fully reviewed and cleared, and creates an arbitrary exception for refugees from "minority" faiths in their country of origin. But most fundamentally, the executive order violates the Establishment Clause of the Constitution. As the Supreme Court has stated in *Larson v. Valente*, 456 U.S. 228, 244 (1982), "The clearest command of the Establishment Clause is that one religious denomination cannot be officially preferred over another." Yet Trump's order singles out only Muslim-majority countries for its outright ban on entry. . . . Trump promised repeatedly during the campaign that he would enact a "Muslim ban," and

---

117. See David Cole, "Trump Is Violating the Constitution," *New York Review of Books*, February 23, 2017, p. 4 (published online on January 26).

118. David Cole, "Trump in Court," *NYR* [*New York Review of Books*] *Daily*, www.nybooks.com/daily /2017/02/10/trump-travel-ban-in-court-ninth-circuit-decision/.

his executive order is clearly aimed at making good on his promise. . . . Trump [has] explained that his executive order was designed to favor Christian refugees and disfavor Muslims. . . . The significance of this growing series of judicial rulings against the executive order can only be fully appreciated when one understands the wide range of opposition that the president's action has engendered. The lawsuit filed by Washington and Minnesota was supported by the states of Pennsylvania, Massachusetts, New York, California, Connecticut, Delaware, Illinois, Iowa, Maine, Maryland, New Hampshire, New Mexico, North Carolina, Oregon, Rhode Island, Vermont, Virginia, and the District of Columbia, as well as some 130 Silicon Valley tech companies, among them several of the largest companies in the world (Google, Apple, Microsoft, Facebook, and Uber). The order has drawn strong criticism from Nobel laureates, the country's leading scientific organizations, as well as dozens of presidents of top American universities. It even saw General Michael Hayden, former head of the CIA and the NSA under George W. Bush, aligned with the American Civil Liberties Union, where I am legal director; the day after the executive order issued, Hayden tweeted "Imagine that. ACLU and I in the same corner." This is the man who defended the CIA's torture and the NSA's warrantless wiretapping. The tweet generated over five thousand likes. Hayden ultimately signed a declaration in the Washington case attacking the president's executive order as undermining national security—a declaration joined by former secretaries of state John Kerry and Madeline Albright, and former CIA directors and deputy directors Leon Panetta, Michael Morell, and John McLaughlin. Among other things, they argued that the order plays directly into ISIS's hands, by reinforcing the narrative that the US is at war with Islam, while it does nothing to single out those who actually pose a threat to the national security. Indeed, as the Ninth Circuit noted, not a single alien from any of the seven countries named in Trump's order has perpetrated a terrorist attack against the United States. Even the most aggressive advocates of executive power have denounced the ban. Former Vice President Dick Cheney said it goes "against everything we stand for," and John Yoo, the author of the notorious torture memo, who has never before seen a Republican presidential action he could not defend, deemed it "executive power run amok."

That Hayden, Cheney, and Yoo would denounce the President's executive order is truly remarkable.

And not to be overlooked is the fact that not only has the United States never been attacked by an alien from any of the seven countries covered by the executive order, but the order omits aliens from Saudi Arabia, Egypt, and the United Arab Emirates—yet according to Marilyn Geewax and Michel Martin "those are the countries of origin of a number of people who carried out terrorist attacks in the U.S. starting with September 11, 2001. *Those countries also happen to be places where President Trump and his family have business interests.*"[119]

A final point about Judge Gorsuch. He has frequently expressed skepticism about the *Chevron* doctrine, which I criticize in Chapter 4. The doctrine, created by the Supreme Court, requires a high degree of deference by federal judges to decisions by administrative agencies interpreting the statutes they administer—a higher degree of deference than federal judges are required to give decisions by federal district judges, though the latter are on average more capable than immigration judges and other Article I adjudicators ("administrative law judges," as they are usually referred to). A further objection to the *Chevron* doctrine has been expressed recently by Professor Dennis J. Hutchinson of the University of Chicago Law School: "The deference [i.e., *Chevron*] doctrine was born out of suspicion that courts might otherwise meddle with agencies' work and override the agencies' superior expertise. There are two sides to deference, however. My guess is that pro-*Chevron* advocates will soon be begging federal courts *not* to defer to the interpretive findings of agencies headed by men and women whose stated goal is to undermine the mission of the very bodies they head (say, perhaps, an official Environmental Protection Agency finding that 'global warming' is a hoax)."[120]

Good for Gorsuch.

Please, no criticizing living Justices! Deference only! Despite abundant criticism of many of the Supreme Court's decisions, there is rather little criticism of individual Justices—especially by law professors. Little is not none; there have been penetrating criticisms of particular Justices by such law professors as Eric Se-

---

119. Marilyn Geewax and Michel Martin, "Countries Listed on Trump's Refugee Ban Don't Include Those He Has Business With," *National Public Radio*, January 28, 2017, www.npr.org/2017/01/28/512199324/countries-listed-on-trumps-refugee-ban-dont-include-those-he-has-business-with (emphasis added).

120. Dennis J. Hutchinson, "Commentary: Crying Wolf over Neil Gorsuch," *Chicago Tribune*, February 8, 2017.

gall—as the reader just saw—and Stephen Wasby. The criticisms I lodge in this book against Roberts, Scalia, Kagan, and Alito will similarly be understood to be criticisms of *them,* as Supreme Court Justices, rather than just of particular decisions.

I understand the reluctance of professors at the elite law schools to criticize Supreme Court Justices; they want the Justices to continue hiring their students to be law clerks. But the cone of silence seems to cover most law schools, though most can't expect any of their students (or only a very small number, spread over many years) to become Supreme Court law clerks. I imagine that one thing that motivates this reticence of law faculty—I am tempted to call it a conspiracy of silence—is a sense that given the prominence of the Justices in the American legal system, denigration of them is denigration of the system and thus hurts all members of it, including all law professors, whatever their institution. Of course it's wrong to think that weakness at the top of the judiciary implies weakness in the middle or the bottom. We mustn't forget the proverb "a fish rots from the head down," and maybe some judicial systems do too. (Yet I have to admit that the proverb is inaccurate: the guts of the fish rot first.)[121]

If one asks not why law professors are, outwardly at least, ostentatiously respectful of Supreme Court Justices but why federal trial and appellate judges are as well, it might seem that the answer would be that they don't want to be reversed. But that's incorrect. The Supreme Court hears so few cases, and affirms so many of the ones it does hear (about a third), that to be reversed by the Court is like being struck by lightning—painful (though the judicial lightning is fortunately not lethal) but infrequent. Also, few lower-court judges are awed by the current Supreme Court Justices. The deference that lower-court judges accord the Justices nowadays is largely ceremonial; the judges want to do their part to maintain the appearance of a rigid hierarchy lest observers—the competing institutions of government, which in the case of the federal judiciary are Congress and the President—sense weakness in the judicial system and decide to pounce.

Apropos the deference of federal judges to Supreme Court Justices, I had a curious experience many years ago involving Judge Henry Friendly, with whom I'd become friends shortly after my appointment to the Seventh Circuit in December 1981, a friendship that lasted until his death in 1986. I happened

---

121. *The Phrase Finder:* "The Origin of the Expression: A Fish Rots from the Head Down," www.phrases .org.uk/meanings/fish-rot-from-the-head-down.html.

one time to be at a dinner with Friendly in Washington presided over by Chief Justice Burger. I knew that Friendly had a very low opinion of Burger, and I was surprised therefore to see him approach and greet Burger in a manner that can only be described as sycophantic. That was so unlike Friendly! (His law clerks thought it ironic that he was named Friendly, because he was very brusque with them—not at all friendly.) I neglected to ask him about his hyperdeferential style of greeting Burger, but I am guessing that it was simply an acknowledgment of hierarchy. I imagine that many of the people who curtsey to Queen Elizabeth II and ooh! and aah! at her beloved corgis have no very high regard for her or them.

And, finally, both the professors and the lower-court judges may feel that Supreme Court Justices are simply too full of themselves to listen to their inferiors, as they probably regard both their institutional inferiors and the law professors and the rest of the legal profession. Justices are likely to feel that any criticisms of them by members of the legal profession, including judges, are motivated by envy. So challenging the Justices is pointless.

A note on precedent. I mentioned textualism, to which Justice Kagan is a self-proclaimed convert. I think it demonstrable that judges (including Justices) pay more, and more honest, heed to precedents—earlier judicial decisions of the same or (in the case of trial and intermediate appellate judges) a higher court—than they do to constitutional and legislative text. Precedents tend to be more recent, to deal with issues likely to recur, and, being in judicial rather than legislative language, to be more accessible to judges.

Yet whether a precedent is recent or ancient, it is entitled to weight apart from its intrinsic merit (which is unrelated to "precedence"—older is not ipso facto better than newer) only if ignoring or rejecting it would upset reasonable expectations without generating offsetting benefits. Justice Scalia was mistaken in thinking that by committing himself to adherence to precedent he made himself a more careful judicial voter because he knew that his vote would return to haunt him should a similar case come before him in the future, and therefore he had better be right the first time.[122] That would have been a ratio-

---

122. I'm not sure he ever said that outright, but I think it consistent with, and maybe even implicit in, his statement that "when, in writing for the majority of the Court, I adopt a general rule, and say, 'This is the basis of our decision,' I not only constrain lower courts, I constrain myself as well. If the next case should have such different facts that my political or policy preferences regarding the outcome are quite the opposite, I will be unable to indulge those preferences; I have committed myself to the governing principle." Antonin Scalia, "The Rule of Law as a Law of Rules," 56 *University of Chicago Law Review* 1175, 1179 (1989).

nal strategy only if he could have predicted the future. Since he couldn't, it was reckless of him to believe that a vote today should bind him in a case a decade hence, by which time the reasons for the earlier vote might have been universally repudiated.

Traditionally the effect of precedent on future cases depended on a distinction between holding and dictum—holding being the part of the opinion that was essential to its outcome, dictum being material in the opinion that was not essential to the decision itself. A holding by the Supreme Court would bind the lower federal courts; dictum would not, the theory being that because it was not essential to the decision it couldn't be assumed to have received sufficient consideration to assure its soundness. Lately, however, as explained in Neal Devins and David Klein, "The Vanishing Common Law Judge?,"[123] the Supreme Court has moved to a more hierarchical mode of judging, in which it directs the lower courts to follow rules stated by the Court even if they're not actual holdings. I doubt that the Court is authorized to issue binding such directions, any more than it can order the lower federal courts to lengthen or shorten their opinions or adopt the Supreme Court's (distinctly unattractive) citation style. Those are issues within the purview of the Federal Rules of Appellate Procedure rather than the Supreme Court.

Devins and Klein also present evidence that, quite apart from the Court's adoption of a hierarchical mode of judging, lower-court judges are more timid than they used to be about distinguishing decisions by higher courts, decisions that relate to cases before these judges but do not constitute holdings and therefore need not be followed by those judges. One reason for this increased timidity that the authors do not discuss, and that may also be related to the Supreme Court's hierarchical mode of judging, is that there are far more district judges and court of appeals judges than there used to be, and therefore fewer standouts. In former times some district judges, such as Charles Wyzanski in Boston, and some court of appeals judges, such as Learned Hand and Henry Friendly (both in New York City), stood out as judicial luminaries and received a good deal of deference from the Supreme Court. It seems a vanished breed.

On candor. I keep coming back to the judiciary's candor deficiency. It would enable a more informed critique of the judiciary if appellate judges, including Supreme Court Justices, were more candid as well as more thoughtful and

---

123. Forthcoming in *University of Pennsylvania Law Review.*

more "with it." But it's a quixotic hope. As Max Weber explained a century ago, politicians can't afford to be candid,[124] and our federal judges are political officials albeit of a somewhat unconventional sort relative to both elected officials and bureaucrats. Still, without jettisoning the conventional manifestations of judgeship (the *gravitas,* the authoritative manner, the robe, the gavel) our judges could eschew jargon and openly premise their decisions largely on common sense, a practical weighing of the relative costs and benefits of alternative decisions, the relevant scientific and academic literature dealing with issues that arise frequently in federal cases, evidence both judicial and extrajudicial (evidence found in Internet searches for example), and precedents only when departing from a precedent though otherwise desirable would impose excessive costs by defeating reasonable reliance on what had been assumed to be a settled rule. Federal judges, even the lofty Justices of the Supreme Court, could do all this without being tarred and feathered.

Indeed, all this and more: were judges, or for that matter lawyers and law professors, candid they would explain to the laity that judges *have* to be political animals (in a broad sense, not necessarily a partisan sense but one that can involve religious, moral, experiential, and / or temperamental elements of thought). They *have* to make moral or pragmatic judgments, owing to the ambiguity of the Constitution and the uncertain meaning and frequent obsolescence of statutes, regulations, precedents, and other orthodox sources of law. The judge can't just say: "sorry, case dismissed, no law to apply, try again some other time."

I don't like pretense, but realism requires acknowledgment that the pretense that a Supreme Court Justice is an umpire (the claim John Roberts made at his Senate confirmation hearing, which no member of the judiciary committee thought to call him on) can't be abandoned. Abandonment would imply acknowledgment that much of what judges do with statutes is better described as amendment than interpretation. Congress would be furious if the judiciary acknowledged that it too was a legislative body, competitive with—indeed maybe superior rather than equal or subordinate to—the formally, explicitly legislative branch.

A court could take the position that if an issue allegedly of statutory interpretation has arisen and there is no evidence that Congress (or whatever other legislative body had promulgated the statute) had foreseen the issue at the time of enactment and made provision for its resolution, the proper judicial re-

---

124. Max Weber, "Politics as a Vocation" (1919), in *From Max Weber: Essays in Sociology* 77 (H. H. Gerth and C. Wright Mills eds. 1991).

sponse would be to dismiss any suit that seeks judicial resolution of the issue, on the ground that there is no law to apply—for otherwise the court would be legislating. And indeed it would be—it would in effect be amending the statute. But judicial abdication would delay resolution of many legal issues and create more work for legislatures that already have difficulty legislating expeditiously.

What do judges and Justices internalize? I disagree with Professor Fallon's claim that "judges and justices are deeply socialized, beginning with their training as law students, to believe that there are legal norms independent of personal preference and that judges have an obligation to do what the law requires. Indeed, legal norms may become so deeply internalized that the prospect of deviating from them would simply never enter a judge's mind in many, perhaps even most, cases. For those who have internalized norms, those norms frequently determine behavior."[125] I don't know where Fallon got this idea; I'm almost certain it's wrong. I sure didn't get socialized, deeply or otherwise, as a student at the Harvard Law School, in the manner that Fallon attributes to all judges and Justices. And in my thirty-five years as a judge I've never participated in, or heard about, a conversation between judges concerning their judicial philosophies, a conversation on which Fallon could have based the claim I just quoted. The judges discuss cases, and learn about each other's leanings, but don't pontificate along the lines suggested by Fallon. Judges tend to be quite guarded in their dealings with each other.

Supreme Court Justices also; Fallon's claim that I quoted above is inconsistent with his stated conception of the Justices' behavior, discussed earlier. For the most part the Justices make their own rules—inescapably so, owing to the vagueness and antiquity of the Constitution—which, in conjunction with the absence of a court above them and the extreme difficulty, bordering on impossibility, of amending the Constitution to overrule a Supreme Court decision or doctrine, vest the Justices with uncanalized political power, legislative in character, that they find impossible to resist exercising. The judges of the lower courts are kept in line less by remembered indoctrination in law school than by having far less power than Supreme Court Justices, making them more likely to reach outcomes that are fair, moral, and sensible rather than outcomes that in effect amend statutes or constitutional provisions. Yet if they internalize norms, they also internalize ideological, religious, moral, and emotional prompts and

125. Richard H. Fallon, Jr., "Constitutional Constraints," 97 *California Law Review* 975, 992 (2009) (footnote omitted).

urges as well, which like norms influence judicial action. Until Justice Scalia's departure from the scene the Supreme Court had four orthodox Catholic Justices—Roberts, Scalia, Alito, and Thomas (and two less orthodox Catholic Justices—Kennedy and Sotomayor); and it showed. In short, law is not found only or even mainly in constitutions and statutes and ordinances and regulations; law is whatever judges *do.*

Result orientation and "hard" cases. I am willing to go so deep into the realm of unorthodoxy as to suggest that "result-oriented" be retired as a term of opprobrium of judges and Justices. All it means is a judicial focus on outcome rather than process—and outcome *should* be the focus. The judge should decide what is the best outcome for a case and then decide whether that outcome is blocked by some authoritative source of law, such as a clear statute or a binding precedent. The outcome is the end, the process merely the means.

Another old saw is "hard cases make bad law,"[126] where "hard" means, not difficult (the current connotation of the word), but tugging at the heartstrings—and judges are advised by the proverb I just quoted to ignore the heartstrings, to be hard-hearted in other words. But while sometimes the "soft" outcome will be blocked by some rule or other, when it isn't it will usually be the right outcome—the humane, the sensible, the civilized, the modern.

Can law professors tell us how judges and Justices think? I imagine that some of my readers, especially if they're law professors, will think I've misconceived judicial thought processes—that when I explain how judges think I'm really just explaining what I and a handful of other judges think. But I'm not impressed by law professors' criticisms based on their conception of how judges think, because, as I mentioned with respect to Fallon, I don't see how law professors can know how we think. Few professors are former (let alone present) judges (Michael McConnell of Stanford, formerly of the Tenth Circuit, is an outstanding exception); many have never practiced law; some have never taken a bar exam and so are not even licensed to practice law. And none except the handful of judges-turned-professors have ever attended postargument conferences among judges, where they (where we, I should say) take a tentative vote on how to decide the cases we've just heard and where the presiding judge assigns the writing of each majority opinion to one of the judges on the panel (including

126. Old, yet still invoked from time to time. See, e.g., J. L. Coté, "A Practical Guide to Appellate Judging," *Journal of Appellate Practice & Process*, vol. 16, no. 1, pp. 15, 17 (spring 2015).

himself or herself). It is there that one learns (where I learned) what interests and motivates judges—learns for example that even conservative judges sometimes vote for liberal outcomes, and liberals for conservative outcomes, for reasons that include the variety of needs and pressures that bear on a judge, such as a desire to maintain good relations with colleagues, to want not to seem rigid, doctrinaire, or unduly political, to manifest whether or not truthfully fidelity to doctrine, to extend sympathy to the occasional litigant in an extreme case, even to angle for promotion—stealth candidature, in other words. The postargument conferences are confidential; no professors are in attendance or receive a transcript or recording of the judges' discussion at the conference.

One doesn't learn how judges think and interact from reading judicial opinions or hearing speeches by judges or even talking one-on-one to them. To repeat and amplify my earlier disagreement with Professor Fallon, judges tend to be secretive except to some extent with each other, and to be self-serving and self-protective, just like most everyone else. And much (often most) of what they produce for public consumption—mainly judicial opinions—is ghost-written by law clerks sworn to secrecy ("what goes on in chambers stays in chamber" is, as I noted in the Introduction to this book, the rule in almost all judges' offices, though not in mine). The judiciary is a guild, a secret society. When I was appointed, a federal judge whom I knew though he was not on my court welcomed me to "the club."

Law professors, not knowing how judges think, tend mistakenly to suppose them weak imitators of law professors, their (often) intellectual superiors. True, not all law professors think that, or at least confess to thinking it. On the day Justice Scalia died, the dean of Georgetown University Law Center, William M. Treanor, delivered a memorial address in which he said that "Scalia was a giant in the history of the law, a brilliant jurist whose opinions and scholarship profoundly transformed the law. Like countless academics, I learned a great deal from his opinions and his scholarship. In the history of the Court, few justices have had such influence on the way in which the law is understood." (Shades of Justice Kagan.) Moreover, "he cared passionately about the profession, about the law and about the future. . . . We will all miss him."[127] And this was just the beginning.

Did Scalia *really* care passionately about the future? Despite being only a

---

127. "Georgetown Law Mourns the Loss of U.S. Supreme Court Justice Antonin Scalia," *Georgetown Law,* February 13, 2016, www.law.georgetown.edu/news/web-stories/georgetown-law-mourns-the-loss-su preme-court-justice-antonin-scalia.cfm.

month short of eighty when he died, he seems to have paid little attention to his health, which was gravely impaired by the remarkable number of ailments from which he suffered at the end of his life: obesity, coronary artery disease, sleep apnea, degenerative joint disease, chronic obstructive pulmonary disease (formerly called emphysema), and high blood pressure. He was considered too weak to undergo surgery required to repair a shoulder injury. He was also a smoker. When he died, he had his sleep apnea machine with him, but not in his mouth, which is where it is supposed to be. That was very careless of him, and may have been the precipitating cause of his sudden death. His neglect of his health is difficult to understand, and I'm surprised it hasn't received more attention. I suppose it's possible that as a devout Catholic he thought he should let God rather than doctors decide when his time was up. But that's pure speculation on my part.

The Georgetown dean's speech out-Kaganed Kagan, out-Minowed Minow. Unsurprisingly "two Georgetown law professors, Mike Seidman and Gary Peller, disagreed with Dean Treanor's glowing assessment of Scalia and said so,"[128] provoking two conservative law professors to respond:

> Although this email [an email by Professor Peller criticizing Scalia] was upsetting to us, we could only imagine what it was like for these students. Some of them are 22-year-old 1Ls [first-year law students], less than six months into their legal education. But we did not have to wait long to find out. Leaders of the Federalist Society chapter and of the student Republicans reached out to us to tell us how traumatized, hurt, shaken, and angry, were their fellow students. Of particular concern to them were the students who are in Professor Peller's class who must now attend class knowing of his contempt for Justice Scalia and his admirers, including them. How are they now to participate freely in class? What reasoning would be deemed acceptable on their exams?[129]

Could Georgetown law students really be such sensitive plants? I am skeptical.

The dean, the conservative professors, and the student "Leaders" and "student Republicans" come out poorly in their exchange with the two professo-

128. This quotation, like my quotation of the dean's statement, is taken from Glenn Greenwald, "Georgetown Law Professors Say Students Are 'Traumatized' by Criticisms of Scalia, Demand 'Remedies,' *The Intercept*, February 23, 2016, https://theintercept.com/2016/02/23/georgetown-law-professors-complain-conservative-students-are-traumatized-by-criticisms-of-scalia-demand-remedies/.

129. Id.

rial critics of Scalia. They sound like crybabies. The dean, like Justice Kagan, probably knows better; his tribute may just be one more example of how little the legal profession values candor or even truthfulness. The Georgetown brouhaha underscores these deficiencies, as well as the frequent lack of knowledge—even of maturity—that afflicts all branches of the legal profession. What is impossible to credit is that Georgetown's conservative students were actually "traumatized, hurt, shaken, and [made] angry" by the professors' remarks. Law students are not children, although these law students' angry reactions (if accurately reported) to criticism of Scalia were childish.

I want to return briefly to the issue of Scalia's health. A strange performance by him at a session of the Court some eight months before his death may have signaled seriously deteriorating health. As reported by the journalist Dahlia Lithwick,[130] who was in the courtroom that day (June 29, 2015) to hear the final decision of the Court in the 2015 term—the decision in *Glossip v. Gross*,[131] an Oklahoma lethal injection case, the decision was read by Justice Samuel Alito and joined by the three other very conservative Justices plus Justice Anthony Kennedy. Alito stated that the use of midazolam, one of three drugs in Oklahoma's lethal-injection protocol, had not violated the defendant's constitutional rights even though midazolam has been involved in multiple botched executions. Alito added that from now on the burden would be on defendants to identify a known and available alternative method of execution. Alito repeated the view that he'd expressed at oral argument that it was "anti-death-penalty advocates" who had made it difficult to use drugs more reliable than midazolam in executions.

After Alito finished, Justice Sotomayor read from her strong dissent in the case, and Justice Breyer from a lengthy dissent joined by Justice Ginsburg, urging abolition of the death penalty altogether. But after listening to Alito and the two dissenters, Scalia announced that he had concurred in the majority opinion but had some things to say about the dissents. He opened his statement—which seemed not to have been written down, and didn't track his concurring opinion—with: "Last Friday five justices of this court took the issue" of same-sex marriage away from the voters based on their "policy preferences," and he added that today two Justices had sought to do that again, by calling for the abolition of the death penalty. (So in case you were wondering, Scalia hadn't

---

130. Dahlia Lithwick, "Scalia Goes Off Script," SLATE, June 29, 2015, www.slate.com.
131. 576 U.S. ___.

gotten over *Obergefell*.) He went on to note that the death penalty is expressly contemplated by the words of the Constitution, and continued with the accusation that maybe it's a good thing that "two justices are willing to kill the death penalty outright rather than just pecking it to death." He concluded by saying that "not often in the law is it the case that so few have changed so much." This may not be as pointed an indictment as the zinger at the end of his written concurrence, which accuses Breyer (but not his partner in crime, Ginsburg) of rejecting "the Enlightenment," but it's an unmistakable echo of Breyer's lament, delivered when he read aloud his dissent in the 2007 Seattle schools case, that "it is not often in the law that so few have so quickly changed so much." Lithwick remarked that Scalia's was a doubly strange accusation because the two dissenters—unlike the majority in the schools case—had not changed anything at all, since they were the only two willing to do away with the death penalty.

The issue of Scalia's deterioration in the months before his death was examined in a blog post by Eric Segall, from which I quote the gist, with a few editorial changes for clarity:

> Justice Scalia is 79 years old and has served on the bench for almost 30 years. In 1995, I wrote an article in part defending his rules-oriented jurisprudence from what I thought were unfair attacks from Professor Laurence Tribe and a budding young scholar named Mike Dorf. But that was then. Now, Justice Scalia has betrayed his own principles, and acted so inappropriately so often, that he should seriously consider retiring from the bench. His own legacy, and the good of the country, are both very much at stake.
>
> As far as his votes and written opinions are concerned, this term alone shows how Justice Scalia has veered far away from any reasonable level of internal consistency. His dissent in the same-sex marriage case was full of wild accusations that the Justices in the majority were failing to act as proper judges by invalidating state laws prohibiting same-sex marriage. For example, he lamented the "practice of constitutional revision by an unelected committee of nine," and said that any "system of government that makes the People subordinate to a committee of nine unelected lawyers does not deserve to be called a democracy." . . . This call for judicial deference, however, is completely inconsistent with numerous other Justice Scalia votes and written opinions this term. In fact, he voted to strike

down so many important laws that he should be embarrassed by his stridency in his same-sex marriage dissent.

Earlier this term, Chief Justice Roberts sided with the liberals in a 5–4 decision upholding Florida's very modest regulation of judicial campaigns. Scalia's dissent alleged that Roberts' decision "flattens one settled First Amendment principle after another," and "was more than one should have to bear." In other words, Scalia would have struck down a state law trying to place just a few reasonable restrictions on the coercive nature of judicial requests for campaign money.

Although he didn't write separately, Justice Scalia also voted with Justice Alito to reverse Texas's decision refusing to issue a special Confederate flag license plate. Neither of these two first amendment cases involved state laws that clearly violated the text or history of the Constitution, yet Justice Scalia in both cases would have reversed the decisions of the people. Perhaps even more strangely (and inconsistently), he wrote a scathing dissent when the Court upheld by a 5–4 vote a ballot initiative in Arizona that created a bipartisan redistricting commission. The case involved a decision by the people of Arizona on a core issue of democratic self-government (the people were tired of partisan posturing when it came to the vital task of dividing the state into voting districts). Once again Justice Scalia would have reversed the decision of the people and replaced it with his own. Although he said there was no proper jurisdiction over the case, he also wrote that the majority's "resolution of the merits . . . is so outrageously wrong, so utterly devoid of textual or historic support, so flatly in contradiction of prior Supreme Court cases, so obviously the willful product of hostility to districting by state legislatures, that I cannot avoid adding my vote to the devastating dissent of the Chief Justice." In reality, Roberts' dissent was "devastating" only to those Justices willing to freely replace the decision of the people of Arizona with the decision "of an unelected committee of nine," on an issue where the constitutional text was in fact ambiguous, its history contestable, and the prior case law on point mixed.

In previous terms Scalia had voted to invalidate affirmative action plans by local school districts (parents, teachers, and board members acting together in true democratic fashion). He had voted to strike down virtually all campaign finance reform laws as well as the key section of the Voting Rights Act that had been re-enacted by a unanimous Senate and an overwhelming majority in the House, and had been signed by President George W. Bush. In none of these cases were the text and history of the relevant constitutional provisions clear. . . .

In addition to his voting record, Justice Scalia has leveled such personal attacks at other Justices that he is becoming, if he has not already become, a caricature of the bitter old man despondent about the "good old days." Here's a quotation from his same-sex marriage dissent: "If, even as the price to be paid for a fifth vote, I ever joined an opinion for the Court that began [quoting Justice Kennedy's majority opinion], I would hide my head in a bag. The Supreme Court of the United States has descended from the disciplined legal reasoning of John Marshall and Joseph Story to the mystical aphorisms of the fortune cookie." The suggestion that one or more of the Justices had to pay a "price" for Justice Kennedy's vote was an irresponsible airing of the Court's dirty laundry. He added that the "opinion is couched in a style that is as pretentious as its content is egotistic." Those charges have nothing to do with proper application of law to facts and everything to do with personality. They are unbecoming of a Supreme Court Justice.

Scalia has also acted in ways that make it reasonable to think that he has lost the ability to perform his job responsibly. On Monday he took the unusual step in a death penalty case of summarizing a concurring opinion from the bench. Not only is this rare, but he also again chastised the Justices who voted to overturn the same-sex marriage bans and, according to Dahlia Lithwick, acted in 'weird' and 'odd' ways by going back and forth between the death penalty case at issue and the same-sex marriage decision *of the week before*. This behavior led law professor Rick Hasen to ask: "Is Scalia losing it?"

He has also made a few mistakes recently that suggest he may not be as careful as he used to be. In an opinion on environmental law, he badly misstated the holding of a previous case that he himself had written, leading law professor Dan Farber to call it a "cringe-worthy blunder." The opinion had to be changed. And in Atlanta, not too long after the Court struck down a formula in the Voting Rights Act, Justice Scalia could not remember a vital part of the rationale for that historic decision.

There was a time when Scalia was a commanding influence on the

Court, urging upon the other Justices an originalist methodology and a rule-like approach to judging, and only occasionally using his nuclear-powered pen to detonate personal insults at the other Justices. But with each passing term, his votes, his rhetoric, his behavior are eating away at that legacy. Other Justices, such as Thurgood Marshall and William Douglas, stayed on too long and Justice Scalia is in danger of making the same mistake. He should retire before it is too late.[132]

Of course, he didn't. Eight months later he was dead.

Returning momentarily to my criticism of Professor Fallon's conjectures about how judges think, I note that law professors were far more attuned to judges in the old days (ending in the 1960s), when most law professors had not only had the same legal education as judges but also had had practical legal experience similar to what most judges had had before they had become judges. Fewer and fewer law professors have such experience today, law school faculties having become top-heavy with professors who earned doctoral degrees in other fields before they entered law school and who never intended to practice law or even to defer their academic career for a few years spent in the practice of law to enrich that career. As a result, a great deal of academic legal writing is pitched at a level of abstraction beyond the grasp or interest of most judges.[133] And that tempts some appellate judges to engage in what is called "independent judicial research" (primarily Internet research by the judge). At the trial level it is feasible to allow rebuttal by the lawyers to evidence presented at trial, so at least there is a contest, though the back and forth of lawyers and witnesses is often unedifying and surely no guaranty of truth. At the appellate level, where the lawyers are onstage only for the time it takes them to make their oral argument, allowing the lawyers to offer support of or rebuttal to an argument discovered on the Internet by a judge would require reargument or supplementary briefs, and either procedure could delay the decision of the appeal significantly. I suggest a solution to the problems posed by independent judicial research in Chapter 4 regarding a recent case in my court named *Rowe v. Gibson*.

---

132. Eric Segall, "Why Justice Scalia Should Seriously Consider Retiring," July 1, 2015, *Dorf on Law,* www.dorfonlaw.org/2015/07/why-justice-scalia-should-seriously.html.

133. An example is a book by Adrian Vermeule, *The Constitution of Risk* (2014). Vermeule is a well-known law professor at Harvard, but his target audience is academic, not judicial.

PART TWO

I have at times drifted from the subject of this chapter, which is the Supreme Court, and let me return to it.

We really do need *a supreme court*—a court empowered, and willing, to create a degree of uniformity among the nation's federal courts, to rein in the other branches of the federal government, and also to rein in state governments— imagine the chaos that would ensue were there no federally enforced limitations on state regulation of personal, political, or commercial behavior. And so there is a difference in degree, as far as the political character of adjudication in the federal judiciary is concerned, between the Supreme Court and the other federal courts—and it's a substantial difference.[134] But it is not a difference in kind.[135] In the words of Justice Robert Jackson, "We [Justices of the Supreme Court] are not final because we are infallible, but we are infallible only because we are final."[136] The cases the Court decides present issues that usually can't be sensibly resolved by reference to prior law, to precedent (a form of prior law), to the canons of statutory construction (which are a joke—a confusion of interpretation with creation),[137] or to constitutional theory (another joke—read

134. See, e.g., Epstein et al., note 44 above.

135. I thus disagree with Professor Segall's statement that "our Supreme Court is not really a court at all." Eric Segall, "What Would You Do If You Were a Supreme Court Justice?," *Dorf on Law,* May 23, 2015, www.dorfonlaw.org/2015/05/what-would-you-do-if-you-were-supreme.html

136. *Brown v. Allen,* 322 U.S. 443, 540 (1953) (concurring opinion).

137. That is, the linguistic canons of construction; the policy canons, such as the rule of lenity—resolve an ambiguous criminal statute in favor of the defendant—are substantive rules, essentially common-law rules, some good, some bad. (The rule of lenity, however, is almost never enforced.) The linguistic canons, such as *eiusdem* [usually misspelled "ejusdem"—there is no *j* in Latin] *generis,* which means that if a general word, such as "animals," is followed by particular examples (such as "dogs, cats, and parakeets"), the general word does not embrace items remote from those examples, such as, in my example, "mosquitoes"—are largely nonsense. See, e.g., Joseph Kimble, "Ejusdem Generis: What Is It Good For?," 100 *Judicature* 48 (2016); cf. Anita S. Krishnakumar, "Dueling Canons," 65 *Duke Law Journal* 909 (2016). *Eiusdem generis* is not the worst of the linguistic canons, but it frequently fails. Consider a sign at the entrance to a store that says "No dogs, cats, or other animals allowed." Although farm animals are very different from dogs and cats, it would be dumb to think that, as implied by *eiusdem generis,* pigs and goats and cows and boa constrictors would be welcome in the store.

Professor Victoria F. Nourse of Georgetown Law School has written a book of comprehensive, devastating criticism (*Misreading Law, Misreading Democracy: Legislative Process and Statutory Interpretation for the 21st Century Lawyer,* Harvard University Press 2016) of how judges, including Supreme Court Justices, interpret (or pretend to interpret) congressional enactments. The canons of statutory construction, plain meaning, textualism, literalism, originalism—all these crutches fall, felled by *her* cannons (particularly chapter 4 of her book). The question left open is the scope of statutory interpretation—what a court is to do if, Congress not having anticipated the issue of statutory meaning that the court is asked to resolve, there is nothing to interpret. The judges are on their own; creation replaces interpretation. Nourse's book should be required reading

on). Legal disputes that can be resolved by reference to existing legal rules usually are resolved at a lower level of the judiciary. Issues that can't be resolved by reference to existing rules can be resolved only by recourse to pragmatic, ethical, or if you will, political values. That's the way it is—and the way it has to be and should be and probably always will be. But still, we ought to note the following:

Priors and politics to the fore. The Supreme Court is insistent that its decisions are the pure product of analysis based on previous decisions and on the interpretation of authoritative legislative sources of law, notably the Constitution. That's rubbish. Everyone knowledgeable about law knows there are conservative and liberal Justices and that in the same cases the former tend to cast conservative votes and the latter liberal ones. The different wings of the judiciary pretend to base their judicial votes on the same sources, the same documents; yet actually, and whether or not consciously, they usually are voting their personal and political, sometimes their religious, preferences (if they are religious; not all the current Justices are, some of their most illustrious predecessors, such as Holmes, Brandeis, and Cardozo, also were not). The Justices' principal guiding star is not legislation, or the Constitution, or precedents; it is the Justices' priors[138]—a mixture of temperament, ideology, ambition, and experience.[139]

An example of a prior that is neither political nor religious nor indeed ideological in any sense is Justice Kennedy's steady support of homosexual rights, culminating in his majority opinion in *Obergefell* creating a constitutional right to same-sex marriage. Kennedy is both politically conservative and a devout Catholic, as well as heterosexual, yet his sympathetic understanding of homo-

---

not only for judges and their law clerks but for legislative staff; likewise Bryan A. Garner's new book *Guidelines for Drafting and Editing Legislation* (2015). Still another must-read is Joseph Kimble, "The Doctrine of the Last Antecedent, the Example in *Barnhart,* Why Both Are Weak, and How Textualism Postures," *Scribes Journal of Legal Writing* 5 (2014–2015)—demonstrating the politicization of statutory interpretation, especially by conservative Justices (led by Justice Scalia). The sheer number of canons, exhaustively catalogued in William N. Eskridge, Jr., *Interpreting Law: A Primer on How to Read Statutes and the Constitution* (2016), assures their practical uselessness.

138. "Priors," as the reader will have grasped by now, is short for prior probabilities—what you bring to a problem, which you want to solve, before you search for evidence relating to a correct solution; the evidence may alter your initial probability assessment.

139. See, e.g., Matthew E. K. Hall, "Judging with Personality: Individual Personality Traits and Decision Making on the U.S. Supreme Court," www.law.uchicago.edu/files/file/personality.pdf.

sexuals was manifest long before he became a Supreme Court Justice.[140] And it is difficult to understand what other than that sympathetic understanding persuaded him to break with his conservative colleagues, who dissented in *Obergefell* as they had in the cases leading up to it—cases in which he'd allied himself with the liberal Justices.

Knowing that Justices are influenced, often decisively, by their priors, conservative Presidents try to appoint conservative Justices and liberal Presidents liberal ones. Yet even if a President faces little opposition from the Senate because it happens to be controlled by the President's party when the vacancy occurs, the President may be mistaken about an appointee's political priors. And even if he isn't mistaken, those priors can change unpredictably over time. The constant is that the Court's decisions are heavily influenced by them. And that is not going to change just because many professors of constitutional law, liberal as well as conservative, profess to believe that constitutional decision making should be guided by what the Constitution was understood to mean when it was (or its amendments were) enacted—an impossibility, as I have insisted and as the most intelligent originalists are beginning to realize, causing adjustments such as those Professor Baude has been making.[141] Society has changed radically since the eighteenth-century Constitution was ratified, and also since the ratification of the mid-nineteenth-century amendments (of which the most important is the Fourteenth Amendment), and has changed in ways unforeseen by the framers and ratifiers of those documents. Originalism has become a mask for deciding cases on ideological grounds, using history as a mirror.

Nevertheless I would not call the Supreme Court a "political court." That would both exaggerate the political element in Supreme Court adjudication[142] and imply that the lower federal courts are apolitical and that a court should not be "political." And that is not realistic or even desirable if I'm right that judges often *must* go beyond legal doctrine to decide a case sensibly. And so it

140. See Sheryl Gay Stolberg, "Justice Anthony Kennedy's Tolerance Is Seen in His Sacramento Roots," *New York Times,* June 21, 2015, www.nytimes.com/2015/06/22/us/kennedys-gay-rights-rulings-seen-in-his-sacramento-roots.html?_r=0.

141. And others—to the extent of rendering originalism incoherent, as implied in James E. Fleming, "The Inclusiveness of the New Originalism," 82 *Fordham Law Review* 433 (2013).

142. Richard A. Posner, "The Supreme Court 2004 Term: Foreword: A Political Court," 119 *Harvard Law Review* 32, 34 (2005). I added a qualification: "viewed realistically, the Supreme Court, at least most of the time, *when it is deciding constitutional cases* is a political organ, and (confining myself to *constitutional law*), I shall develop some implications of this view." Id. at 34 (emphases added).

is self-servingly silly for judges to refer to Congress and the President as "the political branches" of the federal government, as if the judiciary were "apolitical." Not only do most federal judges lean either conservative or liberal, but these classifications are predictive of their votes in many cases. The Supreme Court behaves that way far more frequently than the lower courts, however, both because much more of the Court's docket consists of cases that are either toss-ups so far as legal doctrine is concerned or have a strong political valence as a consequence of the nature of the dispute that the Court is asked to decide, and because there is no higher court to which its decisions can be appealed—which means that while the lower courts are bound by decisions of the Supreme Court, the Supreme Court can if it wishes reject, ignore, or redefine its decisions and by any of these devices free itself not to follow them.

Though there is a considerable political element in the Supreme Court's adjudication, there is a difference between politics in the federal courts and in other branches of government. Politicians are indifferent to most of the decisions of courts because most of those decisions do not affect a politician's workload, influence, or chances of reelection. Conversely, federal judges do not canvass the voters in their jurisdiction to learn how the voters would like the judges to decide cases. Congress can't remove a federal judge except in rare cases of impeachment, and federal judges can't remove members of Congress except in rare cases in which a member is convicted of a crime. Yet the dichotomy I'm sketching dissolves when one is speaking not of the federal judiciary in general but of the Supreme Court, which exerts enormous power, in particular in the name of the Constitution. The power of the Court to check Congress is almost without limits; the power of Congress to check the Supreme Court is minuscule. The lower-court federal judges are petty legislators and petty politicians; not so the grandees of the Supreme Court.

What the Court needs (and needs urgently, but is unlikely to get) is not "depoliticization" (which is impossible) but better appointments and an improvement in how law schools train their students. The training is too formalistic, too prone to indoctrinate students (some of whom will some day be judges, others law clerks, others litigators) in a false belief in law's objectivity, its scientific precision, its doctrinal rigidity, its venerability. And all Supreme Court Justices since Robert Jackson and James Byrnes, both appointed in 1941, have been law school graduates. (Byrnes did not attend law school at all; Jackson attended for just one year.)

But appointments to the Supreme Court (and to the lower federal courts as well) are unlikely to improve as long as the President nominates and the Senate confirms, because Presidents and Senators are politicians. They value their ability to influence through the appointment process the direction of the Court. They will not willingly cede the appointment power to others.

States' rights, and the politics of the Justices. The framers of the Constitution could have created, but did not, a uniform, hierarchical form of government for the entire country, as in France. Had they done so, every government agency, government office, and government employee would be a component of the national government. If some of the subunits were called "states," still they would have no autonomy; they would exist at the will of the national government; there would be no such thing as "states' rights." The Constitution, however, recognized the states as entities distinct from the federal government. The question was how much autonomy the states would have. For my present purposes, the key provisions of the Constitution are Article I, section 8, which lists powers conferred on Congress (of which my focus will be on the powers to regulate commerce among the states and to make all laws that are necessary and proper for executing the listed powers), and the Tenth Amendment, which provides that "powers not delegated to the United States by the Constitution . . . are reserved to the States respectively, or to the people."

It's obvious that the power to regulate commerce that crosses state lines and the power to make laws needed for applying the commerce power combine to confer enormous federal power over activities that have any nontrivial (even if indirect) commercial consequences, thus curtailing the "reserved" powers of the states.[143] The results are frequent collisions that the Supreme Court is repeatedly called upon to resolve between the desire of states to be allowed to govern themselves and the desire of the federal government to regulate activities that have effects in more than one state. The collision reached its modern apogee under the Chief Justiceship of William Rehnquist (1986 to 2005), an emphatic supporter of states' rights. A comprehensive analysis of the Court's commerce-clause adjudications before, during, and since the Rehnquist era would carry me beyond the scope of this book, and I will merely register my belief that there is virtually no merit to challenging federal power over commerce by referring to the Supreme Court's decision in *United States v. Lopez.*[144]

143. For comprehensive analysis, see Tribe, *American Constitutional Law,* vol. 1, chap. 5 ("Federal Legislative Power: Congressional Authority and the Implications of State Sovereignty").
144. 514 U.S. 549 (1995).

In an opinion by Rehnquist (with Breyer, Stevens, and Souter dissenting force-fully), the Court invalidated, as beyond the federal commerce power, a fed-eral statute forbidding the possession of firearms near schools. Firearms are commercial products that are frequently shipped or carried across state lines; schools help prepare children for careers; and regulating the proximity of fire-arms to schools affects both interstate commerce in guns and the ability of schools to protect children to the benefit of their education and hence ca-reers—careers almost certain to involve or affect interstate commerce. The *Lo-pez* decision makes no sense that I can see, and can be explained only as an expression of conservatives' hostility to federal regulation by a Democratic ad-ministration (the President in 1995 was Bill Clinton).

An equally questionable decision from the same era, *Jones v. United States*,[145] held that arson of an owner-occupied home is not within the power of the fed-eral government to regulate interstate commerce because home ownership is not an activity affecting commerce. That is absurd. The owner has to maintain the property, replace fixtures and furniture, pay for gas and electricity and of-ten water, pay property taxes that the state or a municipality may use in part to obtain goods and services from other states, and so on. The Court in *Jones*[146] distinguished an earlier decision, *United States v. Russell*,[147] which had held—splitting hairs—that arson of an apartment building consisting of rental units is within the statute because the rental of real estate is an activity affecting com-merce. I don't see a meaningful distinction between the cases.

In a case of mine, *United States v. Veysey*,[148] we split the split, explaining:

> The house was rented but the renter (Veysey, who burned the house down) was not engaged in a commercial activity, as was the apartment-house owner in *Russell*. The owner was a typical householder, who after living in the house for several years had moved to another state and after trying unsuccessfully to sell the house had decided to rent it. He rented it first to a family for six months and then to Veysey for a year at a monthly rental of $1,300. The lease gave Veysey an option to buy the house at the end of the year for $138,000. Had Veysey burned down the house while the original owner was living in it, or had he burned it down after exer-

---

145. 529 U.S. 848 (2000).
146. Id. at 853.
147. 471 U.S. 858 (1985).
148. 334 F.3d 600 (7th Cir. 2003).

cising his option and buying the house, the arson would have been beyond the reach of the federal statute by virtue of the *Jones* case.

At the [oral] argument [of the appeal], a member of the court remarked the awkwardness of property drifting in and out of interstate commerce. And under pressure of that awkwardness one might have tried to distinguish *Veysey* from *Russell* by noting that the owner of the apartment building in *Russell* was in the business of renting, while the owner of the house that Veysey torched was an accidental renter. He rented the house only because he couldn't sell it at an acceptable price. He didn't *want* to be in the real estate rental business. But he was, and the real estate rental market is interstate, as the case illustrated; the owner was in a different state both when he rented the house to Veysey and when the arson occurred; the arson thus had interstate consequences. To decide the case differently from *Russell* would have implied a need to inquire in every case into the motives for renting, and the inquiry would complicate decision making without offsetting gain. And we repeat that the real estate rental market really is an interstate market and the rental in this case was an interstate transaction.[149]

Needless to say I would like to see *Jones* overruled.

But what of the "second dimension"? A recent article, while acknowledging that Supreme Court Justices are to a significant extent political actors, argues that political scientists and other students of the Court exaggerate the degree to which the Court is politicized.[150] The authors claim that there is a second dimension of the Justices' judicial voting, which they call "legal" as distinct from "pragmatic." That's not a happy choice of terms. Pragmatism, as the reader will recall, is the doctrine that decisions should be based on consequences, but the consequences need not be political. A judge or Justice might be influenced not by the political consequences of voting one way or another in a case but by the consequences for judicial workloads, judicial backlogs, judicial efficiency generally, or comity with Congress or the states. As for describing decisions based on nonpolitical considerations as "legal" rather than "pragmatic," this is to de-

149. Id. at 603.
150. Joshua B. Fischman and Tonja Jacobi, "The Second Dimension of the Supreme Court," 57 *William & Mary Law Review* 1671 (2016). But cf. "Politics, Not Qualifications, Matter Most for Supreme Court [Appointments]," 85 *Bloomberg BNA, The United States Law Week Case Alert & Legal News: Lead Reports,* vol. 85, no. 15, p. 542.

fine "legal" too narrowly. However Justices decide a case—however nakedly political their motivations may seem or indeed be—their decision is legal unless they lacked jurisdiction to hear and decide it or had been bribed to decide it as they did or had committed other grievous faults fatal to the legitimacy of the decision.

The more serious problem with the authors' two-dimensional analysis is the separation of the "legal" from the "political" (or, more neutrally, the "methodological" from the "ideological"). They ignore the fact that what they call the legal grounds of a decision are often the result of political preference. For example, in *Maryland v. King*[151] the issue was the constitutionality of a suspicionless DNA swab of an arrestee. A majority consisting of Roberts, Alito, Thomas, Kennedy, and Breyer, in an opinion by Kennedy, held that the swab did not violate the Fourth Amendment because (I quote from the syllabus of his opinion) "when officers make an arrest supported by probable cause to hold for a serious offense and bring the suspect to the station to be detained in custody, taking and analyzing a cheek swab of the arrestee's DNA is, like fingerprinting and photographing, a legitimate police booking procedure that is reasonable under the Fourth Amendment." Scalia, Ginsburg, Sotomayor, and Kagan dissented. So there were three conservatives, a semiconservative (Kennedy), and a liberal in the majority, and an archconservative (Scalia) dissenting in favor of someone arrested on probable cause for a serious offense.

The dissent reminds the reader that the Fourth Amendment requires that warrants be based on probable cause to believe that the warrant if executed will yield evidence of crime,[152] and since the police had no basis for thinking that the swab would, as distinct from might, yield such evidence, the warrant caused an unjustified "incursion upon the Fourth Amendment."[153] But here's the rub. Justice Scalia claimed to decide constitutional cases on the basis of the text of the Constitution as understood by the American people when the particular constitutional provision in question had been ratified, which for the Fourth Amendment was 1791. His originalism was no doubt more important to him than cheek swabs of arrestees, as we know from many of his decisions and from such public statements of his as that flogging is constitutional because it was an accepted method of punishment when the Eighth Amendment, forbidding cruel and unusual punishments, was adopted. The dissent in *Maryland v.*

151. 133 S. Ct. 1958 (2013).
152. Id. at 1981.
153. Id. at 1989.

King is an emphatic endorsement of an originalist approach to the Fourth Amendment. Had Scalia been an originalist for purely intellectual reasons, his dissent would be evidence that his judicial votes were motivated by "legal" rather than "political" considerations. But I doubt that. Originalism is understood to be a conservative doctrine, and most of Scalia's originalist opinions are conservative, most famously perhaps the *Heller* case recognizing a constitutional right to own guns for self-defense,[154] a decision that, as noted earlier, does obvious violence to the original understanding of the Second Amendment.

Without respect to persons. I applaud an important element of genuine neutrality in federal court adjudication, encapsulated in the following sentence in the federal judicial oath: "I will administer justice without respect to persons." We owe this commitment to Aristotle's concept of "corrective justice," which teaches that "it makes no difference whether a good man has defrauded a bad man or a bad man a good one, or whether it is a good or a bad man that has committed adultery; the law looks only to the distinctive character of the injury, and treats the parties as equal, if one is in the wrong and the other is being wronged and if one inflicted injury and the other has received it."[155] This is a vital principle for a judiciary to embrace. For in its absence persons of high social standing by virtue of wealth, prominence, or achievement would have an undeserved opportunity to escape being sanctioned for wronging a person of inferior social standing. It is a principle fundamental to the concept of the "rule of law," as distinguished from the rule of a person, clique, or class, as in a dictatorship or oligarchy. It doesn't extinguish or even dampen the political element in judging, but it damps down the *personal* element—the fact that a litigant may be more attractive than his opponent for reasons having nothing to do with principles. In my thirty-five years as a federal appellate judge, in which I have participated in thousands of postargument or postsubmission conferences with my judicial colleagues, I have never heard this principle violated.

Judges and Justices as de facto legislators. The power of the Supreme Court and to a lesser extent of the other federal appellate courts is to a significant degree legislative, thus blurring the difference between a legislature and a court. The

---

154. *District of Columbia v. Heller,* 554 U.S. 570 (2008).

155. Aristotle, *Nichomachean Ethics,* Book V, section 2 of *The Complete Works of Aristotle,* vol. 2, p. 1786 (Revised Oxford Translation 1984).

courts resolve disputes but at the appellate level also create rules—which is another reason why courts are and have to be political. For to make rules is to legislate. Legislators are not theorists; neither are judges, as pointed out in an article by Marc DeGirolami and Kevin Walsh[156] that discusses me and Judge Wilkinson of the Fourth Circuit (an excellent judge and very fine person, whom I would have much preferred to see made Chief Justice, rather than John Roberts, upon the death of Rehnquist). The article is too long for me to do it justice but I can give readers the gist by quoting from the article's abstract:

> Judge Richard Posner's well-known view is that constitutional theory is useless. And Judge J. Harvie Wilkinson III has lambasted constitutional theory for the way in which its "cosmic" aspirations threaten democratic self-governance. Many other judges hold similar views. And yet both Posner and Wilkinson—in the popular press, in law review articles, and in books—have advocated what appear to be their own theories of how to judge in constitutional cases. Judicial pragmatism for Posner and judicial restraint for Wilkinson seem to be substitutes for originalism, living constitutionalism, political process theory, and so on. [But this article] exposes the limited influence of judicial pragmatism and judicial restraint on these judges' own constitutional jurisprudence even in those cases where one might expect constitutional theory to exert maximal influence . . . [and] . . . explains how judicial pragmatism and judicial restraint are best understood not as constitutional theories but as descriptions of judicial dispositions—character traits that pertain to judicial excellence—that can and should be criticized on their own terms.

DeGirolami and Walsh are correct. There are constitutional theories, such as originalism, textualism, literalism, seventeenth- and eighteenth-century political and philosophical thought (Locke, Montesquieu, et al.), and the living Constitution, but they don't have much heft. They're either out of date or like the "living Constitution" maintain only the most tenuous connection with the actual document. Constitutional decision making is essentially legislative, hence shaped by Justices' and judges' priors and by practical concerns (such as the political, economic, or social impact of deciding a case one way or another) rather than by theory, professorial or otherwise.

156. Marc O. DeGirolami and Kevin C. Walsh, "Judge Posner, Judge Wilkinson, and Judicial Critique of Constitutional Theory," 90 *Notre Dame Law Review* 633 (2014).

Constitutional vagueness. I have placed so much emphasis on the limitations of judicial interpretation of the Constitution that I risk being misunderstood as implying that constitutional law is a complete fabrication by the judiciary, owing nothing to constitutional text, or at least the text of the original Constitution, the Bill of Rights, and the nineteenth-century amendments. I don't mean to go quite that far. The Constitution contains a number of specific, intelligible provisions. But it also contains a number of provisions that are vague—and importantly their vagueness was not a drafting failure but almost certainly a deliberate effort to minimize the considerable tensions among the thirteen states constituting the nascent United States by applying the balm of compromise. Successful compromise frequently requires the shunning of precision, thereby reassuring the parties to the compromise that their interests have not been rejected by the majority. But the consequence of vagueness is lack of guidance, thereby shifting the burden of specification to the courts.

A confusing picture is further blurred by another reason for the vagueness of many of the original constitutional provisions: the framers' inability to foresee the future, especially the future of a new nation. It would have been foolish to truncate that future by wrapping the branches of the new national government in chains, a procedure that might well have led either to a sequence of short-term constitutions or to a dissolution of the union.

Not that all *the Constitution's provisions are vague.* The framers' embrace of vagueness, a sensible as well as inevitable fixture of the Constitution, predestined the federal judiciary to play a creative role in constitutional adjudication. Over time that was bound to and did produce a body of constitutional law owing little to the original text, which besides being vague in places was often questionable in those places that were not vague. Often but not always: the prohibitions against titles of nobility and religious tests for public office are clear, and are as sensible today as they were in 1788. The detailed provisions ordaining the structure and powers and procedures of Congress have also weathered the test of time, though the entitlement of every state, regardless of size or population, to exactly two Senators could well be questioned.

But as I explained earlier in this chapter, the Seventh Amendment, which entitles a party to a civil case in a federal court (with exceptions for several types of such case, however) to a jury trial if the amount in controversy exceeds twenty dollars, the birthright-citizenship rule of the Fourteenth Amendment if interpreted (as it has been thus far, though it needn't be) to make *every* person born in the United States an American citizen, and the requirement that the President be at least thirty-five years old, are all nonsense provisions and it would be interesting to see what the Supreme Court would do were they to be invoked.

I think the Court would say, or at least I would like it to say, that the twenty-dollar rule is so antiquated that it should be deemed repealed; that the birthright-citizenship clause was intended for the benefit of the recently freed slaves rather than of tourist babies and so should not be deemed applicable to the latter; and that the specification of a minimum age to be President is non-justiciable, as it would be absurd for the Supreme Court to void a Presidential election on the basis of the winning candidate's age.

But I don't call birthright citizenship and the requirement that the President be at least thirty-five years old "nonsense provisions" because I think them downright harmful; tourist babies are not overrunning the United States and should therefore be welcome as citizens and none of our politicians reminds me of the great teenage leaders of yore, such as Alexander the Great (who became king of Macedonia at the age of twenty) and Octavian Caesar (later called Augustus), who was nineteen when his great-uncle Julius Caesar was assassinated and who from that moment on exercised significant and by the age of thirty-two total power over what came to be called the Roman Empire. I call birthright citizenship and the minimum age for President nonsense provisions because they're not important enough to merit constitutional status.

And finally there is as I mentioned earlier the hopeless vagueness of the free-speech clause of the First Amendment. The clause does not define "speech." The judiciary broadened it to include burning the American flag yet sensibly narrowed it to exclude defamation, copyright infringement, threats, revelation of military and other government confidences, a variety of confidential communications, and pornography (today mainly just child pornography). What today we understand to be the constitutional right of free speech is thus a creation of the courts rather than of the authors of the Constitution.

But I don't mean to denigrate the document. The Constitution is imperfect. It has vague provisions that have little or no real content and specific provisions that have the wrong content. Still it may well be the most important legal document in history. It created a novel but workable blueprint for the government of a nation riven with divisions (for example over slavery and over whether to have a standing army) and rightly expected to be vast. It created federalism. It inspired the judiciary. It placed the new nation on the right track and has been an inspiration to many other nations. What it didn't do was provide an adequate blueprint for constitutional law. That's a truth we need to learn to live with. What it provided instead, in its general as distinct from its specific provisions—general provisions such as the guarantees of freedom of speech and of the press and of religious freedom and of due process of law—was stimuli for thought translatable into concrete judicial decisions. It gave general guidance to how the federal courts including the newly created Supreme Court of the United States should resolve legal disputes of national significance. Constitutional law may well be, as Professor Strauss persuasively argues, largely a creation not of the framers but of the judges, but the inspiration and (implicit) authorization for such common-law constitutional lawmaking came from the document's authors.

Foreign constitutions, and how about term limits for Supreme Court Justices or, better, mandatory retirement (and for lower-court federal judges as well) at age eighty? We mustn't go overboard in praise of our Constitution. The United States is no longer the only nation that has a written Constitution, and it is noteworthy that foreign constitutions and the modes of their enforcement often differ substantially from the American model. For one thing they tend to be much longer—on average almost three times longer.[157] From this it may be possible to infer that the courts in those countries have less scope for creating constitutional law; for the longer a constitution is, the greater the number of constitutional issues that it is likely to resolve before the courts get hold of them. Moreover, most other countries' constitutions are far newer than ours, so less likely to contain obsolete provisions (though of course some of the provisions in them may in time become obsolete). This is a further reason to expect courts in those countries to be given, or in any event to exert, less authority to formulate constitutional doctrines that will fill holes created by the passage of time than our courts are given (or take). What is more, as David Law and Mila Versteeg note, "Other countries have, in recent decades, become increasingly unlikely to model either the rights-related provisions or the basic structural provisions of their own constitutions upon those found in the U.S. Constitution."[158] The fact that those countries are not imitating the U.S. model is some evidence that our model may be outdated and that the shift of constitu-

---

157. See *Comparative Constitutions Project,* "Constitution Rankings," April 20, 2016, http://comparativeconstitutionsproject.org/ccp-rankings/.

158. David S. Law and Mila Versteeg, "The Declining Influence of the United States Constitution," 87 *New York University Law Review* 762 (2012).

tional power from the document to the judges may be an inevitable adjustment to the document's growing obsolescence as a result of the passage of time.

Many of those countries, moreover, have constitutional courts—courts that decide *only* constitutional cases. And the judges of those courts, unlike our Supreme Court Justices, have fixed terms of office, commonly ten years (as in Germany for example). On the eve of Justice Scalia's death in February 2016 the average age of U.S. Supreme Court Justices was a few months under seventy; three of the Justices (Breyer, Kennedy, and Ginsburg) were seventy-eight or older; Kagan is in her fifties, and the other Justices are in their sixties. The Court thus has a semi-geriatric cast, which is an argument for term limits, not necessarily for all federal judges but for Supreme Court Justices; for the judges of the courts of appeals and the district courts are eligible for retirement, or if they prefer semi-retirement (that is, senior status) at age sixty-five or later, if they have been federal judges for at least fifteen years, and unlike Supreme Court Justices, who also can retire at sixty-five or later provided they have been federal judicial officers for at least fifteen years, the lower federal court judges generally take it when they become eligible or soon afterward. And though there are many exceptions, like me—just turned seventy-eight at this writing— it is relatively rare for lower-court federal judges (especially district judges) to continue sitting for more than a decade after they became eligible to retire with full pay. (I became eligible twelve years ago.)

Which brings me to the case for imposing term limits on our Supreme Court Justices, argued in an excellent recent piece by Eric Segall[159] from which I quote (with a few minor changes) the gist:

> Let's assume the next President nominates two or three Justices (and the Senate confirms them—which at this writing—mid-October 2016 is a big if). They may well serve for more than a quarter of a century—much more, if they're appointed young. Adding two or three liberals or two or three conservatives could thus determine the course of constitutional law for decades. This problem is serious and has in the past led to Courts dominated by Justices who were out of touch with current societal values. For example Justices who delayed important aspects of the New Deal had come of age in the previous century, when those kinds of executive/federal programs were unthinkable. Arguably the Warren and even

159. Eric Segall, "The 2016 Election, the Supreme Court and the Problems of Life Tenure," *Dorf on Law,* July 23, 2016, www.dorfonlaw.org/2016/07/the-2016-election-supreme-court-and.html.

Burger Courts issued decisions (*Roe* was issued by the Burger Court) that were out of step with the changing values of the American people when the 1960s gave way to the 1970s. . . . I suspect, although conservatives will be loath to admit this, that the perspectives of Justices Alito, Thomas, Roberts, and Scalia on gay rights, faux religious liberty, and voting rights, among other issues, will fifty years from now be universally deemed absurd and antiquated. These Justices generally came of age during the time when opposition (or support of) *Roe, Miranda,* and other Warren Court / Burger Court decisions, for better or worse, generated constitutional crises. But times have changed dramatically since then while the Justices (including Ginsburg and Breyer) often seem rooted in past arguments, values and debates. . . . A good example is gay rights. A necessary condition for those rights having been protected by the Court is that Justice Kennedy received the seat that Bork failed to secure. . . . [Had Bork gotten the seat], gay rights issues could easily have gone the other way, which I am completely confident would have astonished later generations. Justice Stevens served into his 90's and no one is suggesting he was unfit when he retired. But our country is ill-served by an institution staffed by folks who have been doing the same job for 20 to 30 years, or more. My father used to say that CEOs (he was one), after about ten years feel like they have heard it all before, and generally speaking lose the hunger to experiment and accept new ideas. One does not have to be a core legal realist to accept that stale legal doctrine plays less of a role than the Justices' perspectives on the real life consequences of their decisions. Do we really want Justices whose perspectives were often formed 30–40 years *before* they are called upon to decide hard cases? There are good reasons we have constitutional limits on how long the President can serve, why many states have term limits for governors, and most importantly, why 49 of the 50 states (Rhode Island is the exception) do not confer life tenure on their high-court judges. Giving government officials who have serious and largely final decisionmaking power a job for life subject only to their own personal whims and political goals is an exceptionally bad idea, and right now the stakes couldn't be any higher. Conservatives have every reason to fear a Court shaped by Hillary Clinton while the same is true for liberals and Donald Trump. Whoever is elected President will seriously affect the future of this country long after [he or she is] out of office, and that should trouble everyone.

Unlike Professor Segall, however, I don't favor *uniform* term limits for federal judges. Suppose the term limit for a Supreme Court Justice were twenty years. Then a Justice appointed at the age of forty-five would have to step down at sixty-five, while a Justice appointed at sixty-five could remain in office until eighty-five. A superior alternative would be compulsory retirement, say at age eighty; that would bring the term of the Justice appointed at a more advanced age (fifteen years) close to that of the Justice appointed at a much earlier age (twenty years). A more realistic alternative, however, might be to require every judge—including the Justices of the Supreme Court—upon reaching eighty or eighty-five to have a mental-acuity test, geared to the type of oral and written materials germane to the judicial task at the particular judge's level, with the test to be repeated at five-year intervals or upon evidence of diminished mental acuity reported by the judge's chief circuit or district judge.

The suggested combination of term limits and compulsory retirement would increase the turnover of Justices, which would be a good thing. The problem of a court that both decides what cases to hear *and* is composed in part of octogenarians is that its caseload is bound to drop because the octogenarians can't carry as heavy a load as the younger judges, and if they are given a lighter load observers will infer that they lack the energy of the young judges—which means they should retire! The Supreme Court's current very light workload may reflect (though this is pure speculation on my part) the tensions that arise from having old Justices. The Court hears only seventy to seventy-five cases a year, implying an average of 8.33 or fewer majority opinions per Justice (assuming nine Justices), which is a light workload especially when one considers that each Justice has four highly qualified law clerks. Yet the total number of opinions issued by the Court in the 2015 term (which ended at the beginning of October 2016) was 149, meaning that approximately half were concurring or dissenting opinions. This indicates a high level of disagreement (most concurring opinions, while not questioning the decision announced in the majority opinion, question some or even all the analysis in that opinion), amounting to fragmentation, and possibly also a desire to increase the Justices' prominence and significance. The pressure to write separate opinions would weaken if the Court heard ninety cases a year instead of seventy or seventy-five, for then the average number of majority opinions per Justice would be ten, though some Justices might issue far fewer.

Even ninety is not a great number of opinions for a nine-Justice Supreme Court to issue in a term. In the late 1960s the Court heard about 150 cases a year; each judge of my court hears about 200. The reader may say: but the

Court's cases are more difficult. I doubt that. They are more consequential, but that's not the same thing. Because there are nine Justices (normally), each of whom has four law clerks, there are forty-five "judges" on each case, who also have the benefit of an opinion by a lower court and multiple classy briefs, including amicus curiae briefs, and don't have to worry about the risk of reversal by a higher court, though in a statutory as distinct from a constitutional case they may have to worry about being "overruled" by a congressional statute or amendment.

Anent compulsory retirement of federal judges and Justices, it's true that Article III section 1 of the Constitution states that federal "Judges, both of the supreme and inferior Courts, shall hold their Offices during good Behaviour." But this provision need not be interpreted to entitle the Justices or any other federal judges to life tenure unless removed by impeachment and conviction. A number of federal judges and Justices have remained in office beyond their "sell-by" date, usually owing to physical or mental impairment; the Supreme Court Justices have included Rutledge, Field, Holmes, Murphy, Whittaker, Douglas, Blackmun, Rehnquist, and doubtless other. The number of lower-court judge who overstay their welcome is of course much larger, because there are so many more lower-court judges. Senile judges and Justices usually are induced by colleagues or family to retire, but often not until years after they should have retired. A fixed retirement age, predicated on a belief that some degree of mental and physical deterioration after age eighty is common although not universal, would be consistent with the standard of "good Behaviour."

I am mindful that some Justices have performed their judicial duties with distinction into their eighties. Holmes retired in 1932 at the age of ninety, when he was no longer fit; yet he had been eighty-seven when he delivered his notable dissent in *United States v. Schwimmer*.[160] And Brandeis was seventy-nine when he issued his most famous opinion, the majority opinion in *Erie R. Co. v. Thompson*.[161] (He retired the following year.) But we can't expect to see the likes of Holmes or Brandeis ever again. It's eighty-four years since Holmes retired, seventy-seven years since Brandeis retired. Only two great Justices, Cardozo and Jackson, have been appointed in that period, the former to succeed Holmes, the latter two years after Brandeis's retirement. Presidents no longer seek greatness in a Supreme Court Justice. Just study the list of twenty-one judges from which President-elect Trump has promised to pick a successor to

160. 279 U.S. 644, 653–655 (1929).
161. 304 U.S. 64 (1938).

Justice Scalia, and reflect on the (in my opinion disappointing) quality of the Justices appointed by Presidents George W. Bush and Barack Obama.

A considerable curiosity of the Supreme Court tenure system is the perpetual term of the Chief Justice; once appointed, he or she has the position for life. CEOs don't hold their jobs for life, or chief circuit or district judges; why should Chief Justices? The longer a chief judge or Chief Justice serves, the less likely the other judges or Justices are to take him or her seriously, and he or she is likely to become stale in the job after a time and confused by the changing mix of the other Justices. It's not as if the Constitution had conferred lifetime tenure on Chief Justices. There is no mention of a Chief Justice in Article III of the Constitution. The only reference is in Article I, section 3, and consists solely of the statement "When the President of the United States is tried, the Chief Justice shall preside." That has a nice rhyme ("tried . . . preside") but says nothing about how the Chief Justice is selected or what his term is. It would be entirely consistent with the constitutional language for the Justices to be permitted (perhaps by federal statute) to select from their ranks a Chief Justice for a specified term, or for the President to be permitted (again by statute) to select a Chief Justice from the Justices and specify his or her term; or the statute could fix a term. A ten-year nonrenewable term, long enough for a Chief Justice to develop and exercise organizational and leadership skills, would make more sense than life tenure. Upon expiration of the term, the Chief Justice would revert to being one of the Associate Justices.

Because the Chief Justice's term has as yet no prescribed limit, one might expect Presidents to pick as Chief Justices persons with managerial experience and competence. This has been rare, however, consistent with the disdain for efficiency that characterizes many courts and the poor management practices that pervade the federal judiciary. The present incumbent, Chief Justice Roberts, had had some limited supervisory authority in the Justice Department and then in a law firm before becoming a court of appeals judge and then Chief Justice. But basically he'd been an appellate advocate and, as far as I can judge, as Chief Justice he hasn't exercised significant managerial authority either over the Supreme Court or over the federal judiciary as a whole. It has, for example, taken him a decade to require public disclosure of changes made by Supreme Court Justices in their opinions after the opinions have been issued but before they've been published five years later in the U.S. Reports,[162] and he's done

---

162. See Adam Liptak, "Justices Show How Disclosing Revisions Offers (Confers?) Benefits," *New York Times*, July 25, 2016, www.nytimes.com/2016/07/26/us/politics/supreme-court-opinion-edits.html.

nothing to close the five-year publication gap. Nor has he dealt with the Supreme Court's ethical issues that I discuss later in this chapter.

Grievous defaults? Professor Sanford Levinson lists seven "truly grievous defaults"[163] in the U.S. Constitution (not including absence of term limits) that he wishes to see changed by amendments to the Constitution: "the allocation of power in the Senate; the almost certain presidential dictatorship that will follow any catastrophic attack on members of Congress; excessive presidential power; the Electoral College; the hiatus between the repudiation of a sitting president and the inauguration of a successor; the inability to get rid of an incompetent president; the functional impossibility of amending the Constitution with regard to anything truly significant."[164] The list is unduly alarmist. For what Professor Levinson misses is that a constitutional convention (his proposed solution[165]) is not required to prevent the defaults that concern him. Nor are constitutional amendments. Whether working jointly with or independently of the President and Congress, the Supreme Court can be counted on to ward off the disasters that Levinson fears, as it's been doing for the last two hundred odd years—as we saw (and will shortly see again) in reference to the Court's decision in *Bolling v. Sharpe*—by treating the Constitution as authorizing the Court to create and refine a body of constitutional law. The Justices pick up where the framers left off.

Managing the Supreme Court. What could easily be changed for the better regarding the Supreme Court would be its management, which as I've already suggested is mediocre. Forget the spittoon that squats next to each Justice's seat in the courtroom—sheer antiquarian silliness.[166] There is the five-year interval between the rendering of a decision and its publication in the *U.S. Reports,* and I should also mention the Court's refusal to disclose the vote (not the voters) in cases in which certiorari is denied. Such disclosure would convey a sense of the importance of the issue sought to be resolved by the Court and so encourage or discourage future efforts to persuade the Court to hear a case presenting the

---

163. Sanford Levinson, *Our Undemocratic Constitution: Where the Constitution Goes Wrong* (2006).

164. *Comparative Constitutions Project,* note 157 above, at 167.

165. Id. at 174–180.

166. Though one person's silliness can be another's charm—and so we read that "in many ways, the justices . . . live in a bygone era: one of elevator operators, ceramic spittoons, white quill pens and government lawyers in elegant gray morning coats." Joan Biskupic, "Supreme Court Holds to Tradition," *USA Today,* March 19, 2007, http://usatoday30.usatoday.com/news/washington/2007-03-19-court-rituals_N.htm. I know the spittoons are still there; I don't know the status of the other antiquities, which strike me as equally silly.

same issue. Think too about the Justices' refusal to give reasons for recusing themselves from hearing a case, and their refusing to recuse themselves in the face of plausible motions to recuse, and the bunching of opinions at the end of June, rather than making September the deadline so that cases argued late in the term could receive due consideration rather than being rushed out in time for the summer break. Think too of the excessive length of that break; the inordinate length and unlovely jargon of so many of the Court's opinions (including concurring and dissenting opinions, culminating in Justice Alito's tedious forty-page dissent in a recent Texas abortion case).[167] Think of the unmemorability of almost all modern Supreme Court concurring and dissenting opinions (no more gems from the likes of Holmes, Brandeis, and Jackson); the Justices' warring footnotes and occasional lapses into incivility; the antiquarian capitalizations (for example, of "State"); the Justices' excessive reliance on law clerks; the Justices' babble at oral argument; their plagiarism of passages from the briefs filed in the Court; their incestuous practice of appointing former Supreme Court law clerks to participate as amici curiae in cases argued before the Court. These defects could be eliminated by a forceful, aggressive Chief Justice who had management talents and experience. What cannot be changed is the Justices' pretense that they do not make law but merely apply it. They'll never give that up, false though it is.

Although the Justices endeavor to be civil to each other both in their opinions (with the notable though now defunct exception of Justice Scalia's frequently vitriolic dissents) and in person, there is plenty of tension and doubtless some mutual dislike. The characterization by Holmes of Supreme Court Justices as nine scorpions in a bottle remains apt, owing in part to the fact that the Chief Justice assigns the majority opinion in every case in which he is in the majority. The Court's cases differ markedly in importance and a Justice who receives few choice assignments is likely in consequence to be quickly forgotten after he leaves the Court (the fate of Justice Potter Stewart, who complained albeit sotto voce that Chief Justice Burger did not give him good assignments). This problem could be solved or at least alleviated by random assignment, among the Justices in the majority in a given case, of the preparation of the majority opinion. That would emulate the practice of the New York Court of Appeals (the state's supreme court), famously when Cardozo was the dominant figure on the court, of random assignment of the majority opinion in every case.

167. See note 188 below.

A better remedy for the managerial deficiencies of the Court, as suggested by political scientist Timothy A. DeLaune, might be to rotate the Chief Justice-ship among the Justices.[168] This would be effective, however, only if the term of each Chief Justice were short. If it were as long as five years, it would take forty-five years for all nine Justices to have a shot at being Chief Justice, and some would die or retire before their turn had come. This would not happen, or at least not happen very often, if the term were only one or two years, but the re-sulting rapid turnover in Chief Justices might be disorienting.

Another possibility would be for the Court to imitate the practice of the courts of appeals of having appeals heard before three-Justice panels presided over by the senior Justice on the panel (provided that he had not taken senior status, the semi-retired status that among other things disqualifies a judge from presiding if there is an active judge on the panel), subject to rehearing by the full Court should a majority of the Justices disagree with the panel's decision and consider the issue decided by it important enough for the entire Court to resolve. I mentioned the occasional (maybe frequent) failure of Justices (also a common failure of lower-court judges) to explain why they are or are not re-cusing themselves in a case because of a conflict of interest. Recusal of a Su-preme Court Justice is undesirable because he or she can't be replaced by an-other judge or Justice, as the Court always sits en banc (that is, with all Justices eligible to participate who are neither recused nor unavailable because of ill-ness or accident), and never in panels. So this is another argument for the Court's adopting the panel system used by the courts of appeals.

To minimize recusal of Supreme Court Justices because of ownership of stock in a litigant, every Justice should be required to sell all his or her stock holdings when appointed to the Court and having done so permitted to invest the proceeds in a mutual fund or mutual funds, since recusal is not required just because a judge or a Justice owns shares of a mutual fund that invests in the stock of a company that happens to be a party to a case in the judge's court, or in the Supreme Court if the judge happens to be one of the Justices.[169]

---

168. "An Immodest Proposal," 20 *Green Bag* 2d 85, 87–89 (2016).

169. See "Blind Trusts and Recusals: Supreme Court Justices Should Not Own Individual Stocks That Would Trigger a Recusal and Generally [Should] Be More Thoughtful about Potential Conflicts of Interest," in *Fix the Court,* http://fixthecourt.com/fix/blind-trusts-and-recusals/. To minimize the frequency with which I would have to recuse myself, when I was appointed to the Seventh Circuit my wife and I sold all our stocks and placed the proceeds in mutual funds. As a result I have with *very* rare exceptions recused myself only in cases in which the University of Chicago, of which I remain a part-time (a very part-time) employee teaching occasionally in the law school and conducting research there mainly with the help of students, is a party to a case in my court.

Better appointments! The most constructive change in the Supreme Court that could be made without legislation or a constitutional amendment—a change that may seem straightforward but actually is only barely feasible because of the political repercussions it would engender and the long time it would take to effectuate given the relative youth of most of the current Justices—would be to improve the quality of appointees. The President nominates a Justice when a vacancy occurs, and the Senate confirms or rejects (rarely rejects—Presidents for obvious reasons try to avoid nominating candidates likely to be rejected by the Senate) the nominee. Both centers of power act mainly on political grounds—the conformity of a nominee's likely political leanings as a Justice to the political leanings of the President and the Senate majority. This is not a formula for obtaining top quality. The point is not that the Justices aren't competent, aren't fit for the job; they are, after all, screened carefully by both the President's advisers and the Senate Judiciary Committee. But are they super? No, because quality is only one of the criteria that Presidents and Senators consider, and not the most important. They may feel that given the quality of the law clerks and of the Supreme Court bar almost any Justices are likely to be "good enough" at their job, and therefore appointment can be based on race, or sex, or ethnicity, or religion, or ideology, or some other characteristic more likely than quality to seize public attention and serve the political goals of the appointing authorities. But note the paradox: we can expect that as law clerks become better (because the job is more highly valued now that law firms pay huge signing bonuses—$300,000 or more—to former Supreme Court law clerks whom they hire) and also more numerous (there was a time when each Justice had only one clerk; now each has four), the quality of Justices will decline because Presidents in choosing them will be able to pay more attention to the political dividends of an appointment, leaving the smarts to be supplied to the dimmer appointees by their clerks.

Many constitutional law professors, and for that matter many judges, would think it blasphemy to describe the Supreme Court as a "politicized" institution (politicized but also politicizing), as I am doing. Yet its politicization can be traced to the document itself, and specifically to Article II, section 2, which states that the President "shall nominate, and with the Advice and Consent of the Senate, shall appoint . . . judges of the Supreme Court." The President is a politician, the Senators are politicians, the members of the House of Representatives are politicians, and so are the executive and legislative officers of the states; it's inconceivable that no attention would be paid in the appointment of

Supreme Court Justices to the likely political consequences of the appointments. (Article II section 2 also authorizes Presidential appointment, subject to Senate confirmation, of lower-court federal judges.) But if too much attention is paid to these things, the result is bound to be a weak Court.

It's not merely nostalgia that reserves the adjective "great" for a bare handful of Justices, all dead, all of whom were pragmatic, and "political" only in a nonpartisan sense: John Marshall, Holmes, Brandeis, Cardozo, Hughes, Jackson, the two Harlans, perhaps a few others (Story? Black? Rehnquist? Frankfurter?).[170] Given the politics of the appointments process, one can't expect many *great* appointments. Maybe some members of the current Court will be reckoned great, because evaluation must await the completion of their Supreme Court careers, but I am not holding my breath.

The Bushmen cometh, and other reflections on the same-sex marriage controversy and religion in the Supreme Court. I don't have a good feeling about the current Court, impertinent though such an acknowledgment may seem coming from a mere court of appeals judge. But consider Chief Justice Roberts's dissent (joined unsurprisingly by Justices Alito, Scalia, and Thomas, the most conservative of Roberts's colleagues) in the Supreme Court's 2015 decision declaring a constitutional right to same-sex marriage *(Obergefell v. Hodges).* Roberts's dissent contains the following eye-popping passage: "The Court invalidates the marriage laws of more than half the states and orders the transformation of a social institution that has formed the basis of human society for millennia, for the Kalahari Bushmen and the Han Chinese, the Carthaginians and the Aztecs. Just who do we think we are?"[171] It's a painfully easy question to answer: we are not Kalahari Bushmen, Carthaginians, or Aztecs, though some of us are Han Chinese. The Han are the largest ethnic group in China—90 percent of Chinese are Han—and so undoubtedly many of our citizens of Chinese origin are Han, though I'm unaware that they are more opposed to same-sex marriage than other Americans, most of whom are no longer opposed to it. Probably Chinese Americans are on average *less* opposed than other Americans because most of the opposition to same-sex marriage is religious and

---

170. And on the other (including state) courts Roger Traynor, Henry Friendly, Learned Hand, Alex Kozinski, Michael Boudin, Pierre Leval, John Minor Wisdom, Harold Leventhal, Jay Wilkinson, Calvert Magruder, Charles Fried, Charles Wyzanski, Arthur T. Vanderbilt, Edward Becker, Patrick Higginbotham, Harry Edwards, Goodwin Liu, Hans Linde, Robert Katzmann, Thomas Ambro—and many others.

171. *Obergefell v. Hodges,* note 61 above, at 2584, 2612.

more than 50 percent of Chinese Americans report no religious affiliation, compared to only 30 percent of all Americans.[172]

It's true that nonrecognition of same-sex marriage goes back millennia, but so does slavery and, more to the point, so does prohibition of miscegenation, which the Supreme Court invalidated in *Loving v. Virginia*[173] as a denial of the equal protection of the laws. The racism that undergirded those prohibitions differed little from the prejudice against homosexuals that supported prohibitions of same-sex marriage. Both were paeans to bigotry.

So what can Chief Justice Roberts have been thinking when he wrote the passage I quoted? And how did he pick those four ethnic groups to compare to Americans? I have no idea, especially after reading an article in the *Washington Post* that sharply criticizes that part of his dissent.[174] The article points out that the Bushmen, who are hunter-gatherers in sub-Saharan Africa and nearly extinct, don't go in for wedding ceremonies, and that among their ancestors were women warriors who styled themselves polygamists and lesbians. I thus find it exceedingly difficult to imagine the Chief Justice of the United States looking to the Bushmen as allies in the fight against recognition of same-sex marriage in twenty-first-century America.

As for the Han, the largest ethnic group in China, homosexual marriage is indeed forbidden to them as to the other people in China. But in the ancient Han dynasty (roughly 200 B.C. to A.D. 200), homosexual sex was rife, especially among the emperors;[175] and I am guessing that Roberts was alluding to the Han

172. See "Chinese Americans," *Wikipedia,* https://en.wikipedia.org/wiki/Chinese_Americans#Religion; "Religion in the United States," *Wikipedia,* https://en.wikipedia.org/wiki/Religion_in_the_United_States.

173. 388 U.S. 1 (1967). Denouncing *Obergefell,* the *National Review,* on June 26, 2015, in an article entitled "Against Redefining Marriage—and the Republic," www.nationalreview.com/article/420405/against-redefining-marriage-and-republic-editors, stated that "the majority points out how marriage has evolved over millennia—though hardly beyond recognition—and suggests it now must encompass homosexual relationships. But marriage evolved as societies and governments did—not as the result of imperious court decisions. Until the last several years, capped by this decision." The implication is that *Loving v. Virginia* was also an "imperious court decision."

174. Ishan Tharoor, "Justice Roberts Cited the Traditions of Four Cultures in His Dissent on Gary Marriage. Here's What He Didn't Mention," *Washington Post,* June 26, 2015, www.washingtonpost.com/news/worldviews/wp/2015/06/26/justice-roberts-cited-the-traditions-of-four-cultures-in-his-dissent-on-gay-marriage-heres-what-he-didnt-mention/.

175. See Maria Manoli, "Sexuality in Ancient China, pt. 2, *gbtimes,* August 16, 2011, http://gbtimes.com/life/sexuality-ancient-china-part-2, where we read that

homosexuality was not uncommon in ancient China and had no negative connotation. There are many historic sources and depictions in Chinese art praising homosexual love that survived the puritanical book burning of the Cultural Revolution. It is said that same-sex love was particularly popular during the Song, Ming and Qing dynasty. Scholar Pan Guangdan came to the conclusion that many emperors of the Han dynasty had one or more male sex partners in their harem. There is a well

dynasty rather than to the current Han Chinese—which is to say the major Chinese ethnic group today—because he neither suggests, nor have I found any indication, that the 10 percent of the modern Chinese population that is not Han engage in marital or sexual practices different from those of the Han Chinese. Had Roberts been thinking about modern Chinese he probably would have omitted "Han." Of course I have no idea what he was thinking; I'm not sure he did either. If he did, I would have expected him to indicate which Han, the ancient or the modern, he was writing about.

As for Carthage, it was destroyed by Rome in 146 B.C., and not much is known about the marital and sexual practices of its people. According to the Italian scholar Roberto De Mattei, however, Carthage "was a paradise for homosexuals" and after the Roman conquest "the abhorrent presence of a few [Carthaginian] gays infected a good part of the [Roman] people" and led eventually to the downfall of the Roman Empire. That is not easy to credit, so I will "give" the Chief Justice the Carthaginians.

The *Washington Post* article says little about the Aztecs, but elsewhere it's been noted that the soldiers of Cortez's army that conquered Mexico in the sixteenth century were shocked by the prevalence of sodomy among the Aztecs.[176]

There is more that is wrong with the Chief Justice's dissent in *Obergefell*. Recall how the passage I quoted from the dissent begins: "The Court invalidates the marriage laws of more than half the states and orders the transformation of a social institution that has formed the basis of human society for millennia." When he wrote, thirty-seven states—three-fourths of U.S. states—had already legalized same-sex marriage, and so the Court was invalidating the marriage laws of only thirteen states, slightly more than a quarter, rather than more than a half, of the states. Those thirty-seven had already transformed the social institution of opposite-sex marriage, though, granted, many of them had done it as a result of litigation rather than legislation or a popular vote.

Roberts committed a further error in saying that "as the majority acknowledges, marriage has existed for millennia and across civilizations. . . . For all those millennia, across all those civilizations, 'marriage' referred to only one

---

known story about Emperor Ai, who carefully cut off his sleeve in order not to wake his male concubine Dongxian, who had fallen asleep on it. There are also many tales of lesbian love, but to a lesser extent.

176. Google "Aztec sodomy" for relevant websites.

relationship: the union of a man and a woman. . . . As the Court explained two Terms ago, 'until recent years, . . . marriage between a man and a woman no doubt had been thought of by most people as essential to the very definition of that term and to its role and function throughout the history of civilization. . . . This universal definition of marriage as the union of a man and a woman is no historical coincidence.'"[177] Roberts forgot polygamy—marriage as the union of one man with two or more women, not only a widespread historical phenomenon but still common today; it is legal in fifty countries, mostly countries with a Muslim majority.[178] It even continues, albeit *sub rosa*, in parts of Utah today. Does he equate same-sex marriage to polygamy?

The Chief Justice's biggest error, in which he was joined by two of the other three ultraconservative Justices (Alito and Scalia), was to deny that *any* society had *ever*, until the Netherlands broke ranks in 2001, recognized same-sex marriage. At oral argument he said that "every definition I looked up, prior to about a dozen years ago defined marriage as unity between a man and a woman as husband and wife" (note his again forgetting polygamy). Justice Alito chimed in that "as far as I'm aware, until the end of the 20th century there was never a nation or a culture that recognized marriage between two people of the same sex," and Scalia added that "I don't know of any—do you [the lawyer arguing the case] know of any society, prior to the Netherlands in 2001, that permitted same-sex marriage?"—to which the lawyer answered "no." But she was wrong and they were wrong. Same-sex marriage (sometimes between men, sometimes between women) was permitted to elite men in the Roman Empire (Nero for example), to men in many Native-American societies, to women in some pre-colonial African families, and to men, and perhaps also to women, in East Asia.[179]

So history seems not to be the Chief Justice's strong suit, or that of his allies. But one suspected that already, for in an earlier foray into history, in sarcastically "characterizing legal scholarship as something concerned with 'the influence of Immanuel Kant on evidentiary approaches in eighteenth century Bul-

177. *Obergefell v. Hodges*, note 61 above, at 2612–2613, citing *United States v. Windsor*, 133 S. Ct. 2675, 2689 (2013).

178. "Legal Status of Polygamy," *Wikipedia*, https://en.wikipedia.org/wiki/Legal_status_of_polygamy.

179. See Laura Geggel, "Same-Sex Marriage in History: What the Supreme Court Missed," *Live Science*, May 5, 2015, www.livescience.com/50725-same-sex-marriage-history.html. See also "History of Same-Sex Unions," *Wikipedia*, https://en.wikipedia.org/wiki/History_of_same-sex_unions (the references section lists thirty-nine books and articles on the subject); and Gary Ferguson, *Same-Sex Marriage in Renaissance Rome: Sexuality, Identity and Community in Early Modern Europe* (2016).

garia or something,'"[180] the Chief Justice had got his century wrong. In the eighteenth century Bulgaria was not a country at all, but merely a province of the Ottoman Empire, and it remained so until 1908. True, it achieved a significant degree of autonomy in 1878—but 1878 was in the nineteenth century rather than the eighteenth. Conceivably, though improbably, Kant's philosophy could have influenced provincial thought in the Ottoman Empire, and Bulgaria was a province of the empire, but in fact his philosophy did not influence eighteenth-century Bulgarian thought. According to Orin Kerr, "The earliest reference to Kant's work in a Bulgarian journal appeared in 1859. That reference dismissed Kant's ideas as 'obscure and awkward.' . . . European thought in general had little influence on the Bulgarian legal system until Bulgaria became an independent state in 1908. The likelihood of Kantian influence on evidence law is particularly remote. . . . [A] study of Bulgarian evidence law in the 18th century suggests no Kantian influence."[181] The anti-intellectual tone of Roberts's Bulgarian remark should also be noted.

I don't want to leave the impression that Chief Justice Roberts's *Obergefell* dissent and his musings on the impact of Kantian philosophy on Bulgaria when it was a province not a nation and his absurd contention at his confirmation hearing that Supreme Court Justices are the equivalent of sports umpires or referees are his only questionable public pronouncements. Another is his opinion invalidating a Massachusetts rule requiring abortion protesters to stay at least thirty-five feet away from the entrance to an abortion clinic[182] on the ground that streets and sidewalks are important sites for "discussions about the issues of the day"—which was once true but is no longer.

More important is what he did to section 2 of the Voting Rights Act of 1965, which bans any "standard, practice, or procedure" that "results in a denial or abridgement of the right of any citizen . . . to vote on account of race or color"[183] and applies nationwide. Section 4(b) of the Act,[184] defines the jurisdictions covered by section 2 as states or their political subdivisions that maintained tests or devices as prerequisites to voting, and had low voter registration or turnout,

180. Diane P. Wood, "Legal Scholarship for Judges," 124 *Yale Law Journal* 2592, 2594 (2015), quoting *A Conversation with John Roberts*, C-SPAN, June 25, 2011, www.c-span.org/video/?300203-1/conversation-chief-justice-roberts.

181. Orin S. Kerr, "The Influence of Immanuel Kant on Evidentiary Approaches in 18th-Century Bulgaria," 18 *Green Bag* 2d 251–253 (footnotes omitted).

182. *McCullen v. Coakley,* 134 S. Ct. 2518 (2014). See *Divergent Paths: The Academy and the Judiciary* 171–173 (2016).

183. 42 U.S.C. § 1973(a).

184. 42 U.S.C. § 1973b(b).

in the 1960s and early 1970s. Finally section 5,[185] forbids any change in voting procedures in the covered jurisdictions until cleared by the federal government ("preclearance"). In 2006 the Act was reauthorized for an additional twenty-five years, but the coverage formula was not changed. Coverage still turned on whether a jurisdiction had had a voting test in the 1960s or 1970s and low voter registration or turnout then.

In *Shelby County v. Holder*[186] the Supreme Court, in a 5 to 4 opinion by Chief Justice Roberts, invalidated the preclearance statute on the ground that discrimination had declined significantly in the states subject to it since 1965. As Justice Ginsburg explained in a powerful dissent, the majority's reasoning made no sense, since the federal government has, one would have thought, authority under the Fourteenth and Fifteenth Amendments to outlaw racial and other invidious discrimination in voting regardless of *how* invidious it is. Certainly there is no limitation of that authority in either amendment, or anywhere else in the Constitution.

Faced with an insuperable hurdle, Roberts ingeniously but unscrupulously invoked what he called a "fundamental principle of equal sovereignty" among the states, a principle which if it existed would seemingly forbid imposing a preclearance obligation on any state unless it was imposed on every state. But there is no such principle. What is true is that it has long been the understanding that when a state is admitted to the union, it enters "on an equal footing" with the existing states. That is a principle with no application to the Voting Rights Act. *Shelby County* is an unprincipled opinion. The states formerly subject to section 2 took advantage of the decision to strew impediments to voting before members of minority groups that in the pre-preclearance days the states had discriminated against openly.

I want to return briefly to *Obergefell*. All four dissenting Justices were Catholic, as of course were two of the Justices in the majority—Kennedy and Sotomayor; but on the basis of their vote in *Obergefell* and in many other cases as well we know that neither toes an orthodox, *Opus Dei* style Catholic line[187]—which is not surprising because there is as great diversity of religious belief and observance among American Catholics as there is among other American religious groups. The four dissenters were, and the three survivors (that is, the four

185. 42 U.S.C. § 1973c(a).
186. 570 U.S. __ (2013).
187. I don't mean to suggest that any past or present Catholic member of the Supreme Court has ever belonged to *Opus Dei*. Even Scalia had not belonged.

minus Scalia) are, judging from their votes and opinions, deeply orthodox, and it's difficult to believe that their religious beliefs play no role in their votes in cases that have a religious dimension.[188] I don't say that critically, because religious belief is among the priors that exercise strong influence over people's thoughts and actions and so are bound to exert an influence in as nebulous an intellectual realm as constitutional law.

Neither the two Catholic Justices who did not dissent nor the three Jewish ones (Ginsburg, Breyer, and Kagan), seem influenced in their judicial votes and opinions by religion. I assume they're not particularly religious—probably not religious at all, I'm guessing, except Kennedy, whose consistent votes in favor of legalizing same-sex relationships may be influenced by a liberal form of Catholicism now common among Americans. I know devout Catholics who believe that priests should be allowed to marry, that married couples should be allowed to use contraception, and (here I am judging by the two same-sex marriages that I've performed, at which most of the guests were heterosexual Catholics) that persons of the same sex are rightly permitted to marry. Catholicism in modern America is no monolith.

Justice Kennedy seems by the way to have relished the role of swing Justice—it made him the most powerful member of the Court until the death of Scalia deprived him of the role by creating a Court of four liberal Justices (Ginsburg, Breyer, Sotomayor, and Kagan), three conservative ones (Roberts, Thomas, and Alito)—and Kennedy. He will recover his swing position only if the Scalia vacancy is filled by a conservative, for there will then be four conservative Justices—and Kennedy.

Another oddity in the failed attempts of conservative judges and Justices to prevent, in the name of religious freedom, government from recognizing a right of homosexuals to engage in same-sex marriage, and also of women to have abortions and use contraceptives, is a failure to recognize that rejection of religious dogma is itself a manifestation of religious freedom. Would America have more religious freedom if atheism were illegal, or does freedom of reli-

188. All three dissented in the two religion-charged cases that the Court dealt with at the very end of the 2015 term: *Whole Woman's Health v. Hellerstedt*, No. 15-274, June 27, 2016 (involving a Texas abortion statute that was forcing the closure of most abortion clinics in the state), and the denial of certiorari in *Storman's Inc. v. Wiesman*, No. 15-862, June 28, 2016. The length, tedium, unreality, insensitivity, and fussy formalism of the two dissenting opinions in *Whole Woman's Health* (by Alito and by Thomas) make those opinions a remarkable throwback to the nineteenth century. And for powerful criticism of the *Storman's* dissent, see Mark Stern, "One Last Snarling, Tetchy Dissent," *Slate*, June 28, 2016, www.slate.com/articles/news_and_politics /the_breakfast_table/features/2016/supreme_court_breakfast_table_for_june_2016/conservative_justices_pro test_businesses_having_to_sell_plan_b.html.

gion encompass not just freedom to choose *among* religions but also freedom *from* religion? The pledge of allegiance to the United States has since 1954 included the phrase "under God." Many people omit the phrase in pledging allegiance, either because they don't believe in God or think it blasphemous to deem Him the overlord of the United States. In either case aren't they exercising a *religious* right?

Shortly before the Supreme Court decided *Obergefell*, Judge Jeffrey Sutton, a very fine judge on the Sixth Circuit, wrote an opinion (rendered defunct by *Obergefell*) upholding the prohibition of same-sex marriage by the four states in his circuit (the Sixth Circuit, comprised of Michigan, Ohio, Kentucky, and Tennessee). The opinion *(DeBoer v. Snyder)*, which is a good deal more temperate, refined, and sophisticated than any of the four Supreme Court dissenting opinions in *Obergefell*, offered the following alternative to Roberts's cry of "Who do we think we are?": "When the courts do not let the people resolve new social issues like this one, they perpetuate the idea that the heroes in these change events are judges and lawyers. Better in this instance, we think, to allow change through the customary political processes, in which the people, gay and straight alike, become the heroes of their own stories by meeting each other not as adversaries in a court system but as fellow citizens seeking to resolve a new social issue in a fair-minded way."[189] The problem with this reasoning, eloquent though it is compared to the dissenting Justices' opinions in *Obergefell*, is that it implies that courts should never invalidate a state law, for by doing so they prevent "change through the customary political processes." *Loving v. Virginia*, for example, prevented such change by invalidating Virginia's antimiscegenation law as a violation of the equal protection clause of the Fourteenth Amendment. I doubt that Judge Sutton disapproves of *Loving* or for that matter of *Brown v. Board of Education*. He might well have thought the states of his circuit less reactionary than the states in the deep south, but Kansas, the state of the defendant (the Board of Education of Topeka) in the *Brown* case, is not in the deep South.

Anent Roberts's and Sutton's positions, Gary Peeples has reminded me that "the underlying rationale—that states ought to be allowed to conduct social experiments at their own speed—sounds nice until one remembers that (virtu-

---

189. *DeBoer v. Snyder*, 772 F.3d 388, 421 (6th Cir. 2014). I find it very odd that neither Judge Sutton nor Judge Kavanaugh was on President-elect Trump's list of twenty-one judges from which he said he would nominate Scalia's replacement, though in the end he didn't—Gorsuch had not been on the list. I have my disagreements with Sutton and Kavanaugh, but both of them are outstanding federal court of appeals judges and would I am sure be excellent Supreme Court Justices.

ally) no judge would permit a state to conduct the sort of social experiment that would involve reinstituting Jim Crow laws (or their equivalent) against another minority group, such as Sikhs. When it comes to pure bigotry (and its cousin, irrational ignorance), states should not be allowed to serve as laboratories."[190]

Judge Sutton's opinion mentions in passing "judicial restraint." Early in the opinion we read that

> A first requirement of any law, whether under the Due Process or Equal Protection Clause, is that it rationally advance a legitimate government policy. Two words ("judicial restraint") and one principle (trust in the people that "even improvident decisions will eventually be rectified by the democratic process") tell us all we need to know about the light touch judges should use in reviewing laws under this standard. As long as judges can conceive of some "plausible" reason for the law—*any* plausible reason, even one that did not motivate the legislators who enacted it— the law must stand, no matter how unfair, unjust, or unwise the judges may consider it as citizens.[191]

This is the only mention of judicial restraint in Judge Sutton's opinion, and it is not mentioned at all in Judge Daughtrey's dissent—which tells us something about the evolution of constitutional law. In 1893 a Harvard law professor named James Bradley Thayer published an article which argued that a statute should be invalidated on constitutional grounds only if its unconstitutionality was "so clear that it is not open to rational question."[192] The problem with the approach, as I and others have argued,[193] is that it requires the judge to uphold a statute that he is convinced is unconstitutional, provided only that a rational person (Jeffrey Sutton, for example) could disagree.

Anyway, one doesn't hear much about "judicial self-restraint" any more. If it ever existed, it's dead; and even Judge Sutton, though he mentioned it (though without the "self-"), didn't do anything with it. As Larry Kramer explains,

---

190. Gary Peeples, email message to author.

191. *DeBoer v. Snyder,* note 189 above, at 404 (citations omitted).

192. James B. Thayer, "The Origin and Scope of the American Doctrine of Constitutional Law," 7 *Harvard Law Review* 129, 144 (1893).

193. See, e.g., Richard A. Posner, "The Rise and Fall of Judicial Self-Restraint," 100 *California Law Review* 519 (2012)—the first of five articles in that issue of the review, all consistent.

people will let the Justices go further and do more things they dislike if they believe it is the Court, and not they or their representatives, that is supposed to have final authority to decide. Judicial supremacy is an ideology, and its whole purpose and effect is to shift the equilibrium point of public and political acceptance in favor of judicial authority. As . . . judicial supremacy has become taken for granted throughout our political system, the ability of the Court to act without worrying about its authority has naturally grown. . . . [J]udicial authority has, just as naturally, played a smaller and smaller role—until it has become, as Judge Posner notes, little more than a rhetorical tool used opportunistically by pretty much all of the Justices. If that's bad, and I for one think it is, the culprit is not interpretive theory or the idea that there are right answers to constitutional questions. It is our embrace of the strange and counterintuitive notion that determining these answers, and so deciding the ongoing meaning of a democratic constitution, is best left to life-tenured judges whose chief qualification is technical legal training.[194]

But I am left wondering, on the basis of the quoted passage, whether Kramer (who when he wrote this article for the *California Law Review* was dean of the Stanford Law School) would have sided with Judge Sutton had he been a judge on the panel that decided the *DeBoer* case.

Thomas in lieu of Scalia. With Scalia gone, the mantle of judicial ultraconservatism has descended on Justice Thomas, about whom Professor Segall has remarked that

Justice Thomas's America is one where Americans possess strong rights to guns but no rights to abortion; where no government, city, state or federal, may take racial criteria into account when trying to address our racist past and current racial problems; where gays and lesbians are strangers to equal rights under the law; where Congress is prohibited from addressing serious economic issues that plague our country; where the protections for criminal defendants set forth in the 4th, 5th, 6th, and 8th Amendments to our Constitution barely exist; where corporations may spend as much money on elections as they want because money is

---

194. Larry D. Kramer, "Judicial Supremacy and the End of Judicial Restraint," 100 *California Law Review* 621, 634 (2012).

speech and corporations are people; where the President of the United States may fight terrorism without any constitutional check from the other two branches of government; where state and local governments are practically prohibited from regulating private property for the common good; where states may place term limits on members of Congress; and where the rights of majority religions constitute constitutional trump cards authorizing discrimination against minorities and traditionally disadvantaged groups.[195]

Segall later amplified his criticisms of Thomas,[196] noting among other things that

a former law clerk of Thomas' wrote that "it is a shame that in this day and age, a belief in applying the law as written—divorced from the preferences and predilections of the age—makes one a radical." But that description of Justice Thomas is a myth. Far from applying a text and history approach to constitutional cases, Justice Thomas consistently reaches conservative results regardless of whether those results can be justified by reference to the actual words of the Constitution or their original meaning. . . . In 1993, the federal government was working on a comprehensive computer database to use for background checks for gun purchases. As an interim measure, federal law required the Chief Law Enforcement Officers of the states to help implement the measure. The issue in the case was whether the federal government could use its enumerated powers, in this cased the power to regulate commerce among the states, to require state cooperation in a federal program. Justice Scalia's majority opinion conceded there was not one word in the United States Constitution suggesting there was such a limit on federal power. In addition, history was at best unclear on the issue. Nevertheless, the five conservatives including Justice Thomas concocted the rule that Congress could not commandeer state governments in this way.

Regardless of whether as a policy matter such a rule makes sense, it cannot be gleaned from text or history. Justice Thomas' short concur-

---

195. "Justice Thomas' America: Originalist or Republican?" July 2, 2016, in *Dorf on Law,* July 2, 2016, www.dorfonlaw.org/2016/07/justice-thomas-america-originalist-or.html.

196. Eric Segall, "Justice Thomas' 25 Years of Conservative Politics Not Law," in *Dorf on Law,* October 31, 2016, www.dorfonlaw.org/2016/10/justice-thomas-25th-year-of.html.

rence, while joining in full the majority opinion, also argued that Congress' power to regulate "commerce among the states" did not extend to the intrastate purchase and sale of firearms. Thomas was repeating an argument that he, and he alone, has made repeatedly: that Congress' power to regulate "commerce among the states" does not extend to local economic activities that "substantially affect" commerce among the states. Not only is this idea inconsistent with more than a century of Supreme Court precedent (a fact that Thomas brushes aside), but it would deprive the Congress of the ability to do what was the major impetus behind ratification of the United States Constitution—giving Congress the power to regulate the national economy. Justice Thomas' view is much more in tune with the Articles of Confederation, the first document to govern this country, than our current foundational law. In making his argument, Justice Thomas completely ignores a part of the Constitution that has been an integral component of Congress' powers since at least the early 19th century. Article I, Section 8 gives Congress the authority to pass all laws "necessary and proper" to carrying out its enumerated powers. The Supreme Court has consistently held that this provision allows Congress to use all reasonable or rational means to carrying out its lawful authority. Thus, Congress may use a draft to implement its duty to raise an army, and it may punish people who steal the mail so that it can run a Post Office even though neither a draft nor the ability to punish mail-theft is listed in the Constitution. Even Justice Scalia believed Congress has the power to regulate local practices that substantially affect commerce, as he argued when he voted to uphold the federal criminalization of the possession of marijuana that was never bought, sold or moved in commerce. Thus, just as Congress may prohibit the local noncommercial use of marijuana to assist in its overall War on Drugs, Congress may regulate the sale of guns as part of a more comprehensive plan to prevent dangerous people from owning firearms. Thomas' view to the contrary ignores the plain text of the Necessary and Proper Clause, and its original meaning. There are numerous other examples of Justice Thomas ignoring or distorting constitutional text and history.

He has interpreted the phrase "another state" in the Eleventh Amendment to mean the "same state" so that states may be immune from federal lawsuits in ways not supported by the text; he has signed on to a rigid "personal injury" test that all federal plaintiffs must satisfy before having "standing to sue" in federal court even though neither Article III nor its history suggest such a requirement; and he has strongly rejected all affirmative action programs based on a principle of "color-blindness" that is nowhere in the text of the Constitution and is inconsistent with the original meaning of the Equal Protection Clause. The list goes on and on.

At the nadir. When I wrote the present paragraph, on July 17, 2016, just days after Justice Ginsburg's outburst against Donald Trump,[197] the Supreme Court seemed to me to have fallen to a low point (apart from its being undermanned because Justice Scalia hadn't been replaced yet), though I blamed the President, the Senate, and tradition rather than the Justices themselves for the plunge.[198] One can't expect someone to refuse appointment to the Court just because he realizes he has only modest qualifications for the position, which in truth many do. Although members of the legal profession are reluctant to question the competence of Supreme Court Justices out loud, there is considerable such questioning sotto voce, focused primarily on Kennedy, Sotomayor, and Thomas, and secondarily on Roberts,[199] Alito, and Kagan. Even if they are competent, there is considerable doubt whether they were the best choices to be Supreme Court Justices.

The competence of Breyer and of Ginsburg is rarely questioned, though this may change with regard to Ginsburg in light of her comments (discussed further below) during the 2016 Presidential race, first about Donald Trump and then about the black professional football players who kneeled on the playing field while the national anthem was being sung: being guilty therefore, in Ginsburg's view, of *lèse-majesté*.

Considerations of purely legal competence, and of the ability to discipline's

197. See notes 203 to 207 below and accompanying text.

198. On its decline since the early 1960s, see Richard A. Posner, *Divergent Paths: The Academy and the Judiciary*, note 182 above, at 249–251.

199. And not only for his dissent in *Obergefell*, but also for several of his majority opinions, such as *McCullen v. Coakley*, 134 S. Ct. 2518, 2541 (2014), which as I noted earlier invalidated a Massachusetts law requiring abortion protesters to stay at least thirty-five feet away from the entrance to abortion clinics. Roberts's ground was that public streets and sidewalks "have hosted discussions about the issues of the day throughout history"—which may once have been true but certainly is no longer. (See my discussion of his opinion in *Divergent Paths*, note 182 above, at 170–173.) Yet with Roberts the issue may not be competence so much as guile, as evidenced in his testimony at his Senate confirmation hearing that Supreme Court Justices are just like umpires of sports games. He had to know that isn't true, and he probably knows that city sidewalks are no longer public-debate forums either, and he may even know that the remarks in his *Obergefell* dissent about the marital practices of Kalahari Bushmen, Han Chinese, Aztecs, and Carthaginians were—I'll be polite—conjectural. Of course American law has remarkable tolerance for untruthfulness by the members of the legal profession, so Roberts's job remains secure.

one's political and religious yearnings, to one side for the moment, the current Justices are notably deficient in trial and political experience, in educational diversity, and in knowledge of science and technology. They have too much staff for their light caseload—*too* light, which is by their own devising because they decide which and how many cases to hear. The opinions are too long and there are too many separate (concurring or dissenting) ones. Whether majority or separate, the opinions tend to be opaque and loaded with jargon. Despite its light caseload the Court allows too little time for oral argument, since each of the Justices (with the famously mysterious exception of Justice Thomas) apparently wants to use oral argument as an occasion for talking at length rather than for asking real questions. And Presidents (I am thinking of George W. Bush and Barack Obama) are if anything even more shameless than they used to be in basing appointments to the Court on anticipated political benefits. Can one imagine a President today who would appoint to the Court someone as politically remote from himself as Cardozo was from Herbert Hoover, the Republican President who appointed the Democratic Cardozo to the Supreme Court in 1932 to fill the vacancy created by Holmes's retirement? Or for that matter as politically remote as Eisenhower was from Brennan? Those days are gone.

Some months ago a lawyer whom I do not know sent me copies of two letters he'd written raising competence issues about the current Court (including Scalia, who was still living), and later a third letter focused entirely on Scalia. I do not feel at liberty to disclose his name, but he authorized me to quote freely from his letters. Building on the warnings of a British judge, Lord Bingham, against absolute judicial power,[200] he made a number of pointed observations about several of the Justices, and they deserve to be shared with my readers.

My correspondent happens to have been a Harvard Law School classmate of Justice Scalia,[201] and says that

> as a young man [Scalia] was an excellent friend but he was super-self-confident. [He was] one of the "true believers," . . . given to absolutes, no self-doubt, never asking the question, "might I be wrong?" . . . His "originalism" is his vehicle to get rid of *Roe v. Wade.* His "faint hearted" loyalty

200. See note 95 above and accompanying text.
201. I was not. Scalia graduated from Harvard in 1960, I two years later. When I entered law school in 1959, he was a senior and I had no contact with any seniors until I joined the law review in 1960 a couple of months after his graduation.

to originalism is so he can decline to employ it where it might dictate a different result as in honesty it should have in *Heller*. With his intimidating approach to decision making and his corrosive sarcasm, Scalia spurred partisanship in and outside the Court and the steep decline in the Court's reputation. Belligerent with his colleagues, dismissive of his critics, nostalgic for a world where outsiders knew their place and stayed there, Scalia represents a perfect model for everything President Obama should avoid in a successor.

Nobody now believes the Court is just an umpire calling ball and strikes, as Chief Justice Roberts testified before Congress. The Chief Justice's priority of partisanship over building consensus rebuts his testimony. The founding fathers would be aghast and Scalia's conduct belies his attempt to speak for them. . . . [Regarding *Heller,*] despite the almost 250 years of amazing changes, [Scalia] knew with certainty the intended meaning and appointed himself as their spokesperson. . . . [H]e chose whatever rule of construction, facts or non-facts fit his conclusion, a conclusion he ha[d] favored from the outset. . . . He was an advocate, not a judge. . . . In social matters [e.g., abortion and homosexual rights] he could not accept change. . . . In political matters he was pugilistic and taunting. . . . He was corrosively sarcastic to anyone who thought differently, particularly Justice O'Connor. In matters of religion, he was absolute, accepting no separation between church and state and in speeches [he was] a provocateur referring to the United States as a Christian country. . . . Scalia, purporting to speak for the founding fathers, would have it that the proposition that "all men are created equal . . . with certain inalienable rights . . ." in the Declaration of Independence includes not just "men" but "corporations"!

My correspondent also targeted Justice Thomas, who he said "appears to be a rogue justice. Rehnquist and later Roberts recognized that Thomas's views were so extreme that they could not assign controversial opinions to him and expect a majority of his colleagues to agree. . . . Whatever he concludes about the Constitution, he believes should be law. Corporations have freedom of speech for unlimited political contributions but students have no free speech. . . . 'Absolute power is kinda neat.'"[202]

202. Variously attributed to John Lehman or Donald Regan, officials in the Reagan Administration. In refined versions, "kind of neat" is substituted for "kinda neat," but the substitution weakens the remark.

The writer was caustic about Chief Justice Roberts as well, whom he accused of having a political agenda that "he has pursued . . . until in the case of Obamacare he began to appreciate what he was or might be doing to the court's credibility with the public. I had always believed that one of the particular responsibilities of the Chief Justice was to try to build consensus and, if possible, avoid 5 to 4 decisions. That's not for Roberts." Surprisingly my correspondent is equally caustic about Justice Kennedy, of whom he said that "more than any other justice, he had the confidence or arrogance, to trump the other branches of government. . . . [J]udicial modesty . . . was never for Anthony Kennedy. His opinions are declarations of generalities, almost declamations. He revels in them. . . . Kennedy seeks to support his opinions by factual judgments for which there is no evidence in the record before the Court."

That there should be quality issues regarding the Supreme Court may seem surprising, since it would be easy enough for a President and his advisors to find first-class prospective Justices among lawyers, law professors, and lower-court judges who were unusually intelligent, well trained, experienced, hard-working, familiar with the workings of government, ethical, fair-minded, broad-gauged, civil, and willing (not all successful lawyers—not even all lower-court judges—would accept appointment to the Supreme Court). That wouldn't be asking a great deal, considering that there are more than a million American lawyers to choose from—were it not for the politics of the appointment process, which I stressed earlier and in light of which one can't expect the Justices to be the nine best of the million plus, but perhaps they could be chosen from among the hundred best or, more realistically, the thousand or ten thousand best. Maybe some of the current incumbents come from one of those lofty strata; maybe not. I have my doubts but only time will tell.

I am however struck by the number of superb *potential* appointments to the Supreme Court from among lower-court judges and academics (that is, leaving out practicing lawyers and lawyer-politicians) that were never made, though the persons passed over were better qualified to be Supreme Court Justices than those appointed to the Court instead. I will name just a few (omitting judges of my court): in the nineteenth century Francis Lieber and James Bradley Thayer; in the twentieth Learned Hand, Henry Friendly, Roger Traynor, John Minor Wisdom, Robert Bork, Jay Wilkinson, Laurence Silberman, Harry Edwards, Michael Boudin, Pierre Leval, Alexander Bickel, Henry Hart, Hans Linde, Charles Fried, Benjamin Kaplan; in the twenty-first century Thomas Ambro, Robert Katzmann, Alex Kozinski, Goodwin Liu, Kathleen Sullivan,

Jeffrey Sutton. This is a *very* partial list, in part because it omits district court judges. In the largest district court (the Northern District of Illinois, mainly Chicago) in my circuit, a number of the judges would qualify for appointment to the Supreme Court, including Gary Feinerman, Virginia Kendall, Matthew Kennelly, Amy St. Eve, and Andrea Wood—and again that's just a partial list. I should add that each of the three "maverick" district judges whom I mentioned in the Introduction—Kane, Rakoff, and Weinstein—should also have been considered for the Supreme Court.

The Court and the media: The Justices' theatrical bent and inconsistent refusal to allow the televising of Supreme Court arguments. Supreme Court Justices used to be, with rare exceptions, wallflowers. Oral arguments were not recorded or televised (they're still not televised), and it was rare for a Justice to engage in public activities. No longer. And sad to say the current Justices' public activities are not infrequently deficient in dignity. *The Wall Street Journal* posted a picture on its front page several years ago of Justice Ginsburg wearing a Civil War uniform because she was presiding at a posthumous court martial of George Custer for having blown the Battle of the Little Big Horn (posthumous because he had, of course, been killed in the battle). Pretty ridiculous. On the other hand I have no criticism of Justice Sotomayor's appearance on *Sesame Street* adjudicating a dispute between two stuffed animals. That sounds ridiculous but she was doing this for children and there was no pretense that she was engaged in a serious intellectual activity.

But speaking of Justice Ginsburg I was surprised at her public attack, made in an interview during the 2016 Presidential campaign by a *New York Times* reporter (and repeated in two other interviews in the same week), on Donald Trump that culminated in her pronouncing him a "faker."[203] I was also surprised by her obvious relish, reported in the same article, at the Supreme Court's upholding the Texas affirmative-action college-admission system and invalidating the Texas anti-abortion law, and by her urging the Senate to confirm Chief Judge Merrick Garland as Scalia's replacement on the Court—thus marking him, in the eyes of Republicans, as a liberal stealth candidate rather than the moderate that President Obama had declared him to be. Hillary Clin-

---

203. See Adam Liptak, "Ginsburg Has a Lot to Say About Trump," *New York Times,* July 11, 2016, p. A1; Aaron Blake, "In Bashing Donald Trump, Some Say Ruth Bader Ginsburg Just Crossed a Very Important Line," *Washington Post,* July 11, 2016, www.washingtonpost.com/news/the-fix/wp/2016/07/11/in-bashing-donald-trump-some-say-ruth-bader-ginsburg-just-crossed-a-very-important-line/.

ton declined to commit herself to nominating Garland should she be elected President; the election of Trump mooted the issue.

As when impersonating a military judge at Custer's imaginary court martial, Justice Ginsburg didn't sound much like a judge in trashing Trump, though of course she had a lot of company. I suppose I shouldn't complain about a judge's being as candid as she, since I keep complaining about the absence of judicial candor. But it should be possible to be at once reasonably candid and fully judicial, and she was the former but not the latter in the interviews. Her antics exacted a remarkable criticism from the liberal *New York Times,* which in an editorial captioned "Mr. Trump Is Right about Justice Ruth Bader Ginsburg" accused her of "flinging herself into the mosh pit."[204] The day after the editorial appeared she climbed out of the pit, apologizing for trashing Trump, saying that "on reflection, my recent remarks in response to press inquiries were ill-advised and I regret making them. Judges should avoid commenting on a candidate for public office. In the future I will be more circumspect."[205] Yet in an interview she gave three months later she called the refusal of two black professional football players (one being the well-known quarterback Colin Kaepernick) to stand during the playing of the national anthem (instead they kneeled, in protest against police brutality and racial injustice) "dumb and disrespectful"—only to apologize the next day.[206] Her eruption—which was especially strange because kneeling is normally a sign of deference rather than of defiance—raised questions whether at age eighty-three she might have overstayed her welcome.

I doubt by the way that her apologizing for the attack on Trump was a wise tactic; it vindicated Trump and was bound to disappoint Ginsburg's lefty fans. And although it's understood that federal judges are not to intervene in political campaigns, as Ginsburg did when she denounced Trump publicly, I don't think it should be an ironclad rule. I hark back to a remark I made earlier in

204. "Donald Trump Is Right About Justice Ruth Bader Ginsburg," *New York Times,* Editorial, July 13, 2016, p. A18. But what on earth is a mosh pit? Merriam-Webster defines it as "an area in front of a stage where very physical and rough dancing takes place at a rock concert." I imagine that a mosh pit full of Supreme Court Justices would draw quite a crowd.

205. She said her "recent remarks [criticizing Trump] in response to press inquiries were ill-advised. . . ." "Ginsburg Exresses 'Regret' Over Trump Comments," *TPM Lifewire,* July 14, 2016. The reference to press inquiries may have been intended to suggest that the press had been complicit in her plunge into the mosh pit.

206. Adam Liptak, "Ginsburg Says She Regrets Chastising Quarterback," *New York Times,* October 15, 2016, p. A15. I have trouble understanding why kneeling rather than standing while the Star Spangled Banner is being played at a sports event should be regarded as either dumb or disrespectful, or why a Supreme Court Justice, or indeed anyone else, should think that if kneeling is somehow a breach of etiquette, the fact must be remarked on by someone who is not a part of the sports scene.

this chapter, quoting from a previous book of mine: "in national emergencies
. . . law bends to necessity." If Ginsburg thought (as her initial comments made
one think she did) that electing Trump President would be a national disaster
because he was among other things a "faker," she should have stuck to her guns,
not retracted. By retracting she discredited her criticisms of him.

I can imagine some observers of the Ginsburg-Trump imbroglio, followed
by the Ginsburg-football-player imbroglio, wondering whether it mightn't indeed be a good idea, as I suggested earlier, to impose a mandatory retirement
age on federal judges including Supreme Court Justices—a requirement that
Congress might as I also suggested earlier be able to impose, without need for a
constitutional amendment authorizing it, were the Court willing to interpret
"during good Behaviour" in Article III, section 1, of the Constitution broadly.[207]
And why not?

At the risk of being thought a spoilsport I admit to disapproving not only
what seem to me the inappropriate out-of-Court public statements of Kagan
and Ginsburg (inappropriate because of their content, not because I think that
judges should never say anything outside the courtroom), but also mock trials,
presided over by real judges, of historical or fictitious characters and controversies, though I admit to having been a judge in several such trials, albeit none
of the absurd ones (rather, the trials of Antigone, Orestes, and Socrates—the
first two being dramas written by Sophocles and Euripides, respectively, the
last a real trial of a real person, ending in a death sentence). Several of the current Supreme Court Justices have presided at trials of whether Shakespeare was
the actual author of the Shakespearean plays, or instead the Earl of Oxford.
That's crank stuff, like belief in flying saucers or a flat Earth. Anyway the current Supreme Court Justices have no competence to opine on what is an issue

207. Law professor Stephen L. Wasby has been quoted as saying that

one of the potential effects of [Ginsburg's] hostile remarks about Trump will be to provide him with
more ammunition (as if he doesn't manufacture enough all by himself). To the extent that would improve his election chances, it is exactly what she does NOT want. So, assuming some modicum of rational self-interest, she did something that runs counter to her long-run interests in liberal positions
on the Court. And she has hurt the Court institutionally as well. . . . I suggest that this outburst and
its effects should be tied to her earlier refusal to leave the Court a couple of terms ago, while Obama
might still have had a chance to replace her. Doing so would have been more likely to guarantee that
her views would have persisted for quite some time. Further, her not having done so seems to cut
against her interests (if not SELF-interest) in seeing her views prevail. What has happened here? Has
[Ginsburg] notoriously become like Justice Rehnquist in thinking the world (or at least the Court)
depends on them so they stay on too long?

Wasby's insightful criticism of Ginsburg is one of the relatively rare examples of a law professor publicly criticizing a Supreme Court Justice.

for Renaissance historians and literary scholars rather than for judges who lack a literary background. Ginsburg majored in government in college; Breyer, the most cultured member of the Court, in philosophy.

A Justice has presided at trials of Hamlet for murdering Polonius, trials in which Hamlet's defense is insanity. But if you know the play, you know that Hamlet kills Polonius thinking that Polonius is Claudius (Hamlet's uncle, and the king), whom he wants to kill because he suspects Claudius of having killed Hamlet's father, the rightful king, and committed adultery with Hamlet's mother, Hamlet's father's widow and now Claudius's wife—and all his suspicions are correct. Hamlet is not "insane" in killing Polonius; it's a case of mistaken identity. Whatever mental problems Hamlet displays at other times in the play do not figure in that killing.

A favorite of Supreme Court Justices and other judges is conducting a trial to determine whether the wicked and deformed Duke of Gloucester (the future King Richard III) was really responsible for the murder of the little princes (one, the legitimate heir apparent, Edward V, the other his younger brother the Duke of York) in the Tower of London. Edward IV having died, his heir was due to be the next king, but Gloucester intercepted the little princes en route to London, imprisoned them in the Tower of London, and took the kingship himself as Richard III. There is a good deal of historical controversy over just how evil and deformed Richard III was. But recently Richard's skeleton was found in a construction excavation and sure enough it was deformed by scoliosis, though maybe not so badly deformed as depicted by Shakespeare in *Richard III* because the controversy over Richard was a phase of Tudor / Plantagenet rivalry and Elizabeth I was a Tudor and Shakespeare's queen and Richard had been a Plantagenet. So there is a lively historical controversy. But our Supreme Court Justices are incapable of opining responsibly on it. It doesn't create a good impression when by virtue of being prominent in one field a person starts offering irresponsible opinions in another. But it is a common temptation. Success in any field can breed an illusion of omnicompetence.

The biggest objection to the mock trials—an objection forcefully made by Professor Lawrence Douglas of Amherst College[208]—is that they reflect a misunderstanding of what a trial is. It's an odd mistake for a judge to make. Trials are not designed for determining historical truth. Many aspects of the trial

---

208. See Lawrence Douglas, "The Memory of Judgment: The Law, the Holocaust, and Denial," 7 *History and Memory* 100, 110 (1995); also my book *Public Intellectuals: a Study of Decline* 371 (paperback ed. 2003), quoting Douglas.

process subordinate the truth-seeking function of the trial to other social values, such as privacy. Some highly probative evidence is excluded merely because it was obtained illegally or because its probative value is deemed outweighed by the likely prejudicial effect of the evidence on jurors. And because of statutes of limitations and the sheer difficulty of reconstructing the past, few trials deal with events that occurred long ago. Justices who use trials to determine historical truth are perpetuating a misconception of the nature and capabilities of the trial process. But they are encouraged to do this by the backward-looking orientation that is so settled yet so harmful a characteristic of our legal system, as well as by the inflated self-regard bred by prominence. This criticism is inapplicable to performances of fictitious trials, such as those of Antigone and Orestes, where the only relevant facts (made-up facts) are those in the texts of the trial, or real trials of which there is a record, such as the trial of Socrates, although the record of that trial is incomplete.

But what of the Justices' refusal to allow the televising of its hearings? The Court has remained adamantly opposed in the face of strong public support for such televising.[209] In a brilliant article, law professor Sonja R. West explains that "three primary reasons [for the opposition] emerge. First, the Justices express concern that the lawyers, and even the Justices themselves, will begin grandstanding or showboating. Second, they fear the media would use the video to show out-of-context sound bites. Finally, they worry about the public's ability to comprehend the process they are observing."[210] After explaining the advantages to the public of televised Supreme Court hearings (she capsulizes them as "vividness" and "accessibility," and relatedly as enhancing transparency and accountability of government and helping to educate people about government), she takes up the objections, beginning with "grandstanding" by the lawyers in Supreme Court arguments and possibly by the Justices themselves. She points out that, as mentioned earlier in this book, the Ninth Circuit (now joined by the Second and Third Circuits) allows the televising of its oral arguments—in fact has allowed it for twenty years—with no indication that

209. See Coalition for Court Transparency, "New CCT Poll Finds Live Video, Live Audio, Online Disclosures at Supreme Court All Favored by Wide Majority of Americans," September 3, 2014, www.openscotus .com/?m=201409. There were other interesting results of CCT's poll: only 35 percent of those surveyed gave the Justices a positive approval rating, versus 59 percent who gave them a negative rating; 86 percent favored requiring Supreme Court Justices to abide by the Judicial Code of Conduct (from which they currently are exempt); and 61 percent said that lifetime tenure for Justices should be abolished in favor of fixed terms of office. And finally and most relevantly to my present discussion, 71 percent supported "cameras in the Supreme Court," presumably referring to televising the Court's proceedings.

210. "The Monster in the Courtroom," 2012 Brigham Young University Law Review 1953, 1972 (2012).

it's resulted in any grandstanding; almost all the state appellate courts allow televising as well, again without engendering grandstanding. Because of the broad interest in and coverage of U.S. Supreme Court hearings, the risk of lawyer grandstanding exists irrespective of television, yet has not materialized. She quotes one frequent advocate before the Supreme Court as saying that "as someone who is getting ready to argue his twenty-fifth case I can say that our only concern is persuading the Justices, not annoying them and potentially losing votes by grandstanding."[211] There is grandstanding in oral arguments in the Supreme Court, all right, but it is by the Justices. Their volubility has become remarkable.[212]

As for the risk that an ignorant television audience will take thirty-second sound bites out of context, Professor West points to studies of Supreme Court confirmation hearings and of Justices' frequent television appearances, and notes that the thirty-second sound-bite problem has not arisen; that is, Justices have not been embarrassed by statements made by them on television and then taken out of context by journalists or others.

The sound-bite argument against televising the Court's hearings merges into the third concern with televising them, namely the claim "that the television audience will not understand what is happening in the proceedings they are viewing and why it is happening. The Justices fear the public will be confused or fail to grasp why the Justices ask certain questions or focus on one issue over another. They fear that, without being able to see the entire decision-making process, members of the public will reach false conclusions about how the Supreme Court makes its decisions."[213] Again, as Professor West explains, experience with confirmation hearings, the Justices' appearances on televised shows, and the many courts that allow their proceedings to be televised without any adverse consequences show that the Justices' fears are groundless. In fact what they fear is "simply the unknown. . . . The public is right. It is time for the Justices to let the monster out of its box and see that it was never really a monster at all."[214]

The abiding puzzle is why the Court doesn't *experiment* with televising its hearings. Invite C-SPAN to cover a week's hearings and then decide whether to allow its hearings to be covered as a regular matter. The Court's refusal even to

---

211. Id. at 1977.
212. See Epstein et al., note 44 above.
213. "The Monster in the Courtroom," note 210 above, at 1982–1983.
214. Id. at 1987–1988.

experiment casts gave doubts on its competence, and specifically on the managerial ability of the Chief Justice.

The Court obstructs access to its work by means other than forbidding the televising of its hearings. Audios of the Court's arguments, for example, are released weekly on the Court's website, while audios of the bench statements (the reading of opinions announcing the decisions in the Court's cases, together with a reading of any dissenting and concurring opinions) are not made available until the beginning of the following term and only at the National Archives. And while transcripts of oral arguments are released daily on the Court's website, there are no official transcripts of bench statements. The result, as explained by Professor West, is that "through policies that obstruct access by the general public and exploit real-world limitations on the press and practitioners, the justices have crafted a grey area in which they can be 'public,' yet only to select audiences. The effect is that few outside the courtroom ever learn about these moments, even though they technically occurred in public. By operating in this semi-public sphere, the justices have robbed the public of important information about the workings of its Court."[215]

And finally regarding the televising of judicial proceedings I note a questionable intervention of the Court in the televising of such proceedings in the lower federal courts. In January 2010 a trial was about to begin in a federal district court in California to determine the constitutionality of a recently enacted California law forbidding same-sex marriage in the state. The highly regarded district judge presiding in the case, Vaughn Walker (incidentally an outstanding student of mine the year—1968–1969—that I taught at Stanford Law School—my first year teaching), made arrangements to have the trial televised and shown at courthouses in San Francisco, Pasadena, Seattle, Portland, and Brooklyn and also on YouTube. Defendant intervenors in the case asked the U.S. Supreme Court to bar the telecasting of the trial, and the Court in a 5 to 4 per curiam opinion[216] barred the telecasting of the trial to (just) the federal courthouses, primarily on the authority of 28 U.S.C. § 2071(b), which provides so far as relevant to Walker's case that "any rule prescribed by a court, other than the Supreme Court, under subsection (a) [which authorizes all federal courts from time to time to prescribe rules for the conduct of their business] shall be prescribed only after giving appropriate public notice and an opportu-

---

215. Sonja R. West, "The Supreme Court's Limited Public Forum," 73 *Washington and Lee Law Review Online* 572 (2017). My quotation is from the abstract.

216. *Hollingsworth v. Perry,* 558 U.S. 183 (2010).

nity for comment." The majority held that Judge Walker had failed to comply with these requirements. But as Justice Breyer, the author of the dissenting opinion, pointed out, the judge's plans had been disseminated far and wide, providing not only comprehensive public notice but abundant opportunity for comment. The majority was wrong.

The skittishness displayed by the Supreme Court Justices with regard to the televising of their oral arguments has counterparts in the lower federal courts, since only three of the thirteen courts of appeals allow such televising. Recently in another of the circuit courts (mine, as a matter of fact) a meeting of the judges was held to discuss the issue. In preparation for the meeting Professor West's important article was circulated to all the judges. At the beginning of the meeting one of the judges (me), who had read the article, asked how many of the other judges had read it. Answer: none. I summarized the article briefly, eliciting no response. A couple of the judges then voiced their extreme concern for their safety if the court's oral arguments were televised, and a third judge said the safety issue should be taken up with the U.S. Marshals—and so it was agreed, mistakenly because the Marshals would have a strong incentive to advise the court not to allow televising, because of the security risk. For though the risk appears to be negligible, it can't be confidently said to be zero, and the Marshals would be protecting themselves against a possible materializing of the risk by advising against televising, since they would look bad if there were a security problem but not if the court decided not to allow televising of its oral arguments. A committee of judges was appointed by the chief judge to look into the question whether to allow televising of oral arguments; the committee has not yet, at the time of this writing, made a recommendation to the full court.

The Supreme Court on Slate. Earlier I mentioned professorial commentary on the Supreme Court, and I need to say a bit more about it. Every year the online magazine *Slate* sponsors an exchange among law professors and journalists, and one judge—me—in the closing days of the Supreme Court's term, which come in the last week of June. One of the most active professorial participants is Professor Akhil Amar of Yale Law School, whom I mentioned briefly in Chapter 1—a well-known professor of constitutional law. He and I had an exchange in the 2016 end-of-term roundup,[217] which I reproduce here (some of

217. "Supreme Court Breakfast Table," *Slate*, June 24, 2016, www.slate.com/articles/news_and_politics /the_breakfast_table/features/2016/supreme_court_breakfast_table_for_june_2016/the_lack_of_transparency _on_court_boggles_the_mind.html.

our comments were rather long; hence the numerous ellipses in my quotations) in part to contrast academic with judicial outlooks on the Court:

> *Amar.* You see the Court's inability to reach a decisive majority on DAPA [the reference is to the 4–4 vote that upheld a lower court's rejection of President Obama's program of Deferred Action for Parents of Americans and Lawful Permanent Residents to reduce deportation of illegal immigrants] as reflecting the same sort of gridlock and dysfunction that plagues Congress. . . . But deadlock / gridlock is not the worst thing in the world. Yes, it's worse than moving forward, but it's better than moving backward. . . . But I do wonder about transparency. . . . If the Court formally disposes of a case after cert, and full briefing, and full oral argument, why doesn't it at the very least tell us how each justice voted? . . . Why, indeed, aren't 4–4 cases situations where it is especially important to know where each justice stands? In any 9–0, 8–1, 7–2, or 6–3 disposition, the justices' individual votes are nowadays always reported, even though no individual justice was decisive: Had any one justice switched sides, the outcome would have been the same. Yet each justice goes on record, and rightly so. In a 5–4 case, only 5 of the justices' votes (those in the majority) are decisive; had any one of the 4 dissenters switched, the case would still have come out the same. Yet in 5–4 cases, each justice's vote is duly recorded and properly made public. But no official report of votes occurs in 4–4 cases, *even though in these cases, each and every vote is indeed decisive.* If any of the affirming four justices had switched, the case would have come out the other way—a reversal—and if any one of the reversing four justices had switched, the affirmance would have been a national precedent binding on all lower courts. So, to repeat, only in tie-vote situations is each and every justice's vote truly decisive, yet it is in these cases, uniquely, that the Court refuses to officially report each and every justice's vote. . . .
>
> . . . Aren't we, the people, entitled to know who stands . . . where on the great issues of the day? And while we are at it, . . . why shouldn't we have full-blown opinions, even in 4–4 situations? True, the opinions would not be of national precedential significance, because no opinion, by hypothesis, would have commanded a Court majority. But justices write opinions all the time that are not national precedents—dissents, concurrences, dissents from denials of cert, even dissents from grants of cert in some situations. And speaking of cert—why doesn't the Court announce

who voted for and who voted against cert in every case in which cert is in fact granted? Perhaps the Court shouldn't announce these individual cert votes before oral argument, lest advocates draw undue inferences. . . . But on the day the Court announces its disposition on the merits . . . why shouldn't it tell us not just who voted which way in the end, but also who voted which way in the beginning (that is, the cert stage)?

Posner. The Supreme Court is unlikely to accept advice from law professors on administrative issues, such as whether to issue opinions in tie cases and whether to identify the Justices voting for or against cert. The Court is bound to think that law professors are in no position to advise on such issues. I also think there's a growing gap between judges (including the Supreme Court Justices) and the academy, which judges tend to think is increasingly distant from the actual practice of law, staffed as it increasingly is with refugees from other disciplines—the graduate students in classics and history and anthropology and so on who discovering there are very few well-paying positions in such fields nowadays decide to go to law school and afterwards have no time to practice law before getting a law-teaching job.

The law schools should be hiring a higher percentage of lawyers with significant practical experience. Think of Benjamin Kaplan of the Harvard Law School, who went into law teaching after 14 years in practice and became an immensely distinguished law professor and later was appointed to the Massachusetts Supreme Judicial Court. There used to be many like that; there are many fewer now, especially at the leading law schools.

Amar. Some might think that judges are constitutional experts, but in fact they are not. At times, they are merely opinionated lawyers with powerful political connections. At best, they are upright and hardworking generalists who must be ready in short order to rule on any legal issues that might come their way—tort law, property law, commercial law, civil-procedure law, employment law, antitrust law, and so on. . . . Even the Supreme Court, which hears a higher percentage of constitutional law cases than do other courts, consists of generalist lawyers. Despite the justices' familiarity with Supreme Court case law, especially cases in which they themselves participated in years past, few of the justices have spent decades or even years intensely studying the Constitution itself, or the history of its enactment, amendment, and implementation across the centuries. Thus, America's legal and political system is today marred, and for much of our history has been marred, by a wide gap in truly useful constitutional knowledge and expertise.

Truth be told, only a few modern constitutional law scholars [you and who else, Akhil?] aim to bridge this gap. Most professors who teach constitutional law focus on recent Supreme Court case law, not first principles of constitutional text, history, and structure. Many gifted scholars also dream of ultimate appointment to the bench, and these dreams can seduce. Ours is a partisan world, and many a scholar picks a side, hoping that one day the phone will ring when the scholar's preferred party is in power. In the meantime, some of these politically ambitious or merely ideological scholars crank out work that is less objective than one might wish for—just objective (or seemingly objective) enough to neutralize credulous journalists and persuade or provide cover for inexpert judges and politicos who lean in the same ideological direction.

Posner. . . . What is the evidence that Supreme Court Justices are especially hardworking? They have a light caseload and an excessively long summer vacation. And what is meant by calling them "upright"? Merely that they are law-abiding (unlike such predecessors as William O. Douglas and Abe Fortas)? More important, I see no value to a judge of devoting decades . . . to studying the text of the Constitution, the history of its enactment, amendments, and implementation. For eighteenth-century Americans, however smart (several of the Constitution's framers were brilliant), could not foresee the culture, technology, etc., of the 21st century. Which means that much in the original Constitution, the Bill of Rights, and the post Civil War amendments (including the 14th), simply does not speak to today. And so the Supreme Court perforce treats the Constitution as authorizing the Court to create, in the open areas left by the constitutional text, a common law of constitutional law, based on current concerns rather than eighteenth-century or nineteenth-century (or for that matter twentieth-century) insights and beliefs. In short, let not the dead bury the living.

Amar. . . . I do think that we can learn a great deal from constitutional history. It is wise—wiser than even our smartest judges acting on their own instincts, untutored by history. . . . Constitutionalists must attend . . . to all three branches of government, and not just the judiciary, which is the obsessive focus of so many modern constitutional scholars. The constitutional issues of our era, like the constitutional issues of every era, have pulsed through every vital organ of the American body politic. And like blood itself, the Constitution sustains our republic. This compact intergenerational document does not merely limit; it empowers and illuminates. For those skilled in the arts of unlocking its meaning, this document distills and preserves the wisdom of a great people over many centuries. Read right, it guides us and shapes us, giving a raucous and variegated society a common language, a handy metric, a shared set of institutions, a joint history, a collective identity, a national narrative, a genuinely unifying yet pluralist ideology. It might be asked why the current generation of Americans should ever resolve any genuinely difficult and important modern issue by paying close attention to words penned and deeds done long ago by now-dead men. This is hardly a new question. It might also have been asked in 1861. . . . But in general, neither side in the great secession debate claimed that, because all the leading framers were long dead, the Constitution's text and enactment history were simply irrelevant. Instead, both blue and gray invoked the Founding text and Founding deeds. . . . Despite—or perhaps because of—their age, the Constitution's text and traditions provide important sources and resources for modern constitutional conversation and contestation. . . . Also, many of the difficult issues faced by modern constitutional decision-makers are in fact surprisingly similar to those faced by their predecessors, because today's constitutional institutions lineally descend from the Founders' institutions. Presidents still sign and veto bills, the Senate still remains the judge of its own elections, the House continues to enjoy the power of impeachment, and so on. Modern interpreters should attend to various elements of the Constitution's original intent not because these old unwritten understandings always and everywhere tightly bind us today, but rather because we can learn from our constitutional predecessors. The evils that they lived through—that they experienced firsthand at epic moments in American history such as the Revolution and the Civil War—can help us understand why they put certain things in the text, to spare us from having to suffer as they suffered. Various rights emerged from real wrongs, wrongs we ignore at our peril. Simply put, the written Constitution is often wise—typically, wiser than judges acting on [Amar means under] their own steam—because the document distills the democratic input of many minds over many generations. More ordinary people voted on the Constitution in 1787–88 than had ever voted on anything else in world history. In saying yes to the Constitution that year, everyday people up and down the continent wisely insisted that a Bill of Rights be added—a Bill in which the phrase "the people" appears no fewer than five times. Later generations of ordinary Americans mobilized to enshrine in this terse text an end to slavery, a sweeping guarantee of equal birthright citizenship, an emphatic commitment to protecting civil rights against all levels of government, and radical expansions of the rights of political participation—to blacks, to women, to the poor, to the young, and more. . . . We, the people of the twenty-first century ignore the collected and collective wisdom of this old and intergenerational text at our peril.

Posner. This is *corny,* Akhil. Sure, Presidents still sign and veto bills, the Senate still remains the judge of its own elections, the House continues to enjoy the power of impeachment, and so on, but that has nothing to do with the constitutional issues that arise in cases and are resolved by judges. And I don't understand your reference to 1861. There was going to be a civil war regardless of what the Constitution said. And consider the Fourth Amendment. The Supreme Court now says that the amendment requires a warrant to search a person's home or arrest him in his home. There's no basis for that in the amendment; its only mentions of warrants are limits on warrants. The amendment does not require a warrant in *any* situation. This is one of countless examples vindicating David Strauss's thesis. You mention birthright citizenship. The purpose was to give black people, released from slavery, citizenship, because they hadn't been citizens when they were slaves. That has nothing to do with tourist-baby citizenship—foreigners getting citizenship for their children so that the children can if necessary relocate to the U.S. from wherever they live. The Supreme Court should refuse to hold tourist-baby citizenship guaranteed by the Constitution. The Constitution, except in allocating powers among the three branches of government in some other provisions, is *awfully* loose, and is so treated by the courts—as in *Bolling v. Sharp.*

In another part of our exchange, Amar intimated that the citations to his work in Supreme Court opinions are marks of influence on the Court:

Although my academic position was not intentionally designed for the purpose of judging the judges and *keeping them honest,* my job does have the right features. I too have life tenure, which enables me to take a long view about both the Constitution and the court (as well as other organs of government). I have had years of training in constitutional law, and I know how the judiciary works. Like the justices, I have been afforded considerable leeway to define my own agenda. . . . I can credibly adopt a neutral and disinterested stance vis-à-vis competing branches, acting as an umpire of sorts. Because I do not practice law before the justices themselves—because I do not litigate—I do not need to flatter the members of the court in order to put food on my table or win points in a status hierarchy. Instead, I can perform a *useful social function* by both praising and criticizing the justices as I see fit, a sincere and relatively disinterested, albeit fallible, professional observer—a true friend of the court.[218]

Amar writes with eloquence and even passion, as well as with considerable self-importance, but I doubt that the Court pays any more attention to him than it does to me (that is, no attention), though he's not alone among law professors in taking pride in being cited by the Court (Fallon is another[219]). Granted that citation usually signifies approval of the cited work (though sometimes of course the citing opinion is critical), why should a law professor value approval by a Supreme Court Justice (more likely by a law clerk who found the citation and plugged it into the opinion)? Put to one side the possible effect on a Justice's hiring of the professor's protégés as law clerks, a matter of concern only to faculty at the handful of elite law schools. What is mainly involved is the hierarchical structure of the legal profession. Almost all American judiciaries have three clearly demarcated tiers: trial courts, intermediate appellate courts, and a supreme court; and there is a further hierarchy among the fifty-one supreme courts in the United States that situates the U.S. Supreme Court far above the rest. Law professors do not constitute a tier but are conscious of the hierarchy and know that if they did constitute a tier it would be far below the Court. They crave appreciation by their hierarchical superiors if only as displayed in the Supreme Court's occasional citations to their books or articles. At least in cases in which the Court is divided they can hope that one side of the split or the other (rarely both) will cite a book or article of theirs. But they will go out of their way to display respect for *all* the Justices, to demonstrate their recognition of and respect for judicial hierarchy.

218. Akhil Amar, "Who Judges the Judges," in "How to Keep Supreme Court Justices Accountable," *The Breakfast Table, Slate,* June 25, 2016, www.slate.com/articles/news_and_politics/the_breakfast_table/features/2016/supreme_court_breakfast_table_for_june_2016/how_to_keep_supreme_court_justices_accountable.html (emphases added).

219. See note 17 in Chapter 1.

They will also display respect for all the judges before whom they or their students or alumni may appear, in recognition and acceptance of a hierarchy that places judges above lawyers and law professors. Professors will tend to mute their criticism of individual judges out of fear of retaliation against their schools or the schools' students. They may fear that a judge who is annoyed at them may refuse to speak at the school, judge a moot court, or hire law clerks from the school.

Fear of retaliation to one side, respecting or even flattering a judge comes readily to lawyers, including academic lawyers, and does so ultimately because of the adversary system. Lawyers are not expected to be candid, let alone impartial. They are hired guns, expert therefore at displaying enthusiasm for and profound commitment to their clients, whom they may secretly despise. Conscious of the power that judges wield, they kowtow to them without hesitation or even reluctance.

Presidential pushback. An issue I've touched on already but only very briefly is the neglected issue of the propriety of Presidential pushback against Supreme Court decisions. Famously, Abraham Lincoln at the outset of the Civil War defied a writ of habeas corpus issued by the Chief Justice, Roger Taney, ordering the release from federal confinement of a rebel sympathizer. Lincoln got away with his defiance, with no damage to his reputation as one of the two greatest U.S. Presidents in history (George Washington being the other). A similar opportunity was presented to President Obama by the Supreme Court's end-of-term decision in *United States v. Texas* (June 23, 2016) upholding by a 4 to 4 vote a decision by the federal court of appeals in Texas invalidating the President's plan (DAPA—"Deferred Action for Parents of Americans") to provide a kind of amnesty to illegal immigrants who have been in the United States for at least five years, have children who were born here (and therefore are U.S. citizens under the conventional though questionable interpretation of the "birthright-citizenship" clause of the Fourteenth Amendment), and have committed no crimes. It's believed that about five million illegal immigrants would have been eligible for relief under the plan. In invalidating it by affirming the court of appeals, the Supreme Court issued an opinion that states in its entirety, "The judgment is affirmed by an equally divided Court." There were no opinions by individual Justices.

There are oddities associated with the plan that the Court invalidated—one being that Obama had been responsible for more deportations than any previous President, another being the conditioning of his amnesty on an immigrant's having been in this country for at least five years and having a child born here. I don't want to see law-abiding immigrants deported but I have difficulty understanding the criticisms of the judicial invalidation of the plan, as it seems easier for the President to have nullified the invalidation than it was for Lincoln to nullify Taney's grant of habeas corpus. All the President had to do was remind the head of the Department of Homeland Security that the Department does not have the personnel or other resources needed for rounding up millions of harmless immigrants and that especially given the fears of terrorist infiltration of the United States the Department must focus its attention on immigrants who are likely to undermine security or engage in serious criminal activity, and ignore the other illegals even if they don't have U.S. citizen children and haven't lived in the United States for five or more years. Consistent with this policy the Department could have been directed to strengthen its border protection so as to reduce the influx of new illegal immigrants; this could accomplish much that a deportation frenzy would, at less cost to the government or to the economy, which relies heavily on the millions of illegal immigrants employed to do lawful work.

But I want to come back to Lincoln's defiance of Taney, in light of a recent note from my friend Peter Heidenberger, a German lawyer who immigrated to the United States in 1950. He reminded me in his note that when on January 30, 1933, Vice Chancellor Franz Von Papen (who was acquitted at Nuremberg) recommended to German President Paul von Hindenburg that he appoint Hitler Chancellor of Germany, the Nazi Party did not have a majority in the Reichstag (the German parliament) although it was the largest party. Hindenburg accepted Von Papen's proposal and, upon being appointed Chancellor, Hitler took immediate steps to achieve total power: he abolished all German parties except the Nazi Party, and he had the now one-party parliament pass the Equalization Law (*Gleichschaltungs Gesetz*) that decreed legal uniformity for all the German states. Such usurpative actions by a U.S. President would, like Hitler's actions, be unconstitutional. But if in a period of crisis the President had powerful public support, and the military and the police did not attempt to thwart him, might he not get away with his actions notwithstanding the Constitution, just as Lincoln had gotten away with defying Taney?[220] And bearing in mind as well the liberties that the Supreme Court has long taken with the

220. An impressively long and detailed pre-election article on Donald Trump's likely goals if he became President depicts him as a megalomaniac, though without using the word. Evan Osnos, "President Trump's First Term: His Campaign Tells Us a Lot about What Kind of Commander-in-Chief He Would Be," *New Yorker*, September 26, 2016. The author does not suggest that Trump would violate the Constitution or defy

constitutional text, should we perhaps accept that the Constitution is au fond tentative, elastic?

Professor Klarman, in a massive recent study of the drafting, debates over, and finally ratification of the Constitution, reminds the reader toward the end of the book that "every generation must govern itself,"[221] and proceeds to consider the many decisions and compromises in the drafting and ratifying process that resulted in a host of provisions ill adapted to later times, concluding that "as Jefferson would have recognized, those who wish to sanctify the Constitution are often using it to defend some particular interest that, in their own day, cannot in fact be adequately justified on its own merits."[222]

A note on finality. While I'm on the subject of end-of-term decisions and more broadly how Presidents can sometimes nullify Supreme Court decisions, I want to return for a moment to the end-of-term abortion case.[223] Justice Alito's forty-page dissent argued for affirmance (and hence for upholding Texas's law, which if upheld would have shut down three-fourths of the abortion clinics in that vast state) mainly on the ground of res judicata—the doctrine that once a suit is decided the loser can't try to undo the decision by bringing a second, identical suit against the winner. Some of the plaintiffs in the abortion case had earlier filed and lost a very similar suit. But as Justice Breyer's majority opinion pointed out, the previous suit hadn't been identical to the present one, and his argument is convincing despite its brevity relative to the Alito dissent. But had I been in Breyer's shoes I would, the other Justices in the majority agreeing, have added an alternative ground: that given the prevalence of abortion laws like that of Texas (they are of course *anti*-abortion laws, religiously inspired and supported), and the need for at least a roughly uniform national rule invalidat-

the Supreme Court, but the article's characterization of Trump would support an inference that such behavior was likely. Osnos says for example:

> What, exactly, can a President do? To prevent the ascent of what the Anti-Federalist Papers, in 1787, called "a Caesar, Caligula, Nero, and Domitian in America," the founders gave Congress the power to make laws, and the Supreme Court the final word on the Constitution. But in the nineteen-thirties Congress was unable to mount a response to the rise of Nazi Germany, and during the Cold War the prospect of sudden nuclear attack further consolidated authority in the White House. Eric Posner, a law professor at the University of Chicago, is quoted by Osnos as saying that "Congress has delegated a great deal of power to the President, Presidents have claimed power under the Constitution, and Congress has acquiesced." And the courts are slow: "If you have a President who is moving very quickly, the judiciary can't do much. A recent example of this would be the war on terror. The judiciary put constraints on President Bush—but it took a very long time."

221. Michael J. Klarman, *The Framers Coup: The Making of the United States Constitution* 624 (2016).
222. Id. at 631.
223. See note 188 above.

ing those laws, the rule of res judicata—a rule made by judges and therefore one would think alterable by them—should be subordinated to more pressing concerns. Had the Court affirmed on the basis of the rule urged by Justice Alito, the legality of the Texas law and similar laws in other states might have remained unresolved for years before the major national issue of constitutional law presented by the case was resolved.

Finality is an important consideration in a well-run legal system, as I noted in the Introduction. And res judicata is an important doctrine of finality. But it should yield to competing considerations in extreme cases. Even Justice Kagan—Scalia's most prominent hagiographer, remember—would be unlikely to agree with his contention that a defendant convicted of murder and sentenced to death, yet discovered after the sentence was issued but before the sentence was carried out to have been innocent, could still rightly be executed provided only that the proceedings resulting in his conviction and sentence had been procedurally regular.[224] The abortion case is less extreme, yet still a plausible case for making finality bend to justice.

The Garland imbroglio and vacancy issues. The 4 to 4 deadlock in the Texas immigration case (p. 199 above) has been blamed on the Republican Senate's refusal to hold a confirmation hearing for President Obama's nominee to fill the Scalia vacancy, Chief Judge Merrick Garland of the District of Columbia Circuit.[225] But that is a superficial criticism, since it is most unlikely that the Senate, Republican-controlled in a period of fierce partisanship, would have confirmed Garland had it given him a hearing, at least until and unless Hillary Clinton was elected President (which of course didn't happen). Robert Bork had had a confirmation hearing, and had not been confirmed, though he was a far greater eminence than Garland is. As I argued in a short piece published shortly after Scalia's death,[226] the significance of the Senate's refusal to consider Garland lay in reminding us that the Supreme Court is a *politicized* body, influenced in making its decisions by the political beliefs of the judges (which are often the beliefs of the President who nominated them and the Senators

224. See note 47 above.

225. His supporters call him Chief Judge Garland—which is accurate; he's the chief judge of the District of Columbia court of appeals. But persons who are not familiar with the federal judiciary may think that a chief judge is appointed by the President or by the judge's colleagues or by some merit board, whereas as I noted in the Introduction the only criterion for appointment is seniority.

226. Richard A. Posner, "The Supreme Court Is a Political Court. Republicans' Actions Are Proof," *Washington Post,* March 9, 2016, www.washingtonpost.com/opinions/the-supreme-court-is-a-political-court-repub licans-actions-are-proof/2016/03/09/4c851860-e142-11e5-8d98-4b3d9215ade1_story.html?utm_term=.76bb73a f54c7. I have edited it slightly for this book.

who confirmed them). This is not a usurpation of power but an inevitability. Most of what the Supreme Court does or says it does is "interpreting" the Constitution and federal statutes, but I put the word in scare quotes because interpretation implies understanding a writer's or speaker's meaning; and, as I keep insisting, most of the issues that the Court takes up can't be resolved by interpretation because the drafters and ratifiers of the constitutional or statutory provision in question had not foreseen the issue that has arisen years, decades—sometimes centuries—after its enactment and had not made provision for its resolution.

When judges are not interpreting they're creating, and when creating they are as I keep saying bound to draw on their priors—attitudes, inclinations, presuppositions derived from upbringing, from training, from personal and career experience, from religion and national origin and character and ideology or politics—these being unavoidable tools of decision making in fields like law that lack settled principles for resolving the most difficult and consequential controversies.

With Scalia's death there are now three very conservative Justices (Samuel Alito, John Roberts, and Clarence Thomas), four liberal Justices (Stephen Breyer, Ruth Bader Ginsburg, Elena Kagan, and Sonia Sotomayor), and a swing Justice (Anthony Kennedy) who is generally conservative but in several important areas liberal, such as discrimination against homosexuals and capital punishment of minors. Before his death Scalia, a strongly conservative and devoutly Catholic Justice, gave the Court a conservative majority, much as the liberal Justices of the 1950s and 1960s had pushed the court in a strongly liberal direction. President Obama may in Merrick Garland have nominated to the Scalia vacancy a centrist-appearing judge who was actually a "stealth" liberal in the mode of John Paul Stevens, David Souter, Harry Blackmun, and to a lesser extent Sandra Day O'Connor—Justices who seemed and maybe were conservative when appointed but became significantly less so as Justices. (Garland however is better described as a cautious centrist than as a conservative.) This time Republican Senators avoided the embarrassment of confirming a possible stealth liberal by declaring that they wouldn't hold a confirmation hearing for *any* Obama nominee. Their hope was that the next President would be a Republican and appoint someone in Scalia's mold. They went so far as to declare that they'd hold no confirmation hearing for any nominee of Hillary Clinton, should she be elected President. Their behavior was proof (were any needed) of the Supreme Court's politicization. But all this is academic now because Trump won the election.

After Scalia. Liberals are in despair at the thought that Trump will be nominating successors to any Justices who die or retire in the next four, and maybe the next eight, years.[227] The Trump Supreme Court should not be reviled until the Scalia vacancy is filled, and perhaps not until other vacancies are filled and the occupant or occupants can be evaluated on the basis of their performance as Supreme Court Justices.

The preoccupation during the 2016 Presidential campaign with likely appointments to the Court by whichever candidate was elected was fueled by awareness that the new President, especially if he or she served two terms (which is normal, though of course not inevitable), might well have several vacancies to fill besides the Scalia vacancy. Justice Ginsburg turns eighty-four in 2017, Kennedy eighty-one, and Breyer seventy-nine. Six years from now (half way through the second term of President Trump, assuming he's reelected), Ginsburg will be eighty-nine, Kennedy eighty-six, and Breyer eighty-four. It is quite likely that two, or maybe all three, will be gone by then. Suppose all three are; Scalia of course is already gone. Then the new President will have four vacancies to fill. How much freedom of choice he or she will have will depend on the make-up of the Senate. But since both the new President and the new Senate are Republican, we can expect that if there are four vacancies on the Supreme Court during the President's term or terms and the Senate remains Republican there will be four Republican appointees to join the three "young" (under seventy) Republican Justices—Roberts, Thomas, and Alito. Seven of the nine Justices would then be Republican. Although there might be some drift— think of how Blackmun, Stevens, and Souter disappointed their appointing Presidents by drifting Left—and Justices rarely vote a straight party line, it would be naïve to doubt that the filling of several vacancies by the same President would have a significant effect on the Court's political slant. And so one heard it predicted before the election that if "Donald Trump is elected president, the Supreme Court may, seat by vacated seat, move rightward toward its most conservative position in recent memory."[228] But this of course remains to

227. I thought it in the worst possible taste when I wrote this footnote that with the inauguration still seven weeks in the future liberal journalists such as Charles Blow in the *New York Times* and Mark Danner in the *New York Review of Books* should be heaping abuse on Trump. Why not give him a chance to show what he can do as President? Writing today, however—February 9, 2017—I am a good deal more understanding of the abuse.

228. Oliver Roeder, "Clinton and Trump Are Both Promising An Extreme Supreme Court," *FiveThirtyEight,* August 2, 2016, http://fivethirtyeight.com/features/clinton-and-trump-are-both-promising-an-extreme-supreme-court/.

be seen, for as I noted Trump has not been consistently conservative in the past, though surrounding himself, as he seems to be doing at this writing (two months after the 2016 Presidential election), with conservatives, some of them extreme—some of them indeed beyond the pale—may have curbed any liberal inclinations he might otherwise have had.

Should deadlock be welcomed? At this writing, the Supreme Court has an even number of Justices, which creates a risk of deadlock. Yet it is being argued, mainly by Professor Eric Segall of Georgia State University's law school, whom I've quoted several times in this chapter, that the nation is better off with an even number of Justices, which would eliminate most 5 to 4 decisions while increasing the number of deadlocks. Segall argues that there wouldn't be many deadlocks because the prospect of them would cause the Justices to compromise more, and because in any event affirmance by an equally divided Court is fine because it reduces the Court's power, devolving much of it onto the lower courts, more of whose decisions would as in *United States v. Texas* be immune from being overturned by the Supreme Court. And lower-court decisions, having less scope, cause less harm on average—though by the same token do less good.

The argument has weaknesses. Imagine a Republican President required to appoint a Democrat to replace a recently retired Republican Justice. There are many conservative Democrats (there are even some liberal Republicans), and so the Republican President could appoint a token Democrat who was ideologically Republican. Professor Segall's response to this criticism is to require in my example that a Democrat appointed by a Republican President be submitted to the Democrat members of the Senate Judiciary Committee for approval. I find it hard to imagine the Senate agreeing to such a procedure. Furthermore, Professor Segall's proposal if adopted would deal a body blow to all political parties except the Democrats and the Republicans. Yet there are other parties, and some day one of them may produce a President—who under Segall's plan would have, in my example, to appoint a Democrat. That seems very odd.

But whatever the merits of Professor Segall's argument, it's unlikely to gain any traction. Congress—which in default of any reference in the Constitution to the number of Supreme Court Justices has assumed the power to determine the number—is unlikely to legislate an even number of Justices. Anyway the number would turn odd whenever a Justice retired or died, unless two retired or died (or one retired and the other died) in quick succession. For a President would never relinquish the power to nominate a Justice when the Court was evenly divided, since his nominee if confirmed could provide decisive assistance to the President's projects and burnish the President's legacy.

And their opinions are unreadable and too long! Virtually all issues resolved in Supreme Court decisions are first attempted to be resolved by a state court or a lower federal court, so the opinions at the different appellate levels can be expected to resemble each other. But Supreme Court opinions tend to be longer than those of other American courts, which is paradoxical since having no fear of reversal by a higher court because there is none the Court could afford to be briefer, more blunt, and more candid; instead, compounding excessive verbosity by bad writing, it is less blunt, more verbose, and less candid than the other courts. This is a relatively new development. In the old and not-so-old days there were plenty of bold, forthright Supreme Court opinions, by such Justices as Holmes, Taft, Hughes, Brandeis, Cardozo, Frankfurter, Jackson, Black, Douglas, and Rehnquist—not to mention Scalia, whose death may thus have ended an era.

An excellent study of the trend in Supreme Court opinions concludes that

> a comparison of the opinions issued by the Supreme Court in the 1931–1933 terms and the 2009–2011 terms confirms the claims of critics that the Court's decisions are becoming excessively long and unreadable for the public. Today's opinions are three times as long as the Depression era opinions and are twenty-five percent less readable, based on the Flesch Reading Ease formula. However, the transition does not appear to be related to increasing legal challenges spurred by the "statutorification" of law or the expansion of federal administrative programs following the New Deal. Indeed, the Court's opinions are getting longer and less readable in all types of case, with the greatest increase in obfuscation arising in cases involving criminal law. It appears more likely that a cultural change in the Court, the expansion of concurring and dissenting opinions in the 1940s, could have played an important role in changing the nature of the dialogue in the Court's opinions, sparking a more academic and professional tone in the opinions. Regardless of what factors motivated the shift, the Court's opinions today are less likely to achieve the goals identified for them by many commentators: (1) informing the pub-

lic about the rule of law; (2) promoting the legitimacy of courts; and (3) facilitating judicial [re]straint.[229]

The most plausible explanation for the conjoint length and diminished readability of current Supreme Court opinions is the sharp decline noted earlier in the number of cases that the Court decides. There has been no decline in the number of the Justices' law clerks, and the amount of time that each clerk can devote to drafting an opinion has therefore risen markedly. Both the clerk who drafts and the Justice who signs off on the draft (though perhaps after editing it) derive satisfaction from the creation of a larger product—at the double expense of their readers, who must read more in order to be able to understand the Court's decision, not only because the opinion is longer but also because it is apt to be less clearly written, by inexperienced writers as most law clerks are, than a shorter opinion would be. The resulting loss of clarity is important.

I am mindful that a recent study finds somewhat reassuringly that "the Court writes clearer opinions when it faces ideologically hostile and ideologically scattered lower federal courts; when it decides cases involving poorly performing federal agencies; when it decides cases involving states with less professionalized legislatures and governors; and when it rules against public opinion. The data show[] the Court writes clearer opinions in every one of these contexts, and demonstrates that actors are more likely to comply with clearer Court opinions."[230] But clearer isn't a synonym for clear.

Please, bring back the sixties! I clerked for Justice Brennan in the Supreme Court's 1962 term, and later spent two years (1965 to 1967) as an assistant to the Solicitor General. The differences between the Court then and the Court now are striking—and they all cut in favor of the earlier Court. For one thing, al-

229. Stephen M. Johnson, "The Changing Discourse of the Supreme Court," 12 *University of New Hampshire Law Review* 29, 66–67 (2014). See also Ryan C. Black and James F. Spriggs, II, "An Empirical Study of the Length of U.S. Supreme Court Opinions," 45 *Houston Law Review* 621 (2008); and Ryan Whalen, "Judicial Gobbledygook: The Readability of Supreme Court Writing," 125 *Yale Law Journal Forum* 200 (2015), www .yalelawjournal.org/forum/judicial-gobbledygook. Whalen's article discusses an analysis of "the readability of over six thousand Supreme Court opinions by measuring the length of sentences and the use of long, polysyllabic words. The data shows that legal writing at the Court has become more complex and difficult to read in recent decades. On an individual level, writing style tends to become somewhat more complex the more years a Justice spends on the court. We also see substantial variation among opinion writers—with Justices Scalia and Sotomayor penning particularly wordy opinions—and a tendency for conservative opinions to be somewhat more difficult to read than their liberal peers."

230. Ryan C. Black et al., *U.S. Supreme Court Opinions and Their Audiences* (2016).

though the Court heard far more cases then than it does now, each Justice had only two law clerks (in fact Douglas by choice had only one), except the Chief Justice (Earl Warren), who had a third, to assist in the management of the Court. And two law clerks, it turned out, were plenty. There was no "cert. pool," as there is today, where clerks of the Justices alternate in writing a cert. memo (a memo recommending grant or denial of certiorari) for distribution to all the Justices in the pool, which is to say all but Alito. Back in 1962, each law clerk wrote cert. memos just to his (there were no female law clerks) Justice. My co-clerk and I devoted, as I recall, Friday to writing cert. memos for the latest batch of cert. petitions. And we wrote opinion drafts for cases assigned to Justice Brennan, or that he planned to dissent in. And we were not overworked, though the caseload was heavier than it is today.

Another difference is that the Justices had an unwritten rule that no one would be hired as a law clerk who had clerked for a lower-court judge; today virtually all—perhaps it is all—Supreme Court law clerks have clerked previously, almost always for a federal court of appeals judge.

The Justices were more diverse; Warren had been governor of California; Black a Southern trial lawyer and influential Democratic Senator; John Marshall Harlan a prominent lawyer and later a judge of the Second Circuit; Byron White also a prominent lawyer and former deputy attorney general; Tom Clark a former attorney general; William O. Douglas a brilliant though erratic former law professor and head of the SEC; Brennan a very successful labor lawyer, army finance general in World War II, and justice of the New Jersey Supreme Court in its heyday; Potter Stewart a well-regarded legal practitioner; and Arthur Goldberg a prominent labor lawyer. They were not a uniformly distinguished group, but most of them were able and experienced and some of them outstanding (Black, Harlan, White, Douglas [though erratic], and Brennan)—and it was certainly a markedly diverse group, quite unlike today's Court; they had far more varied pre-Court careers; I believe only Stewart had been a federal court of appeals judge. There was delegation by the Justices to their law clerks, but less than today because the law clerks hadn't had previous clerkships and so couldn't do as much of the Court's work as today's clerks can. And finally, except for Douglas, who did a lot of extralegal writing—and well-publicized hiking—the Justices were wallflowers by modern standards. They didn't appear on television, they didn't conduct mock trials, they didn't engage in expensive travel paid for by foreign hosts, they didn't appoint former law

clerks as amici curiae to argue cases before them, they didn't blanket the lawyers at oral argument with questions, and I don't think a Justice would fail to
recuse himself in a case in which he had a financial stake in one of the parties,
although I'm not certain of this; Douglas was involved in some financial shenanigans (his two divorces had been very expensive). In sharp contrast to the
present Court, all of whose members are either Catholic or Jewish, seven of the
nine Justices in 1962 were, I believe, Protestants; Brennan was Catholic and
Goldberg Jewish, though they wore their religion lightly.

I'm unsure whether, like the modern Justices and the other federal judges,
Justices in 1962 considered themselves the owners of their judicial papers.
(Speaking of which, I don't understand why that should be so—why judges
should be considered the owners of papers prepared by or for them for use in
their official work, rather than their employer, the U.S. government.) The case
for regarding these as governmental rather than private property is powerfully
argued by Kathryn A. Watts.[231] At the risk of seeming a complete philistine,
however, I can't imagine why anyone would want to do anything with judges'
or Justices' papers other than discard them. They are the equivalent of an artist's preliminary sketch of what becomes a painting, or the rough draft of a
novel; they are superseded by the finished work; the judges' preliminary work
on a case, such as it is, is superseded by the opinion. I agree that the papers in a
judge's case files, like any other employee's papers used by him in his job, are
the property of the government, who is the judge's employer, rather than of the
judge. But the best thing to do with such papers is to throw them out. There are
about one thousand federal judges, Justices, etc. (not to mention law clerks and
secretaries), and the amount of documentary junk they accumulate must be
staggering, yet holds very little interest.

So, to conclude this discussion of the Supreme Court of 1962, it was not a
perfect Court, maybe not even a model Court, but it was a better Court than
today's Supreme Court.

Continuing: The ethics of today's Supreme Court. A recent posting on a website
called "Fix the Court,"[232] from which I'll quote some of its findings, questions
the ethics of the Court:

231. "Judges and Their Papers," 88 *New York University Law Review* 1665 (2013).

232. Gabe Roth, "The Supreme Court Is Being Hypocritical FTC [Fix the Court] Writes in N.Y. Times
Op-Ed," October 11, 2016; also printed on the same day in the *New York Times*, p. A23, under the title "The
Supreme Court Is Being Hypocritical."

Concerning whether a state judge should have recused himself from a capital case in which he had an earlier involvement, . . . Justice Elena Kagan, who participated in both Supreme Court lawsuits concerning the Affordable Care Act despite having served as solicitor general in the Obama administration, asked what would constitute "significant involvement" in a case—i.e., enough to require a recusal. The answer to that question may not be obvious. But surely Justice Kagan's experience in the Obama administration constituted "significant involvement" in the Affordable Care Act cases. In the end, a majority of justices, including Justice Kagan, ruled that the judge who [had] refused to recuse himself should have stepped aside.

So went another case in what I call the Supreme Court's self-referential docket. Each year, the justices hear a handful of suits that have parallels with how they act as stewards of their institution. But instead of changing their own practices in light of their holdings in these cases, the justices too often carry on as before, as if they can play by their own rules when it comes to transparency and accountability. . . . In recent years there have been a number of such cases concerning money and the potential for judicial corruption. In 2015, for example, the court ruled that the Florida Bar was within its rights to discipline a judge for personally soliciting campaign contributions. The majority opinion, delivered by Chief Justice John G. Roberts Jr., held that there was a "vital state interest in safeguarding public confidence in the fairness and integrity" of the nation's judges. But if there is a vital interest in the integrity of the court, why was Justice Breyer allowed to rule on a case last fall in which his wife held about $33,000 worth of stock in a company whose subsidiary was one of the litigants? Or how about the $400,000 worth of shares that Chief Justice Roberts owned in Intel, Microsoft and Hewlett-Packard, which all signed amicus briefs supporting Wal-Mart in a 2011 class-action lawsuit before the court? Chief Justice Roberts voted in favor of Wal-Mart in that case. . . .

Just a week into the current [2016] term [the Supreme Court's term, by statute, begins on the first Monday in October], there has already been a self-referential case. In *Salman v. United States*, argued on October 5, the justices looked to reconcile two appeals courts' differing standards for what constitutes insider trading. Though the justices may give no thought to their investment portfolios when hearing cases, ample research has shown that their decisions affect financial markets. Yet three justices— Justices Roberts, Breyer, and Alito—own individual stocks rather than placing them in the type of investment account or blended fund that would shield them from any appearance of benefiting financially from their legal decisions. [I give a further example of these Justices' seeming indifference to the ethical issue presented by a judge's or Justice's refusing to recuse himself in a case in which he has a financial stake in the Epilogue to this book.]

If the court wants to regain the respect it has lost in recent years, the Justices should consider how, by acting more consistently with their own rulings, they could help build a more open and accountable institution. [For example, though there is a code of ethics for federal judges, there isn't one for the Justices—and the absence shows.]

I mentioned earlier the Justices' plagiarizing language in briefs. Another long-standing ethical issue concerns the insistence by federal judges, including the Justices of the Supreme Court, that federal judges and Justices, unlike American Presidents, own their working papers.[233] I was surprised to discover this because it has never occurred to me, and I still do not believe, that I own any of my judicial working papers. When I have finished with a case I put my notes and any other papers relating to the case in a case file that is then stored in the courthouse, and I have always assumed that it was the property of the court, and not my property. But apparently most federal judges and all Supreme Court Justices think otherwise. Some of them nevertheless give prompt access to their working papers, others (such as Souter and Burger) embargo them for a substantial period (fifty years from retirement in Souter's case), and Byron White (and maybe others) put many of his papers through a shredder. I find this assumption of private ownership baffling. If you work for a company, your working papers belong to the company. If you're a professor, most of your working papers will be articles or books or drafts thereof, and it's understood that they are your property. I can't see any basis for deeming judges' working papers private property. Treating them as such could be thought a form of embezzlement.

233. For devastating criticism, see Kathryn A. Watts, "Judges and Their Papers," 88 *New York University Law Review* 1665 (2013).

And now for an issue that lies on the border between lack of ethics and lack of competence, flagged in an as yet unpublished article by law professor Eric Berger,[234] which complains about the Court's arbitrarily rejecting factfindings underlying congressional statutes when the Court wants to brush them aside to be able to decide the merits as it wants. Berger notes that

> sometimes . . . the Court brushes facts to the side and offers little explanation for why seemingly crucial facts were legally irrelevant. Perhaps even more remarkably, the Court sometimes rejects the relevance of facts that constitute the very mischief Congress sought to remedy in the first place. In such cases, the veracity of particular facts is less important than their ostensible legal relevance. . . . The decision about which facts "count" is ultimately a *legal* determination. Courts usually decide the salience of particular facts, and legal doctrine usually sheds light on the facts a party must prove to assert a viable legal claim. But in constitutional cases, the Supreme Court often makes crucial and controversial determinations that certain facts don't matter and yet, despite the significance of these determinations, it sometimes offers minimal explanation. Given the Court's assertions of judicial supremacy in such cases as *Dickerson v. United States,* 530 U.S. 428, 437 (2000), and *Cooper v. Aaron,* 358 U.S. 1, 18 (1958), it is unsurprising that the Court would retain for itself the ultimate prerogative to define the law and, with it, the class of relevant facts. More striking, however, is just how undeferential the Court is to Congress's findings and how little the Court says when it casts aside mountains of legislative findings.

Berger gives the example of *Shelby County v. Holder* (discussed earlier in this chapter), where the Court found to be relevant "only evidence that certain kinds of intentional voter discrimination, such as various forms of voter tests, had decreased significantly since the initial passage of the Voting Rights Act (VRA) in 1965."[235] In striking down a provision of the Act, the Court focused on the demise of such barriers to voting and the resulting improvements in minority voter registration and turnout. In so doing, it all but ignored congressional evidence of continued racism and "second-generation" barriers to vot-

---

234. "When Facts Don't Matter: The Roberts Court, Congressional Findings, and Constitutional Decision Making."

235. See *Shelby County v. Holder,* 133 S. Ct. at 2625–2626 (2013).

ing, such as racial gerrymanders and the adoption of at-large voting.[236] Berger comments that

> interestingly, the disagreement between majority and dissent was not so much about whether Congress's factual findings were empirically correct but rather whether they were constitutionally relevant. In the majority's eyes, the VRA represented a grave affront to state sovereignty. Consequently, only naked attempts to prevent racial minorities from casting a ballot could justify the VRA's egregious intrusions on state sovereignty. Other evidence of racial discrimination in voting, such as racial gerrymanders, did not justify the Act's strong medicine.

> The Court's position may be defensible, but it said little to justify its factual priorities. The reader, then, is left to wonder why poll taxes are constitutionally relevant, but racial gerrymanders not. Instead, the Court told us that times have changed and that the Voting Rights Act is no longer necessary and must therefore fall. Congress, however, had found reams of evidence suggesting that voter discrimination still was a problem. How exactly did the Court decide that the problems Congress had identified didn't matter?

And finally and most important, we need a smarter—which incidentally requires a much larger—Supreme Court, and failing that we could use a revision in the confirmation process. In a recent article Professor Jonathan Turley argues persuasively that the Supreme Court is too small: "A better size is 19. The increase could occur slowly with no president filling more than two new positions per term. That would bring the U.S. high court in line with those of other countries, which have purposefully avoided our court's concentration of power (and swing justice) problems. Germany's high court has 16 members; Japan's, 15; the United Kingdom's, 12; India's, 31; and Israel's, 15. On a 19-member Supreme Court, two justices (rotated by order of seniority) would sit each year on lower courts—a tradition from the early days of the Republic that should be resumed. When 'riding circuit' was abandoned, it produced a Supreme Court too easily seen as arrogant and out of touch with real-world issues."[237]

---

236. See id. at 2634–2635 (Ginsburg, J., dissenting).

237. Jonathan Turley, "Battling Over Neil Gorsuch Is Beside The Point: The Supreme Court Needs an Institutional Overhaul," *Los Angeles Times*, February 1, 2017, www.latimes.com/opinion/op-ed/la-oe-turley-su preme-court-reform-20170201-story.html.

I think Turley's suggestion is great, and would add that the enlargement he suggests, besides creating a more diverse, intellectually rich, and experienced Court (more experienced because the Justices would occasionally be sitting in the lower federal courts) would enable it to hear far more cases, some of them in panels of three or six or nine Justices, with review en banc should a majority of the Justices question a panel decision. But I wish to dwell for a moment on the issue of intellectuality. In an age of science and technology, none of the current Justices has a background in either. Were there nineteen Justices instead of eight (at present) or nine (the maximum number at present), there would be room for a Justice with an educational background in physics, one with a background in biology, another with a background in mathematics, others with backgrounds in computer technology, or psychology, aeronautics, economics, finance, chemistry, or criminology—and these are all fields that crop up in litigation in federal courts. A Supreme Court that has no judge or Justice with a scientific or technological background is severely handicapped—and the present Supreme Court is such a court. But the knowledge deficit could be rectified by enlarging the Court along the lines suggested by Professor Turley and appointing ten more Justices, all knowledgeable in one or more of the fields that I have mentioned.

The persons whom Trump named during the campaign as candidates for the Supreme Court were all judges, as were all the present Supreme Court Justices (and likewise Scalia), except Kagan, before their appointment to the Court. The result of limiting (or virtually limiting) eligibility for appointment to the Court to judges is to diminish diversity and probably quality, when one considers some of the notable Justices of yore who had *not* previously been judges: John Marshall, Joseph Story, Melville Fuller, Louis Brandeis, Charles Evans Hughes, Hugo Black, William O. Douglas, Felix Frankfurter, Harlan Fiske Stone, Earl Warren, Robert Jackson, Byron White, Lewis Powell, and William Rehnquist. And further elaborating my suggestion in the preceding chapter, what a shot in the Court's arm it would be to have, along with outstanding Justices plucked from the lower federal courts and the state supreme courts a Justice who had been a first-rate trial lawyer, a Justice who was a technology whiz, a Justice who had been a leading Senator or high-ranking executive-branch official, the nation's foremost law professor, a Justice who had "graduated" from the practice of law to chief executive of one of the nation's largest banks or other businesses, a Justice who had won a Nobel Prize in economics, a Justice who would write his own judicial opinions, a Justice who would not base law-clerk hiring on the applicants' politics. There would be room for all these different types of Justice (all superior to what we have now) in a nineteen-Justice Court.

And if Turley's proposal seems too radical, here is a modest alternative: change the confirmation process in the Senate to require confirmation of a Supreme Court nominee not by fifty-one Senate votes but by sixty-seven.[238] This would diminish the political role in Supreme Court nominations, because one party would be unlikely to have sixty-seven Senators in its pocket.

What a great Supreme Court this nation *could*, but doesn't, have.

Is the Court broken? A checklist. This question is repeatedly asked by my friend, the constitutional-law professor Eric Segall, whom I quote extensively in this book, and by him is answered "yes." For which indeed a good deal of support can be marshaled: the lavish paid-for trips (especially expensive foreign trips); the failure of some Justices to recuse themselves when they have a financial stake in one of the litigants; the nepotistic practices in regard to the Court's choice of amici curiae to appoint; the appointment of the Chief Justice for life, rather than rotating the Chief Justiceship among the Justices; the Justices' sometimes silly extracurricular activities, such as presiding over silly mock trials (such as the trial of Richard III for killing the child prisoners in the Tower, enabling him to substitute himself for the legitimate claimant to the throne of England); the lack of diversity of the Justices; their limited qualifications to *be* Justices—their lack of background in science, technology, mathematics, history, literature, philosophy, economics, other social sciences, business, finance, and politics—in short their lack of relevant diversity (related to the fact that a Supreme Court of only nine Justices is too small); the poor management of the Court; the Justices' antics at oral argument; their dearth of trial experience— the fact that only one of them at present (Sotomayor) has ever presided at a trial; the poor quality and excessive length of many of their judicial opinions; their excessive questioning (often lecturing rather than questioning) at the oral arguments; their refusal to allow the oral arguments to be televised; their too-light caseload and too-long summer vacation; their refusal to report votes to grant or deny certiorari; the lack of an official ethical code for Supreme Court Justices; their excessive dependence on law clerks (and four law clerks per Justice are too many); the lack of geographic diversity; the refusal to allow audio recordings of their bench statements (announcements of their decisions); the claim to own their judicial papers; and their f*** and s*** prissiness (see Conclusion); absence of mandatory retirement or mandatory mental-acuity test at age eighty or eighty-five; and failure to get rid of the spittoons that sit behind the Justices' seats on the bench and to reopen the front doors of the Supreme Court building.

And how about once in a while a little common sense: the fiasco of Clinton v. Jones. In 1994 a woman named Paula Jones sued President Bill Clinton charging him with having made "abhorrent" sexual advances to her prior to his becoming President. He claimed that as President he was immune from civil suits based on acts committed before he became President, because such suits would interfere with the performance of his Presidential duties, and alternatively that if he was not immune, at least the litigation should be deferred until he left office in January 2001. The case wended its way up to the Supreme Court, which in 1997 rejected his defenses unanimously,[239] though Justice Breyer to his credit filed a concurring opinion indicating some doubts about the decision.

The majority opinion, written by Justice Stevens, is a hoot. Although there is nothing in the Constitution about Presidential immunity from suit, the Court had already held sensibly that a President could not be sued for his official acts as President, as that would be disruptive—one can imagine an avalanche of such suits by disgruntled citizens. But in the entire history of the United States there had been only three suits against Presidents based on their private as distinct from their official acts, and Justice Stevens stated in his opinion with stunning inaccuracy that *Clinton v. Jones* "appears to us highly unlikely to occupy any substantial amount of petitioner's [i.e., President Clinton's] time." The case proceeded on remand with perjurious testimony by Clinton and a perjurious affidavit by Monica Lewinsky, and these perjuries led to the Starr investigation of President Clinton and ultimately to Clinton's impeachment by the House of Representatives and his trial before the Senate.

The Court's critical error was its failure to evince any awareness of the significance of the fact that Paula Jones' suit was about sex. It's as if all nine Justices were eunuchs. A sex suit against a President long suspected (indeed long known) to be a promiscuous adulterer was likely to be, and of course proved to

---

239. *Clinton v. Jones*, 520 U.S. 681 (1997). The argument in the text is a compressed version of my discussion of the Supreme Court's decision in my book *An Affair of State: The Investigation, Impeachment, and Trial of President Clinton* 225–230 (1999).

be, explosive, even though it had no actual significance. Presidential promiscuity was nothing new; everyone in government knew that FDR and Kennedy had been adulterers, but this did not detract from the high regard in which these Presidents were and continue to be held; their sexual proclivities were irrelevant to the performance of their official duties, and likewise Clinton's sexual proclivities, which differed mainly in Clinton's inability to conceal them. The Supreme Court could have said that Presidents can't be sued while in office, as such suits are likely to be distractions or to mushroom into *causes célèbres*—both turned out to be consequences of the decision in *Clinton v. Jones*. As the Court should have foreseen.

But I agree with the Court's refusal to grant Clinton immunity from suit—that would have placed Presidents above the law, much like the Roman Emperors, such as Nero, who had a young boy (Sporus by name), whom he fancied, castrated, and then married. All that the Court should have done was order Paula Jones's suit stayed until President Clinton left office. Staying a civil suit for six and a half years (the interval between when she filed her suit and when Clinton left office) is unusual, but by no means unknown.

Am I too negative about the Supreme Court? David Lat has an excellent law blog called "Above the Law." On October 16, 2016, he published a partial transcript of a talk I had given shortly before at a bookstore in Chicago. The talk had been arranged by William Domnarski, who had just published his biography of me. The bookstore event was lightly attended, mainly by University of Chicago Law Students (the bookstore is near the university), and I had not thought of what I would say, and ended up speaking extemporaneously—and, the reader of this book will not be surprised to discover, negatively, also tactlessly through an excess of candor—about the current Supreme Court. Lat's transcription, I am told, aroused considerable criticism of me on various law blogs. Mea culpa! But I do want to correct a couple of errors in Lat's transcription. One was that I had said that none of the current Justices except Sotomayor had any trial experience, the other that none of the current Justices other than Ginsburg and Breyer were "qualified" to be on the Supreme Court. I'm sure these were not Lat's errors, but either errors in my talk or errors in a recording or other source on which Lat based the transcription. I think it worthwhile to correct them:

First, I had never meant to suggest that only one of the Justices has trial experience. My point, rather, or at least my intended point, was that only Sotomayor had been a trial *judge*. I didn't mean to suggest that only former trial judges should be appointed to the Supreme Court, but rather that *all* appellate judges should have tried cases. When I was appointed to the Seventh Circuit in 1981, I had never been a trial judge (or any other type of judicial officer, for that matter). One of the senior judges (a former chief judge) of the court told me that I needed such experience and should therefore volunteer to conduct trials in the district courts of the circuit. I thought that was excellent advice, and I have been conducting trials in those courts (mainly though not exclusively in the district court in Chicago), both civil and criminal, trial and bench, ever since, plus pretrial both in cases that went to trial and cases that didn't. I regard my trial court experience as *extremely* valuable to my appellate court work and I believe that every appellate judge, including Supreme Court Justices, who have not been trial judges should volunteer to conduct trials, because you can't understand the trial process merely by reading transcripts and other documents. You have to have screened jurors, decided on the jury instructions, observed the witnesses and the lawyers, set time limits; and have imposed sentence in a criminal case—the most difficult phase of a criminal trial.

The only appellate judges whom I know to have conducted a trial besides me (though I'm sure there are others) though never having been trial judges, are Judges Bea, Kozinski, and McKeown, all of the Ninth Circuit, Judge Easterbrook of my court, and Chief Justice Rehnquist, who tried one (I believe only one) case—only to be reversed by the court of appeals (I think it was the Fourth Circuit)! (My trial decisions have been reversed a few times also.) Rehnquist didn't try again. Apart from Rehnquist, I don't know the frequency of trials conducted by appellate judges who had never been trial judges.

The second correction I would have liked to make in the transcription of my bookstore talk has to do with my saying that none of the sitting Justices (plus Scalia) is "qualified" for the Supreme Court except Ginsburg and Breyer. This could be misunderstood to mean that I think that the others lack the necessary paper credentials, of which the most important are graduating from a law school and passing the bar exam (though one of our greatest Justices, Robert Jackson, had had just a year of law school and had not graduated). That was not my intention in using the word "qualified" (if I did use it). I meant good enough to be a Supreme Court Justice. There are 1.2 or 1.3 million American lawyers, some of them brilliant, fair minded, experienced, and the like. I sometimes ask myself whether the nine current Supreme Court Justices (I'm restoring Scalia to life for this purpose) are the nine best-qualified lawyers to be Justices. Obviously not. Are they nine of the best one hundred? Obviously not. Nine of the best one thousand? I don't think so. Nine of the best ten thousand? I'll give them that.

I said some harsh things in my bookstore talk about the current Supreme Court. I stand by the content though not the form of my remarks. I think the Court is at a nadir. I don't think it's well managed and I don't think the Justices are doing a good job. Of course that is not a case that I could make in a bookstore talk. But this very long chapter has set forth in detail my views of the current Court and my grounds for those views. I look forward to critique of the chapter.

But am I being impertinent in criticizing my judicial superiors in public? Definitely, but I find my excuse in this charming passage in *Alice's Adventures in Wonderland*:

> "Who are you talking to?" said the King, going up to Alice, and looking at the Cat's head with great curiosity. "It's a friend of mine—a Cheshire Cat," said Alice: "allow me to introduce it." "I don't like the look of it at all," said the King: "however, it may kiss my hand if it likes." "I'd rather not," the Cat remarked. "Don't be impertinent" said the King, "and don't look at me like that!" He got behind Alice as he spoke. "A cat may look at a king," said Alice. "I've read that in some book, but I don't remember where."[240]

And there are the ethics issues, broadly understood, as compactly summarized by Professor Segall in his article "Invisible Justices: How Our Highest Court Hides from the American People:"[241] "Whether it is the lack of cameras, the anonymity of the certiorari votes, the refusal of the Justices to abide by the same ethical and recusal rules as other judges [unlike all other federal judges, the Justices have no ethical code], or the lack of any rules regarding their official papers, the story of the Supreme Court is one of secrecy and mythology instead of accountability and transparency." Consider how many of the Justices' opinions are weak, or verbose, or needlessly and confusingly complex. And consider Katherine Shaw's recent article about amici curiae:[242] About twice a term the Supreme Court invites a lawyer to participate in an argued case as an

240. (Emphasis added, but by the author, Lewis Carroll, whose real name of course was Charles Dodgson.) It's an old English proverb, commending impertinence to one's superiors, as in, "Jill: 'Fred, You shouldn't stare *at me* like that. I'm your boss.' Fred: 'A cat can look *at a* king.'"

241. 32 *Georgia State University Law Review* 787, 838 (2015).

242. "Friends of the Court: Evaluating the Supreme Court's Amicus Invitations," 101 *Cornell Law Review* 1533 (2016).

amicus curiae, both submitting a brief and if he wants participating in the oral argument as well. Almost always these amici curiae are former Supreme Court law clerks, leading Professor Shaw to comment that "what emerges [from the Court's practice] is a picture of a Court that has become increasingly insular and cloistered over time, less and less inclined to invite in outsiders who might approach the law in different, perhaps radically different, ways."[243]

For further criticism of the Court's practices see Adam Liptak, "Justices Disclose Privately Paid Trips and Gifts,"[244] where we learn among other things that in 2015 Justice Breyer made nineteen paid trips, including three to London and two to Paris. Sotomayor was next with sixteen paid trips, but to less exotic places. Alito took paid trips to London and the Dominican Republic, Ginsburg to London, South Korea, and Zurich, Kagan to Jerusalem, Roberts to Japan, and Kennedy to Salzburg. Almost without exception the Justices' financial disclosure forms did not disclose the costs involved, but Ginsburg did say that the Supreme Court of Korea had paid $8,220 for airfare and Sotomayor that she had flown to the University of Notre Dame on a private plane. Liptak also notes that in 2011 the University of Adelaide in Australia paid more than $38,000 for Justice Scalia, his wife, and another couple to fly business class to a 2011 conference. It seems that Supreme Court Justices don't have much work to do and don't like to pay for their boondoggles.

It remains to note the politicization of Supreme Court clerkships. Justices used not to base their clerk hiring decisions on an applicant's politics. No more. Now, and indeed for a decade or more, the Republican Justices hire conservatives to be their law clerks and the Democratic Justices liberals.[245] Since the law clerks draft their Justices' opinions, the politicization of the law clerks increases the politicization of the Justices, enhancing the Court's political divisiveness.

243. Id. at 1592.

244. *New York Times*, June 22, 2016, republished January 26, 2017, www.nytimes.com/2016/06/23/us/poli tics/justices-disclose-privately-paid-trips-and-gifts.html.

245. Adam Liptak, "A Sign of Court's Polarization: Choice of Clerks," *New York Times*, September 7, 2010, p. A1.

THREE

Tier Two of the Federal Judiciary:
The Federal Courts of Appeals

THE PRIMARY FUNCTION of the federal courts of appeals is to review decisions by the district courts, but it is not their exclusive function because the district courts are not the exclusive venue for federal trial-level adjudication. Though there are no Article III judges below the district-judge level, there are magistrate judges, who function as auxiliary trial judges; bankruptcy judges, who conduct bankruptcy proceedings; and, most important, a number of federal administrative agencies, many well known—such as the National Labor Relations Board, the Federal Communications Commission, and the Equal Employment Opportunity Commission—that engage in adjudication through arbiters usually called administrative law judges, and also engage in rulemaking.[1] The agencies that adjudicate are like federal district courts inasmuch as their decisions are subject to judicial review, sometimes by district courts, sometimes by the courts of appeals, and sometimes by both (that is, first the district court and then the court of appeals). But unlike district courts the agencies have a limited subject-matter scope (just labor relations, or just electricity regulation, or just employment discrimination, and so forth), varied procedures, industry-specific expertise, and greater subordination to Congress and a concomitantly greater susceptibility to political pressures. I do not discuss administrative law in this book, as distinct from judicial review of administrative decisions, a focus of the present chapter.

Like the Supreme Court, the federal courts of appeals could benefit from a

---

1. For a list, incomplete because it excludes most adjudicative agencies that are part of Cabinet departments, see United States Government Information Online: "Federal Administrative Agencies," http://libraryguides.law.pace.edu/c.php?g=319332&p=2134043.

number of changes, some of form and some of substance. At the level of form the first thing that can and should be done is to burn all copies of the *Bluebook,* in its latest edition 560 pages of rubbish.[2] It is a terrible time waster: for law clerks employed by judges who mindlessly insist that the citations in their opinions conform to the *Bluebook;* for students at the University of Chicago Law School, who are required to master the *Bluebook* in their first-year writing course even though the school's law review uses a different citation manual, the *Maroonbook;* and for students at Yale Law School who aspire to be selected for the staff of the *Yale Law Journal*—for they must pass a five-hour exam on the *Bluebook.* All this is a colossal waste of time because no serious reader pays more than passing attention to citation format; all the reader cares about is that a citation enable him or her to find the cited material. And it is by reading judicial opinions that law students learn the standard formats for the citation of cases, statutes, books, and articles; they don't need a citation manual.

The *Bluebook* has a zombie-like existence. Look up *"Bluebook"* in *Wikipedia* and you'll find under "reception" a summary of my criticisms of the *Bluebook* but you'll find no defenses of the *Bluebook.*[3] And that's typical of legal academia, which rarely bothers to defend *any* of its antiquated and pointless practices, numerous as they are; and the cone of silence embraces the judges and the practicing lawyers as well. Critics of established practices are generally simply ignored.

Yet if you search carefully enough online you'll find *some* defenses of the *Bluebook,* including the pathetic statement that it has "a signaling value to law firms. Bluebooking proves that the student is willing to work very carefully for hours and hours on a task with very little intrinsic value and of extreme boredom. These skills are valuable to top law firms, and membership in a law review proves that the student has the skills."[4] But why would a top law firm *want* lawyers who work for hours on end on boring tasks of little value? Is the point that for whatever reason the firms *do* want drudges, and that anyone who masters the *Bluebook* is by definition a drudge?

The most common defense of the *Bluebook* is that there would be costs of transitioning to an alternative citation system, and the alternative system might turn out to be no better than the *Bluebook.* Yet my own experience, of limiting

---

2. See, for example, the misleading abbreviations that I quoted on page 000 of this book, plus section R6.1 of the 20th edition of *The Bluebook*—a page and a half of abbreviations, many also misleading, with directions to another twenty-nine pages consisting of "lists of specific abbreviations" in a dozen categories.

3. "Bluebook," *Wikipedia,* https://en.wikipedia.org/wiki/Bluebook.

4. Tom Hynes, in *The Volokh Conspiracy,* May 2, 2016, www.volokh.com/posts/1146606025.shtml.

to five the number of pages in my law-clerk handbook that are devoted to cita-tion formatting (recall "A Miniaturized Substitute for the *Bluebook*" at the end of Chapter 1 of this book), tells me there's no need for a set of citation forms grand enough to be called a "system." The essential elements of a workable guide to legal citations are a few examples of intelligible, informative case cita-tions and a few reminders of citation practices to avoid, such as the use of non-obvious abbreviations of parties' names in citations (a bad practice strongly encouraged by the *Bluebook*—naturally). My opinions and other writings are sometimes criticized, but never (so far as I'm aware) for the style or form of my citations. But I guess ignoring beats refuting as responses to unwelcome pro-posed reforms.

The *Bluebook* to one side, one might expect judges and their law clerks to endeavor to eliminate the superfluous verbiage that mars so many opinions, verbiage that exhibits a remarkable tenacity and weed-like growth. Many an opinion ends with the statement that "for the foregoing reasons the decision of the district court is" affirmed or reversed. If "for the foregoing reasons" were deleted, as it should be, would the reader think the judge was concealing the reasons for his decision? That there were no reasons? That the reasons would be announced at some indefinite time in the future? Sometimes this silly flour-ish is found at the beginning of the opinion, as in "for the reasons set forth below, we affirm [or reverse] the judgment of the district court." Is the judge worried that without the flourish the reader would think the opinion was not going to give reasons for the decision? Another silly expression is "after careful consideration, we [affirm, reverse, or whatever]," implying (unintentionally of course) that usually the judges are careless, but for a change they've given this case "careful consideration."

Some judges, perhaps remembering Polonius's *aperçu* that "brevity is the soul of wit," announce at the beginning of an opinion "We affirm" or "We re-verse," with no amplification. That's bad too, because it is abrupt, peremptory—it makes it seem that the judge is in a hurry to get rid of the case. Better simply to announce at the close of the opinion that "the judgment of the district court [or agency] is affirmed [or reversed]."

Redundancy is a more common vice of judicial opinions than abruptness, as when an opinion states that "a question of fact [is] to be determined from the totality of all the circumstances." "Totality" *means* "all." Grammatical mis-takes are common too, such as "his presentence report . . . recommended that he was subject to an enhanced sentence." Either "recommended that" should be changed to "stated that," or "was subject" should be changed to "be sub-jected." Terms in judicial opinions sometimes have no meaning at all, such as "moral turpitude," typically—and meaninglessly—defined as "conduct that is considered contrary to community standards of justice, honesty or good mor-als" and is therefore illegal. Even worse is the definition of moral turpitude in *Black's Law Dictionary:* "act of baseness, vileness, or the depravity in private and social duties which man owes to his fellow man, or to society in general."[5] This is not how modern Americans speak or should speak.

Apart from being crowded with superfluous flourishes, of which I've given just a few examples, appellate opinions tend to be overlong, crammed with ir-relevant facts and repulsive legal jargon ("subjective prong" is one of my favor-ite examples of judicial illiteracy[6]). They also are crammed with headings and subheadings, like the chapter headings in books, though headings and sub-headings in opinions typically introduce paragraphs that need no headings be-cause of their brevity, and certainly no dull, obvious headings such as "Intro-duction," "Facts," "Analysis," "Conclusion" (often the conclusion is a sentence or less). In part because judicial opinions nowadays are largely ghostwritten by law clerks, the opinions often conceal the judges' thinking—thinking that may be at the level of hunch, common sense, emotion, or ideology (four headings you'll never see in an opinion)—that actually motivated the decision. And the opinions typically are too long, because law clerk and judge have made no ef-fort to prune them of superfluous words and sentences. Would that judges heeded both halves of Polonius's aphorism that "brevity is the soul of wit and tediousness its limbs and outward flourishes."

The judges would do well to follow Rule 28(a)(6) of the Federal Rules of Ap-pellate Procedure, which says that an appellate brief should contain "a concise statement of the case setting out the facts relevant to the issues submitted for review, describing the relevant procedural history, and identifying the rulings presented for review, with appropriate references to the record." That's what a judicial opinion should contain as well, and in addition the opinion's author should strive for brevity and clarity.

My complaint is not that modern appellate opinions lack eloquence. They certainly do lack it, but it's no longer a property of legal writing. Today no Jus-tice and few other judges write eloquently, as Holmes and Hand and Brandeis and Cardozo and Jackson and a few others once did. The literary culture is

5. Page 1008 (6th ed. 2009). More on "moral turpitude" shortly.
6. For other examples see note 16 below.

moribund. Clarity and brevity, not eloquence, are the only attainable, though rarely attained or even attempted, literary goals of modern judicial writing, cultural change being busy killing off the humanities. Among the current Supreme Court Justices only Justice Breyer appears to have genuine cultural breadth. The attainable goal in contemporary judicial opinions comes down to plain talk. I am therefore minded to appropriate a passage from a century-old poem by the great Irish poet William Butler Yeats:

> And I grew weary of the sun
> Until my thoughts cleared up again,
> Remembering that the best I have done
> Was done to make it plain.[7]

I strive to make the thoughts in my opinions plain.

Judge Wiley, from whose review of my book *Divergent Paths* I quoted extensively in the Introduction, has also written (though I don't think has published) a short paper that he entitles "Judge Posner's Advice to Judges: 'Write Clearly and Simply,'" in which he draws on Chapter 8 of my book *Reflections on Judging* (2013) (the chapter is entitled "Make it Simple, Make it New: Opinion Writing and Appellate Advocacy"), and let me quote a few passages from his review:

> Posner states the case for [judges'] writing the first draft ourselves: "the process of writing, which means searching for words, for sentences in which to express meaning, is a process of discovery rather than just of expressing preformed ideas. . . ." Writing it ourselves "reveals analytical gaps [and] gives rise to new ideas." Most fundamentally, "fluency in writing comes largely from—writing."
>
> Posner says to write for the intelligent lay person. He offers specifics. Avoid jargon. "Legal jargon obfuscates, and deceives the legal writer into thinking he's writing with precision, when he's simply writing anachronistically.
>
> "Avoid acronyms and abbreviations other than the obvious ones, such as FBI and etc. They are ugly and distracting, as well as often being opaque to the reader. Even if the opinion writer spells out the acronym or abbreviation when first using it, readers may have difficulty keeping the

---

7. "Words," in William Butler Yeats, *The Green Helmet and Other Poems* (1910).

meaning in mind as they read on." Cut the "turgid prose, footnotes, long quotations, tedious repetition, and the other earmarks of conventional legal writing." Then mercilessly winnow. "Facts, names, dates, procedural details—how often they merely pad out an opinion! Must every opinion list the parties' contentions? For that matter, must all the *parties* be mentioned? No, because often the caption of a case will list parties that have dropped out or were supernumerary from the beginning. Must every opinion . . . repeat the standard of review? Assure the reader that the court has given 'careful' consideration to the issues? (An empty, self-congratulatory flourish.) Demonstrate, in short, that the literary culture in America is indeed dead?"

Dump solemnity and pomposity. Be "simple, nontechnical, colloquial, narrative, essayistic. . . . As Holmes once said, a judge's opinions don't have to be heavy in order to be weighty."

It is hard to discuss writing without examples. Posner gives them. He rewrites an opinion from the prestigious D.C. Circuit. Posner's version is 602 words. The D.C. Circuit version is 3,237 words long. The contrast is devastating. Posner does not target an obvious stinker. The D.C. Circuit opinion is perfectly normal. By contrast, Posner's work is short and sweet. Until you read his trim little masterpiece, it is hard to grasp how used to bad prose we are.

If despite Judge Wiley's efforts and mine good judicial writing is a lost cause, as I believe it is, still a number of common practices of federal appellate courts could easily be abandoned and should be. One is a court's announcing in advance (often months in advance) who the members of the panel will be that will hear a particular case. Such a preannouncement is likely to cause the lawyers in the case to focus on the particular leanings of the panel members, which may result in decisions that reflect the idiosyncrasies of those judges rather than the law of the circuit and by doing so may provoke gratuitous rehearings en banc. Another unsound practice is for one judge on a panel to be assigned by the presiding judge to prepare a bench memo (which means, as a practical matter, have a law clerk of the assigned judge prepare a bench memo) for circulation to all the members of the panel in advance of oral argument. This is bound to give that judge disproportionate influence in the panel's deliberations. And finally, though federal appellate judges' staffs—usually consisting of four law clerks and a secretary—are very small from a managerial standpoint, judicial management, as I noted in the Introduction, is frequently inefficient, even eccentric. Yet given the small size of the judges' staffs, the management of them is readily improvable—one would think,[8] were it not that like the rest of the legal profession federal court of appeals judges tend to be allergic to change.

Indeed the most serious problem with appellate litigation, both at the circuit level and in the Supreme Court, is, as I argued in Chapter 2 and will elaborate briefly here, the stodginess and stuffiness of the American legal culture. Judges are forever looking backward, and not only in constitutional cases, where the rearward glance carries them back mainly to the late eighteenth century (the years of the original Constitution and the Bill of Rights) and to 1868 (the year the Fourteenth Amendment was ratified)—eras too far in the past to provide guidance for the present and the future. The backward focus is also visible in statutory and common-law cases, where judicial precedents tend to be uncritically venerated, as are many constitutional decisions.

An amusing example of the legal profession's resistance to change was brought to my attention recently by Gary Peeples. It is an article in the *Harvard Law Review* by Hampton Dellinger denouncing the inclusion of maps, photographs, and any other pictorial material in Supreme Court opinions and implicitly in any other judicial opinions, on the ground that "their inherent distortions and vulnerability to manipulation make the Justices' reliance on them problematic. . . . The legal documents that have bound and bettered our nation—from the Declaration of Independence to *Brown v. Board of Education*—have been plain and unencumbered, yet clear and powerful. A review of the Supreme Court's use of photographs, maps, replicas, and reproductions shows the items generally to be incompatible with such ideals. Visual attachments are much more likely to obscure the best available legal answer rather than reveal it."[9] Notice the nostalgic invocation of the eighteenth century, the supposition that all important legal documents are "plain" and "clear," the implicit assumption that words deceive less than maps and photos, when surely the opposite is

---

8. See Mitu Gulati and Richard A. Posner, "The Management of Staff by Federal Court of Appeals Judges," 69 *Vanderbilt Law Review* 479 (2016); and my book *Divergent Paths: The Academy and the Judiciary* 222–230, 372–373 (2016). I don't understand why the Federal Judicial Center doesn't have a program in judicial staff management. (I am pretty sure, having searched its website, www.fjc.gov/, that it doesn't.)

9. Hampton Dellinger, "Words Are Enough: The Troublesome Use of Photographs, Maps, and Other Images in Supreme Court Opinions," 110 *Harvard Law Review* 1704, 1753 (1997). At least Dellinger didn't bow to Friedrich Carl von Savigny, the great nineteenth-century German legal scholar who thought the model for modern law should be Roman law. See Oliver Wendell Holmes, Jr., *The Common Law* 164–246 (1881); Richard A. Posner, "Savigny, Holmes, and the Law and Economics of Possession," 86 *Virginia Law Review* 535, 535–540 (2000).

the case, and the conclusion that as there were no photos and few accurate maps in the halcyon days of our constitutional youth, the use of modern photos and accurate maps to illuminate legal issues disrespects the past and must therefore be forbidden. I am reminded that in a couple of my opinions I have said that lawyers think that a word is worth a thousand pictures; Mr. Dellinger may be one of those lawyers.

It's not easy to see where you're going if your head is screwed on backward. Few of our judges today obey T. S. Eliot's command "Not fare well, but fare forward, voyagers."[10] Nor his reminder that "the historical sense involves a perception not only of the pastness of the past, but of its presence. . . . It is not preposterous that the past should be altered by the present as much as the present is directed by the past."[11] Nor Nietzsche's critique of historicism,[12] on which he sarcastically bestowed the slogan "Let the dead bury the living."[13] Nor A. N. Wilson's observation that "the many authors in the nineteenth century who thought they were recovering the historical Jesus" but in fact "were looking down the well of history and catching their own reflections. Jesus-scholars . . . are often writing autobiography and calling it biography."[14] Modern judges and constitutional scholars project their policy preferences onto the hapless framers of the Constitution and call this mirror-gazing history; in Chapter 2 we saw Professor Amar doing this.

But stodginess must not be confused with what I'll call "pastness." We must not overlook, in the passage that I just quoted from T. S. Eliot, the statement that "the present is directed by the past." Or as he said elsewhere, "Our problem being to form the future, we can only form it on the materials of the past; we must *use* our heredity, instead of denying it."[15] It's undeniable that the future

10. "The Dry Salvages," Quartet 3 of Eliot's *Four Quartets*.

11. "Tradition and the Individual Talent," in T. S. Eliot, *The Sacred Wood: Essays on Poetry and Criticism* 47, 49, 50 (1920).

12. Friedrich Nietzsche, "On the Uses and Disadvantages of History for Life," in Nietzsche, *Untimely Meditations* 57 (R. J. Hollingdale trans. 1983). The essay was first published in 1874. I discussed the application of his critique to law at some length in my article "Past-Dependency, Pragmatism, and Critique of History in Adjudication and Legal Scholarship," 67 *University of Chicago Law Review* 573 (2000). Since Nietzsche's article that I am citing approvingly is almost 150 years old, I have to qualify my aversion to the backward judicial glance. I am also mindful that two thousand years ago Aristotle formulated the modern concept of the rule of law: indifference of judges to the social status or individual attractiveness or repulsiveness of a litigant—in other words, seeing litigants as representative parties and thus judging, as the federal judicial oath commands, "without respect to persons." 28 U.S.C. § 453.

13. Friedrich Nietzsche, *Unmodern Observations* 73, 79 (1990).

14. A. N. Wilson, "Two Horses" (review of John Dominic Crossan, *Jesus and the Violence of Scripture*), *Times Literary Supplement*, December 9, 2015, pp. 26, 27.

15. Eliot, "The Humanism of Irving Babbitt," in *Selected Prose of T. S. Eliot* 277, 278 (Frank Kermode ed. 1975)—Eliot's essay was first published in 1928.

builds on the past, and thus that the history of law and much other history (political, economic, etc.) as well are indispensable quarries for the building blocks of the future. In forging the law of the future we mustn't forget Aristotle, Blackstone, Holmes, and the other past masters of law. But neither can we merely repeat the past—which is an undoubted tendency of American legal thought. We mustn't emulate the Bourbon kings, of whom it was said that they learned nothing and forgot nothing. We must shake off judicial stodginess.

That stodginess is connected to the oddity that unlike other decision makers, judges are reluctant to acknowledge responsibility for their decisions. It is the rare judge who will do so. A judge commonly wants to be understood as just applying the "law." He has "discovered" the law. He read those old documents, old cases, etc. and now he knows what the law *is*. That is what judges like to do and say but it doesn't mean that's how they actually decide cases— that "the law made me do it." Is this modesty? No, it's timidity. The judge who says he decided a case one way because he thought it the sensible way invites disagreement; if instead the law made him do it he is blameless.

Stuffiness: herein of "crimes involving moral turpitude." The legal profession's stuffiness, as distinct from its stodginess, is its stubborn adherence to stale legal terminology, some still in Latin.[16] A notable example, though not a Latinate one, concerns the term "moral turpitude" mentioned earlier in this chapter. Stale, antiquated, and, worse, meaningless, it remains a part of American law and plays a particularly malign role in immigration adjudication, because conviction of a crime involving moral turpitude bars the Attorney General from canceling the deportation, or adjusting the status (such as to lawful permanent

16. I offered the following litany of judicial offenses against the English language in my book *Reflections on Judging* 250 (2013): Latinisms (such as *"ambit," "de minimis," "eiusdem generis," "sub silentio"*); legal clichés (such as "plain meaning," "strict scrutiny," "instant case," "totality of circumstances," "abuse of discretion," "facial adequacy," "facial challenge," "chilling effect," "canons of construction," "gravamen," and "implicates" in such expressions as "the statute implicates First Amendment concerns"); legal terms that have an ambulatory rather than a fixed meaning (such as "rational basis" and "proximate cause"); incurably vague "feel good" terms such as "justice" and "fairness"; pomposities such as "it is axiomatic that"; insincere verbal curtsies ("with all due respect," or "I respectfully dissent"); and gruesome juxtapositions (such as *Roe* and its progeny," meaning *Roe v. Wade* and the subsequent abortion-rights cases). To this add: timid obeisance to clumsy norms of politically correct speech; unintelligible abbreviations gleaned from the *Bluebook*; archaic grammatical rules (for example, don't begin a sentence with "But," "And," "However," or "Moreover"—these words are "postpositives," and never say "on the other hand" without having first said "on the one hand"); archaic rules of punctuation, especially placement of commas; and offenses against good English ("choate" for "not inchoate," "pled" for "pleaded" when referring to a complaint or other pleading, "proven" as a verb instead of "proved," "absent" and "due to" as adverbs, "habeas claim" for "habeas corpus claim," "he breached his contract" for "he broke his contract") or against good Latin (*"de minimus"* for *"de minimis"* and *"ejusdem generis"* for *"eiusdem generis"*). Professor Ferguson, at page 209 of his *Practice Extended: Beyond Law and Literature* (2016) notes "Posner's desire and ability to challenge reflexive use of unhelpful but familiar terminology."

resident), of an illegal alien.[17] I had a scrape with the term in a recent immigration case, *Arias v. Lynch*,[18] in which the panel granted an illegal immigrant's petition for relief from an order removing (deporting) her from the United States because she had committed a very minor crime. Though agreeing with the panel opinion's bottom line I wrote a concurring opinion expressing my strong disapproval of the continued use of the concept of "moral turpitude" in federal law. Drawing on my opinion I'll explain the basis of my disapproval and hope by doing so to help turn my readers against legal jargon in general and "moral turpitude" in particular.

The term "crime involving moral turpitude" first appeared in American law more than two hundred years ago, in a case called *Brooker v. Coffin*.[19] Without defining the term the court concluded that prostitution and other disorderly-conduct offenses were not crimes of moral turpitude, and therefore falsely accusing someone of such an offense could not support a suit for slander.[20] The term made infrequent further appearances in case law until legislators became enamored of it in the closing years of the nineteenth century, when in the Act of March 3, 1891 (chap. 551, 51st Cong., 2d Sess.), Congress, worried by the swelling tide of immigration to the United States, forbade the admission of, among other categories of disfavored aliens (such as polygamists), aliens "who have been convicted of a felony or other infamous crime or misdemeanor involving moral turpitude." Why Congress chose the term "moral turpitude" to describe crimes that should bar aliens is unclear because there is no attempt to explain it either in the statute itself or in the legislative history.[21]

Congress has never defined the term "moral turpitude," but courts and the immigration agencies have tended to adopt a slight variant of the definition in *Black's Law Dictionary:* an "act of baseness, vileness, or the depravity in private and social duties which man owes to his fellow man, or to society in general. . . . [An] act or behavior that gravely violates moral sentiment or accepted moral standards of [the] community and is a morally culpable quality held to be present in some criminal offenses as distinguished from others."[22] Thus my court in

---

17. See 8 U.S.C. §§ 1229b(b)(1)(C), 1182(a)(2)(A)(1)(I).

18. 834 F.3d 823 (7th Cir. 2016).

19. 5 *Johns.* 188 (N.Y. 1809); see Note, "Crimes Involving Moral Turpitude," 43 *Harvard Law Review* 117, 118 n. 7 (1929).

20. 5 *Johns.* at 191–192.

21. See Staff of House Committee on the Judiciary, 100th Cong., *Grounds for Exclusion of Aliens Under the Immigration and Nationality Act: Historical Background and Analysis* 10 (Comm. Print. 1988).

22. *Black's Law Dictionary* 1008–1009 (6th ed. 1990).

Lagunas-Salgado v. Holder[23] remarked that "the BIA [Board of Immigration Appeal] has described a crime of moral turpitude as including 'conduct that shocks the public conscience as being inherently base, vile, or depraved, and contrary to the accepted rules of morality and the duties owed between persons or to society in general.'" The most recent edition of *Black's* offers a simpler but broader definition: "conduct that is contrary to justice, honesty, or morality; esp., an act that demonstrates depravity."[24]

It's difficult to make sense of these definitions, which approach gibberish yet are quoted deferentially in countless modern opinions. What does "the public conscience" mean? What does "base, vile, or depraved"—words that have virtually dropped from the vocabulary of modern Americans—mean and what does "inherently" add to the three-word string? And how do any of these terms differ from "contrary to the accepted rules of morality"? How for that matter do the "accepted rules of morality" differ from "the duties owed between persons or to society in general"?

And—urgently—what *is* "depravity"? A partial list of its synonyms turned up by a Google search includes corruption, vice, perversion, deviance, degeneracy, immorality, debauchery, dissipation, profligacy, licentiousness, lechery, prurience, obscenity, indecency, a wicked or morally corrupt act, the innate corruption of human nature caused by original sin, moral perversion, bestiality, flagitiousness, and putrefaction. The definitions constitute a list of antiquated synonyms for bad character, and why does the legal profession cling to antiquated synonyms? Why are we so backward-looking?

The answer lies in the fact that the legal profession revels in antiquity, cherishes jargon, and lacks respect for proper English usage—"base or vile" is not an expression used by sophisticated speakers of modern English or for that matter unsophisticated ones, and the word "turpitude" has disappeared from the language as spoken and written today. The language I quoted from *Black's*— who talks like that? Who *needs* to talk like that? Lawyers apparently, and they go a step further into the lexical mud by intoning an adjectival form of "turpitude": "turpitudinous." Our profession is shameless.

At this point I need to prepare the reader for the mysterious ways in which the federal government classifies crimes against itself (for that is the nature of the crime that the petitioner in *Arias v. Lynch* had committed—a crime against the government) as "turpitudinous" or not. The *U.S. Department of State For-*

23. 584 F.3d 707, 710 (7th Cir. 2009).
24. *Black's Law Dictionary* 1163 (10th ed. 2014).

eign Affairs Manual (FAM),[25] divides crimes against government into those that are, and those that are not, crimes of moral turpitude:

a. Crimes committed against governmental authority which fall within the definition of moral turpitude include:

(1) Bribery;

(2) Counterfeiting;

(3) Fraud against revenue or other government functions;

(4) Mail fraud;

(5) Perjury;

(6) Harboring a fugitive from justice (with guilty knowledge); and

(7) Tax evasion (willful).

b. Crimes committed against governmental authority, which would not constitute moral turpitude for visa-issuance purposes, are, in general, violation of laws which are regulatory in character and which do not involve the element of fraud or other evil intent. The following list assumes that the statutes involved do not require the showing of an intent to defraud, or evil intent:

(1) Black market violations;

(2) Breach of the peace;

(3) Carrying a concealed weapon;

(4) Desertion from the Armed Forces;

(5) Disorderly conduct;

(6) Drunk or reckless driving;

(7) Drunkenness;

(8) Escape from prison;

(9) Failure to report for military induction;

(10) False statements (not amounting to perjury or involving fraud);

(11) Firearms violations;

(12) Gambling violations;

(13) Immigration violations;

(14) Liquor violations;

(15) Loan sharking;

(16) Lottery violations;

(17) Possessing burglar tools (without intent to commit burglary);

25. Volume 9, Visas, 9 FAM 40.21(a) N2.3-2 Crimes Committed Against Governmental Authority (2015).

(18) Smuggling and customs violations (where intent to commit fraud
is absent);

(19) Tax evasion (without intent to defraud); and

(20) Vagrancy.

The division between the two lists is arbitrary. The first, being open-ended,
provides incomplete guidance to how to avoid committing a crime of moral
turpitude. The second list, the list of crimes that do *not* involve moral turpitude, includes such marginal crimes as possessing burglar tools without intent
to commit burglary and committing tax evasion without intent to defraud; and
those are indeed crimes (though probably they shouldn't be) that belong on the
second list. But the list also includes a number of crimes that are as serious, as
"turpitudinous" one steeped in the jargon of crimes of moral turpitude might
say, as those in the first list: desertion from the Armed Forces, escape from
prison, smuggling, firearms violations, loan sharking, breach of the peace, and
failure to report for military induction (that is, draft dodging, when there is a
draft). The pair of lists seems the product of a disordered mind. They make no
sense.

Petitioner Arias's crime was the use of a social security number that had
been assigned to another person by the Social Security Administration. That
was a felony.[26] She had used the number to obtain a job. There is no indication
that had she not done this an American citizen would have gotten the job in
her stead, rather than one of the ten or eleven million other illegal aliens who
live in the United States and like Arias need to work in order to support themselves. The statute does not require proof of intent to cause harm—an absence
that one would think would negate an inference of moral turpitude. Nor is it
required that the violation be material. There was no proof that Arias's crime
had deprived anyone of social security benefits or increased the expenses of
government.

Happily she was punished very lightly by being placed on probation for a
year and assessed $100, the mandatory monetary assessment for felony convic-
tions.[27] So: no incarceration, no fine, just a year's probation and an assessment
equivalent to the amount of money she earns in 9.1 hours of work (for her wage
is $10.97 per hour).

The very light sentence may reflect in part the fact that she has two young

26. 42 U.S.C. § 408(a)(7)(B).
27. See 18 U.S.C. § 3013.

children, has worked without incident since coming to the United States in 2000, and has paid federal income tax. Or maybe the judge thought her crime trivial, as do I. (Has the Justice Department nothing better to do with its limited resources than prosecute a mouse? Has prosecutorial discretion flown out the window?) She did not steal or invent the social security number; it was given to her by the persons who smuggled her into the United States.

After completing her probation she was allowed to resume her employment with the same company she'd worked for until her arrest, and she obtained a glowing letter of support from the company's general manager. She does manual work for the company, described by the general manager as "sealer sanding doors, wear thru and working with specialty paints." It is the kind of work that illegal immigrants typically do, by default, because it is not pleasant work and not well paid and on both accounts unattractive to most American citizens.

To prosecute and deport such a harmless person (to Ecuador, her country of origin)—indeed a productive resident of the United States—would have been a waste of taxpayers' money, but to deport her on the ground that her crime was one of moral turpitude would have been downright ridiculous. Fortunately the crime she committed does not appear in the State Department's list of crimes of moral turpitude and is less serious even than many of the crimes in the second list (crimes that don't rise to the level of crimes of moral turpitude). Her crime might seem to fall in category 13 in the second list—"immigration violations"—but she was not convicted of violating immigration law, only of violating a section of 42 U.S. Code, Chapter 7, Subchapter II, entitled "Federal Old-Age, Survivors, and Disability Insurance Benefits." Her crime could also have been placed in category 10 on that list—"false statements (not amounting to perjury or involving fraud)," since the State Department is explicit that false statements do *not* constitute crimes of moral turpitude.

The government argued that the petitioner's conduct had been "deceptive" and therefore constituted a crime of "moral turpitude." But glance again at the second list, the list of crimes that are not crimes of moral turpitude. In addition to crime 10—"false statements"—which by definition involve deception, crimes 1, 3, 4, 15, 18, and 19 on that list may also involve deception. When a panel of this court said in *Marin-Rodriguez v. Holder*,[28] a case factually almost identical to the *Arias* case, that "crimes entailing an intent to deceive or defraud are un-

---

28. 710 F.3d 734, 738 (7th Cir. 2013).

questionably morally turpitudinous," it was deviating from the *Foreign Affairs Manual* without explanation.

In *Lagunas-Salgado v. Holder,*[29] mentioned earlier in this chapter, an alien had been convicted of making "false Social Security and alien registration cards so that others could find employment."[30] The Board of Immigration Appeals deemed his crime one of moral turpitude and a panel of this court affirmed. It was a more serious crime than Arias's, because Lagunas-Salgado had sold false papers to about fifty people, some for as much as $100; and he was sentenced to five months in prison and two years of probation, a much heavier sentence than Arias received. The panel opinion in *Lagunas-Salgado* remarked with apparent approval the BIA's conclusion "that petty larceny and issuing a worthless check involve moral turpitude" but that "crimes such as importing, selling, or possessing drugs do not involve moral turpitude because evil intent is not an element of the offense."[31] That is an absurd distinction, given that the congressional mandate is to identify crimes that are morally reprehensible and thus a proper ground for deportation and that drug offenses are widely believed to be morally reprehensible—far more so than petty larceny.

Interestingly, the immigration judge in the *Arias* case said that "unfortunately" the Seventh Circuit had ruled in *Marin-Rodriguez* that the type of conviction involved in Arias's case was "inherently turpitudinous." The judge's instincts were sound, but she felt bound by our decision. The Board of Immigration Appeals affirmed her ruling primarily on the authority of *Marin-Rodriguez*. But *Marin-Rodriguez* was wrong and should by now have been overruled but hasn't been. The court had no basis for rejecting what for a change was proper guidance from the State Department's *Foreign Affairs Manual*.

The idea that fraudulent intent makes any crime "turpitudinous" received its authoritative modern statement in *Jordan v. De George,* like the other cases I've been discussing a deportation case, where we read for example that "fraud has consistently been regarded as such a contaminating component in any crime that American courts have, without exception, included such crimes within the scope of moral turpitude."[32] But notice that the word used by the Court to describe a crime of moral turpitude was "fraud," not "deception," and

29. 159 584 F.3d 707 (7th Cir. 2009).
30. Id. at 708.
31. Id. at 710.
32. 341 U.S. 223, 229 (1951).

De George was a fraud case in the core sense of "fraud": it was a conspiracy to defraud the federal government of tax revenues. Yet though it was a much stronger case for deportation than the *Arias* case, the majority opinion evoked a remarkable dissent by Justice Jackson,[33] joined by Justices Black and Frankfurter, which exposed the emptiness of the concept of moral turpitude. Jackson pointed out that

> Congress did not see fit to state what meaning it attributes to the phrase "crime involving moral turpitude." It is not one which has settled significance from being words of art in the profession. If we go to the dictionaries, the last resort of the baffled judge, we learn little except that the expression is redundant, for turpitude alone means moral wickedness or depravity and moral turpitude seems to mean little more than morally immoral. The Government confesses that it is "a term that is not clearly defined," and says: "the various definitions of moral turpitude provide no exact test by which we can classify the specific offenses here involved." Except for the Court's opinion, there appears to be universal recognition that we have here an undefined and undefinable standard.[34]

Jackson went on to argue convincingly that deportation was an extreme sanction to impose on De George, the alien, without a more definite standard guiding its imposition.[35]

Alas, a great dissent by a great Justice has been forgotten. The concept of moral turpitude, in all its vagueness, rife with contradiction, a fossil, an embarrassment to a modern legal system, continues to do its dirty work. Even so, and despite the precedent of *Marin-Rodriguez*, there was a route to justice in the *Arias* case. It was to recognize that it was not a fraud case. Although convicted of a crime against the government, the petitioner, unlike her predecessor De George, was not seeking any money from the government. So far as appears her crime harmed no one, least of all the government though it was the "victim" of her crime, and so even the muddled overbroad FAM provided no defensible basis for classifying her crime as one of moral turpitude.

The case was in fact identical to *Beltran-Tirado v. INS*,[36] where the Ninth

33. Id. at 232–245.
34. Id. at 234–235.
35. Id. at 240–242.
36. 213 F.3d 1179 (9th Cir. 2000).

Circuit held that using a false social security number on an employment verification form in order to obtain employment was *not* a crime of moral turpitude. Consider, too, *In re Delgadillo*,[37] where the BIA held that an applicant for admission to the United States who had "fabricated a property transfer in an unsuccessful attempt to reduce his wife's potential settlement in a divorce action" had *not* committed a crime "so base or vile as to be deemed morally turpitudinous." The Ninth Circuit and the BIA recognized in these cases, as the State Department does in its manual, that deception alone is not enough to make a crime one of moral turpitude.

The approach I'm suggesting derives support from *Lagunas-Salgado*. The panel in that case was emphatic that it was a fraud case,[38] and *Jordan v. De George* had held that crimes of fraud are *ipso facto* crimes of moral turpitude. Lagunas-Salgado gave away some of his false documents but sold others, and was "deceiving the government" because "he knew the persons receiving the false documents would use them in an attempt to obtain work that they could not otherwise lawfully obtain."[39] Arias did not forge documents, let alone for gift or sale to other persons. The impact of her conduct on her "victim," the U.S. Government, was negligible, as reflected in the nominal sentence that she received relative to the heavier (though still light) sentence imposed on Lagunas-Salgado.

Marin-Rodriguez is closer to the *Arias* case, but the alien in that case had been convicted under a different statute, 18 U.S.C. § 1546, entitled "Fraud and misuse of visas, permits, and other documents," which authorizes sentences of up to ten years in prison (even longer if the offense was committed in connection with drug trafficking or terrorism), and thus punishes more heavily conduct more reprobated than the conduct in which Arias engaged. The court in *Marin-Rodriguez* was mistaken, however, as I've said, in assuming that all deceptive acts, no matter how harmless, are crimes of moral turpitude.[40] It based that proposition on *De George*, as well as on *Abdelqadar v. Gonzales*,[41] and *Padilla v. Gonzales*,[42] though none of those cases involved harmless deception, as did the *Arias* case.

The mess that is the contemporary usage of "moral turpitude" illustrates the

37. 15 I. & N. 395, 1975 WL 31528 (BIA 1975).
38. 584 F.3d at 711–712.
39. Id. at 712.
40. See 710 F.3d at 738.
41. 413 F.3d 668 (7th Cir. 2005).
42. 397 F.3d 1016, 1019 (7th Cir. 2004).

fundamental problem that plagues the judiciary: the past lays foundations, but does not contain usable solutions to contemporary problems. Let's not forget that the past is another country and that they do things differently there. The eighteenth-century United States, the nineteenth-century United States, much of the twentieth-century United States, might as well be foreign countries so far as providing concrete guidance (as distinct from inspiration) to solving today's legal problems is concerned. The judges and Justices are unwilling to admit this (often even to themselves), because they feel or sense that their authority is bound up with ancientness, that if they admitted they're constantly remaking the law they would be thought legislators, competing with "the political branches," which are thought to be the primary legitimate sources of law (putting aside the common law—the law that judges create without pretense of merely interpreting or applying law made by legislatures and executive agencies—and those provisions of the Constitution that time has not made obsolete).

Though federal judges are not elected, as legislators are (though not members of federal administrative agencies), they legislate, in effect, whenever their decisions create rules, because those rules have the force of law. The rules sometimes are inspired by orthodox legislative activity, including constitutional provisions, but the principal use to which judges put such provisions is as grants of judicial authority. This *has* to be. The free-speech clause of the First Amendment, for example, *can't* mean what it says, because a society can't function without a degree of censorship. So instead it's treated by judges and Justices as an invitation to second guess legislative and executive regulations of speech—permitting some curtailments, such as defamation law, copyright and trademark law, and laws punishing unauthorized disclosures of sensitive information, and forbidding others. But it's a joke to say, as judges like to, that in deciding what speech to privilege (adult pornography for example) and what speech to allow to be suppressed (such as child pornography), they are implementing decisions by the drafters or ratifiers of the Constitution, though they may well be implementing (mistakenly in my view) judicial decisions that have lost their relevance to contemporary social and economic conditions but not their authority as precedents.

It might seem that federal court of appeals judges would be particularly averse to innovating because of the looming eminence of the Supreme Court. But the Court hears so few cases that lower-court judges have a good deal of freedom—and frequently exercise it, as implied by Professor Corey Yung's discovery of nine judging styles among federal court of appeals judges: collegial, regulating, error correcting, incrementalist, minimalist, consensus building, trailblazing, steadfast, and stalwart.[43] The stalwart judges have "the highest Ideological, Activism, and Partisanship Scores."[44]

Down with the standards of appellate review. Among problems common to appellate courts one of the worst—a genuine horror, on which I feel compelled to dwell at some length—is their preoccupation with standards of appellate review. One gets the flavor of such standards from the introduction to the following primer on the subject (footnotes omitted):[45]

> Appellate courts never perform their magic from an empty hat. Standards of review, once called the appellate court's "measuring stick" by Judge John Godbold of the Eleventh Circuit, are important on appeal and even at trial to frame the issues, define the depth of review, assign power among judicial actors, and declare the proper materials to review. "Unless counsel is familiar with the standard of review for each issue, he may find himself trying to run for a touchdown when basketball rules are in effect." Standards of review have evolved to be, more and more, the essential language of appeals. The various catchphrases associated with standards of review are often difficult for court and counsel to define and apply in practice. Conflicts abound, among circuits and even within them. Yet it is widely believed that standards of review cannot be ignored, that they are essential to effective advocacy. See, e.g., Peter Nicholas, "De Novo Review in Deferential Robes? A Deconstruction of the Standard of Review of Evidentiary Issues in the Federal System," 54 *Syracuse L. Rev.* 531, 531 (2004) ("In federal appellate practice, the standard of review is

43. Corey Rayburn Yung, "A Typology of Judging Styles," 107 *Northwestern University Law Review* 1757, 1780–1781 (2013).

44. Id. at 1784. Yung in a series of articles has presented convincing evidence that ideology plays a significant though not a huge role in federal judicial decision making at the court of appeals level; besides the article cited in the preceding footnote, see, e.g., his article "Judged by the Company You Keep: An Empirical Study of the Ideologies of Judges on the United States Courts of Appeals," 51 *Boston College Law Review* 1133 (2010). In a subsequent article he claims with some evidentiary support that partisanship and independence (willingness to disagree with judges who may not have a different ideology) play a larger role than ideology itself in predicting judicial behavior: "Beyond Ideology: An Empirical Study of Partisanship and Independence in the Federal Courts," 80 *George Washington Law Review* 505 (2012).

45. Steven Alan Childress, "Standards of Review Primer: Federal Civil Appeals," 229 F.R.D. 267, 268–269 (September 2005).

the name of the game"); W. Wendell Hall, "Standards of Review in Texas," 29 *St. Mary's Law Journal* 351, 358 (1998) (they are the "cornerstone of an appeal"). They are integral to any coherent strategy—to speak a language understandable to appellate judges' ears.

It is not just a matter of strategic choice alone. In 1993 the Federal Rules of Appellate Procedure were amended to require a statement of the applicable review standard (as many circuits already had required). Fed. R. App. P. 28(a)(9)(B) and 28(b)(5). Most circuits followed suit with local rules implementing or refining this rule. E.g., 3d Cir. R. 28.1(b); 9th Cir. R. 28-2.5; 11th Cir. R. 28-1(i)(iii). For example, the Fifth Circuit's internal rule was amended to match this requirement, as specified in Fifth Circuit Rule 28.2.6 (further requesting that it be identified in a separate heading up front in the brief). Nevertheless a study by its clerk's office named "failure to state the standard of review" as the number one reason it rejects briefs. Luther T. Munford, "The Most Common Mistakes in the Form of Fifth Circuit Briefs," 14 *Fifth Circuit Reporter* 227 (March 1997). The requirement applies generally to federal appeals in civil, criminal, and administrative cases, but it also sets the tone for many procedural and review issues facing the U.S. district court.

What are we hearing? "Magic," "essential language of appeals," "conflicts abound among circuits and even within them. Yet standards of review cannot be ignored. . . . They are integral to any coherent strategy—to speak a language understandable to appellate judges' ears." "In federal appellate practice, the standard of the review is the name of the game;" it is the "cornerstone of an appeal." The federal rules of appellate procedure require appellate briefs to include "a statement of the applicable review standard." The "clerk's office named a 'failure to state the standard of review' as the number one reason it rejects briefs." All this is nonsense. Even a staunch defender of the standards of review complains that "courts ignore, confuse, and misuse them."[46] But maybe what these rebels are really doing is, having realized that the standards of review are indeed nonsense, bypassing them.

To evaluate the standards of review in detail requires considering them one by one. Here is a serviceable list, which I have slightly edited for the sake of clarity and brevity, from *Wikipedia*,[47] together with my appraisal of each. The

---

46. Amanda Peters, "The Meaning, Measure, and Misuse of Standards of Review," 13 *Lewis & Clark Law Review* 233 (2009).

47. "Standard of Review," *Wikipedia*, https://en.wikipedia.org/wiki/Standard_of_review.

first paragraph of each standard of review is a description of the standard, based on *Wikipedia;* the paragraph or paragraphs below it are my critique.

QUESTIONS OF FACT

Arbitrary and Capricious

In administrative law, a government agency's resolution of a question of fact, when decided pursuant to an informal rulemaking under the Administrative Procedure Act (APA), is reviewed under the arbitrary and capricious standard. A legal ruling is deemed arbitrary and capricious if the appellate court determines that a previous ruling is invalid because it was made on unreasonable grounds or without any proper consideration of circumstances. This is an extremely deferential standard.

But why *extremely* deferential? And what meaning is supposed to attach to "unreasonable grounds" or to "without any proper consideration of circumstances"? What circumstances are being referred to? Fortunately, in the well-known case of *Motor Vehicles Manufacturers Ass'n v. State Farm Mutual Automobile Insurance Co.* the Supreme Court gave some content to "arbitrary and capricious" by saying that "normally, an agency [decision] would be arbitrary and capricious if the agency has [1] relied on factors which Congress has not intended it to consider, [2] entirely failed to consider an important aspect of the problem, [3] offered an explanation for its decision that runs counter to the evidence before the agency, or [4] is so implausible that it could not be ascribed to a difference in view or the product of agency expertise."[48] In other words, if the agency screws up it gets reversed.

Substantial Evidence

Under the "substantial evidence" standard, a finding of fact from a jury, or a finding of fact made by an administrative agency decided pursuant to an APA [Administrative Procedure Act] adjudication or formal rulemaking, is upheld on appeal unless it is unsupported by substantial evidence. The appellate courts will generally not review such findings unless those findings have no reasonable basis. This is a highly deferential standard.

But what is "substantial" evidence? What is "reasonable basis"? How does "highly deferential" differ from "extremely deferential"?

48. 463 U.S. 29, 43 (1983).

Clearly Erroneous

Under the "clearly erroneous" standard, where a trial court (as opposed to a jury or administrative agency) makes a finding of fact, such as in a bench trial, that finding will not be disturbed unless the appellate court is left with a "definite and firm conviction that a mistake has been committed" by that court. For example, if a court finds, based on the testimony of a single eyewitness, that a defendant broke a window by throwing a one pound rock over 20 feet, the appeals court might reverse that factual finding based on uncontradicted expert testimony (also presented to the lower court) stating that such a feat is impossible for most people. In such a case, the appeals court might find that, although there was evidence to support the lower court's finding, the evidence taken as a whole—including the eyewitness and the expert testimony—leaves the appellate court with a definite and firm conviction that a mistake was committed by the Court below.

What does "definite" add to "firm" or "firm" to definite"? What does "clearly" add to "erroneous"? What is an "unclear" error?

Reasonable Suspicion

This is most commonly encountered in *Terry*-stop cases—brief investigative stops of a person or vehicle solely to determine whether probable cause for an arrest can be established.[49] The officer who executes the stop must have "reasonable suspicion" of unlawful behavior.

But what is reasonable suspicion? The courts say that it's more than mere suspicion or hunch—and presumably more than a mere possibility—but less than probable cause. But judges don't know how to split these hairs. An improvement would be to require that the stop be supported by evidence, though of course not necessarily conclusive evidence.

QUESTIONS OF LAW

De novo

Under *de novo* review, the appellate court acts as if it were considering the question for the first time, according no deference to the decisions below. Legal decisions of a lower court on questions of law are reviewed

49. See *Terry v. Ohio*, 392 U.S. (1968). Cf. Timothy P. O'Neill, "Posner Opinion Aims to Put Teeth into 'Reasonable Suspicion' Doctrine," *Chicago Daily Law Bulletin*, June 1, 2016, p. 5. The case referred to in the article is *United States v. Paniagua-Garcia*, 813 F.3d 1013 (7th Cir. 2016).

using this standard. This is sometimes also called the "legal error" standard. It allows the appeals court to substitute its own judgment about whether the lower court correctly applied the law. A new trial in which all issues are reviewed as if for the first time is called a trial *de novo.*

At last, a clear statement! This is the only standard of review I pay attention to, though I'd substitute "plenary" for *de novo.*

Chevron

Questions of statutory interpretation decided by an administrative agency in a manner that has the force of law are subject to *Chevron* review, which is highly deferential, to the point of allowing agencies in effect to define the scope of their powers.

That may seem strange, but apparently Congress prefers that its statutes be "interpreted" by agencies rather than by courts—probably because agencies are more under Congress's thumb than courts are and also because agency staff knows more about the tasks Congress has assigned it than federal judges do.[50] But trial judges know more about their cases than appellate judges do, yet the latter accord only limited deference to the former, and it is not apparent why appellate courts should accord greater deference to agencies. Moreover, while agencies are indeed more responsive to Congress than to courts, they are more responsive to the President than to Congress, so that the effect of *Chevron* has been "to displace *legislative* power into the *executive* branch—a paradoxical result since the authors of these decisions [*Chevron* and also *INS v. Chadha,* 462 U.S. 919 (1983)] defend them by reference to the allocation of powers in the Constitution, which endeavored to lodge the legislative and executive powers in different branches."[51]

Deference should be earned rather than bestowed, one reason being the great variance in the quality of federal administrative agencies. In my experience the two worst are the SSA Disability Office, which adjudicates applications for disability benefits, and the Executive Office for Immigration Review Immigration Court/Board of Immigration Appeals, which adjudicates deportation cases, including cases in which aliens seek asylum in the United States because of acute dangers or hardships in their native lands to which the De-

---

50. On the relation of the federal agencies to Congress, with specific reference to agency interpretation of statutes, see Christopher J. Walker, "Inside Statutory Interpretation," 67 *Stanford Law Review* 999 (2015).

51. Richard A. Posner, "The Rise and Fall of Administrative Law," 72 *Chicago-Kent Law Review* 953, 960 (1997).

partment of Homeland Security wants them deported. The administrative law judges of the SSA Disability Office are overworked because there are too few of them, and because they rely heavily on boilerplate, embrace unsound practices such as inferring an applicant's ability to work from his engaging in "activities of daily living" (which are unavoidable—until they qualify for benefits, persons with disabilities will often force themselves to work harder than is good for them, as they have no alternative), are ignorant about mental disease, fail to give due weight to the disabling effects of severe obesity, fail to evaluate an applicant's disabilities holistically, are serviced by a weak bar because there is little money in social security disability practice, and rely on unreliable statistics regarding the availability of jobs for persons with disabilities.[52] A systemic error is that decisions by the SSA denying disability benefits are appealable in the first instance to district courts rather than to courts of appeals, but an adverse judgment by the district court can then be appealed to the court of appeals. There is no need for a two-tier appellate structure. The district courts should be bypassed, as in appeals from adverse decisions by the BIA.

The worst social security disability case that I have seen is not a case of mine or a case in my court; it is a case that was before my friend Judge John Kane of the federal district court in Denver; I quote the conclusion of his concise and eloquent decision reversing a denial by SSA of benefits to a most deserving applicant:

IN THE UNITED STATES DISTRICT COURT
FOR THE DISTRICT OF COLORADO
CIVIL ACTION NO. 15-CV-1378-JLK

DIANA I. ANDERSON,
Plaintiff,

v.

CAROLYN COLVIN, Acting Commissioner of Social Security,
Defendant.

District Judge Kane:
It is hard to come away from the Administrative Law Judge's extravagant and exhaustive takedown of Ms. Anderson's functional limitations ac-

---

52. On social security disability practice see also *Divergent Paths*, note 8 above, at 135–137, 150–154, and Harold J. Krent and Scott Morris, "Inconsistency and Angst in District Court Resolution of Social Security Disability Appeals," 67 *Hastings Law Journal* 367 (2016). On immigration adjudication see, e.g., *Gutierrez-Rostran v. Lynch,* 810 F.3d 497 (7th Cir. 2016); *Mendoza-Sanchez v. Lynch,* 808 F.3d 1182 (7th Cir. 2015); *Rodriguez-Molinero v. Lynch,* 808 F.3d 1134 (7th Cir. 2015).

cording to the doctor who knew her best without wondering why such pains were taken. The SSA had recognized Ms. Anderson as disabled from 1978 to 2002, had subjected her to a continuing disability review in 1996 that confirmed her disability, and had found, in 2009, that she was again incapable of gainful employment. The insistence, in 2015, that such a person had gained the capacity a dozen years before and was able, for a brief period of time long since gone, to perform full time work as a "small product assembler," "cafeteria attendant," or "cashier II" . . . simply flies in the face of the reality and the agency's own 2009 determinations to the contrary. All of the effort expended engaging in a fictional analysis of facts long past and no longer apt—why do it? The *post facto* reasons the ALJ gave to support a finding of non-disability in 2002 would seem to apply equally in 2009, except, perhaps, Ms. Anderson's then-advancing age. In any event, the consternation Judge Matsch expressed in 2010 is only amplified now, six years later, and I paraphrase it here to conclude: It is difficult to understand how the SSA, having repeatedly recognized a woman as incapable of substantial gainful employment for the entirety of her working life—from the age of 20 on—has spent more than a decade insisting that she suddenly gained the capacity back in 2002, at the age of 43, while conceding she "lost" it again seven years later. The herculean effort expended by ALJ Musseman in writing a 40-page, singlespace typewritten decision, peering back over a dozen years after the fact, to reaffirm that point is even more confounding. There is no purpose to be served in 2016 to remand the case for proper consideration of Dr. Higgins's opinions or to reassess Ms. Anderson's 12-year-old hypothetical "vocational baseline." Ms. Anderson is 58 years old, has never worked, and has been declared incapable of working anymore for the remainder of her work-age life. A remand after the Kafkaesque proceedings revealed by this record would be manifestly unjust.

I remain outraged. Because

"I am involved in mankind.
Therefore, send not to know
For whom the bell tolls,
It tolls for thee."[53]

I reverse ALJ Musseman's March 22, 2015 decision and order.

---

53. John Donne, "Meditation 17" (1624), in *Devotions upon Emergent Occasions.*

*   *   *

Often immigration judges and members of the BIA, both in adjudicating asylum applications and in adjudicating deportation requests by the Department of Homeland Security, lack adequate knowledge of conditions in the country of origin of the applicants (which becomes their country of destination if they are deported).[54] But now an even larger cloud is hanging over the immigration agencies: the possibility that, with a backlog of more than 500,000 cases, the Immigration Court may collapse.[55]

Just a year after the Supreme Court decided *Chevron,* my court, observing that "ALJ's work under great burdens," said that a "sketchy opinion" was adequate if the reviewing court could "trace the path of the ALJ's reasoning," and that "a more extensive requirement sacrifices on the altar of perfectionism the claims of other people stuck in the queue."[56] *Chevron* notwithstanding, I trust we wouldn't say that today; disability applicants deserve better.

I need to connect my discussion of the *Chevron* deference doctrine to the concern I expressed much earlier in this book about the remoteness of so much academic scholarship from the practical realities of law. In a recent article[57] Adrian Vermeule, a well-known Harvard Law School professor[58] who has never practiced law or worked for an administrative agency, applauds the *Chevron* doctrine without grounding his applause in fact. He wants courts to "defer to reasonable agency decisions about the design of procedural arrangements, reviewing the agency's choices for arbitrariness, but not correctness. . . . [C]ourts will relegate themselves to the institutional margins." Why? Why is it worse to be arbitrary than to be wrong? Vermeule quotes with approval a concurring opinion in a Supreme Court case that states that as long as the agency offers a "'facially legitimate and bona fide reason' for its procedural choices, 'courts will neither look behind the exercise of that discretion nor test it by balancing its justifications against the constitutional interests of citizens.'"[59] This is gobbledygook (and "facially," which as used in law is a crude contraction of "on its face," is a vulgarity), which Vermeule makes no effort to explain or justify. But it be-

---

54. As if this were not criticism enough, further cogent criticisms are presented in David Hausman, "The Failure of Immigration Appeals," 164 *University of Pennsylvania Law Review* 1177 (2016).

55. See Julia Preston, "Under Deluge, Migrant Courts Begin to Buckle: Huge Case Backlog Is a Hurdle for Trump," *New York Times,* December 2, 2016, p. A1.

56. *Stephens v. Heckler,* 766 F.2d 284, 287–288 (7th Cir. 1985).

57. "Deference and Due Process," 129 *Harvard Law Review* 1890, 1893 (2016).

58. See note 133 in Chapter 2 and accompanying text.

59. "Deference and Due Process," note 57 above, at 1893, quoting *Kerry v. Din,* 135 S. Ct. 2128, 2140 (2015).

comes clear from the next page of his article that he is reasoning from recent Supreme Court decisions that appear to give the agencies free rein, even suggesting that "*Chevron* may actually give agencies the power to determine the scope of their own jurisdiction."[60] Allow an agency to expand or contract its jurisdiction at will? Crazy!

I have no sense that Vermeule has any first-hand familiarity with administrative agencies, without which, however, his prescriptions are ungrounded conjecture. Other scholars have such familiarity.[61] Even I do, as I mentioned briefly in the Introduction. I worked for the Federal Trade Commission for two years in the early 1960s, was an assistant to the Solicitor General for two years after that, dealt extensively with federal administrative agencies as a consultant in the 1970s, and as a judge have heard a great many appeals from and by such agencies. My judicial experience has taught me that some of the agencies, such as the FTC, the FCC, the NLRB, the EPA, OSHA, and the Corps of Engineers, are highly competent, that others, such as FERC and the IRS, are intermittently competent, and that two, which I've already mentioned and which happen to be the two with which my court has the most experience, are very weak—the Immigration Court and Board of Immigration Appeals (I am treating them as one, since the Board is the body to which disappointed applicants for relief by the Immigration Court appeal before seeking judicial relief), and the SSA Disability Office. Given the competence scatter I can't imagine wanting to limit judicial review of an agency's procedures and rulings and jurisdiction to "arbitrariness," but in any event I find nothing in Vermeule's article to suggest any empirical grounds for the degree of deference that he wants to grant the agencies. In fact, although elegantly written the article is disconnected from the reality of federal administrative structure and process.

It is also of a piece with his notorious (one might even call it bratty, though ignorant will do) disparagement of Judge Friendly in a review of David Dors-

---

60. Id. at 1894. Vermeule has been riding the *Chevron* horse for many years; I criticized him for this years ago in "Reply: The Institutional Dimension of Statutory and Constitutional Interpretation," 101 *Michigan Law Review* 952, 967–978 (2003). On the administrative process in general, see my book *Economic Analysis of Law*, chap. 24 (9th ed. 2014). Vermeule's advocacy of judicial deference to administrative agencies echoes the school of "judicial self-restraint" founded by Harvard law professor James Bradley Thayer, who in his article "The Origin and Scope of the American Doctrine of Constitutional Law," 7 *Harvard Law Review* 129, 144 (1893), urged that a statute should be deemed unconstitutional only if its unconstitutionality is "so clear that it is not open to rational question." If we except the school of Vermeule and his coauthors regarding judicial review of administrative agencies, the doctrine of judicial self-restraint is dead. See the first five articles in 100 *California Law Review* 519–621 (2012).

61. See the scholarly works cited in note 82 below.

en's biography of Friendly for having failed to contribute "ideas of general and lasting significance . . . to law and legal theory."[62] In fact, in addition to his large number of highly influential judicial opinions Friendly wrote two important books (*Benchmarks* and *Federal Jurisdiction*) and a number of important articles, such as "Is Innocence Irrelevant,"[63] which I discuss later in this chapter. His contributions to legal thought exceed those of Professor Vermeule by a wide margin. As I explained in a memorial tribute to Friendly shortly after his death, "He was the greatest appellate judge of his time—in analytic power, memory, and application perhaps of any time. His opinions have exhibited greater staying power than that of any of his contemporaries on the federal courts of appeal."[64] Dorsen's biography confirmed my belief that Judge Friendly was a good deal smarter than I am, and I suspect that he was a good deal smarter than Professor Vermeule is, as well.

A particular irony in Vermeule's disparagement of Friendly is that administrative law was Friendly's principal field, both in private practice and as a judge.[65] Among other involvements with administrative agencies he was vice president and general counsel of Pan American World Airways for many years, in which capacity he litigated frequently before the Civil Aeronautics Board. In contrast, unless Google is deceiving me, Vermeule has never practiced law in any capacity.

Critical as I am of Vermeule's article "Deference and Due Process," I am still more critical of his even more recent article (coauthored with Jacob Gersen) entitled "Thin Rationality Review."[66] The article, building on a literal interpre-

---

62. Quoted and discussed in *Divergent Paths*, note 8 above, at 34–35.

63. "Is Innocence Irrelevant? Collateral Attack on Criminal Judgments," 38 *University of Chicago Law Review* 142 (1970).

64. "In Memoriam: Henry J. Friendly," 99 *Harvard Law Review* 1724 (1986). See also the memorial tributes of three of Friendly's distinguished colleagues on the Second Circuit—John O. Newman, Wilfred Feinberg, and Pierre Leval: Newman, "From Learned Hand to Henry Friendly," *New York Times*, March 24, 1986; Feinberg, "In Memoriam: Henry J. Friendly," 99 *Harvard Law Review* 1713, 1714 (1986) ("Somehow, an unusually high percentage of cases in which Henry wrote opinions involved interesting and important issues. This was because, like other great judges, he carried the full sweep of the law in his mind and saw issues that others might ignore"); Leval, "In Memoriam: Honorable Henry J. Friendly," 805 F.2d XCVI (1987). Friendly and I had a definite affinity. In the almost five years between my judicial appointment (which is when my relationship with him began) and his death, we exchanged letters and opinions at a great rate. William Domnarski has published our correspondence under the title *The Correspondence of Henry Friendly and Richard A. Posner 1982–86*, in 51 *Journal of American Legal History* 395 (2011). Though Friendly was elderly and in poor health, his letters shine and sparkle. www.williamdomnarski.com/article_friendly-and-posner/.

65. See, e.g., A. Raymond Randolph, "Administrative Law and the Legacy of Henry J. Friendly," 74 *New York University Law Review* 1 (1999): "Judge Friendly Laid the Foundation and Mapped the Course for Many of the Modern Doctrines of Administrative Law." Id. at 17.

66. Gersen and Vermeule, "Thin Rationality Review," 114 *Michigan Law Review* 1355 (2016). In the same vein, see Vermeule's forty-one-page article "Deference and Due Process," 129 *Harvard Law Review* 1890

tation of "arbitrary and capricious" that makes it almost impossible to reverse an administrative agency's decision, approves appellate courts' "utiliz[ing] a thinner form of rationality review, one that requires merely that the agency's decision not be pure caprice."[67] But when is an agency's decision ever "pure caprice"? The authors commend judicial "willingness to allow agencies to adopt strategies of second-order rationality that permit *inaccurate, nonrational,* or *arbitrary* action in particular cases."[68] That's rubber-stamping at its worst. The reviewing court is to tell the agency—tell the world—that the agency's rule that it is asked to review is irrational, inaccurate, and arbitrary—and approved. The Gersen-Vermeule formula vitiates the "arbitrary and capricious standard" of judicial review of agency action and comes close to eliminating judicial review of agencies, period.

The authors admit that "agencies must act based on reasons," but quickly retract the admission by declaring that "(1) agencies may *have* reasons they cannot *give,* at least at acceptable cost"[69] and repeating that "(2) the set of admissible reasons includes second-order reasons to act *inaccurately, nonrationally,* or *arbitrarily.*"[70] What are "second-order" reasons? And if an agency has reasons for some action that it has taken or wants to take, why can't it state them? Gersen and Vermeule seem to think that arbitrary actions by agencies are okay as long as they're not capricious as well, but that can't be right. To act arbitrarily or irrationally *is* to act capriciously, since as usually understood "capricious" means impulsive and unpredictable—determined by chance, impulse, or whim.

The authors even approve "rational arbitrariness," by which oxymoron they mean an agency's decision to stop searching for information if the benefits of the search seem unlikely to exceed the costs.[71] There's nothing arbitrary about *that.* But in the conclusion of their article we read that an agency's ruling should be upheld by a reviewing court unless "based on nothing more than caprice," which they define as "a sudden, impulsive, and seemingly unmoti-

---

(2016). For cogent criticisms of *Chevron,* see Brett M. Kavanaugh, "Fixing Statutory Interpretation," 129 *Harvard Law Review* 2250–2254 (2016); Philip Hamburger, *"Chevron* Bias," 84 *George Washington Law Review* 1187 (2016).

   67. Gersen and Vermeule, preceding note, at 1397.

   68. Id. at 1370, emphases added.

   69. Id., emphasis in original.

   70. Id., emphases added.

   71. Id. at 1388. Vermeule amplifies the approach sketched in his articles (including the article with Gersen) in his recent book, *Law's Abnegation: From Law's Empire to the Administrative State* (November 2016), in which, as in his articles, he speaks approvingly of the fact that the administrative state has grown to irreversible proportions with little constraint from the legal system.

vated notion or action."[72] This can't be right, because agency decisions, like judicial decisions, can be demonstrably erroneous even though not sudden, impulsive, or unmotivated.

Of particular concern to me is the authors' failure to grapple with the problem of experimental uncertainty. Agencies inhabit a constantly changing environment, requiring adaptation—often under conditions of uncertainty. Gersen and Vermeule have difficulty seeing any role for judicial review of agency experimentation and initiative. The assumption seems to be that judges are incapable of dealing with either uncertainty or technology (which may well be true of Gersen and Vermeule). But that isn't true, for these are things that judges deal with frequently in cases filed in district courts, as distinct from cases challenging agency action; and there is also the underutilized authority of the appellate court to appoint a neutral expert to help it understand the reasonableness of challenged agency action.

Some years ago I wrote a book dealing with prediction and assessment of catastrophic risk, and became acquainted with the relevant scientific tools, an acquaintance that should be within the capacity of any competent judge.[73] Can't judges be asked to stretch their minds a little? Don't they need more in their noggins than legal doctrine?

Fortunately most risks that agencies run are not catastrophic, and are both easier to understand and assess and easier to avert. But most are not all. My book dealt at length with an experiment conducted at Brookhaven National Laboratory involving a very powerful particle accelerator called the Relativistic Heavy Iron Collider (RHIC). The experiment was believed by several reputable scientists to have a positive though very small probability of destroying the entire planet.[74] By colliding and shattering gold nuclei, which are massive, RHIC produced an unprecedented volume of quarks (the constituents of protons and neutrons), which could have created "strange quarks," which could in turn have "transform[ed] the entire planet Earth into an inert hyperdense sphere about one hundred meters across."[75]

My book identified a number of other catastrophic risks as well, including

72. Gersen and Vermeule, preceding note, at 1407.

73. *Catastrophe: Risk and Response* (2004). For a brilliant fictional account of catastrophic risk see Margaret Atwood, *Oryx and Crake* (2003); see also the index references to Atwood's book in *Catastrophe: Risk and Response* at 318.

74. Again see the index references, in id. at 320; also the brief discussion of the experiment in id. at 30–32.

75. Id. at 30, quoting Martin Rees, *Our Final Hour: A Scientist's Warning: How Terror, Error, and Environmental Disaster Threaten Humankind's Future in This Century—on Earth and Beyond* 120–121 (2003).

(and this is not a joke) mouse pox. A team of Australian scientists, while trying to invent a contraceptive vaccine for mice as a method of pest control, created a lethal virus that could be the basis of a devastating weapon of bioterrorism.[76] It and RHIC illustrate the danger of allowing agencies carte blanche to determine how much risk to take, as advocated by Gersen and Vermeule.

I am mindful that decisions by federal administrative agencies frequently are technologically dense and therefore difficult for judges to understand, but that is also true of many district court decisions, and I therefore don't see why there should be a fundamental difference between judicial review of district courts and of agencies. It behooves federal appellate judges, even the eminences of the Supreme Court, to familiarize themselves with science and technology—it should not be beyond their and our capacity to do, albeit within limits.[77] Nor beyond the capacity of Harvard Law School faculty.

With Gersen-Vermeule contrast a recent article by Jonathan Masur and Eric Posner, sensibly suggesting that agencies be required (and this is a requirement that reviewing courts could enforce) to conduct rigorous cost-benefit analysis, where feasible, before promulgating a new regulation.[78] That will not always be feasible: requisite data may not exist, a degree of guesswork by an agency should certainly be permitted, but the reviewing court should insist on as much analytical precision by the agency as is feasible.

There is more that is wrong with Gersen and Vermeule's "thin rationality" thesis. They ignore regulatory capture (equivalently, the revolving door)—the not infrequent ability of a regulated industry to dominate the regulators, as by offering them good jobs in the industry on the implicit condition that as regu-

76. Again see the index references in *Catastrophe: Risk and Response*, note 73 above, at 319; also the discussion in id. at 77–81.

77. I acknowledge the complexity of many regulatory issues, however. See, e.g., Robert C. Lind et al., *Discounting for Time and Risk in Energy Policy* (1982). Faced with them, judges and Justices would be well advised to appoint experts to advise them, as authorized by Rule 706 of the Federal Rules of Evidence. Here I should mention that judicial review of agency rulings is not the only area of potential tension between courts and agencies. Another is antitrust enforcement; efforts by the Department of Justice to suppress anticompetitive practices in regulated industries may collide with administrative regulation of competition in those industries. Cf. Arup Bose, Debashis Pal, and David E. M. Sappington, "On the Merits of Antitrust Liability in Regulated Industries," 59 *Journal of Law and Economics* 359 (2016).

78. Jonathan S. Masur and Eric A. Posner, "Unquantified Benefits and the Problem of Regulation Under Uncertainty," August 17, 2015, forthcoming in volume 102 of the *Cornell Law Review*. Paul Rogerson, in an unpublished article, "Reversibility and Judicial Review of Policy Experiments" (February 20, 2015), suggests the following, much in the spirit of the Masur-Posner article: "It isn't always easy to tell what the consequences of a regulation will be before it is issued, so a regulatory system with high ex ante review requirements will miss out on some good regulations. One idea that might be able to help, in at least some cases, is the idea of a policy experiment, where an agency tries out a policy on a temporary basis in order to gather more information about its effects."

lators they protect the industry against effective regulation. The authors ignore as well mission orientation, whereby the regulatory agency's leadership imbues staff with agency goals that may not correspond to the aims of Congress or the President. And they ignore the frequent heavy hand of influential members of Congress, who may deflect an agency from its statutory goals.

The Gersen-Vermeule article is fifty-seven pages long—too long, too complicated (yet also too abstract), too remote from the actual practice of judicial review and the realities of administrative regulation to guide or improve judicial review of agency action.

There is a simple way to cut through the fog with which Gersen and Vermeule have engulfed the administrative process; it is found in *Mathews v. Eldridge*,[79] the case in which the Supreme Court adopted a simple cost-benefit test for deciding whether the government's depriving a person of his property should be deemed a violation of due process of law. The test is to compare the cost of the procedural safeguard against error to the likelihood that the error will materialize if the safeguard is withheld and to the gravity of the error if it does materialize. The test is a variant of Judge Learned Hand's formula for determining tort liability: $B < PL$, where B is the cost of a precaution that will prevent an accident, L the loss to an accident victim if the precaution is forgone and the accident occurs, P the probability of the accident's occurring if the precaution is not taken, and PL therefore the expected cost of the accident if the precaution is forgone. If PL is greater than B and an accident occurs, the defendant is deemed negligent for having failed to take the precaution that would have prevented the accident at a cost lower than the accident cost.

Now consider, as I discussed in *Economic Analysis of Law*,

> whether the owner of an apparently abandoned car should be notified, and given an opportunity for a hearing, *before* the car is towed away and sold for scrap. The probability that the car wasn't really abandoned, but broke down or was stolen, is not trivial, and the cost of a hearing is modest relative to the value of the car; so maybe, as most courts have held, the owner should be entitled to the hearing. But suppose we're speaking not of abandoned but of illegally parked cars. Since the cars are not about to be destroyed, the deprivation . . . is much less than in the case of the abandoned car. The probability of error is also much lower,

79. 424 U.S. 319 (1976). See also chapter 22 of my book *Economic Analysis of Law* (9th ed. 2014), pp. 773–774, and also chapter 24 of that book, which discusses administrative agencies in detail.

because ordinarily the determination of whether a car is illegally parked is cut and dried. And the cost of a pre-deprivation hearing is high; if the owner has to be notified before the car is towed, he'll remove it and the deterrent effect of towing will be eliminated. So courts hold that due process does not require a predeprivation hearing in the case of illegally parked cars.[80]

The approach just sketched is readily transferable to judicial review of the decisions of administrative agencies. Administrative error is not uncommon, not only because administrative agencies deal with complex regulatory issues but also because, as I suggested earlier, the agencies operate under considerable political pressure from Congress, the President, and interest groups ("regulatory capture"; they also are distracted by rivalry with agencies with which they overlap).[81] These are compelling grounds for giving the appellant in an administrative case a fair judicial hearing, rather than just rubber-stamping the administrative decision. The cost of the judicial hearing is bound to be much lower than the costs of error by the administrative agency.

I can imagine, albeit not without some difficulty, President Trump appointing Vermeule to the Supreme Court. The federal administrative agencies are tools of the President, and the President has no interest in subjecting their decisions to judicial review. He should therefore be delighted to see judicial review of the agencies' decisions curtailed, as urged by Vermeule.

Much of the academic writing emanating from the leading law schools is of the sterile character of Gersen and Vermeule's "Thin Rationality Review."[82] I am put in mind of an essay by the great American literary critic Edmund Wilson in

---

80. See id. at 774.

81. See id., §§ 24.3–24.6, pp. 866–879. On standards of evidence applied in administrative proceedings and in judicial review of such proceedings, see William H. Kuehnle, "Standards of Evidence in Administrative Proceedings," 49 *New York Law School Law Review* 829 (2005).

82. The article might be renamed "Thin Academic Review." In contrast to Vermeule, "Judge Posner is urging the current crowd of federal lawyers and judges (yours truly would add state lawyers and judges) to see further into the facts, that they may achieve more than what they say they want now." James L. Robertson, "Variations on a Theme by Posner: Facing the Factual Component of the Reliability Imperative in the Process of Adjudication," 84 *Mississippi Law Journal* 471, 682 (2015). Moreover, there is a rich, concrete, critical literature on the *Chevron* doctrine that contrasts sharply with Vermeule's articles. See, e.g., Stephen Breyer, "Judicial Review of Questions of Law and Policy," 38 *Administrative Law Review* 363 (1986); Cass R. Sunstein, "Chevron *Step Zero*," 92 *Virginia Law Review* 187, 191 n. 19 (2006); Lisa Schultz Bressman, "*Chevron's* Mistake," 58 *Duke Law Journal* 549 (2009); Jack M. Beerman, "End the Failed Chevron Experiment Now: How Chevron Has Failed and Why It Can Be Overruled," 42 *Connecticut Law Review* 779, 832 (2010); Jennifer Nou, "Agency Self-Insulation Under Presidential Review," 126 *Harvard Law Review* 1755 (2013); Jennifer Nou, "Regulatory Textualism," 65 *Duke Law Journal* 81 (2015).

which he expressed disappointment with American poetry of the first quarter of the twentieth century,[83] remarking that "one gets the impression that, if it
is true that the manner of it is often more interesting than the matter, this is
perhaps because the poets themselves do not lead very interesting lives. Does it
really constitute a career for a man to do nothing but write lyric poetry? Can
such a man expect the world to be concerned with what he has to say?"[84]
And he contrasts these poets with such English poets as Milton, Waller, and
Prior (to whom could be added, among others, Shakespeare, Donne, Marvell,
Shelley, and Byron), who had careers apart from their poetry writing and led
very interesting lives. Can it not also be said that law professors who in their
maturity have always and only been law professors are missing something in
not having had careers outside the professoriate? In not having practiced law
whether in a private firm or for the government? Aren't the "pure" law professors missing something by (again I quote Wilson's essay) not "try[ing] to im-
merse themselves . . . in the common life of their time"?[85]

Skidmore

Questions of statutory interpretation to which the agency's answer does
not have the force of law are subject to *Skidmore* review. Such review, too,
is supposed to be deferential.

I wish someone would explain—maybe someone *has* explained—what exactly
it means for appellate review to be "deferential." That a tie (the appellate court
thinks the appellant and the appellee have equally good or equally bad cases)
means the appellate court should affirm? That makes sense. Or must the appellate court affirm unless it is certain, or nearly so, that the district court erred?
Federal Rule of Civil Procedure 52(a)(6), which governs bench trials (trials
by judge rather than by jury), substitutes "clearly erroneous" for "deferential"
—but is there any real difference? And what does "clearly" add to "erroneous"? Rule 52(a)(6) commands "deference" to district judge credibility findings,
which is a discredited reference to "demeanor cues" (of which more in Chapter
4) mistakenly thought to enable judges to make reliable credibility determinations. And in the next sentence of the rule, what, to repeat an earlier point,
does "definite and firm conviction" mean, as distinct from "is convinced"?

---

83. "The Muses Out of Work" (1927), in Wilson, *Literary Essays and Reviews of the 1920s and 30s* 166
(2007).
84. Id. at 170.
85. Id. at 171.

"Deference" as a standard of appellate review is so nebulous that it invites the appellate courts to brush over serious defects in trial courts' analyses. Eric Berger, moved by this concern, has mounted a powerful argument against the Supreme Court's recent decision in *Glossip v. Gross* upholding execution by lethal injection of a drug, midazolam, found erroneously by the Court to be an effective anesthetic that would assure a painless death.[86] Berger argues persuasively that the Court "ignored the State's manifest lack of expertise, care, transparency, and oversight," and he describes the notion of "deference" invoked by the Court to justify what it did as "atmospheric spin."[87] "The Court viewed deference not as a legal issue to be figured out, but rather as a rhetorical arrow in the advocate's quiver. . . . *Glossip* epitomizes judicial deference gone berserk."[88]

But problems of this sort inhere in *all* the standards of appellate review, except of course *de novo* review—review, typically of an issue of law unmixed with factual issues, that accords no deference to the district court's decision. The other standards of appellate review should be replaced by the following simple rule for appellate judges to follow: reverse the lower court if you have a robust disagreement with that court on an issue material to the outcome of the case. That would rid us of "deference" as a governing standard of appellate review—and high time, too. What an appellate court can say about a district court or agency decision that it wants to affirm is that the decision is careful, well informed, embodies expertise about which the appellate judges know even less than the district court or the agency, and for all these reasons the appellate court can't improve on the decision that the appellant has challenged.

In other words, as I noted earlier, a tie goes to the district judge or the agency, as it should. But to call this "deference" is potentially misleading. The word originally meant kowtowing to one's social superiors, such as aristocrats. It meant in other words acknowledging inferiority. Deference as used in modern American law turns the concept on its head: it now denotes deference to one's judicial inferiors! Where once the word denoted recognition of hierarchy—we "defer" to our social or economic superiors—we now have, in administrative review for example, the opposite—Article III judges deferring to an immigration judge, to an administrative law judge, to a bankruptcy judge. Why "defer" to them?

There is sometimes an answer. Many years ago I had a case involving very

---

86. 135 S. Ct. 2726 (2015). See Eric Berger, "Gross Error" (*Washington Law Review* forthcoming), http://papers.ssrn.com/sol3/papers.cfm?abstract_id=2752690.

87. Id.

88. Id.

strict standards imposed by OSHA on dental staff because of fear of AIDS infection by patients.[89] The standards seemed to us judges on the reviewing panel too strict, but OSHA's opinion justifying the standards was thorough and well written and revealed a level of medical and other technical understanding that we judges respected. And so we affirmed.[90] But we were not deferring to OSHA as such, but rather to a particular decision. We didn't say to ourselves or to each other—oh well, this is OSHA's business, we have no business interfering. We were reviewing OSHA's decision as we would a district judge's decision that so far as we could determine was a reasonable solution to a complex issue that we the appellate judges might not fully understand. And that is how it should be.

In short, I sense no fundamental difference between federal appellate review of district courts and federal appellate review of agency rulings. All the appellate court has to do is decide whether the agency's challenged ruling is reasonable and not in patent conflict with a statute, the Constitution, or a governing precedent, etc. When I need to make such a decision I ask myself whether the agency was behaving reasonably in issuing the challenged ruling and if so I'm very reluctant to reverse, while if I decide that it's behaving unreasonably I'm very reluctant to affirm on the authority of statutes or precedents that I doubt were intended to compel the reviewing court to behave unreasonably.

MIXED QUESTIONS OF LAW AND FACT

Court and jury decisions concerning mixed questions of law and fact are usually subject to *de novo* review unless factual issues predominate, in which event the decision will be subject to review for clear error. When made by administrative agencies, decisions concerning mixed questions of law and fact are subjected to arbitrary and capricious review. Addi-

89. *American Dental Association v. Martin*, 984 F.3d 823 (7th Cir. 1983).
90. We explained at id., 830–831, that OSHA's

rule must be vacated insofar as it applies to sites not controlled either by the employer or by a hospital, nursing home, or other entity that is itself subject to the blood borne-pathogens rule. The other objections lodged by the health personnel industry against the rule, however, either duplicate those of the dental association or plainly lack merit. So in the main the rule must be upheld. Which is not to say that it is a good rule. It may be unnecessary; it may go too far; its costs may exceed its benefits. Concern with the cost of health care in the United States is growing, and OSHA has received a steady drumbeat of criticisms even from supporters of public regulation of occupational health and safety. . . . But our duty as a reviewing court of generalist judges is merely to patrol the boundary of reasonableness, and, with the exception we have noted, OSHA's blood borne-pathogens rule—accepted as it has been by most health care industries and based as it is on the recommendations of the nation's, perhaps the world's, leading repository of knowledge about the control of infectious diseases—does not cross it.

tionally, in some areas of substantive law, such as when a court is reviewing a First Amendment issue, an appellate court will use a standard of review called "independent review." The standard is somewhere in between *de novo* review and clearly erroneous review. Under independent review, an appellate court will reexamine the record from the lower court in making its legal determinations.

But what *is* a "mixed question of law and fact"? A typical definition is "a mixed question of law and fact arises when the historical facts are established, the rule of law is undisputed, and the issue is whether the facts satisfy the legal rule." A mixed question thus "exists when primary facts are undisputed and ultimate inferences and legal consequences are in dispute. Mixed questions of law and fact generally require the consideration of legal concepts and the exercise of judgment about the values that animate legal principles."[91]

I get *nothing* out of this. To me it's a *complete garble.*

QUESTIONS OF TRIAL OVERSIGHT

Abuse of Discretion

Where a lower court has made a discretionary ruling (such as whether to allow a party claiming a hardship to file a brief after the deadline), that decision will be reviewed for "abuse of discretion" and won't be reversed unless the lower court committed a "plain error." One consideration in deciding whether an error is "plain" is whether it was "unpreserved"—that is, not objected to in the lower court as the law generally requires for the objection to the error to be allowed to be pressed in the appellate court. In such a case the appellate court may still choose to look at the lower court's mistake even though there was no objection, provided that the appellate court determines that the error was plain (meaning "evident, obvious, and clear") and that it materially prejudiced a substantial right, meaning the mistake probably affected the outcome of the case in a significant way. If a party forfeits a complaint about an error by failing to raise a timely objection, on appeal the burden of proof will be on that party to show that the error had been plain. If the party had raised a timely objection but it had been overruled, then on appeal the burden of proof is on the opposing party to show that the error was harmless. This

91. *Standards of Review-U.S. Courts,* http://cdn.ca9.uscourts.gov/datastore/uploads/guides/stand_of_review/I_Definitions.html.

approach is dictated by Federal Rule of Criminal Procedure 52, which states that "any error, defect, irregularity, or variance that does not affect substantial rights must be disregarded, [while a] plain error that affects substantial rights may be considered even though it was not brought to the court's attention." The appellate court has discretion as to whether or not to correct plain error. Usually the court will not correct it unless it led to a brazen miscarriage of justice.

But why is a mistake called an "abuse"? And what is a "plain" error? Or stated differently what is or should be the status of an error that is not plain? Are there murky errors? If so, do they not count? Should an error ever be ignored if it's not "harmless"? And what does it mean to affect the outcome of a case in a "significant" as distinct from "insignificant" way? And is "miscarriage of justice" anything more than a pompous term for an erroneous judicial decision? What is a "brazen" miscarriage of justice? Must we live with such muddle?

Section 1252(b)(7) of Title 8 of the U.S. Code states that "the Attorney General's discretionary judgment whether to grant relief under section 1158(a) [asylum] of this title shall be conclusive unless manifestly contrary to the law and an abuse of discretion." This is a garble. What does "manifestly" add to "contrary to the law"? A judgment contrary to law should be reversed. And why, in addition to being not only contrary but "manifestly" contrary to the law, must the judgment *also* be denoted "an abuse of discretion"? Stated differently, if it is an abuse of discretion, why must it also be manifestly contrary to the law? That really is nonsense.

QUESTIONS OF CONSTITUTIONALITY

Questions of constitutionality are considered a type of question of law, and thus appellate courts always review *de novo* (that is, without any deference to the lower court) decisions that address constitutional issues. But the focus is different from what it is in the application of the normal standards of review because reviewing a law for its constitutionality means deciding how much deference the judiciary should give *Congress* in determining whether legislation is constitutional. It's as if Congress were the trial court, and in a sense it is, because it is deciding in the first instance whether a statute that it would like to enact is constitutional. It's understandable however that as applied to Congress rather than a trial court or an agency the standards of review have been renamed levels of scrutiny, dependent on the nature of the congressional action under review. The levels are rational basis, intermediate scrutiny, and strict scrutiny.

Rational Basis

Generally the Supreme Court bases a judgment of the constitutionality of legislation on whether the legislation is grounded in a legitimate state interest. This is called rational-basis review. For example, a statute requiring the licensing of opticians is permissible because it has the legitimate state objective of ensuring the health of consumers and licensing statutes are reasonably related to ensuring their health by requiring that opticians receive certain training. *Williamson v. Lee Optical Co.*, 348 U.S. 483 (1955).

But why "rational"? Why would a state law not reasonably related to a legitimate state interest be thought "irrational" rather than merely improper, unauthorized?

Intermediate Scrutiny

When the equal protection clause of the Fourteenth Amendment is invoked to challenge a law based on a "quasi-suspect" classification, such as gender, the courts apply intermediate scrutiny, which requires that the law be substantially related to an important government interest. Intermediate scrutiny is more strict than rational-basis review but less strict than strict scrutiny, discussed next. Other forms of intermediate scrutiny are applied in other contexts. For example, content-neutral time, place, and manner restrictions on speech are subject to a form of intermediate scrutiny on the authority of the First Amendment's free-speech clause.

But what does "strict" mean in this context and what is the difference between "reasonably related" (rational-basis scrutiny) and "substantially related"?

Strict Scrutiny

If a statute impinges on a fundamental right, such as a right listed in the Bill of Rights or the Fourteenth Amendment, courts apply "strict scrutiny," which requires that the statute must be "narrowly tailored" to ad-

dress a "compelling state interest." For example, a statute that seeks to reduce public corruption by limiting the funds that a candidate for public
office may receive may be deemed unconstitutional because it is overly
broad and impinges on the right to freedom of speech. For it affects
not only corrupt individual, corporate, and other institutional contributions, but also non-corrupt expenditures from candidates' own personal
or family resources or genuinely public-interested individuals or institutions. *Buckley v. Valeo,* 424 U.S. 1 (1976). The courts also apply strict scrutiny if the law targets a suspect classification, such as race. For example,
there is no fundamental right to be an optician (as explained above), but
if the state requires licenses of African Americans but not of opticians of
other races that double standard would receive strict scrutiny and undoubtedly be ruled unconstitutional. But why is gender only "quasi-
suspect" (see under "intermediate scrutiny," above) yet race "suspect"?

I find the levels of scrutiny no more illuminating than I do the standards of appellate review. They just don't sort for me. I'll illustrate with my same-sex marriage case, *Baskin v. Bogan,*[92] a precursor to *Obergefell* that invalidated Indiana's
and Wisconsin's prohibitions of such marriage. I noted in my opinion that homosexuals do not choose to be such, that there is a long and vicious history of
discrimination against them, that they *want* homosexual marriage, that refusing to allow such marriage is hard to square with the common exception for
allowing first cousins to marry if but only if at least one of them is sterile, that
after the Supreme Court in the *Lawrence v. Texas* decision had invalidated sodomy laws there was no remaining argument except the religious one against
homosexual marriage, and—what I particularly stressed—that marriage is important, psychologically and financially, to children adopted by homosexuals
(which has long been legal). In short, I thought and think that the reasons for
invalidating the Indiana and Wisconsin bans (and those of the other states that
had such bans, all later invalidated in *Obergefell*) were compelling.

I would have stopped there but a member of my panel urged me to say
something about levels of scrutiny. It was the counsel of prudence, so I did. But
doing so didn't and doesn't affect my thinking about the constitutional basis for
invalidating the same-sex marriage bans. My view of judging may seem sim-

92. 766 F.3d 648 (7th Cir. 2014). Discussed in Daniel R. Pinello, *America's War on Same-Sex Couples and
Their Families and How the Courts Rescued Them* 278–279 (2017)—the definitive book on the subject.

pleminded to some, insubordinate and even radical to others, but I do insist that judging is basically about picking a commonsense result in a case, checking to make sure it's not blocked by some precedent or procedural concern or what have you that outweighs the commonsense result, and if it isn't blocked, then going with that result.

My worry about the standards of appellate review is not new; I've worried about them for decades—ever since my opinion in a case called *Mucha v. King*[93] where I discussed at some length the rule that findings of fact by a trial judge or a jury can be reversed by the appellate court only if clearly erroneous. The question was whether findings of fact included "legal characterizations (negligence, possession, ratification, principal place of business, and the like)"[94] as well as determinations of raw fact. In a negligence case the raw facts might be a collision, a driver who'd fallen asleep, an injured pedestrian, etc. Yet negligence itself could be, I said in my opinion, a "fact" too, "for purposes of separating the trial judge's function from our own. . . . Facts of this sort, which are found by applying a legal standard to a descriptive or historical narrative, are governed by the clearly-erroneous rule."[95] And why? Not because of

> the appellate court's lack of access to the materials for decision but [because] its main responsibility is to maintain the uniformity and coherence of the law, a responsibility not engaged if the only question is the legal significance of a particular and nonrecurring set of historical events. This set will not recur—that is for sure. Once Rule 52(a) is understood to rest on notions of the proper division of responsibilities between trial and appellate courts rather than just on considerations of comparative accessibility to the evidence, the concern expressed by Judge [Henry] Friendly[96]—that it is shocking to imagine that two identical cases might be decided in opposite ways by two different district judges, yet each decision be affirmed—subsides. Review is deferential precisely because it is so unlikely that there will be two identical cases; the appellate court's

---

93. 792 F.2d 602 (7th Cir. 1986).
94. Id. at 605.
95. Id.
96. In *Mamiye Bros. v. Barber S.S. Lines, Inc.*, 360 F.2d 774 (2d Cir. 1966).

responsibility for maintaining the uniformity of legal doctrine is not triggered.[97]

This comes close to saying—as I would *not* say today—that the appellate court should not review the trial court's factfindings at all; that the only business of the appellate court is to maintain the uniformity and coherence of legal doctrine. That can't be right, for the court is supposed to reverse factfindings by the trial court that it finds to be clearly erroneous. To refuse to do that is to perpetuate error and injustice. But what is the force of "clearly" in this formula? Posing that question makes the entire body of law governing standards of review unravel. For what is an error that is not clear? A murky error? A maybe error? Is it enough that the appellate court thinks there's a 51 percent probability that a trial judge's, or a jury's, ruling was incorrect? But it's unrealistic to think an appellate court could make such a precise estimate. Why not just say: if the appellate court thinks the district judge or the jury erred on a point material to the outcome of the case, it should reverse.

One can ask similarly unsettling questions about the opaque wording of the other standards of appellate review. What does it mean for a trial judge or a jury to be arbitrary? To be capricious? To be both? Is there an actual difference between the terms? The first item on the list of synonyms for "arbitrary" at Thesaurus.com is "capricious" and the first item on the list of synonyms for "capricious" is "arbitrary." So what is added by conjoining them? And what is "substantial" evidence? Or a "mixed" question of law and fact? Is the latter term what negligence for example might be understood to be, as a finding of negligence requires both a factual determination and a legal standard? And what exactly is the appellate judge supposed to do when faced with such a mixture? Review part of it *de novo* and the rest of it for error or clear error?

And what is an "abuse of discretion"—how does one "abuse" discretion? Actually in law "abuse of discretion" just means committing a procedural error; why not say that, rather than accuse the lower-court judge of "abusive" behavior? What for that matter does it mean for a judge to *exercise* discretion? To "use discretion" just means to make a choice, for a judge, to make a ruling. But we know that judges *have* to make rulings. Is that all that "judicial discretion" amounts to? Isn't it time to scrap that term too? Where *do* these terms come from, anyway? Why are lawyers and judges so *comfortable* with jargon?

---

97. 792 F.2d at 605–606.

The most innocuous-appearing standard of review is "plain error." It's an offshoot of the principle of finality—that a litigant should not be permitted to relitigate a case that he's lost, lest the courts be swamped with cases, as in legal systems that do not enforce finality. Plain error is an exception in our system; if the district court commits a plain error in the sense of an error that should have been completely obvious but was somehow missed by both parties as well as by the judge, and the error caused one of the parties to lose the case, that party can challenge the error on appeal despite having failed to challenge it in the district court. Ordinarily of course a litigant must have pressed a claim in the district court in order to be allowed on appeal to challenge that court's denial of the claim. The plain-error rule thus compromises the principle of finality in a narrow set of cases. Maybe too narrow; better might be a more flexible rule that would authorize the appellate court to reverse the district court even if the error overlooked in that court was not "plain." I would like to see the interest in finality balanced against the magnitude of the error sought to be corrected, if the balancing can be done without an undue judicial burden.

I should note for completeness that just as the "plain" in "plain error" means "obvious," so the "plain" in "plain meaning"—a common term in cases involving statutory meaning but one that lawyers and judges tend to misuse—means the same thing. Think back to the ambulance case discussed in the Introduction to this book. If you ask anyone whether an ambulance is a vehicle, the answer you'll get is "of course; it's an emergency vehicle used to transport sick or injured persons to and from hospitals." But to use that "plain meaning" to authorize ticketing the ambulance driver who drives into a park posted with "no vehicles in the park" signs would be asinine. The fact that a word has a plain meaning doesn't give us its statutory meaning.

The proper limits of plain error are illustrated in another recent case in my court, in which I found myself dissenting (together with three of the other judges) from the court's decision not to hear a criminal case en banc. At the defendant's trial the prosecutor had told the jury (truthfully) that the defendant had refused to take a polygraph test. The prosecutor should not have done that, as the panel decision[98] (the decision I would have liked the full court to review) acknowledged. But the panel refused to order a new trial.

My dissent argued as follows (I have made a few minor stylistic adjustments, to enhance clarity):

---

98. *United States v. Resnick,* 835 F.3d 658 (7th Cir. 2016).

The majority opinion makes two damaging admissions. The first is its statement that "our decisions have, in practice, pointed in only one direction: affirming the *exclusion* of polygraph evidence. There is no scientific consensus that polygraph testing is reliable, and there is a significant possibility of unfair prejudice if it is introduced into evidence at trial" (emphasis in original). The second [admission in the majority opinion] is a statement, citing *Garmon v. Lumpkin County,* 878 F.2d 1406, 1410 (11th Cir. 1989), that "because a criminal defendant's constitutionally protected silence may not be used against her, the natural corollary to that rule is that generally a defendant's refusal to submit to a polygraph examination cannot be used as incriminating evidence." See also *United States v. St. Clair,* 855 F.2d 518, 523 (8th Cir. 1988) (noting, without stating grounds, that "the Eighth Circuit has held [that] it is improper for a witness to testify whether or not a criminal defendant refused to submit to a polygraph test)."

Because polygraph (i.e., lie-detector) evidence is unreliable, its introduction in a trial creates a significant possibility of unfair prejudice, and a defendant has a constitutional right not to have his refusal to submit to a polygraph used in evidence against him as an admission of guilt. The government is "prohibit[ed] . . . from 'treat[ing] a defendant's exercise of his right to remain silent at trial as substantive evidence of guilt,'" *United States v. Ochoa-Zarate,* 540 F.3d 613, 617 (7th Cir. 2008), quoting *United States v. Robinson,* 485 U.S. 25, 34 (1988). Therefore if a defendant refuses to testify, or invokes his *Miranda* rights, the prosecutor is forbidden to comment to the jury on the defendant's refusal to take a polygraph test. Most people, moreover, would be made nervous at the thought of having to take such a test and we now know that being nervous cannot be treated as a confession of guilt—that there are nervous truthtellers as well as confident ones, and confident liars as well as nervous ones. These principles, accepted by the majority [in this case], require that the judgment be vacated and the case remanded for a new trial. Against this conclusion, all that the majority can marshal is the doctrine of "plain error," an ambiguous term used to enforce finality in litigation, where finality takes precedence over other values—as it shouldn't in this case; there is too much at stake, not only for the defendant but for criminal procedure in general. What can be a simpler or more effective or more disreputable prosecutorial tactic than simply to ask the defendant whether he'll agree to take a polygraph test, and if he refuses, as he is likely to do whether under his own steam or by advice of counsel, parade his refusal before the jury, arguing that it amounts to a confession of guilt—and if he appeals cite the decision [in this case] as a controlling precedent.

We need not go so far as to ban all polygraph evidence from criminal trials. The fact that it's unreliable doesn't distinguish it from a lot of other evidence—eyewitness evidence for example—that frequently turns out to be unreliable. But if a suspect refuses to take a polygraph examination, the government shouldn't be allowed to introduce the refusal as substantive evidence, or to comment on the refusal to the jury. Adopting the narrower rule that I'm suggesting would align our court with the prevailing judicial recognition of an expansive right against self-incrimination, see, e.g., *Griffin v. California,* 380 U.S. 609 (1965); *Miranda v. Arizona,* 384 U.S. 436 (1966), coupled with concern that polygraphs are unreliable trial evidence. See, e.g., *United States v. Scheffer,* 523 U.S. 303, 309–10 (1998); *United States v. Lea,* 249 F.3d 632, 639 (7th Cir. 2001).

The government argues that because of the "overwhelming evidence of guilt, the defendant in this case can't prove that admitting and commenting on his refusal to submit to a polygraph test affected the verdict." The implication is that if the government presents enough evidence of guilt it can top it off with evidence that violates a constitutional right, ignores evidentiary rules, and tempts the jury to abdicate its role as factfinder. There is no evidentiary demarcation line that when traversed with enough damning evidence of guilt permits the government and the court to deny a criminal defendant the right to a fair jury trial.

That the polygraph is at the center of this controversy is important. A polygraph is an instrument designed to determine whether the person examined is telling the truth. But polygraphs are not reliable truthtelling tools, and determining credibility is the jury's duty. Introducing and commenting on evidence that a suspect refused to take a polygraph tells the jury that polygraph evidence is reliable when it is not and that his refusal to talk evidences consciousness of guilt—though courts have consistently held that to be an impermissible inference. It could also signal to the jurors that their own instincts do not matter when determining credibility—the presence of a polygraph supersedes their common sense—and so they might as well ignore their duty as factfinders. The potential for this effect contradicts the government's assertion that the defendant cannot show that its tactics affected the jury. Those tactics infected the trial and rendered it unfair, no matter how "overwhelming" the evidence against the defendant. Such tactics should not be tolerated. Reversal would send the right signal; this affirmance sends the wrong one. Resnick deserves a new trial.

I would go further. In cases in which the appellate court discovered significant factual errors in the district court's disposition of a case that has been appealed, I would give the appellate court the option of taking evidence and making factfindings itself, rather than having to remand the case for further evidentiary proceedings in the district court likely to delay the final decision in the case indefinitely. I would also be more emphatic about the unreliability of eyewitness identification: on the positively dreadful record of eyewitness identification in criminal cases see *Dennis v. Secretary,*[99] well discussed in Timothy O'Neill's article "As Times Change, the Law Proves to Be a Living, Breathing Thing."[100]

I conclude my discussion of standards of appellate review with brief remarks about two questionable standards that until recently I hadn't even heard of. One is appellate review for "objective evidence." My court has held that "'a mere allegation by the defendant that he would have insisted on going to trial [had he known that his lawyer was not going to present mitigating evidence at his sentencing hearing after his plea of guilty] is insufficient to establish prejudice.'"[101] The defendant must go further and "establish through objective evidence that a reasonable probability exists that he would have gone to trial."[102]

But what *is* "objective" evidence? Had the defendant previously insisted on going to trial, and in fact taken that step, would that satisfy the requirement of objective evidence? Ordinarily testamentary evidence can be believed by the trier of fact, and therefore accepted, without any "objective" backup; so if the defendant testifies that he would have insisted on going to trial, shouldn't the judge try to determine whether he's telling the truth? And what was "prejudice" doing in the quotation from the *Berkey* case?

99. Pennsylvania Dept. of Corrections, 834 F.3d 263, 313 (3d Cir. 2016) (Chief Judge Theodore A. McKee, concurring).

100. Timothy P. O'Neill, "As Times Change, the Law Proves to Be a Living, Breathing Thing," *Chicago Law Bulletin,* January 3, 2017, p. 4.

101. *Berkey v. United States,* 318 F.3d 768, 772 (7th Cir. 2003), quoting *Barker v. United States,* 7 F.3d 629, 633 (7th Cir. 1993).

102. *Berkey v. United States,* preceding note, at 773; see also *United States v. Cieslowski,* 410 F.3d 353, 359 (7th Cir. 2005).

The other questionable standard new to me—"extraordinary circumstances" —has been used by my court to affirm decisions by the Immigration Court and the BIA rejecting claims by illegal immigrants to be allowed to remain in the United States, the basis for affirmance being that the immigration judge's "credibility determinations are questions of fact and should only be overturned under extraordinary circumstances, although they must be supported by specific, cogent reasons that bear a legitimate nexus to the finding."[103] This can't be taken seriously as a standard of judicial review of agency action. It can't be right to say that an immigration judge (or the BIA) can be reversed only in "extraordinary circumstances," for they can and should be reversed if they're wrong; we have reversed countless immigration cases without invoking "extraordinary circumstances." Appellate courts don't require "extraordinary circumstances" to reverse Article III district judges; so what is the basis for requiring extraordinary circumstances when the trial judge is an Article I judge in an agency with a deservedly bad reputation in this court, which reverses decisions by the Immigration Court and the BIA at a higher rate (more than a third) than any other federal court of appeals? And what does "bear a legitimate nexus" mean? Is this English, or gibberish?

In another embarrassing opinion of my court we read that "immigration judges can base an adverse credibility finding on any inconsistency, whether it goes to the heart of the applicant's claim or not."[104] The implication is that by for example confusing the names of two people who have nothing to do with the immigration authorities' case against him, the applicant forfeits a meritorious claim for relief from deportation. Can this make any sense?

I have come to believe that there are no satisfactory answers to my questions about the meaning of familiar legal phrases commonly invoked by lawyers and judges without any clear idea of their meaning. This belief is based not only on my experience as an appellate judge but also on my not infrequent forays into the district courts of my circuit to conduct pretrial and trial proceedings in civil, and latterly in criminal, cases. I have arrived at the conclusion that all that can sensibly be said about appellate review is that if the appellate court disagrees with any ruling or other act of the trial judge (which might include a ruling on jury selection or a refusal to set aside a jury verdict)—substantive, procedural, factual, or legal—it should reverse the district court unless the rul-

---

103. E.g., *Rama v. Holder*, 607 F.3d 461, 465 (7th Cir. 2010). Notice the poor English: "only" should follow not precede "be overturned," and "nexus" is a Latin word meaning (approximately) "connection." So why don't judges and lawyers say "connection" rather than "nexus"? They say "court" rather than its Latin counterpart "curia."

104. *Georgieva v. Holder*, 751 F.3d 514, 520 n. 2 (7th Cir. 2014).

ing or other complained-of act is certain or at least highly likely to have had no effect on the outcome of the district court proceeding—to have been therefore a "harmless error." But the appellate court should bear in mind that it prevails when it disagrees with the trial court not because it necessarily is right but because it is on a higher rung of the judicial hierarchy. The analogy is to a parent disciplining a child.

The appellate court should also affirm the trial court if it can't decide whether it agrees or disagrees with some challenged ruling or act of that court (this will often be the case with sentencing), and *a fortiori* if it agrees with the district court. And likewise it should affirm if though it disagrees with the district judge's ruling it respects the particular judge's superior relevant knowledge, experience, or attention to the facts and other aspects of the case, and the appellate court as a result lacks confidence that its disagreement with the district judge is well founded. If the case is highly fact intensive and the district judge experienced and respected, reversal will be especially unlikely. I was once criticized for daringly suggesting that the scope of appellate review of district court decisions is related to the respect in which the appellate judges hold particular district judges. That's true, but is considered impolitic to acknowledge.

What is clear is that in deciding whether to affirm or reverse a district court (or for that matter an administrative agency), the appellate court will get no help from the "standards" of appellate review. They should be ignored, and certainly not required to be stated in the appellant's brief, as they are by Fed. R. App. Proc. 28(a)(8)(B). I expressed these concerns in a separate opinion in a case called *United States v. Dessart*,[105] where I said:

> I agree with the outcome but have reservations about some of the verbal formulas in the majority opinion. I do not criticize the majority for reciting them, because they are common, orthodox, even canonical. But they are also inessential and in some respects erroneous, and on both grounds ripe for reexamination. First is the proposition that when a judge issues a warrant, whether to search or to arrest, the appellate court "must afford 'great deference' to the issuing judge's conclusion" that there was probable cause. *United States v. McIntire*, 516 F.3d 576, 578 (7th Cir. 2008). This proposition derives from *Illinois v. Gates*, 462 U.S. 213, 236 (1983), where we are told that the Supreme Court has "repeatedly said that after-the-fact scrutiny by courts of the sufficiency of an affidavit should not take

---

105. No. 14-2686, 823 F.3d 395 (7th Cir. 2016).

the form of *de novo* review. A magistrate's 'determination of probable cause should be paid great deference by reviewing courts.'" Why *great* deference? Because, we're told in *Ornelas v. United States,* 517 U.S. 690, 698–99 (1996), the Fourth Amendment demonstrates a "strong preference for searches conducted pursuant to a warrant," *Illinois v. Gates, supra,* 462 U.S. at 236, and the police are more likely to use the warrant process if the scrutiny applied to a magistrate's probable-cause determination to issue a warrant is less than that for warrantless searches. Were we to eliminate this distinction, we would eliminate the incentive.

This is a curious passage in three respects. First, why should a reviewing court accord "great" deference to a magistrate's determination of probable cause? The term "magistrate," often used in place of "judge" to designate the judicial officer who issues warrants, is an acknowledgment that warrants usually are issued by the most junior judicial officers—and often police or prosecutors can shop among magistrates for one who is certain or almost certain to respond affirmatively to a request to issue a warrant. Second, the Fourth Amendment does not express a preference for searches conducted pursuant to warrants. As I keep reminding the reader, warrants are mentioned only in the amendment's second clause, which forbids general warrants and warrants not supported by both probable cause and an oath or affirmation. Nothing in the amendment requires warrants—ever.

And third, the proposition, whether or not correct, that police are more likely to resort to warrants if more deference is given to a magistrate's finding of probable cause than to an after-the-fact assertion by police or prosecutors that a search without a warrant is supported by probable cause, implies confidence by the police that the magistrates from whom they seek warrants can be depended upon to find probable cause to issue the warrants. Otherwise warrants would be abjured. In short, the more warrants, the more searches because searches pursuant to warrants are less likely to be challenged than warrantless searches.

The passages from judicial opinions that I've quoted thus far invite judicial haste and carelessness. But wait a minute—I am objecting to propositions enunciated by the Supreme Court. That may seem impertinence on my part, forcing me to invoke the old proverb that "a cat may look at a king," one meaning of which [as I noted in Chapter 2 of this book] is that an inferior should be allowed to criticize a superior.

Another reservation I have concerning the majority opinion relates to the defendant's request that the district judge conduct a hearing (called a *Franks* hearing, see *Franks v. Delaware*, 438 U.S. 154 (1978)) to determine the likelihood that an agent had lied in the affidavit submitted to the magistrate in support of the agent's request for a warrant. The district court refused to hold a hearing, and in affirming the refusal our majority opinion says that "determining the likelihood that [an investigator] lied in his warrant affidavit . . . involve[s] essentially the same process as fact-finding, so our review of this issue, too, is deferential, for clear error only," quoting *United States v. Pace*, 898 F.2d 1218, 1227 (7th Cir. 1990). Doubtless the majority would also agree with the statement in *Pace* that "where the district court has reasonably and conscientiously reviewed the defendant's [claim for a hearing], and has properly applied the law, its decision should stand even if we, as an original matter, would have ordered the hearing." *Id.* This is a conventional appellate-court statement, but it's puzzling. What could it mean to say that the district court's decision "should stand even if we, as an original matter, would have ordered the hearing"? It could just mean that we haven't been given all the facts, and the district court *was* given them, so its decision is more likely to be correct than ours would be. Or it could mean that the case is a toss-up and—rightly—a tie goes to the district court. Which is it? I'd really like to know.

I am puzzled too by the remark in *Pace* that "even if de novo review is more likely to catch and correct more 'mistakes' by the district courts in denying *Franks* hearings, those mistakes do not go to a defendant's actual guilt or innocence. . . . [W]here mistakes do not go to guilt or innocence, de novo review imposes too great a cost for the benefits it might obtain." *Id.* There is first the question what "actual guilt" and "actual innocence" mean that "guilt" and "innocence" without the adjective do not mean. The next question is when there are mistakes that do not relate to the defendant's guilt or innocence what reason could there be for paying *any* attention to them? A partial answer is that while a warrant procured by a lie is unlawful (it may violate a statute, or a judicial gloss that has been placed on the Fourth Amendment), it need not signal that the defendant is innocent of the crime with which he's charged—the crime that led to the application for a warrant. Yet one would have expected a dishonest application, being a serious procedural violation, to invite as close (or almost as close) judicial scrutiny as an erroneous conviction. Otherwise there would be bound to be false convictions. Police who procure a search warrant by lying to the magistrate may also have no scruples about planting contraband in the house they are searching, or pretending that the person they arrested had resisted arrest violently. It makes sense to exclude the fruits of such warrants even if the error often doesn't mean that the defendant is innocent.

Three-fourths of the way through the majority opinion we read that "any challenge to the sufficiency of the evidence [that the defendant acted with 'deceptive intent'] comes with 'a heavy, indeed, nearly insurmountable burden,'" quoting *United States v. Warren*, 593 F.3d 540, 546 (7th Cir. 2010). To prevail the defendant "must convince us that even after viewing the evidence in the light most favorable to the prosecution, no rational trier of fact could have found him guilty beyond a reasonable doubt." *Id.* I have trouble understanding why an appellant should have to overcome "a heavy"—a "nearly insurmountable"—burden of proof. As explained in *United States v. Curescu*, 674 F.3d 735, 741 (7th Cir. 2012), "to say that a jury verdict can be set aside only if 'wholly irrational' (which would indeed be a 'nearly insurmountable' proposition to establish) is the kind of hyperbole that sometimes creeps into opinions. . . . A jury verdict of guilt can be set aside—must be set aside—if, even though the verdict is not 'wholly irrational,' the evidence would not have justified a reasonable juror in finding guilt beyond a reasonable doubt."

And why is evidence in a criminal trial to be viewed "in the light most favorable to the prosecution"? It's been said that when an appellant "challenges the sufficiency of the evidence to convict him . . . by expressing his disagreement with the state trial judge's [or the jury's] decision to believe one of the eyewitnesses against him, we cannot reverse the conviction unless given some 'basis to suppose that the trial judge was irrational to credit this witness's testimony.'" *Johnson v. Gramley*, 929 F.2d 350, 351 (7th Cir. 1991). Yet often the study of a trial transcript reveals not that the judge was irrational but that there was no basis for his believing or disbelieving the witness—the judge was guessing, and while the guess was rational it can't realistically be thought to have determined guilt or innocence.

And why must a conviction be affirmed even if it is apparent that the trier of fact (judge or jury), while not irrational, was mistaken? Why in short are the dice so heavily loaded against defendants? And finally can the extraordinary burden of proof placed on defendants be squared with the requirement (unchallenged) that a defendant must be proved guilty beyond a reasonable doubt in order to be convicted?

I also question the statement near the end of the majority opinion that "claims of [jury-]instructional error" are to be "review[ed] . . . for abuse of discretion." The term "abuse of discretion" is defined a few lines further along as including, among other missteps, "material errors of law." Of course material errors of law are potentially very serious, but what has that to do with discretion or its abuse? Common as the term "abuse of discretion" is in opinions dealing with appeals from district court decisions, I find it opaque. If the appellate court is persuaded that the trial court erred in a way that makes the trial court's decision unacceptable, it reverses. What has discretion to do with it? And "abuse" seems altogether too strong a term to describe what may be no more than a disagreement between equally competent judges—the trial judge and the appellate judges—that the appellate judges happen to be empowered to resolve as they see fit.

All this said, I didn't disagree with the decision to affirm the district court in the *Dessart* case; I disagreed only with the rhetorical envelope in which the majority opinion was delivered to the reader. Judicial opinions are littered with stale, opaque, confusing jargon—unnecessarily. For everything judges do can be explained in straightforward language, and should be—but won't be. The standards of review, and other opacities of judicial procedure, exist for a reason, though not the stated reason, which is to pressure judges to decide cases without recourse to ideological and other priors. The real reason is to equip judges with plausible, neutral-appearing, and malleable, though not necessarily sound or motivating, reasons for their decisions. The judge is thereby left free to base decision (without public acknowledgment, and often without awareness) on his ideological or other preferences or intuitions.

I don't want to go overboard; I acknowledge that it's unrealistic to expect judges to be entirely candid in their opinions—candor is not in the legal DNA. Lawyers are not candid when negotiating on behalf of a client, or when representing a client in court, though they usually are when simply advising a client—but in other settings candor would amount to disloyalty. And judicial candor would make for a very insulting, repulsive judiciary. I therefore see nothing wrong, in a case in which there is both a neutral and a personal or ideological reason for affirming or reversing a district court or agency decision, in the appellate court's stating only the neutral reason. But judges should not be allowed the total disguise enabled by hiding behind the standards of appellate review, which, to be blunt, are phony.

Those standards by the way exemplify not only concealment and indirection but also sheer superfluity in legal discourse. Brevity has no appeal to lawyers or to most judges. A striking instance is a term that I mentioned earlier—"actual innocence"—which appears in many cases. I discussed it, together with another questionable term, in my separate opinion in a case called *Blackmon v. Williams*,[106] where I said that

> an example of what troubles me is the majority opinion's numerous iterations of the phrase "actual innocence," and its occasional invocations of the cognate term "actually innocent." These phrases are misleading. A defendant is either innocent or guilty. There is no separate state of being actually rather than just—just what?—innocent. So what work is "actual" or "actually" doing? None. But something in the legal genome causes lawyers and judges to want to speak in pairs, as in "arbitrary and capricious" and "clear and convincing." Ask yourself: what does "arbitrary" add to "capricious" or vice versa, "clear" to "convincing" or vice versa, "actual" to "innocence."
>
> The history of the term "actual innocence" is revealing. Its remote origin is a famous article by Judge Henry Friendly, "Is Innocence Irrelevant? Collateral Attack on Criminal Judgments," 38 *University of Chicago Law Review* 142 (1970). He argued that for collateral attacks (as by seeking federal habeas corpus) on criminal convictions to succeed—attacks based for example on federal constitutional violations in the state proceeding—generally the petitioner should be required to present evidence that he probably was innocent of the crime for which he had been convicted. Three Justices of the Supreme Court adopted Judge Friendly's suggestion in *Kuhlmann v. Wilson,* 477 U.S. 436 (1986), where Justice Powell, writing for a plurality of the Justices, added "factual" before "innocence." Later the full Court adopted this formulation, minus the "f," thus creating the "actual innocence" exception to procedural default, at issue in this case. See *Murray v. Carrier,* 477 U.S. 478 (1986). The term is

---

106. No. 14-3059, 823 F.3d 1088 (7th Cir. 2016).

understood to distinguish not having committed the crime of which one was charged from having been entitled to acquittal on some ground unrelated to the merits, such as lack of jurisdiction. See *Bousley v. United States*, 523 U.S. 614, 623 (1998) ("'actual innocence' means factual innocence, not mere legal insufficiency"). It would have been more accurate to say that some acquittals are based on the defendant's having been found innocent of the crime or crimes with which he was charged, and others on reasons unrelated to guilt or innocence, such as expiration of the applicable statute of limitations. Fair enough. But the adjectives "factual" and "actual" add nothing to the distinction. The defendant who gets off merely because the statute of limitations has expired is guilty rather than innocent, but just cannot be convicted.

Another familiar term in legal discourse that appears in the majority opinion in this case and that I would like to see purged is "procedural default," a cumbersome substitute for "forfeiture." The failure of a petitioner for federal habeas corpus to have given the state courts a chance to rule on the claim he seeks to vindicate in the habeas corpus proceeding normally forfeits his right to press the claim in federal court. But the petitioner can be relieved of his forfeiture . . .—if [as in this case] he has strong though not necessarily conclusive evidence of his innocence.

But I didn't explain the term "actual innocence" clearly enough in my opinion. The essential distinction is between innocence, sometimes paraphrased as a state of facts that no reasonable jury would have thought justified convicting the defendant, and gaps in the prosecution that might have convinced the jury that the prosecutors had failed to prove the defendant's guilt beyond a reasonable doubt—which unlike my first example would not establish the defendant's innocence—would not *prove* that he hadn't committed the crime for which he'd been prosecuted, but only lower that probability into the realm of uncertainty.

The reason for the distinction is the concern with finality of litigation. If a prison inmate can prove that he's innocent in the strong sense of not having committed the crime for which he's been convicted and punished, he certainly should have a shot at submitting his proof in a lawsuit, normally a federal habeas corpus suit, even though that will delay the final decision. But if he wishes to premise the second suit on errors in the first that may well not have determined the outcome in the first, and so he has less to gain from relitigation than

in our first example, the pressure to relax finality is itself relaxed. So the concept of "actual innocence"—of a situation in which no reasonable jury would
have convicted—is defensible, but the word-doubling is as usual *de trop*. Better
to say that seeking to upset a finding of guilt by means of a habeas corpus action requires proof of innocence, which is to be distinguished from a procedural error that should have led to an acquittal but would not have established
the defendant's innocence.

In my concurrence in the *Dessart* case I had mentioned "actual innocence"
but not discussed it; I had said "there is first the question, which I'll leave for
another day, what the terms 'actual guilt' and 'actual innocence' mean that
'guilt' and 'innocence' without the adjective 'actual' do not mean." For this I was
criticized—specifically for forgetting that I had said in an earlier opinion that
(this is the critic's paraphrase, but is accurate enough) that "if the court or jury
finds the defendant not guilty, that simply means that the prosecutor did not
prove its case. The court or jury may have rendered the verdict because the
court had to exclude a crucial piece of evidence, or because the conviction violated double jeopardy. In such cases, the defendant is not 'actually' innocent,
which becomes crucial for many courts if the defendant seeks to sue his lawyer
for malpractice."[107]

The critic missed the point, explained in my *Blackmon* opinion discussed
above and my subsequent discussion of the meaning and utility of the term
"actual innocence." To recapitulate, to be innocent is to mean not to have committed the crime one is being prosecuted (and perhaps convicted) for. It does
not mean to be acquitted, because guilty people are sometimes acquitted as a
result of prosecutorial errors, defense counsel brilliance, mistakes by jurors, or
jury nullification. These lucky defendants are not innocent! It is silly jargon
(apparently commended by my critic) to say that that the innocent defendant is
"actually innocent," but the guilty defendant who is mistakenly acquitted is "innocent."

Notice that in both jargony examples that I've just been discussing—"actual
innocence" and "procedural default"—the terms, while not denoting a standard of appellate review, function like one. Habeas corpus is not an appellate
procedure, but like an appeal is a procedural device for trying to reverse a previous decision—most commonly an attempt to persuade a federal court to set

107. Ronald D. Rotunda, "Excoriating Other Judges for Using Terms of Art They Don't Like: The Comments of Richard Posner," *Verdict, Justia*, August 1, 2016, https://verdict.justia.com/2016/08/01/judges-excor
iating-judges-using-terms-art-dont-like-comments-richard-posner.

aside a conviction or a sentence imposed in a state-court proceeding against the defendant now turned habeas-corpus applicant.

Given the meaningless doubling of terms used to denote a litigant's status or chances, one should not be surprised by the tendency of opinions of the federal courts of appeals (and of the Supreme Court as well) not only to offend the English language in the ways I've suggested but also to be larded with unnecessary, even fatuous, subheadings (such as Introduction, Background, Factual Background, Procedural Background, Facts and Procedural History, Discussion, Analysis, Conclusion—not all in the same opinion, however), or, what seems entirely pointless, to include subheadings consisting only of a letter or number, such as I, II, IA, or A, B, etc. And as I noted earlier judges love to end an opinion with "For the reasons stated" the judgment is affirmed (or reversed), though it should be perfectly obvious that the opinion gives reasons for the court's judgment. And not infrequently the opinion will have started off with "for the reasons to be given, the judgment is affirmed [or reversed]," thus telegraphing the punch. No reader has to be told that a judicial opinion contains reasons (true or false) for the court's decision.

Many federal judicial opinions are awash in loquacity, repetition, jargon, and excessive citation of previous judicial opinions; and when these faults are found in opinions that recite standards of review as well, contain subheadings, and tell the reader at the beginning or the end of the opinion (or at both the beginning and the end) that there are reasons for the court's judgment affirming or reversing the district court or federal agency, the opinions become unreadable. Brevity as I keep saying has no appeal to the legal profession, including its judicial branch. Think back to Justice Alito's painfully long, painfully dull, res-judicata-drenched dissent in the Texas abortion case decided at the end of the Supreme Court's 2015 term.

The underlying problems are tradition—the judges constantly looking over their shoulders at the receding past for guides to the future, though rarely finding them—and also ghostwriting. For as I noted in the Introduction most federal judicial opinions are initially drafted by law clerks. The judge will then edit, though often only lightly, the law clerk's draft. Even with conscientious editing the opinion will primarily be the product of the clerk (rarely is a first draft effaced by an editor), who will be reluctant, given his humble status, to depart from the format, structure, vocabulary, and conventions of the typical federal appellate opinion, stale though they so often are.

But we shouldn't ignore the minority of judges, tiny though it is, who do write their own opinions and whom Professor Gulati and I referred to in our article on judicial staff management as "writing judges" as distinct from "editing judges."[108] Writing judges provide a more candid, a more authentic, product. Theirs (or perhaps I should say "ours," since I am a member of that small breed) is the superior approach. And it's not that difficult; the judge can learn to write by writing; can learn he doesn't have to be long or complicated, just clear; and the clerks can clean up, add citations, criticize, and in these ways improve the product—without being the authors. But the low value that modern American culture places on writing continues to make the writing judge a rarity, perhaps en route to becoming a fossil remnant.

The fact that at present all the Supreme Court Justices have their law clerks write an initial opinion draft (though Breyer and Kagan then write their own drafts, though doubtless influenced by the clerk's drafts) is surprising as well as deplorable when one considers how light the Court's workload is. The average Justice (when there are nine Justices) writes only eight majority opinions a year, and majority opinions are on average far more important than concurring or dissenting ones. The Justices' large staffs, long summer vacations, and light caseloads may, as I intimated in Chapter 2, be factors in the diminished public respect for the institution. Justice Brandeis liked to say that Supreme Court Justices differed from other government officials in that they did their own work; they weren't just supervisors. For the most part that is no longer true of appellate judges, though it remains true of many trial judges.

Professor William D. Popkin is a distinguished law professor with a deep interest in judicial writing about which he makes cogent observations in a new book,[109] He points out that "traditional styles of judicial opinion-writing are ill-suited to conveying the reality that judging is discretionary and the law is uncertain. . . . Is there an alternative style of writing judicial opinions that is more suited to the contemporary understanding of judging?" A style neither "magisterial" nor "oracular"? Popkin argues that there is: writing in "a personal voice familiar to a lay public." An opinion written in such a voice is "well-suited to an exploratory tone that does not claim authority by reference to objectively verifiable criteria but which draws the audience into a participatory community with the judge by honestly acknowledging the uncertainty that characterizes judging." Popkin explains, "Voice refers to the judges' relationship to the source of law"; "tone" to "the relationship of the judge to the audience."

108. Gulati and Posner, note 8 above.
109. *Judgment* (January 2017).

He flatters me by saying that I "exemplif[y] a style of writing opinions that is both personal and exploratory. . . . Posner's personal voice is evidenced by his use of colloquial language, reducing legal language to everyday usage, and by his employment of a conversational style." Popkin goes on to say

> Posner's *exploratory tone* is evident in his sharing with the audience the difficulty of reaching a decision rather than speaking down to the reader. There are two ways in which Posner opinions are exploratory. The first is to share doubts with the reader about how to find the right answer. . . . The second way relates to the substantive criteria used to reach a decision, illustrated by his rejection of clear-sounding rules for deciding a case (such as textualism or statutory interpretation). Indeed, Posner often prefers more fuzzy standards (such as the purpose of the underlying rule) or rules-with-exceptions.
>
> We might suppose that a personal voice and exploratory tone are ill-suited to the kind of judicial command of an audience's assent that is associated with a judge's reliance on subjective universals. But that is not true, at least not in Posner's case. He typically commands the agreement of the audience he has wooed.

The obvious objection to the "personal voice and exploratory tone" that Popkin advocates and that I indeed try to embody in my opinions is that there is no point in writing for lay persons because unless they're litigants (and often even if they are litigants) they don't read opinions; besides the occasional litigant, only lawyers do. Adam Liptak, the very fine lawyer-journalist who covers the Supreme Court for the *New York Times,* is widely read by lay persons, I am sure. But I am also sure that few of them bother to dig up and read any of the opinions he writes about. And I'm sure that my audience is composed almost entirely of lawyers, including judges, law professors, law clerks, staff attorneys, and law students, with a smattering of college students (colleges and even high schools sometimes offer law courses). But as I tried to explain earlier in this chapter in discussing standards of appellate review, the formal "law diction" to which most judicial opinions adhere is harmful to the law because it is confusing to the point of being gibberish. It's time the legal community learned to speak and read and understand clearly, simply, and intelligently, bury the jargon and cultivate in its place a "personal voice" and an "exploratory tone."

FOUR

Tier Three of the Federal Judiciary:

The Federal District Courts

It is difficult to recapture the agonizing drama
of trial, its triumphant flow and its
humiliating ebb.

ALAN MOSES, 2016

Meanwhile declining from the noon of day
The Sun obliquely shoots his burning ray;
The hungry judges soon the sentence sign,
And wretches hang that jurymen may dine.

ALEXANDER POPE, 1712

THERE ARE MANY MORE CASES in the federal district courts than in the courts of appeals or the Supreme Court, and many more federal district judges than federal appellate judges—and the only federal trials conducted by Article III judges take place in the federal district courts. But only a minority of federal appellate judges, including just one Supreme Court Justice (Sotomayor), have been trial judges—either federal district judges (which is what Justice Sotomayor was) or their state counterparts (or sometimes both). Of the seventeen Chief Justices in the history of the Supreme Court, only eight had *any* prior judicial experience.[1]

Yet it's difficult to see how one could be a fully competent appellate judge without understanding the trial process—broadly understood to consist both

1. J. Gordon Hylton, "Most United States Supreme Court Justices Have Lacked Prior Judicial Experience," Marquette University Law School Faculty Blog, http://law.marquette.edu/facultyblog/2012/03/08/most-united-states-supreme-court-justices-have-lacked-prior-judicial-experience/.

of district court proceedings and of trial-level proceedings in other courts or in administrative agencies—at first hand. Very few proceedings before trial judges actually go to trial, the vast majority being decided by pretrial motions or settled out of court, but those proceedings can still be very complex. And the understanding of trial-level procedure must be at first hand rather than filtered by an appeal. For though there is a good deal of academic research on the trial process for appellate judges to draw upon, reading isn't the same as seeing; as with many activities in life, one can't obtain a deep understanding of the trial process without becoming involved in it—without ever conducting trial-court proceedings, including not only trials but also pretrial proceedings and settlement conferences. I don't think that even an experienced trial lawyer can fully understand the trial process, because he doesn't have the judge's perspective. And so every appellate judge should have trial-court experience as a judge, and therefore every federal court of appeals judge should hear cases in the district court unless he has been a district judge, or its state-law equivalent, before becoming an appellate judge. And that includes the eminences of the Supreme Court.

When I became a judge of the U.S. Court of Appeals for the Seventh Circuit on December 4, 1981, I had briefed and argued appeals, mainly in the Supreme Court, but I had never been a trial judge or conducted a trial or participated in trial-level proceedings except as a consultant or expert witness during my time as a law school professor (1968 to the end of 1981). Luther Swygert, the seniormost judge on the court that I had just joined, suggested that I volunteer to conduct trials in the district courts of the circuit. I took his advice, and in the ensuing thirty-five years have conducted numerous civil (and lately a few criminal) trials, many of them jury trials, and I have also conducted a number of pretrial proceedings and settlement negotiations.[2] I regard this range of experiences as a significant part of my judicial education, and I believe it should be *required* of all federal appellate judges (not excluding Supreme Court Justices) who like me had become appellate judges without ever having been trial judges. I noted at the end of Chapter 2 that I'm not the only appellate judge who, never having been a trial judge, conducts trials as a volunteer in the district courts, but I believe that it's only a small minority of appellate judges who do this.

Because of the opacity of trial-level process, the conduct of federal trials, both criminal and civil, requires more research than it's received. Interviews

2. I discuss my trial-court experience up to 2012 at some length in chapter 9 of my book *Reflections on Judging* (2013).

with district judges (also bankruptcy and magistrate judges) are a largely unexplored research technique that needs to be exploited. Other promising techniques include observation of trials, the study of court records, and the conduct of mock trials, including mock trials utilizing the highly realistic case folders published by the National Institute for Trial Advocacy, which include complaints, deposition summaries, diagrams, photographs, and other materials simulating the record of a real trial.[3] Such trials can be the core of a law-school evidence course as well—they were the core of the evidence course that I taught for several years at the University of Chicago Law School some years back. A spinoff of this method of teaching evidence was that I was able to identify the students who had an instinct for the trial process and whom I could therefore recommend enthusiastically to law firms interested in hiring potential litigators.

I've learned a great deal about the trial process from my forays into the district court (and from my "realistic" style of teaching evidence that I just described), and not just that *all* appellate judges who like me had not been a trial judge before their appointment as an appellate judge should (if necessary be ordered to) handle trials and other trial-court-level proceedings. I've also learned that there is a great deal of room for improvement in federal trial and pretrial process. Below I sketch my approach to each of the key stages of that process, with the principal aim of stimulating more systematic research concerning those stages, research in which I would hope law professors with trial experience would collaborate with social scientists and perhaps even with judges. Any reader familiar with the American trial process will note several respects in which my approach differs from the conventional one.

Here are the key stages of the civil jury trial as conducted by me:

The judge not the lawyers conducts the voir dire, asking a maximum of twenty questions of the prospective jurors. The judge is more likely than the lawyers to ask truthful, relevant questions rather than ones aimed at disqualifying a qualified juror whom a questioning lawyer might try to trick into giving a disqualifying answer. My twenty-to-a-customer limit on questions is intended to avoid boring the prospective jurors.

The preliminary instructions, read by the judge to the jury before the opening arguments of counsel in order to orient the jurors to trial procedure, can't

---

3. On the promising field of mock jury research, see works listed at http://scholar.google.com/scholar?as_sdt=0,9&q=mock+jury+research&hl=en. Mock trials used for research and training should of course be distinguished from the mock trials presided over by judges and Justices that I discuss in Chapter 2.

avoid the issue of Internet research by jurors, which occurs and indeed seems to be common. There may well be valid objections to such research, but it isn't a valid objection that there are frequent errors in websites; for live witnesses make many errors as well, often deliberate. The problem with Internet research by jurors is that the lawyers and the judge will not know what the jurors have found, even if what they've found is erroneous, misleading, or incomplete and so if revealed could be refuted or at least placed in a perspective that might alter the inferences to be drawn from it.

All this should be explained to the jurors at the outset. But judges rarely do that. Instead the judge will simply tell the jurors that they are forbidden to conduct such research. Unsurprisingly the prohibition is often ineffectual. An article by Caren Myers Morrison[4] quotes jurors as saying that *of course* they conduct Internet research even though the judge has told them not to; they do it when they don't feel that the lawyers or the judge are giving them information essential to their deciding on the verdict. Who can blame them? The judge should tell the jury in advance (I do) that if they feel the trial isn't giving them information they need in order to arrive at a sound verdict, they should send a note to the judge explaining what they feel they're missing, and the judge should then make sure they get that information.

To economize on trial time and help focus the trial, the judge should hold both a hearing on objections to documentary evidence, and a preliminary instructions conference, with the lawyers *before* the trial. And he or she should instruct them that verbal objections to testimony at the trial should be limited to one word (e.g., "hearsay"), or a few words (e.g., "asked and answered"), to save time. The judge should also set a time limit (in hours) for the trial, to keep the lawyers, jurors, and witnesses on their toes and reduce boredom and fatigue.

The judge should warn the jury about giving weight to "demeanor cues"— that is, about trying to infer truthfulness or lying from eye contact, posture, accent, hesitation, or other observable characteristics of a witness. The utility of such cues has as we'll see been discredited.

The jury should be permitted to discuss the case during recesses rather than having to wait till the trial is over. But the judge should instruct them not to make up their minds about the verdict until, the trial having ended, they begin their formal deliberations. And a juror who has a question during the trial

4. "Can the Jury Trial Survive Google?," 25 *Criminal Justice* 4 (winter 2011).

should be permitted to submit it in writing to the judge, who if he thinks it a proper question should direct the lawyers to address it, or address it himself.

I recently came across an interesting discussion of efforts being made by the federal district court in Connecticut to improve trial by jury.[5] I learn that judges there are working with lawyers to identify firm trial dates before a jury summons is mailed to prospective jurors. This enables prospective jurors with scheduling conflicts to notify the court in advance by email, thus avoiding the drive to the courthouse and sitting for hours to request to be excused: "We'll look at a similar case from a few months prior, and remind the judges how many jurors were brought in, and how many weren't used. . . . We'll then suggest that they summon fewer jurors for the current case. . . ." Court officials also have focused on improving the juror experience. "To give jurors a sense of involvement, . . . the court makes a point of bringing all jurors into the courtroom for voir dire, even if more prospective jurors report than necessary. In addition, light refreshments, such as coffee, pastry, and healthy snacks are made available during trial breaks, and court staff are quick to explain unexpected delays. [And] . . . judges meet with jurors after the conclusion of the trial, so that jurors can ask questions about the proceedings and provide feedback about their experience. Most of them find that very valuable."

Rule 706 of the Federal Rules of Evidence authorizes federal judges to appoint their own expert witnesses ("neutral experts" as opposed to party experts). This is an important grant of authority with respect to cases, such as patent cases, that involve science or technology or other arcane bodies of knowledge certain to be unfamiliar to most judges and jurors. The use of neutral experts is greatly underutilized (though not by me, in my forays into the district court), in part because it requires an investment of time by the judge in picking the expert and in presiding at his deposition, as unlike a party expert the court-appointed expert will not have a lawyer to defend him at his deposition, and in part because it is inconsistent with adversary procedure, in which all witnesses are designated by the lawyers. To which my response is: so much the worse for adversary procedure, which is overvalued and in acute need of modification.

The time spent by the judge in picking an expert witness can be minimized by the simple expedient of directing the lawyers for each side to tell their party experts to confer with the other side's experts with the aim of agreeing on sev-

5. United States Courts, *Judiciary News,* September 29, 2016, "Court's Focus on Jurors Saves Time, Money and Frustration," www.uscourts.gov/news/2016/09/29/courts-focus-jurors-saves-time-money-and-frustration.

eral neutrals from whom the judge can pick one to be his expert. (This works—I've done it.) This will usually be the neutral who seems best able to communicate with a jury—often that will be a professor who has taught first-year college students and thus knows how to communicate with novices. At the trial the judge will tell the jury how a neutral expert is selected and that his fee for testifying will be split 50/50 between the parties (as otherwise his neutrality would be compromised). The neutral expert should be the first expert witness to testify but the jury should be told to listen carefully to the party experts as well, who will testify afterward.

What makes the appointment of neutral experts particularly important is that the party's expert witnesses have a conflict of interest. On the one hand a party expert wants to avoid damaging his reputation by giving false or incomprehensible testimony. So far so good. But on the other hand he wants to give testimony helpful to the party that has hired them; if he fails to do that, thereby failing to help the client, he is unlikely to be hired as a party expert in future cases. I don't doubt that expert testimony is frequently "bent" in favor of the client, and this is a compelling reason for the appointment by the judge of a truly neutral expert in any case in which expert testimony is likely to be decisive.

Recently I was asked for my views on neutral experts. Here are the questions I was asked, and my answers.

> *Why do you think judges are reluctant to use court-appointed "neutral" experts?*
> Because it is inconsistent with the pure adversary system, in which all witnesses are lawyer-provided. And it makes more work for the judge—he has to preside at the deposition of the neutral expert, since the neutral does not have the protection of any of the lawyers in the case because he isn't employed by any of the parties.

> *Do you foresee an increase in the next five years in the use of court-appointed "neutral" experts?*
> I don't know, but I would welcome such an increase.

> *There is some question whether there is such a thing as a "neutral" or independent" or "impartial" expert witness. What do you think?*
> Yes, unquestionably. I conduct trials as a volunteer in the district court, though I'm an appellate judge, and if the case has significant technologi-

cal aspects I ask the lawyers to have their experts get together and nominate a few neutrals, whom I then interview and choose one. With both sides' experts agreeing on a neutral, one can be confident that he or she is indeed neutral.

Are there litigation areas (i.e., intellectual property, antitrust) or certain types of case (i.e., valuation disputes) in which court-appointed experts are more / less likely to work? Or should these experts be considered only for certain specialties (i.e., economics). Avoided in certain specialties (i.e., medial causation)?
The question should be: will the jurors understand the party experts? If there is significant doubt that they will, the appointment of a neutral expert is essential. The area of law involved is not important.

Should court-appointed experts be agreed-upon by the parties? If so, what qualities would you look for that differ from those of party experts?
I answered the first question earlier. As for the second, the qualities the neutral should have are similar to those the parties' expert should have—competence, and ability to communicate effectively with jurors.

Should the testimony of a court-appointed "neutral" expert be subject to the same admissibility / reliability standards used for party experts?
I can't think why not.

What are some of the pros and cons regarding the use of court-appointed "neutral" experts?
I don't think there are any cons. The pro is the neutral expert's neutrality.

How should litigators approach potentially damaging testimony by a court appointed "neutral" expert?
That's their business, not mine as the judge.

At what stage in the process should a court-appointed "neutral" expert be appointed?
As early as possible, to give him or her time to prepare and to be deposed. Should juries be informed that an expert has been appointed by the court? Absolutely!! Otherwise they'd be baffled.

Should the expert be subject to vigorous cross-exam at trial? If the "neutral" expert testifies, should it be before or after that of party experts?
I think he or she should testify first, but of course be subject to cross-examination just like any other witness.

Should the parties be responsible for a court-appointed expert's fees and expenses? Does this raise concerns?
Yes they should be responsible and the costs should be split 50/50 between the parties. I don't see what possible objection could be made to this approach.

What challenges do reviewing courts face in challenges to rulings/verdicts based on the testimony of court-appointed "neutral" experts?
None that I know.

Moving on: pattern jury instructions, which are drafted by committees composed of judges and trial lawyers, are popular with judges because adherence to them is unlikely to prompt a finding by the appellate court of instructional error. But they should never be given (I never give them), because they are too legalistic, or sometimes just too complex, to be fully intelligible to most jurors. Professor Jeremy Paul has given a great example, a California jury instruction that states, "Failure of recollection is common. Innocent misrecollection is not common" (the second sentence is nonsense); and a rewritten version, vastly superior because transparent: "People often forget things or make mistakes in what they remember."

So I draft my own instructions,[6] and my friend Judge Kane[7] likewise—but with a twist unknown to me until he told me about it. He subjects drafts of his instructions (before instructing the jury) to the Flesch Reading Ease Test, available on the Internet, which calculates the difficulty of understanding a passage of English text.[8] On the basis of the test results of his first draft Judge

6. For cogent criticisms of judicial failure to understand the difficulty that jurors have in understanding instructions commonly given by judges, see Judith L. Ritter, "Your Lips Are Moving . . . But the Words Aren't Clear: Dissecting the Presumption That Jurors Understand Instructions," 69 *Missouri Law Review* 163 (2004); Robert P. and Veda R. Charrow, "Making Legal Language Understandable: A Psycholinguistic Study of Jury Instructions," 79 *Columbia Law Review* 1306 (1979).

7. See note 6 in Chapter 1.

8. I mentioned the Flesch Reading Ease Test in passing in Chapter 2. The Flesch Reading Ease Readability formula is $RE = 206.835 - (1.015 \times ASL) - (84.6 \times ASW)$, where RE = Readability Ease; ASL = Average Sentence Length (i.e., the number of words divided by the number of sentences); and ASW = Average num-

Kane will often decide to simplify his instructions further before submitting them to the jury. He reports that since adopting this procedure no juror has asked questions about the instructions given. He also reports that the lawyers find that the simplified instructions (Judge Kane prepares them before trial, as do I, and shows them to the lawyers) help them to communicate better with the witnesses as well as with the jurors. I intend to use the Flesch Reading Ease Test the next time I conduct a jury trial.

So far so good, I would say: adequate solutions to common problems of jury trials. Now for the bad solutions or the no solutions.

Demeanor cues. The term refers to inferring the truthfulness or untruthfulness of a witness's testimony from impressions other than those created by his or her words: impressions made by physical appearance, ease or anxiety in speaking, confidence versus hesitation, facial expression, posture, relaxed versus nervous appearance, articulateness, friendliness. Most judges think that these "demeanor cues" are essential to determining the truthfulness or falsity of a witness's testimony. But a growing psychological literature suggests that the cues are largely worthless, for there are confident liars as well as nervous ones, nervous truth tellers as well as confident ones: and so "demeanor cues do not lead to accurate lie detection"[9] but instead distract the trier of fact (or triers of fact if it's a jury trial) from the cognitive content of the witness's testimony.[10] The literature implies that the best way to infer the truthfulness or untruthful-

---

ber of syllables per word (i.e., the number of syllables divided by the number of words). The formula's output, i.e., RE, is a number ranging from 0 to 100. (Note that the higher that number, the easier the text is to read, the reason being that RE is higher the longer the average sentence and the more syllables per word.) Sentences that score between 90.0 and 100.0 are considered easily understandable by an average fifth grader; scores between 60.0 and 70.0 are considered easily understandable by eighth and ninth graders; and scores between 0.0 and 30.0 by college graduates. Judge Kane (see note 6 in Chapter 1) aims for a score above 60 for his jurors. See generally Flesch Reading Ease Readability Formula, in *Readability Formulas*, October 1, 2016, www.read abilityformulas.com/flesch-reading-ease-readability-formula.php.

9. Max Minzer, "Detecting Lies Using Demeanor, Bias, and Context," 29 *Cardozo Law Review* 2557, 2566 (2007); see also *Divergent Paths: The Academy and the Judiciary* (2016), at 141–142.

10. See, e.g., Amina Memon et al., *Psychology and Law: Truthfulness, Accuracy and Credibility* (2d ed. 2003); Scott Rempell, "Gauging Credibility in Immigration Proceedings: Immaterial Inconsistencies, Demeanor, and the Rule of Reason," 25 *Georgetown Immigration Law Journal* 377 (2011); Guri C. Bollingmo et al., "The Effect of Biased and Non-Biased Information on Judgments of Witness Credibility," 15 *Psychology, Crime & Law* 61 (2009); Jeremy A. Blumenthal, "A Wipe of the Hands, a Lick of the Lips: The Validity of Demeanor Evidence in Assessing Witness Credibility," 72 *Nebraska Law Review* 1157 (1993). A related concern, also growing, is with the reliability of eyewitness testimony. See, e.g., Steven P. Garmiza, "Court Takes New Look at Eyewitnesses: *People v. Lerma*," *Chicago Daily Law Bulletin*, May 11, 2016, p. 1, and cases (in addition to *Lerma*) cited there.

ness of a witness's testimony is not to hear or see him at all but instead to read a transcript of his testimony. To most judges and lawyers this is heresy. As Viktoras Justickis explains, "The law has its own set of psychological principles that permeate all its activities. By keeping these independent of 'basic legal psychology' its statements are protected from any criticism from scientific psychology. Therefore, the law can regard its basic psychological statements as valid *even if scientific verification qualifies them as invalid.*"[11] We are no longer in the nineteenth or even the twentieth century. It's high time that law caught up with science. Three cheers for heresy.

By a "no" solution to a legal problem I mean not a bad solution but a good solution that will never be adopted. I'll discuss just one, which resembles both Internet research and the appointment of neutral experts under Rule 706 in being a challenge to the adversary system. Often the opposing lawyers in a trial differ greatly in quality. The inequality distorts the adversary process, which presupposes at least a rough equality of the adversaries. Often, too, one of the parties to a case—the plaintiff if it's a civil case and the defendant if it's a criminal one—has no lawyer at all, which shifts the odds of victory enormously in favor of the represented party regardless of the merits of his case. Differences in the quality of lawyers wouldn't matter a great deal if, for example, they were compensated as judges are: with a uniform government salary unrelated to outcomes or to the relative wealth of dueling litigants. (The analogy is to a "single payer" system of medical care.) There would then be no contingent fees and no $1,100 an hour billing rates. My pay isn't docked if I'm reversed by the Supreme Court; neither do I get a bonus if I'm affirmed. But few lawyers in our system besides public defenders are compensated in that way. As Paul Collier explains, "The rule of law is a huge public good, but no commercial lawyers are working to achieve 'justice': they work to win a case in a zero-sum tournament. The last hour of legal effort purchased by a party to a legal dispute yields its return not by generating more justice, but by increasing the chances of winning the tournament. There are simply too many people spending their time on these zero-marginal-social-product activities. Worse, many of them are highly talented."[12]

The sixty-four-dollar question, which I won't attempt to answer, is whether improvements in the civil jury system such as I've just described will save the

11. Viktoras Justickis, "Does the Law Use Even a Small Proportion of What Legal Psychology Has to Offer?" in *Psychology and Law: Bridging the Gap* 223 (Canter and Žukauskienė eds. 2008) (emphasis added).

12. Paul Collier, "Wrong for the Poor: A Clearer Alternative to Thomas Piketty: and the Problem When Capitalists Make Nothing But Money," *Times Literary Supplement,* September 25, 2015, p. 3. I would not limit his criticisms to commercial lawyers.

federal civil jury from eventually disappearing. In 1962, 5.5 percent of federal civil cases were decided by juries; the rate has since fallen below 1 percent.[13] The causes are various;[14] let me leave it at that.

Criminal procedure. Most of what I've been saying (other than in the immediately preceding paragraph!) is applicable to criminal as well as civil trials. But in addition I'm troubled by a number of features of the federal criminal process that until recently I had been only dimly aware of, such as that in the federal system only "probable cause" is required to indict a person[15] and probable cause does not require even a "preponderance of evidence" of the defendant's guilt—in other words doesn't require that the defendant be more likely to be guilty than to be innocent. Suspicion thus being enough to warrant indictment, a prosecutor can in good faith ask a grand jury to indict even though he himself doesn't believe the defendant guilty of the crime that the indictment charges him with. If the grand jury indicts in such a case (and it is rare for a grand jury to turn down a request to indict), the consequence is likely to be plea bargaining that culminates in the defendant's pleading guilty to some lesser crime and the prosecutor's agreeing to propose a lighter sentence to the judge. The possible result—punishment of an innocent person—would, if it materialized, be traceable to the low standard for indicting.

The jury is given the indictment when it retires for its deliberations, which is worrisome because invariably the indictment is shorter, and often contains more severe accusations, than the jury instructions; it may therefore increase the likelihood of conviction—improperly.

Federal prosecutors tend to be very able—the job is highly coveted—and sometimes they are quite fierce. And it's not uncommon for there to be two of them at the trial and only one (and sometimes no) lawyer for the defendant. The built-in bias in favor of conviction by the jury, based simply on the fact that the government is the plaintiff, is enhanced when skillful prosecutors confront a less skillful defense attorney (and *a fortiori* a defendant representing himself), as they often do because most criminal defendants can't afford a first-rate lawyer and no public defender (a "federal defender" in federal criminal cases)

13. New York University School of Law, Civil Jury Project, "The Civil Jury Is in Decline. What Are the Implications?" (2016), http://civiljuryproject.law.nyu.edu/.

14. See, e.g., Ashby Jones, "Why Have Federal Civil Jury Trials Basically Disappeared?" *Wall Street Journal*, September 21, 2010 (Law Blog); Richard A. Posner, "Juries on Trial," *Commentary*, March 1995, p. 49.

15. *Kaley v. United States*, 134 S. Ct. 1090, 1103 (2014); see also *Gerstein v. Pugh*, 420 U.S. 103, 121 (1975); William Ortman, "Probable Cause Revisited," 68 *Stanford Law Review* 511, 559–560 (2016).

may be willing to take the case if the likelihood of an acquittal, or a favorable plea bargain, is remote.

A related problem is the right of the criminal defendant to refuse to be represented by a lawyer at trial, held in *Faretta v. California*,[16] to be a defendant's *constitutional* right unless he's mentally incapable of defending himself. The fact that though not insane or retarded he is almost certain to be incapable of mounting an effective defense, and so is almost certain to be convicted even if the government can't prove him guilty beyond a reasonable doubt, does not entitle the trial judge to appoint counsel for him. This is a bad rule, which grants the defendant a "right" that disserves his interest in an acquittal and makes a mockery of the adversary system. And like many other constitutional rights, the right created in *Faretta* has no basis in the Constitution. The failure of the Supreme Court to have overruled *Faretta* is inexplicable.

I recently conducted a criminal trial in which the defendant refused to allow me to obtain a lawyer for him. He was convicted. Although I have no doubt that he was guilty, and the government's two prosecutors were superb, he just might have been acquitted had he had a lawyer.

The judge can appoint standby counsel for an unrepresented defendant, and often the defendant in the course of the trial will decide to turn his defense over to that lawyer, but not always; and, as it happens, not in the trial that I just mentioned.

While I'm on the subject of *Faretta* let me express my doubts that corporations should be forbidden (as they have been held to be) to litigate pro se. They would be unlikely to do so unless they had employees who though not lawyers were competent to handle litigation. A corporation, especially a large one, can't sensibly be equated to a lone unrepresented criminal defendant.

A practice of which I had not been aware was brought to my attention recently by Judge Kane: the practice of sometimes having two juries at one trial of two defendants. In *United States v. Muhtorov*, Criminal Case No. 12-cr-33-JLK, the two defendants were charged in a single indictment with separate and overlapping counts of providing, and conspiring to provide, material support to a foreign terrorist organization. Rule 8(b) of the Federal Rules of Criminal Procedure permits such joinder if defendants are alleged to have participated in the same act or transaction or series of acts or transactions constituting an offense or offenses, but Rule 14(a) permits severance in such a case if joinder would prejudice one or more of the joined defendants.

16. 422 U.S. 806 (1975).

Judge Kane decided to sever. He noted that "the pivotal circumstance in this case is the omnipresence of language differences that require at the very least two simultaneous translators, one in Russian and the other in Uzbek, complicated by some references to Kyrgyz and possibly Arabic and Urdu. I hasten to observe that combinations of these languages occur in the same conversations, indeed some interspersed in the same statements. I am already advised that due to inherent ambiguities in the Uzbek language some statements will require an interpreter to question a defendant as to precise meaning and it is clear that the same meaning might very well not be understood by both defendants." As for the government's suggestion "that one trial may be had before two juries, one for each defendant," Judge Kane said,

> I have seriously considered this option, but given the language problems described above, the complexity of the evidence to be adduced, the number of witnesses to be called and the likelihood that one or the other jury would have to leave the courtroom on numerous occasions makes management and presentation of the case unnecessarily difficult. I am also mindful of other inchoate factors that must be given close attention in this case. These include the nature of the charge and the current public arousal regarding terrorism, the religions espoused by the defendants, their ethnicity, and inflammatory language that potentially may be admitted. While I strongly believe that our best efforts, already underway, will produce exemplary jury instructions, I think the foregoing factors make this case too fragile under the circumstances to justify a joint trial.

I add that having two juries in the same courtroom would be likely to confuse all the jurors, and quite possibly the lawyers and the judge as well.

Moving on again: murders of police officers have been increasing lately, and one of the explanations offered is that policy brutality has inflamed the black community, stimulating thoughts and acts of revenge. A recent case in my court, *United States v. Johnson*,[17] poses a subtle issue regarding the motivation for such revenge. Milwaukee police took the unusual (one hopes unusual) step of treating a trivial parking violation of a type usually ignored (stopping a few feet closer than sixteen feet from a pedestrian crosswalk) as a criminal act. They had no reason to deem it criminal. The car was parked next to a liquor store, and the natural assumption would be that the driver or a passenger was

---

17. 823 F.3d 408 (2016). There was a forceful dissent by Judge Hamilton, and rehearing en banc was granted in the case, but at this writing the decision of the en banc court has not yet been issued.

in the liquor store buying liquor and would soon return to the car, which would then drive off. It was a wintry night, with snow on the ground, which helps to explain why an occupant of the car or more than one occupant wanted to buy liquor without having to walk through icy, snowy streets.

Had the police desired to verify this, the natural assumption of what was going on, one of them could have entered the liquor store to see whether a transaction was in progress, or could have shone a flashlight into the car or knocked on a car door and asked an occupant why the car was stopped, or the police could have driven around the block a couple of times in the thought that by then probably the liquor transaction would have been completed and the car would have gone. Instead they blocked the car with their two squad cars and shone the squad cars' bright lights into the car's windows, doubtless alarming the passengers.

The neighborhood in which this occurred is described, I assume accurately, as a high-crime neighborhood. The police may have believed, not unreasonably, that in such a neighborhood a search of even an innocuous vehicle may enable an arrest, as in fact happened. But that is not a good reason for treating parking violations as potential crimes. Indeed this one was not; for while Johnson, the driver, was discovered to have a gun with him (for which he had no license—and couldn't obtain one, because he was a felon) there is no evidence that the gun bore any relation to the decision to stop the car next to the liquor store. In these circumstances not only Johnson but the other occupants doubtless thought the police were overreaching.

The panel majority seems to have thought that police can act on the slightest suspicion of possible illegal activity, even if the illegality (a parking violation) does not rise to the level of a crime. And suspicion is more likely in a high-crime neighborhood. What the majority ignored, surprisingly in a period in which the murder of police officers in the United States has soared, is the cost *to the police* of heavy-handed police activity in high-crime, typically predominantly black, communities, and to the residents of those communities as well. Heavy-handed policy activity in such communities, well illustrated by this case, breeds anger and resentment among the residents. The occupants of the car were hardly likely to be mollified by learning that the driver had an unlicensed firearm. They are likely to have thought that in a high-crime neighborhood being armed is the height of prudence; and often because of a criminal record or for other reasons residents may find it very difficult to obtain a gun license. In an ideal world there would be no unlicensed guns, but that is not our world.

So, the police engaged in gratuitous heavy-handed police behavior in the very type of community in which such behavior is likely to spark violence, including violence against the police. That is foolish behavior; and foolish police behavior, when it takes the form of unreasonable searches and seizures (the search of the car and the seizure of Johnson), engenders violence. Such behavior should be discouraged and one way to do that is to require the police, before taking steps that may well violate the Fourth Amendment as well as poison the relations between the police and the community, to employ nonprovocative investigatory methods, which happen in this case to have been well suited to deal with a car parked a few feet nearer to the crosswalk than it should have been—though still well back (eight feet) from it.

I am mindful that in *Wren v. United States*,[18] the Supreme Court held that when the police have probable cause to believe that a driver has committed a traffic violation, there is a legitimate legal basis for the stop even if a reasonable officer would not have stopped the car in the absence of some additional law enforcement objective. But the stop in *Wren* was for unambiguous traffic violations: making a turn without signaling and then speeding.[19] As the facts of *Johnson* demonstrate, however, mere pretextual stops lack a veneer of a traffic-safety justification: the obscurity of and uncertainty surrounding the supposed parking violation and the show of force by which the seizure was effectuated made it apparent to everyone that the stop was made to give the police an opportunity to search the vehicle. Sociological research supports this distinction: although "being stopped for unambiguously running afoul of the law has no effect on trust (and, consequently, legitimacy of law enforcement), . . . when [a] stop was for a minor infraction and led to the officer asking prying questions and requesting to search the vehicle, the stops engendered hostility and resentment."[20]

Moving on once again: judges tend not to be well informed about the sophisticated literature on recidivism and other factors that should influence a criminal sentence. The Federal Judicial Center should focus on educating federal judges about sentencing, emphasizing the limited value of long sentences for both general deterrence (deterring other potential criminals) and specific deterrence (deterring the sentenced criminal from committing crimes when released from prison). Many criminals have "high discount rates"—in other

---

18. 517 U.S. 806 (1996).

19. Id. at 808.

20. Jonathan Blanks, "Thin Blue Lies: How Perpetual Stops Undermine Police Legitimacy," 66 *Case Western Reserve Law Review* 931, 933–934 (2016).

words are shortsighted and tend therefore not to be influenced significantly by the portion of a prison term that will be served in the far future, and for the further reason that the prospect of a longer sentence may have little deterrent effect on criminals who think the likelihood of their being caught is slight, as it may be; for the length of the prospective sentence is unlikely to affect the likelihood of their being caught.

I have expressed these concerns at greater length elsewhere, for example in *United States v. Presley*,[21] where the district judge in sentencing the defendant pointed out that he was a career offender who had begun his criminal career when he was sixteen, was a large-scale heroin dealer, and had committed disciplinary violations in previous incarcerations. What the judge failed to consider was the appropriateness of incarcerating Presley for such a long time that he would be elderly when released. Criminals, especially ones engaged in dangerous activities such as heroin dealing, tend to have what economists call a "high discount rate"—that is, they weight future consequences less heavily than a sensible, law-abiding person would.[22] Just as $1,000 to be received thirty years from today is worth less to a person than $1,000 received today (at an annual discount rate of 10 percent its present value is only $57), so the prospect of being in prison at age sixty is less worrisome to a thirty year old than the prospect of being in prison today—and the higher his discount rate, the less worrisome the prospect.[23] The length of a sentence therefore has less of a deterrent effect on such a person than the likelihood that he'll be caught, convicted, and imprisoned. An increase in sentence length may therefore add little additional deterrence, since every sentence increment is an increment in future, not present, punishment.[24] The sentencing judge in *Presley* referred to none of this literature and gave no reason to think that imposing a thirty-seven-year sentence would have a greater deterrent effect on current or prospective heroin dealers than a twenty-year or perhaps even a ten-year sentence, or that incapacitating Presley

21. 790 F.3d 699, 701–703 (7th Cir. 2015).

22. John Bronsteen et al., "Happiness and Punishment," 76 *University of Chicago Law Review* 1037, 1060 n. 115 (2009); Yair Listokin, "Crime and (with a Lag) Punishment: The Implications of Discounting for Equitable Sentencing," 44 *American Criminal Law Review* 115, 124 (2007); Stephanos Bibas, "Plea Bargaining Outside the Shadow of Trial," 117 *Harvard Law Review* 2463, 2504–2506 (2004).

23. A. Mitchell Polinsky and Steven Shavell, "On the Disutility and Discounting of Imprisonment and the Theory of Deterrence," 28 *Journal of Legal Studies* 1, 4–6 (1999); see also Paul H. Robinson and John M. Darley, "The Role of Deterrence in the Formulation of Criminal Law Rules: At Its Worst When Doing Its Best," 91 *Georgetown Law Journal* 949, 954–955 (2003).

24. Linda S. Beres and Thomas D. Griffith, "Habitual Offender Statutes and Criminal Deterrence," 34 *Connecticut Law Review* 55, 62–65 (2001).

in his sixties was necessary to prevent his resuming his criminal activities at that advanced age.

In short, sentencing judges need to consider the phenomenon of aging out of risky occupations. Violent crime, which can include trafficking in heroin, is generally a young man's game. Elderly people tend to be cautious, often indeed timid, and averse to physical danger. Violent crime is far less common among persons over forty, let alone over sixty, than among younger persons. According to the Bureau of Justice Statistics,[25] only 1.18 percent of persons entering federal prisons in 2012 for drug crimes were in the sixty-one to seventy age group. That is another reason to doubt that very long sentences reduce violent crime significantly. There needs finally to be considered the cost to the government of imprisonment, which is not trivial. The U.S. prison population is enormous by world standards—about 1 percent of the nation's entire population—and prisons are costly to operate because of their building materials (steel especially is very expensive) and large staffs. If the deterrent or incapacitative effect on criminal propensities fades sharply with time, the expenses incurred in the incarceration of elderly persons may be a social waste.

The Bureau of Prisons reports that 17.5 percent of the federal prison population is over the age of fifty, 2.7 percent between 61 sixty-one and sixty-five, and 2.2 percent older than sixty-five.[26] "Aging prisoners," defined as prisoners fifty years old or older, cost the federal prison system about 8 percent more than younger prisoners, and these excess costs, mainly medical, rise with age. The Inspector General's study also finds that only 8 percent of inmates aged sixty to sixty-four who were released between 2006 and 2010 were rearrested for new crimes within three years, compared to 19 percent who were fifty to fifty-four.[27]

I am not suggesting that sentencing judges (or counsel, or the probation service) should conduct a cost-benefit analysis to determine how long a prison sentence to give. But the considerations listed above should be part of the knowledge base that judges, lawyers, and probation officers consult in deciding on the length of sentences to recommend or impose. There is no indication that these considerations received any attention in the *Presley* case. I do not criticize the district judge or the lawyers or probation officers for the oversight, however; recognition of the downside of long sentences is recent and is just

25. "Prisoners Entering Federal Prison," www.bjs.gov/fjsrc/var.cfm?t=new.

26. Federal Bureau of Prisons, *Inmate Statistics: Inmate Age,* www.bop.gov/about/statistics/statistics _inmate_age.jsp.

27. See Office of the Inspector General, U.S. Dept. of Justice, "The Impact of an Aging Inmate Population on the Federal Bureau of Prisons," May 2015, https://oig.justice.gov/reports/2015/e1505.pdf.

beginning to dawn on the correctional authorities and criminal lawyers. Neither the Justice Department nor the defendant's lawyer (or the probation service) evinced awareness in *Presley* of the problem of the elderly prison inmate. Some judges, however, have drawn attention to the problem in their opinions.[28]

There is much else that federal district judges are required to consider in deciding on a sentence to impose on a convicted defendant—maybe too much: the federal Sentencing Guidelines and statutory sentencing factors,[29] the statutory and regulatory provisions relating to conditions of supervised release, presentence reports, briefs and arguments of counsel, statements by defendants and others at sentencing hearings. In thinking about the optimum sentence for a prisoner who is no longer young, the judge's primary focus should be on the traditional triad of sentencing considerations: incapacitation (which prevents the defendant from committing crimes against persons other than prison personnel and other prisoners until his release), general deterrence (to repeat, that's the effect of the sentence in deterring other persons from committing crimes), and specific deterrence (its effect in deterring the defendant from committing crimes after he's released). A sentence long enough to keep the defendant in prison until he enters the age range at which the type of criminal activity in which he engaged is rare should, as I discussed earlier, be sufficient to achieve the aims of incapacitation and specific deterrence. A problem is that law enforcement rarely publicizes criminal punishments (an omission that could well be thought a form of entrapment), and as a result criminals accustomed to the usually lighter state-law criminal penalties are often unaware of federal penalties, and the lack of notice weakens the deterrent effect of those penalties.

And finally the heinousness of a defendant's crime may argue compellingly for a sentence longer than needed to achieve the goals served by incapacitation and general and specific deterrence.

Emphasis needs also to be placed on cautious, sensible administration of "supervised release," the substitute, brought about by the Sentencing Reform Act of 1984, for federal parole—a substitution rich with problems[30]—and on

28. See, e.g., *United States v. Johnson*, 685 F.3d 660, 661–662 (7th Cir. 2012); *United States v. Bullion*, 466 F.3d 574, 577 (7th Cir. 2006); *United States v. Howard*, 773 F.3d 519, 532–533 (4th Cir. 2014); *United States v. Payton*, 754 F.3d 375, 378–379 (6th Cir. 2014); *United States v. Craig*, 703 F.3d 1001, 1002–1004 (7th Cir. 2012) (concurring opinion).

29. 18 U.S.C. § 3553(a).

30. I discuss the problems of supervised release at some length in *Divergent Paths*, note 9 above; see index references at p. 414 of that book.

inequality of the opposing lawyers in civil as well as criminal cases. Many civil plaintiffs are prisoners complaining about their treatment in prison, and they rarely have or are given lawyers. Criminal defendants have lawyers unless they invoke their *Faretta* right, but often as I have noted their lawyers are outnumbered and outgunned by the prosecutors. Judges should do what they can to even the balance, for example by appointing an additional lawyer for a defendant who is up against two experienced, aggressive prosecutors. Judges must also be on the lookout for federal prosecutorial misconduct, which is—to put it mildly—not unknown.[31]

The excessive severity of federal (and to a considerable extent as well of state) criminal laws[32] needs also to be corrected; in many cases it constrains the sentencing judge to impose an unduly harsh sentence and as a result is primarily responsible for the enormous prison population in this country (2.3 million as of June 2016). Judges have no direct control over criminal legislation that doesn't violate a constitutional provision, but they can express their views in their opinions and speeches and other writings (as I am doing here), and in these ways encourage the states and Congress to continue a trend now underway to reduce the prison population by, for example, eliminating or reducing "three strikes and you're out" (i.e., mandatory life imprisonment for your fourth felony) and scaling back punishment for dealing in crack cocaine to the lesser punishment for dealing in powder cocaine. These and other reforms have at least stopped the growth in the prison population and even scaled it back some.

The abolition of parole for federal crimes was responsible for a steep increase in the prison time actually served by convicted defendants, and it is time for Congress to scrap supervised release (which does not affect sentence length) and restore parole, including parole of lifers. And finally the states need to improve the medical care they provide to their prison inmates.[33]

31. See, e.g., Sidney Powell, *Licensed to Lie: Exposing Corruption in the Department of Justice* (2014), which includes an approving foreword by Judge Alex Kozinski—whose important critique of federal criminal law, "Preface: Criminal Law 2.0," 44 *Georgetown Law Journal Annual Review of Criminal Procedure* iii (2015), notes federal (as well as state) prosecutorial misconduct. See id., viii, xxii–xxxii, xxxv–xl. Solomon Wisenberg, "Too Much Skin in the Game? A Review of Sidney Powell's Licensed to Lie," *White Collar Crime Prof Blog*, October 27, 2014, http://lawprofessors.typepad.com/whitecollarcrime_blog/2014/10/too-much-skin-in -the-game-a-review-of-sydney-powells-licensed-to-lie.html, notes some exaggerations in Powell's book but on the whole commends it.

32. See David Garland, "Land of the Unfree: How and Why the United States Sends Millions of Men, Mostly of Colour, to Prison," *Times Literary Supplement*, July 22, 2016, p. 14, for an excellent summary and analysis of the problem.

33. See discussion of *Rowe v. Gibson* in the next chapter.

But I would go further; I would (if I were President and Congress rolled into one) abolish the federal laws against illegal drugs, with the possible exception of fentanyl because of its extreme lethality. The presently illegal drugs, once legalized, should still be regulated to warn users, should probably be taxed (as marijuana is now being taxed in states that have legalized it), and also should be forbidden to be sold to minors. But if adults want to risk life and health by taking drugs such as heroin and cocaine, and know the risks, I can't see how that distinguishes them from people who drink alcohol in dangerous quantities, or smoke heavily, or engage in risky sports—all activities that we permit adults to engage in. Anyway it's plain that criminalizing drug trafficking has failed to make much of a dent in the trade and consumption of drugs and the violence that goes with the trade, and I agree with my colleague Judge William Bauer that instead we should be searching for medical solutions to drug addition.[34] Decriminalizing the drug trade would have the incidental benefit for federal authorities of reducing the federal prison population substantially and by doing so reduce prison costs markedly.

Some of my concerns about federal sentencing are reflected in an order I issued in a fascinating recent criminal case that I conducted. The order upheld, with misgivings, the jury's findings of guilt. The basis of my misgivings was not that I was convinced that the defendant was innocent but that I was dubious that her alleged criminal conduct was serious enough to warrant criminal punishment as distinct from administrative discipline. I reprint my order here, despite its length, in order to give the reader a better feel for modern federal criminal proceedings:

MAY 3, 2016: MY DENIAL OF THE DEFENDANT'S MOTION TO ACQUIT OR IN THE ALTERNATIVE FOR A NEW TRIAL

After a four-day jury trial, the defendant, Enkhchimeg Ulziibayar Edwards (who goes by "Eni Edwards"), was found guilty of two counts of attempted obstruction of justice (also described as "witness tampering") in violation of 18 U.S.C. § 1512(b)(3), and two counts of making false statements to her employer, U.S. Customs and Border Protection (CBP), an agency of the Department of Homeland Security, in violation of 18 U.S.C. § 1001(a)(2). (The State Department's Diplomatic Security Service has also been involved in this case, as will be noted.) Before the jury ren-

---

34. William J. Bauer, "The War on Drugs," 2014 Wisconsin Law Review 1 (2014).

dered its verdict, the defendant moved for a judgment of acquittal pursuant to Rule 29 of the Federal Rules of Criminal Procedure, which provides relief "if the evidence, viewed in the light most favorable to the
government, would not justify any rational trier of fact in finding the elements of the crime charged beyond a reasonable doubt." *United States v.
Rahman*, 805 F.3d 822, 836 (7th Cir. 2015). I deferred ruling on the motion
until the jury rendered its verdict, after which the defendant moved for a
judgment of acquittal or in the alternative for a new trial, pursuant to
Rules 29(c) and 33(a) respectively. I conducted a hearing on the defendant's motion on April 27. I now must decide whether to grant or deny, in
whole or in part, the motion.

Mrs. Edwards, born in Mongolia in 1977, came to the United States in
the late 1990s, became a lawful resident of this country in 2003 or 2004
and an American citizen in 2005. She attended several American colleges, graduating from Roosevelt University in Chicago. In 1998 she had
married an American named Kenneth Edwards (whose name she took)
who happens to be an agent of CBP. Fluent in Russian and Polish as well
as in English and Mongolian, Mrs. Edwards long aimed at becoming a
CBP agent herself, though she did not attain this goal until 2009, having
formally applied the previous year. In the meantime she worked mainly
at the "Gate Gourmet" at O'Hare Airport (in an executive capacity, rather
than as a waitress or kitchen worker) and became friends there with an
employee named Michael Rosel.

Enter Tsasanchimeg Erdenekhuu, a young cousin of Mrs. Edwards.
Tasha, as the parties refer to Ms. Erdenekhuu, had come to the United
States on a temporary visa in 2001 as a teenager and decided to stay,
though without obtaining the permission of the U.S. government to do
so. In 2002, at age 17, she was arrested by immigration officers, and the
following year was ordered deported from the United States (i.e., air-
mailed back to Mongolia). She was placed in a detention center pending
deportation. After turning 18 that summer, she was eligible for bail while
awaiting deportation, and Mrs. Edwards' parents (who, by the way, now
live in Chicago too) sent Mrs. Edwards the $4,000 in bail money re-
quired to get her cousin released from the detention center. Although
ordered deported in 2003, thirteen years later Tasha remains in Chicago,
living with her third American husband. Although she lives openly in
Chicago and a document placed in the record by the government gives a

Chicago street address for her and the deportation order issued in 2003 has never expired or been withdrawn, the government has yet to make any move to deport her. The reason for this forbearance is unexplained, but probably it's that she has, so far as anyone has suggested, never been involved in any criminal activity. Noncriminal illegal immigrants in the United States are rarely deported; given the estimate that there are 10 or 11 *million* such persons in the nation at this time, that they constitute at least 5 percent of the American work force, that they have a lower crime rate than American citizens, and that law enforcement agencies have their hands full with more pressing problems than that of law-abiding though unauthorized immigrants, it is not surprising that persons such as Tasha generally are left alone.

When arrested by the immigration authorities and later ordered deported, Tasha could not feel entirely secure. It occurred to Mrs. Edwards (doubtless to Tasha as well) that Tasha would be completely secure only if she became a lawful U.S. resident, a status she would be likely to attain if she entered into a marriage with an American citizen that was either bona fide, or, if not, nevertheless a marriage that would not be exposed as fraudulent. Opportunity struck in 2003, when Mrs. Edwards suggested to her friend Michael Rosel—a divorced man in his late forties who testified in this case that he finds Asian women attractive—that he consider marrying Tasha. Doubtless Mrs. Edwards mentioned the possibility to Tasha as well. Tasha and Rosel were soon married—and after ten months divorced. The marriage had been a flop, largely it seems because of the large age difference between the spouses (about 30 years), Tasha's English, which apparently was very poor at the time, and her apparent unwillingness to have sex with Rosel. Indeed, there is reason to think that she found Rosel a totally unsuitable husband. The marriage ended before Tasha had obtained any change in her immigration status; she was, as she remains to this day, under an order, though never enforced or, it seems, intended to be enforced, of deportation.

The government believes or professes to believe that the marriage of Tasha and Rosel was fraudulent, and points us to the federal statute that provides that "any individual who knowingly enters into a marriage for the purpose of evading any provision of the immigration laws shall be imprisoned for not more than 5 years, or fined not more than $250,000, or both." 8 U.S.C. § 1325. However, the statute of limitations for marriage fraud is five years, see 18 U.S.C. § 3282(a); *United States v. Rojas,* 718 F.3d 1317, 1319 (11th Cir. 2013), and starts to run on the date of the marriage. *Id.* at 1319–20; *United States v. Ongaga,* No. 14-20235, 2016 WL 1458942, at *3–4 (5th Cir. Apr. 13, 2016). Therefore no one—not the cousin, not Mrs. Edwards, not Mr. Rosel—could be prosecuted for the alleged marriage fraud after July 21, 2008, and no one *has* ever been prosecuted for it.

U.S. Immigration and Customs Enforcement (ICE), which like CBP is an agency of the Department of Homeland Security, has tried to warn the public that "Terrorists and other criminals can use marriage fraud as a vehicle to enter the United States, often due to the willingness of U.S. citizens. They can then hide their identity, gain unlawful employment, access government buildings, and open bank accounts and businesses to conduct further criminal activity." ICE, "Marriage Fraud Is Not a Victimless, Innocent Crime," www.ice.gov/sites/default/files/documents/Document/2014/marriageFraudBrochure.pdf. There is no indication, however, that Mongolians who enter the United States engage in that type of activity.

Fast forward to 2008, when the U.S. Embassy in Ulan Bator, the capital of Mongolia, began worrying about a number of Mongolian "throat singers" (see "Mongolian Throat Singing—Batzorig Vaanchig," *YouTube,* www.youtube.com/watch?v=1rmo3fKeveo) who requested performance visas to allow them to visit Chicago—when two years previously several other throat singers, having obtained such visas and come to Chicago, did not return to Mongolia but instead vanished (presumably they are living somewhere in the United States, all or most of them perhaps in Chicago, home to some 3000 or 4000 persons of Mongolian origin—in addition Chicago is a "sanctuary city," meaning that it doesn't assist federal authorities to hunt down illegal immigrants). In retrospect the concern of the embassy officials seems strange—I call their anxiety about a Mongolian influx to the United States the "Mongolian Panic." There are very few Mongolians in the United States (probably no more than 20,000, though there are no hard statistics)—for that matter there aren't many Mongolians in Mongolia, which has a population of only about 2.8 million, which is just 100,000 more than the population of Chicago. And while doubtless many of the few Mongolians in the United States are, like Tasha, illegal aliens, they do not appear to be involved in criminal activities, and therefore, one would think, would be of no interest to the authorities, just as Tasha quickly ceased to concern the authorities, who could but have never bothered to deport her.

Officials from the U.S. Embassy in Mongolia referred their concerns to the State Department's Diplomatic Security Service office based in Chicago, whose agents began to investigate visa applications filed by Mongolian nationals. Their concern focused on the American Mongolian Association, a tiny Chicago civic organization (apparently it has only 1 to 4 employees) that the State Department believed had been trying to smuggle Mongolians into the United States via Chicago, never to return to Mongolia, though there is no proof of such smuggling. No one knows whether the AMA assisted the throat singers to remain in the United States in 2006 after their performance visas expired.

Mrs. Edwards, it turns out, was involved with the American Mongolian Association, though in what capacity is unclear—there is evidence that she was a vice president of the organization for a time, but she testified that she had stopped participating in AMA events in 2008 though continued to have a social relationship with the organization's president. The fact that many Mongolians seeking visas to visit Chicago listed her phone number as their contact in Chicago aroused federal agents' suspicions, though it must be emphasized that she has not been charged with smuggling Mongolians into the United States or with visa fraud. As I noted at the beginning of this order, she is charged, rather, and was convicted by the jury, of two counts of attempted obstruction of justice and two of making false statements on employment forms and in interviews, demanded of her by CBP. An oddity of her involvement with the AMA is that one would expect CBP to have *wanted* to plant one of its agents in that suspect organization to report on its nefarious activities (if they were nefarious, which has not however been proved).

The two counts of attempted obstruction of justice are based on recordings of two phone calls made to Mrs. Edwards by Tasha's first husband, Michael Rosel, on successive days early in January 2013. Agents from the Diplomatic Security Service had gotten wind of Rosel's marriage to Tasha and suspected that it had been a fake marriage arranged by her cousin, that is, by Mrs. Edwards, of whom they were already suspicious because of her involvement with the AMA. To nail down their suspicions concerning the marriage, agents persuaded Rosel to call Mrs. Edwards and, by asking questions that the agents instructed him to ask, seek to elicit an admission that she had arranged the allegedly fake marriage. Rosel did not elicit any such admission, but did extract what the government has contended proved that the marriage was indeed fake and Mrs. Edwards complicit in it along with Tasha and Rosel. Her conversations with Rosel were secretly recorded by the agents and played at the trial.

Now as I noted earlier Mrs. Edwards cannot be prosecuted (no one can be) for marriage fraud concerning Rosel's marriage to Tasha. The charge is that by encouraging Rosel to lie in her two phone conversations (totaling more than fifty minutes) with him she interfered with governmental investigative activity. Such interference can be, and in this case was charged as, the crime of attempted obstruction of justice (alternatively called, in a case such as this, in which the alleged obstruction is of a potential witness, "witness tampering"). One element of that crime—the one critical to the obstruction charges in this case—is, as I instructed the jury, that "the defendant [Mrs. Edwards] attempted to persuade another person [Mr. Rosel] to interfere with the government's investigation or prosecution of illegal activity." See 18 U.S.C. § 1512(b)(3).

I can set to one side attempted interference with a prosecution. There was no possibility of prosecuting Tasha five years after the statute of limitations applicable to the allegedly fraudulent marriage had expired. Nor is it apparent that lying to Rosel about the marriage was likely to or did interfere with an investigation of the marriage, as there would have been no point to such an investigation, especially since Tasha could be deported any time the government decided to do so, whether or not the marriage had been fraudulent.

In fact the investigative activity that Mrs. Edwards may have interfered with in her conversations with the agents was not an investigation of the allegedly fake marriage as such; it was an investigation of Mrs. Edwards' likelihood of involvement in the suspected (though never proved) scheme, possibly (if there really was such a scheme) devised by the American Mongolian Association with which Mrs. Edwards was as I said connected, to smuggle Mongolians into Chicago. She had not, it is true, smuggled Tasha into Chicago, but knowing that Tasha was an illegal immigrant who had been ordered deported Mrs. Edwards had tried to protect her from being deported by urging Mr. Rosel to marry her, which he did.

The prosecutors in this case seem, however, to have an imperfect understanding of marriage fraud. They think that endeavoring to secure a person from deportation by helping him (or in this case her) find a spouse is ipso facto marriage fraud. That is false; marriage fraud, as I quoted from the marriage-fraud statute earlier, requires that the marriage have been made "for the purpose of *evading* any provision of the immigration laws" (emphasis added). Only "a marriage entered into *solely* to obtain immigration benefits not otherwise available without the marriage has as its purpose the evasion of immigration laws." *Eid v. Thompson*, 740 F.3d 118, 124 (3d Cir. 2014) (emphasis added). Marriage fraud is *evading* immigration laws, rather than seeking to obtain *lawful* permanent U.S. residence for a person by finding a mate for her, provided that the marriage is bona fide. The typical fraudulent marriage is one in which an illegal immigrant pays an American citizen money to induce him to marry her, with the mutual understanding that they will not live together or otherwise behave like a married couple and will divorce as soon as the immigrant has, on the basis of the marriage, obtained lawful U.S. residence. See *U.S. Dept. of Justice, Offices of the United States Attorneys*, "1948. Marriage Fraud—8 U.S.C. 1325 and 18 U.S.C. 1546," www.justice.gov/usam/criminal-resource-manual-1948-marriage-fraud-8-usc-1325c-and-18-usc-1546.

True, as the government emphasizes, money need not change hands for a marriage to be fraudulent, though such cases (illustrated by *King v. Holder*, 570 F.3d 785, 788 (6th Cir. 2009)) appear to be rare. The most famous was not an American case at all, but a British one. When the Nazis seized power in Germany in 1933, Thomas Mann, the great German writer and an outspoken anti-Nazi was, fortunately for him, in Switzerland. His daughter Erika however was in Germany, and wanted out. She wanted to relocate to Britain, but couldn't without being married. This was a problem for her, because she was a lesbian. She solved it by marrying the English poet W. H. Auden—a homosexual. Unsurprisingly, they never lived together. The marriage, though certainly for a good cause and never questioned by the British authorities, was thoroughly fraudulent.

It is unclear whether the marriage of Rosel and Tasha was fraudulent. No money changed hands, and Rosel, who remember was divorced, did testify at the trial that sex was one of the considerations that induced him to agree to marry Tasha. (In one of the phone conversations he told Mrs.

Edwards that "the only thing he got out of [the marriage] was the sex part.") But he also testified that the main inducement for his agreeing to the marriage was his wanting to do a favor for Mrs. Edwards, a friend and coworker—the favor consisting not of the marriage as such but of obtaining lawful U.S. residence for Mrs. Edwards' cousin. It may be that no "real" marriage was ever in the contemplation of Rosel, Tasha, or Mrs. Edwards.

Knowing that Rosel had been questioned by federal agents, but not knowing that his calls were at their behest and were being recorded, Mrs. Edwards endeavored to persuade him to tell anyone who asked that it was a perfectly normal marriage—that Rosel and Tasha had dated (he testified that they hadn't, though it must be borne in mind that these calls were made ten years after the marriage, and memories might have faded), had gotten married, had lived together (true, though only for a few months), the marriage hadn't worked out, Tasha had obtained no change in her immigration status, they divorced, and such sequences are not uncommon and need not involve fraud. She may have been telling the truth, but Rosel testified to the contrary (though he fudged some on cross-examination—and was one of the most uncomfortable witnesses whom I have ever seen), and the jury was entitled to believe him. And to believe him was to believe that Mrs. Edwards had arranged a fake marriage, and more important that she was now covering it up, and by covering it up trying to make it difficult for federal agents to determine whether it *had* been a fake marriage. And while she couldn't be prosecuted for such illegality because the statute of limitations had run, it could be thought to cast doubt on her character and her loyalty to the government agencies, including her own agency (CBP), that are responsible for enforcing the nation's immigration laws.

Remember that at the time of the calls (2013), the Diplomatic Security Service suspected that Mrs. Edwards was involved in smuggling Mongolians into the United States. Although as I said she had not smuggled Tasha into the United States—Tasha had shown up on her doorstep, as it were, unexpectedly back in 2001—and for all we know may never have smuggled anyone into the United States—a willingness to assist an illegal immigrant to avoid deportation by contracting a fake marriage could be thought to imply willingness to assist other illegal immigrants from Mrs. Edwards' country of birth. The investigation of the marriage, though it could not lead to a fraudulent-marriage prosecution, might therefore have assisted in an investigation of Mrs. Edwards' possible involvement in smuggling Mongolians into Chicago. If so, the investigation of the 10-year-old marriage was legitimate, and Mrs. Edwards could be found by the jury to have interfered with the investigation by trying to persuade Rosel to tell the agents that the marriage had been on the up and up, though it is important to bear in mind that there is no actual evidence that she ever smuggled anyone into the United States; nor has she been charged with doing so.

Although the phone calls didn't lead anywhere, she is not entitled to be acquitted of the first two counts—the obstruction of justice counts, which are based on the calls. I say this with regret, as I think the fake-marriage issue is actually quite inconsequential, and should not have been a charge in the indictment. The jury could easily have found that either the marriage was genuine, or at this late date that its genuineness or lack thereof could no longer be determined, in which event "finding" it to be a fake marriage would be no more evidence-based than flipping a coin. The jury could have found that since Mrs. Edwards had not been charged with smuggling or concealing immigrants or engaging in visa fraud, the investigation of the alleged marriage fraud would have yielded no evidence that was relevant to the case.

A possible-seeming exception to my disparagement of bringing the marriage into the case, discussed in the second part of this order, is Mrs. Edwards' failing to list Tasha as a "foreign-national contact" as required by her employment forms. But this is another nothing, because her association with Tasha in all these years since Tasha first appeared on the scene led to no alteration in Tasha's status as an illegal immigrant. The deportation warrant issued in 2003 is still in force. There is no evidence that apart from the marriage Mrs. Edwards has ever done anything to alter Tasha's status—and certainly the marriage failed to alter her status in the slightest, as she and Rosel abandoned the application for a green card (proof that the holder is a lawful permanent resident of the United States) for her that they had filed.

Her lies (if they were lies) through Rosel to the agents in the two phone calls did no harm to the United States, but harm is not required for a conviction of attempting to obstruct justice. Harm is relevant—but to the sentence, not to the conviction, and I will reserve judgment on the proper sentence to impose on Mrs. Edwards to the sentencing hearing. I will listen carefully to what the prosecutors and the probation service advise on sentencing, but as of now I incline to the view that the alleged attempt to obstruct justice (or equivalently to tamper with a witness—namely Rosel) was inconsequential, and not worth the time and effort that the government, Mrs. Edwards' lawyer, and court staff have devoted to it.

I need to discuss, however, an alternative contention by her lawyer—that Edwards is entitled if not to an acquittal of the charges of attempted obstruction of justice or witness tampering (which mean the same thing) then to a new trial of those charges, as well as of the false statement charges. The arguments in support of this claim are weak, such as that the indictment (which as is commonplace was shown to the jury) included surplusage—namely unnecessary and potentially misleading material consisting of the allegations concerning the Mongolian performers who had been sponsored by the American Mongolian Association to come to the United States on temporary visas and had promptly vanished. Although Mrs. Edwards was not accused of being responsible for their failure to return to Mongolia when their visas expired (or at any later time, for that matter), the attempted obstruction of justice and the concealment on her employment forms of any involvement with Mongolian immigrants (counts 3 and 4, discussed below) presupposed *some* involvement on her part with illegal Mongolian immigrants—even if only Tasha.

"[S]urplusage may be stricken from the indictment if the court finds the language to be immaterial, irrelevant, or prejudicial." *United States v. Marshall,* 985 F.2d 901, 905 (7th Cir. 1993); see also *United States v. O'Connor,* 656 F.3d 630, 645 (7th Cir. 2011). But the evidence that the defense had asked me to strike was relevant to both the false statement and obstruction of justice counts. The government was investigating a broad suspected scheme of immigration fraud, and was entitled to present evidence about the AMA and the performers who overstayed their visas as background to how Edwards' name had cropped up in their investigation. Remember that most of those performers had listed Edwards' phone number on their visa applications as their American contact, which supported the government's claim that the false statements on her employment forms were intentional.

Also unpersuasive is the argument that the obstruction and false statement counts should have been charged and tried separately. . . . [T]hey were properly joined, because they were "of the same or similar character," Fed. R. Crim. P. 8(a), all four counts having pertained to Mrs. Edwards' alleged concealment of relationships with foreign nationals from her employer, a federal agency concerned with illegal immigration. . . .

The defense motion further insists that the word "corruptly" in the phrase "corruptly persuades another person" in the witness-tampering statute, 18 U.S.C. § 1512(b), is unconstitutionally vague. It's not vague, although it is surplusage; it signals the absence of any lawful excuse for trying, as relates to this case, to "prevent the communication to a law enforcement officer . . . of information relating to the commission or possible commission of a Federal offense." *Id.,* subsection (b)(3). As explained in *United States v. Farrell,* 126 F.3d 484, 488 (3d Cir. 1997), "attempting to *persuade* someone to provide *false* information to federal investigators constitute[s] 'corrupt persuasion' punishable under § 1512(b)."

Remarkably, while arguing that "corruptly" is unconstitutionally vague, the defense motion argues that it should have been included in the instructions! I don't get it. Moreover, I had proposed the following instruction: "The defendant attempted to persuade another person to interfere with the government's investigation or prosecution of illegal activity, *without justification* for interfering" (emphasis added). "Without justification" was meant to convey the meaning of "corruptly" in section 1512(b). See *United States v. Matthews,* 505 F.3d 698, 706 (7th Cir. 2007); *Arthur Andersen LLP v. United States,* 544 U.S. 696, 705 (2005). The government asked that "without justification" be removed, because no justification for such an interference had been suggested. Defense counsel agreed to the removal of the phrase.

The defense also complains about my refusal to give six jury instructions that it submitted, but they either duplicated material in the instructions that I did give or were irrelevant to the charges.

I move now to counts 3 and 4, the false-statement counts, which required the prosecution to prove that the defendant had "knowingly and willfully . . . ma[de] any materially false, fictitious, or fraudulent statement or representation" to the federal government. 18 U.S.C. § 1001(a) (2). These counts are better supported by the evidence adduced at trial than the obstruction of justice counts—so much better that Mrs. Edwards' lawyer devotes less than two-thirds of a page in his 12-page motion to discussion of the issue, and the discussion is perfunctory.

The defendant argues that the exclusion of "knowingly," "willfully," and "materially" from the false-statement instruction was erroneous. I instructed the jury that it must find "the defendant deliberately made a statement that she *knew* was false or misleading" (emphasis added), in order to convict, and "deliberately" is the equivalent of "knowingly." I substituted "deliberately" for "willfully" because "deliberately" has the same meaning and is more understandable to a jury. Edwards' argument that the substitution of "material" with "capable of influencing the agency's actions" was an erroneous departure from the pattern jury instructions is also unpersuasive, because that is how the pattern instructions define "material." Nor must jury instructions be based on the pattern instructions.

Regarding the sufficiency of the evidence to support the false-statement counts, I note that employment forms that Mrs. Edwards was asked to fill out in 2014 asked among other questions whether she had ever provided financial support for any foreign national, and she had answered "no" though in fact she'd provided such support for Tasha. She also falsely denied having "had close and / or continuing contact with any additional foreign nationals within the last 7 years with whom you, your spouse, or your cohabitant are bound by affection, influence, and / or obligation"—another question to which the correct answer was Tasha, who had actually lived with the defendant for a time in the early 2000s and with whom Mrs. Edwards had kept in close contact, as evidenced by the detailed information about Tasha that Mrs. Edwards shared with Rosel during their recorded conversations—information such as that Tasha was pregnant and engaged to be married and planning to expedite the marriage because of the pregnancy. The two cousins were also depicted together in photos posted on social media and for a time shared a bank account. Mrs. Edwards stated in a supplemental interview that she had never helped anyone enter or stay in the United States illegally, but clearly she had helped Tasha remain illegally.

So the challenge to her conviction on counts 3 and 4, as to her conviction on counts 1 and 2, fails. But I need to say a bit more about all four counts in anticipation of the sentencing hearing. There is, to begin with counts 3 and 4, no evidence that the false statements that she made to

CBP about her contacts with foreign nationals such as Tasha did any harm to the agency or to the United States. Remember that the principal foreign national with which she had contacts, and so far as appears the only one with whom she had extensive contacts, was Tasha, a relative; and remember that it was Mrs. Edwards' parents who by sending the bail money to their daughter involved her with Tasha. Families in Mongolia are famously tight knit, see, e.g., "Family First," *The Washington Diplomat,* January 2008, www.washdiplomat.com/index.php?option=com_content&view=article&id=6588:-family-first-&ca=985:january-2008&Itemid=272, so it wouldn't be surprising if Mrs. Edwards felt a moral obligation to assist a cousin. That is not an excuse but it is a mitigating factor. Neither CBP nor any other government agency appears to have the slightest interest in this illegal immigrant who has been living openly in Chicago for many years, totally ignored by the government. Had the government thought Tasha had some sinister influence over Mrs. Edwards, it would have deported her to Mongolia years ago. So I find it impossible to see how the contacts between the two women have or could have harmed the United States, and hence how Mrs. Edwards' attempt to conceal those contacts could have harmed the United States.

The same can be said about counts 1 and 2. I anticipate the government's arguing to me that *of course* an attempted crime need not inflict any harm to be punishable, and no doubt many attempts do not inflict any harm, especially if the intended victim is unaware of the attempt, and yet the perpetrators are rightly punished. But if one asks why attempts are punished, one may be inclined to doubt that Mrs. Edwards should be punished, or at least punished severely, for the attempts, of which I have concluded her conviction must be upheld, charged in the first two counts.

There are two reasons for punishing attempts that do no harm, either physical or psychological or financial. One is that an attempt constitutes a revelation of character. Someone who shoots at another person out of enmity rather than fear, though he misses, shows himself to be a dangerous person, and punishing him is intended to (and in some cases is likely to) deter him and similar persons from engaging in such behavior in the future. The punishment thus contributes to both specific and general deterrence. I have difficulty envisioning Mrs. Edwards becoming involved in the future either in fake (or possibly fake) marriages, or in making false claims on federal employment forms, as it is unlikely that she will ever again be employed by the federal government, let alone by a government agency concerned with protecting the nation's borders from illegal immigrants. The investigation leading up to the trial, the trial itself, and now the certainty of sentencing are bound to have a dampening effect on any illegal impulses that remain with Mrs. Edwards. But these are issues to be considered further at sentencing.

Speaking of sentencing, I originally fixed May 26, 2016, as the date of the sentencing hearing. At the April 27 hearing I asked the lawyers to agree on an earlier date; I didn't and don't want to leave Mrs. Edwards, who has three young children and is pregnant with a fourth, twisting in the wind indefinitely. The lawyers promised they would agree to an earlier date, they have kept their promise, and one of the dates and times they have proposed, being the one most compatible with my schedule— namely May 17 at 2:45 P.M.—I hereby adopt. . . . In summary, the defense motions to acquit or in the alternative for a new trial [docket nos. 109 and 112] are denied.

The sentence I imposed in May 2016 departed dramatically from the Guideline Range. Earlier I mentioned in passing the federal Sentencing Guidelines, which are sentencing ranges promulgated by the United States Sentencing Commission *within* the statutory ranges. (The Commission has no authority to recommend a sentence above the statutory maximum sentence or below the statutory minimum sentence). A federal criminal statute might set a minimum prison sentence for the crime forbidden by the statute at ten months and the maximum sentence at forty months, but the guideline range might be, say, twenty to thirty months. A guidelines sentence is usually more lenient than a sentence based solely on statute; it can't, as I just noted, be more severe.

The two crimes of which Mrs. Edwards was convicted—making a false statement to the government, 18 U.S.C. § 1000(a)(2), and tampering with an informant (Mr. Rosel)—are punishable by maximum prison sentences of five and twenty years, respectively, and / or by fines in an unspecified amount; there is no minimum prison sentence under either statute. But the total guideline prison range was only twenty-four to thirty months; and taking advantage of the absence of any statutory minimum, I imposed no prison sentence at all but instead two years of probation (placing minimal restrictions on Mrs. Edwards during the two years) and a fine (payable in installments and affordable by her and her husband) of $2,000 (when probation is imposed but no prison sentence, imposing a fine is mandatory). I explained that "the nature and circumstances of the offense support the sentence imposed; specifically, the violations of law found by the jury caused no harm to the government. The history and characteristics of the defendant also support the sentence imposed; the defendant has young children and is a first-time offender. Additionally, the sentence imposed is sufficient to deter the defendant and others from committing similar crimes."

Enough about the Edwards case. But an interesting issue concerning sentencing guidelines arose recently and merits discussion. A federal criminal statute defines a "violent felony" (which is punishable more severely than a nonviolent felony) to include "burglary, arson, or extortion, . . . use of explosives, or otherwise involves conduct that presents a serious potential risk of physical injury to another."[35] In *Johnson v. United States*[36] the Supreme Court held that the last clause in the statutory provision that I just quoted—"otherwise involves conduct that presents a serious potential risk of physical injury to another"—was unconstitutionally vague. It was a sensible ruling, because the clause fails to specify the gravity of the threatened injury necessary to trigger the provision. But as it happens there is an identical guideline provision,[37] and the question has arisen whether it too should be deemed unconstitutionally vague. At this writing the issue is unresolved, the Supreme Court not yet having addressed it, but a court of appeals decision in a case called *United States v. Matchett*[38] has ruled—very sensibly in my judgment—that it is not unconstitutionally vague. Not only are sentencing judges not bound by the guidelines; they are not permitted to impose a guideline sentence without considering the sentencing factors in 18 U.S.C. § 3553(a). A sentencing judge might sensibly reason that to conform to those factors (in particular the requirement in subsection (a)(2)(A) that the judge consider "the need for the sentence imposed to reflect the seriousness of the offense"), he should understand "serious" potential risk in 18 U.S.C. § 924(e)(2)(B) to imply "serious physical injury"; and so understood the

---

35. 18 U.S.C. § 924(e)(2)(B).
36. 135 S. Ct. 2551 (2015).
37. U.S.S.G. § 4B1.2(a)(2).
38. 802 F.3d 1185, 1193–1195 (11th Cir. 2015).

clause is not vague and should therefore be considered applicable in an appropriate case.

So far my discussion of the guidelines has not criticized the *concept* of sentencing guidelines, but criticisms of the concept by Judge Kane[39] have gotten me thinking critically about them. On reflection I am not convinced of the competence of the U.S. Sentencing Commission to establish guideline ranges for particular federal crimes. The proper sentence for a criminal defendant depends on the particulars of his crime and of his character and mentality, depends also on his upbringing and the circumstances, choice of victim, and other characteristics that vary from criminal incident to criminal incident, and are not captured by the guidelines. For example the robbery guideline (U.S.S.G. § 2B3.1) provides:

> (1) If the property of a financial institution or post office was taken, or if the taking of such property was an object of the offense, increase by 2 levels; (2)(A) If a firearm was discharged, increase by 7 levels; (B) if a firearm was otherwise used, increase by 6 levels; (C) if a firearm was brandished or possessed, increase by 5 levels; (D) if a dangerous weapon was otherwise used, increase by 4 levels; (E) if a dangerous weapon was brandished or possessed, increase by 3 levels; or (F) if a threat of death was made, increase by 2 levels. (3) If any victim sustained bodily injury, increase the offense level according to the seriousness of the injury: for bodily injury, increase by 2 levels, for serious bodily injury, by 4, and by permanent or life-threatening bodily by 6, *Provided*, however, that the cumulative adjustments from (2) and (3) shall not exceed 11 levels. And (4)(A) If any person was abducted to facilitate commission of the offense or to facilitate escape, increase by 4 levels; or (B) if any person was physically restrained to facilitate commission of the offense or to facilitate escape, increase by 2 levels. (5) If the offense involved carjacking, increase by 2 levels. (6) If a firearm, destructive device, or controlled substance was taken, or if the taking of such item was an object of the offense, increase by 1 level. (7) If the loss exceeded $10,000, increase the offense level as follows (add 1 level for $10,000 up to 7 levels for more than $5 million). [I have omitted the intermediate levels in part 7 of the guideline.]

39. See note 6 in Chapter 1.

What possible utility could such a mélange have for a sentencing judge? And how could a rational analytical process generate the number levels I quoted? They are surely arbitrary. And recently I have seen cases in which, as is inevitable given the mélange, the sentencing judge computed the applicable guideline range inaccurately, requiring the court of appeals to vacate the sentence the judge imposed and remand for resentencing—even though the sentence the judge did impose was entirely appropriate given the specific character of the defendant's crime as well as *his* history and character. In addition, as Judge Kane has pointed out to me in correspondence, the guidelines give the prosecutors another means of hammering defendants into pleading guilty (which prosecutors much prefer because it avoids the potential embarrassment of an acquittal) rather than going to trial even if they would have a chance of acquittal, because in exchange for a defendant's pleading guilty the prosecutors can recommend that the judge impose a within-guidelines sentence likely to be significantly more lenient that the statutory maximum sentence. Indeed so much more lenient to make a plea agreement highly attractive to the defendant.

FIVE

Civil Litigation Revisited

FOR COMPLETENESS I NEED TO DISCUSS several facets of civil procedure that so far in this book I've either ignored or touched on only lightly: Internet research at the appellate level (the touchiest issue); the hearsay rule; some questionable devices that litigants employ in an effort to manipulate district court litigation, including forum-selection clauses and class actions; the scope of judicial review of arbitration awards; and the puzzle of nominal damages.

Internet research. I have read somewhere that forty million websites can be accessed through Google (elsewhere that the figure is now one billion), only two million of which are cat videos, whose value to the legal system is, I reluctantly acknowledge, severely limited. It is an open question whether the other thirty-eight million websites are less accurate on average than documents admitted into evidence at trial or than witnesses who testify at trial, both lay witnesses (including of course parties) and expert witnesses. I mentioned in Chapter 4 that we are learning that demeanor cues are unreliable; we are also learning that cross-examination is of limited utility in exposing error and, as is implicit in the earlier discussion, that expert witnesses do frequently earn their popular sobriquet of "paid liars."

Because the contents of websites are not systematically less accurate, informative, or useful in litigation than paper documents are, they should be treated the same: that is, as evidence the admissibility of which is to be determined by the judge at a pretrial conference. I mentioned in the preceding chapter that in the course of a trial, jurors' questions may invite further investigation, by the lawyers or the trial judge, of possible Internet sources of relevant evidence.

The question whether a trial judge (or for that matter an appellate judge) should ever do his own Internet research in a case before him is controversial because any evidentiary initiative by a judge makes inroads into the adversary system, which has sacred-cow status in the American legal system. But it is possible to allay the concerns with such research to some extent by distinguishing among three possible uses of the Internet by a judge: taking judicial notice (for example of darkness on a particular time on a particular day); providing background and context (for example a description, often omitted by the lawyers, of the scale, focus, and workforce of a party to the lawsuit); and finally using material found in Internet research as evidence, which if it is important evidence may require supplementary briefing, or if the evidence is first presented at the appellate level a remand to the trial court for further evidentiary proceedings.

Use as evidence is at once the most controversial and the most important potential use of the Internet by judges, raising as it does, in acute form, the fundamental question mooted by Judge Kavanaugh (see Chapter 2) and others whether judges should be more than umpires. My answer is that they are and should and must be. Remember that real umpires are not responsible for the outcome of the games they umpire. They enforce rules that if violated cost teams points, but the points may not determine which team wins the game. Litigation is not like that (as John Roberts failed to remind the Senate Judiciary Committee at his confirmation hearing, or for that matter since—a remarkable oversight). A judge or a jury decides which side wins. A judge who, perhaps prompted by a juror's questions, thinks the parties are overlooking potentially crucial evidence has in my view a duty to arrange for the presentation of that evidence, whether the evidence is to be found online or elsewhere.

I presided over an appeal in 2015 in which the plaintiff-appellant, a prison inmate who had had neither a lawyer nor an expert witness in either the district court or my court, was alleging dangerously incompetent medical treatment. On reputable medical websites I found what I considered strong evidence to support his complaint. On the strength of that and other evidence the panel I was presiding over remanded the case *(Rowe v. Gibson)*, in an opinion I wrote, to the district court for a further evidentiary hearing.[1] That was a proper response to the undoubted limitations of the adversary system as demonstrated by the case, but also to the limitation of Internet research. Yet it stirred up a storm in my court. David Hamilton, one of the three judges on the panel, wrote

---

1. 798 F.3d 622 (7th Cir. 2015). I understand that the case was later settled, though I have no idea on what terms.

a fierce dissent, and a motion to rehear the case en banc failed by the narrowest of margins: the eight judges eligible to vote on whether to hear it en banc split 4 to 4 (shades of the Supreme Court's current deadlock, but our deadlock was due to a recusal by one of the judges of our court). In view of the importance of the case to the issue of appellate reliance on the Internet, I am going to quote my opinion along with Judge Hamilton's dissent—a clear statement of the orthodox view. Because of the length of the opinions I have taken the liberty of editing them slightly, indicating the deletions of text by ellipses but also deleting, without ellipses, all citations other than the names of cases or of other sources. From my opinion I have deleted a longish appendix taking issue with several points made in Judge Hamilton's dissent. I have also deleted the concurring opinion of the third judge on the panel, again to save space but also because I had (with her permission) incorporated the principal points in her concurrence in my opinion. All three opinions can of course be read in their entirety online, or in the Federal Reporter.[2]

My opinion has the further utility of revealing the serious deficiencies in the medical care of prison inmates; the propensity of some district judges (some appellate judges as well) to brush aside prisoners' complaints, however serious, as unworthy of serious judicial attention; and above all the limitations of purely adversary procedure.

I could of course merely summarize my opinion and ask Judge Hamilton to do likewise with his. But as in the case of several other long quotations in this book, I want the reader to taste the flavor of the opinions and by doing so get closer to the judges, the better to feel rather than just read about the judicial process.

Without more ado, here are the opinions:

POSNER, *Circuit Judge:* An Indiana prison inmate named Jeffrey Rowe, the plaintiff in this suit under 42 U.S.C. § 1983, accuses administrators and prison staff (actually employees of Corizon, Inc., which provides medical services to the inmates at Pendleton Correctional Facility, Rowe's prison) with deliberate indifference to a serious medical need—that is, with *knowing* of a serious risk to inmate health or safety but responding ineffectually (as by departing substantially from accepted professional judgment) or not at all. See, e.g., *Farmer v. Brennan; Sain v. Wood.* Such

2. At the volume and page cited in the preceding note.

conduct was held in *Farmer* to violate the cruel and unusual punishments clause of the Eighth Amendment, deemed by the Supreme Court to be applicable to state action by interpretation of the due process clause of the Fourteenth Amendment. Rowe charges gratuitous infliction of physical pain and potentially very serious medical harm—cogent examples of cruel and unusual punishment. . . . The district judge granted summary judgment in favor of the defendants. . . , dismissing Rowe's suit and precipitating this appeal.

In 2009, already an inmate at Pendleton, Rowe was diagnosed with reflux esophagitis, also known as gastroesophageal reflux disease (GERD). . . . The Mayo Clinic explains that "a valve-like structure called the lower esophageal sphincter usually keeps the acidic contents of the stomach out of the esophagus. If this valve opens when it shouldn't or doesn't close properly, the contents of the stomach may back up into the esophagus. . . . [GERD] is a condition in which this backflow of acid is a frequent or ongoing problem. A complication of GERD is chronic inflammation and tissue damage in the esophagus." "GERD can . . . produce persistent, agonizing pain and discomfort. It can also produce 'serious complications.' Esophagitis can occur as a result of too much stomach acid in the esophagus. . . , [and] may cause esophageal bleeding or ulcers. In addition, a narrowing or stricture of the esophagus may occur from chronic scarring. Some people develop a condition known as Barrett's esophagus. This condition can increase the risk of esophageal cancer." *WebMD, Heartburn / GERD Health Center,* "What Are the Complications of Long-Term GERD?"; *Miller v. Campanella,* 794 F.3d 878 (7th Cir. 2015). Rowe complains of pain based on neglect of his need for symptomatic relief; continued neglect will endanger him more profoundly.

The prison physician who diagnosed Rowe with GERD told him to take a 150-milligram Zantac pill twice a day. Zantac inhibits the production of stomach acid and is commonly used to treat esophagitis (as we'll abbreviate the name of Rowe's disease). Although technically merely the trade name for ranitidine manufactured by GlaxoSmithKline (in prescription strengths) and Boehringer Ingelheim (in over-the-counter strengths), . . . Zantac is the only word for the drug that appears in the briefs, and so we too will call the drug that Rowe received Zantac.

After the diagnosis, Rowe was given Zantac pills and was permitted to keep them in his cell and take them when he felt the need to. This regimen continued for more than a year. But in January 2011 his pills were confiscated and he was told he'd be allowed to take a Zantac pill only when a prison nurse gave it to him, and that would be at 9:30 A.M. and then at 9:30 P.M. He complained that he needed to take Zantac with his meals, which were, oddly enough, scheduled by the prison for 4 A.M. and 4 P.M. (why these times, we are not told). The prison had decided that inmates such as Rowe who take psychiatric medications should not be allowed to keep any pills in their cells—yet the head of health care at the prison told Rowe that he could keep in his cell (and thus take whenever he wanted) any Zantac pills that he bought at the prison commissary—which, however, as we're about to see, he couldn't afford. No reason has been articulated for forbidding him to keep Zantac given him by prison staff while permitting him to keep Zantac that he buys at the commissary and take it whenever he needs to in order to prevent or alleviate pain. There is no suggestion that Zantac is a narcotic or is otherwise consumed for nonmedical as well as medical reasons; it's a psychiatric medicine only in the sense that it can have psychiatric side effects, such as depression, though these are rare.

The defendants question Rowe's alleged inability to pay for the pills. They point out that in one 13-month period he spent approximately $60 at the commissary. But the prison commissary charges $3.28 for just four 75-mg Zantac pills (and recall that Rowe was to take two 150-mg pills daily), meaning that he would have to pay almost $1300 for a 13-month supply. And he was forbidden to buy more than eight days' worth of Zantac a month from the commissary, which was only about a quarter of the amount that he needed.

. . . [A]t the beginning of July 2011, a month after he filed suit, he ceased receiving Zantac because his "prescription" (that is, his authorization to receive over-the-counter Zantac free of charge on a continuing basis) had lapsed. He made a series of requests for the drug beginning on July 3, but the nurse defendants denied all of them because he had no prescription. When he complained, he was told by the administrative director of the medical staff: "Your chronic care condition does not warrant the continued use of Zantac. The continual use of over-the-counter medications can create further health problems in many instances. You will have to purchase this off of commissary if you wish to continue taking it." Notice the contradiction (illustrating the run-around to which Rowe was continually subjected) in denying Rowe free Zantac because it could create "further health problems" but permitting him to buy it and, if he bought it, to use it at will, though he couldn't afford to buy it. There is no suggestion that Zantac is one of the over-the-counter medications that create health problems if taken daily for a protracted period of time. And finally, if over-the-counter medicines are to be barred, why wasn't Rowe given a prescription for 300-mg Zantac pills? These not only are prescription rather than over-the-counter drugs, but one such pill a day may be sufficient to control one's GERD, compared to two or more when an over-the-counter strength Zantac is prescribed.

On July 13, 2011, in response to Rowe's continued requests for a renewed prescription for Zantac, a physician who works at the prison (though employed by Corizon, a company of dubious reputation that provides contract medical staff to state prisons) named William H. Wolfe, whose professional specialty is preventive medicine rather than gastroenterology and who is a frequent defendant in prisoner civil rights suits, reviewed Rowe's medical records and opined that his condition didn't require Zantac at all—this despite the fact that Rowe had been continuously prescribed Zantac for almost two years and that Wolfe himself had been the prescribing doctor for a quarter of that period. But though initially refusing to provide a new prescription for Zantac, Wolfe later relented and on August 2 prescribed it, though he later said in an affidavit that he had done so as a "courtesy" to Rowe and not out of medical necessity. (Prescribing drugs for prison inmates as a "courtesy" seems very odd; it is not explained.) The upshot was that Rowe had no access to Zantac between July 1 and August 3—a significant deprivation. Even after Zantac was restored to him, he continued to be allowed to take it only at 9:30 A.M. and 9:30 P.M.—both times many hours distant from his meals.

In another affidavit Wolfe stated that "it does not matter what time of day Mr. Rowe receives his Zantac prescription. Each Zantac pill is fully effective for twelve hour increments. Zantac does not have to be taken before or with a meal to be effective." However, according to Boehringer Ingelheim, the manufacturer of over-the-counter Zantac, while Zantac can be taken at any time "to relieve symptoms," in order "to prevent symptoms" it should be taken "30 to 60 minutes before eating food or drinking beverages that cause heartburn," *Zantac,* "Maximum Strength Zantac 150," and this advice is repeated on the labels of the boxes in which over-the-counter Zantac is sold. Were Zantac equipotent whenever taken, the manufacturer would not tell consumers to take it 30 to 60 minutes before eating, for having to remember when to take a pill adds a complication that the consumer would rather do without. There is thus no reason for the manufacturer to be lying, and it would be absurd to think that Dr. Wolfe, a defendant who is not a gastroenterologist, knows more about treating esophagitis with Zantac than the manufacturer does.

Rowe's aim was pain prevention, so having to take Zantac six and a half hours before a meal did not do the trick. It left him in pain for five and a half hours during and after the meal, until he got his next Zantac pill. Wolfe's statement that "each Zantac pill is fully effective for twelve hour increments" is . . . contradicted by the Zantac website, which states that one 150-mg pill "lasts *up to* 12 hours" (emphasis added). Thus a pill taken six and half hours before a meal might not be effective in alleviating the pain caused by acid secretions stimulated by the meal.

It might be thought that a corporate website, such as that of a manufacturer of Zantac, would be a suspect source of information. Not so; the manufacturer would be taking grave risks if it misrepresented the properties of its product. In any event, the Mayo Clinic's website, as we'll see in a moment, confirms the manufacturer's claims.

Wolfe's affidavit states that Rowe was complaining just of "alleged heartburn [that] was not a serious medical condition warranting a prescription for Zantac"—but if so why did Wolfe prescribe Zantac for Rowe during the very period in which, according to the affidavit, Rowe's condition was not serious? (The affidavit fails to mention that it was Wolfe who had prescribed Zantac for Rowe, but that's conceded.)

It's true that the Mayo Clinic's website, after listing various drugs (including ranitidine) for treatment of the cluster of ailments that includes esophagitis, states that "for this class of drugs . . . patients taking two doses a day are instructed: 'Take one in the morning and one before bedtime.'" But this dosing, Mayo goes on to state, is appropriate "only for patients taking the prescription strengths of these medicines." The 150-mg pills that Rowe was taking are available over the counter; a prescription is required only for the 300-mg version. Both the Boehringer Ingelheim and Mayo websites also say that the patient shouldn't take Zantac for more than two weeks unless directed by a doctor—but Rowe was of course directed by Wolfe, as well as by other doctors earlier, to take Zantac on a continuing basis.

Not only wasn't Rowe allowed to take Zantac with his meals; he was not, as the Mayo website recommends, allowed to take it with water a half hour or an hour before eating a meal or drinking beverages that might cause him esophageal pain. As the Mayo website explains, for "adults and teenagers—150 mg with water taken *thirty to sixty minutes before eating a meal* or drinking beverages you expect to cause symptoms. Do not take more than 300 mg in twenty-four hours" (emphasis added).

Stomach acid is of course integral to the digestion of food, and indeed thirty percent of total gastric acid secretion is stimulated by the anticipation, smell, and taste of food, before the food ever reaches the stomach. Thomas A. Miller, *Modern Surgical Care: Physiologic Foundations and Clinical Applications* 344–45 (2006). "The foods you eat affect the amount of acid your stomach produces," and "many people with GERD find that certain foods trigger their symptoms." *Healthline,* "Diet and Nutrition for GERD." So it is no surprise that Rowe experiences painful symptoms when he eats without having been allowed to take a Zantac pill shortly before the meal.

The *Physicians' Desk Reference,* "PDR Search: Full Prescribing Information: Zantac 150 and 300 Tablets," states that a 150-mg dose of Zantac inhibits 79 percent of food-stimulated acid secretion for up to three hours after it's taken. This implies that the drug's efficacy decreases over time and so supports Rowe's claim that a 150-mg dose does not suppress his food-stimulated acid secretions when taken six and a half hours before a meal. The *Desk Reference* also says that "symptomatic relief commonly occurs within 24 hours after starting therapy with ZANTAC 150 mg twice daily," which could be misread to mean that it does not matter what time of day the pills are taken, but which actually means that it takes a day for the body to recognize Zantac as a source of relief from esophageal distress. This interpretation is confirmed by Mayo, which states (at the website cited earlier): "It may take several days before this medicine begins to relieve stomach pain."

The evidence that Rowe was in pain for five and a half hours after eating is his repeated attestation—in his verified federal complaint and his declarations—that he experienced pain for that length of time when he was not allowed to take Zantac with or shortly before his meals. For purposes of summary judgment his attestations of extreme pain must be credited. See 28 U.S.C. § 1746; Fed. R. Civ. P. 56(c). There was no plausible contrary evidence. The affidavits of the only expert witness on the proper times at which to take Zantac, defendants' witness Wolfe, were highly vulnerable. Wolfe is not a gastroenterologist. He says that Rowe didn't need Zantac yet prescribed Zantac for him. He opined with confidence about what Rowe needed or didn't need—yet never examined him—and offered no basis for his off-the-cuff medical opinion. A court should not "admit opinion evidence that is connected to existing data only by the ipse dixit of the expert." *General Electric Co. v. Joiner;* see also *Finn v. Warren County* ("the 'knowledge' requirement of Rule 702 requires the expert to provide more than a subjective belief or unsupported speculation"); *Guile v. United States* ("we look to the basis of the expert's opinion, and not the bare opinion alone. A claim cannot stand or fall on the mere ipse dixit of a credentialed witness"); *McClain v. Metabolife International Inc.*

Remember that Rowe had been diagnosed with esophagitis back in 2009 and that for the ensuing two years physicians had prescribed Zantac to treat his condition. Furthermore, the Indiana Department of Correction permits such continuous treatment only to treat a *serious* health condition, so presumably the prescribing physicians thought Rowe's condition serious. None of this evidence or inference is undermined by Dr. Wolfe's evidence.

A member of a prison's staff is deliberately indifferent and thus potentially liable to an inmate if he "knows of and disregards an excessive risk to inmate health," *Williams v. O'Leary,* quoting *Farmer v. Brennan, supra;* see also *Miller v. Campanella.* Rowe makes two distinct claims of deliberate indifference; the evidence that we've reviewed tends to substantiate both. There is both evidence that defendants Wolfe, Deborah Dotson, Melissa Bagienski, Chris Deeds, and Lisa Gibson were deliberately indifferent to his pain when they denied him access to free Zantac for thirty-three days, and that defendants Mary Mansfield, Gibson, and Dr. Michael Mitcheff were deliberately indifferent to his pain when they insisted—for many months—on giving him Zantac only at 9:30 A.M. and 9:30 P.M., instead of at his prescribed mealtimes. Regarding the first claim, if the nurse defendants to whom Rowe complained about reflux pain were not authorized to give him the free Zantac they should have promptly referred the matter to a doctor.

The evidence of Wolfe's deliberate indifference to Rowe's pain and resulting need for Zantac is, as we've shown, substantial, and likewise the evidence that limiting Rowe's taking Zantac to 9:30 A.M. and 9:30 P.M. for a protracted period exhibited deliberate indifference to a serious medical need. Wolfe never told anyone, so far as appears, when would be the best times for administering Zantac to Rowe. In very large doses Zantac will remain in your blood stream long enough to affect the stomach acid produced by meals eaten many hours later, but the Mayo and Boehringer Ingelheim timing recommendations suggest that this isn't true for 150-mg doses. Wolfe's assertion that "it does not matter what time of day Mr. Rowe receives his Zantac prescription" is implausible as well as vigorously contested. Rowe's pain and the Mayo Clinic's timing recommendations suggest that giving 150-mg doses of Zantac five and a half hours after one meal and six and a half hours before the next (and only other) meal of the day may be a substantial departure from accepted professional practice, preventing summary judgment for defendants regarding Rowe's claim of deliberate indifference to avoidable pain caused by the timing of his medication. See *Sain v. Wood*. Since Rowe's pain strongly indicated that he was experiencing reflux, the reflux could have had serious medical consequences (up to and including cancer) in addition to inflicting chronic pain on him. Prisoners aren't supposed to be tortured.

In citing even highly reputable medical websites in support of our conclusion that summary judgment was premature we may be thought to be "going outside the record" in an improper sense. It may be said that judges should confine their role to choosing between the evidentiary presentations of the opposing parties, much like referees of athletic events. But judges and their law clerks often conduct research on cases and it is not always research confined to pure issues of law, without disclosure to the parties. We are not like the English judges of yore, who under the rule of "orality" were not permitted to have law clerks or other staff, or libraries, or even to deliberate—at the end of the oral argument in an appeal the judges would state their views *seriatim* as to the proper outcome of the appeal. Furthermore there was no meaningful evidentiary presentation by Rowe, since he has no medical knowledge and had no expert witness (there is nothing to suggest he could either afford one, or find one)—in fact had no witnesses at all.

We don't insulate judges, as the English used to do, but we must observe proper limitations on judicial research. We must acknowledge the need to distinguish between judicial web searches for mere background information that will help the judges and the readers of their opinions understand the case, web searches for facts or other information that judges can properly take judicial notice of (such as when it became dark on a specific night, a question we answered on the basis of an Internet search in *Owens v. Duncan*, 781 F.3d 360 (7th Cir. 2015)), and web searches for facts normally determined by the factfinder after an adversary procedure that produces a district court record or an administrative record. When medical information can be gleaned from the websites of highly reputable medical centers, it is not imperative that it instead be presented by a testifying witness. Such information tends to fall somewhere between facts that require adversary procedure to determine and facts of which a court can take judicial notice, but it is closer to the second in a case like this in which the evidence presented by the defendants in the district court was sparse and the appellate court need only determine whether there is a factual dispute sufficient to preclude summary judgment.

Rule 201 of the Federal Rules of Evidence makes facts of which judicial notice is properly taken conclusive, and therefore requires that their accuracy be indisputable for judicial notice to be taken of them. We are not deeming the Internet evidence cited in this opinion conclusive or even certifying it as being probably correct, though it may well be correct since it is drawn from reputable medical websites. We use it only to underscore the existence of a genuine dispute of material fact created in the district court proceedings by entirely conventional evidence, namely Rowe's reported pain.

There is a high standard for taking judicial notice of a fact, and a low standard for allowing evidence to be presented in the conventional way, by testimony subject to cross-examination, but is there no room for anything in between? Must judges abjure visits to Internet web sites of premier hospitals and drug companies not in order to take judicial notice but to assure the existence of a genuine issue of material fact that precludes summary judgment? Are we to forbear lest we be accused of having "entered unknown territory"? . . . Shall the unreliability of the unalloyed adversary process in a case of such dramatic inequality of resources and capabilities of the parties as this case is be an unalterable bar to justice? Must our system of justice allow the muddled affidavit of a defendant who may well be unqualified to be an expert witness to carry the day against a pro se plaintiff helpless to contest the affidavit?

This is not the case in which to fetishize adversary procedure in a pure eighteenth-century form, given the inadequacy of the key defense witness, Dr. Wolfe, who refused to continue Rowe's Zantac prescription in July 2011 while Rowe was being kept waiting for three weeks before being seen by a doctor. Wolfe knew Rowe had esophagitis: he reviewed Rowe's medical records, which contained the 2009 diagnosis and revealed nearly two years of physicians' having prescribed Zantac for him continuously. Wolfe had *personally* prescribed Zantac for Rowe for six months of those two years and must have known that the Department of Correction authorizes such treatment only for a *serious* health condition. Rowe was complaining of continuing reflux pain; and while Wolfe denied a prescription renewal on July 13, he demonstrated his awareness that Rowe might need treatment by scheduling him for a later appointment (the August 2 appointment) to evaluate his request to resume taking Zantac.

Against this background, to credit Wolfe's evidence that it doesn't matter when you take Zantac for relief of GERD symptoms (evidence that may well have failed to satisfy the criteria for the admissibility of expert evidence that are set forth in Fed. R. Evid. 702) just because Rowe didn't present his own expert witness would make no sense—for how could Rowe find such an expert and persuade him to testify? He could not afford to pay an expert witness. He had no lawyer in the district court and has no lawyer in this court; and so throughout this litigation (now in its fourth year) he has been at a decided litigating disadvantage. He requested the appointment of counsel and of an expert witness to assist him in the litigation, pointing out sensibly that he needed "verifying medical evidence" to support his claim. The district judge denied both requests, leaving Rowe unable to offer evidence beyond his own testimony that he was in extreme pain when forbidden to take his medication with his meals.

The web sites give credence to Rowe's assertion that he was in pain. But the information gleaned from them did not *create* a dispute of fact that was not already in the record. Rowe presented enough evidence to call Dr. Wolfe's assessment into question—Rowe claims that after his medication was switched to the 12-hour schedule he was in extreme pain and Dr. Wolfe, without examining Rowe or disclosing the basis for his opinion (as we require experts to do), stated cursorily that the medicine would be effective for 12 hours. It will be up to the factfinder to decide, on a better-developed record, who is right.

Nor is pain the only concern. Esophageal reflux disease can lead to serious damage of the stomach or esophagus, and even to cancer.

It is heartless to make a fetish of adversary procedure if by doing so feeble evidence is credited because the opponent has no practical access to offsetting evidence. To say for example that however implausible Dr. Wolfe's evidence is, it must be accepted because not contested, is to doom the plaintiff's case regardless of the merits simply because the plaintiff lacks the wherewithal to obtain and present conflicting evidence. Rowe did not move to exclude Wolfe as an expert witness on the ground that Wolfe was neither qualified to give expert evidence in this case (because he is not a gastroenterologist) nor, as a defendant, was likely to be even minimally impartial. But Rowe does not have the legal knowledge that would enable him to file such a motion.

We have decided to reverse the judgment. We base this decision on Rowe's declarations, the timeline of his inability to obtain Zantac, the manifold contradictions in Dr. Wolfe's affidavits, and, last, the cautious, limited Internet research that we have conducted in default of the parties' having done so. We add that the judge erred not only by giving undue weight to Wolfe's internally contradictory affidavit but also by relying on a defendant (Wolfe) as the expert witness. There are expert witnesses offered by parties and neutral (court-appointed) expert witnesses, but *defendants* serving as expert witnesses?—and in cases in which the plaintiff doesn't have an expert witness because he doesn't know how to find such a witness and anyway couldn't afford to pay the witness? And how could an unrepresented prisoner be expected to challenge the affidavit of a hostile medical doctor (in this case *really* hostile since he's a defendant in the plaintiff's suit) effectively? Is *this* adversary procedure?

Esophagitis is a common disease for which Zantac is a common treatment, and it makes common sense as well as medical sense that a drug for treating symptoms of stomach acid backing up into the esophagus would be administered shortly before or shortly after meals unless the massive 300-mg pill was being administered to the patient, and it was not in this case. . . . But without his own expert Rowe couldn't counter Wolfe's assertion that Zantac does not need to be taken shortly before, or with or shortly after, a meal in order to be effective. As Rowe explains in his brief, while he "provided evidence that Zantac does not 'prevent' reflux during its 12 hours of effectiveness, and that it was not effective at relieving

Rowe's symptoms, the district court accepted the word of a defendant [i.e., Dr. Wolfe], who was speaking as an 'expert,' that the treatment Rowe received was adequate and effective. Had an expert been appointed, the expert would have been likely to confirm Rowe's factual representations and supported his objection that the defendants lack personal knowledge of Rowe's condition because Wolfe never examined Rowe or had diagnostic testing done on him."

Rowe's allegations alone were sufficient to preclude summary judgment, and were enhanced by the defendants' own evidence, which included both Wolfe's contradictory evidence (among other things, he asserted that Rowe does not need Zantac and yet prescribed it for him) and the absurd opinion by the medical director that over-the-counter medications should not be provided to prisoners. Allowing Wolfe to be an expert witness in the case despite his being a defendant and not practicing the medical specialty at issue is another boost to the plaintiff's case, though again not one that an unrepresented, indigent prisoner could exploit. . . .

Although reversing, we are not ordering that judgment be entered in Rowe's favor. As we've explained, we are not invoking Fed. R. Evid. 201 and thus are not taking judicial notice of any facts outside the district court record. The remaining defendants are entitled to try to rebut any evidence whether or not presented in the district court, including any evidence found on the Internet. Like the conventional forms of evidentiary inquiry, Internet research must be conducted with circumspection. In particular it must not be allowed to extinguish reasonable opportunities for rebuttal.

Pure adversary procedure works best when there is at least approximate parity between the adversaries. That condition is missing in this case, in which a pro se prison inmate, incapable of retaining an expert witness (expert witnesses usually demand to be paid—and how would this inmate even *find* an expert witness?), confronts both a private law firm and the state attorney general.

Because of the profound handicaps under which the plaintiff is litigating and the fact that his claim is far from frivolous, we urge the district judge to give serious consideration to recruiting a lawyer to represent Rowe, see *Miller v. Campanella; Perez v. Fenoglio* and appointing a neutral expert witness, authorized by Fed. R. Evid. 706, to address the medical issues in the case. We are mindful that district courts don't have budgets for paying expert witnesses. But the medical issues in the case are not complex; there should be no difficulty in the judge's persuading a reputable gastroenterologist to speak to Rowe and some of the prison medical personnel (Rowe's prison is only 30 miles from Indianapolis, and there are 128 gastroenterologists in or near Indianapolis, *healthgrades,* to sit for a deposition, and, if necessary, to testify.) Rule 706(c)(2) states that a court-appointed expert "is entitled to a reasonable compensation, as set by the court," and that "the compensation is payable . . . in any . . . civil case [not involving just compensation under the Fifth Amendment] by the parties in the proportion and at the time that the court directs—and the compensation is then charged like other costs." In light of Rowe's indigency, the court if it appoints its own expert witness will have to order the defendants to pay the expert a reasonable fee if the expert is unwilling to work for nothing. Most prisons are strapped for cash, and this is something for the district court to bear in mind in deciding on whether and how large a fee to order the defendants to pay a court-appointed expert witness in a case (such as this case) that has sufficient merit to warrant such an appointment.

A substantial academic literature identifies serious deficiencies in the provision of health care in American prisons and jails,[3] including by Corizon,[4] the employer of Dr. Wolfe and the other medical staff members sued by Rowe. The present case illustrates the problems this literature has identified.

Judgment Affirmed in Part, Reversed in Part, and Remanded

HAMILTON, *Circuit Judge,* concurring in part and dissenting in part. I agree with the majority's disposition of most claims and issues: affirming summary judgment for defendants on several claims and reversing on Rowe's retaliation claim and his claim for complete denial of his Zantac medicine for 33 days in July and August 2011.

I must dissent, however, from the reversal of summary judgment on

---

3. See, e.g., Andrew P. Wilper et al., "The Health and Health Care of US Prisoners: Results of a Nationwide Survey," www.ncbi.nlm.nih.gov/pmc/articles/PMC2661478/ and the studies sponsored by the *Academic Consortium on Criminal Justice Health,* www.accjh.org/.

4. See David Royse, "Medical Battle Behind Bars: Big Prison Healthcare Firm Corizon Struggles to Win Contracts," *Modern Healthcare,* April 11, 2015; also Human Rights Defense Center, *Prison Legal News,* March 15, 2014, "Corizon Needs a Checkup: Problems with Privatized Correctional Healthcare."

Rowe's claim regarding the timing for administering his medicine between January and July 2011 and after August 2011. On that claim, the reversal is unprecedented, clearly based on "evidence" this appellate court
has found by its own internet research. The majority has pieced together
information found on several medical websites that seems to contradict
the only expert evidence actually in the summary judgment record. With
that information, the majority finds a genuine issue of material fact on
whether the timing of Rowe's Zantac doses amounted to deliberate indifference to a serious health need, and reverses summary judgment. (The
majority denies at a couple of points that its internet research actually
makes a difference to the outcome of the case, see ante at 629, 630, but
when the opinion is read as a whole, the decisive role of the majority's
internet research is plain.)

The majority writes that adherence to rules of evidence and precedent
makes a "heartless . . . fetish of adversary procedure." Yet the majority's
decision is an unprecedented departure from the proper role of an appellate court. It runs contrary to long-established law and raises a host of
practical problems the majority fails to address. . . .

On Rowe's claim that the timing of his Zantac doses showed deliberate indifference to his health, the evidence *in the record* consists of two
items. First, plaintiff Rowe asserts in his verified complaint and in several
affidavits that he believes the prison's schedule for giving him two 150 mg
Zantac pills each day left him in unnecessary and avoidable pain for
hours every day after meals. Second, defendants filed an affidavit from
defendant Dr. William Wolfe, who was a career physician in the United
States Air Force and is now a contract physician for the Indiana Department of Correction. Dr. Wolfe testified: "It does not matter what time of
day Mr. Rowe receives his Zantac prescription. Each Zantac pill is fully
effective for twelve hour increments. Zantac does not have to be taken
before or with a meal to be effective. Providing Mr. Rowe with Zantac
twice daily as the nursing staff makes their medication rounds, whatever
time that may be, is sufficient and appropriate to treat his heart burn
symptoms."

The record thus shows a prisoner's diagnosed disease and complaints
of pain that prison staff treated with an appropriate medicine. The prisoner is not satisfied with details of the treatment's timing, but a physician
testified that the timing change the prisoner wanted was not called for

because the medicine was equally effective as long as he was receiving two doses per day. This evidence does not support a reasonable inference of deliberate indifference.

Proof of deliberate indifference is much more demanding than proof of even medical malpractice. . . . This record evidence would not let a reasonable jury find that the prison's schedule for giving Rowe his medicine departed so far from professional standards to find that any prison staff acted with deliberate indifference to his health. The district court therefore properly granted summary judgment for defendants on this claim. . . .

As noted above, the majority claims twice that its decision does not actually depend on its independent factual research, at pages 629 and 630. . . . These denials contradict the rest of the majority opinion. If they were accurate, the majority's long discussion of its research and its justifications for it would amount to a long essay not necessary to the court's decision. If the denials were accurate, moreover, the majority decision would amount to a significant rewriting of the Eighth Amendment law governing health care for prisoners.

Where prison medical staff just refuse to treat serious pain or disease, a prisoner may well have a viable claim that should go to trial. . . . Where the evidence shows, however, that medical staff have provided at least some treatment for pain we almost always hold that the prisoner is not entitled to a jury trial on a claim for deliberate indifference based on a claim that the pain treatment was not adequate.

If the majority decision did not depend on its own factual research, then the majority would be holding that the prisoner's dissatisfaction with pain treatment is enough to require a jury trial on whether the prison's medical staff were deliberately indifferent to his pain. We have not found before this case that such evidence is sufficient to infer deliberate indifference. But we will see a lot more cases like this one. As the average age of the prison population increases, so will the incidence of painful, chronic conditions that cannot be treated to the complete satisfaction of the prisoners. The fact that a treatment for pain is not as effective as the prisoner would like should not be enough to support an inference that the prison staff are deliberately indifferent to his pain.

In fact, the majority's reversal on this claim is based on a small but important category of cases in which prisoners have shown that medical staff persisted in obviously inadequate courses of treatment. In those cases, we have found triable issues of deliberate indifference. . . . [T]hese decisions were based on evidence showing that the need for specialized expertise or different treatment was either known by the treating physicians or would have been obvious to a lay person.

The problem for the majority here is that Rowe himself has made no comparable showing. Only by relying on its independent factual research can the majority establish an arguable basis for applying this theory that the course of treatment was so clearly inadequate as to amount to deliberate indifference. The majority decision to reverse summary judgment on this claim thus depends on that independent factual research.

The ease of research on the internet has given new life to an old debate about the propriety of and limits to independent factual research by appellate courts. To be clear, I do not oppose using careful research to provide context and background information to make court decisions more understandable. By any measure, however, using independent factual research to find a genuine issue of material, adjudicative fact, and thus to decide an appeal, falls outside permissible boundaries. Appellate courts simply do not have a warrant to decide cases based on their own research on adjudicative facts. This case will become Exhibit A in the debate. It provides, despite the majority's disclaimers, a nearly pristine example of an appellate court basing a decision on its own factual research.

The majority's factual research runs contrary to several lines of well-established case law holding that a decisionmaker errs by basing a decision on facts outside the record. If a district judge bases a decision on such research, we reverse for a violation of Rule 201. . . . If jurors start doing their own research during a trial, a new trial is likely. . . .

We are in no better a position to go outside the record for decisive facts. Our job is to reverse in cases where the decision-maker has gone outside the record. The majority in this case, however, not only does what we treat as reversible error when others do it; it holds in essence that the district judge erred by *not* doing such independent factual research. What was forbidden is now required.

In addition to the case law holding that a decision-maker is not permitted to base a decision on evidence outside the record, another body of law is relevant to this issue: Federal Rule of Evidence 201 and the law of judicial notice. The majority opinion runs contrary to that law and misunderstands how Rule 201 and judicial notice fit together with the ordinary, adversarial presentation of facts.

The vast majority of facts that courts consider when deciding cases comes from the familiar, adversarial presentations of evidence by opposing parties. The foundation of our legal system is a confidence that the adversarial procedures will test shaky or questionable evidence: "Vigorous cross-examination, presentation of contrary evidence, and careful instruction on the burden of proof are the traditional and appropriate means of attacking shaky but admissible evidence." *Daubert v. Merrell Dow Pharmaceuticals, Inc.* Those protective procedures are not available when a court decides to do its own factual research and bases its decision on what it finds.

The law of evidence allows a narrow exception permitting some judicial research into relevant facts, under Federal Rule of Evidence 201 and the concept of judicial notice. Judicial notice "substitutes the acceptance of a universal truth for the conventional method of introducing evidence," and as a result, courts must use caution and "strictly adhere" to the rule before taking judicial notice of pertinent facts.

The majority says twice it is *not* taking judicial notice of all the cited medical information from the internet. I agree it could not properly take judicial notice of this information under Evidence Rule 201(b) and (e). The proper timing of a patient's doses of Zantac is not "generally known within the trial court's territorial jurisdiction" and is not beyond "reasonable dispute," nor can it be "accurately and readily determined from sources whose accuracy cannot reasonably be questioned," as Rule 201(b) requires. And the majority has made no effort to comply with the procedural requirements of Rule 201(e), essential to basic fairness, of giving the parties an opportunity to be heard on the evidence.

If the majority is not taking judicial notice, what exactly is it doing? It seems to have created an entirely new, third category of evidence, neither presented by the parties nor properly subject to judicial notice. The majority writes:

"When medical information can be gleaned from the websites of highly reputable medical centers, it is not imperative that it instead be presented by a testifying witness. *Such information tends to fall somewhere between facts that require adversary procedure to determine and facts of which a court can take judicial notice,* but it is closer to the second in a case like this in which the evidence presented by the defendants in the district court was sparse and the appellate court need only determine whether there is a factual dispute sufficient to preclude summary judgment."

In other words, the majority acknowledges that its "evidence" neither comes from adversarial presentation by the parties nor meets the strict substantive and procedural standards for judicial notice under Rule 201.

Before this decision, American law has not recognized this category of evidence, which might be described as "non-adversarial evidence that the court believes is probably correct."

The usual method of establishing adjudicative facts is through the introduction of evidence, ordinarily consisting of the testimony of witnesses. If particular facts are outside the area of reasonable controversy, this process is dispensed with as unnecessary. *A high degree of indisputability is the essential prerequisite.*

In other words, the Federal Rules of Evidence allow no room for the majority's innovation. Adversarial evidence and judicial notice are not opposite poles on a wide spectrum, with a middle ground for the majority's evidence that has neither been subjected to adversarial testing nor a proper subject of judicial notice. These are two distinct categories. To be admissible, evidence must fall within one or the other. "Close" to judicial notice does not count.

The majority has not offered any precedent from the law of evidence to support its reliance on its own factual research. Instead, it tries to downplay the unprecedented step it takes, including its emphasis that it is "not ordering that judgment be entered in Rowe's favor" and that defendants will be entitled to rebut the majority's factual research on remand. The majority's modest demurrer loses sight of the stakes. The issue on summary judgment is whether the evidence *in the record* would allow a reasonable jury to find in favor of the non-moving party. . . . By reversing, the majority is necessarily finding that this record is sufficient to support a jury verdict for Rowe. I disagree.

The majority also points out that "judges and their law clerks often conduct research on cases without disclosure to the parties." Such research has long been understood to involve only *legal research*. The majority's effort to compare long-accepted judicial research into case law and statutes to its independent *factual* research shows the majority has entered unknown territory.

To justify this venture, the majority asks a number of rhetorical questions and invokes the courage of the barons at Runnymede in 1215. With respect, we are an intermediate appellate court. The Federal Rules of Evidence and Federal Rules of Civil Procedure that we apply are adopted and amended through processes established by the Rules Enabling Act, 28 U.S.C. § 2071 et seq. We simply do not have authority on our own to take the law into this unknown territory.

The majority points out correctly that prisoners must depend entirely on the government for their health care. If they turn to the federal courts for help, the combination of the constitutional standard under the Eighth Amendment, deliberate indifference to a serious health need, and the system of personal liability under 42 U.S.C. § 1983 can make it very difficult for a prisoner to hold anyone accountable for serious wrongs. . . . When a prisoner brings a pro se suit about medical care, the adversary process that is the foundation of our judicial system is at its least reliable. Few prisoners have access to lawyers or to expert witnesses needed to address medical issues.

These conditions pose important challenges to federal courts doing their best to decide these cases fairly. Yet the majority's solution—to research available medical information on its own and find a genuine issue of material fact on that basis—raises problems much more serious than a possible error in the resolution of one prisoner's case.

The majority's approach turns the court from a neutral decision-maker into an advocate for one side. The majority also offers no meaningful guidance as to how it expects other judges to carry out such factual research and what standards should apply when they do so. Under the majority's approach, the factual record will never be truly closed. This invites endless expansion of the record and repetition in litigation as parties contend and decide that more and more information should have been considered.

In addition to the abandonment of neutrality, consider the problems from the district judge's point of view. The majority clearly implies, while denying it is doing so, that the district judge herself should have done the independent factual research the majority has done on appeal, questioning an unchallenged expert affidavit by looking to websites of the drug manufacturer, the Mayo Clinic, the Physician's Desk Reference, and Healthline.

The practical questions are obvious: When are district judges supposed to carry out this independent factual research? How much is enough? What standards of reliability should apply to the results? How does the majority's new category of evidence fit in with a district judge's gatekeeping responsibilities under Rule 702 and *Daubert*? The majority offers no answers.

The majority essentially orders the district judge on remand to find an expert witness on the medical issues, either for plaintiff or as a neutral expert under Rule 706. That might well be helpful, but as the majority concedes, district courts do not have budgets for that purpose. Even if a few experts might be willing to volunteer in unusual cases, the demand of prisoners for free medical or other expert witnesses will far exceed the supply, especially in the rural areas where so many prisons are located and smaller towns where the nearest district courts are located.

The majority's solution for this problem is to have the district court use Federal Rule of Evidence 706 to order defendants, and only the defendants, to pay for an expert witness for the plaintiff or the court. That approach is not foreclosed by the language of Rule 706, and there is some case law supporting it. Nevertheless, the majority's reliance on this solution in this ordinary case further threatens the neutrality of the courts. It is worth recalling that damages under 42 U.S.C. § 1983 must be sought from state employees only in their individual capacities. Indemnification by their employer is a matter of state law and policy, and sometimes grace. Is it fair to impose on individual guards, prison administrators, staff, nurses, and doctors the cost of finding evidence to build a case against them? At the very least, such one-sided burdens should be imposed only in extraordinary cases.

Further, if the case goes to trial, how is the district judge supposed to present to a jury the information the majority has found? My colleagues and I agree it is not suitable for judicial notice because it is not indisputable, as required under Rule 201(b). Without an expert witness qualified to present the facts and opinions the majority finds persuasive, that information does not come into evidence. On appeal would the majority's approach lead us to remand for a new trial with instructions to look harder for the right evidence? Or what should we do if the district judge did not find or rely on the information that our research turns up? As long as the factual record remains open for judicial supplements, parties will try to use the quest for the perfect record to keep any loss in litigation from being final.

Then consider the problems parties and their lawyers will face. If we permit such independent factual research by district judges—even *expect* such research from them—parties will need to plan for it. Responding to the evidence actually offered by the other side is often the biggest challenge and expense in a lawsuit. Now parties need to anticipate the evidence the judge might turn up on her own and prepare to meet it. The time and expense devoted to such preventive measures will be substantial and should be unnecessary. And if the district judge does her own research and gives the parties an opportunity to respond to it, the majority's approach here is an open invitation for parties to add to the record on appeal. The parties will also need to anticipate on appeal that our court will undertake its own factual research, opening up opportunities to save any losing case by offering new evidence on appeal.

From the larger perspective of our judicial system, the independent factual research the majority endorses and even requires here is not something that federal courts can carry out reliably on a large scale. History is probably the academic field closest to the practice of law and judging. Yet historians regularly scoff at the phenomenon called "law-office history." "[J]udges do not have either the leisure or the training to conduct *responsible* historical research or *competently* umpire historical controversies. The term 'law-office history' is properly derisory and the derision embraces the efforts of judges and law professors, as well as of legal advocates, to play historian. . . . Judges don't try to decide contested issues of science without the aid of expert testimony, and we fool ourselves if we think we can unaided resolve issues of historical truth."

Law-office or judicial-chambers medicine is surely an even less reliable venture. The internet is an extraordinary resource, but it cannot turn judges into competent substitutes for experts or scholars such as historians, engineers, chemists, psychologists, or physicians. The majority's instruction to the contrary will cause problems in our judicial system more serious than those it is trying to solve in this case.

Thus far I have avoided debating the details of the majority's research, but they deserve closer attention. The specific details highlight the more general criticisms I have directed at such factual research by judges.

First, on the websites the majority relies upon, we find important disclaimers that emphasize the need for filtering their information through qualified medical advice, which no member of this court is qualified to provide. The Physician's Desk Reference site says it is to be used "only as a reference aid. It is not intended to be a substitute for the exercise of professional judgment. You should confirm the information on the PDR.net site through independent sources and seek other professional guidance in all treatment and diagnosis decisions." www.pdr.net (last visited August 19, 2015, as were all websites cited here). The Mayo Clinic and Zantac websites have similar disclaimers advising readers to talk to a physician or other health care provider before acting on the information on the websites.

Second, after we get past the disclaimers, the content of the majority's websites simply does not give clear support to the majority's views (a) that Dr. Wolfe was wrong in saying that the 150 mg pills Rowe was receiving twice a day could be equally effective even if not given shortly before meals, let alone (b) that Dr. Wolfe was *so thoroughly and obviously* wrong that a jury could infer that prison staff were deliberately indifferent to Rowe's health needs. The majority's websites instead show that some degree of medical judgment is needed to decide when best to administer which size pills for patients with different needs, especially patients like Rowe with chronic conditions.

The Mayo Clinic site says that patients taking prescription strength Zantac twice a day should take one in the morning and one at bedtime. The majority discounts that advice because Rowe was taking an over-the-counter dosage of 150 mg pills rather than the prescription dosage of 300 mg pills. Ante at 626. Yet that explanation overlooks the advice from both the manufacturer and the Mayo Clinic that a patient should not take the over-the-counter pills for more than two weeks *unless directed by a doctor.* For patients like Rowe, taking Zantac long-term to treat GERD, the Mayo Clinic offers more specific guidance. It advises that adult patients with GERD take the 150 mg pill two times a day without specifying that the pills should be taken shortly before meals.

Similarly, the PDR advises that for treatment of GERD, "Symptomatic relief commonly occurs within 24 hours after starting therapy with

ZANTAC 150 mg twice daily," again without indicating any need to take the pills before meals.

The "full prescribing information" on the Physician's Desk Reference website says that for treatment of GERD with the 150 mg and 300 mg pills, "Symptomatic relief commonly occurs within 24 hours after starting therapy with ZANTAC 150 mg twice daily," again without saying anything about taking pills before meals.

The majority draws on the PDR website and "common sense" regarding how long the pills remain effective. The PDR website, however, simply does not provide sufficient data on absorption and clearance rates for the medicine to allow us to exercise our own (non-expert) judgment about whether the timing of Rowe's pills was appropriate. It certainly does not allow us to conclude that the timing could have amounted to deliberate indifference to his serious health needs or to find that Dr. Wolfe's uncontradicted affidavit did not support the district court's entry of summary judgment on this claim.

Of course, the point of this discussion of the websites is not to debate the majority on the medical fine points. The websites the majority relies upon tell us themselves that their information needs to be interpreted by a qualified physician. None of this information is in the record. None was before the district court, nor is it properly before us.

The majority's interpretation of its internet research is not a reliable substitute for proper evidence subjected to adversarial scrutiny. And while Dr. Wolfe's affidavit is far less detailed than the information the majority has explored on the internet, I also see no basis for the majority's harsh criticism of him . . . .

In the end, whether Dr. Wolfe's testimony about the timing for Rowe's doses was right or wrong in some pure and objective sense, or in a case tried with ample resources and talent on both sides, is not the question for us. For purposes of summary judgment, Dr. Wolfe's testimony was undisputed. We have no business reversing summary judgment based on our own, untested factual research. By doing so, the majority has gone well beyond the appropriate role of an appellate court. I respectfully dissent from the reversal of summary judgment on Rowe's claims based on the timing of his medication.

Whew!

* * *

It may surprise some readers to learn that Judge Hamilton and I are friends, and that no animosity attended our disagreement, profound as it was, over Rowe's case. (The Seventh Circuit has a tradition of cordiality—a very valuable asset for an appellate court!) What is most interesting about the case is the sharp cleavage that it illustrates between the conventional approach to prisoner civil rights suits, which is the approach taken in Judge Hamilton's dissent, and the approach taken in my majority opinion. The main theme of the dissent is the deference that Judge Hamilton (who was a district judge for fifteen years before being appointed to the court of appeals) believes that the appellate courts owe to district courts, owing to a trial judge's greater proximity to the parties, the witnesses, and hence the evidence. And this is a widely held view, though mainly I think because it's the traditional view. As with much that is traditional in law (that is, backward-looking), a rethinking of the traditional view is overdue, in light of such advances in knowledge as the discrediting of demeanor cues as reliable grounds for assessing witness credibility, the growing technical complexity of litigation, the enormous intellectual resources available online, and what appears to be a growing inequality in opposing litigants' resources that seems attributable in part to the long-term increase in the prison population, which in combination with the efforts of the states to reduce prison costs (an effort evident in the medical attention paid, or rather not paid, to Rowe's disease) has resulted in a high rate of prisoner civil litigation.

Judge Hamilton's statement that the "foundation of our legal system is a confidence that the adversarial procedures will test shaky or questionable evidence: Vigorous cross-examination, presentation of contrary evidence, and careful instruction on the burden of proof are the traditional and appropriate means of attacking shaky but admissible evidence" is outdated. He should know by now that adversarial procedure is not the panacea we used to think it was. There is no better example of the judiciary's reluctance to innovate, to reform, to *wake up* from its centuries-old intellectual slumbers than the continued reverence for an unmodified adversary system. Anyway there was no meaningful adversarial procedure in Rowe's case because Rowe had neither a lawyer nor a witness nor any knowledge of medicine. The district court threw him under the bus and Judge Hamilton wants to leave him there. That's the case in a nutshell.

But in emphasizing Internet research—because it's new, because it's undervalued by most judges and lawyers, because it has enormous promise—I don't mean to denigrate legal research of a more conventional character. In areas such as antitrust and regulation, research based on economics and statistics has had profound positive effects on how judges interpret and apply the statutes and common-law principles that govern, or at least are supposed to govern, those fields. Legal research into the punishment and possible rehabilitation of child molesters and other compulsive sex offenders holds some hope for progress toward the reform of the law's treatment of such offenders; and the role of psychology in that research is fundamental.[5] Psychology has also contributed importantly to undermining the belief that the truthfulness of a witness can be inferred from observing his appearance and manner on the witness stand—the demeanor cues I keep referring to. As I noted earlier, truthfulness and falsity can be inferred better from reading a transcript of a witness's testimony than from observing the witness testify. The demeanor cues are not clues; they are distractions.

Statistical research has illuminated many facets of judicial behavior, ranging from the role of law clerks in writing their judges' opinions to the effect on the behavior of lower-court judges of aspiring for promotion, for example to the U.S. Supreme Court, to variation across circuits in reversal rates in politically sensitive cases, to regional variance in sentencing, and to much else besides. Political science has contributed significantly to understanding the role of politics, political ideology more broadly, religion, sex and race, and other influences similarly remote from "the law" (legal doctrine) on judicial voting. Political science and psychology are jointly illuminating such facets of judicial psychology as the authoritarian personality of some judges, which can influence criminal sentencing.

Another point worth noting is the role of summary judgment in the *Rowe* case. The defendants moved for summary judgment and the district judge granted the motion, thus denying Rowe the right to a trial. Summary judgment is—summary. A party who moves for summary judgment is, as explained in Rule 56(a) of the Federal Rules of Civil Procedure, entitled to judgment (that is, a decision in his favor ending the case in the district court) only if the movant "shows that there is no genuine dispute as to any material fact and the movant is entitled to judgment as a matter of law." A motion for summary judgment has to be handled with great care by the judge, as the district judge in the *Rowe* case failed to do. Trial judges generally want to minimize the number of trials they preside over, especially jury trials, because such trials are often time-

---

5. See, e.g., *Schmidt v. McCulloch*, 823 F.3d 1135 (7th Cir. 2016).

consuming and complicated, with opening and closing arguments, examination and cross-examination of witnesses with frequent interruptions for objections, and jury selection and jury instructions and jury deliberations, all supervised by the judge. So granting summary judgment is tempting, but because it's tempting there is a danger that the judge will conclude that there is indeed no genuine dispute as to any material fact and the movant is entitled to judgment as a matter of law, where the finding of no genuine dispute as to any material fact will usually be all that's needed to avoid a trial because trials are basically a mode of resolving factual disputes. But to make such a finding in advance of (and eliminating) a trial will often be no better than a hunch, for how is the absence of a "genuine dispute" to be determined, other than in an extreme case, in the absence of a trial? As Professor Arthur Miller has argued in an important article on the overuse of summary judgment,[6] judges seem often to be placing their interests in the efficient (that is, time-saving) resolution of disputes and doubts about jury capability above litigants' right to a jury trial.

There was a genuine dispute in *Rowe* and no basis for the district judge's refusal to recognize that and her consequential grant of summary judgment for the defendants.

Still another facet of the *Rowe* case that I need to emphasize was the role of the concept of "deliberate indifference"; recall the statement in Judge Hamilton's dissent that "where prison medical staff just refuse to treat serious pain or disease, a prisoner may well have a viable claim that should go to trial. . . . Where the evidence shows, however, that medical staff have provided at least some treatment for pain we almost always hold that the prisoner is not entitled to a jury trial on a claim for deliberate indifference based on a claim that the pain treatment was not adequate." As usually understood, "deliberate indifference" is the equivalent of common-law recklessness, which differs from negligence in that negligence just means carelessness, whereas recklessness (and hence deliberate indifference) means that the defendant knew that someone to whom he owed a duty of care was in danger, knew that he (that is, the defendant) could eliminate or at least alleviate the danger at no danger or substantial cost to himself, yet did nothing, thereby imposing cruel and unusual punishment, in violation of the Eighth Amendment, on the prisoner. This is such a case. Dr. Wolfe knew that Rowe was suffering; must as a physician have known

6. Arthur R. Miller, "The Pretrial Rush to Judgment: Are the 'Litigation Explosion,' 'the Liability Crisis,' and Efficiency Clichés Eroding Our Day in Court and Jury Trial Commitments?" 78 *New York University Law Review* 982 (2003).

(though he is not a gastroenterologist) that gastroesophageal disease is potentially very serious, even life-threatening; could readily have alleviated Rowe's suffering by changing the timing of his receiving Zantac; yet did nothing. Wolfe was reckless, and recklessness equals deliberately indifferent.

Judge Hamilton's contention that as long as "medical staff have provided at least some treatment for pain we almost always hold [yes, but we shouldn't] that the prisoner is not entitled to a jury trial on a claim for deliberate indifference based on a claim that the pain treatment was not adequate" was repeated in even stronger form by Judge Easterbrook, another colleague of mine, in his dissenting opinion in a case called *Petties v. Carter.*[7] I will spare the reader the facts of the case and focus on Judge Easterbrook's Hamiltonish understanding of deliberate indifference. His dissent, based on the Supreme Court's decision in *Estelle v. Gamble,*[8] states that

> palliative medical treatment (pain relief without an effort at cure) . . . satisfies the constitutional minimum even if the care is woefully deficient. . . . The Justices (in *Estelle v. Gamble*) said that deliberate indifference to a prisoner's pain violates the Constitution if it leads the staff to do nothing, but that medical care meets the constitutional standard. Gamble received care. He received *wretched* care, but the Court held that a claim based on deficient care depends on state medical-malpractice law. . . . The Justices disapproved the . . . conclusion (of the lower court) that the Constitution entitles prisoners to "adequate" care. . . . [And] why should we *want* to federalize the law of medical malpractice? Prisoners such as Petties have a tort remedy under state law.

But Judge Easterbrook was splitting hairs in limiting deliberate indifference to failure to provide any care at all. Suppose Dr. Wolfe had directed the medical staff to provide Rowe with just one Zantac pill a month. That would be deliberate indifference within the meaning of footnote 3 of the majority opinion in *Petties,* which states that deliberate indifference can be found where "the defendants deliberately refused to pursue care they knew [the plaintiff] needed."

Furthermore, as the last sentence I quoted from Judge Easterbrook's dissent reveals, like Judge Hamilton he misses the difference between the ordinary citizen, who is responsible for his own health care, and a prison inmate. The free

7. 836 F.3d 722 (2016) (en banc).
8. 429 U.S. 97 (1976) (emphasis added).

citizen has a range of health-care alternatives—a doctor of his choice, a hospital emergency room, health insurance, Medicaid if he's indigent, and if he's sixty-five years of age or older Medicare. If he receives inadequate care from one treatment source or center he can switch to another. If he receives negligent treatment and suffers from it he can bring a malpractice suit. This range of opportunities is as a practical matter denied a prison inmate. The Supreme Court noted the significance of this in *Estelle v. Gamble,* remarking that "an inmate must rely on prison authorities to treat his medical needs; if the authorities fail to do so, those needs will not be met."[9]

It's true that *in principle* an inmate can sue for medical malpractice in state court, but he may find it impossible to hire a reputable lawyer to handle the case for him and suing pro se is highly likely to be ineffectual (as the prisoner is unlikely to have any medical knowledge) and hiring an expert witness may be as a practical matter impossible because of the prisoner's lack of money and lack of contacts in the medical profession. These are problems discussed neither in *Estelle v. Gamble* nor in the Hamilton dissent in *Rowe* or the Easterbrook dissent in *Petties.* The prisoner is likely to receive a warmer reception from a federal district judge (though Rowe didn't) and from a federal court of appeals panel than from their counterparts in a state judiciary, which is unlikely to be sympathetic to a suit brought against another department of state government. In addition most state judges are elected, and elected judges tend to be sensitive to public opinion, which is hostile to criminals and prison inmates. A number of states, moreover, including Indiana (Rowe's state), but not Illinois (Petties's state), cap damages awards for medical malpractice.[10] And furthermore it's easier to recruit a good lawyer for a prisoner who has a constitutional suit than for one who has just a malpractice suit.

And finally I'm curious how Judge Easterbrook would interpret the Eighth Amendment in prisoner medical cases if the state had repealed its medical malpractice law.

I don't want to leave the impression that I always prevail in disagreements with the other judges of my court over the rights of prison inmates to proper medical care, as I did in *Rowe* and *Petties.* Here is a recent case in which Judge Easterbrook wrote the majority opinion and I a dissent:

9. Id. at 103.

10. David Goguen, "State-by-State Medical Malpractice Damages Caps," *Nolo,* www.nolo.com/legal-ency clopedia/state-state-medical-malpractice-damages-caps.html.

NO. 15-1497, U.S. COURT OF APPEALS FOR THE SEVENTH CIRCUIT

ESTATE OF WILLIAM A. MILLER,
Plaintiff-Appellant,

v.

HELEN J. MARBERRY and GARY ROGERS,
Defendants-Appellees.

———————

APPEAL FROM THE UNITED STATES DISTRICT COURT FOR THE
SOUTHERN DISTRICT OF INDIANA, TERRE HAUTE DIVISION.
NO. 2:11-CV-JMS-DKL — JANE MAGNUS-STINSON, *CHIEF JUDGE.*

———————

ARGUED NOVEMBER 29, 2016 — DECIDED JANUARY 30, 2017

———————

Before POSNER, EASTERBROOK, and SYKES, *Circuit Judges.*

EASTERBROOK, *Circuit Judge.* While confined at the federal prison in
Terre Haute, Indiana, William Miller fell out of an upper bunk and broke
his back. Contending that he should have been in a lower bunk, Miller
seeks compensation in this *Bivens* action. Miller died in June 2016; the
record does not show why. His estate has been substituted as the plaintiff,
but we use his name to make the exposition easier to follow.

Miller's principal problem is the identity of the two defendants: Gary
Rogers, a guard, and Helen Marberry, then the Warden of Terre Haute.
Miller does not seek relief from any physician or nurse, even though the
prison's medical department is responsible for deciding who has a medical need for a lower bunk. (He named nurse Trisha Haddix in his complaint but has abandoned his claim against her.) Nor did Miller sue the
guard responsible for making bunk assignments. That guard sits in a pod
containing a computer with access to the prison's SENTRY database that
identifies medical restrictions. Rogers, by contrast, roamed the cells on
foot.

The events underlying this suit began on January 6, 2009, when Miller
was moved from the prison's general population to the more restrictive
"special housing unit" and assigned to an upper bunk. Miller contends,
and we assume, that when Rogers made his rounds later that day Miller
told Rogers that he had a brain tumor and was entitled to a lower bunk.

Rogers replied that Miller must follow his assignment or be put on report for disobedience.

Five days later Miller fell from the ladder between the upper bunk and the floor. He hit his head and lost consciousness. Miller does not contend that Rogers (who apparently was not working that shift) or anyone else responded inadequately. Miller was carried on a backboard with a cervical collar to an examination room, where a nurse noted that he reported pain in his neck, back, and left foot. He was transported by ambulance to a hospital's emergency room. The hospital conducted a CT scan that did not detect any fall-related problems. Miller returned to the prison within a few hours and was again assigned to an upper bunk. He does not contend that either Rogers or Marberry played a role in that assignment. Nor does he contend that any of the many medical personnel he saw that day issued, or should have issued, a lower-bunk-only directive. He does not contend that he then (or ever) went to the guard responsible for bunk assignments and either asked for a lower bunk or told that guard that he had a medical pass for one. He does say, however, that once he had retuned to the special housing unit he told Rogers that he had fallen and repeatedly asked him for a lower bunk, and that Rogers did not respond.

On February 14, 2009, Miller rolled over while asleep in the upper bunk and fell approximately six feet to the cement floor. This time he broke his back and suffered other serious injuries. Once again Miller does not contend that the care he received was substandard. He was carried on a backboard, with a cervical collar, to a hospital for a CT scan, which revealed injuries that led to surgery. When he returned to the prison he was *again* placed in an upper bunk, where he remained until December 1, 2009, when the medical staff directed that he be assigned to a lower bunk. Miller does not contend that Rogers played any role in his assignment to an upper bunk between his return from the hospital and December 1—nor does he contend that any of the prison's medical staff is liable for failing to ensure that he had a lower bunk then, or earlier. Finally, Miller does not contend that either Rogers or Marberry is liable for failing to ensure that upper bunks have railings, nets, or other devices to prevent inmates from falling out while asleep.

The district court granted summary judgment to Rogers and Marberry, giving two principal reasons. The first, to which we have alluded, is that neither Rogers nor Marberry was responsible for bunk assignments.

The second is that if Rogers had consulted the SENTRY database he would not have discovered a lower-bunk directive. The district judge found it uncontested that an earlier pass had expired and that a new one was not issued until December 1, 2009. The judge stated that guards and wardens are entitled to rely on the medical staff to make medical decisions about medical problems.

Miller sees this second reason as his opening. He contends that there is a material dispute about what Rogers would have found had he consulted the SENTRY database. When denying a post-fall grievance about his bunk assignment, Warden Marberry wrote that Miller had had authorization for a lower bunk since early 2008 and should have brought this to the attention of the guard responsible for placement decisions (that is, the guard in the pod). Miller observes that this contradicts affidavits filed by Rogers and others relating that in January and February 2009 the SENTRY database did not contain a lower-bunk notation. Both statements could be correct; a lower-bunk assignment may have been issued but not added to the database. But there is still an apparent inconsistency, and Miller maintains that this requires a trial.

Yet the first problem remains—Miller has not sued the people responsible for bunk assignments. Miller supposes that it is enough to tell someone about a problem; anyone told must fix the problem, he insists. He told Rogers that he had a brain tumor and a lower-bunk assignment, and Rogers did nothing. He maintains that, while Marberry was walking through the special housing unit, he tried to tell her too, though she turned her back and left before he was finished. That makes her as much responsible as Rogers, Miller believes.

That line of argument is deficient on multiple levels. One is that it supposes that every federal employee is responsible, on pain of damages, for not implementing the decision of any other federal employee, so that all Miller need show is the existence of a lower-bunk order. Yet the Supreme Court has never held that *Bivens* actions can be used to enforce administrative orders. Nor has the Court held that every public official has a duty to carry out every other public official's decisions. To the contrary, *Castle Rock v. Gonzales*, 545 U.S. 748 (2005), holds that police and prosecutors are not liable for their failure to enforce a judicial no-contact order. Why would a lower-bunk permit receive greater status? To get anywhere, Miller needed to establish that Rogers and Marberry violated his constitutional rights—which for a medical claim under the Eighth Amendment means knowing of (or being deliberately indifferent to) a serious medical condition, then not taking minimally competent steps to deal with that condition. See *Estelle v. Gamble*, 429 U.S. 97 (1976); *Farmer v. Brennan*, 511 U.S. 825 (1994); *Petties v. Carter*, 836 F.3d 722 (7th Cir. 2016) (en banc).

A lower-bunk permit does not supplant that framework for Eighth Amendment claims. Miller does not contend that the very existence of a lower-bunk assignment would convey to any conscientious prison employee the existence of a serious medical condition, something that is a *sine qua non* of an Eighth Amendment medical-care claim. For all this record shows, medical personnel issue lower-bunk directives for reasons that do not imply the existence of a "serious" health problem; Miller did not ask in discovery for the criteria that the prison uses to issue lower-bunk directives. His statement to Rogers that he had a brain tumor likewise falls short of demonstrating a serious medical condition. Brain tumors come in many sizes and locations; they have a range of effects, including none; benign tumors can last decades without causing adverse consequences. So to say "I have a brain tumor" would not necessarily imply to every guard or warden the need for medical care, let alone the particular accommodation (a lower bunk) that Miller demanded. What's more, Rogers was not obliged to believe Miller's assertion that he had a brain tumor and a lower-bunk pass. Prisoners can be manipulative, using deceit to obtain advantages; guards are accordingly entitled to be skeptical. *Riccardo v. Rausch*, 375 F.3d 521, 525 (7th Cir. 2004).

Prisons respond to the risk of manipulative conduct by exploiting the division of labor—for example, by allocating bunk-assignment duties to guards who have computer terminals that enable them to check prisoners' assertions. Miller made his assertions about a brain tumor and a lower-bunk pass to Rogers, who could not verify them, while never complaining to the guard with bunk-assigning duties and access to the SENTRY database. This record shows that Miller *did* have a thalamic brain tumor, diagnosed before he entered prison, that reduced sensation on the left side of his body. A lower-bunk assignment may have been well justified, but neither Rogers nor Marberry knew the details, consequences, and appropriate accommodations of Miller's medical condition.

Liability under *Bivens* is personal rather than vicarious. See, e.g., *Iqbal v. Ashcroft*, 556 U.S. 662, 677 (2009); *Vance v. Rumsfeld*, 701 F.3d 193, 203-05 (7th Cir. 2012) (en banc). One consequence of this rule was spelled out in *Burks v. Raemisch*, 555 F.3d 592 (7th Cir. 2009), which holds that prison officials who reject prisoners' grievances do not become liable just because they fail to ensure adequate remedies. That's a fair description of Rogers's and Marberry's situations. Indeed, Rogers did not have any grievance-adjustment responsibilities, and Marberry, who was the ultimate grievance adjuster, did not receive a formal grievance from Miller until 18 months after his second fall. Defendants' brief in this court relies on *Burks* and two similar decisions, *Arnett v. Webster*, 658 F.3d 742, 755 (7th Cir. 2011), and *King v. Kramer*, 680 F.3d 1013, 1018 (7th Cir. 2012), but Miller's briefs do not discuss any of the three.

Although *Iqbal*, *Vance*, and *Burks* all hold that inaction following receipt of a complaint about someone else's conduct is not a source of liability, Miller seeks support from *Hay- wood v. Hathaway*, 842 F.3d 1026 (7th Cir. 2016), in which the majority of a divided panel thought that allegations against a state prison's warden created a triable Eighth Amendment issue. Haywood contended that he had been held for 60 days in freezing conditions. The panel's majority stressed that the warden had given instructions to the prison's engineering staff, received a report, visited the scene, and declared that all was well. That personal involvement permitted an inference that the warden's own conduct was unconstitutional. Miller's allegation, by contrast, is that Rogers and Marberry brushed off his complaints, leaving them to be handled through the chain of command. That brings Miller's claim within the scope of *Iqbal*, *Vance*, and *Burks* rather than *Haywood*.

AFFIRMED.

POSNER, *Circuit Judge*, dissenting. In November 2006 William Miller was convicted of bank robbery and sentenced to 120 months in prison. Between then and his imprisonment, which began thirteen months later in the Federal Correctional Complex in Terre Haute, Indiana ("FCC Terre Haute" as the prison is more commonly known), he was diagnosed with a thalamic brain tumor (more commonly referred to in the medical profession as a thalamic glioma) that impaired the feeling in the left side of his body—a typical symptom of the disease.

A month after entering prison, Miller was given a "lower-bunk restriction": his doctor ordered that he be assigned to a lower bunk because of his medical condition, and a notation to that effect was added (or should have been added) to his profile in the prison's electronic record-keeping system. A year later, for unknown reasons (but there is no indication that the reasons were disciplinary), he was assigned to a more restrictive housing unit in the prison than he'd originally been in, called the Special Housing Unit. He was initially given a lower bunk, but within hours was moved to an upper one. He complained to Gary Rogers, the number-one guard in the unit, that because of his brain tumor he had a lower-bunk restriction, but Rogers told him he wouldn't be switched to a lower bunk and if he refused the upper bunk he would "receive a disciplinary report for refusing a direct order."

Yet just five days after this contretemps, climbing down the ladder from his upper bunk Miller became dizzy, slipped, and fell to the concrete floor, hitting his head and losing consciousness. According to the prison's report of the incident, Miller was found "lying in [on?] [the] floor of [his] cell at [the] bottom of [the] bunk stairs" with "blood noted to [at?] top of head with a small . . . laceration." He was taken to a hospital, treated, and given a CAT scan, but upon his return to the prison was again assigned an upper bunk. He complained about the assignment, without effect, both to Rogers and to an attending nurse.

At about this time the prison's warden, defendant Marberry, on one of her weekly walks through the Special Housing Unit, stopped at the door to Miller's cell, and he told her he'd recently fallen from the upper bunk and should be placed in a lower bunk. As warden she could of course have taken up the issue of lower versus upper bunk for Miller with the prison's medical staff, but she didn't; she merely "walked away from [Miller's] cell door leaving him in mid-speech" (according to the complaint)—and this despite the fact that before he entered the Special Housing Unit, Miller had repeatedly discussed his brain tumor with the warden on her visits to prisoners during their lunch period.

The following month (February 2009) Miller while sleeping fell from his upper bunk at about 2:30 A.M. and remained lying on the floor for an hour or two until noticed by staff, who placed him on a back board with a cervical collar around his neck and took him to the emergency room of a nearby hospital, where a CAT scan revealed that Miller had severely compacted (that is, compressed) the cervical segment of his spine and sustained a fracture in the thoracic region. He was placed in a hard clam-shell back brace.

Upon his return to the prison so accoutered, he again requested a lower-bunk assignment and it was again refused without reasons given. Warden Marberry walked through the Special Housing Unit many times in 2009 and saw Miller lying on the upper bunk in his cell wearing his clamshell back brace and a cervical brace. Each time she approached his cell he asked her for a lower bunk, but she did nothing in response to his request; and Rogers, who in making his rounds also saw Miller frequently, also did nothing. Throughout this period Miller was in acute pain.

Finally on December 1, 2009, Miller was given a new lower-bunk restriction for one year. Eleven days later, however, the day after a nurse removed surgical staples in Miller's back that had been placed there during his most recent surgery, the wound that had been stapled burst open, discharging a large amount of a yellowish fluid consisting mainly of blood. He was taken to a hospital and remained there for four months until the wound healed. It appears that after returning from the hospital Miller was at last given a lower-bunk assignment.

Miller filed an administrative complaint with the prison the following year, complaining about all the time he'd been made to sleep in an upper bunk despite its serious consequences for his health. His complaint was denied on the ground that—although he'd had a lower-bunk restriction since January 29, 2008—he had never submitted a document confirming that restriction to a member of the prison's staff, as required by a notice to the prisoners that "It is your responsibility to have all medical restrictions on your person to present to staff." Although he'd had a lower-bunk restriction since January 29, 2008, he had lost the document confirming the restriction and had been unable to obtain a new one from the prison's medical staff until well into the following year.

He continued complaining about having to sleep in an upper bunk, all to no avail, and culminating in this remarkable brush-off by the Federal Bureau of Prisons Office of Regional Counsel: an "investigation of your claim did not reveal you suffered any personal injury as a result of the negligent acts or omissions of Bureau of Prisons employees acting within the scope of their employment." In fact he had suffered severe injuries as a result of the negligence—indeed the deliberate indifference—of Rogers and Marberry, both of whom were aware of his problems, could not have failed to realize that they had resulted from his being sentenced to an upper bunk, and could readily have alerted the prison's medical and administrative staff to the need to give him a lower bunk. They did nothing. That's what's called deliberate (that is, knowing) indifference to a serious medical need.

Judge Easterbrook's majority opinion speculates that medical personnel might issue lower-bunk restrictions for reasons that don't imply the existence of a serious medical need; points out that not all brain tumors are serious; and reminds the reader that guards are not obliged to believe whatever a prisoner tells them. All true—but whether Rogers or Marberry was aware of the serious health risk to Miller from being assigned to an upper bunk is an open question that needs to be addressed at a trial. The record contains facts that support Miller's claim that he had a serious medical need and that the defendants knew it and did nothing despite their responsibilities.

His administrative claims denied, Miller brought this civil suit pro se against Rogers, Marberry, and a nurse named Mattix (whom we can ignore however because there is no evidence that she neglected any of Miller's needs), charging them with deliberate indifference to his medical problems in violation of the Eighth Amendment. The district judge granted summary judgment in favor of the defendants, however, mainly on the basis of the defendants' claim that Miller was not listed in the prison's electronic database as having a lower-bunk restriction. This as I'll show is almost certainly incorrect.

He appealed to our court, again pro se, but while the appeal was pending the court recruited counsel for Miller and struck all the briefs that had been filed thus far with the court. Four months later Miller died, causes unknown—so far as appears no autopsy was performed. Miller's lawyer was permitted to substitute Miller's estate as the appellant, and the appeal was argued to this panel on November 29 of last year.

Now it's true that Rogers and Marberry, not being medical personnel, were entitled to "rely on the expertise of medical personnel," *Arnett v. Webster*, 658 F.3d 742, 745 (7th Cir. 2011), but nonmedical prison personnel "cannot [be permitted to] simply ignore an inmate's plight" of which they're aware, *id.*—which a jury could well find was what happened in this case. The defendants knew after Miller's first fall from an upper bunk, and from his complaints to both of them, that he was in danger of a serious injury if he remained in an upper bunk, and it would have been the simplest thing in the world for either or both of them to have conveyed his complaints to the prison's medical staff for confirmation of whether he already had, and if not should be given, a lower-bunk restriction.

Warden Marberry's reactions to Miller's complaints made to her repeatedly in person as she made her rounds through the Special Housing Unit were grossly insensitive—so callous that they could have been expected to cost her her job. All she would have had to do in response to Miller's complaints was alert the prison's medical staff to them; the staff would have responded with alacrity to a directive *by the warden* to determine whether Miller should be given (or indeed already had, as indeed he did have after January 2008) a lower-bunk restriction. It would have taken her no time, no effort, and no detailed knowledge of Miller's condition to respond intelligently to his repeated and plausible complaints (plausible given his brain tumor and his falls from the upper bunk). After his first fall, and certainly after his second, it must have been obvious to Marberry and Rogers and any other prison personnel who knew of Miller's condition that he should not be consigned to an upper bunk.

And finally we know that Miller had been given a lower-bunk restriction in January 2008, before both of his falls from his upper bunk, which occurred early the following year; he just didn't have a paper copy of it and so couldn't prove to Rogers' satisfaction that he had such a restriction. Warden Marberry confirmed in writing that Miller had been given the restriction then and that it was recorded in the prison's database. As a defendant's statement against interest, that confirmation was sufficient to create a factual dispute that could not be resolved by the district judge on summary judgment. The contrary evidence was in fact weak, for remember that it was the warden who said that Miller had had a lower-bunk restriction since January 2008; and Rogers testified weakly that "it would have been" his practice to rely on the number two officer in the Special Housing Unit to check the database if an inmate complained that he had a bunk restriction that wasn't being honored. And more weakly still: "I vaguely remember this inmate [Miller] and do not specifically recall what his medical issues were or may have been on January 6, 2009."

Marberry also pleaded forgetfulness. She claimed no recollection of what if anything she'd done in response to Miller's repeated complaints about being denied a lower bunk. (Obviously, nothing.) No defendant has argued that all the lower bunks were filled by inmates who, like Miller, could not be safely assigned to upper bunks, so that there was no room for him. Most important, there is no evidence that anyone checked the database to see whether, as Miller repeatedly said, he had a lower-bunk restriction.

The insouciance of Rogers and Marberry is remarkable, as well as deplorable, when one recalls that both knew about Miller's brain tumor, about his wanting a lower bunk for medical reasons, and about at least his first fall from the upper bunk and his resulting hospitalization. (Almost certainly they knew of the second fall as well.) True, Rogers is just a guard, but as we said in *Dobbey v. Mitchell-Lawshea*, 806 F.3d 938, 941 (7th Cir. 2015), "prison guards have a responsibility for prisoners' welfare. If a prisoner is writhing in agony, the guard cannot ignore him on the ground of not being a doctor; he has to make an effort to find a doctor, or in this case a dentist or a technician, or a pharmacist—some medical professional." See also *Smego v. Mitchell*, 723 F.3d 752, 757 (7th Cir. 2013). If that's true of a mere guard, it is *a fortiori* true of a warden who knows that a prisoner's potentially very dangerous health condition is being ignored by the prison's guards and medical staff that she—the warden—supervises.

I note that the Bureau of Prisons is required by law to "provide suitable quarters and provide for the safekeeping, care, and subsistence of all persons charged with or convicted of offenses against the United States. . . . " 18 U.S.C. § 4042(a)(2). The Bureau failed in this case. Quarters with an upper-bunk assignment are not suitable for someone with the kind of brain tumor that Miller had; he was denied both safekeeping and care. This is a classic case of turning a blind eye "to a substantial risk of serious harm to a prisoner." *Perez v. Fenoglio*, 792 F.3d 768, 781 (7th Cir. 2015).

Judge Easterbrook's opinion cites *Iqbal v. Ashcroft*, 556 U.S. 662, 677 (2009), for its rejection of a theory of "supervisory liability" that would make supervisors liable for "knowledge and acquiescence in their subordinates' use of discriminatory criteria to make classification decisions among detainees." The Court in *Iqbal* thus rejected the proposition that a supervisor's mere knowledge of a subordinate's discriminatory purpose amounts to the supervisor's violating the Constitution. "[P]etitioners may not be held accountable for the misdeeds of their agents. . . . Absent vicarious liability, each Government official, his or her title notwithstanding, is only liable for his or her own misconduct. In the context of determining whether there is a violation of [a] clearly established right to overcome qualified immunity, purpose rather than knowledge is required to impose . . . liability on the subordinate for unconstitutional discrimination; the same holds true for an official charged with violations arising from his or her superintendent responsibilities."

I have no quarrel with that. But knowledge and duty can be entwined. "A prison official's knowledge of prison conditions learned from an inmate's communications can, under some circumstances, constitute sufficient knowledge of the conditions to require the officer to exercise his or her authority and to take the needed action to investigate and, if necessary, to rectify the offending condition." *Vance v. Peters*, 97 F.3d 987, 993 (7th Cir. 1996). Both Rogers and Marberry were responsible for the safety of prison inmates and were on notice that Miller's safety was jeopardized as a consequence of confining him to an upper bunk. They were complicit in his suffering and may have hastened his death.

I am depressed by the majority's decision. A dog would have deserved better treatment than Miller got. Should not judges have a soul? Should they not heed *Micah* 6:8: "He hath shewed thee, O man, what is good; and what doth the Lord require of thee, but to do justly, and to love mercy, and to walk humbly with thy God?" Or if not *Micah*, then William Blake's poem On Another's Sorrow, which begins: "Can I see another's woe / And not be in sorrow too?"

We should reverse.

The hearsay rule.[11] As should be apparent to the reader of this book by now, I don't like legal jargon or doctrinal complexity and I certainly don't consider law a science—I think of it rather as a methodology of dispute resolution created by simple people for simple people. Therefore I want it to be simple and commonsensical. I want judges to be well informed, curious, experienced, and empathetic. I borrow the credo of the poet Yeats (quoted more fully in Chapter

11. See "The Philip D. Reed Lecture Series Advisory Committee on Evidence Rules: Symposium on Hearsay Reform," 84 *Fordham Law Review* 1323 (2016), for a comprehensive discussion and analysis of the hearsay rule.

3) that "the best I have done / Was done to make it plain." Judges too should endeavor to "make it plain," and in the words of another though lesser poet, Ezra Pound, also "MAKE IT NEW!"

Coming closer to my immediate topic—the hearsay rule—I need first to provide some context. The rule and its numerous exceptions are normally though I think incorrectly considered to be inseparable from the adversary system, which as normally practiced is, as I've argued throughout this book, unsatisfactory because it relies too heavily on such dubious aids as demeanor cues and cross-examination to separate truth from falsity. Cross-examination is not, as lawyers and trial judges like to think (and as many lawyers and judges *do* think), the greatest engine ever invented for determining truth. It is often ineffectual when deployed against expert witnesses and intelligent well-briefed lay witnesses. More broadly, judges leave too much of the development of facts to the lawyers, for example by reluctance to appoint neutral expert witnesses as authorized by Rule 706 of the Federal Rules of Evidence, or by letting the lawyers draft the jury instructions, or by giving pattern instructions, which are concocted by committees of lawyers and judges and as a result are too legalistic for the understanding of the average juror.

And coming still closer to the hearsay rule I note that the federal judiciary has allowed the rules of evidence to balloon excessively. There are now 68 federal rules of evidence, of which the 7 involving hearsay consume 28 pages of West's immense volume of federal rules of procedure and evidence. The volume devotes 117 pages to the rules of evidence, of which the hearsay rules (for the hearsay "rule" is actually a composite of separate rules relating to hearsay) have a big share: 28 pages is 24 percent of 117 pages. There is also an academic literature on evidence that despite some notable contributions is staggering in its length, indecision, and obscurity.

And yet in my experience the hearsay rule plays little role in the federal trial process. Hearsay objections are rare and usually can be circumvented ("counsel, could you rephrase the question," works almost every time). The hearsay rule is a rule of exclusion riddled with exceptions. But what is perhaps most interesting about the rule is that it is further evidence of the incompleteness of the adversary system as a system of trial procedure. For reliable hearsay is admissible in a trial even when the out-of-court declarant can't be cross-examined. (The frequent inequality of the lawyers on the two sides of a case, an inequality that reaches its apogee in pro se cases, where by definition one side has no lawyer at all, is further evidence that the adversary system does not completely describe our procedural system.)

Here I pause to note that although many of the rules of evidence could be discarded without loss, such as the hearsay rule, not all could be. Not Rule 403, for example ("Although relevant, evidence may be excluded if its probative value is substantially outweighed by the danger of unfair prejudice, confusion of the issues, or misleading the jury, or by considerations of undue delay, waste of time, or needless presentation of cumulative evidence").[12] Ideally it would be the only rule of evidence; but realistically some others will, and probably should be, retained: Rule 407 (subsequent remedial measures ordinarily are not admissible to prove negligence, as otherwise post-accident remedial measures would be discouraged) is one. Rules 412 to 415, which allow the introduction of evidence of prior sex crimes committed by a defendant, because sex offenders tend to be obsessive, are others; and the already mentioned Rule 706 authorizing court-appointed expert witnesses is still another.

Back to hearsay: Rules 801 to 807 are the hearsay rules (or compendiously the hearsay rule), and to understand them one needs first to understand the legal meaning of hearsay. Essentially it is a report by one person of what some other person said or wrote. If I say that someone told me it's going to rain this afternoon, my statement is hearsay (I am "telling" what I "heard" = "my testimony is hearsay"). Hearsay evidence is presumptively inadmissible in a trial because the source of a hearsay statement (repeated by a witness at the trial)— the "someone"—is a nonparty to the litigation, being the person from whom the witness heard the statement that the witness has been asked to repeat in court. And often the nonparty source simply is unavailable to be called as a witness and thus to be cross-examined.

Barring hearsay evidence may seem strange since almost all the knowledge that we have is based on hearsay. It is knowledge that was imparted to us by strangers, in school, on the job, in books and increasingly in electronic media; often by long-dead strangers. It is hearsay that Julius Caesar was stabbed to death in the Roman Capitol, that Cleopatra committed suicide, and that Jesus Christ was crucified. Hearsay is by definition not the fruit of our own firsthand investigation. Some of it is reliable, as in the ancient examples I just gave, but much of it is not, and because reliability is critical it's sometimes argued that there should be no hearsay rule—that the main criterion for the admissibility of evidence should be whether it is reliable, not whether it is firsthand or sec-

---

12. In Richard A. Posner, "An Economic Approach to the Law of Evidence," 51 *Stanford Law Review* 1477, 1522 (1999), I offered an economic interpretation of Rule 403, pointing out that it requires determining whether the benefits of particular evidence are likely to exceed the costs of admitting it into the trial. The article recasts most of the law of evidence in economic terms, consistent with my remark in the Introduction to this book that economic analysis of law continues to be a fruitful component of legal analysis.

ondhand.[13] (I say "main" not "sole" because length, materiality, and intelligibility are other criteria of admissibility.)

I am sympathetic to the suggestion. I can imagine benefits from allowing Rule 807 (the "residual exception" to the exclusion of hearsay evidence, which allows the admission of hearsay evidence on the basis of reliability) to swallow much of the content of Rules 801 through 806 and thus many of the exclusions from evidence, exceptions to the exclusions, and notes of the Advisory Committee on the federal rules of evidence.

With its multitude of exceptions, the federal hearsay rule is simply too complicated. Trials would go better with a simpler rule the core of which would be the proposition (essentially a simplification of Rule 807) that hearsay evidence should be admissible when it is reliable, when the jury can understand its meaning, strengths, and limitations, and when it will materially enhance the likelihood of a correct outcome without taking up too much time at trial. Without such a standard too much knowledge is excluded from legal proceedings in misplaced deference to the traditional reliance on adversary procedure (which receives too much deference in general, considering its many weaknesses as an engine of truth). I am mindful too of studies that find that jurors tend to be skeptical of hearsay evidence,[14] which if true implies that its admission may do little harm even when it's unreliable.

But I am not yet ready to endorse the total abolition of the hearsay rule. Precisely because most of our knowledge is hearsay, to abolish the rule in favor of Rule 403, which in essence requires weighing the costs versus the benefits (shorthand for weighing probative value against prejudicial effect, potential for confusion, etc.) of evidence to determine its admissibility, might require a trial judge to make an enormous number of rulings on whether to admit or exclude hearsay evidence. Without limitations on the admissibility of such evidence trials would sprawl. Not only would there be countless attempts to introduce such evidence but rulings on objections to it would be difficult for the judge to make because often it's very difficult to estimate the reliability of a hearsay statement. The fact that jurors tend (it appears) to discount hearsay evidence

13. Professor Richard A. Friedman comes close to advocating this approach in his important article "Jack Weinstein and the Missing Pieces of the Hearsay Puzzle," 64 *DePaul Law Review* 449 (2015); see also his article "The Mold That Shapes Hearsay Law," 56 *Florida Law Review* 433 (2014). For outright advocacy of the abolition of the hearsay rule, see Ronald J. Allen, "Commentary: A Response to Professor Friedman. The Evolution of the Hearsay Rule to a Rule of Admission," 76 *Minnesota Law Review* 797 (1992).

14. See Justin Sevier, "Popularizing Hearsay," 104 *Georgetown Law Journal* 643 (2016); Jeffrey Bellin, "The Case for eHearsay," 83 *Fordham Law Review* 1317 (2014).

would act as some check on lawyers' eagerness to present such evidence, but probably not enough of one to prevent weighing down of too many trials with too much hearsay.

So we need a hearsay rule; and only that—we don't need *all* the exceptions to it. The first hearsay rule in the federal rules of evidence, Rule 801, defines hearsay as a statement that "a party offers in evidence to prove the truth of the matter asserted in the statement." Two exceptions are listed: one for the case in which the defendant testifies and is subject to being cross-examined about a statement that he made out of court, the other where the out-of-court statement was made by the opposing party in the litigation. The limitation of hearsay to statements is important to note because many communications don't take the form of a statement. An example is unfurling an umbrella. The action communicates the fact that it's raining, but because there is no statement the communication is not subject to the hearsay rule.[15]

Rule 803, the next rule I'll discuss, is a list of twenty-three exceptions to the hearsay rule (a bad sign). Two of these—"present sense impression" and "excited utterance"—I'll discuss briefly later, together with an exception found in Rule 804—"dying declaration." Other exceptions in Rule 803 include various types of record (including a record of something the witness doesn't recall) —records kept in the regular course of business, public records, records of baptism and similar ceremonies, some types of reputation evidence, and legal judgments.

Rule 804 contains five more exceptions (so I'm up to thirty hearsay exceptions in the rules I've discussed so far). These include former testimony, dying declarations ("statements under the belief of imminent death"), and statements "against interest," that is, statements that are actually harmful to the persons making them, the theory being that a person would be unlikely to make a *false* statement that harmed him—to say for example "I must have been drunk when my car hit the lamp post," if he doesn't drink.

The last hearsay rule is Rule 807, entitled as I noted earlier "residual exception," which allows the admission of hearsay evidence if "(1) the statement has equivalent circumstantial guarantees of trustworthiness [equivalent, that is, to hearsay statements permitted by other hearsay exceptions to be admitted in[to] evidence]; (2) it is offered as evidence of a material fact; (3) it is more probative on the point for which it is offered than any other evidence that the proponent

---

15. See Christopher G. Miller, "Implied Assertions in Evidence Law: A Retrospective," 33 *Mississippi College Law Review* 1, 3–6 (2014).

can obtain through reasonable efforts; and (4) admitting it will best serve the purposes of these rules and the interests of justice."

There thus are a total of thirty-one exceptions to the exclusion of hearsay evidence. The first thirty are specific, and there is value in such a list—otherwise a judge would have to decide in each case whether proffered hearsay evidence satisfied the balancing test in Rule 403 (the probative value of the evidence versus the prejudicial or other adverse effects of admitting it). The problem is Rule 807, quoted above. It is essentially open-ended, and stripped of what amounts to ornamental verbiage allows the admission of hearsay evidence *whenever* it is both reliable and important to the case. So the federal hearsay rule taken as a whole amounts to declaring that reliable hearsay evidence is admissible when necessary to a full adjudication of a case, and in addition thirty specific forms of hearsay evidence are routinely admissible. The bar to hearsay evidence is thus full of holes. But in practice the bar usually is limited just to unreliable or superfluous hearsay evidence. And maybe that's the best we can do.

Those thirty exceptions seem to me on the whole sound, but with at least three exceptions.[16] One of them, found in Rule 803(1) and captioned "present sense impression," allows into evidence "a statement describing or explaining an event or condition, made while or immediately after the declarant perceived it." The stated rationale is that if the event described and the statement describing it are near each other in time, this "negate[s] the likelihood of deliberate or conscious misrepresentation," as the Advisory Committee Notes to the rule state. I don't get it—especially when "immediacy" is interpreted to encompass periods as long as twenty-three minutes,[17] sixteen minutes,[18] and ten minutes.[19] Even genuine immediacy is not a guarantor of truthfulness. For it's false that people can't make up a lie in a short period of time. Most lies in fact are spontaneous.[20]

The "present sense impression" exception to the hearsay rule never had any grounding in psychology. It entered American law in the nineteenth century,[21] before there was a field of cognitive psychology. It has neither a theoretical nor

16. My discussion of the first two is based on my concurring opinion in *United States v. Boyce*, 742 F.3d 792, 799–802 (7th Cir. 2014).

17. *United States v. Blakey*, 607 F.2d 779, 785–786 (7th Cir. 1979).

18. *United States v. Mejia-Velez*, 855 F. Supp. 607, 614 (E.D.N.Y. 1994).

19. *State v. Odom*, 341 S.E. 2d 332, 335–336 (N.C. 1986).

20. See, e.g., Monica T. Whitty et al., "Not All Lies Are Spontaneous: An Examination of Deception Across Different Modes of Communication," 63 *Journal of American Society of Information Science & Technology* 208–209, 214 (2012).

21. See Jon R. Waltz, "The Present Sense Impression Exception to the Rule Against Hearsay: Origins and Attributes," 66 *Iowa Law Review* 869, 871 (1981).

an empirical basis; it's not even common sense. As remarked in *Lust v. Sealy, Inc.,*[22] "as with much of the folk psychology of evidence, it is difficult to take this rationale [that immediacy negates the likelihood of fabrication] entirely seriously, since people are entirely capable of spontaneous lies in emotional circumstances"; "old and new studies agree that less than one second is required to fabricate a lie."[23] (I wish the court in *Lust* had left out "entirely," which undermined what it was trying to say.)

The "excited utterance" exception of Rule 803(2) allows into evidence "a statement relating to a startling event or condition, made while the declarant was under the stress of excitement that it caused." The Advisory Committee Notes provide the following justification: "circumstances *may* produce a condition of excitement which temporarily stills the capacity of reflection and produces utterances free of *conscious* fabrication." The two words I've emphasized drain the attempted justification of content. And even if a person is so excited by something that he loses the capacity for reflection (which doubtless does happen), how can there be any confidence that his unreflective utterance, provoked by excitement, is reliable? As Robert Hutchins and Donald Slesinger contended, "One need not be a psychologist to distrust an observation made under emotional stress; everybody accepts such statements with mental reservation."[24]

The Advisory Committee Notes acknowledge that the exception has been criticized but defend it on the ground that "it finds support in cases without number." That is less than reassuring. Like the exception for present sense impressions, the exception for excited utterances rests on no firmer ground than judicial habit, in turn reflecting judicial incuriosity and reluctance to reconsider ancient dogmas. Socrates famously said (at his trial for corrupting the youth of Athens and disrespecting the gods) that "the unexamined life is not worth living." The Advisory Committee ought to consider doing some examining of those old "cases without number."

The dying-declaration exception to the hearsay rule, an exception of medi-

---

22. 383 F.3d 580, 588 (7th Cir. 2004).

23. Id., quoting Douglas D. McFarland, "Present Sense Impressions Cannot Live in the Past," 28 *Florida State University Law Review* 907, 916 (2001); see also Jeffrey Bellin, "Facebook, Twitter, and the Uncertain Future of Present Sense Impressions," 160 *University of Pennsylvania Law Review* 331, 362–366 (2012); I. Daniel Stewart, Jr., "Perception, Memory, and Hearsay: A Criticism of Present Law and the Proposed Federal Rules of Evidence," 1970 *Utah Law Review* 1, 27–29 (1970).

24. Robert M. Hutchins and Donald Slesinger, "Some Observations on the Law of Evidence: Spontaneous Exclamations," 28 *Columbia Law Review* 432, 437 (1928). For an excellent analysis of the excited-utterance exception, see Alan G. Williams, "Abolishing the Excited Utterance Exception to the Rule Against Hearsay," 63 *University of Kansas Law Review* 717 (2015).

eval origin based on the Latin expression *nemo moriturus praesumitur men-tiri*—"no one about to die is presumed to be lying," as he would be jeopardizing his immortal soul—is also dubious. Many people nowadays do not believe they have souls, or, if they do believe that, they're dubious that a dying declaration will smooth their way to heaven. And as Professor Aviva Orenstein explains, "physical or mental weakness consequent upon the approach of death, a desire of self-vindication, or a disposition to impute the responsibility for a wrong to another, as well as the fact that the declarations are made in the absence of the accused, and often in response to leading questions and direct suggestions, and with no opportunity for cross-examination: all these considerations conspire to render such declarations a dangerous kind of evidence."[25] And of course there are many sudden deaths and many deaths of people whose minds are confused in the hours or days or weeks or months before their death. And finally if a soul can be jeopardized, how can it be immortal?

Enough about hearsay! Time for another litigation topic, or rather three such topics:

Avoiding litigation: forum-selection clauses. A recent case of mine[26] illustrates the use of forum-selection clauses to deprive unsophisticated litigants of their day in court. The defendant, a company named Pushpin, was an assignee of leases of credit-card processing machines. The leases required that all disputes over them be litigated in Cook County, Illinois, and governed by Illinois law. Having acquired the leases and thus the right to sue to enforce them, Pushpin brought several *thousand* suits in Illinois small-claims courts against guarantors of leases that the lessees had defaulted on. Because the vast majority of the guarantors lived in other states and the amounts sought in the suits were small (otherwise the suits couldn't have been filed in small-claims courts), Pushpin was counting on most of the defendants' simply defaulting rather than going to the expense of hiring lawyers to defend against its suits.

The question presented by such a case is whether forum-selection clauses should be enforceable when used to induce defaults by specifying an inconvenient forum for the litigation of disputes involving unsophisticated signatories of such clauses (which may describe many of the sole proprietors and other small businesses that had leased the credit-card processing machines in

---

25. Aviva Orenstein, "Her Last Words: Dying Declarations and Modern Confrontation Jurisprudence," 2010 *University of Illinois Law Review* 1411, 1460 (2010). As Bellin, note 14 above, at 1331, remarks, "the dying declaration exception . . . is (1) based on untested spiritual assumptions and (2) presumes a counterintuitive measure of lucidity on the part of the dying that science does not support" (footnote omitted).

26. *Johnson v. Pushpin Holdings, LLC*, No. 15-2771 (7th Cir. May 6, 2016).

question). Although the obvious answer is "no," in a much-criticized decision (*Carnival Cruise Lines, Inc. v. Shute*)[27] the Supreme Court upheld a forum-selection clause printed on the "contract" pages attached to a cruise ticket. The clause had not been negotiated; it had simply been imposed by the cruise line on the passengers, who were unlikely to appreciate its significance—the prospect of bringing a lawsuit against the line was not something many passengers would have been thinking about when they bought their tickets. The same may have been true in the *Pushpin* case with regard to the individuals and small businesses that leased credit-card processing machines. But even if in the face of *Carnival* it were possible for a lower court to invalidate forum-selection clauses in a case such as *Pushpin*, the court would have to deal with the objection that *any* forum-selection clause is an inconvenience to a nonresident signer of the contract containing the clause, implying that the challenge to the forum-selection clauses in *Pushpin* if successful would have implied a blanket prohibition of such clauses. But of course that might be a good thing, at least if limited to contracts with an individual or a small firm; but it may well be blocked by *Carnival*.

Avoiding litigation: class actions.[28] I have judged many appeals in class action cases in my thirty-five years as a federal court of appeals judge and have learned that while some of them provide warranted relief unavailable in any other type of proceeding because of the small stakes of the individuals making up the class, others are little (sometimes no) better than rackets. I will illustrate with two recent cases of mine, in the more recent of which[29] I used the word "racket" to describe the class action at issue. A class consisting of the shareholders of Walgreens sued the company contending that it had failed to disclose enough information about a prospective merger with a large foreign firm to enable the shareholders to make an intelligent decision on whether to vote for the merger; the merger could not go through unless shareholders owning a majority of the shares voted for it. The district court approved a settlement whereby Walgreens agreed to make six additional disclosures to the shareholders and to pay class counsel $370,000 for their efforts in obtaining that concession. A member of the class who objected to the settlement appealed, and we reversed, holding

27. 499 U.S. 585 (1991); for criticism, see for example Linda S. Mullenix, "*Carnival Cruise Lines, Inc. v. Shute*: The Titanic of Worst Decisions," 12 *Nevada Law Journal* 549 (2012).

28. Two comprehensive up-to-date studies are Richard Marcus, "Bending in the Breeze: American Class Actions in the Twenty-First Century," 65 *De Paul Law Review* 497 (2016), and Robert H. Klonoff, "Class Actions in the Year 2025: A Prognosis," forthcoming in *Emory Law Journal*, vol. 65, no. 6.

29. *In re Walgreen Co. Stockholder Litigation* (7th Cir. August 10, 2016).

that the disclosures were worthless to the shareholders because they added nothing of any importance to disclosures that Walgreens had already made to them voluntarily; and that having done nothing to benefit the shareholders, class counsel wasn't entitled to a dime from Walgreens. The merger was a multi-billion dollar transaction, and Walgreens was happy to get class counsel off its back for the piddling sum (to a firm of Walgreens' size) of $370,000. We thought the case a good example of extortionate class litigation. And not an isolated one.

Indeed such litigation abounds. The typical class action is the brainchild of lawyers, who select a member of the potential class (sometimes several members) to be the named plaintiffs; yet it is the lawyers who control the litigation and often their interest is limited to the amount of fees they can obtain from the litigation, normally by a settlement with the defendant that the district court (and if there is an appeal the court of appeals) will approve. Although the Walgreens case was an extreme example, it is commonly the case that the fees sought by the plaintiffs' lawyers, though substantial, are peanuts compared to the resources of the defendant. The goal of negotiations is to limit the defendant's settlement expense to the fees sought by the class action lawyers, for that is the deal that makes both sides content—though it gives nothing, or very little, to the members of the class. In the Walgreens case the class got no money, just worthless disclosures; often in a consumer class action the class gets coupons of too little value to be worth cashing in, so again the class action lawyers are the winners, and the loss to the defendant is again minimal—making all the *effective* parties to the litigation, because the class members are powerless, content.

There are blackmail settlements of class actions, where the potential liability of the defendant (owing to the number of class members) is so great that the defendant is forced to settle even if the probability of the class prevailing if the case goes to trial is slight. Algebraically the expected gain to the class (meaning largely to class counsel) can be expressed as PJ, where P is the probability that the class will prevail if the case is litigated and J is the amount of money the class will receive if it prevails. If J is very great, PJ may be very great even if P is small, creating a risk to the defendant that it may be unwilling to take, thus compelling it to settle.[30]

In short: class counsel wants fees, doesn't care about the welfare of the members of the class; the defendant cares only about cost, not how it's split between

---

30. See, e.g., *In re Rhone-Poulenc*, 51 F.3d 1293 (7th Cir. 1995). See also Henry J. Friendly, *Federal Jurisdiction: A General View* 120 (1973).

fees and class compensation. The optimal deal from the standpoint of the opponents—not of society as a whole, however—therefore combines high fees for
class counsel with meager compensation for the class, and that is the deal that
opposing counsel (having settled their differences) will propose to the court.
The fact that court approval of a class action settlement is required for the settlement to be valid demonstrates concern with class counsel's selling out the
class, but tends often to be ineffectual because nonadversary—and judges love
settlement! To try to plug this hole, we have the objectors—class members who
challenge a phony settlement in the district court and may even appeal to the
court of appeals if the district court approves the settlement. Objectors complicate and delay the litigation and make it more costly, but their role as watch-
dogs is essential.

The second case of mine that I want to use to illustrate the class action problem is a consumer class action case, *Pearson v. NBTY, Inc.*[31] The opinion is
long so I will excerpt it. NBTY and its subsidiary (also named as a defendant)
Rexall manufacture vitamins and nutritional supplements, including glucosamine pills, which are dietary supplements designed to help people with joint
disorders, such as osteoarthritis. The suits (six in number) charge the defendants with violating several states' consumer protection laws by making false
claims for glucosamine's efficacy.

Eight months after the suits were filed, class counsel in all six cases negotiated a nationwide settlement with NBTY and Rexall (for simplicity, I'll pretend
there was a single defendant and call it "Rexall") and submitted it to the district court for approval. The judge approved the settlement, though with significant modifications. As approved, the settlement required Rexall to cough
up approximately $5.63 million—$1.93 million in fees to class counsel, plus
an additional $179,676 in attorney expenses, $1.5 million in notice and administration costs, $1.13 million to the Orthopedic Research and Education Foun-
dation (of which more shortly), $865,284 to the 30,245 class members who
submitted claims, and $30,000 to the six named plaintiffs ($5,000 apiece) as
compensation for their role as the class representatives.

The parties agreed that any part of the $4.5 million that the district judge
thought excessive compensation for class counsel would revert to Rexall (such
an agreement is called a "reversion" or more commonly a "kicker" clause),
rather than becoming available for distribution to the class members or to the
Orthopedic Research and Education Foundation, which was to receive the dif-

31. 772 F.3d 778 (7th Cir. 2014).

ference between $2 million and what the class members received if they received less than that amount, which they did. The approved settlement also included an injunction against Rexall's making certain claims (alleged to mislead) in the advertising or marketing of its glucosamine products, for thirty months.

The district judge valued the settlement at the maximum *potential* payment that class members could receive, which came to $20.2 million. That valuation, which played a critical role in the judge's decision as to how much to award class counsel in attorneys' fees, comprised $14.2 million for class members (based on the contrary-to-fact assumption that every one of the 4.72 million class members who had received postcard rather than publication notice of the class action would file a $3 claim), $1.5 million for the cost of notice to the class, and $4.5 million for fees to class counsel (the judge cut this amount but allowed the amount cut to revert to Rexall pursuant to the kicker clause and adhered to the $20.2 million estimate of the overall value of the settlement).

The $20.2 million figure had (and this is a recurrent problem in consumer class action cases) no connection to the settlement's value to the class. Notice and fees, which together accounted for $6 million of the $20.2 million, are costs, not benefits. The attorneys' fees are of course not paid to the class members; and as we said in *Redman v. RadioShack Corp.,*[32] "administrative costs should not have been included in calculating the division of the spoils between class counsel and class members. Those costs are part of the settlement but not part of the value received from the settlement by the members of the class. The costs therefore shed no light on the fairness of the division of the settlement pie between class counsel and class members." The $14.2 million "benefit" to the class members was a fiction too. Only 30,245 claims were filed, yielding total compensation for the class members of less than $1 million.

Because the amount of the attorneys' fees that the judge wanted to award class counsel—$1.93 million—was only 9.6 percent of $20.2 million, he thought the amount reasonable. But as we said in the *Redman* case, the "ratio that is relevant . . . is the ratio of (1) the fee to (2) the fee plus what the class members received."[33] Basing the award of attorneys' fees on this ratio, which shows how the aggregate value of the settlement is being split between class counsel and the class, gives class counsel an incentive to design the claims process in such a way as will maximize the settlement benefits actually received by the class, rather than to connive with the defendant in formulating claims-filing procedures that discourage filing and so reduce the benefit to the class. But $20.2

32. 768 F.3d 622, 630 (7th Cir. 2014).
33. Id.

million was of course not the value of the settlement, defined as the sum of the awards to the class and to its lawyers. The class received a meager $865,284. This means the attorneys' fees represented not 9.6 percent of the aggregate value but an outlandish 69 percent.

Had the judge approved class counsel's request for $4.5 million in attorneys' fees, those fees would have soared to 84 percent of the pot to be divided between class members and class counsel. Moreover, $4.5 million in attorneys' fees would equal an average of $1,254 per hour of time put in by the lawyers and paralegals employed on the case by the law firms representing the class. Even $538 per hour, the average fee allowed by the district judge in cutting the total fees from $4.5 million to $1.93 million, would have been excessive. It would have implied that few if any associates or paralegals had actually been used on the case, even though most of the legal work was routine pretrial preparation. This is a further indication (if any were needed) that class counsel sought and were awarded excessive compensation.

In regard to sizing the benefit of the settlement to the class, it is true that an option to file a claim creates a prospective value, even if the option is never exercised. *Boeing Co. v. Van Gemert*,[34] remarks that the right of class members "to share the harvest of the lawsuit upon proof of their identity, whether or not they exercise it, is a benefit in the fund created by the efforts of the class representatives and their counsel." But in that case the "harvest" created by class counsel was an actual, existing judgment fund, and each member of the class had "an undisputed and mathematically ascertainable claim to part of a lump-sum judgment recovered on his behalf. Nothing in the court's order made Boeing's liability for this amount contingent upon the presentation of individual claims."[35] The class members were known, the benefits of the settlement had been "traced with some accuracy," and costs could be "shifted with some exactitude to those benefiting."[36] There was no fund and no litigated judgment in *Pearson* and no reasonable expectation in advance of the deadline for filing claims that more members of the class would submit claims than did.

I can imagine a case in which a lawyer sets to work diligently to make a powerful argument for his client, agrees to a fee that compensates him for the work necessary to litigate the case to a successful conclusion, and has a reasonable expectation of obtaining a judgment that will exceed the agreed-upon attorney's fee, but unforeseeable developments result in a judgment smaller than

34. 444 U.S. 472, 480 (1980).
35. Id. at 480 n. 5.
36. Id. at 480–481.

the agreed-upon fee, or even in a judgment for the defendant. In such an event the lawyer would have a right to his fee. But especially in consumer class actions, where the percentage of class members who file claims is often quite low (in *Pearson* it was 30,245 ÷ 12 million = .0025, or one quarter of one percent),[37] the presumption should be that attorneys' fees awarded to class counsel should not exceed a third or at most a half of the total amount of money going to class members and their counsel. That range would be between $436,642 and $865,284—a far cry from the $1.93 million that the judge awarded, and absurdly far from the $4.5 million that class counsel requested, with the connivance of Rexall, which doubtless looked forward to recapturing, as it did, a big chunk of that amount. The parties could not have thought that the attorneys' fees that they agreed to pay class counsel, even if reduced by the district judge by almost one-half, would be commensurate with the modest award to the clients, which is to say the class members. The parties may not have expected only 6.4 claims per each one thousand class members who received postcard notice to file claims. But they didn't claim to have been surprised by the low rate. They did say that the settlement they negotiated was indistinguishable from consumer class actions in which the claims rate has been much higher, but those may have been cases in which the parties did not structure the claims process with an eye toward discouraging the filing of claims, as appears to have happened in this case.

As experienced class action lawyers, class counsel must have known that the notice and claim forms, and the very modest monetary award that the average claimant would receive, were bound to discourage filings. The postcard sent to each of 4.72 million class members would have informed each recipient that to file a claim he would have to click www.GlucosamineSettlement.com on his laptop or cell phone or call a toll-free phone number. The website would direct him to a "Claim Form" that required the claimant to list cash register receipts or other documentation indicating the date and place at which he or she had bought the product. The form advised the claimant that "the Claims Administrator and the Parties have the right to audit all claims for completeness, waste, fraud, and abuse. Filing a false claim may violate certain criminal or civil laws." Further, the claimant was—in boldface—required to "certify under penalty of perjury that the foregoing is true and correct to the best of my knowledge."

---

37. See, e.g., Daniel Fisher, "Odds of a Payoff in Consumer Class Action? Less Than a Straight Flush," *Forbes*, May 8, 2014, www.forbes.com/sites/danielfisher/2014/05/08/odds-of-a-payoff-in-consumer-class-action-less-than-a-straight-flush/.

One would have thought that given the low ceiling on the amount of money that a member of the class could claim, a sworn statement would be sufficient documentation, without requiring receipts or other business records likely to have been discarded. The requirement of needlessly elaborate documentation, the threats of criminal prosecution, and the fact that a claimant might feel obliged to wade through the five other documents accessible from the opening screen of the website besides the claim form, help to explain why so few recipients of the postcard notice bothered to submit a claim. Rexall obviously was trying to minimize the number of claims that class members would file, in order to minimize the cost of the settlement to it. Class counsel also benefited from minimization of the claims, because the fewer the claims, the more money Rexall would be willing to give class counsel to induce settlement. Rexall had no reason to care about the allocation of its cost of settlement between class counsel and class members; all it cared about as a rational maximizer of its net worth was the bottom line—how much the settlement was likely to cost it. When the parties to a class action expect that the reasonableness of the attorneys' fees allowed to class counsel will be judged against the potential rather than actual or at least reasonably foreseeable benefits to the class, class counsel will lack any incentive to push back against the defendant's creating a burdensome claims process in order to minimize the number of claims. Class counsel could have done much better by the class had they been willing to accept lower fees in their negotiation with Rexall. But realism requires recognition that probably all that class counsel *really* cared about *was* their fees—for $865,284 spread over twelve million class members is only seven cents apiece.

The Orthopedic Research and Education Foundation was to receive the difference (which turned out to be $1.13 million) between $2 million and what the class members received if they received less than that amount, which they did. The Foundation was not a class member; anything it received would be a "cy pres" award.[38] The award did not benefit the class, except insofar as armed with this additional money the foundation may contribute to the discovery of new treatments for joint problems—a hopelessly speculative proposition.

Since the joint problems that glucosamine is supposed to alleviate are the

38. *Cy pres* (properly *cy près comme possible*, an Anglo-French term meaning "as near as possible") is the name of the doctrine that permits a benefit to be given other than to the intended beneficiary or for the intended purpose because changed circumstances make it impossible to carry out the benefactor's intent. A familiar example is that when polio was cured, the March of Dimes, a foundation that had been established in the 1930s at the behest of President Roosevelt to fight polio, was permitted to redirect its resources to improving the health of mothers and babies.

domain of orthopedic medicine, the choice of an orthopedic institute as a recipient of money left over after all approved class members' claims are paid was consistent with *cy pres*. But there was not basis for the $1.13 million *cy pres* award in this case. A *cy pres* award is supposed to be limited to money that can't feasibly be awarded to the intended beneficiaries, here consisting of the class members. Notice costing $1.5 million reached 4.72 million class members. Granted, doubling the expenditure would not have doubled the number of class members notified. The 4.72 million who received postcards were all those whom Rexall knew (through pharmacy loyalty programs and the like) to have bought its glucosamine pills, while notice by publication or via the Internet tends to be ineffectual when the class consists of consumers. But the claims process could have been simplified; or knowing that 4.72 million people had bought at least one bottle of its pills, Rexall could have mailed $3 checks to all 4.72 million postcard recipients. The Orthopedic Research and Education Foundation seems perfectly reputable, but it was entitled to receive money intended to compensate victims of consumer fraud only if it was infeasible to provide that compensation to the victims—which was not demonstrated.

We reversed. But unfortunately the shenanigans that we identified in the *Pearson* case are common in class action suits; such suits require extreme care on the part of the district judges who preside over them. At this writing (November 15, 2016), the Federal Trade Commission is embarked on an investigation of class action suits that may reveal that, on average, fewer than 1 percent of class members in such suits bother to file claims.[39]

Avoiding litigation: arbitration.[40] As should be apparent to the reader by now, my conception of litigation in the American context is as a form of common-sense dispute resolution; I therefore regard many of the substantive and procedural rules in which the adjudication of civil disputes comes wrapped as window dressing. But if this is right, the question arises why we have courts to decide *any* such disputes; why not leave them all to arbitration? The answer is several-fold. First, arbitration is often more expensive to the parties than litigation, because they have to pay not only their lawyers but also the judges—that is, the arbitrators—and many disputants couldn't afford the added expense. Second, arbitrators have a tendency to "split the difference"—that is, to avoid awarding complete victory to either party. The reason is that the parties must

39. Allison Frankel, "FTC's Class Action Claims Investigation Could Be 'Bombshell' for Consumer Cases," *Reuters*, November 15, 2016, www.reuters.com/article/us-otc-ftc-idUSKBN13A2MU.

40. For some useful background, see William W. Park, "Explaining Arbitration Law," reprinted from *Defining Issues in International Arbitration* (Julio César Betancourt ed. 2016).

agree on arbitrators, and if risk averse they are more likely to agree to have their dispute resolved by an arbitrator who is, or arbitrators who are, moderate and therefore unlikely to impose a crushing loss on either party. A third reason, related to the second, is that when an agreement to arbitrate is in effect forced on one of the parties, as is often the case if one of the parties is a consumer and the other a seller, and the consumer signs without reflection a form in which he agrees to arbitrate any dispute arising from his purchase, the seller may decide to seek out an arbitrator known to favor sellers, while it may never occur to the consumer to seek out an arbitrator who favors consumers. The seller exploits his superior sophistication, much as when a seller inserts a forum-selection clause in a contract with a consumer—a practice that should probably be forbidden. Recall the discussion above regarding the much-criticized *Carnival Cruise Lines, Inc. v. Shute,* in which the Supreme Court upheld a forum-selection clause that being simply printed on the "contract" pages attached to a cruise ticket was unlikely to be noticed let alone challenged by any of the passengers.[41]

Back to arbitration: the loser in an arbitration may sometimes be able to obtain judicial review of the arbitration award; if so, a principal value of arbitration—the avoidance of tiers of review—may (depending on the time consumed by judicial review) be sacrificed.

The problem of exploitive arbitration is well illustrated in a recent *New York Times* article. I quote the first two paragraphs:

> The federal agency that controls more than $1 trillion in Medicare and Medicaid funding has moved to prevent nursing homes from forcing claims of elder abuse, sexual harassment and even wrongful death into the private system of justice known as arbitration.
>
> An agency within the Health and Human Services Department on Wednesday issued a rule that bars any nursing home or assisted-living facility that receives federal funding from requiring that its residents resolve any disputes in arbitration, instead of court.[42]

A challenging issue presented by arbitration is the scope of judicial review of an arbitrator's or arbitration panel's decision. I had occasion recently to con-

---

41. See Mullenix, note 27 above.

42. Jessica Silver-Greenberg and Michael Corkery, "No Arbitration, U.S. Agency Tells Nursing Homes: Day in Court Restored: New Rule Is Latest Effort to Rein in a Private System of Justice," *New York Times,* September 29, 2016, p. A1. See Myriam Gilles, "The Day Doctrine Died: Private Arbitration and the End of Law," 2016 *University of Illinois Law Review* 371 (2016), on how arbitration can freeze legal doctrine.

sider the issue[43] and, for the last time in this book, present the reader with the fruits of my consideration of the issue, though in severely abbreviated form. An insurance company named Bankers wanted to sublease its space in a building in Chicago and relocate to another building, and hired a real estate company named CBRE to arrange the two deals. CBRE agreed among other things to "answer [Bankers's] questions relating to the offers, counteroffers, notices, and contingencies." Bankers told CBRE that it wanted to net $7 million from its deals with its sublessee and the lessor of the space that Bankers would obtain to replace the space it would be vacating. The $7 million would be the consequence of the generous income that Bankers would receive from its sublease combined with Bankers's inexpensive relocation elsewhere. CBRE responded with a cost-benefit analysis that showed a net savings to Bankers from the deals of $6.9 million, close enough to $7 million to be acceptable to Bankers. The cost-benefit analysis turned out to be incorrect; the correct figure for the net benefit of the deals to Bankers was only $3.8 million.

The parties had agreed to arbitrate any dispute arising from their agreement, and Bankers sought arbitration and asked the arbitration panel to order CBRE to remit the lost $3.1 million ($6.9 million – $3.8 million) to it. The panel turned Bankers down. It acknowledged that the parties' deal had "obligated CBRE to answer questions accurately," but denied relief on the ground that the cost-benefit analysis had "included a disclaimer that provided that CBRE was not guaranteeing that there were not any errors contained in the CBA. Here, there was an arithmetic error, or an error in aligning the columns of numbers. The disclaimer clearly provides that CBRE was not responsible for errors."

Bankers challenged the arbitrators' decision in the district court, lost, and appealed to us. We reversed, on the ground that the arbitration panel had exceeded its authority. It was authorized to interpret only the contract, and the contract did not include any cost-benefit analyses. The panel's reliance on the disclaimer in the cost-benefit analysis that had erred to the tune of $3.1 million was therefore unjustified. The disclaimer was not part of the parties' deal; it was not negotiated by the parties but merely inserted by CBRE unilaterally.

But here's the kicker: an error by the arbitrator or arbitrators does not normally invalidate an arbitration award; otherwise such awards would have no greater immunity from judicial review than decisions by district judges or administrative agencies. The governing assumption is that by electing arbitration the parties have chosen to bypass the judicial system. And indeed there was a

---

43. See *Bankers Life & Casualty Ins. Co. v. CBRE, Inc.* (7th Cir. July 29, 2016).

time when commercial arbitration awards contained *no* reasoning, in order to avoid attracting the scrutiny of judges, who were fiercely hostile to arbitration, which they viewed (correctly) as a competitor of adjudication. But increasingly parties to arbitration insist on "reasoned awards," whereby "arbitrators' authority is limited by the unambiguous contract language," depriving them of "authority to ignore the plain language of the contract and to alter the agreement, as the ultimate award must be grounded on the parties' contract."[44] And so when "arbitrators ma[k]e an evident miscalculation of figures in arriving at the award, the reviewing court will modify or correct the award."[45] In the Bankers case the arbitrators made, or more precisely endorsed, a $3.1 million miscalculation, based on a document outside the parties' contract—the cost-benefit analysis. The arbitrators confused the cost-benefit analyses with the contract. That invalidated their award.

The nominal-damages puzzle. Suppose a person I'll call Mr. T commits a violation of tort law against Mr. V by negligently colliding with V's car, which is parked on the street outside V's house. Before V discovers the damage to his car, his house is struck by lightning and its front façade falls on the car, destroying it. As a result V has sustained no damages from T's tort, because, given the lightning strike, V would be no better off had T committed no tort. Nevertheless he can sue T and if he succeeds in proving T's negligence he'll be awarded nominal damages, usually just a dollar or two. The entitlement to nominal damages in such a case is unquestioned,[46] having the priceless advantage, in a backward-looking legal system, of a pedigree stretching back several hundred

44. *First Merit Realty Services, Inc. v. Amberly Square Apartments, L.P.,* 869 N.E. 2d 394, 399 (Ill. App. 2007). The substantive law governing the case was Illinois law.

45. *Shearson Lehman Brothers, Inc. v. Hedrich,* 639 N.E. 2d 228, 232 (Ill. App. 1994).

46. F. Andrew Hessick, "Standing, Injury in Fact, and Private Rights," 93 *Cornell Law Review* 275 (2011). Cf. *Carey v. Piphus,* 435 U.S. 247, 266 (1978), where we read:

> By making the deprivation of such rights [procedural due process, in *Carey*] actionable for nominal damages without proof of actual injury, the law recognizes the importance to organized society that those rights be scrupulously observed; but at the same time, it remains true to the principle that substantial damages should be awarded only to compensate actual injury or, in the case of exemplary or punitive damages, to deter or punish malicious deprivations of rights. Because the right to procedural due process is "absolute" in the sense that it does not depend upon the merits of a claimant's substantive assertions, and because of the importance to organized society that procedural due process be observed, we believe that the denial of procedural due process should be actionable for nominal damages without proof of actual injury. (citations omitted)

Notice that this could be read as limiting nominal damages to cases in which the plaintiff had been deprived of a constitutional right though with no resulting harm to him, but I still wouldn't understand the point of awarding essentially nothing damages rather than just excoriating the defendant for having violated the Constitution. The nominal-damages doctrine is pure clutter.

years.[47] Yet I don't get it. It's a case of *damnum absque injuria*—a wrong without an injury. Why waste judicial resources on such a case? The answer the courts give is that the plaintiff was wronged and the law recognizes that fact by awarding him nominal damages. But since the issue is recognition rather than compensation, why doesn't the judge dismiss the case with a simple notation that the case is being dismissed because the plaintiff incurred no damages from the defendant's act, wrongful though it was? Why mention damages when there are none?

But maybe I'm being too hasty. Professor Dobbs offers three reasons for awarding nominal damages in cases in which there is a wrong but not a harm.[48] The first is that "some suits might be brought much as declaratory judgment suits are brought, to determine a right. A money recovery would not be the real object in such a suit. . . . Relatedly a plaintiff might seek vindication of a right which is not economic in character and for which no substantial nonpecuniary award is available. A plaintiff might, for example, wish to establish a constitutional right, even if a large damage verdict is not possible." I don't find this explanation satisfactory. A jury verdict that awards nominal damages is not a small rather than a large damages award; functionally it is no damages award at all. If the plaintiff goes around bragging that he won his suit, and is asked what exactly he won and replies "one dollar," he'll be laughed at.

Professor Dobbs's second explanation for awarding nominal damages is that such an award "is, realistically, a rescue operation. The plaintiff has established a cause of action but has no damages or has been unable to prove the damages she does have. If that led to a judgment for the defendant, the plaintiff would normally be required to pay the court costs. To avoid that and put the cost burden on the defendant, nominal damages are awarded."[49] That's okay. But there is a simpler, straightforward alternative: skip the nominal damages and simply rule that the defendant must pay the court costs if the plaintiff prevails on the merits but can't prove that he incurred any monetizable harm from the defendant's wrongdoing.

The third explanation for nominal damages, similar to the second, is based on the fact that some federal statutes, such as the Civil Rights Fee Award Act,

47. See id., *passim;* Arthur G. Sedgwick and Joseph H. Beale, Jr., *A Treatise on the Measure of Damages,* chap. 3 (8th ed. 1891); J. G. Sutherland and John R. Berry, *A Treatise on the Law of Damages,* chap. 2 (2d ed. 1898). These treatises were published more than a century ago and provide examples from even earlier eras of cases in which nominal damages were awarded.

48. Dan N. Dobbs, *Law of Damages* § 3.3(2), pp. 295–296 (2d ed. 1993).

49. Id.

authorize awarding to the "prevailing" party in a suit attorneys' fees as well as court costs.[50] Although to be deemed the "prevailing party" it's not enough for the plaintiff to persuade a judge or a jury that his rights were violated,[51] he may be deemed the prevailing party if he obtains an award of nominal damages.[52] And some courts hold that while a plaintiff cannot be awarded punitive damages without obtaining actual damages,[53] nominal damages are "actual enough" to satisfy the actual-damages requirement and thus permit the imposition of punitive damages.[54]

The alternative to all these types of nominal-damages award, an alternative that would make the life of the law a little more livable, would be a rule that a party that establishes a violation of a legal right is entitled to an award of court costs and/or attorneys' fees, period—that is, even if he incurred no harm from the violation of his right, but in that event he would be entitled to no damages at all. Such a rule would reduce paperwork, and the time of judges and jurors, without disserving any deserving plaintiffs.

50. 42 U.S.C. § 1988(b).
51. *Hewitt v. Helms*, 482 U.S. 755 (1987); *Rhodes v. Stewart*, 488 U.S. 1 (1988).
52. See *Fast v. School District of City of Ladue*, 728 F.2d 1030 (8th Cir. 1984); Dobbs, note 48 above, § 3.10.
53. Id. § 3.11(10), pp. 512–514.
54. See, e.g., *Carey v. After the Gold Rush*, 715 P. 2d 803 (1986).

Conclusion

It is time for the destruction of error.
w. h. auden, 1929

Grant me an old man's frenzy,
Myself must I remake
Till I am Timon and Lear
Or that William Blake
Who beat upon the wall
Till truth obeyed his call.
w. b. yeats, 1938

Such is the character of human language,
that no word conveys to the mind, in
all situations, one single definite idea.
john marshall, 1819

————————

THE DOMINANT THEME OF THIS BOOK has been judicial standpattism—more precisely, the stubborn refusal of the judiciary to adapt to modernity. One sees it in the antiquated management methods used by the federal judiciary from bottom to top. And one observes that with notable but few exceptions the methodology and rhetoric employed by almost all federal judges, at whatever level in the judicial hierarchy, are stuck in the past. Their declared methods, their modes of expression, their heroes, their guiding lights are throwbacks to the eighteenth, nineteenth, and early twentieth centuries —sometimes to even earlier periods—to the thirteenth century, for example. The year 2015 was the eight-hundredth anniversary of Magna Carta (Latin for

"Great Charter"), widely misunderstood to this day—most notably by the multitude of lawyers who celebrated the anniversary—as a protection of ancient personal liberties. No, it was the result of a struggle within England's political class, in which the nobles wrested certain privileges from an unpopular king (John). The reference in Magna Carta to the judgment of one's peers, for example, was not a reference to trial by jury. In 1215 the jury trial as we know it did not exist, guilt often being determined by whether defendants survived ordeal by fire or by immersion in water. The reference to "one's peers" was meant to establish that nobles could not be tried by commoners—who might include judges appointed by the king.[1] Magna Carta eventually fell out of English law; in America it was superseded by the Constitution. If one wants (but why should one want?) a remote antecedent of modern law, ancient Athenian democracy is a surer bet than Magna Carta.

Fortunately, the judicial standpattism that I have been inveighing against throughout this book is to some extent a surface phenomenon, for it is apparent that judicial decisions, as distinct from the articulation of the decisions, are influenced to a great and often a decisive extent by the judges' political, ethical, emotional, and other lived history, including career and familial experience, and not—certainly not *just*—by doctrine and habit, let alone by history-book history. The tension is reconciled to the satisfaction of most judges by the adoption of a discourse of strict professional neutrality. Passion swirls unnoticed, hidden beneath a frozen surface of conventional legal language, driving decision not in every case but in many cases. Yet when the decision that may have been brewing for months is finally made public, it is seen to be clothed in a rhetoric of cold rationality.

Not the cold rationality of scientific discourse, however. Law is not a science. There is no architecture of legal thought that has only to be given a descriptive terminology to make law clear. We saw in the discussion of standards of appellate review in Chapter 3 that legal discourse is *systematically* unclear—the standards are nebulous, overlapping, and to a large degree meaningless. No one knows how to distinguish "clear and convincing" from "[not] arbitrary and capricious," or "abuse of discretion" from "procedural error," or "rational basis" from "we agree with the trial court (or agency), so: we affirm." And while constitutional and statutory "interpretation" seems, and is represented to be, a ma-

---

1. See Tom Ginsburg, "Stop Revering Magna Carta," *New York Times,* June 14, 2015, www.nytimes.com /2015/06/15/opinion/stop-revering-magna-carta.html?_r=0. My discussion in the text is a paraphrase of one paragraph of Ginsburg's very fine article.

jor activity of the judiciary, much so-called judicial interpretation is legislative in the sense of making law (as acknowledged by Justice Holmes in the *Missouri v. Holland* opinion, from which I quoted in Chapter 2), for often there is nothing to interpret. For example a right to burn the American flag to protest a government policy can't be derived from the free-speech clause of the First Amendment, but the judiciary's pretense is that it can be.

One reason that federal judges shy away from acknowledging their lawmaking role is that they don't want to offend members of Congress, who claim to be the only authorized federal legislators and have a degree of power over judges: judges want raises, which they can get only from a friendly Congress. Another reason is that judges don't want to be seen "dissing" the Constitution.

But I want to be more careful than I've been up to now about distinguishing between judicial "legislating" (better termed judicial "lawmaking," as explained earlier) and judicial "interpreting." I have treated interpretation largely as recovery of an intended meaning and legislation as the creation or adoption of a brand-new meaning unrelated to an originator's thoughts or intentions. But there is an intermediate position, sometimes also described as interpretation, in which the latecomer tries to *imagine* what the legislator or the constitution maker would have done had he foreseen the issue that has arisen. The ambulance example in the Introduction illustrates this point. Probably the way one decides whether the police officer was right to ticket the ambulance driver is to ask: had the authors and promulgators of the "no vehicles in the park ordinance" been asked whether they meant to include emergency vehicles in "vehicles" forbidden to enter the park, would they have answered "of course not"? Probably so; and this plausible conjecture can be thought a form of interpretation and proper guide to decision.

A notable example of interpretation so understood can be found in a book by the illustrious nineteenth-century German-American jurist and philosopher Francis Lieber. He offered the following example of what *he* called "interpretation":

> Suppose a housekeeper says to a domestic: "Fetch some soupmeat," accompanying the act with giving some money to the latter; he will be unable to execute the order without interpretation, however easy, and, consequently, rapid the performance of the process may be. Common sense and good faith tell the domestic, that the housekeeper's meaning was this: 1. He should go immediately, or as soon as his other occupations are

finished; or, if he be directed to do so in the evening, that he should go the next day at the usual hour; 2. that the money handed him by the housekeeper is intended to pay for the meat thus ordered, and not as a present to him; 3. that he should buy such meat and of such parts of the animal, as, to his knowledge, has commonly been used in the house he stays at, for making soups; 4. that he buy the best meat he can obtain, for a fair price; 5. that he go to that butcher who usually provides the family, with whom the domestic resides, with meat, or to some convenient stall, and not to any unnecessarily distant place; 6. that he return the rest of the money; 7. that he bring home the meat in good faith, neither adding any thing disagreeable nor injurious; 8. that he fetch the meat for the use of the family and not for himself. Suppose, on the other hand, the housekeeper, afraid of being misunderstood, had mentioned these eight specifications, she would not have obtained her object, if it were to exclude all *possibility* of misunderstanding. For, the various specifications would have required new ones. Where would be the end? We are constrained then, always, to leave a considerable part of our meaning to be found out by interpretation.[2]

The order given the domestic worker was too terse to be "interpreted," in the ordinary sense of reconstructing an original meaning from a statement. The worker nevertheless interpreted the statement correctly, as in the ambulance example, by imagining what the speaker would have said had she realized she had to offer an explanation.

Doubtless much of what I have described as judges' imposing meaning on ambiguous statutes and constitutional provisions could be restated as interpretation in Lieber's sense, which I consider a valid meaning of the word "interpretation." But not all. As Judge Easterbrook has pointed out, the meaning of a constitutional or statutory provision may simply be lost in the sands of time[3]— or have been inscrutable *ab initio*. When either condition prevails, a third mode of "interpretation" (in a very loose sense of the word) may come into play: interpretation as the assignment of a commonsense meaning to a consti-

---

2. *Legal and Political Hermeneutics or Principles of Interpretation and Construction in Law and Politics, With Remarks on Precedents and Authorities* 18 (3d ed. 1880) (emphasis in original). The Lieber approach is endorsed by Professor Nourse in her important book *Misreading Law. Misreading Democracy: Legislative Process and Statutory Interpretation for the 21st Century Lawyer* 183 (2016), and in William Eskridge, "Textualism, the Unknown Ideal?" 96 *Michigan Law Review* 1509, 1549 (1998).

3. See note 14 in Chapter 2 above and accompanying text.

tutional or statutory provision the original or intended meaning of which can no longer be discerned or recovered. That is a legitimate, if only loosely "interpretive," method of assigning statutory meaning if the net social benefits are positive; I will give an up-to-date example shortly.

And finally (though in my view illegitimately) there is what might be called "interpretation by rules." The so-called "canons of construction" are rules of interpretation of statutory and constitutional provisions. A book by Justice Scalia and Bryan Garner cited earlier in this book discusses seventy-five of the canons and approves fifty-seven of them.[4] An example is the series-qualifier canon: "when there is a straightforward, parallel construction that involves all nouns or verbs in a series, a prepositive or positive modifier normally applies to the entire series."[5] I barely know what that means; and while I know that some judges think that by application of such rules the meaning of a statutory provision can be determined, the reader will recall that in the Introduction to this book I expressed skepticism that judges' statutory interpretations are really the result of applying interpretive rules.

Anyway I don't believe in the rules, and thus can understand judicial "interpretation" in only the three senses suggested above. One is the extraction of an original meaning, and corresponds to interpretation in ordinary discourse; knowing English, I can usually determine swiftly and straightforwardly the meaning of a statement made to me in English (not always, because the statement may be garbled, grammatically intricate or inaccurate, obtuse, or complex beyond my ability to understand). The second form of interpretation, illustrated by Lieber's analysis and also by the ambulance example, is discernment of meaning by understanding the context of a statement. The statement is incomplete, but if the context is understood, the meaning of the statement can, as in those examples, be discerned. And finally and most controversially, interpretation can be understood as giving a fresh meaning to a statement (which can be a constitutional or statutory text)—a meaning that gives the statement life and utility today.

That last form of interpretation is illustrated by a case decided recently in my court, on April 4, 2017, called *Hively v. Ivy Tech Community College* (7th Cir. No. 15-1720). The case had been brought by a woman who claimed she'd been fired because she's a lesbian. She argued that firing her on that ground violated a provision of Title VII of the Civil Rights Act of 1964 that forbids an employer

4. Antonin Scalia and Bryan A. Garner, *Reading Law: The Interpretation of Legal Texts* 147 (2012).
5. Id. at 147.

"to fail or refuse to hire or to discharge any individual, or otherwise to dis-criminate against any individual with respect to his compensation, terms, con-ditions, or privileges of employment, because of such individual's race, color, religion, *sex,* or national origin."[6] The argument that firing a woman on account of her being a lesbian does *not* violate Title VII is that the term "sex" in the stat-ute means man or woman and a lesbian is a woman, so if she's fired because she's a lesbian she's not being fired for being a woman.

That is doubtless what the word meant to most Americans, including the members of Congress who voted for the law, in 1964; and a diehard "original-ist" would argue that what was believed in 1964 defines the scope of the statute, the meaning of which will therefore remain unchanged until changed by Con-gress's amending or replacing the statute. But as should be clear from the ear-lier discussions of statutory and constitutional interpretation in this book, that is a misunderstanding of interpretation as actually practiced by the Supreme Court and the other courts in this country. Statutes and constitutional provi-sions frequently are interpreted on the basis of present need and understand-ing rather than original meaning. Take the Sherman Antitrust Act, enacted in 1890. As remarked earlier, today it is interpreted on the basis of modern economic understandings of competition, monopolization, and cartelization. Those understandings did not exist in 1890.

Hively's lawyer gave us a neat sarcastic summation of the employer's case: "You can't discriminate against a woman because she rides a Harley, had Bears tickets or has tattoos, but you can if she's lesbian."[7]

And remember Justice Scalia's vote to hold that burning the American flag as a political protest is protected by the free-speech clause of the First Amend-ment, provided that it's your flag and is not burned in circumstances in which the fire might spread? Burning a flag is not speech in the ordinary sense, and there is no indication that the framers or the ratifiers of the First Amendment thought they were using the word "speech" to include flag burning, or other nonverbal methods of communicating. Note too the oddity of Justice Gins-burg's excoriation of the two football players for kneeling on the field during the playing of The Star-Spangled Banner. That was a lot more civilized form of "speech" than burning the American flag.[8]

6. 42 U.S.C. § 2000e-2(a)(1) (emphasis added).
7. Id.
8. On verbal versus nonverbal communication, see the interesting article by J. Gregory Sidak, "Some Economics of Flag Burning and Jimi Hendrix," *The Criterion: Journal on Innovation* vol. 1, p. 563 (2016).

Or consider—another example from earlier in this book—the Supreme Court's holding that the Fourth Amendment requires the issuance of a warrant as a precondition for searching a person's home or arresting him in his home. In fact there is nothing in the amendment about requiring a warrant ever. All that the amendment does so far as warrants are concerned is forbid general warrants and warrants that are vague or issued without probable cause. And finally think of how the term "cruel and unusual punishments" has morphed over time. Or think how the Second Amendment, which is about arming the members of the state militias (now the National Guard), has been interpreted to confer gun rights on private citizens.

So over and over again, old statutes, old constitutional provisions, are given new meaning, as explained so eloquently by Holmes in the *Missouri* case. And so should discrimination on grounds of "sex" in Title VII, a statute enacted more than a half century ago, be given a new, a broader, meaning? Nothing has changed more in that period than attitudes toward sex. The year 1964 was more than a decade before Richard Raskind underwent male-to-female sex reassignment surgery and took the name Renée Richards. In those days, and in some states until the *Obergefell* decision, male homosexuals were not allowed to marry each other; nor were lesbians. If in those days an employer fired a lesbian because he didn't like lesbians, he was not firing her because she was a woman (he would not have fired her had she not been a lesbian), and so he was not discriminating on the basis of sex. Today "sex" has a broader meaning than the genitalia you're born with. In *Baskin v. Bogan*[9] my court, anticipating *Obergefell* by invalidating statutes in Indiana and Wisconsin that forbade same-sex marriage, discussed at length whether homosexual preference (including therefore lesbianism) is innate or chosen, and found that the scientific literature strongly supports the proposition that it is innate, whether biological or a response to events in early childhood, and in either event not a choice like deciding how to dress.[10] The position of a woman discriminated against on account of being a lesbian is thus closely analogous to a woman's being discriminated against on account of being a woman. That woman didn't choose to be a woman; the lesbian didn't choose to be a lesbian. Their identities as woman or lesbian (lesbian being both) are innate, and I can't understand why firing a lesbian because she's a lesbian should be regarded as any less a form of sex discrimination than firing a woman because she's a woman.

9. 766 F.3d 648 (7th Cir. 2014).
10. See id. at 657–658.

Life is easier for heterosexuals, though not because we're a nobler class of human beings. In fact homosexuals (and bisexuals, who have both homosexual and heterosexual preferences) tend to have higher IQs than heteros, have made many outstanding intellectual and cultural contributions to society (think for example of Tchaikovsky, Walt Whitman, Oscar Wilde, Thomas Mann, Leonard Bernstein, Jane Addams, Alec Guinness, Marlene Dietrich, Alan Turing, Bayard Rustin, James Baldwin, and Tammy Baldwin), commit fewer crimes than heteros, and play an essential role, in this country at any rate, as adopters of children from foster homes—another point emphasized in our *Baskin* decision.[11] They should be entitled to the same freedom from employment discrimination as any other minority that has biological traits different from those found in the majority. Nothing in the language of Title VII, and nothing in an interpretation updated to the present, precludes relief in a case such as *Hively*.

(Timothy Terrell mentions "pragmatism" in statutory interpretation and attributes it to "the judiciary's general interest—shared by all good citizens—in contributing productively to the common good,"[12] thus taking an approach similar to the one I take in my concurring opinion in the *Hively* case.)

Yet this last sense of "interpretation" that I've been discussing, the reparative sense—the statutory or legislative provision, damaged by time, requires amending by the judges called on to "interpret" the provision (to "apply" it, would be more accurate)—clashes with the persisting pretense that judges do not legislate.[13] The pretense causes them to do handsprings in their statutory opinions in order to disclaim a creative role, while respect for conventional though inaccurate understandings of the Constitution causes them to do further handsprings in constitutional cases, pretending to be interpreting when they are creating.

On page 126 I noted that Judge Neil M. Gorsuch calls himself an originalist and may be one in light of his statement in an opinion of his that I quoted on that page that "ours [he means federal judges, including Supreme Court Justices] is the job of interpreting the Constitution. And that document isn't some

11. See 766 F.3d at 654–663, 671.

12. Timothy P. Terrell, *The Dimensions of Legal Reasoning: Developing Analytical Acuity from Law School to Law Practice* chap. 10: "The Never-Ending Disagreement over Statutory Interpretation: The Primacy of Subtext," 252 (2016).

13. A slight variant—too slight I think to warrant separate consideration—is James Madison's concept of "liquidation": "All new laws, though penned with the greatest technical skill, and passed on the fullest and most mature deliberation, are considered as more or less obscure and equivocal, until their meaning be liquidated and ascertained by a series of particular discussions and adjudications." *The Federalist* No. 37, at 236 (Jacob E. Cooke ed. 1961). It is another example of the judges' reparative role in the legislative process.

inkblot on which litigants may project their hopes and dreams for a new and perfected tort law, but a carefully drafted text judges are charged with applying according to its original public meaning. If a party wishes to claim a constitutional right, it is incumbent on him to tell us where it lies, not to assume or stipulate with the other side that it lies, not to assume or stipulate with the other side that it must be in there *somewhere*."[14]

Gorsuch is also the author of what has become a notorious dissent that is notably incongruous with my court's decision in *Hively* and the theory of interpretation that it illustrates. *TransAm Trucking, Inc. v. Administrative Review Board, United States Department of Labor*[15] was a suit by a trucking company against the Department of Labor, which had ruled that the company had unlawfully fired one of its truck drivers, a man named Maddin, for abandoning his trailer. He was driving his truck, to which a trailer was attached, in extremely inclement winter weather. It was so cold that the brakes on the trailer froze, stranding him because, as both the majority and dissenting parties appear to have agreed, the brakes being "locked in," the trailer could no longer be dragged by the truck. He notified the company, which promised to send a repair truck to fix the brakes. But hours passed without the arrival of the repair truck, the temperature inside the truck fell to seven degrees below zero, and fearing that he'd freeze to death Maddin detached the trailer and drove the truck to safety.

It seemed obvious to the government and to the majority of the appellate panel, and seems obvious to me as well, that to fire Maddin for refusing to allow himself to freeze to death rather than abandon the trailer would have been unjustified; it could not have been deemed permissible conduct by an employer, given the provision of the Surface Transportation Assistance Act that makes it unlawful for an employer to discharge an employee who "refuses to operate a vehicle because . . . the employee has a reasonable apprehension of serious injury to the employee or the public because of the vehicle's hazardous safety or security condition."[16] Judge Gorsuch argued in dissent, however, that Maddin hadn't been fired for refusing to operate his vehicle, but for refusing to operate it in the way the employer desired, namely by sitting tight until help came, though help might have come too late. Gorsuch's pièce de résistance was

---

14. *Cordova v. City of Albuquerque*, 816 F.3d 645, 661 (10th Cir. 2016) (concurring opinion) (emphasis in original).

15. 833 F.3d 1206 (10th Cir. 2016).

16. 49 U.S.C. § 31105(a)(1)(B)(ii).

that "there is simply no law anyone has pointed us to giving employees the right to operate their vehicles in ways their employees forbid. . . . When the statute is plain it simply isn't our business to appeal to legislative intentions."[17]

This kind of literalism is just what my court rejected in *Hively*, and what the majority rejected in the *TransAm Trucking* case. In neither case had the statute anticipated the exact harm that ensued; in both cases a flexible interpretation was required to give the statutes, which are not recent (Title VII was enacted in 1964, STAA in 1982), continued effectiveness.

One can at least understand the motives for the type of contortion engaged in by Judge Gorsuch in the *TransAm Trucking* case. What is difficult to understand is the felt need of the judiciary (and of the legal profession in general) to embrace meaningless jargon (typified by the standards of appellate review, all of which except *de novo* review of rulings on pure issues of law could be discarded without being missed), and, silliest of all, complex rules of citation—the domain of the *Bluebook*, a monstrosity. The profession, including its judges, is no more able to shake off the *Bluebook* than to shake off the standards of appellate review, or legislating in the guise of interpreting, or antiquated trial procedures, or obsolete methods of office management ("call me 'Judge'"; "what goes on in chambers stays in chambers"), or ghastly jargon culminating in that most absurd of legal clichés, "actual innocence." ("Judge, I may not be *actually* innocent, but I am innocent—really.")

But if I'm right that the superstructure of doctrine and scholarship that dominates judicial and academic discussion of statutory interpretation is largely superfluous to an understanding of what judges do when they "interpret" statutes, the question arises why the superstructure has been erected and remains upright.[18] There are multiple answers. One is that judges tend to tread cautiously when dealing with legislatures, because legislatures—Congress, if one is speaking of federal judges—have considerable power over judges with respect to appointment, removal, salary, and tenure. Legislators do not bridle at common law, because, though it is judge-made "legislation" in a realistic sense, it is subject to legislative revision. What they don't cotton to is aggressive judicial interpretation of their handiwork. They are likely to consider it an encroachment on legislative prerogatives, thus diminishing legislators' power. So to avoid ruffled feathers, judges pretend when they interpret a statute to

17. See note 15 above, at 1216.

18. The discussion of statutory interpretation that follows borrows from my "Comment on Professor Gluck's 'Imperfect Statutes, Imperfect Courts,'" 129 *Harvard Law Review* 11 (2015).

merely be articulating what the legislature intended but may have expressed imperfectly.

Another cause of the judicial pretense (for I think it is largely pretense) of judicial deference to Congress is a desire of judges to hide behind the "law"— "the law made me do it" might be a judicial motto. Many judges would be profoundly uncomfortable having to explain that they had "interpreted" a statute in a particular way because an issue had arisen that the legislators had not envisaged when they enacted the statute and so the judges resolved it in what they thought a sensible way that was at least roughly congruent with what the statute seemed to be concerned with. In short, judges prefer for reasons of self-protection to be thought of as agents rather than as principals.

Another obstacle to frank statutory interpretation that judges are reluctant to acknowledge is that a statute is the output of a group rather than of an individual. The legislators who voted for the statute may not have agreed on its scope of application, so that if a new and unforeseen issue within the statute's semantic scope arises it may be impossible to say how the legislature would have resolved it had they foreseen it. But the judges still have to decide, though the decision cannot be "interpretive" in a meaningful sense.

Regarding judicial review of statutory issues, there are, as counterparts to the confusing medley of standards of review, the multiple canons of statutory construction and other supposed aids to interpretation. Yet if one considers the interpretation of difficult literary and historical texts (the Bible for example), one discovers that it's done by critics and scholars without the aid of a system of rules. For interpretation is a natural process; we do it any time we hear someone speak our language and any time we read anything in our language (or in another language that we understand). Interpretation can be difficult but it isn't made easier by bringing a formal apparatus to bear; it is made easier by linguistic competence and familiarity with the texts to be interpreted. And cases must be decided even if interpretation is impossible and the judges must bluff their way to a decision—which is often.

Confronted with a novel issue to resolve, one often will have an intuitive, even an unconscious, response; and while that response may be modified or even abandoned as one gathers evidence bearing on the issue, it often will still have an impact, sometimes a decisive impact, on one's final decision. And that is true in judging. Judging as I keep saying is not a hard science, a soft science, or any kind of science; law is not a scientific discipline even to the extent that the social sciences are scientific. And the result is that judges' priors, which include but are not exhausted by the judges' political or ideological leanings, are bound to influence many of their decisions. This need not be a bad thing, because their priors will often be fruits of experience and insight. My point is only that the more difficult it is to gather evidence to challenge one's priors, the more likely the priors are to determine the outcome of a case. Because interpretation is so natural, instinctive, and unsystematized an activity, notably in law, priors, including political or ideological ones, are bound to influence many decisions involving the application of statutes. Nothing is going to change that.

So the federal judiciary needs to straighten out its understanding of statutory interpretation. It needs a lot else in the way of reform. (But by now you know that.) It needs to shake off the complacency expressed by Dean David Levi of the Duke Law School (as he then was; on May 17, 2017, he is to be installed as the president of the American Law Institute) when he said that "because of the training provided by our law schools, and by the experience of practice, we have a Bar of great skill and character, a Bar that has a tradition of democratic leadership that continues to inspire. . . . There is no wall between the academy and the profession or between the Bar and the judiciary."[19] I suppose that's the sort of thing that deans are expected to say; we saw examples of tongue-in-cheek "dean speak" in Chapter 2 by the Harvard Law School dean (Martha Minow) and her predecessor (Justice Kagan). But let's be clear that it's false—the wall that Levi denies still stands; the democratic leadership he extols does not exist and never has. His remarks are unhelpfully self-congratulatory. May bragging about our legal system cease, and attention shift to improving the system.

The bragging is a reminder of the legal system's lack of candor. Lawyers are advocates; one can't expect candor from them. Law school deans today, like academic administrators generally, are promoters of their schools. That is the sense in which we should take Dean Levi's comment, but also Dean Minow's exaggerated and, I am guessing, insincere encomium of Justice Scalia that I quoted in Chapter 2. And as for law professors as distinct from deans, think back to the liberal Harvard professors who joined Minow in an encomium frenzy for Scalia. The legal system, even at its highest levels, is permeated by a casual attitude toward truth, as if the advocacy culture of practicing lawyers had penetrated to the profession's judicial and academic branches—as to a degree it has done, with the result that the sincerity of statements by lawyers,

---

19. David F. Levi, "From Judge to Dean: Reflections on the Bench and the Academy," 70 *Louisiana Law Review* 913, 922 (2010).

judges, and law professors is often in question. That's a problem worth a good deal more attention than it is receiving, or has ever received. Complacent profession: wake up!

The federal judiciary needs shaking up along a number of other axes as well as those I've been discussing. It needs, as I discussed at some length in the Introduction, much better management by judges of their small staffs, by chief judges of their courts, and by the Supreme Court. It needs better judicial appointments as well, but this means that better methods of evaluating judges are needed than simply counting the number of citations to a judge's opinions, or the number of opinions, or the frequency with which the judge is affirmed and reversed.

The judiciary needs to rid itself and its staff of style guides. Judges need to learn to write—to learn by writing, but also by reading great literature. They need to learn modern managerial techniques in order to get the most out of their staffs. They need to jettison the standards of appellate review and the levels of scrutiny, to forget Latin[20] and eschew legal jargon, to abandon the linguistic canons of construction, such as *noscitur a sociis*—general words that follow specific words in a statute should be interpreted to include only things of the same "class" as the things denoted by the specific words. The need for such a rule presupposes a real intellectual deficiency on the part of lawyers and judges. For suppose you ask a bartender for a Tom Collins and he hands you a glass of skimmed milk. Would you say he was a dope or a jokester, or that he had forgotten *noscitur a sociis*? The linguistic canons are already the unconscious possessions of normal speakers of the English language. The policy canons are different—they are judicial legislation. The rule of lenity for example cannot be attributed to Congress, which has not enacted such a rule because it does not believe in lenity. Nor do most judges.

The judiciary needs to become comfortable with science and math and technology and also, so it can learn to write, literature, as well as with such social sciences as psychology, sociology, and criminology (which is a branch of psychology and sociology with an admixture of economics—the one social sci-

---

20. I fear this is another lost cause; a recent article recounts the passionate embrace of Latinized legal phrases by federal judges and Justices. Steven Rinehart, "Regula Pro Lege, Si Deficit Lex: The Latin Sapience of High Judges," *Federal Lawyer*, September 2016, p. 52. I'm embarrassed to find myself included among these Latin lovers, see id. at 54—but (whew!) for only one phrase: *de minimis non curat lex* ("the law does not concern itself with trifles"). In truth I prefer it to its normal English translation—just given—which strikes me as pompous. *"Minimis"* just means small things, for which "trifles" is a correct translation but a better one would be unimportant things, and the best translation of the entire phrase would be "the law does not take notice of unimportant things."

ence with which the federal judiciary has to its credit become comfortable). It needs a large dose of common sense. It needs better management, which means it needs a Chief Justice of the United States who can manage (not alone of course) the *entire* federal judiciary and incidentally lay off amateurish historical speculation (leave the Aztecs and the Carthaginians and the Kalahari Bushmen and the Han Chinese in peace, *please,* Chief Justice Roberts). It needs a commitment to truthfulness. It needs simplification of the rules of procedure and evidence. It does *not,* however, need conservative Chief Justices (there's been no liberal Chief Justice since Warren, who retired in 1969—forty-seven years ago), who stack the Advisory Committee on Civil Rules and the Committee on Rules of Practice and Procedure with conservatives sympathetic to the desire of big business to alter the rules to make pretrial discovery more difficult for plaintiffs' lawyers.[21]

The federal judiciary needs lots of help from the law schools, and there are encouraging signs that it is at last getting a little more than in the recent past. I am told of a teacher at one of the leading law schools who does not insist on the students' mastering the *Bluebook,* including its opaque abbreviations that I criticized earlier in this book, or their forswearing the italicization of periods, and who does not require that citations do more than enable a reader to find the cited materials. The law schools need to hire more teachers who have practical legal experience. They need to take over management of the law reviews (which need by the way to be winnowed—there are 980 of them![22]) and the moot courts. They need to teach students how to write jargon-free legal documents, they need to recognize that courses like civil procedure and evidence should be taught not out of the rule books but as simulations of trial and pretrial proceedings, and they need to provide relevant continuing education to judges. A neglected advantage of hiring law professors from the practice of law is not only that they can make legal education more realistic than professors who lack practical experience but also that, especially if they are litigators, they are likely to have a keener insight into the judicial mentality and to be able to convey their insight to students, thereby helping to prepare the students for jobs as law clerks, as practicing lawyers whether in private practice, in government service, as in-house corporate counsel, and (some of them, eventually) as judges. The law schools nowadays seem to think that lawyers who have actually

---

21. See Elizabeth Thornburg, "Cognitive Bias, the 'Band of Experts,' and the Anti-Litigation Narrative," 65 *De Paul Law Review* 755 (2016).

22. See Thomas W. Merrill, "The Digital Revolution and the Future of Law Reviews," 99 *Marquette Law Review* 1101 (2016).

practiced law are thereby spoiled for academia. Yet I was a practicing lawyer for six years before I became a law professor, and my practical experience was an asset, not a liability, in my academic career.

I give up on judicial candor. But an alternative that may be feasible is what I'll call authenticity and Jean-Paul Sartre called "engagement" (*engagée* in French). By that he meant accepting responsibility for the political consequences of one's actions, and, if one was a writer (a journalist, a novelist, or—I add—a judge), committing oneself to socially responsible writing *(littérature engagée)*. Candor taken to an extreme means spouting whatever occupies your mind at the moment, and is not a feasible recipe for a judge, or probably for anyone. But engagement in the Sartrean sense should be both a feasible and a worthy ideal for a judge to strive for. It implies among other things that judges should write their own opinions, not edit law clerks' drafts, and should endeavor (though this will not always be feasible) to purge from their opinions anything they do not believe, however orthodox and expected, normal but stale.

I have criticized the judiciary for verbosity, particularly but not only with reference to the standards of review. But until very recently I was unaware that the judiciary (or at least the federal judiciary, as I do not know whether any of the state judiciaries are similarly afflicted) has a vice that is almost the opposite of verbosity—namely prissiness, or, more precisely, federal judicial prissiness. I became aware of this vice in August 2016 when I received an email from a journalist who said she was writing an article on profanity in judicial opinions, and asked me what my view of the matter was.[23] I took her to be asking whether I made profane remarks in my opinions—for example, calling a party's lawyer, or the party himself or herself, a moron. I replied truthfully that I'd never done anything like that in a judicial opinion or oral argument or other public venue. She responded that there was in fact profanity in some of my judicial opinions. She cited four opinions of mine, of which a typical one was *FAL-Meridian, Inc. v. Department of Health & Human Services.*[24] The opinion upheld an order by HHS penalizing a nursing home for negligence resulting in the death of one of its patients, an insane woman referred to only as "B." Here is the principal "profane" passage in the opinion:

23. The article has now been published: see Zoe Tillman, "In Quoting Profanity, Some Judges Give a F#%&. Others Don't," *Law.Com*, August 25, 2016, www.law.com/sites/almstaff/2016/08/25/in-quoting-profanity-some-judges-give-a-f-others-dont/?slreturn=20160725173640. The article makes the absence of a consensus on the issue clear.

24. 604 F.3d 445 (7th Cir. 2010).

B yelled [to a member of the institution's staff], "Go to hell bitch. I remember you and you are wrong." One hour later B was caught drinking
from the water fountain and a nurse asked her to stop and again reminded her of the danger that forbade her to have food or water in her
mouth and B yelled "You are a fucking liar and fuck the doctor too." She
then locked herself in a bathroom and when she emerged it was apparent
that she had been drinking out of the sink. A nurse asked her not to lock
herself in the bathroom. B laughed.

I could not see any impropriety in my including this material in my opinion,
as B's bizarre behavior (which ended in her death) was central to the legal issues in the case. I did think that my concealing her identity for the sake of privacy appropriate, just as the names of children who are victims of sexual mo-
lestation are typically omitted from judicial opinions, as are trade secrets and
other sensitive business information. But I could and can think of no argument
for omitting the description of an unnamed woman's behavior, and this led
me to reply to the journalist rather rudely, as follows: "With all due respect, I
think you're seriously confused. It is one thing for a judge to use profanity—to
call the defendant an asshole, for example. It is another thing for a judge to
quote profanity used by a party or witness, if the profanity is relevant to the
case. That kind of quotation is routine and unexceptionable. The idea that the
judge should search for an anodyne synonym and substitute it for the profanity
is absurd."
    She responded, I am sure truthfully, that many judges disagree, and take
pains to conceal or disguise profane (which often means obscene) language in
their opinions. I was surprised to hear this; I couldn't imagine a judge omitting
from an opinion profanity that was material to the case, out of squeamishness
or fear of a hostile reaction by readers. Yet she even cited a Supreme Court
opinion—*FCC v. Fox Television Stations, Inc.*[25]—in which we learn that "the
singer Cher exclaimed during an unscripted acceptance speech: 'I've also had
my critics for the last 40 years saying that I was on my way out every year.
Right. So f*** 'em.' . . . Fox broadcast the Billboard Music Awards again in 2003.
There, a person named Nicole Richie made the following unscripted remark
while presenting an award: 'Have you ever tried to get cow s*** out of a Prada
purse? It's not so f***ing simple.'" What strikes me as absurd about this passage

25. 132 S. Ct. 2307, 2314 (2012).

in the *Fox Television* opinion is the asterisks, as every reader would understand that the asterisked words are "fuck," "shit," and "fucking." There doubtless are still a few innocents in this country who would be shocked to see such words in print, but they are not the people who read judicial opinions. Incidentally, on the same page of its opinion the Supreme Court quoted the FCC as having said that the word ["fuck"] was "one of the most vulgar, graphic and explicit descriptions of sexual activity in the English language" and "any use of that word or a variation, in any context, inherently has a sexual connotation." Nonsense! In such common phrases as "fuck you" and "go fuck yourself" and "it's a fuckin' shame" and "fuckin' asshole" the word "fuck" or "fucking" has no sexual connotation at all. Indeed it rarely does. Shame on the Supreme Court and the FCC for displaying such prissiness.[26]

Worse than the asterisks and the other disguises of obscene words in judicial opinions is the substitution by some judges of "[racial epithet]" for the actual racial epithet in a racial discrimination case. This is a worse mutilation of the opinion than the asterisked profanities because racial epithets vary a great deal in their hatefulness, and without knowing what the racial epithet, or epithets, in a particular case is, the reader of the judicial opinion will have difficulty understanding the *seriousness* of the claim of discrimination.

Moving on: The federal judiciary can do without prissiness, but it can't do without good financial management, at present lacking. It's a scandal that there is no cost of living differential among the different districts and circuits, even though the cost of living varies greatly across our vast country. The judiciary needs to dispel another scandal as well—the senseless pay differences between tiers of federal judges. At present the annual salary of the Chief Justice of the United States is $263,300, which is $11,500 more than the other Justices are paid. Circuit judges—my tier—are each paid $217,600, and district judges $205,100. Chief Justice Roberts is therefore paid 28.38 percent more than a district judge. But why? As one moves up the judicial ladder one doesn't work harder (probably doesn't work as hard, on average), and one's power, which is a form of compensation highly valued by ambitious people, increases significantly, along with opportunities for extracurricular activities that may be lucrative (think of Justice Sotomayor's autobiography, or the late Justice Scalia's coauthorship with Bryan Garner of a major treatise on statutory adjudication)—including boondoggles. The salary differences understate the real compensation differences between the levels. I don't know what the federal judicial

26. In a very general sense, this prissiness is of a piece with the Court's refusal to allow its proceedings to be televised.

salary should be, but I can't think of a good reason why it shouldn't be uniform across the ranks.[27]

But above all, the judiciary needs to come to grips with modernity—to think present and future, not just past. To heed Nietzsche's warning against letting the dead bury the living, and T. S. Eliot's command "Not fare well,/ But fare forward, voyagers!" I'm not optimistic, though. The legal profession's resistance to change is massive and ingrained. Even discarding the preposterous *Bluebook* is unthinkable; even stopping the insistence on romanizing italicized periods; even giving up gibberish phrases like "actual innocence." We're reliving *Invasion of the Body Snatchers,* the great 1956 horror movie (greatly superior to the 1978 version) that ends with the majority of the residents in a California town transformed into extraterrestrials—the mindless "pod people"—and the rest unmoved by the shouted warnings of Dr. Miles J. Bennell, the movie's lone hero. I am his descendant in the following sense. I'm a pretty well-known judge; my skepticism about much of the conventional apparatus of legal analysis and judicial decision making is well known; but that skepticism is very largely ignored—not rebutted, ignored—especially the aspects of it that I believe irrefutable, such as that the *Bluebook* must go, along with the refusal to tolerate the italicized period and the insistence by judges that they be called "Judge" by their law clerks rather than "Jack," or "Sally" or whatever else they're called by their friends and colleagues, and that the spittoons behind the bench in the Supreme Court's courtroom should go, along with a lot of other antique silliness. Criticisms by me that seem irrefutable are seemingly not even noticed,[28] as if I were exhibiting paintings to a blind man or singing to a deaf one—indeed as if I were warning the citizenry about an invasion by extraterrestrial body snatchers.

But that's too dark (or maybe too hysterical) a note on which to conclude. I want to top off my criticisms of the federal judiciary by asking to what extent the federal judiciary despite its abundant flaws meets the essential needs of a

---

27. There are of course many federal judicial officers besides the three tiers of Article III judges: law clerks and staff attorneys, other staff, magistrate judges, bankruptcy judges, and adjudicative officers (such as administrative law judges) in federal agencies. I don't know what a proper salary structure embracing the entire federal adjudicative apparatus would look like.

28. Of course that's not always true. There are the criticisms of my bookstore talk, which I mentioned at the end of Chapter 2. I've sometimes received hate mail, of which the outstanding example was a postcard from a man in California who said that if my decision in *Baskin* (the same-sex marriage case) was correct, it would mean that he could if he wanted dig up his grandmother's grave and have sex with her corpse.

national court system. I will break down my discussion into eight parts, each concerned with a different need that a judiciary should be expected to satisfy: selection, independence, rule of law, finality, structure, management, understanding and training, compensation, and looking ahead, to the future. I will grade each part (I was after all a full-time law professor for a number of years).

Selection. There is careful screening of candidates for federal judgeships, but it is screening for adequacy rather than for distinction. Many federal judges are more than adequate, but considering how few federal judges there are (about one thousand) relative to the American lawyer population (well in excess of a million), a higher threshold for appointment would yield a significantly higher average quality. The underlying problem is that the President who nominates and the Senators who confirm a prospective federal judge are more concerned with the political consequences of an appointment than with the appointee's sheer ability. So I'll give "selection" of federal judges a grade of B.

Independence. We don't want judges to show gratitude for their appointment by kowtowing to the appointing politicians, and we don't want politicians to exert pressure on judges to decide cases in a way that will enhance the political influence or career prospects of the politicians. And this is a desideratum that I think is generally achieved, as I suggested in the Introduction. A problem arises however when the judge is angling for promotion—from district judge to court of appeals judge, or from court of appeals judge to Supreme Court Justice. The judge's promotion will depend on the goodwill of the President and the Senate, and if he is very ambitious this dependence may influence his judicial behavior.

Napoleon sought to incentivize the soldiers of the *Grande Armée* by saying that "every French soldier carries a marshal's baton in his knapsack." But I think that only a distinct minority (but not a negligible minority) of federal judges think they carry a certificate of appointment as a Justice of the Supreme Court in their attaché case, so I give the federal judiciary a grade of A– on judicial independence.

Rule of law. Recall that Aristotle taught and the federal judicial oath states that judges shall treat the parties to litigation before them as representative parties, abstracting from their wealth, social standing, and other indicia of wealth, influence, or poverty; in the language of the federal judicial oath judges shall decide cases "without respect to persons." My experience has been that federal judges honor this principle without exception. I give them (us) an A on this element of judicial structure.

Finality. As also noted earlier in the book, finality is essential in order to avoid courts' becoming swamped with cases, and therefore the entry of a final judgment should preclude relitigation, though with the important exception discussed in the Epilogue that follows this Conclusion of postconviction remedies, such as habeas corpus for those rare criminal cases in which after conviction the defendant is able to present definite proof of innocence, or when a serious procedural bobble in the initial proceeding is discovered that dispels confidence that the trial judge or jury made a correct determination of guilt. Because of the resistance put up by a number of federal judges to reopening criminal cases, I give the federal judiciary only a B grade for this aspect of judicial performance.

Structure. As explored in earlier chapters, the federal judiciary has a definite structure: three Article III tiers (district courts, courts of appeals, and the Supreme Court) and below them roughly three tiers of Article I judicial officers: magistrate judges, bankruptcy judges, and administrative law judges and other adjudicators in federal agencies. And of course there are secretaries to the judges, plus law clerks and interns and externs. Besides this adjudicative structure, however, there is an administrative structure comprising the Administrative Office of the U.S. Courts, the Federal Judicial Center, the U.S. Probation and Pretrial Services System, the U.S. Marshals Service, and the U.S. Judicial Conference together with a number of committees that report to it; and there are also the numerous federal courts and courthouses and their staffs. The judges' staffs, though on average poorly managed (see next section, and recall the discussion of this problem in the Introduction to this book), are of high average quality, as are the probation officers and the marshals. I'm somewhat dubious about the other components, though I won't try to explain my dubiety in this book, beyond noting that the mediocre judicial staff management is a failure of structure. On balance I give the federal judiciary a grade of only B for structure.

Management. As explained in the Introduction, judges' management of their tiny staffs is seriously impaired by the judges' failure to implement modern managerial methods. This is a result of the judicial stodginess that I've been criticizing throughout this book, but it is abetted by the failure of the Federal

Judicial Center and of the chief judges of the district and circuit courts, and of the Chief Justice, to help the rest of the federal judges improve their managerial skills and methods. The chief judges do little to prevent lengthy delays by the judges of their courts to render decisions. Some district judges allow (and are allowed by their chief judges to allow) their cases to drag on interminably, defending their procrastination by reference to a heavy caseload, though they could avoid long delays simply by setting reasonable deadlines for each stage of a case. Some court of appeals judges, though they usually have a lighter caseload than district judges, issue decisions a year or two years or even (in one case I know of) four years after oral argument, which is inexcusable. Interminable delay is not a problem in the Supreme Court, because with the rare exception of a case held over to the next term of Court all its cases are decided within no more than nine months of when they were argued; the Court's term begins in October and ends at the end of June. But overall I give the federal judiciary only a grade of C for management.

Understanding and training. How well do federal judges understand their job? Not well enough. They know the rules, the jargon. But what they (I should say what we) tend not to know well are the transactions, behaviors, institutional structures, psychologies, and scientific and technological aspects of many of their (of our) cases. These deficiencies can be traced in part to the nature of college and legal education in the United States, and in part to the deficiencies of continuing or remedial judicial education, whether by law schools or by the Federal Judicial Center.[29] I give the judges a C for understanding and training.

Compensation. Article III judges, each paid more than $200,000 a year, with excellent health benefits, retirement eligibility at sixty-five (if they've served at least fifteen years) or seventy (with ten years of service) and retirement pay equal to the retiree's judicial salary, seem to me adequately compensated, though there is no doubt that some attractive judicial candidates decline appointment because the salary cut would be too painful for them. The most successful lawyers in private practice make millions of dollars a year, and few of them will give up that income just to be a federal district or federal court of appeals judge. Congress isn't going to raise the judicial salary to a million dollars to attract a handful of partners from Sullivan and Cromwell; Cravath,

---

29. These are problems addressed at length in my *Divergent Paths: The Academy and the Judiciary* (2016).

Swaine, and Moore; Skadden Arps; Kirkland and Ellis; and other, comparable firms, of which there are many. I think the federal judicial compensation structure is about as good as can reasonably be expected, though far from perfect, given (as I mentioned earlier) the absence of cost of living differentials and the unjustifiable pay differences among the three tiers of the Article III judiciary (district judges, courts of appeals judges, and Supreme Court Justices). So I give it a B+.

It remains to compute an overall score, which can be done by converting the letter grades to numbers, weighting the eight graded elements of the federal judicial process equally (which could however be criticized as an oversimplification), scoring A as 95, A– as 92, B+ as 85, B as 80, and C as 75,[30] and averaging the grades—the A, the A–, the B+, the three B's, and the two C's. The average as thus computed is 82.75, which is halfway between B and B+.

We could do worse, but we should be able to do better.

30. See, e.g., "Letter Grades Converted to Numbers—Hofstra," https://people.hofstra.edu/Ann_Marie_Burlein/REL_10/Grade%20conversion.doc.

Epilogue

March 6, 2017

I FINISHED—OR RATHER THOUGHT I HAD FINISHED—this book on December 10 of last year, and as mentioned in the Preface emailed the book that day to the publisher (Harvard University Press) for editing. The book was not scheduled to be published for some months, however, and I knew it would seem incomplete if it stopped on December 10. For that was only a month after the Presidential election, and it was obvious that in coming months there would be significant developments of importance to the federal judiciary involving issues central to the book, including though not limited to key judicial appointments (such as the appointment of a successor to Justice Scalia, who had died in February 2016, and the filling of an estimated 103 vacancies on the district courts and the courts of appeals), tugs of war in the Senate between Republicans and Democrats concerning confirmation of judicial nominees, and continued debate, academic and otherwise, concerning a variety of controversial issues of federal (including federal constitutional) law. I have made changes in the body of the book to reflect the recent developments, and the purpose of this Epilogue is to complete the bringing of the analysis in the book up to date with reference not only to events (such as the nomination of Scalia's successor) occurring after December 10, 2016, but also to discoveries I've made since then, and let me begin there.

I mentioned in Chapter 2 the duty of federal judges and Justices to recuse themselves in cases in which they have a financial interest in a party. An article by Adam Liptak,[1] the *New York Times*'s Supreme Court correspondent,

---

1. "On Conflicts, Clumsiness by the [Supreme] Court," *New York Times*, January 10, 2017, p. A16.

highlights what appears to be a careless attitude by some of the Justices to this duty. (The duty, surprisingly, appears to be flouted by a number of lower-court judges as well.[2]) According to Liptak's article, Roberts, Alito, and Breyer have all failed to recuse themselves in cases in which they owned stock in a party to the case. As I mentioned in Chapter 2, a judge doesn't have to recuse himself if the stock is not owned directly by him but instead is an asset of a mutual fund or index fund that the judge owns shares in. That is why when I became a federal judge in 1981 my wife and I sold all our stocks in individual companies and put the proceeds in mutual funds, where they remain to this day. Other judges, and the Justices, should do likewise.

Recently my friend Gary Peeples referred me to a book I'd never heard of by Joseph C. Goulden called *The Benchwarmers: The Private World of the Powerful Federal Judges* (1974). It turns out that this very interesting book is replete with devastating criticisms of a number of federal district judges in Chicago, some of whom I got to know after my appointment to the court of appeals in 1981 because they were still sitting—and I realize from my personal knowledge of them that Goulden's criticisms were well grounded. He also levied in his book powerful criticisms of the judicial selection process, and of the ethics of a number of judges of other federal courts. The book has helped me see that the average quality of federal judges improved significantly after Reagan became President in 1981; and though there is considerable room for further improvement—and it remains to be seen whether there will be any—the fact that the average quality of the federal judiciary has improved in the last thirty-five years or so is a qualification of the criticisms of the judiciary that I have made at such length in the previous chapters—and continue making in this Epilogue.

Recently, too, I learned to my surprise—though I shouldn't have been surprised—that in discussing shortly after Scalia's death the qualifications for a successor, President Obama had said he'd nominate someone "who understands that a judge's job is to interpret the law, not make the law."[3] It was a nonsense statement, as Obama, a lawyer, should have known and probably did know, but he was speaking as a politician rather than as a lawyer. A great deal of law, not only the common law (which is explicitly judge-made) but also

2. See Reity O'Brien, Kytja Weir, and Chris Young, "Justice Obscured: Federal Judges Plead Guilty: Juris Imprudence: Litigants Reeling after Judges Admit Conflicts of Interest," *Center for Public Integrity*, August 5, 2014, https://www.publicintegrity.org/2014/04/28/14630/federal-judges-plead-guilty.

3. President Barack Obama, "A Responsibility I Take Seriously," SCOTUSblog, February 24, 2016, www.scotusblog.com/2016/02/a-responsibility-i-take-seriously/.

much of constitutional and statutory law (the Sherman Antitrust Act was an example I've given in this book; I've given many constitutional examples also), is made by judges rather than by legislators. But because appointment to a federal judgeship requires confirmation by the Senate, a body of legislators, it behooves a President to give assurances, whether or not sincere, that he will nominate to be a judge or Justice only someone who he can be sure will not try to "make law." No member of the Supreme Court, not even the two Obama appointees (Sotomayor and Kagan), fits the bill.

A book of several years ago about judges mistakenly attributes the above quotation from Obama to the statement he made announcing his nomination of Elena Kagan to the Supreme Court.[4] That statement[5] deserves attention only for its extravagance. Obama said among other things, "Elena is widely regarded as one of the nation's foremost legal minds. She's an acclaimed legal scholar with a rich understanding of constitutional law." Not true; her distinction was the managerial skills that she had displayed first as a White House official toward the end of the Clinton Presidency and then as dean of the Harvard Law School. "And [Obama continued exaggerating] she is a superb Solicitor General, our nation's chief lawyer representing the American people's interests before the Supreme Court, the first woman in that position as well. And she has won accolades from observers across the ideological spectrum for her well-reasoned arguments and commanding presence." And "Elena had a brilliant career in academia." No.[6] "She is a great lawyer." Again no. As I explained in Chapter 2, the current Court is weak; Ginsburg and Breyer, both appointed by President Clinton, alone have claims to excellence, in my opinion, and Ginsburg may be fading.

Shifting gears: Almost ten months after Obama's pronunciamentos that I've been quoting, forty-two constitutional law professors wrote an open letter to President-elect Trump expressing a number of concerns about Presidential judicial policy. The letter is serious and sober, powerful and convincing:

4. James E. Whitehead, *Judging Judges: Values and the Rule of Law* 1, 147 n. 3 (2014).
5. The White House: Office of the Press Secretary, "Remarks by the President and Solicitor General Elena Kagan at the Nomination of Solicitor General Elena Kagan to the Supreme Court," May 10, 2010, https://www.whitehouse.gov/the-press-office/remarks-president-and-solicitor-general-elena-kagan-nomination-solicitor-general-el.
6. She had taught at the University of Chicago Law School before joining the White House staff, and sought reappointment by the law school when the Clinton administration ended, but the law school declined to reappoint her.

AN OPEN LETTER FROM CONSTITUTIONAL LAW SCHOLARS
TO PRESIDENT-ELECT DONALD TRUMP

DECEMBER 13, 2016

Dear President-Elect Trump:

On January 20, 2017, you will recite the presidential Oath of Office and pledge to "preserve, protect and defend the Constitution of the United States." As constitutional law scholars, we write to underscore what this profound commitment entails. Specifically, we urge you to uphold and adhere to the rule of law; to take responsible positions on constitutional issues; to make appointments to the executive branch and the courts that will unify, rather than further divide, our nation; and to denounce emphatically the hate crimes and other hateful acts that people have been committing with increasing frequency since your election.

Some of your statements and actions during the campaign and since the election cause us great concern about your commitment to our constitutional system. The following list illustrates, but does not exhaust, our concerns.

1. The First Amendment protects the rights of free speech and a free press, both of which are critical to preserving a functioning democracy. Yet you have demonstrated extreme hostility toward the press, including by denying access to your campaign events to media outlets that you have perceived as antagonistic, threatening to sue journalists, and calling for changes to our nation's libel laws that would seriously hinder the ability of the media to report on matters of public importance. Your conduct and rhetoric fail to register that the institutional role of the press in the United States is to check candidates for office and government officials, the President paramount among them. Once you are in office, it will be critically important for you—like your predecessors from both political parties—to ensure that the press is able to report and opine candidly on your activities, positions, and decisions without fear of politically motivated reprisal or restrictions on access to the White House. We urge you to allow the press to do its job, and we call upon you to commit to honoring First Amendment principles more broadly. For example, your recent threats to punish and revoke the citizenship of Americans who burn the American flag are flatly inconsistent with the modern cross-ideological consensus that flag burning is protected political expression—as the Su-

preme Court has twice held in majority opinions joined by your model Justice, Antonin Scalia—and with longstanding Court holdings that the state may not strip persons of citizenship for being acutely critical of, or even deeply antagonistic to, the government.

2. In December of last year (2016), you proposed prohibiting all Muslims from entering the United States. When asked about Muslims serving in our military abroad who want to come home, you suggested that you were calling for "vigilance." Although your exact position was difficult to pin down, your identification of an entire group of people for differential treatment based only on their religious upbringing, affiliation, or beliefs raises extraordinarily troubling questions about how your administration will understand the rights of religious minorities. These rights are expressly protected by the Free Exercise Clause of the First Amendment, and respecting them is a value fundamental to our constitutional tradition. Moreover, following the Paris terrorist attack last November, you suggested that you would "strongly consider" closing mosques in response. We urge you to renounce this and other poisonous anti-Muslim rhetoric, which threatens our First Amendment guarantee of freedom of religious exercise and the Fifth Amendment's promise of equal protection of the laws.

To make matters worse, your proposed national security advisor, Michael Flynn, has described what he calls "Islamism" as a "vicious cancer inside the body of 1.7 billion people" that "has to be excised." Such rhetoric is shocking in its ignorance and bigotry; it must not become normalized. We continue to hear talk of a "Muslim registry" being created by your administration—or a nationality-based registry that would be a proxy for religious discrimination. To our national shame, the federal government during World War II carried out—and the Supreme Court's discredited *Korematsu* decision upheld—the mass internment of Japanese Americans based upon no individualized suspicion of wrongdoing; the federal government under President Ronald Reagan subsequently apologized and paid reparations. We urge you to reconsider your naming of Flynn and to renounce a Muslim registry or anything like it.

3. Our Constitution creates a system of separated powers and checks and balances. As James Madison wrote in *Federalist No. 51*, the "separate and distinct exercise of the different powers of government . . . [is] essential to the preservation of liberty." A fundamental component of this sys-

tem is the independence of our judiciary. In May, you asserted that a judge presiding over civil litigation to which you are a party should recuse himself because he has "an absolute conflict" on account of his "Mexican heritage" and your promise to "build a wall," even though the case had nothing to do with either the judge's heritage or your immigration proposals. In keeping with the Judicial Code of Conduct, the judge properly did not respond to your attack, which House Speaker Paul Ryan correctly condemned as "racist." These sorts of unjustified attacks have the potential to undermine the public's confidence in the judiciary, and we remain concerned about what this episode may signal about your administration's respect for the independence of the judicial branch.

4. Your comments during and since the election that you would accomplish the overruling of *Roe v. Wade* through the appointment of Supreme Court Justices causes further concern about your commitment to an independent judiciary and reveals a lack of understanding of what an overruling of *Roe* would mean. When asked what pregnant women would then have to do in order to obtain an abortion, you said that they would have to go to another state. While that highly problematic option would remain available to some women, it would be illusory to many other women whose economic, health, work, family, and other life circumstances would not support their ability to travel interstate and who would instead be compelled to resort to unsafe, illegal abortions. Your statement betrays a disturbing lack of awareness of, or insensitivity to, this reality for many women in our country. Your suggestion also ignores past and promised future efforts to enact federal legislation that would restrict abortion nationwide. Unless you mean to oppose any such efforts, your suggestion that the permissibility of abortion restrictions should be decided at the state level is disingenuous in addition to harmful to women. We urge you to renounce your commitment to appointing Justices with the aim of denying women their long-established, fundamental constitutional rights.

5. Your nominee for U.S. Attorney General, Senator Jefferson Sessions of Alabama, had a troubling history on voting rights and civil rights from when he served as the U.S. Attorney for the Southern District of Alabama and as Attorney General of Alabama, and he continues to have one of the worst records on those issues of any Senator. More recently, he expressed incredulity about the Court's protection of same-sex marriage,

and he appears far more likely to pursue charges of voter fraud that lack any evidentiary basis than to protect the voting rights of all Americans. His appointment as Attorney General threatens to erase years of progress in ensuring equal citizenship in the United States. We urge you to withdraw his nomination for Attorney General and to appoint a less polarizing person who enjoys broad bipartisan support.

6. You recently stated: "In addition to winning the Electoral College in a landslide, I won the popular vote if you deduct the millions of people who voted illegally." You have offered no evidence to support this extraordinary allegation. We urge you to cease making baseless charges concerning voter fraud and to communicate with the American people honestly and responsibly about threats to the integrity of our election system, the maintenance of which is crucial to the stability of our political system.

7. Hate crimes and other hate-filled speech and actions against racial, ethnic, and religious minorities have been rampant since your election. Your inflammatory rhetoric during the campaign has been taken as an invitation to discriminate and to act out in all kinds of hate-filled ways. Neo-Nazi and white supremacist groups feel legitimated and empowered to make their presence publicly known, and some of them invoke your name in the apparent belief that your election vindicates their hatred. Rather than strongly condemn such groups, you have offered only half-hearted criticism in response to questions from the media, and you have appointed as your chief strategist Steve Bannon, who has described himself as having close ties to the "alt-right," a euphemism for individuals and groups that spout hatred and bigotry. We urge you to reconsider your close association with Bannon. We also urge you to strongly and unequivocally condemn—and use the power of your future office to combat—racism, sexism, misogyny, homophobia, xenophobia, Islamophobia, and anti-Semitism.

Although we sincerely hope that you will take your constitutional oath seriously, so far you have offered little indication that you will. We feel a responsibility to challenge you in the court of public opinion, and we hope that those directly aggrieved by your administration will challenge you in the courts of law. We call upon legal conservatives who cherish constitutional values to join us in speaking law to power. And we call upon citizens, lawyers, educators, public officials, and religious leaders to use every legal means available to protect the most vulnerable members of our society and our constitutional guarantees. At no point that any of us can remember has this need been more imperative than it is now.

Moving on: Recall that in Chapter 3 I took strong exception to Professor Adrian Vermeule's contention that "thin rationality" is all that a court should demand from an administrative agency, implying that judicial review of administrative decisions should be conducted with considerable laxity. Recently I learned of an article[7] that casts further doubt on his position. I quote the abstract:

Congressional enactments and executive orders instruct agencies to publish their anticipated rules in what is known as the Unified Agenda. The Agenda's stated purpose is to ensure that political actors can monitor regulatory development. Agencies have come under fire in recent years, however, for conspicuous omissions and irregularities. Critics allege that agencies hide their regulations from the public strategically, that is, to thwart potential political opposition. Others contend that such behavior is benign, perhaps the inevitable result of changing internal priorities or unforeseen events. To examine these competing hypotheses, this Article uses a new dataset spanning over thirty years of rulemaking (1983–2014). Uniquely, the dataset is drawn directly from the Federal Register. The resulting findings reveal that agencies substantially underreport their rule-making activities—about 70 percent of their proposed rules do not appear on the Unified Agenda before publication. Importantly, agencies also appear to disclose strategically with respect to Congress, though not with respect to the president. The Unified Agenda is thus not a successful tool for Congress to monitor and influence regulatory development. The results suggest that legislative, not executive, innovations may help to augment public participation and democratic oversight, though the net effects of more transparency remain uncertain. The findings also raise further inquiries, such as why Congress does not render disclosure requirements judicially enforceable.

7. Jennifer Nou and Edward H. Stiglitz, "Strategic Rulemaking Disclosure," 89 *Southern California Law Review* 733 (2016).

There is also a Congressional Review Act,[8] which empowers Congress to review and, if it wants, to void agency rules, but the Act appears to be rarely enforced. But then who, if not Congress, reviews federal agencies' work? The White House, for one, which contains OIRA (Office of Information and Regulatory Affairs): "OIRA has approximately 45 full-time career civil servants who work with agency officials on specific issues and regulations. All OIRA career staff possess graduate level degrees and have historically come from backgrounds in economics, law, policy analysis, statistics, and information technology. With the growth of science-based regulation and information-quality issues, *several* staff members also have expertise in public health, toxicology, epidemiology, engineering, and other technical fields."[9] Several is not enough!

Now it's true that federal agencies other than OIRA also engage in review of administrative rules, but the agencies appear to be skilled in insulating their rules and decisions from executive-branch review.[10] So a heavy burden of *careful* review of administrative action inevitably falls, or should fall, on the courts, for the further reason that there are far more rulings by agencies on the application of administrative rules than there are promulgations of new rules. Those rulings are judicially reviewable and should be reviewed by the courts *carefully,* rather than in the rubber-stamp fashion urged by Vermeule and his coauthor Gersen.

Chapter 2 dealt at length with the continuing controversy over Justice Scalia, a controversy surprisingly intensified rather than calmed by his death on February 13, 2016, and unabated a year later. The controversy flared with the publication on December 25, 2016, of an article by Emily Bazelon,[11] which I shall paraphrase, and expand upon slightly:

In *Edwards v. Aguillard*[12] the Supreme Court by a vote of 7 to 2 invalidated a Louisiana law that the Court deemed to breach the constitutional wall between

---

8. 5 U.S.C. §§ 801–808.

9. See White House, Office of Management and Budget, "About OIRA," https://www.whitehouse.gov /omb/oira/about (emphasis added).

10. See Jennifer Nou, "Agency Self-Insulation under Presidential Review," 126 *Harvard Law Review* 1755 (2013).

11. Emily Bazelon, "He Claimed Objectivity When It Came To Originalism, But He Was a Skeptic about Science," *New York Times Magazine,* December 25, 2016, p. 34.

12. 482 U.S. 578 (1987).

church and state by forcing religious belief into the science curriculum of public schools. Scalia (joined by Thomas) dissented on the ground that there was "ample uncontradicted testimony that 'creation science' is a body of scientific knowledge, rather than revealed belief." He chided his colleagues for treating the evidence for evolution as "conclusive."

Creation science is scientific nonsense. It substitutes what the Old Testament says about the creation of the universe, the earth, animals, and human beings for what science teaches. Rather than accepting abundant scientific evidence for the evolution of human beings from earlier forms of life in Africa and the migration of many of the new species to the rest of the world, creation science teaches that the universe was created some six thousand years ago (Scalia said "about 5000 years ago") in a six-day period culminating in the creation by God of Adam and Eve, from whom all other human beings descend. (So much for Neanderthals, who can have no place in creation science, having preceded Adam and Even, and hence creation, by hundreds of thousands of years.)

Scalia's commitment to creation science reflected both his passionate, literal, though largely discredited version of Catholicism—for Pope Pius XII made peace with evolution in 1950—and also his (related) confessed ignorance of science, of which he appears to have been skeptical. When in an oral argument in a case about climate change in 2006 a lawyer corrected Scalia for referring to the stratosphere when the correct referent was the troposphere, Scalia responded: "I told you before I'm not a scientist. That's why I don't want to have to deal with global warming, to tell you the truth."[13] A majority of the Justices agreed that "the harms associated with climate change are serious and well recognized,"[14] but Scalia, dissenting, held fast to doubt: "The court's alarm over global warming may or may not be justified."[15]

Bazelon points out that in the oral argument of a 2013 case in the Supreme Court the lawyer defending California's ban on same-sex marriage gave no examples of how allowing gay couples to marry could be harmful. "I don't know why you don't mention some concrete things," Scalia prodded him. "There's considerable disagreement among sociologists as to what the consequences of raising a child in a single-sex family, whether that is harmful to the child or

13. The case was *Massachusetts v. Environmental Protection Agency*, argued on November 29, 2006.
14. *Massachusetts v. Environmental Protection Agency*, 549 U.S. 497, 521 (2007).
15. Id. at 560 (dissenting opinion).

not."[16] No, as Bazelon points out there was already a large body of evidence showing that children on average fare as well with gay parents as they do with straight ones.

Bazelon notes in her article that in another case[17] Scalia contradicted scientific consensus by declaring it "very likely" that the death penalty deters murder. In so saying he dismissed the findings of a panel of the National Research Council,[18] which had concluded unanimously in 2012 that the death penalty does not have a deterrent effect. Bazelon goes on to report that "to support his claim to the contrary, Scalia cited three articles. Two were statistical studies that the National Research Council had discredited," while "the lead author of the third . . . had previously stated that his paper did *not* claim that the death penalty had a deterrent effect. 'Scalia was willing to cite work that was thoroughly refuted by an accepted scholarly institution, without feeling any need to buttress his position,' says John Donohue, a Stanford economist and law professor who conducts empirical research on the death penalty."

Scalia refused to join part of a 2013 opinion by his frequent ally Justice Thomas that laid out basic principles of human genetics in textbook fashion such as that "sequences of DNA nucleotides contain the information necessary to create strings of amino acids."[19] Scalia said he could not affirm the facts based "on my own knowledge or even my own belief." That last bit ("my own belief") could contain multitudes; Scalia didn't explain it. The accuracy of Thomas's discussion of genetics has been questioned,[20] but Scalia did not question it but merely acknowledged his lack of understanding of it.

Bazelon's article about Scalia caused an uproar among extreme conservatives. Harvard law professor Adrian Vermeule, that recent convert to Catholicism whom I discussed at several points earlier in this book, tweeted in response to Bazelon's article: "in fact the Catholic Church has never had a problem with evolution. Nor did Justice Scalia."[21] Wrong on both counts—and typical of Scalia's admirers, who rarely remark even his patent falsehoods. The Church had had a "problem" with evolution until Pius XII had made his peace

16. Oral argument on March 26, 2013, in *Hollingsworth v. Perry,* 113 S. Ct. 1652 (2013).

17. The botched execution of Clayton Lockett by Oklahoma in 2014.

18. See www.nap.edu/catalog/13363/deterrence-and-the-death-penalty.

19. *Association for Molecular Pathology et al. v. Myriad Genetics Inc., et al.,* 133 S. Ct. 2107 (2013).

20. Ian Samuel, "Did Justice Scalia Believe in Dinosaurs? An Investigation," December 24, 2016, https://medium.com/@isamuel/did-justice-scalia-believe-in-dinosaurs-an-investigation-79cd99e3559#.ddd7nm4t4.

21. Adrian Vermeule, Twitter post, December 21, 2016.

with it in 1950. Scalia never made his peace with it, never to my knowledge said he believed in evolution, told me in person many years ago that he did *not* believe in evolution because he thought the eye of a fish too complex to be produced in a finite time by evolution (wrong as usual[22]), and implicitly rejected evolution by his repeated assertions that the earth (indeed the universe), and therefore humanity, is only five thousand to six thousand years old.[23] That leaves too little time to enable human beings to evolve, but this was not a problem for him because he believed that on the sixth day of creation God had created Adam and Eve, from whom he believed all human beings had descended, but not evolved; to believers, Adam and Eve, having been created by God, were not precursors of homo sapiens; they were homo sapiens *par excellence*. Scalia could recognize no possibility of evolution from lower primates to human beings. Adam and Eve, having been created (Scalia believed) directly by God, were the *ne plus ultra* of humanity; their descendants, including the author and readers of this book, must in his view have been inferior in intelligence and fitness to those distant ancestors, not having been created by God. And when Adam and Eve were created, there were already (if one believes *Genesis,* as Scalia must have in order to have come up with his estimate of the earth's age) a variety of animals in the Garden of Eden, created by God days earlier, and the many complex animals of today would not have been able to evolve from simpler ones in a mere six thousand or so years.

The notion that the earth and/or human beings are at most six thousand years old is preposterous, as there is abundant evidence that homo sapiens is at least one hundred thousand years old, and cave paintings have been found that can be dated to thirty thousand years ago.

Unsurprisingly given his rejection of science, Scalia was an emphatic believer in the devil. In an interview published in *New York Magazine,*[24] after say-

---

22. "[A] fairly good eye could evolve in maybe a third of a million years. It is thought that animal life has been on earth for at least 600 million years. That is certainly enough time for eyes to have evolved many times over." *How Long Would the Fish Eye Take to Evolve?,* March 15, 1998, www.don-lindsay-archive.org/creation /eye_time.html. See also, for another illustration of an extensive literature, Carl Zimmer, "How the Eye Evolved," *New York Academy of Sciences Magazine,* October 9, 2009, www.nyas.org/publications/detail.aspx ?cid=93b487b2-153a-4630-9fb2-5679a061ffff7.

23. The Anglican bishop James Ussher (1581–1656) calculated the first day of creation as having been Sunday, October 23, 4004 B.C., and that Adam and Eve (created on the sixth day after the creation) had been driven from the Garden of Eden on Monday, November 10, of the same year. That would date the creation to 6,013 years ago, a dating congenial to Scalia, though I don't think the Catholic Church ever accepted Ussher's dating (he wasn't a Catholic after all), or that many Christians today would agree with Scalia's dating of the creation. It is certainly not a Catholic dogma today.

24. Jennifer Senior, "In Conversation: Antonin Scalia," *New York Magazine,* October 6, 2013.

ing "I even believe in the Devil," to which the interviewer asked, "You do?," Scalia replied, "Of course! Yeah, he's a real person. Hey, c'mon, that's standard Catholic doctrine! Every Catholic believes that. . . . If you are faithful to Catholic dogma, that is certainly a large part of it." This prompted the interviewer to ask him, "Isn't it terribly frightening to believe in the Devil?" Scalia replied, "You're looking at me as though I'm weird. My God! Are you so out of touch with most of America, most of which believes in the Devil? I mean, Jesus Christ believed in the Devil! It's in the Gospels! You travel in circles that are so, so removed from mainstream America that you are appalled that anybody would believe in the Devil! Most of mankind has believed in the Devil, for all of history. Many more intelligent people than you or me have believed in the Devil." Childish nonsense.

As explained by Mary Ann Case,

in [his] dissents, Scalia behaves somewhat like the Trojan princess Cassandra, whose gift of prophecy came with the curse that she would not be believed, and whose clear-eyed warnings as a consequence went unheeded until the later point in time when what they predicted came to pass. Like Cassandra, Scalia is on the losing side of many of his prophecies—what he is predicting is the exact opposite of what he wants to see happen. Every battle, however, is necessarily both "lost and won," so that what is bad news for the Trojans is good news for the Greeks, and what Scalia sees as the catastrophic consequences of a decision are most welcome from the perspective of his ideological opponents. In describing what for him are the horrors that will follow from the majority's logic, he often paints a prophetic picture which in time comes true, perhaps in part because of rather than in spite of his dramatic articulation of an opinion's implications. [Case uses] another Greek myth, that of Procrustes, to shed light on a tendency in Scalia's majority opinions. Just as Procrustes forced his guests to fit snugly into an iron bed, stretching out their bodies or chopping off their limbs as necessary, so Scalia frequently forced all prior doctrine in a given area of law into the shape he needed for the new rule he announces in a majority opinion. As with Procrustes's unfortunate guests, so with Scalia's procrustean majority opinions, the result . . . is often that the operation is a success, but the patient dies: subsequent decisions, whether by courts or legislatures, tend to back away from the implications of the categorical rule Scalia had gone through such pains to fashion. The paradoxical result is that Scalia as Cassandra dissenting has sometimes been more effective in illuminating the path to results he deplores than Scalia as Procrustes has been in bringing about results he favors. This is so notwithstanding that Scalia in procrustean mode does his rhetorical best to minimize the innovative or controversial character of his holding for the majority, whereas Scalia in dissent seeks rhetorically to maximize the unprecedented and revolutionary character of the majority position to which he objects.[25]

For other thoughtful assessments of Scalia's strengths and weaknesses as a Supreme Court Justice, see Erwin Chemerinsky, "The Jurisprudence of Justice Scalia: A Critical Appraisal," 22 *University of Hawaii Law Review* 385 (2000); Stephen B. Presser, *Law Professors: Three Centuries of Shaping American Law,* chapter 20 ("Towards Originalism and Textualism: Late Twentieth Century: Antonin Scalia") (2017); and Joseph Kimble, "The Doctrine of the Last Antecedent, the Example in Barnhart, Why Both Are Weak, and How Textualism Postures," 16 *Scribes J. Legal Writing* 5, 30–35 (2015) (summarizing six empirical studies, and citing eleven other sources, that show a strong ideological bent in Scalia's opinions). And notice also the perceptive remark in Allan C. Hutchinson, *Toward an Informal Account of Legal Interpretation* 68 (2016), that for Scalia "originalism . . . [was] less an interpretive methodology than a convenient tool for advancing a partial political agenda."

All this said, credit should be given to Scalia for his excellent writing style, his sense of humor, his independence, and above all his surprising concern with the rights of criminal suspects and defendants.[26] Furthermore, despite my many criticisms of Scalia's jurisprudence, I am equally or more critical of some of his colleagues on the Court, including not only Chief Justice Roberts, whom I have hammered several times in this book, but also, among others, Justices Kagan and Alito—as I'll now illustrate with an opinion by each of them.

25. Mary Ann Case, "Scalia as Procrustes for the Majority, Scalia as Cassandra in Dissent," University of Chicago Law School, December 2016, forthcoming in *Jahrbuch des öffentlichen Rechts der Gegenwart.*
26. See, e.g., Robert J. Smith, "Antonin Scalia's Other Legacy: He Was Often a Friend of Criminal Defendants," *Slate,* February 16, 2016, www.slate.com/articles/news_and_politics/jurisprudence/2016/02/antonin_scalia_was_often_a_friend_of_criminal_defendants.html. A recent article by David M. Dorsen, in the January 26, 2017, issue of the *Washington Post,* entitled "The Unexpected Scalia: Liberal Opinions from a Conservative Justice," elaborates on this theme, while acknowledging that "Scalia was personally a committed conservative and originalist. He relied on that pair of approaches to render conservative opinions on abortion, the right to die, women's rights, rights of gays and lesbians, obscenity, the death penalty, habeas corpus, the exclusionary rule relating to illegal searches and seizures, regulatory takings of private property, gun rights, establishment of religion, states' rights, standing to challenge federal regulatory statutes, the scope of the commerce clause, the Freedom of Information Act and more."

In Justice Kagan's majority opinion in *Kimble v. Marvel Entertainment, LLC,*[27] a patent case, we read that

> in *Brulotte v. Thys Co.,* 379 U. S. 29 (1964), this Court held that a patent holder cannot charge royalties for the use of his invention after its patent term has expired. The sole question presented here is whether we should overrule *Brulotte*. Adhering to principles of *stare decisis,* we decline to do so. Critics of the *Brulotte* rule must seek relief not from this Court but from Congress. . . . The *Brulotte* rule, like others making contract provisions unenforceable, prevents some parties from entering into deals they desire. As compared to lump-sum fees, royalty plans both draw out payments over time and tie those payments, in each month or year covered, to a product's commercial success. And sometimes, for some parties, the longer the arrangement lasts, the better—not just up to but beyond a patent term's end. A more extended payment period, coupled (as it presumably would be) with a lower rate, may bring the price the patent holder seeks within the range of a cash-strapped licensee. (Anyone who has bought a product on installment can relate.) . . . Or such an extended term may better allocate the risks and rewards associated with commercializing inventions—most notably, when years of development work stand between licensing a patent and bringing a product to market. . . . Overruling precedent is never a small matter. *Stare decisis*—in English, the idea that today's Court should stand by yesterday's decisions—is "a foundation stone of the rule of law." *Michigan v. Bay Mills Indian Community,* 572 U. S. ___, ___ (2014) (slip op. at 15).[28] Application of that doctrine, although "not an inexorable command," is the "preferred course because it promotes the evenhanded, predictable, and consistent development of legal principles, fosters reliance on judicial decisions, and contributes to the actual and perceived integrity of the judicial process." *Payne v. Tennessee,* 501 U. S. 808, 827–28 (1991). It also reduces incentives for challenging settled precedents, saving parties and courts the expense of endless relitigation. Respecting *stare decisis* means sticking to some wrong decisions. The doctrine rests on the idea, as Justice Brandeis famously wrote, that it is usually "more important that the applicable rule

27. 576 U.S ___ (2015).

28. The reason for the incomplete citation of this case and two others in this paragraph is that they have not yet been published in the U.S. Reports and therefore do not have a page number in that official publication of Supreme Court opinions.

of law be settled than that it be settled right." *Burnet* v. *Coronado Oil & Gas*, 285 U. S. 393, 406 (1932) (dissenting opinion). Indeed, *stare decisis* has consequence only to the extent it sustains incorrect decisions; correct judgments have no need for that principle to prop them up. Accordingly, an argument that we got something wrong—even a good argument to that effect—cannot by itself justify scrapping settled precedent. Or otherwise said, it is not alone sufficient that we would decide a case differently now than we did then. To reverse course, we require as well what we have termed a "special justification"—over and above the belief "that the precedent was wrongly decided." *Halliburton Co. v. Erica P. John Fund, Inc.*, 573 U. S. ___, ___ (2014).

What is more, *stare decisis* carries enhanced force when a decision, like *Brulotte*, interprets a statute. Then, unlike in a constitutional case, critics of our ruling can take their objections across the street, and Congress can correct any mistake it sees. See, *e.g.*, *Patterson v. McLean Credit Union*, 491 U. S. 164, 172–173 (1989). . . . And Congress has spurned multiple opportunities to reverse *Brulotte*—openings as frequent and clear as this Court ever sees. . . .

[Furthermore] overturning *Brulotte* would . . . upset expectations, most so when long-dormant licenses for long-expired patents spring back to life. Not true, says Kimble: Unfair surprise is unlikely, because no "meaningful number of [such] license agreements . . . actually exist." . . . To be honest, we do not know (nor, we suspect, do Marvel and Kimble). But even uncertainty on this score cuts in Marvel's direction. So long as we see a reasonable possibility that parties have structured their business transactions in light of *Brulotte*, we have one more reason to let it stand. As against this super powered form of *stare decisis,* we would need a super special justification to warrant reversing *Brulotte*.

So Kagan gives three reasons for not overruling *Brulotte:* to do so would undermine *stare decisis* (Latin for to stand by what has been decided), second it would infringe on Congress's responsibility for correcting judicial misinterpretations of statutes (in this case the Patent Act), and third it would upset reliance interests created by the decision sought to be overruled. The first two reasons are no good. The fact that a judicial decision is on the books is no reason to adhere to it after it becomes clear that the decision is either recognized to have been erroneous when rendered or no longer fits current circumstances. *Bru-*

lotte was a mistake when rendered because it confused the length of patent protection (usually twenty years) with the timing of patent license fees. A licensee who cannot afford the annual license fee that the patentee wants to charge may suggest, and the patentee may accept, that the annual fee be reduced but the deficit made up by extending the payment term from twenty to say thirty years. This does not violate the twenty-year limit of patent protection; at the end of the twenty years anyone can copy the patented product, but the licensee must continue paying the license fee for another ten years. There is no interference with the ending of the patentee's monopoly of the patented product.

As for the role of Congress, nowhere is it written that only Congress can overrule a judicial decision. Most overrulings are by the court that issued the decision, rather than by Congress. The court is more likely to understand the deficiencies of its former case.

The third ground given in the *Kimble* majority opinion for not overruling *Brulotte*—the importance of reliance interests—is valid for many cases, but not for *Kimble*. If an industry, say, has come to rely on a decision—has made investments or done other things in order to comply with it—the overruling of the decision may impose costs on the industry that exceed whatever benefits the overruling would confer. In that event simple cost-benefit analysis argues for invoking *stare decisis*. Justice Kagan admitted that she didn't know whether there were reliance interests that would justify adherence to *Brulotte*. She said there might be. One would have expected the Court therefore to remand the case for a factual determination of whether there were compelling reliance interests.

In sum, the opinion is completely unconvincing.

The *Alito* opinion I want to discuss is his dissenting opinion in *Walker v. Texas Division, Sons of Confederate Veterans*.[29] Automobile owners in Texas are permitted by the state government to choose between having what is called a general-issue license plate, that is, a plate designed by the state government, and a specialty license plate chosen or created by the owner. The specialty plate must however be approved by the Texas Department of Motor Vehicles Board. The majority opinion held that any message conveyed by a Texas license plate, whether general issue or specialty, is "government speech," and the department may therefore refuse to allow a private person or organization to post a specialty plate that conveys a message that the board disapproves of. The heart of the Alito dissent is as follows:

> The Texas Division of Sons of Confederate Veterans . . . is an organiza-
> tion composed of descendants of Confederate soldiers. The group ap-
> plied for a Texas specialty license plate in 2009 and again in 2010. Their
> proposed design featured a controversial symbol, the Confederate battle
> flag, surrounded by the words "Sons of Confederate Veterans 1896" and a
> gold border. . . . The Board . . . voted unanimously against approval and
> issued an order stating: . . . "The Board has considered the information
> and finds it necessary to deny this plate design application, specifically
> the confederate flag portion of the design, because public comments
> have shown that many members of the general public find the design of-
> fensive, and because such comments are reasonable. The Board finds that
> a significant portion of the public associate the confederate flag with or-
> ganizations advocating expressions of hate directed toward people or
> groups that is demeaning to those people or groups." . . .

Alito concedes that "the Confederate battle flag is a controversial symbol. To the Texas Sons of Confederate Veterans, it is said to evoke the memory of their ancestors and other soldiers who fought for the South in the Civil War. . . . To others, it symbolizes slavery, segregation, and hatred. Whatever it means to motorists who display that symbol and to those who see it, the flag expresses a viewpoint. The Board rejected the plate design because it concluded that many Texans would find the flag symbol offensive. That was pure viewpoint discrimination." In so saying Alito is denying that a Confederate battle flag on a license plate would be "government speech." And that is certainly correct. Government permits a great deal of private behavior; by doing so it doesn't transform the behavior from private to public. By allowing a person to own a parakeet the government does not make the parakeet a government bird. But if it were discovered that parakeets spread disease, the government could then prohibit their sale.

And that seems to me to be the proper analogy to the board's prohibiting the Confederate specialty license plate. The Southern states that formed the Confederacy proceeded to secede from the United States, precipitating a civil war that resulted in somewhere between 620,000 and 750,00 combat deaths. The confederates were traitors. Their descendants, and other fans, do have a constitutional right to praise the Confederacy, to venerate Jefferson Davis and Robert E. Lee and Stonewall Jackson and its other military leaders, but they cannot be permitted, it seems to me, to *compel* a state government to advertise the Confederacy and its symbols, such as the Confederate battle flag, on government property, here the license plates that the Texas government issues to the owners of motor vehicles. The plates are the property of the government. It can't be compelled to inscribe them with slogans that celebrate treason, albeit treason that ended more than 150 years ago. Does Justice Alito think that the board would have to accept a specialty license plate that contained Nazi slogans, racial epithets, adult pornography, hangings, or mutilated corpses? Would the prohibition of such a license plate really be forbidden "viewpoint discrimination"? Please tell us, Justice Alito.

And speaking of Justice Alito, earlier in the book I remarked what seemed to me his very strange, and indeed offensive, endorsement of the use of the drug midazolam in executions. Recently, we learn from Manny Fernandez that

officials in Arizona agreed to stop using a controversial lethal-injection drug that has been at the center of botched or prolonged executions in several states, including a 2014 execution in Arizona that took nearly two hours and that experts called one of the longest executions ever conducted in the United States. The decision by the Arizona Department of Corrections to abandon the drug, a sedative known as midazolam, came in a settlement agreement as part of a lawsuit over the state's execution drugs and procedures [that was] brought against the state by seven death-row inmates. Midazolam was one of two drugs given to Joseph R. Wood III in July 2014 in Arizona's death chamber in Florence. . . . Wood was injected with 15 times the standard dose of midazolam and a painkiller during a procedure that lasted one hour 57 minutes. Some witnesses described Wood gasping more than 600 times. The unusual length of a procedure that typically takes about 15 minutes prompted the Arizona attorney general to temporarily halt executions in the state. The hiatus remains in effect under a court order. An assistant federal public defender who represented Wood noted that "time after time, midazolam has failed to keep condemned prisoners adequately anesthetized and to bring about a quick, humane death." Death-penalty experts and lawyers representing death-row inmates in those cases applauded the action by Arizona officials, but it was unclear if the decision would lead to changes in the drugs used by other states, some of which use midazolam but many of which do not.

Yet in Virginia, officials planned to execute a death-row inmate, Ricky Gray, using compounded midazolam on January 18, 2017. I don't know whether the execution was carried out and if so whether compounded midazolam was used. Gray's lawyers sought to block his execution over the use of compounded midazolam, which they said no state had used in an execution before. "Remarkably, Virginia is poised to take the risks of midazolam to another level," said one of Gray's lawyers.[30]

We know from the discussion of the *Glossip* case in Chapter 2 that in 2015 in an opinion by Justice Alito the Supreme Court upheld midazolam's use in Oklahoma's three-drug protocol. Even so, many states have discontinued use of the drug ever since its use in a high-profile botched execution in Oklahoma in 2014 in which the condemned man, Clayton D. Lockett, died forty-three minutes after the injections had begun and appeared to moan and struggle in his death throes.

New topic: Last fall I asked the chief judge of the federal district court for Chicago and environs to give me a criminal case to try (as mentioned earlier in the book, I have been trying cases as a volunteer in the district courts of the Seventh Circuit since my appointment as a judge more than thirty-five years ago). He replied that there are now so few criminal trials in his court that they have to be reserved for the district judges. I learned the reason for this dearth recently from my friend Jed S. Rakoff, a very experienced and distinguished federal district judge in Manhattan who in an article in 2014[31] explained that defendants are induced to plead guilty by prosecutors who, not wanting to risk losing a trial, offer defendants sentences the defendants can't resist because they're so far below the maximum sentences that might be imposed if they went to trial and were found guilty. Only about 1 percent of federal criminal prosecutions go to trial nowadays, in 8 percent the government dismisses the indictment, and the rest end in guilty pleas, some by defendants who are innocent but are afraid of being found guilty in a trial and given a sentence much longer than the sentence offered them by the government if they agree to plead guilty.

30. Manny Fernandez, "Arizona Agrees to Stop Using Drug Tied to Botched Executions," *New York Times,* December 20, 2016, p. A3.

31. "Why Innocent People Plead Guilty," *New York Review of Books,* November 20, 2014.

Judge Rakoff's article reminded me of an article by Judge Kozinski of the Ninth Circuit that contains a remarkable list of deficiencies of federal (but also of state) criminal procedure, thus amplifying Judge Rakoff's critique.[32] The article is forty-two pages long; I will not try to summarize it, but will merely list first the propositions of judges and prosecutors that Judge Kozinski debunks and second his suggestions for improvements:

I. The Debunking

> Eyewitnesses are highly reliable.
>
> Fingerprint evidence is foolproof.
>
> Other types of forensic evidence are scientifically proven and therefore infallible.
>
> DNA evidence is infallible.
>
> Human memories are reliable.
>
> Confessions are infallible because innocent people never confess.
>
> Juries follow instructions.
>
> Prosecutors play fair.
>
> The prosecution is at a substantial disadvantage because it must prove its case beyond a reasonable doubt.
>
> Police are objective in their investigations.
>
> Guilty pleas are conclusive proof of guilt.
>
> Long sentences deter crime.

II. The Suggestions for Improvement

> Give jurors a written copy of the jury instructions.
>
> Allow jurors to take notes during trial and provide them with a full trial transcript.
>
> Allow jurors to discuss the case while the trial is ongoing.
>
> Allow jurors to ask questions during the trial.
>
> Tell jurors up-front what's at stake in the case.
>
> Give jurors a say in sentencing.
>
> Require open-file discovery.

32. See Alex Kozinski, "Preface: Criminal Law 2.0," 44 *Georgetown Law Journal Annual Review of Criminal Procedure* (2015). I won't attempt to indicate which of his points are applicable to state judges (except the most important one); but they are a distinct minority, though this may because as a federal judge he is much more attuned to federal than state criminal procedure.

Adopt standardized, rigorous procedures for dealing with the government's disclosure obligations.

Adopt standardized, rigorous procedures for eyewitness identification.

Video record all suspect interrogations.

Impose strict limits on the use of jailhouse informants.

Adopt rigorous, uniform procedures for certifying expert witnesses and preserving the integrity of the testing process.

Keep adding conviction-integrity units.

Establish independent prosecutorial integrity units.

Enter *Brady* compliance orders in every criminal case.

Engage in a *Brady* colloquy.

Adopt local rules that require the government to comply with its discovery obligations without the need for motions by the defense.

Condition the admission of expert evidence in criminal cases on the presentation of a proper *Daubert* showing.

When prosecutors misbehave, don't keep it a secret.

Abandon judicial elections [this recommendation is directed of course exclusively to the states, since no federal judges are elected].

Abrogate absolute prosecutorial immunity.

Repeal AEDPA § 2254(d).

Treat prosecutorial misconduct as a civil rights violation.

Give criminal defendants the choice of a jury or bench trial.

Conduct in-depth studies of exonerations.

Repeal three felonies a day for three years.

Though all of Judge Kozinski's suggestions merit close attention, I want to discuss just one of them—his proposal to repeal 28 U.S.C. § 2254(d), a provision of the Antiterrorism and Effective Death Penalty Act of 1996. This pernicious subsection, passed with the full approval of the great liberal President Bill Clinton (what a joke),[33] states that

An application for a writ of habeas corpus on behalf of a person in custody pursuant to the judgment of a State court shall not be granted with respect to any claim that was adjudicated on the merits in State court

33. See Liliana Segura, "Gutting Habeas Corpus: The Inside Story of How Bill Clinton Sacrificed Prisoners' Rights for Political Gain," *The Intercept,* May 4, 2016, https://theintercept.com/2016/05/04/the-untold-story-of-bill-clintons-other-crime-bill/.

proceedings unless the adjudication of the claim—(1) resulted in a decision that was contrary to, or involved an unreasonable application of, clearly established Federal law, as determined by the Supreme Court of the United States; or—(2) resulted in a decision that was based on an unreasonable determination of the facts in light of the evidence presented in the State court proceeding.

Why should it matter whether the decision of the state court that is challenged in a federal habeas corpus proceeding is contrary to or an unreasonable application of law deemed by the Supreme Court "established"; for if it is contrary to a law that though not "established" is unsound, the defendant should be allowed to challenge it in federal court—why not? And why, proceeding to subsection (2), should the evidence presented in the state proceeding be determinative? Why shouldn't it be enough that the facts were not reasonably determined by the state court? I don't think there are any answers to those questions. Habeas corpus should be available to any criminal defendant who has a good chance of being able to prove that he was unjustly convicted and as a result is unjustly imprisoned and should therefore be released.

Subsection (a) of section 2254(d) provides that "the Supreme Court, a Justice thereof, a circuit judge, or a district court shall entertain an application for a writ of habeas corpus in behalf of a person in custody pursuant to the judgment of a State court only on the ground that he is in custody in violation of the Constitution or laws or treaties of the United States." Which is fine, and enough. A federal court should not order a prisoner discharged because the court thinks that the state court that convicted and sentenced him made errors of state law; but if his conviction and sentence violate federal law—suppose he was a federal officer whose state "crime" was in fact the lawful discharge of his federal duties—he is entitled to relief by a federal court, because compliance with federal law preempts violation of state law; and this regardless of whether the Supreme Court happens to have spoken to the particular conduct involved in the case.

But as explained in a recent concurring opinion by Judge Stephen Reinhardt of the Ninth Circuit—*Curiel v. Miller*[34]—the Supreme Court has narrowed a state prisoner's access to the federal courts for relief from an unconstitutional conviction brutally. I quote a portion of the opinion:

---

34. 830 F.3d 864, 872–881 (2016).

Recent decisions of the United States Supreme Court . . . have placed an almost impossible burden on state courts: to be the final decision-maker in an overwhelming number of cases involving fundamental constitutional rights of criminal defendants. Although recognizing that the California Supreme Court "disposes of close to 10,000 cases a year, including more than 3,400 original habeas corpus petitions," *Harrington v. Richter,* 562 U.S. 86, 99 (2011), the United States Supreme Court has virtually eliminated the ability of federal courts to enforce the Constitution when reviewing state court convictions, holding instead that under AEDPA [the Antiterrorism and Effective Death Penalty Act of 1996, 110 Stat. 1214], federal courts must defer to state court decisions regarding questions of federal constitutional law, even though the state courts often have neither the time nor the resources to fully and carefully consider those questions or even to explain their rulings. . . . Not only must the Supreme Court have previously decided the constitutional question at issue, but the "precise contours" of the rule must have been established by the Supreme Court. *Lockyer v. Andrade,* 538 U.S. 63, 75–76 (2003). Further, slight factual differences between cases have been enough for the Court to determine that no "clearly established" law existed on a particular question. *E.g., Carey v. Musladin,* 549 U.S. 70, 75–77 (2006). The Supreme Court, of course, hears only about 80 cases per year, most of which are not criminal cases, and it therefore addresses applications of constitutional law in that area far less frequently than circuit courts. Moreover, it generally does not consider cases when the circuit courts are in agreement and no conflict exists. Thus, in those instances in which developments in the law are generally agreed upon, there is likely to be no clearly established Supreme Court law at all, simply because the law is so clear as not to require intervention by the Court. For these reasons and others, although a constitutional violation may be clear, federal courts will often be unable to grant habeas relief as there is no "clearly established" Supreme Court law governing the question—certainly a counterintuitive, if not a counterproductive, result.

In addition to the restrictive "clearly established" Supreme Court law doctrine, *Williams* began a march by the Supreme Court toward a narrow and regressive definition of the phrase "unreasonable application." In that case, the Court held that federal courts may not grant relief even though the state courts *erroneously* applied clearly established Supreme

Court law. Rather, it said, any erroneous application of the Constitution must also be objectively unreasonable. See 529 U.S. at 410–13. . . . Subsequently, the Court held that a decision could be objectively unreasonable only "in cases where there is *no possibility* [that] fairminded jurists could disagree that the state court's decisions conflict with [the Supreme Court's] precedents." *Harrington v. Richter*, 562 U.S. 86, 102–03 (2011) (emphasis added). . . . [And] if the state court's rejection of the petitioner's claim is "unaccompanied by an explanation," federal courts must attempt to conjure up a plausible, though not necessarily correct, hypothetical basis for the state court's decision, and, if they can, that will suffice. *Id. at 98–99.* Thus, even if every imagined basis that the federal court can think of is clearly incorrect, the court may still not grant relief so long as any of the reasons, while wrong, could be deemed "reasonable." In short, even though an individual has erroneously been deprived of his constitutional rights, he must remain in prison, perhaps for life, or even possibly suffer capital punishment, if there is no pre-existing Supreme Court case that has recognized the specific error involved *or* if the state court's ruling, although erroneous, could have been arrived at by a "fairminded jurist," however that term may be defined.

There is much more to bemoan in the judicial system, such as the dreadful record of eyewitness identification in criminal cases,[35] the continuing decline in the utilization of juries (grand and petit) in both criminal and civil cases,[36] and the sentencing judge's loss of control over the sentence once it is imposed. Joel Cohen explains:

Once a federally prosecuted defendant is sentenced, except in extremely unusual cases . . . the ballgame is over for him in terms of his sentence. . . . [J]udges are flatly unable . . . to decide what prison a defendant should be placed in and whether it is near or far from family who, the judge believes, would visit if they could. . . . [W]hen a defendant is sentenced, the judge has virtually no ability whatsoever to follow up or add to the discussion of that defendant's future even in compassionate release scenar-

35. Flagged by Chief Judge Theodore A. McKee in his superb concurring opinion in *Dennis v. Secretary, Pennsylvania Dept. of Corrections*, 834 F.3d 263, 313 (3d Cir. 2016), which I cited in Chapter 3.

36. See Suja A. Thomas, *The Missing American Jury: Restoring the Fundamental Constitutional Role of the Criminal, Civil, and Grand Juries* (2016).

ios. . . . Federal judges are appointed by the president and confirmed by the Senate for life—they are not political hacks. . . . Congress should have confidence in their ability to rethink their earlier sentencing decisions, and to take action consistent with that rethinking, if they think it is justified. This is a nation of second chances.[37]

I am particularly perplexed by Congress's refusal to allow federal judges "to rethink their earlier sentencing decisions." Suppose a convicted defendant wants to challenge just his sentence, and not his conviction. 28 U.S.C. § 2255(a) states that "a prisoner in custody under sentence of a court established by Act of Congress claiming the right to be released upon the ground that the sentence was imposed in violation of the Constitution or laws of the United States, or that the court was without jurisdiction to impose such sentence, or that the sentence was in excess of the maximum authorized by law, or is otherwise subject to collateral attack, may move the court which imposed the sentence to vacate, set aside or correct the sentence." But in subsection (h) we learn that "a second or successive motion [to set aside the defendant's sentence] must be certified . . . by a panel of the appropriate court of appeals to contain—(1) newly discovered evidence that, if proven and viewed in light of the evidence as a whole, would be sufficient to establish by clear and convincing evidence that no reasonable factfinder would have found the movant guilty of the offense; or (2) a new rule of constitutional law, made retroactive to cases on collateral review by the Supreme Court, that was previously unavailable."

Suppose a defendant files a section 2255(a) motion, giving reasons why his sentence should be reduced, and the motion is rejected by the district judge and there is either no appeal or the court of appeals affirms the judge's ruling. Sometime later, the defendant discovers another ground for seeking a reduction in his sentence, and moves the district court to reduce his sentence accordingly. Suppose the ground he is asserting is entirely valid. Nevertheless for him to be allowed to file the motion it must first be "certified . . . by . . . the appropriate court of appeals to contain . . . newly discovered evidence that, if proven and viewed in light of the evidence as a whole, would be sufficient to establish by clear and convincing evidence that no reasonable factfinder would have found the movant *guilty of the offense.*"[38] But he is not challenging the of-

37. Joel Cohen, "Federal Inmates Need Second Chances and Congress Can Act," January 12, 2017, *The Hill,* http://thehill.com/blogs/pundits-blog/crime/314009-federal-inmates-need-second-chances-and-congress-can-act.

38. 28 U.S.C. § 2254(h)(1) (emphasis added).

fense; in effect he is acknowledging his guilt. His only objection is to the sentence. He has, I'm assuming, a compelling basis for the challenge yet can get nowhere with it—for not having challenged an irrelevancy. As my court said in *Hope v. United States*,[39] "a successive motion under 28 U.S.C. § 2255 . . . may not be filed on the basis of newly discovered evidence unless the motion challenges the conviction and not merely the sentence." This makes no sense.

Three days before the inauguration of President Trump, the *New York Times* published an article that includes an account of efforts by the Justice Department to civilize the federal criminal justice system:

> They set up a school system in federal prisons. They put in place new oversight for halfway houses. They created a new, centralized mental health facility for women at the federal prison in Danbury, Conn. They stopped using private prisons to house federal offenders because of safety and security concerns. And they issued a report in conjunction with the Urban Institute concluding that fairer and "more enlightened" prison sentencing policies at the state level—where the bulk of prisoners are held—had succeeded both in bolstering public safety and in cutting many millions in costs for strapped states. Many of the recent initiatives have not made headlines, but they have contributed to what Justice Department officials see as a cultural shift that began under Mr. Obama's first attorney general, Eric H. Holder Jr., who instituted a policy in 2013 meant to lessen potential sentences for nonviolent drug offenders. Deputy Attorney General Sally Yates, who has led many of the prison initiatives [yet was fired by President Trump early in his Administration], has sought to send the message that locking people up is not the department's sole mission. "We're not the Department of Prosecution," aides said she often reminded them. "We're the Department of Justice for a reason."[40]

I want to pick up for a moment on the reference in the preceding paragraph to the setting up of a school system in federal prisons. There are many juvenile offenders, and yet from the standpoint of criminology "children are different."[41] Increased recognition of the difference is leading to serious reform. In 2015, the

39. 108 F.3d 119, 120 (7th Cir. 1997).

40. Eric Lichtblau, "Trump May Reverse Obama Policy of Freeing Inmates," *New York Times*, January 16, 2017, p. A12.

41. The title of an important article by Elizabeth S. Scott in 11 *Ohio State Journal of Criminal Law* 71 (2013).

U.S. Department of Justice released a report from a seven-year study of more than 1,300 "serious juvenile offenders," those who had committed felony-level violent, property, or drug crimes. The study reported that more than 90 percent of the juvenile offenders "grew out" of such antisocial behavior by young adulthood and did not reoffend. The report concluded that "[m]ost juvenile offending is, in fact, limited to adolescence."[42] And while the number of juveniles in adult prisons dropped 82 percent between 1997 and 2016 and those in juvenile detention facilities dropped more than 50 percent,[43] during a similar period—between 1994 and 2014, when rates of incarceration of juveniles were plummeting—the number of murders committed by juveniles fell 72 percent.[44]

For other ongoing efforts to reform our criminal justice system in recognition of the limited efficacy of and necessity for the exceedingly harsh punishments that typify American criminal justice, see Holly Harris, "The Prisoner Dilemma: Ending America's Incarceration Epidemic,"[45] who explains that there is much reform at the state level but we need it at the federal level as well—need less incarceration of minor offenders, as incarceration tends not to reduce recidivism by the incarcerated when they are released. See Duaa Eldeib and Steve Mills, "New Hope, New Lives: Illinois Inmates Sentenced as Juveniles to Life Without Parole Are Getting New Hearings, and in Some Cases, Second Chances."[46]

Whether all or indeed any of these reforms will survive the Trump Presidency is an open question. Missing from the reforms, moreover, is recognition of the need to curtail imprisonment of violent offenders, a need stressed in an excellent recent article by John Pfaff,[47] a professor at Fordham Law School, an article amplified in a forthcoming book by him: *Locked In: The True Causes of Mass Incarceration and How to Achieve Real Reform*, summarized by David

42. Laurence Steinberg, et al., "Psychosocial Maturity and Desistance from Crime in a Sample of Serious Juvenile Offenders," *OJJDP* (March 2015), www.ojjdp.gov/pubs/248391.pdf.

43. The Marshall Project, *What We Can Learn from the Amazing Drop in Juvenile Incarceration* (January 24, 2017), www.themarshallproject.org/2017/01/24/what-we-can-learn-from-the-amazing-drop-in-juvenile-incarceration?utm_medium=email&utm_campaign=newsletter&utm_source=opening-statement&utm_term=newsletter-20170125-679#.17pQdRfhX.

44. *OJJDP Statistical Briefing Book* (May 25, 2016), http://www.ojjdp.gov/ojstatbb/offenders/qa03105.asp?qaDate=2014.

45. *Foreign Affairs* (March/April 2017 issue).

46. *Chicago Tribune*, February 22, 2017, p. 1. [The juveniles had been sentenced to life without parole mainly for having committed murderers as teenagers.]

47. "Imprisoned by Violence: If We're Going to End Mass Incarceration in the U.S., It Will Mean Figuring Out Better Ways to Prevent Violent Crimes and to Deal with Those Who Commit Them." *Wall Street Journal*, January 28, 2017 p. C1.

Scharfenberg in a recent article,[48] from which I quote excerpts: One concern of Pfaff, Scharfenberg points out, is the high discount rates of the typical violent offender, though Scharfenberg doesn't use the phrase "high discount rates" but instead says that "those contemplating crime often don't know how long sentences are, or even that sentences have gotten longer." More important, "those who are most likely to engage in violence and antisocial behavior tend to be very present-minded. They don't think a lot about tomorrow. What really deters them, if anything does, is the risk of getting caught in the first place: policing and arrests, not prison sentences." Moreover, many violent offenders age out of crime, often as early as their mid- to late twenties. "[A] long prison sentence also undermines someone's ability to find the stabilizing influence of a job or a spouse, thus increasing the long-run risk that he will reoffend." Among other alternatives to prison for dealing with violent criminals, Scharfenberg's article mentions that "hot-spot policing identifies . . . high-risk blocks and significantly increased patrols and community involvement there . . . ha[ve] produced significant results."

President Trump appears to want to go in the opposite direction, inviting criticism from—of all unexpected sources—police chiefs. Timothy Williams and Richard A. Oppel, Jr. point out[49] that "Mr. Trump has shifted the focus from civil rights to law and order, from reducing incarceration to increasing sentences, from goading the police to improve to protecting them from harm. Last week, he swore in a new attorney general, Jeff Sessions, who has said that the government has grown 'soft on crime,' and helped block a bipartisan bill to reduce sentences. Mr. Sessions said that a recent uptick in crime in some major cities is a 'dangerous, permanent trend,' a view that is not supported by federal crime data, which shows crime remains near historical lows." Some day we'll learn who's right.

I have been so critical of the federal judiciary in this book that I wish to end on a positive note, lest I be thought just a curmudgeon. And the positive note is this: the doctrine of "standing to sue." Article III, section 2, clause 1 of the Constitution authorizes the federal judiciary to decide cases or controversies (these

---

48. "Why We Should Free Violent Criminals," *Sentencing Law and Policy*, February 6, 2017, http://sentencing.typepad.com/sentencing_law_and_policy/2017/02/why-we-should-free-violent-criminals.html.

49. In "Police Chiefs Contend Trump's Law Enforcement Priorities Are Out of Step," *New York Times*, February 13, 2017, p. A8.

appear to be synonyms) arising under federal law. The term "cases or contro-versies" appears to (and has long been held to) exclude advisory opinions (au-thorized under state law in some states), as where a governor asks the state su-preme court to advise him on the constitutionality of a proposed statute, a situation in which there is not yet a case.

But even if there is a case—a lawsuit—it is not considered justiciable under federal law unless the plaintiff has a tangible interest in the case—in legal par-lance, unless he (or she or it) has "standing to sue." So consider the following hypothetical case:[50] a provider, which I'll call KingCable, of residential cable television programming has violated 47 U.S.C. § 551(e), a section of the Cable Communications Policy Act (47 U.S.C. § 551) that commands a cable operator to "destroy personally identifiable information if the information is no longer necessary for the purpose for which it was collected and there are no pending requests or orders for access to such information [by a cable provider] under subsection (d) or pursuant to a court order." KingCable has violated the statute by failing to destroy the personally identifiable information (date of birth, home address, home and work telephone numbers, social security number, and credit card information) of a person who had subscribed to its service a decade earlier and canceled his subscription after a year. Knowing of the viola-tion (for he had inquired of KingCable whether it had destroyed his personal information and KingCable had replied that it had not), and fearing that de-spite its denial his personal information may have been stolen from KingCable or sold or given away by it and if so the recipient or recipients of the informa-tion may be using it, or planning to use it, in a way that will harm him, the ex-subscriber sues the cable company.

There is unquestionably a risk of harm to him from the violation. But sup-pose the plaintiff has no evidence that KingCable has ever given away or leaked any of his personal information, or intends to do so, or is at risk of having the information stolen from it. It's true that section 551(f)(1) of the Cable Commu-nications Policy Act provides that "any person aggrieved by any act of a cable operator in violation of this section may bring a civil action in a United States district court," but the plaintiff in my hypothetical case has presented no evi-dence of having been "aggrieved" by KingCable's violation of section 551(3)—no evidence that in the decade since he subscribed to the company's residen-tial services any of the personal information that he supplied to the company

---

50. Based on a real case, not yet decided when this Epilogue was written, pending in my court.

when he subscribed has ever leaked and caused financial or other injury to him. So a claim for damages will get him nowhere, and as for the alternative of seeking injunctive relief, he could no more prove irreparable harm (the condition for obtaining such relief) than he can prove a harm reparable by an award of damages.

In short, our hypothetical cable customer lacks standing to sue because he can't prove he was harmed by the statutory violation that he seeks to challenge. He can no more sue than someone who, though he has never subscribed and means never to subscribe to a cable company, nevertheless is outraged by the thought that KingCable and perhaps other providers are violating a federal statute with apparent impunity.

So, much like the finality rule that I discussed briefly in the Conclusion, the standing rule reduces the workload of the federal judiciary, but does so more innocently, because the "victims" of the rule are persons or organizations who suffer no significant deprivation if denied the right to sue, as persons barred by the finality rule frequently are (as we just saw). Nor does the standing rule leave the government without means to enforce its rules, in the present example the requirement that the cable company destroy its subscribers' (or former subscribers') personal information. Although I'm not aware of a law that authorizes the government to enforce section 551(e) of the Cable Communications Policy Act, or to provide bounties to private enforcers not harmed by the Act, either law could be enacted by Congress, and presumably would be if the limited private enforcement that the doctrine of standing permits proved unable to achieve reasonable compliance with the Act.

But there is a rub. The Supreme Court has ruled that a lawsuit is not valid under federal law unless the plaintiff has a "concrete" interest in prevailing in the case—has in other words suffered a "concrete injury" that can be redressed by the judgment in a lawsuit brought by him. Such an interest is the sine qua non of "standing to sue"—that is, the right to sue. The plaintiff in our hypothetical case might well be able to prove a violation of section 551, yet be unable to prove risk of harm to himself definite and substantial enough to be deemed "concrete,"[51] and as a result not be entitled to sue. The concern behind this rule, and it is not an unjustified concern, is that without it the federal courts would be flooded with cases based not on proof of harm but on an implausible and at worst trivial risk of harm. The concern with the rule is that the Supreme Court

51. See *Spokeo, Inc. v. Robins*, 136 S. Ct. 1540, 1549 (2016); *Braitberg v. Charter Communications, Inc.*, 836 F.3d 925 (8th Cir. 2016).

and the lower federal courts have been unable to specify what constitutes a claim of concrete injury, or other basis for a lawsuit.[52]

In *Lujan v. Defenders of Wildlife*—one of Justice Scalia's most impressive majority opinions—the Supreme Court, explaining the outer bounds of standing to sue, said that standing is not

> an ingenious academic exercise in the conceivable, but as we have said requires, at the summary judgment stage, a factual showing of perceptible harm. It is clear that the person who observes or works with a particular animal threatened by a federal decision is facing perceptible harm, since the very subject of his interest will no longer exist. It is even plausible—though it goes to the outermost limit of plausibility—to think that a person who observes or works with animals of a particular species in the very area of the world where that species is threatened by a federal decision is facing such harm, since some animals that might have been the subject of his interest will no longer exist.[53]

Sounds sensible. But as noted above, the Supreme Court's latest word on what constitutes a "concrete injury" is rather confusing, leaving unclear at this writing what exactly the current Court's concept of standing to sue is.[54]

Coda (the end of a musical or other composition): Perhaps this book, now finally ended, will remind some readers of a remark that Robert Graves, the great British (half-Irish, half-German) poet, novelist, critic, classicist, and World War I British combat officer, made to Gertrude Stein in June 1929 about his book *Good-Bye to All That: An Autobiography* (1929). He called it a "quite ruthless" book, though written "without indignation."[55]

52. As explained in Craig Konnoth and Seth Kreimer, "Spelling Out Spokeo," 165 *University of Pennsylvania Law Review Online* 47 (2016), noting how confused is *Spokeo, Inc. v. Robins*, 136 S. Ct. 1540 (2016), the Supreme Court's latest effort to define "concrete injury."

53. 504 U.S. 555, 566–567 (1992).

54. For a helpful recent discussion of the uncertainties of standing to sue, see Eric J. Segall, "Op-Ed Let the Emoluments Case Against Trump Go Forward," *LA Times*, January 25, 2017, www.latimes.com/opinion /op-ed/la-oe-segall-emoluments-case-should-go-forward-20170125-story.html.

55. Jean Moorcroft Wilson, "The Old Trench-Mind at Work: How Siegfried Sassoon's Animus against a 'Profit-seeking Book' Turned His Own Copy into Art," *Times Literary Supplement*, February 3, 2017, p. 15.

Index